THIRD EDITION

ACHIEVER

Exam Prep Guide for AP* European History

by Christopher Freiler

SHERPALEARNING
GUIDING YOU TO EVEN GREATER HEIGHTS

Sherpa Learning is dedicated to helping high-achieving learners gain access to high-quality, skills-based instruction that is created, reviewed, and tested by teachers. To learn more about Sherpa Learning and our vision, or to learn about some of our other amazing products and upcoming projects, please visit us at

www.sherpalearning.com

Publisher/Editor: David Nazarian
Copy-Editor/Permissions: Christine DeFranco
Proofreader: Haley Myers
Administrative/Research: Abeer Aslam
Map Design: Kushan Kalpa
Graphic Design: Syed Rashid Minhas

The publisher would like to thank the big-box publishers for consistently dropping the ball so we can pick it up. Also, Eleanor and Olive Nazarian for their support throughout the development of this text. And 2020, for ending.

Cover Image: Grand Canal in Venice at Dawn
© Sergii Kolesnyk - Dreamstime.com

* AP is a registered trademark of the College Board, which was not involved in the production of, and does not endorse, this product.

ISBN 978-1-948641-40-1

Sherpa Learning, LLC.
West Milford, New Jersey
www.sherpalearning.com

ACKNOWLEDGMENTS

Writing can be a lonely business, yet I wish to thank those in the background who have supported my endeavors, both immediately and at the distance of time. First, I'd like to David Nazarian of Sherpa Learning for taking on this (complex) project and for his unflinching expertise and congeniality. Next, I wish to thank my teachers and mentors who modeled the craft of history and who have assisted me on my career trajectory. Lloyd Kramer sparked my interest in European history; it has been gratifying to continue our historical dialogue over the years. Lloyd projects a down-to-earth authenticity that is not always common among intellectuals. Peter Hayes from Northwestern University taught me the value of historical rigor and to appreciate the joy in attempting to capture the complexity of the past as a mirror to see contemporary concerns more clearly. Without the mentorship and support of Diego Gonzelez-Grande, it's no sure thing I'd be writing this book. My friend and colleague, John Naisbitt, deserves thanks for providing me with a rewarding and often hilarious collaboration of over 20-plus years. Further, I wish to thank all of my peers from the AP reading; their friendship, patience, and ideas are expressed in this text in one form or another. One of the greatest rewards in teaching a challenging course like AP European History has been witnessing the transformation of students in their skills, self-discipline, and sense of their own capabilities. The following students have kindly shared their essays as samples: Zaina Ahmed, Sophie Brown, Katie Cernugel, Andrea Collins, Alice Ding, Tara Entezar, Jayne Gelman, Amy Guo, Minna Hassballa, Sophia Horowicz, Riya Jain, JoonSoo Kim, Nikolai Kowalchuk, Milen Spegar, Sherman Thompson, Nick Tienken, Scott Watson, Meghna Mitra, Keona Schaller, and Ivy Shen. Finally, I extend warmth and gratitude to my family: daughter Megan, my favorite young scientist; son Kyle, a budding teacher in his own right, who provided feedback on key portions of the text; and lovely wife Michele, for her editorial expertise, logistical support, and emotional sustenance.

ABOUT THE AUTHOR

Christopher Freiler has taught Advanced Placement European History at Hinsdale Central High School in Hinsdale, IL, since 1993. Additionally, he has taught Philosophy Honors since 2003, a course he proposed and developed. He has been involved with the national AP program since 1997, serving as a workshop consultant and in leadership positions for the annual exam scoring, the re-design of the AP European History course curriculum, and in test development. Chris earned his B.A. in History at Northwestern University, M.A. in History at University of Virginia, and M.A. in Philosophy at Northern Illinois University.

PREFACE

You, the AP student, will find several products on the market designed to help prepare you for the Advanced Placement European History exam. The author, a former co-chair of the committee that designed the current curriculum and exam, as well as a leader at the annual exam scoring, designed this review guide to be the most representative and comprehensive test preparation manual available. The following features make it stand apart:

➢ This book mirrors the curriculum framework and exam format that define the course, providing an inside look at how to approach European History as an apprentice historian.

➢ This review guide addresses the required content of the course briefly but substantively, ensuring that you will not be left in the dark for any possible item on the AP exam.

➢ "Theme Music," "Skill Set," and "Example Base" features throughout the guide are designed to help students link content meaningfully to course themes, reinforce historical thinking skills (HTS), and connect illustrative examples to broader developments.

➢ Practice exam questions were developed to closely follow both the content and types of questions you will encounter on the exam. If you compare the stimulus-based multiple choice (MC) questions from the actual AP exam, I am confident you will find those in this guide the most realistic replication.

➢ Document-Based (DBQ), Short-Answer (SAQ), and Long Essay (LEQ) Questions follow the format and approach of those on the AP exam.

You have a choice in selecting a review guide, and we are confident the ACHIEVER will provide the guidance needed for success in the course and on the exam.

A NOTE FROM THE AUTHOR

Welcome to your study of Advanced Placement European History. You should find the course content challenging yet rewarding, as the curriculum covers significant developments and events that shape our lives still today. Though the sheer amount of material—the people, places, events, art works, and literature—may seem overwhelming, you will not be expected to recall everything. Rather than approaching the course as a retainer of facts, think of yourself as an apprentice historian—engaging with historical interpretations and employing a set of important historical thinking skills (HTS) in constructing and evaluating arguments with the evidence from primary and secondary sources, as well as content knowledge.

My experience as a teacher has shown me that virtually any motivated student can succeed in the course and on the AP exam. Two keys to success are: (1) a commitment to develop your historical thinking skills and (2) a toolkit of proven strategies to prepare for the exam. You will supply the first key; this guide will provide you with the second.

This book is organized into three sections. In the first section, you'll learn how the exam is structured and scored. This section also surveys important strategies for increasing comprehension in your daily studying and in meeting the tasks required by the various items on the exam, particularly those that involve writing. The second section comprises the crux of this review guide, with chapters surveying essential content, divided into the four chronological periods of the course. Each chapter provides helpful study tips, a brief discussion of interpretive issues, and review questions. You will also find a concise list of suggested readings, websites, and films. At the end of each time period, a diagnostic test is offered, so that you can apply your content knowledge and practice your HTS on the various test item types. Complete answers and explanations, as well as sample responses with analysis, can be found on the Achiever companion website: https://www.sherpalearning.com/achiever.

This review guide can be used on its own or in conjunction with any textbook. It is recommended that you consult outside resources—such as historical interpretations, primary sources, and works of art—whenever useful to your understanding of content or to practice the HTS.

The final section provides two full practice examinations, complete with 55-question multiple-choice sections, 3 SAQS (choice of 4), a DBQ, and an LEQ (choice of 3). In all, you will find over 350 multiple-choice questions with substantial answer explanations, as well as sample DBQ, SAQ, and LEQ responses. Sample essays have been included in the belief that seeing writing that succeeds, and also that which is lacking, serves as the best way to hone your own writing skills. Finally, in the belief that chronology is important for understanding the skills of historical thinking, I have included three different timelines in the appendix to this volume.

Good luck in your review of the course!

Christopher Freiler

TABLE OF CONTENTS

SECTION II   CONTENT REVIEW

CHAPTER 4: THE RENAISSANCE AND REFORMATION

CHAPTER 5: ECONOMIC EXPANSION, SOCIAL CHANGE, AND RELIGIOUS WARS, 1550–1650

CHAPTER 6: THE SCIENTIFIC VIEW OF THE WORLD

CHAPTER 10: THE FRENCH REVOLUTION AND NAPOLEONIC ERA, 1789–1815 156

PERIOD 2 — DIAGNOSTIC EXAM

CHAPTER 11: INDUSTRIAL SOCIETY AND THE STRUGGLE FOR REFORM, 1815–1850 184

CHAPTER 12: REALISM, NATIONALISM, AND IMPERIALISM, 1850–1914 202

SECTION III   PRACTICE EXAMS

THE ACHIEVER COMPANION WEBSITE

Go to the web address shown below for complete answers and explanations for the Diagnostic Exams, including sample essay responses with analysis. You can also register to be notified when new resources and content updates are added to the companion site.

https://www.sherpalearning.com/achiever

COURSE ABBREVIATIONS

The following abbreviations will be referenced throughout the text.

ARG	Argumentation
CAUS	Causation
CCOT	Change and Continuity over Time
CED	Course and Exam Description
CES	Claims and Evidence in Sources
CID	Cultural and Intellectual Developments
COMP	Comparison
CPX	Complexity
CTX	Contextualization
DAP	Developments and Processes
DBQ	Document-Based Question
ECD	Economic and Commercial Developments
HIPP	Historical Situation, Intended Audience, Purpose, Point of View
HTS	Historical Thinking Skills
INT	Interaction of Europe and the World
KC	Key Concept
LO	Learning Objective
LEQ	Long Essay Question
MAC	Making Connections
MC	Multiple-Choice
NEI	National and European Identity
RP	Reasoning Processes
SAQ	Short-Answer Question
SAS	Sourcing and Situation
SCD	Social Organization and Development
SOP	States and Other Institutions of Power
TH	Thesis
TSI	Technological and Scientific Innovations

SECTION I
STUDYING FOR THE EXAM

❧ CHAPTER 1 ❧
The Structure of the AP Exam

Overview of the Test Structure

Each year's exam is designed by the AP European History Development Committee and covers the period from 1450 to around 2001. Knowing the parameters of the exam can guide your study strategy; given the terminal date of 2001, you are discouraged from focusing on current events, though making connections between present and past is, of course, always recommended to develop your analytical abilities. However, material from the post-1945 period *will* appear on the exam, even if your particular class struggles to complete the course in the time before testing. The test writers will aim to provide *roughly* equal treatment to the following four time periods:

- **Period 1** – 1450–1648
- **Period 2** – 1648–1815
- **Period 3** – 1815–1914
- **Period 4** – 1914–ca. 2001

The exam consists of four parts. In Part A of Section I there are 55 stimulus-based multiple-choice (MC) questions (see below). Students are provided 55 minutes to complete this multiple choice section, or about 1 minute per question (for pacing purposes). Once you complete Section I, Part A, you will not be able to return to it; the proctors will collect your test and scan sheet and start you immediately on the next section. Section I, Part B comprises 3 (choice of 4) Short-Answer Question (SAQs), 2 of which will involve stimulus material. Once completed with this part of Section I (40

minutes), the proctors will provide a 5- to 10-minute break, during which they will prepare the room for the next section. Upon resuming, you will have 100 minutes to complete Parts A and B of Section II, which includes the Document-Based Question (DBQ) and Long Essay Question (LEQ). This portion of the exam includes a 15-minute "reading period," intended for looking through the DBQ documents and planning out your response; however, you may divide your time any way you wish. Because the DBQ is the more complex task, you are strongly encouraged to begin with this question.

For many of you, AP European history will be your first AP exam. If so, you will find it to be not only an intellectual test, but a physical and psychological one. It is important, therefore, to pace yourself and come to the exam well-prepared and well-rested.

Section I, Part A: Multiple-Choice Questions (MC)

The multiple-choice questions on the AP exam are designed to test the following: 1) required content knowledge (see the Unit Guides of the College Board Course Exam and Description for European History), 2) the 6 historical thinking skills (HTS) and 3 reasoning processes (RP), 3) the 7 course themes, and 4) any of the relevant 19 key concepts (KCs). As such, it is vital that you do not approach this portion of the test as merely a regurgitation of what you've encountered throughout your course. To put it simply—you *will* be reading, processing, and thinking throughout the MC section. Because these stimulus-based questions draw from different types of source materials and involve more moving parts than content-only items, it is critical to your overall success that you have practice with them.

Section	Part	Number & Type of Questions	Time	% of Score
I	A	55 Multiple-Choice Questions	55 minutes	40%
	B	4 Short-Answer Questions	40 minutes	20%
Scheduled break of 5–10 minutes				
II	A	1 Document-Based Question	60 minutes	25%
	B	1 Long Essay Question (Choice of 2)	40 minutes	15%
		TOTAL:	**3 hours, 15 minutes**	

Even with 55 questions, there will be some gaps of material covered, and thus, one of the topics you studied may not appear on the exam. However, if you've focused strongly on the essential narratives and overarching questions presented through the themes and KCs, you will be prepared to apply your understanding to this portion of the exam. All of the questions will come in sets, oriented around a specific source. Sets will consist of at least 2 and no more than 5 questions, generally testing several of the HTS and RP. Despite a set being centered on one source, your inability to answer one question of the set correctly should not affect your ability to answer others. Each correct answer stands on its own and is not dependent on previous questions. The last question of the set may include a question that tests "skills only," meaning that it does not require content knowledge but simply your ability to think historically, such as evaluating the reliability of a source. In addition, this last question of a set may be "content only" or "stimulus not required," which means you can merely draw from what you know. The former type of question will likely only appear 2-4 times, and the latter about 6–10 times on an exam format.

Each question will have four possible choices, consisting of the key (correct answer) and 3 distractors (wrong answers). As you practice the MC questions in this guide, you will notice that the distractors often seem appealing. This is by design. Compared to previous test formats, you will encounter less "made-up history," or developments that never happened. Instead, you will probably be faced with 3–4 accurate statements; your job is to consider which one is most applicable to the source and the "stem" (what the question asks). At first, this may strike you as difficult and more time-consuming, but you will improve your ability on these items the more you practice them—especially in recognizing the HTS and RP involved with the question, reading the sources efficiently, and familiarizing yourself with the Unit Guides.

Section I, Part B: Short-Answer Questions (SAQs)

The four short-answer questions (SAQs) measure your understanding of important content topics and 1 or 2 historical thinking skills. Of the four prompts you'll be given, 2 will include stimulus material, and they will cover Periods 2–4 (1648–2001). One stimulus will be a primary source (e.g., a political cartoon from the Cold War) and one a secondary source (e.g., historian's interpretation of the effects of the Reformation). For the third question, you will be given a choice of 2 questions with no stimulus, one of which will draw from the period before 1600. The other question will address any period after 1648. Thus, it is possible, though not necessarily recommended, to avoid writing about the period prior to 1600.

Given there are 40 minutes and 3 questions in this section, you will have about 13:20 for each, and considering the pur-

pose of the SAQs, this should be plenty. In fact, you will write each response on a designated template (one side of a sheet of paper), with a box that must contain your entire answer. If you go beyond the box, that portion of your writing will not be scored. Unlike the other written portions of the exam, the SAQs do not have a formal rubric. Since each question comprises three parts, you can earn only three points for each SAQ. Going beyond what earns you the point will not add any bonus or qualitative points to your overall score. Also, simply recalling facts is unlikely to help you on the SAQs; however, always try to include one specific example and connect it to the main idea of the prompt. With appropriate preparation and practice, the SAQs may be the least taxing and stressful portion of the exam.

Section II, Part A: Document-Based Question (DBQ)

If this is your first Advanced Placement history class, you may be unfamiliar with the concept of a document-based question. Responding to a DBQ involves interpreting sources and applying your content knowledge to the development of an argument. Since the question requires content knowledge, the prompt will address a mainstream topic, i.e., one found explicitly in the Unit Guides, often ranging over several KCs or periods. All DBQs will require you to apply the HTS of 1) argumentation, 2) use of evidence in support of an argument, 3) analyzing evidence—sourcing and situation, and 4) contextualization. In fact, you will notice sections on the DBQ rubric (see page 4) where these skills are directly assessed. In addition, each DBQ may be focused on a targeted reasoning process (RP), such as causation, change and continuity over time, or comparison. Look for key phrases in the prompt to determine the targeted skill, like "transformed," "extent to which," "caused by," or "reaction to."

Each DBQ will include 7 documents (one of which will be a visual source, like a chart or image), and you are strongly urged to use all of them in support of your argument. The rubric calls for use of at least 6 documents to earn 2 points, but if you make a major misinterpretation with one document, you will be left with no margin for error. Total time for the DBQ is 60 minutes, made up of 10–15 minutes for reading through the documents and planning your response, and 45–50 minutes to write your response.

Your practice with the DBQ is vital to your effective time management and ability to juggle the various tasks on the rubric to write a focused and coherent argument. To that effect, you will find seven DBQs in this guide, including sample essays and analysis. Just as with any skill—like playing a musical instrument or sport—the DBQ is best approached as a craft that is mastered through deliberate practice and reflection on one's areas of weakness.

Section II, Part B: Long Essay Question (LEQ)

The Long Essay Question (LEQ) measures your ability to use your content knowledge to make an argument on a major theme or topic. You will choose from three prompts, generally focused on the same Targeted RP (e.g., causation) and likely on the same theme (e.g., Interaction of Europe and the World). Each prompt will involve the same number of tasks, so there should be no advantage for students in choosing one over the other. One of the choices will draw from Period 1 (1450–1648), one from Periods 2/3 (1648–1914), and one from Periods 3/4 (1815–2001).

You are allotted approximately 40 minutes to write your LEQ, but you can take a few extra minutes if you like. The directions recommend taking 5 minutes to organize your response, and you are strongly encouraged to apply this advice. Many students on the national exam demonstrate knowledge of the topic but score weakly on their essays, for three main reasons: 1) lack of a clear argument or direction, 2) merely narrating events and content, and 3) making errors in defining the parameters of the question (e.g., geographic, chronological, or topical scope). Most of these errors can be attributed to panicked rather than measured writing. Remember: a briefer, more focused essay that addresses the question will earn higher marks than a lengthy, rambling one.

How the Exam Is Scored

All AP exams employ the same overall scoring system:

- **5** – Extremely well qualified
- **4** – Well qualified
- **3** – Qualified
- **2** – Possibly qualified
- **1** – No recommendation

To calculate your overall total, a complex formula converts the raw score of each section of the exam toward 140 points total. However, you should not think of these points in terms of the standard 90–80–70–60% scale. Break points between each of the above overall scores are determined after the test is administered based on historical standards and how well students performed that particular year on the exam. It is best not to think of the exam by an unreasonable standard of perfection based on points, but with each item as an opportunity to demonstrate your understanding of what you've learned and its application to the course.

Scoring of the Multiple Choice Section

There is no penalty for guessing on this section, so you should make sure you answer each question. Even if you can only narrow the choices down to 2, it is in your best interest to guess. After all, if you do that 10 times (of 55 questions), you are likely by averages to get 5 of them correct.

Scoring of the Essays

Both the DBQ and LEQ are scored with a rubric that awards points based on a measure of student proficiency with the historical thinking skills. Both essays will always measure: 1) Argumentation, 2) Use of Evidence, and 3) Contextualization. In addition, the DBQ will measure a student's ability to provide sourcing and situation analysis for the DBQ documents *as evidence*, in addition to *their use as support for an argument*. Both the DBQ and LEQ will be oriented on one targeted reasoning process (RP), though this will not constitute a separate point on the DBQ rubric, as the skill is measured under the portions of the rubric dealing with argumentation. However, the LEQ rubric calls out two specific points for the RP, with a qualitative distinction between 0, 1, and 2 points, depending on how well students address and extend the Targeted RP with their argument. The Targeted RP for the LEQ are: 1) Comparison, 2) Causation, and 3) Change and Continuity Over Time (CCOT). The generic rubrics below provide a clearer sense of how essays are scored. It is vital that you know these rubrics and practice the skills suggested by them so that you can demonstrate your mastery as you write your essays.

DBQ Rubric

Category	Scoring Criteria	Explanation
A. THESIS/ CLAIM (0–1 pt)	**1 pt.** Responds to the prompt with a historically defensible thesis/claim that establishes a line of reasoning	To earn this point, the thesis must make a claim that responds to the prompt, rather than merely restating or rephrasing the prompt. The thesis must consist of one or more sentences located in one place, either in the introduction or the conclusion.
B. CONTEXTU- ALIZATION (0–1 pt)	**1 pt.** Describes a broader historical context relevant to the prompt.	To earn this point, the response must relate the topic of the prompt to broader historical events, developments, or processes that occur before, during, or continue after the time frame of the question. This point is not awarded for merely a phrase or a reference.
C. EVIDENCE (0–3 pts)	**Evidence from the Documents** **1 pt.** Uses the content of at least **three** documents to address the **topic** of the prompt. **OR** **2 pts.** Supports an **argument** in response to the prompt using at least **six** documents.	To earn one point, the response must accurately describe—rather than simply quote—the content from at least three of the documents. To earn two points, the response must accurately describe—rather than simply quote—the content from at least six documents. In addition, the response must use the content of the documents to support an argument in response to the prompt.
	Evidence Beyond the Documents **1 pt.** Uses at least one additional piece of evidence (beyond that found in the documents) relevant to an argument about the prompt.	To earn this point, the response must describe the evidence and must use more than a phrase or reference. This additional piece of evidence must be different from the evidence used to earn the point for contextualization.
D. ANALYSIS AND REASONING (0–2 pts)	**1 pt.** For at least **three** documents, explains how or why the document's point of view, purpose, historical situation, and/or audience is relevant to an argument.	To earn this point, the response must explain how or why (rather than simply identifying) the document's point of view, purpose, historical situation, or audience is relevant to an argument about the prompt for each of the three documents sourced.
	1 pt. Demonstrates a complex understanding of the historical development that is the focus of the prompt, using evidence to corroborate, qualify, or modify an argument that addresses the question.	A response may demonstrate a complex understanding in a variety of ways, such as: • Explaining nuance of an issue by analyzing multiple variables • Explaining both similarity and difference, or explaining both continuity and change, or explaining multiple causes, or explaining both cause and effect • Explaining relevant and insightful connections within and across periods • Confirming the validity of an argument by corroborating multiple perspectives across themes • Qualifying or modifying an argument by considering diverse or alternate views or evidence This understanding must be part of the argument, not merely a phrase or reference.

On Accuracy: The components of this rubric each require that students demonstrate historically defensible content knowledge. Given the timed nature of the exam, the essay may contain errors that do not detract from the overall quality, as long as the historical content used to advance the argument is accurate.

On Clarity: These essays should be considered first drafts and thus may contain grammatical errors. Those errors will not be counted against a student unless they obscure the successful demonstration of the content knowledge and skills described above.

LEQ Rubric

Category	Scoring Criteria		Explanation
A. THESIS/ CLAIM (0–1 pt)	**1 pt.** Responds to the prompt with a historically defensible thesis/claim that establishes a line of reasoning.		To earn this point, the thesis must make a claim that responds to the prompt, rather than merely restating or rephrasing the prompt. The thesis must consist of one or more sentences located in one place, either in the introduction or the conclusion.
B. CONTEXTU-ALIZATION (0–1 pt)	**1 pt.** Describes a broader historical context relevant to the prompt.		To earn this point, the response must relate the topic of the prompt to broader historical events, developments, or processes that occur before, during, or continue after the time frame of the question. This point is not awarded for merely a phrase or a reference.
C. EVIDENCE (0–2 pts)	**1 pt.** Provides specific examples of evidence relevant to the topic of the prompt.	**OR** **2 pts.** Supports an **argument** in response to the prompt using specific and relevant examples of evidence.	To earn one point, the response must identify specific historical examples of evidence relevant to the topic of the prompt. To earn two points, the response must use specific historical evidence to support an argument in response to the prompt.
D. ANALYSIS AND REASONING (0–2 pts)	**1 pt.** Use historical reasoning (e.g., comparison, causation, CCOT) to frame or structure an argument that addresses the prompt.	**OR** **2 pts.** Demonstrates a complex understanding of the historical development that is the focus of the prompt, using evidence to corroborate, qualify, or modify an argument that addresses the question.	A response may demonstrate a complex understanding in a variety of ways, such as: • Explaining nuance of an issue by analyzing multiple variables • Explaining both similarity and difference, or explaining both continuity and change, or explaining multiple causes, or explaining both cause and effect • Explaining relevant and insightful connections within and across periods • Confirming the validity of an argument by corroborating multiple perspectives across themes • Qualifying or modifying an argument by considering diverse or alternate views or evidence This understanding must be part of the argument, not merely a phrase or reference.

On Accuracy: The components of this rubric each require that students demonstrate historically defensible content knowledge. Given the timed nature of the exam, the essay may contain errors that do not detract from the overall quality, as long as the historical content used to advance the argument is accurate.

On Clarity: These essays should be considered first drafts and thus may contain grammatical errors. Those errors will not be counted against a student unless they obscure the successful demonstration of the content knowledge and skills described above.

Registration and Fees

Registration for AP exams is now handled on-line, as an option for students when they are officially enrolled in a course section (created by your teacher) through AP Classroom. AP Classroom can also be used by your teacher to create quizzes/exams and, of particular benefit, to assign Progress Checks for feedback to students on their success in learning the content and applying the skills of the course. Any questions about registration may be answered at: https://apstudents.collegeboard.org/register-for-ap-exams.

Fee Reductions

The current fee for taking the exam is $95. If this presents a hardship for you or your family, you may qualify for a fee reduction from the College Board and/or a federal or state subsidy depending upon the state in which you reside. For more information about eligibility criteria, and how to claim fee reductions, please visit:

https://apcentral.collegeboard.org/ap-coordinators/exam-ordering-fees/exam-fees/reductions

For more information about financial aid, contact the AP coordinator at your school.

For more information on anything related to the AP program, visit https://apcentral.collegeboard.com or contact AP Services:

AP Services

P.O. Box 6671

Princeton, NJ 08541-6671

Email: apstudents@info.collegeboard.org

Phone: 877-274-6474 (toll-free in the US and Canada) or 212-632-1781

Fax: 610-290-8979

Homeschoolers

Homeschoolers and other alternative learners can take advantage of the AP Program the same way on-site students can. For more information on how homeschoolers or alternative learners can participate in the AP program, including access to fee reductions and financial aid, visit https://blog.collegeboard.org/college-planning-help-homeschoolers

What to Bring to the Exam

To reduce anxiety, it is important that you come prepared on the day of the exam. Here is a list of items you will need:

- **Several sharpened No. 2 pencils** (with erasers) for all responses on their multiple-choice answer sheet
- **Pens with black or dark-blue ink** for completing areas on the exam booklet covers and for free-response questions in most exams

- **A current government-issued or school-issued photo ID** (Additional ID may be required by authorized test centers outside the United States)
- **A watch** that does not beep or have an alarm (in case the exam room does not have a clock that can be easily seen)
- If applicable, **SSD Student Accommodation Letter** which verifies that you have been approved for a testing accommodation such as Braille or large-type exams

Prohibited Items on AP Exam Day

- **Electronic equipment:** phone, smartphone, smartwatch, laptop, tablet computer, portable listening or recording devices (MP3 player, iPod, etc.), cameras or other photographic equipment, devices that can access the Internet, and any other electronic or communication devices
- **Unapproved aids:** books, compasses, protractors, mechanical pencils, correction fluid, dictionaries, highlighters*, notes or colored pencils*
- **Scratch paper:** notes must be made on portions of the exam booklets
- **Watches that beep** or have an alarm, or smartwatches
- **Computers***
- **Reference guides, keyboard maps** or other typing instructions
- **Clothing with subject-related information**
- **Food or drink***

* Unless this has been preapproved as an accommodation by the College Board Services for Students with Disabilities office prior to the exam date.

Additional Resources to Help You Prepare

Using Your Textbook Effectively

For most students, their first content resource will be their textbooks. Textbooks convey material in a standard manner, though they often differ in their areas of emphasis as well as the features they offer. Many texts now come standard with access to a website where you can get chapter summaries, take quizzes, find links to other useful resources, and even obtain feedback on practice essays that you write.

Just because a textbook is your main resource shouldn't prevent you from employing other useful resources, such as reference works, additional readings, periodicals, online materials, or even literature. For your convenience, each chapter in this text includes a list of carefully cultivated resources to raise your interest and understanding, and help you get that extra point. Certainly, it is possible for you to succeed on the exam simply by making effective use of your textbook, but if you find other sources enlightening, convenient, or interesting, your teacher will probably not discourage and is likely to encourage them as a way to get a better feel for what you are learning. **NOTE:** It is NOT your textbook that defines the parameters of the course but the College Board Course and Exam Description (see below). Any material in the Unit Guides (except for the illustrative examples in the left margin) is fair game for a test item. However, this works in your favor too: if the specific term is not in the Unit Guide, it cannot be the answer for a MC question.

AP Central

Your contact point for the latest information regarding the AP program is the official site of the College Board: apcentral.collegeboard.org. Any basic questions you have related to the administration of the exam, its scoring, policies, and others can be found at this website. If you are a senior or would simply like to know policies of particular universities related to AP credit, the site features links to hundreds of colleges that can guide your decision making regarding AP credits you've earned.

In addition, you can access subject specific materials through the course home pages (easily found from the general home page). Some of the materials and sites are geared to teachers, but you will find materials of benefit to students as well.

Internet Resources

Many students find that they are savvier Internet users than their teachers. Certainly, the Internet has opened new sources of information, particularly related to history, unknown to historians and students of history in years past. However, the Internet is a tool like any other and should be used judiciously to meet the appropriate need. Before you rely too heavily on any specific site—say one that you found using one of the major search engines like Google or Bing—you should ensure that the site is reliable and authoritative. Those sites affiliated with a known college or university, or perhaps sponsored by a teacher of the course, may prove useful to your studying. With that in mind, I have listed below some websites that have been helpful to me and my students in the past.

⌨ **https://apstudents.collegeboard.org/ap/pdf/ap-european-history-course-and-exam-description.pdf** — From the College Board site, this Course and Exam Description is the official statement of the curriculum of the course. It is your go-to source for required knowledge and skills.

⌨ **http://www.historyteacher.net/APEuroCourse/APEuroCourseMainPage.htm** — This site is one of the best by a teacher of the course—Susan Pojer, from Horace Greeley High School in Chappaqua, NY—and contains extensive review materials, practice DBQs, and links to other sources.

⌨ **http://eudocs.lib.byu.edu/index.php/Main_Page** — This site offers a thorough collection of primary sources organized by nation, and also includes a section titled "Europe as a Supranational Region" for those applicable to the continent as a whole.

⌨ **https://sourcebooks.fordham.edu/mod/modsbook.asp** — Perhaps the best resource for primary sources related to European history. You will find the site more user-friendly than the one above and the chronological organization easier to follow. The site carries classics, like Luther's Ninety-Five Theses, but also includes interesting nuggets you're unlikely to find elsewhere.

⌨ **http://www.phschool.com/curriculum_support/map_bank/** — This site provides blank maps from a variety of historical eras that can be used to chart the shifting political balance of power in Europe.

⌨ **https://omniatlas.com/** — An interactive site that allows users to chart most changes of the map of Europe (and the world) in the modern era.

⌨ **http://spartacus-educational.com/** — An encyclopedic database for modern history; this site is easy to navigate and effective for research projects.

⌨ **http://www.johndclare.net/** — This site provides interpretations and sources on major topics in twentieth-century diplomatic and political history. Can be simplistic at times.

⌨ **www.wga.hu/index.html** — Even if art isn't one of your favorite areas of history, you will find this easily searchable site a treasure of visual images. You can search chronologically or alphabetically by artist for paintings, sculpture, or architecture. In addition, you can use a special feature to place images side-by-side for comparison. The site, however, is limited to the period before 1900.

⌨ **http://www.artchive.com/** — Excellent searchable site for art that covers the ground thoroughly, if you can stand the prevalence of ads and pop-ups.

Of course, the above list is only a small sampling of sites available. As you read through the content review in Section II, you will find additional suggestions for resources. With modern search engines at your fingertips, many more sites are waiting to be discovered for the motivated. Though these sites can be fun and useful, keep in mind that the rules of citation and rendering proper credit still apply. If you use one of these sites for research, make sure that you supply a bibliography and give proper credit, advice that applies to all of your studies and academic work. Help in formatting bibliographies can be found at **easybib.com** or at the Purdue Online Writing Lab, **https://owl.purdue.edu/**.

Companion Resources from Sherpa Learning

As a small, independent publisher, Sherpa Learning is focused on developing high-quality resources specifically for the Advanced Placement History and English courses. Check out these other amazing resources for AP Euro.

NEED MORE HELP...

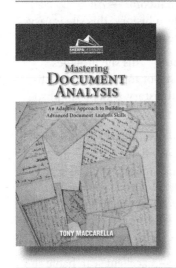

CHAPTER 2

Strategies for Success

How to Use This Review Guide

This review book is intended to supplement, not replace, your textbook. Yet, you will find that any major topic covered within the course or on the exam will be addressed here. As you read and study, make sure that you connect content (e.g., key persons, events, artworks, books, etc.) to the course themes, historical thinking skills (HTS), and key concepts (KCs). The study strategies covered here should improve your comprehension as you move through your daily reading and prepare for quizzes and exams.

Another way you can employ this guide is to use the content review in Section II prior to any assessment, particularly the AP exam. To test your knowledge and apply HTS, try the sets of MC questions and the SAQ or LEQ at the end of each chapter. Following each historical period, you will encounter a diagnostic exam, including 30 MC questions, 2 SAQs, a DBQ, and an LEQ. To help you develop critical writing skills, you will also find sample essays that provide insight into how the exam is scored, as well as indicators of effective strategies and common errors. As you read these essays, your skill in determining the score for each sample should improve, an indication that you are understanding the features of a powerful essay.

As you approach the exam, perhaps starting with your spring break or around late March, you should become more serious about breaking down what you have learned into more manageable chunks for review. Go back to those chapters that you have already covered and refresh your memory with some practice questions. As you near the test date, you should attempt one or both of the full practice tests, using the timing guidelines indicated in Chapter 1. This practice will help you get a feel for the emotional and psychological stresses of the test and be better prepared on the day of the exam. Finally, one of the last items you should review is the full chronological scope of the course, including the timelines in the Appendix. Make sure you can place art movements, social developments, intellectual changes, wars, etc. in the appropriate chronological period, as well as explain the rationale for such periodization schemes. As with any resource, this review guide should prove as helpful as you are willing to make it.

The Historical Thinking Skills

All three AP history subjects (US, European, World) now share the same language of historical thinking skills (HTS) and reasoning processes (RP). These skills are used both to shape test construction and to guide your approach to the subject. Warning: It is not sufficient simply to know content without the ability to apply that content knowledge in demonstration of deeper thinking about the discipline of history. In short, you should consider yourself an apprentice historian rather than a mere reciter of information. On one hand, the focus on HTS creates challenges, but on the other, it makes the course more engaging, especially in that you are expected to approach history as a contested argument over interpretations and evidence. Let's look at the HTS and RP and how they will shape your approach to the subject matter.

Just as science takes as its raw material the natural world, history similarly engages with a "raw material" to drive its investigation. For historians, these materials are both the primary sources of the past (letters, government documents, art, speeches, objects, etc.) and also other historians' interpretations on a topic of study. If you were to investigate, say, the reform of cities around the turn of the twentieth century, it would make sense to begin with relevant sources—maps, architectural treatises, grievances from urbanites, data on infectious diseases. Before focusing your research, you'd want to situate your investigation and subsequent writing in the ongoing literature produced by other historians on that topic, known as historiography. Then you would attempt to answer a question in that field or even pose a new question. Though you won't likely complete this process in the AP European History course, you will simulate that methodology in your studies and on the AP exam. Below you will find explanations and demonstrations of each of the HTS and RPs that will be used to organize the course content and drive test items. (Please take note of the abbreviations that follow for future use.)

Developments and Processes (DAP)

As you progress through the course, you will notice that specific terminology and concepts will emerge and recur. These terms transcend isolated people and events, instead indicating developments and processes in need of specific conceptual definitions and an understanding of their role in driving human activity over time. To make that abstraction more concrete, let's consider the notion of a "commercial revolution." Some historians argue that an early revolution in commerce occurred during the High Middle Ages (twelfth and thirteenth centuries), others that it emerged along with exploration and colonization in the fifteenth and sixteenth centuries. Whatever the timing, you will need to articulate, *specifically*, what features comprise the commercial revolution, such as the expansion in the type and volume of goods exchanged; the institutions that promoted the expansion; and the way in which this trade impinged upon cultural transmission, consumer habits, social dynamics, and how these changed over time. As a practical matter, rather than focusing on the mere accumulation of facts (what I call a "flashcard" mentality), instead try defining as precisely as possible, the critical points around which each unit of study revolves. In testing terms, you will be expected on a multiple-choice question, for example, to recognize in the stimulus the characteristics of the commercial revolution (or the Renaissance, *Realpolitik*, feminism, etc.) to determine the correct answer. Moreover, when you are conceptually defining developments and processes, you will be well on your way to writing a strong introductory paragraph to your DBQs and LEQs, as they will be centered on one of these critical historical trends. As you read through this text, you will notice that I have tried to provide such definitions to aid your conceptual construction of history.

Sourcing and Situation (SAS)

Very few historical documents speak for themselves; they require interpretation and context. Prior to using a document as *evidence for a claim*, historians first consider the document's source and type. For example, if investigating the origins of the French Revolution and examining letters from the monarch as evidence, you would not consider the source as a *fact in itself*. After all, monarchs may provide only a perspective from above, without knowledge of how their policies affect various groups or individuals. And of course, they will view government policy from the perspective of dynastic rule and what's best for their or the state's interests. Documents from monarchs are useful to the historian, but more so to reveal the attitudes and perceptions of decision-makers, maybe even to reveal the discrepancy between their perspectives and those of their subjects, rather than a straightforward identification of cause. More will be shared below on specific strategies for analyzing sources in the DBQ section.

Claims and Evidence in Sourcing (CES)

Both primary and secondary sources make arguments or claims. For example, Martin Luther's famous 95 Theses makes claims regarding the situation and teachings of the Catholic Church in the sixteenth century. A secondary source, like Daniel Headrick's history of European imperialism, attempts to portray the negative political and cultural effects on Africa and Asia resulting from the introduction of new technologies, such as railroads. In each case, the historian's job is not to treat these assertions as *facts*, but as *claims*, albeit claims relying on (often substantial) evidence. Approaching sources (both primary and secondary) with this type of critical posture reminds us that history is primarily an *interpretive* discipline. Whenever encountering an argument in this course, you should always consider the other evidence you've learned to weigh and evaluate those claims. On any of the test items you are presented, you will be asked to make and evaluate historical claims and the evidence that is used to both support and to modify or contradict those claims. Though this and the SAS skill may sound very similar, CES deals with how a source serves as *evidence for a claim*, whereas SAS considers a source as *evidence per se*.

Contextualization (CTX)

Contextualization is both the most basic and subtle of the historical thinking skills. Whenever a historian encounters a source or new fact, they will survey (probably without even being aware of the process) what they know on the topic, attempting to place it within an already existing structure of knowledge. For example, let's suppose you come across a source from a Spanish official (known as a *corregidor*) to the Spanish monarch, around 1550, regarding local grievances directed against high taxes and inflation. In interpreting this source, you may consider developments at the local, national, regional, and global levels. The chart below provides a shorthand version of this process.

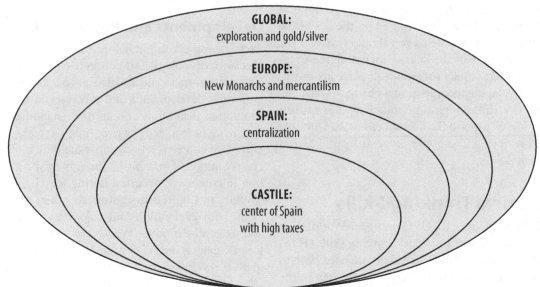

GLOBAL:
exploration and gold/silver

EUROPE:
New Monarchs and mercantilism

SPAIN:
centralization

CASTILE:
center of Spain
with high taxes

As you progress through the course and attend to its themes and key concepts, this subtle inferential process will become more ingrained and apparent to you. Can you see how the chart above may help with interpreting and understanding the hypothetical document above?

Making Connections (MAC)

Whenever you encounter a person, event, or document in a history course, you should consider: Why is it important? To what developments in this or other eras does it relate? How does this fact reveal an ongoing issue or conflict in my course? When you address these types of questions, you are making connections, the heart and soul of historical thinking. For the purposes of test items, you establish your connections through making comparisons, drawing on context, and synthesizing your understanding into a coherent, broader picture. Historians make relevant (and interesting) connections across time, geographic regions, themes, and source types, all in an effort to detect patterns in the past and as a guide to understanding present conditions. As you become more familiar with argumentative writing, you will practice strategies designed to earn you the "complexity" point on the DBQ and LEQ. To earn this point, you must establish a connection that extends, amplifies, or modifies your thesis by considering its application in a related setting. Imagine you are writing a constructed response (DBQ or LEQ) on the issue of absolutism during the seventeenth century and you now want to extend your thesis. The diagram below illustrates several strategies you can use to do this.

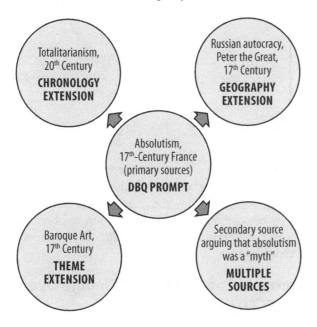

Any of these strategies, if clearly and substantively explained, will demonstrate your skill in making connections and thinking outside of the limited parameters of the prompt.

Argumentation (ARG)

The primary task of historians is to engage with and generate arguments, not to write textbooks. We can compare historical arguments to scientific theories. Arguments in both fields take a position (as in testing a hypothesis), defend the argument with evidence (science uses natural observations while history uses documents and artifacts), and must be falsifiable. This last point means that another historian could theoretically challenge the original historian's argument, just like a scientific hypothesis might be disproven with experimental evidence. For example, a historian might claim that the Industrial Revolution produced economic, social, and political problems; however, though patently true, this claim would generally not constitute an argument, at least not among historians who study industrialization. Why? Because this statement is obvious to even the casual reader of reports of early factory conditions. If, on the other hand, a historian were to claim that by 1850, Britain experienced an increased standard of living due to industrialization, this statement would establish an argument, as it is a contested topic among historians. Further, the truth or falsity of this argument will depend on the type of evidence consulted—statistics on prices of products, accounts of working conditions, maps charting the spread of disease, census data, reform legislation, et al. In other words, if you were to take a position on this question, you would be producing a historical argument.

For both the DBQ and LEQ, you will be expected to establish a position (or argument) that you can defend, with evidence, throughout your essay. Once again, it should be a position with which another writer could disagree. To cite one more instance: take the question of war guilt and the First World War. Article 231 from the Versailles Treaty established Germany's sole guilt for the war—the first "official" historical interpretation on the war's causes and one with profound political implications (e.g., rise of the Nazi Party and World War II). If you were acting as an amateur historian, you could clearly take issue with the "war guilt" clause and establish a rival interpretation. Perhaps you might emphasize the buildup of tensions over decades, consider diplomatic correspondence of other powers, or better yet, go beyond "responsibility" and emphasize the arms race, the dysfunctional structure of diplomacy, or growing tensions in the Balkans. Whatever position you take, your choice will dictate the type of evidence you consider or stress.

The primary task of historians is to generate arguments and interpretations, not simply chronicle the past. Take the Cold War, for example. A highly charged event, it was first interpreted in the 1940s and 1950s by American historians as attributable to traditional Russian expansionism, a Marxist inclination toward world revolution, and perhaps the paranoia of Stalin. However, as classified documents from the early Cold War were released and American foreign policy in Vietnam came under increasing criticism, historians developed a revisionist perspective emphasizing American economic dominance (exercised through the Marshall Plan), its nuclear monopoly, and the weakness of the Soviet Union. By the end of the Cold War (1989–1991), historians moved beyond the question of mere responsibility (US vs. Soviet) to focus on the process of competition between two rival ideologies and politico-economic systems and the cycle of misperception and overreaction. On the exam, you will not be required to know any one particular viewpoint or school of interpretation, but you need to be prepared to recognize and evaluate various historical arguments on major events and developments.

Reasoning Processes

To effectively employ the HTS discussed above, students will need to hone essential reasoning processes, or cognitive abilities, as explained below.

Comparison (COMP)

In comparing two items, we learn more about both of them, as many of the features we had taken for granted when viewed in isolation now become more prominent by being placed side-by-side with another relevant item. Historical thinking means drawing comparisons between nations or regions, between different periods or eras, and between contemporaneous developments or trends. If you are charged with comparing two or more items, make certain that you address both <u>similarities</u> and <u>differences</u>, though you may emphasize one or the other. Also, appropriate comparisons should be between "apples and apples," i.e., explaining economic causes of the French and Russian Revolution, rather than, say, economic causes for one and intellectual causes for the other. Though basic, a standard Venn diagram will help to organize your thoughts before setting out with your analysis. Consider the following example:

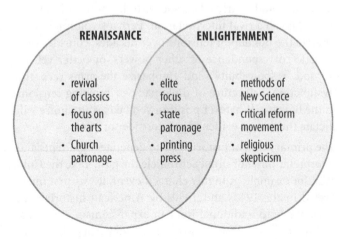

With these similarities and differences briefly and quickly established, you are now prepared to respond to a possible SAQ, DBQ, or LEQ comparing these two key cultural movements.

Causation (CAUS)

We live in a world of causation (excluding quantum physics), and it is the job of the historian to examine the often complex processes that give rise to important events or developments. Given its nature, the skill of causation can be applied to almost any historical inquiry. Historians often divide causation into long- and short-term causes. It is not enough merely to identify a range of causes, rather you should provide a persuasive account of how such causes interacted to produce an event. Let's look at one of the most important and highly charged debates over historical causation—the French Revolution. The chart below provides a high-level overview of what the historian might consider in analyzing this issue.

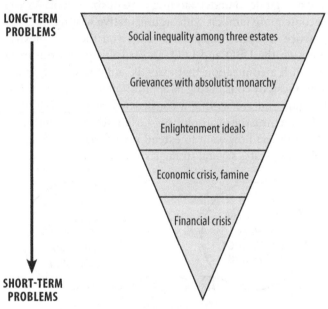

So, if the financial crisis sparked the French Revolution, it remains for the historian to explain the manner in which events unfolded, and how the course of events was influenced by the combination and interaction of other causes that underlay the immediate problems the monarchy attempted to address in 1788–1789.

Patterns of Continuity and Change Over Time (CCOT)

We tend to emphasize change in considering the past; after all, we are eager to explain how we arrived at our current state from what seem like differing circumstances centuries ago. However, as the course themes will remind us, many issues echo throughout the centuries, just in differing contexts. For example, let's consider the issue of industrialization. If you traveled Europe around 1840, you would find pockets of widespread transformation (Britain, Belgium, parts of Germany, cities in France) in the methods of manufacturing and transporting goods. These new patterns of production marked a seismic shift for some in the nature of work—not simply conditions, but also control over the pace and manner of work. However, for many areas of Europe (Russia, southern Italy, central Spain), these new trends seemed remote because agricultural practices continued much as they had for centuries. Even within moments of change, much can remain guided by traditional practices and ideas. Though women participated in the Renaissance, Reformation, and Scientific Revolution, these movements of intellectual and cultural change left attitudes toward gender relatively unaffected, despite sparking debates over women's nature and proper role in society. When you encounter a question of CCOT, remember to note both what changed, what remained the same, and, most importantly, provide an explanation for the diverse outcomes.

The reasoning process of CCOT also bears on the issue of periodization—that is, the way in which historians characterize or label the past. A popular term for the eighteenth-century Enlightenment is the "age of reason," a label which privileges the changes occurring, particularly in the lives of those wealthy enough to partake in salons, coffeehouses, and printed materials common to mostly urban areas. The traditional religious or other belief systems of other, perhaps marginalized, groups in society will be overlooked by this label as unworthy of study or an artifact of a retrograde mindset. When you come across such labels, do not accept them without critical analysis or without considering a range of evidence from varying perspectives.

Reading Strategies

Your primary content source for this course is likely to be your textbook. Chances are, you will find yourself spending about 30–60 minutes per day reading about 7–10 pages in it. It is important that you get the most out of the time you spend reading. My experience as a teacher has shown me that many students do not read as effectively as possible because they lack strategies that can increase their comprehension. Such strategies need not add significantly to your homework, but the extra 5 minutes or so that you spend with them will pay dividends in the long run, both in your performance and in saving time later.

First, you will need to find a time and place that is conducive to your studying. For many students, this is a quiet place with few distractions, but not necessarily the most comfortable, such as your bed, where you are liable to become drowsy or lose concentration. Many studies confirm that multitasking is a myth, so I strongly recommend that when reading, you shut off/down your laptop, phone, social media, and other electronic devices. Do no try to multitask while you study. Several years ago, one of my students raised his grade in my class from a B to an A and reduced his homework time in

all of his classes by 50% simply by focusing with all of his attention on the task directly in front of him. Beyond the improvements in performance, you may find that bringing focus and intensity to what you're doing produces the side benefit of enhancing your enjoyment of it as well.

One way to make reading and studying more engaging is to avoid reading passively, as if history were a story that "speaks for itself." Certainly there is an element of story and drama in history, particularly at its best, but this is usually not the format of most textbooks. Most are written in a fairly standard format with a set of analytical cues, which with some practice, you can pick up on and become adept at deciphering.

A textbook chapter often begins with a hook—a story, personality, event, work of art—that is designed to grab the reader's attention. Beneath the flowery language, the authors are trying to convey the themes, or main ideas, of the chapter. Challenge yourself to identify what the big picture is before you continue with your reading. Other texts begin with a more standard introduction to the chapter content and themes. Perhaps it would be helpful to write out 1–2 sentences based on this introduction that summarize the key points covered in the chapter. This could be done immediately after reading the introduction or after completing the entire chapter. It is vital in your reading that you focus on the Big Picture—defining key terms, identifying cause and effect, linking to previous topics, practicing HTS, and connecting specific content to course themes and period key concepts.

Though there are numerous strategies, not all work as well for each student. Feel free to experiment with strategies until you find those that work well for you. Whatever you do, make sure that you are actively reading your text, much as a builder constructs a scaffolding or framework of a house, before moving on to the siding, roof, interior. The difference is that your scaffolding acts as an analytical structure for your understanding of the entire chapter. To assist you in this process, I have included several specific strategies below to get you started. Keep in mind that there is nothing magical about these strategies; their positive effect depends on your perseverance in developing skills of historical analysis and working at connecting the specific content of the course to the Big Picture.

Scaffolding and Annotating

How do you get started with a scaffold? History revolves more around asking productive questions than having the right answers. Again, you are encouraged to focus on the interpretive issues prompted by historical moments and, further, to anticipate possible essay prompts (including DBQs) by thinking of arguments that you could make with the evidence that you encounter. Begin your reading each night with an overarching question that you will attempt to answer when you've finished with the reading. For example, you may be reading about the religious wars of the sixteenth and seventeenth centuries; a good place to begin would be to ask "what caused the religious wars?" This question will generally lead to further sub-questions. Remember, you will invariably find the answers to your questions within the text itself.

Suppose that you are reading about the Italian Renaissance. In the passage below, from a former course textbook, the authors introduce some interpretive issues, provide an explanation of cause and effect, and identify important conceptual terms. I've marked up the passage to provide an idea of how to engage a text. Keep in mind that what follows is *one* way to approach a text and should not be considered a foolproof formula. (The selection has been taken from Kishlansky, Mark, Patrick Geary, and Patricia O'Brien, *Civilization in the West*, 6/e (New York: Pearson/Longman, 2006), p. 324. It has been streamlined for this exercise.)

Perhaps the most surprising result of the Black Death was the way in which European society revived itself in the succeeding centuries. Even at the height of the plague, a spirit of revitalization was evident in the works of artists and writers.[1] **Petrarch** (1304–1374), the great humanist poet and scholar, was among the first to differentiate the new age in which he was living from two earlier ones: the **classical world of Greece and Rome**, which he admired, and the subsequent Dark Ages, which he detested.[2] That spirit of **self-awareness** is one of the defining characteristics of the Renaissance.[3] "It is but in our own day that men dare boast that they see the dawn of better things," wrote Matteo Palmieri (1406–1475). Like many others, Marsilio Ficino (1433–1499), a Florentine physician and philosopher who translated Plato and dabbled in astrology, dubbed his times a golden age: "This century, like a golden age, has restored to light the **liberal arts**, which were almost extinct: grammar, poetry, rhetoric, painting, sculpture, architecture, and music."[4] The Renaissance was a new age by **self-assertion**. In that self-assertion, wave after wave of artistic celebration of the **human spirit** found its wellspring and created a legacy that is still vibrant 500 years later.[5]

What was the Renaissance? A French word for an Italian phenomenon, renaissance literally means "rebirth." The word captures both the emphasis on humanity that characterized Renaissance thinking and the renewed fascination with the classical world.[6] But the *Renaissance was an age rather than an event. There is no moment at which the Middle Ages ended, and late medieval society was artistically creative, socially well developed, and economically diverse.*[7] Yet eventually the pace of change accelerated, and it is best to think of the Renaissance as an era of rapid transitions. Encompassing the two centuries between 1350 and 1550, it passed through three distinct phases. The first, from **1350 to 1400**, was characterized by a declining population, the uncovering of classical texts, and experimentation in a variety of art forms. The

NOTES

1 Many AP textbooks begin with a chapter on the Late Middle Ages. Here the authors attempt to connect a major defining event of that period with the topic they wish to explain—the Renaissance. This introduces the reader to one of reasoning process of CCOT throughout the passage.

2 If you were to consult the AP Course and Exam Description (CED), you would see that Petrarch is required content and therefore someone you should recall, in this case, not just for what he did or wrote but how he influenced and reflected the Renaissance. Considering the text itself, a good measure of importance is the space dedicated to a person or other example.

3 Petrarch introduces an interesting interpretive question: Did the Renaissance represent a genuine break from the Middle Ages? When you read through your textbook chapter on this topic, it will be useful to keep this question in mind and consider the content as evidence for whatever claim you might make on that issue. It's always a good idea to consider moments of transformation and be able to evaluate the extent to which they may (or may not) have altered the course of history.

4 The figures and their quotes call attention to the thematic focus of this section: Cultural and Intellectual Developments. In fact, the topic of the Renaissance will form the basis for many of the issues addressed by this theme throughout the course: secularism, relation to the classical past, and artistic techniques and motifs.

5 A student could bog down in the second half of this paragraph. No need to memorize the quotes; instead, connect them to the bolded terms, which provide definitions of the Renaissance. Further, the brief reference to astrology reminds us that not all ideas revived during the Renaissance would be considered "modern" today.

6 Here the authors provide further definitions of the Renaissance, suggesting the word most associated with it: "humanism," or an emphasis on human achievement and secular concerns of this world.

7 Almost all generalizations can be qualified, and your ability to do that will not only show your sophistication in historical analysis, it will also earn you points on the writing rubrics. In the italicized section, we return to the interpretive question of whether the Renaissance represents a distinct break with the medieval cultural legacy.

second phase, from **1400 to 1500**, was distinguished by the <u>creation of a set of cultural values and artistic and literary achievements that defined Renaissance style</u>. The large Italian <u>city-states developed stable and coherent forms of government</u>, and the warfare between them gradually ended. In the final period, from **1500 to 1550**, <u>invasions</u> from France and Spain <u>transformed Italian political life</u>, and the <u>ideas and techniques</u> of Italian writers and artists <u>radiated to all points of the Continent</u>. Renaissance ideas and achievements spread throughout western Europe... but they are best studied where they first developed, on the Italian peninsula.[8]

8 To conclude this passage, the authors provide a chronological division and identify the characteristics of each, ending with the connection between Italy and the rest of Europe. Once again, this attention to historical periodization reminds you of the interpretive question of CCOT: Is the relationship between medieval and renaissance more accurately viewed as an "era of rapid transitions" or "the creation of a set of [new] cultural values..."? As you read the remainder of this theoretical chapter, your attention is best focused on these analytical questions—where you can annotate or outline—rather than merely accumulating isolated terms, which will confuse you and mire your reading.

In the chapter introduction above, I have underlined important terms and analytical statements that help home in on the main points of the chapter. At first, these may be more difficult for you to locate, particularly if you are accustomed to thinking of history as "fact-driven" rather than "analysis-" and "interpretation-driven" as historians do. Though many students rely on highlighting texts, I strongly urge you to annotate instead. The underscoring above was used to draw your attention to the relevant portions of the text, but if reading for myself, I would selectively underline and then make margin notes, in an effort to keep a running outline that demands my continuous engagement with the text. Though the annotations beside the introduction above are fairly detailed, try your hand at using basic phrases, such as "classical world" or "human spirit" that will serve to remind you of these concepts when you later return to study this material. Think of yourself as *creating* meaning rather than *absorbing* it. Comprehension relies on asking productive questions and then seeking the answers to those questions.

Let's anticipate some possible essay prompts by creating some questions based on both the passage and perhaps subsequent material in a chapter on this topic:

- To what extent and in what ways did the Renaissance differ culturally from the Middle Ages?

- Why did the Renaissance begin first and take root in Italy?

- To what extent did the Renaissance change the arts, politics, and culture?

- What social factors, such as class or gender, limited the reach of the Renaissance?

- In what ways did the Renaissance anticipate or lay the foundations for the modern world?

These questions represent a high level of analysis and thinking for a student just beginning this course. Think of them as a goal at which to aim. Keep in mind that you need not specifically write out the answers to each question, though

as you can see from the annotation above, questions of this nature were in mind as I marked up the text. As a general rule, you should spend 2–3 minutes prior to reading, constructing such questions and about 5 minutes when you've completed the reading creating a brief outline to review what you have read. Rushing through the reading and flipping your book closed is of little use in the long run. Reviewing immediately after reading will reinforce what you have learned and help you more easily erect future scaffolding for the next reading assignment. Studies show that unless you both focus while reading and reinforce by studying, your comprehension and retention will not likely transfer from your working memory (the cognitive tasks at hand) to your long-term memory. To assist you in your efforts at creating useful yet easily managed outlines, I have included a sample at the end of this imagined chapter section with connections to HTS and course themes (see Chapter 3 for theme narratives and abbreviations).

Middle Ages to Renaissance (HTS: CCOT; Theme: CID)

+ Role of Black Death

+ Petrach as key figure

+ Defining features: self-awareness, liberal arts, humanism

+ Astrology as qualification to Renaissance as "modern"

Definition of Renaissance (HTS: DAP)

+ Rebirth

+ Emphasis on humanity and its potential

+ Classical world

Chronological and Geographical Scope (HTS: CCOT, CAUS, MAC)

+ "Age rather than event"

+ "Series of rapid transitions"

+ 1350–1400: declining population, recovery of classics, artistic experimentation

+ 1400–1500: new set of cultural values and achievements, stable city-states

+ 1500–1550: warfare, decline in Italy, spread to north

An outline of this type can be completed briefly as you read, though you should avoid making it too extensive, as this will render it less effective as a subsequent study tool, and, at some point, adding to it defeats its purpose as a distillation of what you have read. Please take note of the multiple times I've called out and connected the content to the HTS/RP and Themes. Not only will this help build your mastery of the course, it will also render your reading and studying more interesting by orienting you toward connections and analysis, rather than painful and fruitless memorization and recall.

Before we move on to other strategies, we need to address another often-neglected feature of most textbooks—visuals, such as maps, charts, cartoons, primary sources. Many students tend to view these items as pleasant breaks from the monotony of a full page of double-column text. Though they do offer a break, they also serve an important purpose in reinforcing the major themes of the unit. It is a truism that we learn best by what we hear *and* see, rather than either by itself. Think of these non-text items as visual cues for the historical era under study. Again, you can ask useful questions and jot down answers next to the sources themselves:

- How does this map represent the political situation of Europe in _____?

- What about this painting reflects the concerns of the era?

- How does this political cartoon show conflicts or issues important to this period?

- What data in this chart helps me understand the developments of this chapter?

- Why was this primary source chosen as a representation of chapter themes?

Primary sources, such as those noted above, drive test items on the AP exam, which makes it imperative for you to practice interpreting them. In fact, if you engage with the sources and visuals in your text substantively, you are very likely to encounter these or similar sources on exam items, either in your class or on the AP exam.

Consider what use you might make of the following chart.

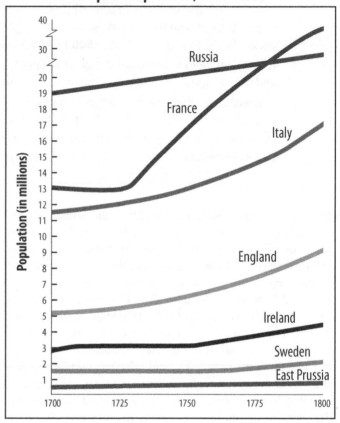

European Population, 1700–1800

This simple population chart provides you with some essential information regarding demographic changes over a century. Population movements coincide with economic, political, and social developments. Try to identify and explain the factors that caused the patterns on the chart, both over time and also by geography. By linking visuals to content in this way, you both sharpen your skills of visual analysis and reinforce your thematic understanding of a particular period in history. Finally, you can anticipate questions that might arise from this chart based on the HTS:

- What factors caused the population patterns in the eighteenth century (CAUS)?

- Compare and contrast population trends based on nation or region (COMP).

- Explain how these patterns changed over time, e.g., why a stronger increase after about 1720 (CCOT).

- What other developments during the eighteenth century do these trends reflect (CTX)?

- What historical eras might be defined, in part, by these trends, e.g., the Enlightenment (MAC)?

Timelines and the Importance of Chronology

Perhaps like my students, one of the first questions you asked in your AP European history class was, "Do we have to know dates?" There are two parts to the answer. First, the course and the exam do *not* test your knowledge of trivia. Dates and the events that occurred on them are generally not important in and of themselves. That's the easy answer. The second part is more nuanced. Chronology is essential to the understanding of history; in fact, without it, the fundamental historical tasks of analyzing cause-effect relationships, making connections across topic areas, and dealing with historical periods would be impossible. So yes, you must have a strong grasp of chronology to perform well in the course and on the exam. This will involve knowledge of historical eras, as well as some dates.

To see why chronology plays this key role in your understanding, let's look at a Long Essay Question:

Analyze the impact of global trade on European diplomacy and society in the period, 1650–1763.

Clearly if you have little or no knowledge of the developments in this period, you will be unable to address this question. There are few cues in the prompt itself, other than an assumption that global trade influenced diplomacy and society. The dates in the question were chosen with a purpose, probably to encompass a particular historical era. What is the significance of 1650? This is approximately when the last of the religious wars (Thirty Years' War) ended, and it marks the beginning of the Age of Absolutism, also named after its dominant personality—the Age of Louis XIV. The latter date (1763) ends the Seven Years' War, the last of the major colonial conflicts prior to the French Revolution. Note also that this is a Causation question, since it asks you to explain how and why global trade *affected* two areas of life.

If you happened to remember that the seventeenth and eighteenth centuries corresponded with the Commercial Revolution, then you would be well-positioned to handle this prompt. This question, then, wants you to deal with the effects of the Commercial Revolution on diplomacy and society in the Age of Absolutism. With the competition for colonies and resources, along with the economic philosophy of mercantilism that emphasized scarcity, nations engaged in near-constant warfare to advance their power. These conflicts are often called the Commercial Wars. You needn't remember all of them, simply their nature and general results, e.g., on the balance of power. For the second part of the question (effects on society), you should think in terms of demographics (the study of populations); changes in class, family, and gender; and the development of a consumer culture.

Don't be concerned if you can't recall all of the details. It is enough for you to begin your essay with some specific historical context. This context serves as a useful way to ground your introductory paragraph and establish your control of the question, as well as earn you the Contextualization point on the DBQ and LEQ rubrics. A good portion of your studying, then, should involve reviewing the events and developments that define historical eras. For example, if you were asked, "What significant intellectual development occurred in the eighteenth century?" you should be able to answer: "the Enlightenment." This knowledge will act as your key to entering any given DBQ or LEQ.

To assist you in your mastery of historical chronology, the Appendix includes three different timelines, one of which is divided into topic areas, so that you can see not only the important developments, but also how these topics are connected. As you review the timelines, you will find it helpful to define the characteristics of a historical era (e.g., explain how Baroque art reflected the religious and political climate of seventeenth-century Europe). Remember that dates are markers—important primarily for how they delineate and define historical eras. Also keep in mind that questions may refer to centuries rather than dates. A century refers to the hundred years numerically prior to the number of the century (e.g., the sixteenth century covers the 1500s). It seems basic, but many students blunder on their essays owing to chronological lapses.

The timeline on the next page is a slice of chronology, about 70 years in length, which highlights developments for the seven course themes. As you peruse the data, look across the chart to establish connections, or threads, that tie together developments. For this example, I have already cross-referenced the themes with the Key Concepts (see Chapter 3 for further description) for Period 1 at the bottom of the timeline.

This timeline, which could be filled with more or less detail, provides cues that help you place the major events and developments in time and that characterize this particular slice of chronology. As is clear, the events and developments here mark those important movements that began your course—the Renaissance and Protestant Reformation. Just as you use landmarks and maps to guide your movement around geographical space, dates and timelines will assist you in marking historical eras, cause-and-effect patterns, and the themes of a historical period. You will find it helpful to make your own timelines, varying from general (perhaps for broad social developments) to more specific (the religious wars and French Revolution). Just keep in mind that the goal is always for you to see the big picture and how the trees make up the forest.

Timeline (1450–1535)

Theme	Events (with dates)
Interaction of Europe & World (INT)	Navigational and mapmaking advances; Portuguese exploration of African coast; 1492, Columbus's "discovery" of Americas; 1498, Vasco da Gama reaches India; 1519–1521, Cortez conquers Aztecs
Economic & Commercial Developments (ECD)	Decline of manorialism; Rise of commercial agriculture; COLUMBIAN EXCHANGE; Global trade begins with exploration; Price Revolution
Cultural & Intellectual Developments (CID)	1452, da Vinci born; 1473, Sistine Chapel built; High Renaissance-centered in Rome; Michelangelo's masterpieces; Erasmus' & More's Christian humanism; Spread of Renaissance to northern Europe; 1513, Machiavelli's *The Prince*; 1517, Luther's 95 Theses
States & Other Institutions of Power (SOP)	1417–1540s, RENAISSANCE PAPACY; 1453, Fall of Constantinople; 1453, End of the Hundred Years' War; 1478, Spanish Inquisition established; 1479, Ferdinand and Isabella unite Spain; 1492, *Reconquista* completed; RISE OF NEW MONARCHS; 1519–1556, Charles V as HRE
Social Organization & Development (SCD)	1454, Peace of Lodi; Decline of feudalism; POPULATION INCREASE (to ca. 1600); 1492, Jews expelled from Spain; Rise of nobility of the robe; Men and women occupy differing but complimentary productive tasks
National & European Identity (NEI)	Regional and noble opposition to central power; Colonial empires established; Growth of national churches
Technological & Scientific Development (TSI)	1450s, Development of printing press; Advances in cartography, ship design, navigation; MILITARY REVOLUTION

Year scale: 1450, 1455, 1460, 1465, 1470, 1475, 1480, 1485, 1490, 1495, 1500, 1505, 1510, 1515, 1520, 1525, 1530, 1535

KC 1.1: A humanist revival of classics introduced new artistic values and methods of knowledge.

KC 1.2: A weakened Church faced growing criticism and calls for reform.

KC 1.3: Driven by profits and technology, Europeans expanded overseas and established colonies.

KC 1.4: Medieval social and economic structures persisted despite the growth of global trade and a money economy.

KC 1.5: States attempted to centralize power within a competitive diplomatic structure.

Strategies for the Multiple-Choice Questions

Though Section I, Part A takes only 55 minutes of the exam's total time, the multiple choice questions count for 40% of your overall score. For some, this is a source of comfort; for others, fear. If you struggle with objective assessments, the goal of this review guide is not to persuade you to prefer them to writing, only that you can gain confidence and achieve higher scores with the right approaches.

All of the MC questions (for all three history subjects) are now based on stimulus material, meaning a source (either primary or secondary) that forms the basis for a set of questions (between 2 and 5). The source might be a text (pamphlet, speech, diary entry, treatise, etc.), chart or graph, photograph, artwork, map, political cartoon, drawing/etching, or an interpretation by a historian. Occasionally one of the set may not require the stimulus or assess skills only; however, these are exceptions. Given this structure, it is in your interest to practice reading and interpreting sources and work with stimulus questions before you take the AP exam, not to mention any unit tests in your course. Here is a Top Ten list of tips before we try a set:

1. Consider glancing briefly at the stem of each question *before* you engage the source, so that you can hunt for the answers as you read the stimulus.

2. Read the source attribution and source carefully and entirely before you determine its perspective. Look for nuances and subtleties, as these will often be referenced as the set unfolds.

3. Before even looking at the choices, quickly survey what you know about the topic or theme. This will become more intuitive as you practice.

4. Each question tests a specific HTS, so try to identify that skill and bring any strategies you've learned to the process of settling on the key.

5. Pick the BEST answer. All of the choices may appeal to you, since they are likely based on actual history, but go with the one that reflects BOTH the perspective of the source AND your content knowledge.

6. Don't worry about getting 100%; that's highly unlikely, and if you're a perfectionist, this expectation will only create anxiety and derail your intuitive thinking process for the test as a whole.

7. How many times have you changed an answer based on doubt, only to find later that you had the right answer the first time? Trust your gut!

8. Before you take MC exams, study from the Unit Guides of the Course Description. Every right answer must arise from the top and right section of the blue boxes—either directly, by paraphrase, or through inference.

9. Practice the many questions in this guide. Peruse the answer explanations (see Chapter 18) to help you sharpen your powers of deduction.

10. Outside-the-box suggestion: Find a source, and try to write your own set of questions, using the Unit Guides and HTS. This will help you gain insight into how the tests are constructed and provide you with "insider" strategic thinking.

Now let's try a set based on the visual prompt at the top of the next page. Consider what you see in and can infer from this image—content, style of presentation, purpose, symbolism, historical context, etc. When you're ready, read the set of 5 questions based on the image. Note: Each question has been correlated with the relevant HTS, course themes, and period key concepts.

Execution of witches, Germany, 1550s

1. The event depicted above best reflects which of the following intellectual features of early modern Europe?

   A. Belief in social hierarchy based on a Great Chain of Being

   B. Persistence of folk beliefs in supernatural causation

   C. Spread of Bible-reading due to the printing press

   D. Revival of classical texts that emphasized civic humanism

HTS: Developments and Processes (DAP) and Contextualization (CTX); Theme: CID; KC: 1.4. This is a standard contextualization question, since it asks you to draw on what you know about the period to determine the ways in which the image reflects, in this case, the intellectual atmosphere of early modern Europe, a CID course theme. If you consult the Unit Guides, you'll see that the correct answer (B) is drawn from Topic 2.6 and KC 1.4, specifically V.C. You may notice that choices A, C, and D are all true of the period, but they don't explain directly why witches were persecuted. For example, it is true that increased Bible reading reasserted belief in demons, but D is not as directly related to the image as is B.

2. All of the following social and economic developments contributed to the phenomenon portrayed above EXCEPT:

   A. the price revolution, which disrupted traditional patterns of economic activity.

   B. a significant increase in poverty and the associated problem of begging.

   C. leisure activities oriented around the agricultural cycle and church calendar.

   D. migration to cities that strained resources and challenged traditional elites.

HTS: Causation (CAUS); Themes: ECD and SCD; KC: 1.4. Here you have an EXCEPT question, of which there will likely be no more than 5–6 on any given test form. For this item type, you are looking for the one explanation that does not fit, which in this case is C. Again, all of the choices represent features of early modern economic and social life, but C does not relate directly to causing witchcraft accusations. Can you see why this is a Causation question? All of these factors helped, mostly indirectly, to create social dislocation and deepen the sense of crisis that found expression in witchcraft accusations.

3. A historian would most likely use the source above to make conclusions regarding:

    A. early modern attitudes toward women and magic.

    B. the impact of the religious wars on social stability.

    C. how artistic styles developed among the lower classes.

    D. the effect of centralized monarchies on the legal system.

HTS: Claims and Evidence in Sources (CES); Themes: CID and SCD; KCs: 1.1 and 1.4. This question involves your judgment, a faculty that will become more sharply honed with your practice in the course. You are asked to think like a historian and consider what type of evidence works best to answer particular historical questions. All of the choices might be related to the image; however, since the image addresses belief in magic and perceptions of women—the most common victims of witchcraft accusations—those constitute the most likely use of this piece of evidence (A). The other choices would require further historical context and corroboration from other sources to be of much use to a historian. Based on the choices, the question addresses both culture (CED) and gender (SCD) attitudes.

---

4. The situation of the main subjects in the image is most similar to:

    A. artistic geniuses, such as Michelangelo.

    B. religious minorities, such as the Anabaptists.

    C. humanist scholars, such as Machiavelli.

    D. new economic elites, such as the gentry.

HTS: Comparison (COMP) and Making Connections (MAC); Themes: CID and SCD; KC: 1.2. We deal with a historical comparison in this question: What other group might have faced a similar situation and perception as women did during the witchcraft phenomenon? One of the elements of the SCD course theme addresses the notion of "the Other," i.e., how groups can be alienated from the larger society through depictions, symbols, and forms of expression. Women were often targeted as witches because of gender beliefs emphasizing their lack of reason, credulity, and power over the human body. All but B represent individuals or groups of power and prestige. Anabaptists experienced persecutions by both Protestants and Catholics because their religious beliefs were considered outside the mainstream and a threat to the integrity of the state, similar to witches.

---

5. Which of the following most directly caused the end of the phenomenon depicted?

    A. Cessation of religious wars

    B. Columbian Exchange

    C. Scientific Revolution

    D. French Revolution

HTS: Change and Continuity Over Time (CCOT); Theme: TSI; KC: 1.1. This question asks how and why the witchcraft accusations ended, simply by listing several important developments or events. It counts on your implicit thinking process regarding change and continuity over time and also transformative moments, i.e., events that changed the way in which the world was viewed. Though all four choices can be argued as such moments, it was the Scientific Revolution (C) that most altered the explanation of causation, replacing supernatural explanations with materialism and mathematics. In this case, the question relates to the TSI theme and KC 1.1, the variation of that theme in Period 1.

In retrospect, you'll notice that this set of MC questions covers almost all of the HTS; however, most sets you encounter on the AP exam will likely involve 3–4 questions and cover a more limited range of HTS as in the example above. Here are the most common types:

- *Causation* – The content of the document will be either the result of a previous cause or itself the cause of a subsequent effect. Notice how Questions 2 and 5 in the set above function in this fashion.

- *Contextualization* – You are asked about how a source "reflects" or "demonstrates" features of an event, period, or development.

- *Developments and Processes (DAP)* – These types test your ability to recognize a historical process or development, like the existence of folk beliefs in Question 1.

- *Comparison* – Comparisons involve similarities and/or differences between two geographic areas, periods, or groups. These questions focus on your ability to make connections.

- *Change and Continuity Over Time (CCOT)* – Less common than the above types, these items ask you to consider how features of a topic might have remained the same or been altered chronologically.

- *Claims and Evidence in Sources (CES)* – Question 3 above represents this type, in which you are asked to think like a historian and also draw on your content knowledge to test the link between evidence and conclusion.

- *Making Connections (MAC)* – In these item types, you are asked to think outside the box and recognize a pattern, issue, or question in the stimulus and apply it to another setting or situation, as in Question 4.

- *Sourcing and Situation (SAS)* – Such types will be less common, but urge you to think like a historian when it comes to evidence, such as the bias or reliability behind the stimulus itself.

- *Argumentation* – Since argumentation involves the ability to make and evaluate arguments, this skill is generally not tested on the MC section of the exam.

Strategies for the Written Section of the Exam

Short-Answer Questions (SAQs)

With Short-Answer Questions (SAQs), you have an opportunity to demonstrate your facility with 1–2 targeted HTS and a course theme while drawing *briefly* on your content knowledge to address a three-part prompt. For these items, do *not* write an essay—avoid introductions, thesis statements, and conclusions. Don't elaborate your response beyond what is necessary to establish your grasp of the key concept and the content involved in the prompt. In fact, your response must be limited to one side of a sheet of paper defined by a lined box. Spare your energy and time for the set of 3 questions (not to mention the later DBQ and LEQ) by maintaining your focus on *what the item format demands*—brevity and concision.

SAQs may or may not involve stimulus. At least 2 of the set of 4 will be stimulus-based; since these tend to be more complicated, let's examine an example of such below. Read the following prompt, consider how you might respond, and then read the sample provided. Remember that each SAQ involves 3 score points, with no qualitative dimension, meaning you get the point or you don't. No extra points, no half-points, just 0 or 1.

Article 231

"The Allied and Associated Governments affirm and Germany accepts the responsibility of Germany and her allies for causing all the loss and damage to which the Allied and Associated Governments and their nationals have been subjected as a consequence of the war imposed upon them by the aggression of Germany and her allies."

Treaty of Versailles, between Allied Powers and Germany, June 1919

---

1. a) Describe one example from European diplomacy or politics in the period 1871–1914 that <u>supports</u> the interpretation above.

   b) Describe one example from European diplomacy or politics in the period 1871–1914 that <u>contradicts</u> the interpretation above.

   c) Explain one specific effect of the treaty provision above on European politics and diplomacy, 1919–1939.

As you consider this question, notice that it involves mainstream topics from your course: World War I, the Treaty of Versailles, and pre- and post-war diplomacy. You are presented with the "war guilt" clause from the Treaty of Versailles and asked to assess the validity of Article 231 by considering the origins of WWI *and* the effect of the treaty on postwar diplomacy. Notice that the question comprises 3 parts (as each SAQ will), and it is strongly suggested that you letter your response accordingly, as a clear indication to the AP reader and yourself that you are addressing all parts of the question. Now consider the following sample response and commentary:

a) Germany was mostly to blame for WWI, as Article 231 states. After Bismarck was dismissed, Germany was led by Kaiser William II, who tried to match England's traditional naval supremacy and aggressively pursued colonies. Because of the Kaiser's reckless diplomacy, Germany was feared by the other powers, except the weak Austria. The war was caused when Germany gave Austria a "blank check" in 1914 to deal with the Serbian threat.

b) Though Article 231 blamed Germany for WWI, this was based on the Allies' desire to punish Germany and make it pay for reparations. However, all nations had responsibility for the war. France wanted to retake Alsace-Lorraine and thus backed Russia's full mobilization when Austria declared war on Serbia, Russia's ally.

c) Versailles was a disaster for diplomacy after 1919. German anger over the unfair treaty led to the rise of Hitler and the Nazis, who were determined to overturn the hated treaty. This led directly to WWII, despite the failed efforts of the League of Nations.

There is no formal rubric for the SAQ; points are awarded based on whether or not the student adequately answers the three parts of the prompt. This question tests the HTS of 1) Claims and Evidence in Sources and 2) Causation. Notice how briefly this response addresses the question, and in so doing, earns all three points. The student takes a position in Parts A and B, providing at least one specific example to support their claim. Then in Part C they connect Versailles to the diplomatic failures of the interwar period that led to World War II. However, the student resists the urge to turn the exercise into an essay question. There are no intros, conclusions, or body paragraphs; just an immediate jump into answering what the prompt asks.

Certainly this response might have been longer (or briefer), but once you've earned the point by responding adequately to that part of the prompt, extending your argument or attempting to be comprehensive will not serve your interests. You will find many more SAQs throughout this review guide, and it is recommended that you build your facility through practice. With such practice, you will find the SAQs one of the easier parts of the course and exam to master.

Strategies for the Essay Questions

Dissecting the Prompt: Answer the Question Asked!

Having read thousands of essays as an AP exam scorer and leader, I can attest that the main reason that students underachieve in writing is their inability to effectively address the question that was asked. As your quivering hands grasp the newly opened booklet of essay prompts (DBQ and LEQ), there is a tendency to fly right into the writing process. Resist this impulse. If planning a road trip, you would consult a map or GPS, and only *then* decide on a route. Writing is no different.

Before writing, spend 5 minutes for the LEQ and 15 minutes for the DBQ planning out your approach. First, make sure

you understand what the question is asking you to *know* and to *do*, especially in relation to 1) chronological scope, 2) geographic scope, and 3) topical scope (basically which course theme(s)). Both the LEQ and DBQ will always measure the HTS of: 1) Argumentation, 2) Use of Evidence, 3) Contextualization, and 4) Making Connections ("complexity" point). Each question will also test a targeted Reasoning Process (RP). The prompts below represent examples of questions based on these targeted skills:

- *Causation* – Evaluate the most important cause for the emergence and continuation of the Cold War, 1943–1961.

- *Comparison* – Analyze the most significant difference in the political development of France and England in the period, 1640–1763.

- *Change and Continuity Over Time (CCOT)* – Evaluate the extent to which Napoleon continued the principles of the French Revolution in politics and religion.

Each of these prompts might form the basis for either a DBQ or an LEQ, but let's imagine that you were confronted on an exam with the CCOT question as an LEQ.

> *Evaluate the extent to which <u>Napoleon continued</u> the <u>principles</u> of the <u>French Revolution</u> in <u>politics</u> and <u>religion</u>.*

To ensure that you understand what you must know and do with this question, underline the relevant tasks and terms as I have done above. This should lead to the identification of a thesis and any appropriate examples as you take 5 minutes to organize your approach. The question asks you to make an assessment regarding the *extent* to which Napoleon continued (or changed) the ideals of the French Revolution. For your argument, avoid statements of degree, such as "to a great extent." Instead, be more specific regarding the ways in which and *why* Napoleon may have altered these ideals. If you consult the rubric on page 5, you will notice that you must establish a "line of reasoning," meaning that you must provide reasons for your claims, not merely assertions. For example, you might claim that Napoleon promoted religious tolerance but violated equality through a chauvinistic Napoleon Code. Though the chronological scope is not specified, it is implied—i.e., the reign of Napoleon I (1799–1815). In addition, you will need to make reference to the French Revolution, if only broadly, to pick up the *principles* part of the question.

Organize Your Ideas

Once clear on what the question is asking, you can begin organizing your response. Keep in mind that this is a brainstorming process of limited time, not a research paper. Think of all the examples and specifics related to the topic. If you end up with an unmanageable amount of information, select those most relevant to the prompt and consider how you can use them to support a thesis. Here is an example of what your notes might look like:

Principles of French Revolution

"Liberty, equality, fraternity"—the last can be construed as "nationalism"

Napoleon's policies

Liberty—secret police, censorship, manipulation of public opinion, allowed freedom of worship, conquest of foreign lands, ending of feudalism and serfdom in conquered lands

Assessment: on balance, Napoleon did not promote liberty, ruled dictatorially, posing as a "man of the people"

Equality—Napoleonic Code, restricted rights for women, abolition of feudalism and serfdom, establishment of schools, creation of uniform bureaucracy, "careers open to talent," nepotism, reestablished slavery in colonies

Assessment: in general, Napoleon's life and policies represent commitment to equality, but excluded women and compromised when it suited his power

Fraternity—Promoted nationalism in army, used revolutionary warfare, rewarded service with Legion of Honor, indirectly fed nationalism in conquered foreign lands

Assessment: Napoleon used nationalism effectively to gain and maintain power, but his indirect promotion of nationalism in foreign lands led to his downfall

This outline may be more detailed than time or your immediately recalled knowledge will allow. Don't worry. A student could easily write a top-notch essay with less detail than is given here. More important than merely mentioning facts is that you demonstrate an understanding of the question and provide a clear and direct thesis in response to the prompt. In fact, the rubric specifies only that you use "examples" to support your thesis, which could mean as few as two. However, these examples must not be merely cited; they must be deployed in support of an argument.

The Introduction and Thesis: Start Strong

You've probably heard it from your teachers before: "Make sure your essay provides a thesis." "Where's your thesis?" "Your thesis needs to be clearer." An explicit thesis statement gives your response direction and acts as a magnet to attract your evidence. A thesis is a (usually) one-sentence statement of the main arguments or points you will develop in your essay. Further, to earn the rubric points, it must be in either your introduction (preferred) or conclusion. Unfortunately, many essays lack such specificity and direction. As you practice your writing, work to develop your skills in articulating a thesis for your responses.

What makes for a powerful thesis? First, a strong thesis does more than simply restate the question. Let's say you are responding to this essay prompt:

> *Evaluate the most important factor that led to Great Britain's industrialization in the period 1750–1850.*

In their rush to get into the question with examples, many students may produce a generic statement, like: "There were many economic, geographic, and social factors that led to the Industrial Revolution in Great Britain." This statement merely provides obvious categories and makes no direct claim, or at least not one anyone could challenge. Your thesis must be *informative*, which means the reader should know something more about the topic in question than they did before reading your introduction. Also, just like a scientific theory, your thesis must be *falsifiable*, meaning that another historian could theoretically use evidence to contradict your claim. Notice that the imaginary thesis above is neither informative nor falsifiable. Finally, consider incorporating essential terms and concepts into your thesis to demonstrate your *specific* grasp of the topic under consideration.

A strong thesis provides clear reasons for its claims. In the above prompt, you are asked (implicitly) to identify the factor that most directly promoted British industrialism, so your introduction should explain how and why that factor proved critical. Since you are asked to "evaluate" or provide a judgment, make sure you concentrate on the *how* and *why* of causation to make your case. It is not enough to simply line up events in chronological order and leave the work of explanation to the reader. For the introduction, numerous examples are not necessary; save them for your body paragraphs. Stop and allow yourself time to recollect what you know about the topic. Consider the following outline for the level of detail and explanation at which you might aim:

Economic: Britain boasted important institutions that helped raise capital and promoted industry— Bank of England, strong navy, commercial empire, productive agriculture

Geographic: abundant natural resources, easy access to the sea, security from invasion

Social: mobile and surplus labor force, elites open to money-making, strong inventive tradition from Scientific Revolution and Enlightenment

Make sure to allow time for this brainstorming process. Again, do not be concerned if you generate less in the way of examples. Try to identify for each area in one sentence *how* developments there contributed to Great Britain's advantage. Keep in mind that for purposes of the prompt, you need only develop one of these categories; however, you might be able to earn the complexity point by acknowledging another of these factors, while still maintaining the primacy of one. Once this process is completed, you are ready to formulate your thesis. But first, let's look at how to structure an effective introduction.

No one strategy works like magic, yet there is a formula that can serve you well. Begin your introduction with two to four sentences of relevant historical context. Avoid philosophizing or taking your question too far outside the time period. Your goal here is to earn the Contextualization point by providing relevant background from the period before or during 1750–1850. For the question above, you might begin like this:

Prior to 1750, Great Britain was a major commercial power, passing rivals like the Dutch and Spanish. It developed a strong navy, which it used to defeat rivals in commercial conflicts, like the Seven Years War. While most of Europe, 1750–1850, was upset by revolutions, Great Britain focused on its internal and imperial economic development.

This context serves as a trajectory into the question and establishes with solid chronological foundations that you have control of the question, as well as earning the Contextualization point. Now you are ready to take the brainstorming above and formulate a thesis—in this case, one that makes a case that one of the causal factors proved pivotal:

Though Great Britain possessed a variety of geographic and social advantages, its economic institutions, like the Bank of England and a strong navy, provided the capital and markets to make it the world leader in manufacturing and industry.

For added punch, finish off your introduction with a clincher that pulls the thesis together with an interpretation and perhaps signals the complexity strategy you may develop later. In this case, Britain influenced other nations to adopt similar production strategies, leading eventually to Europe's economic dominance and imperial control of world trade:

Over the next century, other European nations followed the British example and developed their own economies to compete for trade and power all across the world.

Remember that this model is a process that you will hone in your class and as you use the practice questions in this book. The most important lesson you should take from our discussion is not that your thesis needs to be beautifully articulate (though that's an added bonus), but rather that, in addressing the question that is being asked, you are specific and provide a *line of reasoning*.

The Body Paragraphs: Fleshing Out Your Argument

Though an introduction provides the foundation to your essay, you build the structure of your argument in the body paragraphs. As you write the body of your essay, always have one eye on your argument. Often, students get caught up in telling a story or "data dumping," which has no relation to the ultimate point of the essay. All AP prompts are designed to gauge your understanding of the Targeted RP and the relevant content, not your ability to recall facts. Keep focused on *making and modifying your argument*, avoiding tangential issues and commentary.

An effective body paragraph always begins with a strong topic sentence that connects back to your essential claim. If we take the essay above on Britain and industrialization, our first body paragraph would tease out how economic institutions played the key role in British industrialization. Keep in mind that you need to show *how* and *why*, not merely *who* and *what* led to the phenomenon in question. Statements like "Now I will talk about economics" or "Economic factors also helped Great Britain to industrialize" are insufficient. You must aim to capture the primary role that factor played: "Great Britain's supportive economic institutions provided the capital it needed to industrialize." This claim now gives the remainder of the paragraph, and your examples, the direction you need to analyze, rather than simply list or describe. After all, you are making an *argument*, not merely describing or summarizing. An argument is a claim with which another historian could theoretically disagree, e.g., if you were to claim that social, rather than geographic or economic, factors served as the most important factor in promoting British industry.

In supporting your argument select evidence purposefully. More is not necessarily better. Several well-chosen examples that are clearly and explicitly connected to the topic sentence, and ultimately the thesis, are preferable to an unorganized or unexplained catalogue. As you write, try to think of yourself as establishing connections between the examples and the concept. Schematically, the body paragraph will appear as below, with explanations running along each line that connects the example to the topic sentence. For example, along the line from "strong navy" to the central idea of the paragraph, we might have: "England's strong navy allowed it to establish new colonies and defeat rival powers. The trade that resulted from England's colonial empire allowed entrepreneurs to finance industry in the home isles."

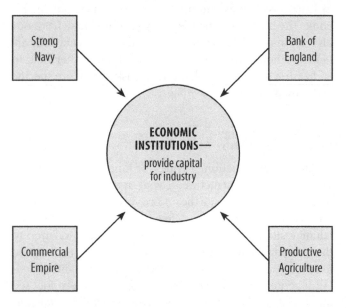

These four examples provide ample support for this paragraph. In fact, for each body paragraph, aim for approximately 2–3 examples as support. Fully explained examples show your control of the question and ability to develop a central idea—the argument—as well as demonstrate your application of the targeted HTS (in this case, Causation). Finally, to conclude your body paragraph, write a transitional sentence that sets up your next paragraph, such as: "While these institutions were critical, they were supplemented by Britain's favorable geographic location." Sentences like this help guide a reader systematically through an argument and show how each component fits with the others. If you made it this far, sometimes, as with speaking, the most important task is knowing when and how to stop.

The Conclusion: Sew Up the Rubric

Think of the conclusion of your essay as a dismount in a gymnastic routine—a last chance to influence the scorer positively. It is important here that you *add* to what you've already written. Therefore, avoid merely repeating the introductory paragraph or reiterating a point already made. For both the DBQ and LEQ, the conclusion is an ideal spot to earn your Complexity point. The most difficult point on the rubric, Complexity involves the ability to make deep historical connections—from your argument to other periods, geographic areas, and issues OR to extend your argument with an additional category of analysis. Both the DBQ and LEQ rubrics specify several strategies for earning the Complexity point:

1. Integrate multiple perspectives or modify or qualify your argument by addressing an opposing point of view.

2. Extend or apply your argument to a development in a different historical period, situation, era, or geographical area.

3. Address the counterpoint to the HTS; so for the question above on *causation*, you might discuss the *effects* of British industrialization on subsequent developments or events.

4. Extend your argument by connecting to a course theme or a topic not addressed by the prompt (e.g., history of art or culture).

At least for the conclusion, most students tend to rely on 2 and 3, with 4 being the least common way to earn Complexity. Keep in mind that you can earn the point in the body paragraphs—as many students do—with 1. Whichever strategy you adopt, make sure you explain your reasoning adequately. Name-dropping an example, without explanation, will not earn you the point.

Let's make this advice more concrete by looking at a specific example from another question:

> *Evaluate the most significant reason for the failure of the German Weimar Republic, 1918–1933.*

First, the dates in the question cue up both the introduction and conclusion. The year 1918 marks the end of the First World War, and 1933, the appointment of Adolf Hitler as Chancellor of Germany. This chronological context will form the structure of our response, as the topic is bracketed by the two world wars of the twentieth century. In fact, the question would have been written by the Test Development Committee to address the SOP theme, which, if you notice, will help you strategize your concluding paragraph for the Complexity point.

Your recognition of the question's link to related issues across chronology should make its way into your conclusion. Let's take our starting point as 1933 and consider how that date represents the failure of the Weimar Republic and context of the two world wars. Here is one way we might approach the conclusion of this essay.

> The Weimar Republic was born amid chaos and revolution after the First World War. Economic problems, along with Germany's lack of a democratic history and anger over the Versailles Treaty, proved unsolvable. The Weimar Republic's failure was significant. Because Germany was unable to establish democracy, Hitler came to power in 1933 and quickly overthrew the Versailles treaty. These policies led to a larger and more violent conflict—the Second World War. However, after WWII, the western Allies realized that they needed to rebuild Germany and reintegrate it into an alliance, rather than punishing it for causing yet another war. Thus Germany was reintegrated into European diplomacy and politics, unlike in the period after 1918.

At this point in the exam, you may feel pressed for time, so practice being economical with your Complexity strategy, as demonstrated above. Notice how the conclusion connects the topic of the question to a similar diplomatic situation—the way in which the Allies treated Germany differently after World War II. Though brief, this paragraph effectively establishes and explains a meaningful connection to a related issue in a subsequent chronological period, as well as considering the results of the republic's failure (Strategies 2 or 3 above). As you read through the sample essays in this volume, you will encounter additional strategies for Complexity—both those that work and those that fall short.

How long should your essay be? As already mentioned, longer essays do not necessarily equate with higher scores. With that in mind, most LEQs responses comprise 2 handwritten pages. Of course, this suggestion should serve as a guideline, not a hard-and-fast rule. After all, the time limit of 40 minutes (for the LEQ) will ultimately shape the length of your response.

Mastering the Long Essay Question (LEQ)

What Should I Expect?

For the Long Essays, you will be presented with three question choices. These questions will test your knowledge of the same targeted Reasoning Process (e.g., Causation), usually the same course theme (e.g., Economic and Commercial Developments), involve parallel tasks, and be drawn from three different chronological eras. Choice 1 will draw from the period 1450–ca. 1700, Choice 2 from 1648–1914, and Choice 3 from 1815–2001. Since the content addressed by the Long Essay prompts must be addressed within the Unit Guides of the Course Description, the questions should address mainstream topics. Of course, you may encounter creative applications of this notion. For example, a question may ask you to pull together content from a broad chronological span focusing on a recurring issue, such as attitudes toward gender or artistic representations.

Look at the set below and try to identify the targeted HTS and course themes.

> **Question 1** *Evaluate the extent to which the religious wars transformed politics and society.*

> **Question 2** *Evaluate the extent to which the French Revolution transformed politics and society.*

> **Question 3** *Evaluate the extent to which the First World War transformed politics and society.*

These questions target the Reasoning Process (RP) of CCOT, since they ask you to deal with the idea of a transformation. To write an effective essay, you must explain the characteristics (with examples) of politics and society either before and during each event, or during and after each event. Also, you'll notice that each question addresses the course themes of States and Other Institutions of Power (SOP) and Social Organization and Development (SCD).

Managing Your Time

Keep in mind that the second phase of the AP exam (following the 10-minute break) requires you to write the DBQ and LEQ in a total of 100 minutes. Of this time, you should spend approximately 40 minutes on the LEQ. Although there is a designated 15-minute reading period for this phase of the exam, you are not required to divide up your time on the two essays in any particular way. Given the tasks you have to juggle, you may find it helpful to spend the first 5 minutes of the reading period organizing your LEQ (settling on a thesis, surveying content, determining paragraph structure, identifying synthesis strategy) and *then* turning to the DBQ.

After you finish the DBQ (in roughly 60 minutes), you can return to the LEQ. Having already planned out your response, you can go right into the writing process. This will make up for the 5-minute lag with the proctor's instructions (since you likely started the DBQ 5 minutes "late" because you outlined your LEQ). By using this strategy, you can create a plan of action for both essays and reduce your anxiety.

Also, by this time in the exam, you may be experiencing mental and physical fatigue, which tend to produce mistakes. By organizing your ideas at the beginning of the 100 minutes—when your mind is still fresh—you're less likely to experience the pitfalls of chronological errors and misinterpreting the required tasks of a question. To manage your time, it is suggested that you bring a watch (no alarms or data allowed) and consult it throughout this and the previous sections of the exam.

Final Tips for Writing an Effective Essay

Before moving on to the unique features of the Document-Based Question, let's pull together the suggestions for effective writing, some of which apply to both the LEQs and DBQ. AP readers will consider your essays as a first draft, so spelling errors, grammar, and less-than-elegant penmanship generally do not detract from your score. With that said, there is no doubt that a clear, cogent writing style can only assist in conveying your understanding. It is in your interest, then, to work at making your writing as tight as possible, that is, making every word count with no wasted motion. AP readers want to see your performance, not your warm-up routine. To assist in improving your writing style, a brief yet essential resource is William Strunk and E.B. White, *The Elements of Style* (Boston: Allyn & Bacon, 2000). This short primer on usage and style will lend your writing power and clarity. So should the following suggestions:

- Allow yourself about 5 minutes (LEQ) to organize your ideas and establish a clear direction for your essay.

- Get to your points as quickly as possible; avoid flowery prose, rhetorical questions, dramatic scene-setting.

- Be specific in identifying your thesis; do not simply restate the question; make an argument.

- Make sure you engage both the RP and course theme(s) on which the question is based. Draw on the strategies you've developed and address the RP explicitly.

- Provide topic sentences to your body paragraphs that relate directly to your argument.

- *Apply* examples to the thesis, rather than simply mentioning or listing them.

- Steer clear of value judgments or opinions. Your role is as an impartial historian.

- Write directly and clearly. Try to avoid complex prepositional phrases. Employ action verbs, such as "advanced," "opposed," and "established," whenever possible.

- Manage your time effectively. Don't get bogged down on side issues; focus on your argument.

- Finish strong. Use the conclusion to establish strong historical connections and earn your Complexity point (if you haven't already).

Even if you lose track of time or are rushed, don't panic. Some years ago, I had a student who found himself with only 12 minutes at the end of our final exam (a full AP exam) to complete his long essay. He approached me and asked, "What should I do?" I responded, "Go back and write as much as you can in those 12 minutes." He did and earned a solid score on his response. Not that I would recommend putting yourself under this time pressure, but it might boost your confidence to know that you don't have to be perfect on all components of the exam to earn a high score. However, you should try to make the most of your opportunities.

An Example

Before we move on to the DBQ, let's look at a sample essay. As you read the response below, you'll notice that I've added commentary as to how the student earned their points on the rubric (see page 4 from Chapter 1 to follow along with the scoring requirements). The following essay is in response to the CCOT question above on the French Revolution (*Evaluate the extent to which the French Revolution transformed politics and society.*)

SAMPLE ESSAY 1

Before its revolution, France had been ruled for decades by a monarchy that imposed an unequal tax and social system. It suffered from poor economic conditions and bankruptcy due to expensive wars and paying for Versailles. From 1789 to 1799 in France, there was massive upheaval in an attempt for the French citizens to replace the Old Regime[1] with a new political and social system where equality and legal rights were exercised. The French Revolution transformed European history because it got rid of the inequalities of the social classes and it established natural law that granted more equality to the citizens.[2]

NOTES

1 A brief but relevant background on features of the Old Regime, earns the CTX point.

2 The response provides a line of reasoning ("got rid of inequalities" and "established natural law") in supporting its claim that the French Revolution did transform politics and society.

One reason that the French Revolution transformed France was because it attempted to abolish the inequalities between social classes.[3] Before the French Revolution, the three estates were not granted equal rights, as the nobles and clergy had many privileges and tax exemptions. However, since a great portion of the revolution was promoted by the overlooked Third Estate, it led to efforts to establish equal social rights. This was especially important during the Liberal phase of the Revolution, where all privileges were abolished, as were any remnants of serfdom and feudalism. These changes were made by the National Assembly in the Declaration of Rights of Man and Citizen. The Revolution also attempted to abolish class distinctions by making positions available by merit rather than birth, something that was continued during the rule of Napoleon. During the Revolution, other social classes needed the right to seek military ranks and high offices, especially the sans-culottes in the Reign of Terror.[4]

The Revolution was also a major turning point in history because it attempted to legally grant equality to its citizens through democratic reform.[5] Prior to the Revolution, France was a monarchy where the king had a significant amount of say over its citizens. Although it wasn't entirely an absolute monarchy, it did have some remnants of that type of rule. However, this changed dramatically because of the input of ordinary citizens during the revolution. The revolution was mostly led by the Third Estate, the common citizens. They created a new constitution and documents such as the Declaration of Rights of Man and Citizen. Later on during the Reign of Terror, the sans-culottes influenced the Committee of Public Safety, which promoted equality through many reforms. This shows that the balance of power changed from one in which only the highest classes had the most rights to one in which the lower classes had a chance to rule.[6] However, this was only true to some extent. Women were still left out of governments and, during the radicalization and Reign of Terror, even forbidden to join women's groups and associations. Although women's roles in the revolution were decreased, their participation during the Liberal phase, especially during the October Days and the storming of Bastille, played a significant role in creating feminist attitudes.[7]

Overall, the French Revolution transformed European history because it changed the balance of social power and showed the power the lower classes could have when given equality. The topic of the French Revolution also was both impacted and had an impact on the rest of the world. In the United States, the American Revolution had just taken place, increasing the revolutionary spirit and admiration of Enlightenment policies, such as equality and liberty, both of which had an impact on France and inspired the trend of revolution. On the other hand, France impacted other states to reform their governments. This was especially evident during the Haitian slave revolt, the first successful slave revolt in history. Here the Haitian slaves overthrew the slave-keepers, fighting for equality and liberty as well. This goes to show how a revolutionary spirit can make lasting changes.[8]

3 This topic sentence refers back to the relevant RP and establishes the student's focus on explaining changes.

4 This paragraph offers several examples. Though limited in number, the student applies them to their argument regarding the French Revolution as a transformation. The response even makes a connection to the rule of Napoleon (after 1799).

5 Again, this topic sentence, while somewhat general, effectively returns to CCOT and the argument.

6 In this section, the student introduces several examples and suggests a grasp of the chronological scope of the revolution. Also, they note how a specific social group—the sans-culottes—were affected by the revolution's policies.

7 This is one of the more impressive features of this essay: the student notes a limitation on the revolution as a transformation by analyzing its (lack of) impact on women. But they also note its future effects. Taken alone, this reference would likely earn the Complexity point.

8 With references to the Enlightenment, American Revolution, and Haitian slave revolt, the student amply demonstrates their ability to make historical connections by introducing a new theme, Interaction of Europe and the World (INT) (which was not part of the prompt), as well as other geographic regions and events. If the Complexity point was in doubt, the student clinched that point with their ability to extend their argument in the conclusion.

This essay overall earned a 6, the highest possible on the LEQ. It earned the points for Contextualization and Thesis (see intro), 2 points for Use of Evidence in supporting the thesis with multiple examples, 1 point for addressing the Reasoning Process of CCOT through substantive analysis of the French Revolution as a transformation, and the Complexity point for modifying/extending the argument by showing limitations to change and the connection of France to other revolutions. Is this a perfect response? By no means. It might be enhanced by a more developed introduction and 1–2 more specific examples. However, it should remind you that with a strong grounding in the chronology of European history, attention to the course themes, practice with the skills and reasoning processes, and a focused approach, you too can write essays that earn top scores. A professional historian of the French Revolution would certainly write a much more impressive essay, yet it would still only earn a 6, as did this one. "Excellence is risk. Perfection is fear. Excellence is confidence. Perfection is doubt." ~Thomas Greenspon

How to Approach the Document-Based Question (DBQ)

Purpose of the DBQ

The document-based question is designed to test your skill in using historical sources and content as evidence to make an argument. With the 7 documents provided, you will detect patterns from the sources; evaluate evidence for bias; note multiple perspectives on an issue; detect nuance, irony, and purpose in documents; and apply varying techniques of analysis depending on the type of source. In the current age of social media and a divided political dialogue, we are bombarded by images and claims, many connected to product sales, lofty advertising promises, high political rhetoric, and unsubstantiated assertions by bloggers. As a citizen, you need to be able to sort well-reasoned from spurious claims, recognize the agendas behind the words, and appreciate that there can be many ways of looking at an issue. By practicing such skills with historical sources, it is hoped that you will not only appreciate how historians arrive at explanations and interpretations, but translate these skills into both your professional and civic lives.

Before delving into DBQ strategies, let's consider an actual question. After you note the general directions below, I recommend reading through the DBQ question that follows. If this is your first foray into DBQs, don't worry if you find the task confusing. We'll go through it step-by-step, and then you can try the question as an exercise.

General Directions

1. You have 60 minutes to complete the DBQ, of which 15 minutes is allotted for reading the documents and planning your response.

2. Read the question precisely, underlining key words and tasks.

3. Read the documents completely and carefully; oftentimes, you will encounter a document that shifts tone or that outlines an argument with which the author *disagrees*, and then lays out his own perspective.

4. As you read the sources, consider how the evidence from the documents AND your content knowledge (Evidence Beyond the Documents) can be used to develop an argument.

5. Pay careful attention to each source—its type, information about the author, historical context, etc. Brainstorm approaches on how to use this information for source analysis.

6. When you are finished reading the documents, make a brief outline that includes: paragraph topics, organization of documents, content examples, and strategies for source analysis.

7. As you begin writing, keep referring back to the question to ensure that you are addressing it explicitly, with the documents and content examples.

Document-Based Question

Total Time—60 minutes; 1 Question

Directions: Question 1 is based on the accompanying documents. It is suggested that you spend about 15 minutes reading the documents and 45 minutes writing your response. The documents have been edited for the purpose of this exercise.

In your response you should do the following:

- Respond to the prompt with a historically defensible thesis or claim that establishes a line of reasoning.
- Describe a broader historical context relevant to the prompt.
- Support an argument in response to the prompt using at least six documents.
- Use at least one additional piece of specific historical evidence (beyond that found in the documents) relevant to an argument about the prompt.
- For at least three documents, explain how or why the document's point of view, purpose, historical situation, and/or audience is relevant to an argument.
- Use evidence to corroborate, qualify, or modify an argument that addresses the prompt.

Question 1 *Evaluate whether or not Charles Darwin's theory of natural selection contributed to the idea of progress in the period 1859–1914.*

Document 1

Source: Samuel Wilberforce, English bishop and writer, *On Darwin's Origin of Species*, 1860

Mr. Darwin declares that he applies the principle of natural selection to man himself, as well as to the animals around him. Now, we must say at once and openly, that such a notion is absolutely incompatible not only with expressions in the word of God on the subject of man's natural condition, but more importantly, with the whole representation of the moral and spiritual condition of man which is the Bible's proper subject matter. Man's supremacy over the earth; man's power of articulate speech; man's gift of reason; man's free will and responsibility; man's fall and man's redemption; the incarnation of the Eternal Son; the indwelling of the Eternal Spirit—all are equally and utterly irreconcilable with the degrading notion of the brute origin of humans who were, in fact, created in the image of God, and redeemed by the Eternal Son assuming to Himself man's nature.

Document 2

Source: Clémence Royer, female French translator of Darwin, anthropologist, and feminist, Preface to *On the Origin of Species*, 1866

The doctrine of Mr. Darwin is the rational revelation of progress, pitting itself in logical antagonism with the irrational revelation of Man's fall*. These are two principles, two religions in struggle, a thesis and an antithesis of which I defy any who is proficient in logic to find a reconciliation. It is a categorical 'yes' and 'no' between which it is necessary to choose, and whoever declares himself for the one is against the other.

For myself, the choice is made: I believe in progress.

*A reference to the account of Adam and Eve from the Old Testament.

Document 3

Source: Charles Darwin, biologist and developer of theory of natural selection in evolution, *Autobiography*, 1876

Disbelief in God crept over me at a very slow rate, but was at last complete. The rate was so slow that I felt no distress and have never since doubted even for a single second that my conclusion was correct. I can indeed hardly see how anyone ought to wish Christianity to be true.

The old argument of design in nature, as given by [William] Paley*, which formerly seemed to me so conclusive, fails, now that the law of natural selection has been discovered. We can no longer argue that, for instance, the beautiful hinge of a bivalve shell must have been made by an intelligent being, like the hinge of a door by man. There seems to be no more design in the variability of organic beings and in the action of natural selection, than in the course the wind blows. Everything in nature is the result of fixed laws.

The mystery of the beginning of all things is insoluble to us; and I for one must be content to remain an Agnostic.

*William Paley was an early nineteenth-century natural theologian who devised a famous argument for intelligent design.

Document 4

Source: "Man is But a Worm," *Punch's Almanack for 1882*, satirical magazine addressing social and political issues

Document 5

Source: Herbert Spencer, British philosopher and sociologist, *Social Statics*, 1896

Pervading all nature we see at work a stern discipline which is a little cruel that it may be very kind. Meanwhile, the well-being of humanity and its unfolding into ultimate perfection are both secured by the same beneficial though severe discipline to which animals are subject.

It seems hard that a laborer, incapacitated by sickness from competing with his stronger fellows, should have to bear the resulting sufferings. It seems hard that widows and orphans should be left to struggle for life or death. Nevertheless, when regarded not separately but in connection with the interests of universal humanity, these harsh fatalities are seen to be full of beneficence—the same beneficence which brings to early graves the children of diseased parents, and singles out the intemperate and the debilitated as the victims of an epidemic.

Document 6

Source: Karl Pearson, British mathematician and scientist, professor of eugenics,* *National Life From the Standpoint of Science*, 1900

History shows me one way, and one way only, in which a high state of civilization has been produced, namely, the struggle of race with race, and the survival of the physically and mentally fitter race.

The struggle means suffering, intense suffering, but that struggle and that suffering have been the stages by which the white man has reached his present stage of development, and they account for the fact that he no longer lives in caves and feeds on roots and nuts. This dependence of progress on the survival of the fitter race, terribly dark as it may seem to some of you, gives the struggle for existence its redeeming features; it is the fiery crucible out of which comes the finer metal.

*Eugenics is the supposed science of studying and classifying racial characteristics.

Document 7

Source: Friedrich von Bernhardi, German general and writer on military affairs, *The Next War*, 1912

This aspiration for universal peace is directly antagonistic to the great universal laws which rule all life. War is a biological necessity of the first importance, a regulative element in the life of mankind which cannot be dispensed with, since without it an unhealthy development will follow, which excludes every advancement of the race, and therefore all real civilization. 'War is the father of all things.' (Heraclitus*) The sages of antiquity long before Darwin recognized this.

*Heraclitus was an ancient Greek philosopher.

Interpreting the Question

Once you look at the DBQ, make sure you understand what the prompt is asking you to know and to do. In fact, not only should you re-read it and underline key terms, you should also look back at the question after you write your introduction—to make sure you've addressed *all* parts of the question. In this case, the markup of the question might look like this:

> *Evaluate* whether or not Charles *Darwin's theory of natural selection contributed* to the *idea of progress* in the period *1859–1914*.

The above process will reinforce the topical (Darwin's theory), geographical (Europe as a whole), and chronological (1859–1914) scope of the question. In this case, you can consider progress in multiple areas, such as culture, society, economics, politics, and diplomacy. Also, try to use the dates as a cue for organizing your essay and considering content examples. Darwin published *On the Origin of Species* in 1859, and the end date marks the onset of World War I. Knowledge of that span should help you survey relevant content and employ helpful historical context.

For the DBQ, you may not always notice from the prompt what reasoning process is targeted. It's possible that the question is open to several; for the question above, you could theoretically deploy Causation or CCOT analysis. Either can work, as long as you are explicit about making an argument. Notice how the question forces you into taking a position, but remember that your thesis must provide a <u>line of reasoning</u>, not merely an assertion.

As you read the documents, make connections to what you know about the period. Remember, you only need one specific content example (*not* related to source analysis) to earn the Evidence Beyond Documents (EBD) point. To remind yourself about the EBD point, brainstorm content ideas <u>as you read the documents</u> and make note of them. Don't worry about being comprehensive. There will be a range of choices; the more important task is linking the content explicitly to your argument. Here are some content examples suggested by the period:

- Social and Racial Darwinism
- Religious divisions between modernists and fundamentalists
- "White Man's Burden" (Kipling poem)
- Marx's use in history of Darwin's notion of evolution
- Theories challenging traditional ideas, such as Freud, Nietzsche, Einstein, quantum physics
- Scramble for Africa

- Nationalism and national unification campaigns (esp. Germany), including wars
- Arms race
- Increased nationalist tensions on eve of World War I

As you develop your outline and consider use of documents, strategize where you can integrate 1–2 examples like those listed above.

Interpreting the Documents

All DBQs will include different types of documents—letters, speeches, books, articles, pamphlets, diaries, cartoons, charts, and illustrations. In one way your task is the same for each document: explain how it relates to your argument. In another way, each document offers a different opportunity to engage in substantive source analysis. These strategies can vary based on the type of document. In which situation—making a speech before a political gathering or writing a personal letter—would a politician be more forthright in explaining their true motives and intent? Political cartoonists boast a rich history of poking fun at the high and mighty. Illustrators and even photographers (in the manner of how they choose and compose their subjects) act as effective propagandists for and against political movements.

Each of the above scenarios highlights an essential theme of your AP European history course: history is not simply "facts" but a contested story seen from multiple perspectives. Your job in the DBQ is to demonstrate that you can see through the smokescreen of bias and hidden motives, as well as consider the purpose and intended audience of the document. When addressing point of view, you may speculate as to authors' motives and reliability. Just make sure that you *explain* the reasons for your assertions. Simply stating that "the author of Document 3 is biased because she's a woman" is insufficient and will not earn you credit for point of view. As revealed in the DBQ rubric, there are four specific source analysis strategies identified. We will look at them in general terms before examining specific uses in this particular DBQ.

- **Historical Situation:** Any document reflects the time period in which it was created, either obviously or subtly. Look at the source attribution and note the date or era of the document's provenance. Most likely the source reveals concerns or issues from the period in which it was recorded. For example, imagine a pamphlet on crime and punishment written in 1762. Since the document was produced during the Enlightenment, it may reveal the influence of ideals of reason, reform, progress, or humanitarianism—all features of enlightened thought.

- **Intended Audience and Purpose:** The intended audience may be called out specifically by the author, or you may infer it based on the type of document. In either case, try to use your determination as to the intended audience to analyze the tone and reliability of the source. Two documents can address the same topic and make similar points, yet they may differ widely in purpose and tone, and thus reliability. Imagine an autobiography recounting events that occurred decades before its writing. The more removed in time we are from our memories, the more unreliable they become. Also, autobiographies are often written to "set the record straight" or "tell my side of the story." All these considerations should matter. Though it may not be evident, every document was originally created for some purpose, perhaps merely for a chronicler to record his thoughts in a personal diary. To infer this purpose, you can consider the type of document as you analyze its meaning and reliability. For example, a speech by a political leader before an assembly aims at persuasion, so as you read this type of document, pay attention to the rhetoric of the speaker.

- **Point of View:** Here you take a known fact about the author's identity and use it to consider (or speculate as to) how that factor may have influenced the content or manner in which they present their ideas. Such factors of identity can include 1) class/status, 2) gender, 3) age, 4) occupation, 5) ethnicity/race, 6) political affiliation, and 7) religion.

Many teachers and students will use the acronym HIPP to encompass the strategies available for earning the Source Analysis point. Before we look at each document individually, let me add two cautions. First, every document included is relevant to the exercise; there are no "trick" documents. Though the relevance of some documents may be harder for you to see than others, each can be related to your argument and other documents, which leads to the next point. In any DBQ, two or three more subtle and nuanced documents will be included. Their purpose is to separate the average response from those that offer sharp and detailed insight into how the documents support a thesis. Now's look at the content of each document, its possible relation to an argument, and possible strategies for source analysis.

Document 1: Samuel Wilberforce, English bishop and writer, *On Darwin's Origin of Species*, 1860—The first document provides a clearly negative perspective on Darwin's theory. The author, an English bishop, sets up a repeated contrast between the qualities of humans (as created in the image of God) and the "degrading" implications of humans' origins from lower forms of life. Wilberforce finds natural selection to be scandalous, not simply because it seems to contradict the Bible, but also for what it implies about the moral status of humans. This document appears to be a treatise or pamphlet, written the year after *On the Origin of Species*. One may wonder whether Wilberforce even read Darwin's book, and certainly his standing as a bishop indicates his point of view as an advocate for a predominantly moral and religious view of the world.

Document 2: Clémence Royer, female French translator of Darwin, anthropologist, and feminist, Preface to *On the Origin of Species*, 1866—Royer's perspective contrasts sharply with that of Wilberforce above. Though she accepts Wilberforce's dichotomy between religion and science, she opts for the opposing side, or progress as she sees it. Considering that this is the preface to Royer's translation of Darwin, her intended audience will be those either interested in or supportive of natural selection. Royer aims to convince her readers of Darwin's accomplishment and to accept the theory as a valid scientific law. Finally, it makes sense that a woman (and feminist), having been subjected to inferior treatment, may convey antagonism toward the traditional political and social order, as well as sympathize with those viewed as outcasts.

Document 3: Charles Darwin, biologist and developer of theory of natural selection in evolution, *Autobiography*, 1876—Darwin explains the course of his theological beliefs due to his involvement in biological studies. The document addresses many of the same religious issues as Documents 1 and 2, though Darwin's adopts a more subtle tone. For him, the acceptance of the randomness inherent in natural selection leads to agnosticism, i.e., the removal of the explanatory power of a Supreme Being to account for the existence of humans, or any biological change over time. As an autobiography, written almost twenty years after *On the Origin of Species*, we may wonder whether Darwin's account of his intellectual journey overlooks the inner and outer conflict that his theory produced.

Document 4: "Man is But a Worm," *Punch's Almanack for 1882*, satirical magazine addressing social and political issues—A complex image, this source offers multiple possibilities for interpretation. You may note first that the source comes from a magazine with a satirical approach, though it may not be obvious what is being mocked in the cartoon—the validity of natural selection and the idea of man's lowly roots OR those who may be unwilling to accept that humans do not hold the lofty place in Creation they once believed (as expressed in Document 1). If unsure, you can make explicit those multiple ways of interpreting the source in your argument. In the bottom left, you'll notice what look like letters. These spell out "CHAOS," and then following the time arc, this process leads to present-day humans, all with Darwin watching over, sitting on what seems to be a classical throne. Whatever the interpretation, it is clear that Document 4 demonstrates the consequences of rethinking the origins of humans.

Document 5: Herbert Spencer, British philosopher and sociologist, *Social Statics*, 1896—Spencer helped develop the field of sociology and advocated for the position we now call Social Darwinism. Spencer's use of "survival of the fittest" is starkly evident in this passage, as he discusses the situation of the working classes and poor, issues which would have gained increased attention during the Second Industrial Revolution. As an academic and a respected member of society, Spencer probably lacked first-hand knowledge of the situation of poverty. Also, the source seems to be a scholarly volume designed for fellow intellectuals, hence his tone of academic distance. Spencer's application of Darwin influenced government policy and political debates, as evidenced in the following two documents.

Document 6: Karl Pearson, British mathematician and scientist, professor of eugenics, *National Life From the Standpoint of Science*, 1900—Though less scholarly in tone, Pearson's treatise echoes that of Spencer's in Document 5. Again, we see the emphasis on struggle, except in this instance, with a decidedly racial tone. The phrase "fitter race" may have jumped out and reminded you that this was an age of imperialism and competition among the great powers in the Scramble for Africa. Pearson justifies this conquest as the natural outcome of competition among civilizations, a process that results in the advance of the human race. Please note the gloss on eugenics: though the field claimed the mantle of scientific credibility, it has since been discredited (after the Nazis) as a pseudo-science motivated more by racism than disinterested inquiry into human characteristics. We may conclude that Pearson wished to justify intellectually the expansion and height of the British Empire under Queen Victoria.

Document 7: Friedrich von Bernhardi, German general and writer on military affairs, *The Next War*, 1912—In this brief source, a German military theorist justifies war as a "biological necessity," certainly a phrase taken from Darwin, not to mention that von Bernhardi invokes him later in the paragraph. Since war is the business of a general, von Bernhardi deems military affairs vital to a nation's survival and natural advance. If you consider the historical context, von Bernhardi writes two years prior to the outbreak of the First World War, as tensions grew among the great powers and amidst the arms race and mad pursuit of colonies.

The Scoring Rubric

It is unlikely a student could score well on the DBQ without knowing the scoring rubric. The rubric is not difficult to learn, and your continued practice with DBQs will build mastery and fluency. In fact, if there is one area of the AP exam where practice can do the most to improve your score, it is on the DBQ. Since the DBQ comprises many moving parts, it is vital that you practice, review areas of struggle, and then use strategies to develop mastery. As you practice the DBQs in this review book, make sure you keep referring back to the rubric on page 4 (Chapter 1) and assess the sample essays. In fact, you might try rewriting parts of deficient samples to raise their scores to a 7. Before we take a first look at several such samples for the Darwin question, let's go more in-depth on two areas that are likely to present the strongest challenge to students in earning top scores on this exercise.

General Strategies for Source Analysis

You will have noticed some strategies in addressing source analysis in the previous examples. Here are some general questions to ask about the documents you encounter, which should lead you to effective HIPP strategies:

1. How might the author's identity (race, ethnic background, occupation, social class, age, nationality, religion) have impacted their position?

2. Does this source have first-hand knowledge about what it is they are reporting? In other words, how reliable is the source?

3. What seems to be the purpose of the source or its intended audience? Is this a public or private document? Does the document have a clear purpose, perhaps as propaganda (especially useful for visual sources)?

4. How close in time to the events being reported was this document written or published? Could the author's memory be faulty or idealized by nostalgic reflection?

5. What is the tone of the document? Are there strong words that suggest an explicit bias?

6. What historical events or processes might have influenced the content or manner of presentation in the document?

One way to demonstrate your mastery of point of view is to employ adjectives or verbs, other than "says" or "states," to capture the tone of the document. Try some of these to characterize the tone of the document:

condemned	typified	observed
encouraged	implied	criticized
praised	postulated	showed
sarcastic	exhorted	modified
extolled	idealized	adapted
satirized	stereotyped	issued
ridiculed	generalized	decreed
informed	ignored	suggested
patronizing	overlooked	categorized
dismissive	glorified	classified
speculated	contrasted	defended
condoned	recorded	represented
mocked	noted	excoriated
attacked	depicted	embraced
questioned	exalted	rejected
doubted	claimed	challenged
exemplified	rationalized	contrasted
upheld	compared	berated

Remember, to receive credit on the rubric for source analysis, you must provide three explicit examples. Your source analysis must provide adequate explanation of its rationale to earn points. Many students simply make assertions, like "Since he's a noble, he would think that way." This statement represents only a first step, i.e., noting that the author's status as a noble likely affected his stance on the issue in question. However, the statement lacks sufficient explanation; in contrast, the following assertion *would* earn credit: "Since nobles controlled positions in government and the army, Duke Charles fears the entrance of the middle-class into political power and thus denounces the proposed law."

Writing the Introduction and Thesis

The introduction to your DBQ sets you up for success; in fact, you can easily earn two points on the rubric even before embarking on the body of your essay! To set up the specific topic, be sure to provide background on developments or processes that offer historical context to it. For example, in the Darwin question above, you might mention the general advance of scientific theories and prestige of science and technology, including positivism. Or you might explain the role of imperialism, nationalism, or secularism to help set the stage for your later discussion of how natural selection affected or was affected by these ideas. With 2–3 sentences of substantive linkage to the DBQ prompt, you will earn your Contextualization point.

After establishing the chronological and geographical setting, you turn to your thesis. Under no circumstances should you merely restate the question or provide vague references to whatever reasoning skill is being assessed, such as "changed politics a lot," "made culture more progressive," or "had a big impact on ideas." With the Darwin question, you are dealing with its impact on the notion of progress, suggesting a Causation or CCOT focus. Be specific, clear, and precise: "Darwin's theory of natural selection supported the idea of progress through secularism and challenging religious authorities. At the same time, in promoting struggle and warfare in politics, it undermined progress." Notice, first, that this thesis employs two sentences (which is acceptable), and second, that it provides a line of reasoning ("idea of progress," "challenging religious authorities") for its complex assertions regarding progress. More importantly a specific thesis like this will provide direction to your analysis of the sources and the development of your argument.

Don't get bogged down in the introductory paragraph; it should be no more than 4–6 sentences. Resist the temptation to provide extensive background or commentary on the topic. The focus of your essay will be the body paragraphs and treatment of the documents.

Effective Body Paragraphs Using the Documents

It is in the body paragraphs where you make your argument. In my view, the Complexity point (or 2nd point for Analysis and Reasoning) is the hardest to earn. You must adopt one of the six strategies noted above for LEQs, but you might consider the strategy inherent to the DBQ: showing how <u>the documents</u> "corroborate, qualify, or modify one another." Many students fall into a pattern of summarizing or quoting a document, adding analysis that is merely a paraphrase, and then unceremoniously moving on to the next source. If you adopt this approach, you will not demonstrate complexity in your argument through examining multiple perspectives. To help you internalize these requirements, we will use some basic formulas, which you can practice and adapt as you develop your skills on the DBQ.

First, begin your body paragraphs with a powerful topic sentence that indicates how the paragraph supports your thesis. Avoid simply stating the topic: "Darwin's ideas affected culture." Give the reader more direction: "The theory of natural selection opened further rifts between religious and scientific views of the world and ethics." Next, move into your documents. When you use a document, cite the author and the title or type of source. This is the first step toward addressing source analysis. It is also a good practice to put the document number in parentheses after using it, e.g. (Doc. 4), to make it easy for the reader to count the documents should they be in doubt whether you used the required number. When you use a document, you should 1) indicate how it supports the topic sentence of the paragraph, 2) consider opportunities for source analysis with it, and 3) explain how it juxtaposes with other documents.

Think of the documents as being part of a conversation on the issue. If you can get the evidence to interact, you will be moving toward fulfilling the Complexity point (see above). Before looking at specific techniques, let's define some of the features of this point:

Corroboration: If you think of a trial, one type of evidence (e.g., DNA) can confirm or support another type of evidence (e.g., eyewitness testimony). This is corroboration. Though sources may provide differing perspectives and evidence, they may still arrive at a similar conclusion. In Document 5, Spencer applies Darwin's notion of "survival of the fittest" to government policy as it relates to internal issues of poverty and inequality. Pearson (Document 6) agrees with Spencer's conclusion, except that he applies the struggle inherent in nature to foreign policy, justifying imperial domination.

Qualification: We often make generalizations that need to be qualified in recognition of complexity, and in the same way, sources can be in general agreement but provide differing justifications for their conclusions. Moreover, when we consider certain types of sources, we pick up on nuances or shades of meaning not noticed in other types of evidence.

Darwin explains his path from belief to unbelief (Document 3) as a slow process of replacing one set of explanations (religious) with another (scientific). The Punch cartoon (Document 4) seems also to realize this implication of natural selection; however, as a cartoon, it employs exaggeration (in the depiction of the figures and the compression of time) and humor (from CHAOS to worms to reptilian creatures to monkeys to the "missing link" to humans). All this unfolds while Darwin, like God, watches over the process. There is similar recognition of the issues involved, but divergence on what this means for humanity.

Modification: As you read the sources, look for how documents modify or even contradict one another on a similar point. For example, Documents 1 and 2 on the Darwin question offer two opposing perspectives on the theological implications of natural selection. Try to capture this tension by using an appropriate transition, e.g., "In Document 2, Royer challenges Wilberforce's denunciation of Darwin, instead arguing that…." If you are taking a position (e.g., that Darwin's ideas promoted progress), then you will need to address evidence that runs counter to your claim. Don't ignore such evidence; your engagement of it demonstrates your recognition of complexity.

To capture these three features of documents, employ transition words as you move from one document to the next. Think of the phrases below as a template for placing your evidence in a conversation. They will lend your writing power and indicate your awareness of the complexity involved in argumentation.

- "This document is supported by…"
- "On the other hand,…"
- "His view is directly contradicted by…"
- "The author agrees, but with differing reasoning…"
- "This perspective is echoed by…"
- "This viewpoint receives confirmation from…"

As you develop your argument in this way, pay attention to possibilities for source analysis—the rubric requires 3 explicit examples—and attend to this task as well. Like those above, the following phrases will serve as indicators of your analysis of the sources:

- It is not surprising that X should take this view, given that Y...
- Considering their position/status as X, this source is a reliable account of Y because of Z.
- Since the document was created during X, the perspective was likely influenced by Y.
- X probably created this document for the explicit purpose of Y, which implies that Z.

- This speech/writing/visual/etc. was aimed at X to convince them that Y.
- Taking into account their X, the source is (un) biased because Y.
- Because of the gap in time between the writing of this source and X, it cannot be considered reliable.

Phrases and transitions like these are not specifically required by the rubric, nor should they be considered to have magical properties. They act as reminders to you and your reader that the DBQ is about making an argument, using and recognizing the complexities of evidence. For further examples and insight into these strategies, please see Gerald Graff and Cathy Birkenstein's *They Say, I Say: The Moves that Matter in Academic Writing*, 4th ed. (New York: W.W. Norton, 2018).

The Conclusion

Your conclusion offers an ideal chance to hammer home your Complexity point, assuming you have not already earned it through document interaction. Remind the reader of your argument, but then connect the topic to related historical issues (from a different period or nation/region). You can also add another category of analysis with the course themes (e.g., economic), or you might explicitly address the opposing side of the argument by saving a specific document as evidence. As you read through the DBQ samples throughout this guide, please take note of the varying Complexity strategies.

The "Ten Commandments" of DBQ Writing

1. Avoid long quotations from the documents. They add nothing to source analysis and waste time you might spend on higher-level tasks. Paraphrase specific information in the documents or use brief quotes and/or phrases.

2. The question is designed to gauge your skills of historical analysis, not serve as a platform for your own position on the issue. Avoid indicating your own opinion and using "I" references.

3. Make sure you address *all* parts of the question (if it has parts) throughout your essay.

4. Cite the documents appropriately. Identify the author, source (this can be abbreviated if it's lengthy), and place the document number in parentheses.

5. Make the structure of your argument clear by employing a direct thesis, strong topic sentences, and transitional phrases.

6. Use the documents *explicitly* to advance your argument. Avoid simply summarizing or paraphrasing without connecting to an argument.

7. Be explicit in explaining your rationale for source analyses. Simply stating, "The author is biased," is insufficient. Aim for at least 3–4 examples of source analysis and try to vary your strategies.

8. Try to use all of the documents to support your response. If you make a major error of interpretation, that document will not count toward your total. You should be aiming for 6 (to earn 2 points), so using 7 provides a margin for error. It is acceptable to spend more time on a document that offers rich opportunities for analysis, but avoid getting bogged down with any particular document. Try to be efficient in using the documents to support your answer.

9. Refer to appropriate content beyond the documents: as background to introduce your thesis, as historical context to analyze sources, and as additional content evidence that advances your argument.

10. The question will ask you to take a position; make sure you use the key phrase from the prompt ("progress") in your evaluation as well as a line of reasoning for that evaluation. Address evidence that modifies your argument (to show complexity) and work toward engaging the documents in an ongoing conversation/debate on the topic.

Practice Writing

Now you should be ready to begin writing the sample DBQ on Darwin. Take about 15 minutes to read through the documents and plan your response. Once you begin writing (you have 45 minutes), stay focused on the question. When you are finished, compare your response to the samples that follow, which include commentary. Use the scoring rubric (on page 4) to evaluate your essay. Remember that this is a first effort, so you may feel a time crunch. Don't worry, that's common and you will improve your efficiency with each effort.

Sample Essays with Commentary

The essay below demonstrates how to approach the writing of the DBQ. You can follow along with the commentary to see how the student earned all points in the rubric.

SAMPLE ESSAY 2

Charles Darwin's theory of natural selection and evolution developed during a time period of great changes in many fields. Advances in scientific research during the Second Industrial Revolution produced new technologies, like the railroad and telegraph. With greater wealth, many people embraced the idea of never-ending progress, known as positivism.[1] Natural selection changed European cultural ideas, challenging the traditional Christian view of intelligent design, which marked progress. However, Darwin's ideas also caused the development of eugenics, a pseudo-science that provided "scientific" support for nationalism and racism, which was not progressive.[2]

Christians in Europe traditionally believed in a God who, being perfect in every way, created the world to be perfect, like Himself. As evidenced by Document 1, Darwin's ideas presented a contradiction to this theory of intelligent design by a perfect God. Wilberforce, who was a bishop, and therefore wished to preserve his traditional beliefs about religion in writing this document,[3] wrote that mankind's power over all other species on Earth could not have been an accident, and that man's creation must have been done by

NOTES

1 Though brief, the references to the Second Industrial Revolution, railroad, telegraph, and positivism provide enough specific content to earn the Contextualization point.

2 These two sentences earn the Thesis point, as the response takes a position on the question of progress, provides a clear line of reasoning, while also noting complex outcomes from natural selection.

3 A brief but adequate source analysis for Document 1 using point of view.

some perfect Master Being. This document shows that Darwinism indeed did not agree with traditional Christian doctrine. Although Bishop Wilberforce was not convinced that evolution should replace intelligent design as the theory of choice, Clemence Royer, the author of Document 2, was. She wrote that anyone who used evidence should most definitely recognize that Darwin's theory was superior to the "irrational" happenings of the Bible. Royer wrote this document to preface "On the Origins of Species," Darwin's definitive work on evolution, and that is probably why she spoke with so much praise about Darwin's ideas; she wanted to sell more books.[4] Corroborating Document 2, Document 3, written by Darwin himself, continues the idea that natural selection and religion came into direct conflict.[5] Darwin wrote that he became an agnostic because of his ideas of natural selection. Since nature came about entirely by accident, according to him, there must be no God to perfectly design everything. Darwin, of course, as the original developer of the theory of evolution, would wish to believe in its truth, and would defend his theory against detractors. Though Christians were upset with Darwin's ideas, these documents show how society could progress from science based on religious text to science based on observations.[6]

The period 1859–1914 was the great age of European imperialism. Not only did Darwinism cause the development of eugenics and a further increase in nationalistic fervor, but it also provided "evidence" for the superiority of Europe and the need to colonize. With racism and domination, the effects of Darwin's ideas on politics show a step backward, not progress.[7] In Document 6, Pearson, a professor of eugenics, wrote that history reveals that the survival of the fitter and stronger race is why Europe was so advanced at the time. Since Pearson was, after all a professor of eugenics, it makes sense that he firmly believed in its truth, and wished to prove it and influence others to believe in it as well by writing this document.[8] Eugenics, which taught such ideas as this, provided evidence for the superiority of Europeans, thus justifying colonization and imperialism. Rudyard Kipling, a British poet, wrote the famous poem, "White Man's Burden," which demonstrated, satirically, many popular European political attitudes of the time. The poem discusses the superiority of the titular "white man" and said that it would forever be the burden and responsibility of the white men, or Europeans, to civilize inferior races, who were compared to devils or children.[9] Darwinism, which morphed into social Darwinism, provided fodder for nationalism.[10] In Document 7, Friedrich von Bernhardi argued that war is beneficial to civilization, as presumably it impedes the development of weaker races and allows the stronger to come out on top. Bernhardi's ideas were written during the height of nationalism, right before World War I, which demonstrates the effects of natural selection on politics and explains his war-mongering. As he was

4 Source analysis for Document 2; uses purpose strategy.

5 This transition effectively connects Documents 2 and 3.

6 Source analysis for Document 3 with point of view, as well as a link to the argument for the documents in the paragraph.

7 Not only a topic sentence, this preface to the body paragraph also suggests that the student is aiming to show complex results; in this case, the contradiction to progress in Darwin's ideas.

8 Source analysis for Document 6, identifying and explaining its purpose.

9 With this example and full explanation, the student earns the Evidence Beyond Document point.

10 An effective transition to the next document.

German, he was probably extremely nationalistic, as that country had only recently been unified, and in writing about superior races, he wished probably to justify the warlike tendencies of his Kaiser, Wilhelm II.[11] Nationalism in conjunction with natural selection is also seen in Document 5,[12] in which a British philosopher, Spencer, argues that the hardships of life, including war, disease, and hard work, are ultimately beneficial to humanity, as these trials help weed out the weaker members of society and leave only the strong to survive. These documents may be explained in the context of industrialization. With the poor working and living conditions that came along with industrialization during this time period, many workers lived short, miserable, sickly lives.[13] This document may have been trying to justify some of these conditions by calling them ultimately good. The rise in nationalism and imperialism that was also justified by natural selection was additionally part of this movement of industrialization. Since Europeans possessed more advanced weaponry and technology, such as ships, guns, and cures for diseases like malaria, they were easily able to conquer and subdue native inhabitants of their colonies, thus leading them to point to natural selection as the cause of their victory but also crushing native peoples in the process, which would not have been "progress" for them.[14]

Europe during 1859–1914 was greatly influenced by Darwin's ideas, both culturally and politically. Natural selection also affected European attitudes and policies toward the non-European world. Europeans took evolution and used it to justify the brutal colonization of areas in Africa, Asia, and the Middle East. Imperialism forever changed the way Europe interacted with the world. Instead of being equals or the inferior party in negotiations, as Europeans were during the time of the Silk Road, Europe was most definitely the master of the world because of its superior attitudes and technology. During this period, Europe dominated much of the world, but this ultimately created poverty and discontent within those societies, leading to colonial rebellion and chaos, the price of "progress" for the new secular ideas.[15]

11 With this use of historical situation, the student establishes their 4th source analysis for a document, surpassing the Source Analysis point on the rubric.

12 The student's 6th document, earning 2 points for Using Documents as Evidence. Note that each document is used in some way to advance or modify the argument, sometimes subtly.

13 Another effective link to historical context, though the student has already earned Evidence Beyond the Documents.

14 To conclude the paragraph, the student once again draws on their extensive knowledge of historical context and then makes a connection back to the argument.

15 The concluding paragraph uses a strong Complexity strategy, effectively linking the topic to an additional theme and suggesting a sense of CCOT by anticipating subsequent events.

As you read the essay and comments, you may have noticed the student's mastery of the scoring rubric and deliberate effort to earn all of the points. Their response earned the Complexity point by consistently playing the documents off one another in service of a sophisticated argument, as well as by integrating an additional strategy in the conclusion. **Score:** 7. Let's look at one more sample.

SAMPLE ESSAY 3

The theory of natural selection created by Charles Darwin created great uproar in the European aspects of culture and religion. As a result of his theory, the reliability of the church came into question and who was to trust between the two—the church or natural selection and evolution? The argument for the church being that the moral and spiritual aspects of man cannot be developed, while those who supported Darwin argued natural selection and evolution created humans today.[1]

The spread of Darwin's theory had great impact on Europe, and promoted aggressive beliefs in life for "survival of the fittest."[2] It ranged from day-to-day life actions to business operations. Document 5, written by a social Darwinist, Herbert Spencer, explains how natural selection is positive for Europe. He explicitly states how natural selection is able to remove the weak and promote a stronger species. The possible purpose of the statements by Herbert Spencer might be him attempting to promote his own belief, social Darwinism, in an attempt to gain popularity.[3] Many agreed with Herbert Spencer's beliefs,[4] such as Karl Pearson from document 6. Throughout document 6, Karl Pearson, a professor of eugenics, points to the fact that class and racial struggle exists. His reasoning for white supremacy is simply stated by the fact that Europeans developed sooner than others, and how any nation that experienced horrors and poor living conditions is because they are inferior and it is only a matter of time before natural selection removes them. A very similar situation also took place, when North American slavery grew in numbers. It is very likely that Karl Pearson would also support that.[5] Document 3 also promoted Darwinism, as it was written by Darwin himself. Darwin argues that his belief in god disappeared slowly, but he felt no distress. He then argues on the fact that natural selection is good for mankind and gives progress. His belief is that everything in nature has resulted from something else, and has formed in a positive way from its previous generation. Darwin might have written this book to promote his theory.[6] Friedrich von Bernhardi also agreed with Darwin, on the premise that war promoted natural selection. Bernhardi believed that war is a necessity to mankind. It promotes regulation and if it does not take place, unhealthy developments may occur. Friedrich von Bernhardi might've said this as a preface to the looming First World War.[7]

However not everyone agreed with Darwin that his ideas gave progress. As an attempt to promote the church, Samuel Wilberforce explicitly states how it's impossible for Darwinism to exist, as physical developments have nothing to do with the spiritual and moral aspects of a man. Samuel Wilberforce's beliefs in document 1 are likely biased, as he was a bishop of the church.[8] Though document 4 does appear to have promoted evolution, it is actually sarcastic.[9] The political cartoon represents man's evolution from

1 There is an attempt at the Thesis point, but the student does not take a position on the question of progress nor indicate a line of reasoning, seeming unsure of what the question asked. Also, no Contextualization is provided in the intro or elsewhere.

2 An effort at a topic sentence, but it could be more specific in what it means by "aggressive."

3 Minimal but adequate source analysis, using purpose, for Document 5.

4 Effective transition to the next document.

5 An effort at Evidence Beyond the Documents (slavery) but it requires further explanation.

6 An attempt at source analysis, but the student provides no real explanation for what is suggested already in the source attribution (given to the student).

7 This attempt at source analysis (through historical situation) does not provide adequate explanation.

8 This source analysis for Document 1 also falls short, as there is no explanation as to why a bishop would be biased on the issue.

9 This is the student's 6th document used, earning 2 points for Use of Evidence with Documents.

a worm into modern day man, but the cartoon takes place in a satirical magazine. Though the magazine does address social and political issues, it is likely that it is throwing a jab at all the arguing that has occurred as a result of Darwin's theories. Also, the fact that the final "evolve" that takes place is from man to god, also points to the fact that it should not be taken seriously.[10]

It is very clear that the opposing beliefs of the church and Darwin did cause great uproar and resulted in many new beliefs and aspects on life. Some people viewed these as progress. A similar development that took place earlier in history is between the Catholic Church and Lutheranism. The spread of Luther's ideas caused controversy in politics (like religious wars) and culture (the decline of the Church's power over education), just like Darwin's ideas. In both cases, many people were forced to choose sides, and this led to conflict within society, but also progress.[11]

10 Here the student earns source analysis for the purpose of the magazine and the cartoon; probably the best analysis provided in this response.

11 Solid connection between Darwin and Luther in how their challenges to established religious authorities produced conflict but also progress, earning the Complexity point.

This student provides some effective analysis but also seemed shakier than the first sample on the application of the rubric. Unfortunately, the introduction earned neither the Contextualization nor Thesis points, as the background proved too general and no positions on the question or line of reasoning were given. Though the student earned Use of Evidence with Documents (for 6 accurate uses), the response's attempt at Evidence Beyond the Documents did not offer adequate explanation or connect to an argument. Further, the student fell just short of the Source Analysis point, with 2 examples and several near-misses. Finally, the response offered an appropriate albeit brief connection to another period to earn Complexity. **Score: 3** (+2 for Use of Evidence with Documents, +1 for Complexity)

Conclusion

As you read through the content review section, keep practicing both your writing and application of the historical thinking skills and reasoning processes. It is especially important that you refer back to the rubrics (for the DBQ and LEQ) whenever you attempt to answer essay questions, as well as evaluate the various samples provided, which like those above, highlight excellent responses and those that might have been easily improved with clearer direction and an explicit application of skills. Good luck!

❧ CHAPTER 3 ❧
The Rise of Europe

Introduction

The following chapters review the content of the AP European History course. The material may correspond in content and organization to your textbook. When warranted, I have reorganized the material to provide a stronger focus on the format of the official curriculum framework for the course. The AP European History course is organized around four time periods of roughly equal distribution for test items:

- **Period 1** – 1450–1648
- **Period 2** – 1648–1815
- **Period 3** – 1815–1914
- **Period 4** – 1914–ca. 2001

This guide will employ the same chronological scheme, but you'll notice that each period will be subdivided into more focused topics, such as the Enlightenment or Industrial Revolution, each of which will offer test items to check your understanding. Furthermore, the introduction of each content chapter will indicate clearly its correlation with the relevant content of the Unit Guides from the official course framework (CED). Within each chapter, you'll find connections called out to link the content review to features of the curriculum framework (**Theme Music**, **Skill Set**, and **Example Base**). Further, at the end of each of the four periods, you will have the opportunity to practice with a full DBQ, 30 multiple-choice questions, 2 SAQs, and choice of 2 LEQs.

Seven course themes provide a narrative of the recurring issues across this time span. As you look over the themes, you may notice that they correspond to the categories that are used to drive test items, like social, economic, cultural, or diplomatic history. You are strongly advised to draw on the themes to create a narrative framework for the course and to employ them in your writing. Moreover, the themes serve to remind you that this course is *not* primarily oriented toward memorizing content, but instead for you to demonstrate an understanding of the overarching issues and interpretive questions that have marked European history. With the themes that follow, I have included the 19 Key Concepts that provide the narrative structure for each of the 4 Periods above. Each Key Concept can be connected either primarily or secondarily to the course themes. As you study the content review, thematic and key concept connections will be called out to ensure that you are keeping your attention focused on the big picture. I strongly recommend that you not only familiarize yourself with the narrative arc of these themes but also consider dedicating time and space throughout the course to enhancing the outline provided here with further content examples.

Themes and Key Concepts (KCs)

Theme 1: Interaction of Europe and the World (INT)

Summary: If you've taken World History before this course, then you have a leg up for this theme. If not, don't worry, as this theme is the most straightforward of the seven. As of 1450, Europe had already begun its outward reach toward Africa and Asia in pursuit of gold and silver, luxury products, and spices. These motives coincided with the goal of spreading Christianity and states seeking political advantage over rivals. Since the Crusades, Europeans gradually accumulated knowledge of new navigational and ship-building techniques from Arab traders and China. The establishment of European colonies—first as trading outposts, then as territorial empires—helped create a global trading network by the end of the seventeenth century. These endeavors resulted in a two-way causal stream, with Europe gaining access to new commodities as part of the Columbian Exchange, as Native Americans experienced demographic disaster through disease and mistreatment, while Africans were subjected to the transatlantic slave trade.

Interaction with the non-European world also generated cultural and intellectual reassessments. Europeans responded in a variety of ways to contact with the outside world—by articulating theories of racial superiority and cultural relativism, writing travel literature, and developing new commercial and financial practices. The slave trade, in particular, had by the eighteenth centuries raised questions of natural rights and citizenship that coincided with the Enlightenment and the age of revolutions. With the Industrial Revolution of the nineteenth century, European states sought global resources with a renewed vigor and established more direct and expansive empires, the pursuit of which only heightened national rivalries while prompting internal debates and anti-colonial movements. By 1914, a new player, the United States, had emerged on the world scene and as a European power. The world wars and Cold War reoriented Europe's position in the world and affirmed the importance of the United States to the European balance of power as the superpowers erected an Iron Curtain that divided East from West. The destructive wars and economic upheaval of the twentieth century engendered, first, movements for indigenous liberation, and then, outright independence for former colonies. Decolonization also contributed to new patterns of immigration and conflict, raising further issues regarding European identities and the continent's position in the world.

- Why have Europeans sought contact and interaction with other parts of the world?

- What political, technological, and intellectual developments enabled European contact and interaction with other parts of the world?

- How have encounters between Europe and the world shaped European culture, politics, and society?

- What impact has contact with Europe had on non-European societies?

🔑 Key Concepts

KC 1.3: Europeans explored and settled overseas territories, encountering and interacting with indigenous populations.

KC 2.2: The expansion of European commerce accelerated the growth of a worldwide economic network.

KC 3.5: A variety of motives and methods led to the intensification of European global control and increased tensions among the Great Powers.

KC 4.1: Total war and political instability in the first half of the twentieth century gave way to a polarized state order during the Cold War, and eventually to efforts at transnational union.

⊕ Major Topics and Developments

- Motives, means, and consequences of European exploration (15ᵗʰ–16ᵗʰ centuries)

- Establishment of gunpowder and colonial empires (15ᵗʰ–18ᵗʰ centuries)

- Global trading network → Commercial Revolution (16ᵗʰ–18ᵗʰ centuries)

- Slave trade, slavery, and race (15ᵗʰ–19ᵗʰ centuries)

- Travel literature and the Enlightenment (17ᵗʰ–18ᵗʰ centuries)

- Revolutionary ideas and anti-colonialism (18ᵗʰ–19ᵗʰ centuries)

- Imperialism in Asia and Africa (19ᵗʰ–20ᵗʰ centuries)

- Impact of interaction on the arts, culture, and ideas (18ᵗʰ–20ᵗʰ centuries)

- World Wars and decolonization (20ᵗʰ century)

- Guest workers and issues of dependency and immigration (20ᵗʰ–21ˢᵗ centuries)

Theme 2: Economic and Commercial Developments (ECD)

Summary: After 1450 Europe gradually, and with wide regional variations, developed away from subsistence and preindustrial toward commercial and money-oriented economic activities. The Price Revolution—caused primarily by rising population bidding up the price of land and goods—privileged the development of cash crops for sale on the market. Rising prices paralleled the enclosure movement and the breakdown of communal agriculture practices, all of which encouraged the growth of larger landholding and a new rural elite. Pre-industrial economic operations had been subject to the control of traditional institutions such as guilds and villages. The transformation toward a money and commercial economy corresponded with: 1) trade in goods from the Americas and other colonies, 2) a rising standard of living, 3) efforts by governments to promote commerce and accumulate hard money (mercantilism).

Despite the increase in wealth during the period 1500–1750, Europe continued to confront a Malthusian Trap whereby limited resources restrained population growth. Enlightenment thinker Adam Smith formulated a systematic critique of mercantilism with his free-market theories of capitalism. Capitalist principles and practices supported the growth of industry in the eighteenth century, first in Britain and spreading to the continent in the nineteenth century. Industrialization revolutionized production through the factory system and application of machinery, but at the same time produced new class inequalities and a range of social problems, such as overcrowded cities and child labor. Stimulated by these problems and the legacy of the French Revolution, socialism and then Marxism developed throughout the nineteenth century, reaching political power with the Bolshevik Revolution in 1917.

Two world wars and a Great Depression ended the European-dominated world economic system, allowing new centers of production and economic powers to arise, particularly the United States. The economic crisis of the twentieth century led to experimentation with new theories and policies in western Europe, such as Keynesianism and then the growth of a more extensive welfare state. During the Cold War, the Soviet Union and Eastern Europe offered a rival system of centralized control and collective ownership of property. The imperatives of the Cold War facilitated Europe's recovery from the Cold War, in the form of American aid and new policies of political and economic integration. The latter were highlighted by the formation of the European Union and euro currency around the turn of the twenty-first century, which were joined by the former Eastern bloc satellites following the collapse of communism. These policies of unity and the growing costs of the welfare state have been criticized from both the left and right of the political spectrum, highlighting the perennial issue of organizing production efficiently while addressing issues of inequality and status of labor.

❓ Overarching Questions:

- How has capitalism developed as an economic system?
- How has the organization of society changed as a result of or in response to the development and spread of capitalism?
- What were the causes and consequences of economic and social inequality?
- How did individuals, groups, and the state respond to economic and social inequality?

🔑 Key Concepts

KC 1.4: European society and the experiences of everyday life were increasingly shaped by commercial and agricultural capitalism, notwithstanding the persistence of medieval social and economic structures.

KC 2.2: The expansion of European commerce accelerated the growth of a worldwide economic network.

KC 3.1: The Industrial Revolution spread from Great Britain to the continent, where the state played a greater role in promoting industry.

KC 4.2: The stresses of economic collapse and total war engendered internal conflicts within European states and created conflicting conceptions of the relationship between the individual and the state, as demonstrated in the ideological battle among liberal democracy, communism, and fascism.

⊕ Major Topics and Developments

- Traditional economy and subsistence agriculture (15th–17th centuries)
- Renaissance recovery (15th century)
- Price Revolution and money economy (16th–17th centuries)
- New financial and trading institutions (15th–18th centuries)
- Mercantilism → Capitalism (17th–18th centuries)
- 1st and 2nd Industrial Revolutions overcome Malthusian Trap (18th–19th centuries)
- Inequality—reform and socialism (19th–20th centuries)
- Effects of World Wars—Great Depression (20th century)
- Economic miracle and unity (20th–21st centuries)

Theme 3: Cultural and Intellectual Developments (CID)

Summary: Classical and medieval learning began with authoritative texts and institutions, such as Aristotle's writings, the Bible, and the Catholic Church. After 1450, this approach was increasingly challenged by a new methodology of inquiry that involved more systematic investigation of the natural world and a quantitative, rather than the classical qualitative, perspective. During the Renaissance and Reformation, classical texts and standards of value continued to hold sway; however, these movements' attitude of questioning set the stage for the Scientific Revolution. The new science not only produced new conceptions of the cosmos and human body, it also adopted a radically simple new method of investigation involving empirical evidence, a reliance on mathematics, and the articulation of natural laws.

The Scientific Revolution reached its culmination with Newton's mechanical view of the universe and set the stage of the application of "natural" laws to human affairs, the eighteenth-century movement known as the Enlightenment. The philosophes of the Enlightenment, such as Voltaire and Diderot, expressed skepticism toward religious authority with new ideas ranging from deism to outright atheism. All human endeavors, from education to politics to economics, came under the aegis of reason and science, producing an impulse toward reform and a belief in progress. The new attitude of progress and confidence in reason reached fruition with the French and Industrial Revolutions, aimed at applying Enlightenment principles to political systems and its technologies to production. Along with impressive accomplishments in the technology and the social sciences, the revolutionary era also sparked new ideologies aimed at providing systematic accounts of the human condition.

Despite the powerful appeal of the new science, many continued to adhere to a religious worldview and subjective interpretations of reality and knowledge. Romanticism reacted to the Enlightenment's perceived overemphasis on rationalism by countering it with emotion, intuition, and a more subjective attitude toward the natural world. Just as science and technology seemed to reach their apogee during the nineteenth century—particularly with the development of positivism, which asserted that only observable objects and forces could exist—new theories in science and social science called objective truths into question. Freudian psychology, relativity theory, and quantum physics reinforced the subjective nature of reality and laid the foundations for movements in philosophy and the arts that questioned the possibility of absolute paradigms. After two world wars and the threat of nuclear destruction during the Cold War, intellectuals and artists greeted claims of objectivity with skepticism, instead embracing a plurality of intellectual perspectives and an eclectic blending of styles.

❓ Overarching Questions:

- What roles have traditional sources of authority (church and classical antiquity) played in the creation and transmission of knowledge?

- How and why did Europeans come to rely on the scientific method and reason in place of traditional authorities?

- How and why did Europeans come to value subjective interpretations of reality?

🔑 Key Concepts

KC 1.1: The rediscovery of works from ancient Greece and Rome and observation of the natural world changed many Europeans' view of the world.

KC 1.2: Religious pluralism challenged the concept of a unified Europe.

KC 2.3: The popularization and dissemination of the Scientific Revolution and the application of its methods to political, social, and ethical issues led to an increased, but not unchallenged, emphasis on reason in European culture.

KC 3.6: European ideas and culture expressed a tension between objectivity and scientific realism on one hand, and subjectivity and individual expression on the other.

KC 4.3: During the twentieth century, diverse intellectual and cultural movements questioned the existence of objective knowledge, the ability of reason to arrive at truth, and the role of religion in determining moral standards.

🔍 Major Topics and Developments

- Authoritative (classical and ecclesiastical sources) → objective knowledge (15th–17th centuries)

- Renaissance and Scientific Revolution— from qualitative to quantitative approaches (15th–17th centuries)

- Enlightenment—"science of man" (18th century)

- Romanticism and subjectivity (18th–19th centuries)

- Positivism and modernism (19th–20th centuries)

- Questioning of rationality—Freud, Darwin, Einstein, quantum physics (19th–20th centuries)

- Age of Anxiety—effects of World Wars (20th century)

- Post-modernism and plurality of intellectual frameworks (20th–21st centuries)

Theme 4: States and Other Institutions of Power (SOP)

Summary: By 1450, Europe was just beginning to develop the modern conception of nation-states. Previous political thinking focused on the ideal of reviving the ancient Roman Empire around Christianity. Spurred by new secular political theories and the imperative of warfare—now dominated by gunpowder and the foot-soldier—states developed new institutions and policies to centralize power around the monarch and curb the prerogatives of traditional groups like nobles, estates, and local assemblies. The Renaissance, exploration, and the Protestant Reformation inadvertently facilitated the centralizing trend—by providing a cadre of literate office-holders drawn from the middle class, opening a range of new wealth and resources, and strengthening control over religious institutions. The Peace of Westphalia of 1648, which followed over a century of religious warfare, confirmed the sovereignty of the nation-state over internal religious policy and created a secular order of competing states seeking to maintain the balance of power.

By the seventeenth century, differing types of states had evolved—from city-states to multiethnic empires—but the dominant trend was toward absolutism, as exemplified by France under Louis XIV (1643–1715). Some states, such as the Netherlands and Britain, developed into constitutional regimes, running counter to the centralizing trend. Nations also patronized the arts, sciences, and commerce in an effort to lend tangible and emotional props to their power. Commercial expansion supported the growth of the middle class and the creation of a civil society, or public spaces outside the control of the government, such as coffeehouses, salons, and libraries. Drawing from the New Science and embracing secular progress, the Enlightenment stoked the articulation of new political theories, which culminated in the French Revolution's fundamental attack on the Old Regime in favor of natural rights. Though incomplete, the French Revolution inspired new ideals of popular legitimacy and mass politics, and acted as a touchstone for critics of existing governments. Moreover, the revolution and subsequent wars of Napoleon threatened the state system created at Westphalia.

Despite the efforts of diplomats to close the Pandora's box of revolution in 1814–1815 at Vienna, new ideologies arose to articulate blueprints for change and motivate political action. In combination with the issues raised by industrialization, revolutionary politics sparked development of a political spectrum ranging from socialism to Liberalism to Conservatism. Perhaps the most powerful ideology in the nineteenth and twentieth centuries proved to be nationalism, particularly since it was stymied by the Vienna settlement. After the breakdown of Metternich's Concert of Europe with the revolutions of 1848 and Crimean War, the door opened to the unification of Italy and Germany, the creation of which disrupted the balance of power in Europe.

With pursuit of colonies added to the mix, the system of alliances failed to integrate Germany into a stable diplomacy, leading to the two world wars of the twentieth century. Diplomats in Versailles attempted to reconstruct a new order of collective security with the League of Nations; however, economic crisis and diplomatic instability—complicated by the existence of the first Marxist state in the Soviet Union—led to extremist political ideologies. The Second World War ended even more destructively than the First, with Europe now divided between the superpowers of the United States and Soviet Union. However, Western Europe recovered quickly with the help of American aid and new policies of economic and political integration. The new ideal of a unified Europe has been stimulated, on one hand, by the collapse of communism after 1989, but also challenged, on the other, by a revival of nationalism in the Balkans and elsewhere and tensions over the euro currency.

❓ Overarching Questions:

- What forms have European governments taken, and how have these changed over time?

- In what ways and why have European governments moved toward or reacted against representative and democratic principles and practices?

- How did civil institutions develop apart from governments, and what impact have they had upon European states?

- How and why did changes in warfare affect diplomacy, the European state system, and the balance of power?

- How did the concept of a balance of power emerge, develop, and eventually become institutionalized?

🔑 Key Concepts

KC 1.2: Religious pluralism challenged the concept of a unified Europe.

KC 1.5: The struggle for sovereignty within and among states resulted in varying degrees of political centralization.

KC 2.1: Consolidation of different models of sovereign states defined the relationship among states and between states and individuals.

KC 3.3: Political revolutions and the complications resulting from industrialization triggered a range of ideological, governmental, and collective responses.

KC 3.4: European states struggled to maintain international stability in an age of nationalism and revolutions.

KC 4.1: Total war and political instability in the first half of the twentieth century gave way to a polarized state order during the Cold War, and eventually to efforts at transnational union.

KC 4.2: The stresses of economic collapse and total war engendered internal conflicts within European states and created conflicting conceptions of the relationship between the individual and the state as demonstrated in the ideological battle among liberal democracy, communism, and fascism.

🔍 Major Topics and Developments

- Rise of centralized states and decline of empires (15th–17th centuries)
- Military revolution (15th–17th centuries)
- Theories of absolutism and resistance (16th–18th centuries)
- Great power system and balance of power (17th–18th centuries)
- Civil society and public opinion (17th–18th centuries)
- Enlightenment—social contract, natural rights, limited government (18th century)
- Revolutionary movements and ideologies (18th–19th centuries)
- Nationalism and unification (19th century)
- World Wars and totalitarianism (20th century)
- Cold War and transnational unity (20th–21st centuries)
- Decolonization (20th–21st centuries)

Theme 5: Social Organization and Development (SCD)

Summary: Though the SCD theme may seem primarily descriptive and cover many different groups or issues, it is best to consider the details under the guidance of some prevailing issues, namely (in)equality, role of social institutions (marriage, family, village, guild), gender norms and behavior, and effects of economic changes on social life. In addition, you may find it instructive to use the chronological division of medieval legacy (fifteenth and sixteenth centuries), early modern (sixteenth through eighteenth centuries), modern (nineteenth through twentieth centuries), and postmodern (twentieth and twenty-first centuries).

Individuals in European society were traditionally defined by status, e.g., the three estates used in feudal France of the clergy, nobles, and commoners. Between and within these ranks, inequality, hierarchy, and privilege informed attitudes and behaviors, such as with the Body Politic metaphor. Religious authority reinforced class and gender expectations. However, the revival of the classics during the Renaissance and new religious ideals of the Reformation prompted an ongoing debate over the extent to which intellectual and cultural movements should alter society, particularly in relation to women, known as the "woman question." The pre-industrial economy of limited resources reinforced the importance of household and village production. Women and men worked in complementary tasks to raise crops or manufacture products; though gender norms guided productive and reproductive activities, the idea of strictly separate spheres would not arise until mechanization. Supposedly revolutionary intellectual movements often reaffirmed negative stereotypes of women, which, in addition to social and economic instability, promoted the witchcraft phenomenon of the sixteenth and seventeenth centuries.

With the Enlightenment and revolution in politics and industry in the eighteenth and nineteenth centuries, traditional social norms were fundamentally called into question. Supported by a rising standard of living and the notion of progress, the upper classes embraced new attitudes and practices toward children. The French Revolution led to the abolition of serfdom and feudalism in many states and introduced new conceptions of government, stressing individualism and equality. With the First and Second Industrial Revolutions of the nineteenth and early twentieth centuries, women gained the means of economic independence, stimulating the modern feminist movement, but mechanized production also created the notion of domesticity, or separate spheres for women (private) and men (public). A rising standard of living and increasing leisure time helped to create a new consumer culture and, in urban areas, a mass society involving access to newspapers, education, and redesigned city landscapes.

The two world wars of the twentieth century called for the mass mobilization of society, altering the relationship between the state and the individual. In some cases—as with women gaining the vote—warfare promoted equality, but in others—as with the forced industrialization of the Soviet Union under Stalin or the racial policies of fascist governments—the organized violence of the state meant repression or, worse, mass murder. Totalitarian regimes generally overlooked the rights of individuals—women, kulaks, ethnic minorities—in pursuit of a "higher" ideal of complete equality or racial purity. The postwar economic recovery and Cold War fears produced Second Wave feminism and new movements for equality, especially among immigrant populations. Though Europe has become more pluralistic since 1945, issues of equality and identity—whether over the extent of the welfare state or the status of immigrants—continue to generate conflict and change.

❓ Overarching Questions:

- What forms have family, class, and social groups taken in European history, and how have they changed over time?

- How and why have tensions arisen between the individual and society over the course of European history?

- How and why has the status of specific groups within society changed over time?

🔑 Key Concepts

KC 1.4: European society and the experiences of everyday life were increasingly shaped by commercial and agricultural capitalism, notwithstanding the persistence of medieval social and economic structures.

KC 2.4: The experiences of everyday life were shaped by demographic, environmental, medical, and technological changes.

KC 3.2: The experiences of everyday life were shaped by industrialization, depending on the level of industrial development in a particular location.

KC 3.3: The problems of industrialization provoked a range of ideological, governmental, and collective responses.

KC 4.4: Demographic changes, economic growth, total war, disruptions of traditional social patterns, and competing definitions of freedom and justice altered the experiences of everyday life.

⊕ Major Topics and Developments

- Pre-industrial economy and traditional social structure (15th–17th centuries)

- Family, village, guild, and the individual (15th–17th centuries)

- Intellectual and cultural movements—impact on society (15th–17th centuries)

- Concerns over marginal social groups—poverty and witchcraft (16th–17th centuries)

- Effects of commercial agriculture and expanding commerce (17th–18th centuries)

- Movements of equality—Enlightenment and French Revolution (18th–19th centuries)

- First and Second Industrial Revolutions—effect on gender and class (19th–20th centuries)

- Feminism and movements of liberation (19th–20th centuries)

- Effects of Great Depression and World Wars on state power and individual (20th century)

- Changing identities in post-1945 Europe (20th–21st centuries)

- Second Wave Feminism (20th–21st centuries)

Theme 6: National and European Identity (NEI)

Summary: Prior to the development of modern nation-states, European life in the early modern era centered around local and personal loyalties and identities. In Renaissance Italy, the peninsula remained divided into city-states, which served as the focal point of identity and the growth of civic humanism. Though nation-states in the fifteenth and sixteenth centuries worked to centralize power through new administrative bodies and courts, these efforts were often resisted or even thwarted by the diversity of languages or corporate groups, such as town charters, guilds, or aristocratic estates. In some cases, as with Spain unified under Isabella and Ferdinand, identity was hammered out on an anvil of religious identity and a crusading mindset against perceived common enemies (e.g., Jews and Muslims). Imperial dynasties, such as the Habsburgs, advanced their power through marriages and promoting loyalty to family as well as to emerging notions of national identity. However, national identity was often limited by the diversity of traditions and territories controlled by rulers such as Charles V.

Before the development of popular ideologies of nationalism, rulers in the seventeenth and eighteenth centuries focused their attention on the development of institutions of centralization. Rulers like Louis XIV of France and Peter I of Russia relied on both culture and customs on one hand, and coercion and war, on the other, to achieve national greatness and power. Once again, efforts at centralization often met resistance in the form of noble protest, peasant revolt, or even efforts at regional independence. Modern nationalism arose out of the combination of Enlightenment social contract theories, partially realized during the French Revolution. Revolutionaries attempted to replace the patchwork of provincial loyalties and institutions with a uniform government based in Paris along with a new system of standardized weights and measures, including a new calendar. The success of French mass citizen armies under Napoleon revealed the power of nationalism.

During the Age of Ideologies in the first half of the nineteenth century, Romantic writers and artists explored and glorified national traditions in word, song, and image. Nationalism became one of the most powerful ideologies of change, especially since the map of Europe did not correspond with linguistic and/or ethnic divisions. After 1848, nationalism ultimately led to the unification of Italy and Germany, stimulating a further sense of destiny among national groupings. Nonetheless, many Europeans held to regional or class identity over and above the claims of newly powerful states. For the former, long-oppressed groups like the Basques, Slavs, and Irish clamored for autonomy and challenged the national identities foisted upon them by larger states or empires. For the latter, many members of the working class, attracted to ideas of socialism, raised class consciousness over and above states based on racial identity.

Nationalism led to imperialism in the late-nineteenth century. States began to envision their identity as part of a larger "civilizing mission" in the pursuit of colonial empires. The subsequent interactions often confirmed in the minds of Europeans their identity as superior nations and peoples. These nationalist attitudes led Europeans into the world wars of the twentieth century, traumatic events which created new identities and challenged old ones. Efforts to create a new international order through the League of Nations failed to overcome national self-interest. In addition, Soviet communism emerged to attract workers to a movement that transcended national boundaries. At the same time, fascist ideology emphasized race as its organizing principle, persecuting Jews and other ethnic and political minorities considered a threat to the purity of the state. Out of the ashes of the world wars and amid Cold War division, Western Europe moved toward a new identity through institutions such as NATO and the European Union; however, these efforts have often been met with reluctance or resistance by those holding to national and regional identities, as evidenced by the Brexit vote in Britain. After 1945, increased immigration from the Middle East, Africa, and South Asia has only added complexity and conflict to questions of European identity, as well as revealed the constantly shifting boundaries and ways in which peoples find meaning and solidarity.

❓ Overarching Questions:

- How were national identities created, developed, and challenged over time?

- How and why have cultural, regional, and other social identities coexisted with national identities and challenged the idea of a unified nation or empire?

- How and why have political, economic, and religious developments challenged or reinforced the idea of a unified Europe?

- How have overseas expansion, warfare, and international diplomacy affected Europeans' identities as part of national, cultural, regional, or transnational groups?

🔑 Key Concepts

KC 1.2: Religious pluralism challenged the concept of a unified Europe.

KC 1.5: The struggle for sovereignty within and among states resulted in varying degrees of political centralization.

KC 2.1: Consolidation of different models of sovereign states defined the relationship among states and between states and individuals.

KC 3.4: European states struggled to maintain international stability in an age of nationalism and revolutions.

KC 4.1: Total war and political instability in the first half of the twentieth century gave way to a bipolar state configuration during the Cold War, and eventually to efforts at transnational union.

Major Topics and Developments

- Expansion and enhancement of state power (15th–18th centuries)
- Religious reform and religious division of Europe (16th–17th centuries)
- Development of social contract theory and nationalism (17th–19th centuries)
- Revolutions and spread of nationalism/mass citizen armies (18th–19th centuries)
- Industrialization and development of class identities (18th–20th centuries)
- National unification and pursuit of empires (19th–20th centuries)
- Racial ideologies and totalitarian movements (19th–21st centuries)
- Movements toward collective security and transnational unity (20th century)
- Immigration and shifting religious and ethnic identities (20th–21st centuries)

Theme 7: Technological and Scientific Innovation (TSI)

Summary: In the fifteenth century (1450), Europeans began to expand outward, beginning with exploration in the fifteenth century and culminating with the new imperialism in the early twentieth century. However, along with greater control over the environment, new scientific and industrial techniques produced great destruction and raised moral and ethical questions. Through cultural contact with advanced civilizations, Europeans adapted and improved existing technologies and ideas. In the fifteenth and sixteenth centuries, this process of cultural transmission was exemplified by the development of the printing press and navigational technologies that allowed for blue water voyages and trading empires. Gutenberg's invention stimulated the spread of Renaissance ideals of humanism, as well as promoted the religious reforms of the Protestant Reformation. Given Europe's political division, states competed with one another to promote and deploy new technologies, particularly those that would aid navigation, commerce, and warfare. From the end of the Hundred Years' War (1453) through the end of the Thirty Years' War (1648), Europe experienced a military revolution that left the tradition of feudal knights and chivalry behind to be replaced by firearms, the foot soldier, and artillery. These new technologies rendered warfare more complex and expensive, requiring the centralization of military affairs, taxation, law, and administration.

Starting in 1543 with the publication of Copernicus's heliocentric theory, the Scientific Revolution represents a watershed in European science and technology. A traditional epistemology (theory of knowledge) and cosmology (model of the universe), dependent on classical and church authority, was gradually but decisively replaced by one based on empirical evidence and mathematics aimed at discovering and articulating natural laws. Though traditional approaches toward knowledge, such as alchemy and astrology, continued to influence popular and even elite thinking, the new science sparked a range of new technologies and an effort to apply these new principles to human affairs, with the Enlightenment. Monarchs patronized this "scientific" approach toward governance ("enlightened absolutism"), while reformers invoked empiricism and rationalism to criticize the old regime for inequality and backwardness. In the nineteenth century, the goals of those embracing scientific approaches toward human affairs seemed to reach a culmination with the First and Second Industrial Revolutions, which introduced efficient systems of mechanization and advanced European control of the environment, extending to the globe, with the new imperialism.

As the Enlightenment project seemed to be realizing its ultimate objective with the nineteenth-century theory of positivism—that all knowledge can be reduced to and is based on the observation of material objects—new scientific ideas and technologies were also having unintended consequences. New models, such as natural selection in biology and Freudianism in psychology, provided powerful new understandings of nature and humans, yet also called into question the notion of an orderly universe and the exalted status of humans. As of 1914, most Europeans embraced notions of cultural superiority based on the previous centuries of scientific creativity. This assumption was to be fundamentally challenged by the world wars, Holocaust, and threat of nuclear destruction, all of which defined the twentieth century. After the experience of total war, many Europeans expressed disillusionment and cynicism toward the former tokens of progress. Postwar Europe continues to highlight the tensions in this theme. On one hand, the twentieth century has seen the largest increase in life expectancy with new medical technologies, democratization of knowledge with computers, access to world markets and culture through globalization, and new forms of leisure and entertainment with television and high-speed travel. At the same time, these technologies have come under criticism for their destructive potential.

Overarching Questions:

- How have new ideas in science developed over time and challenged existing systems of knowledge and ethics?
- How have new technologies addressed human problems and provided benefits and, at the same time, produced destruction and unintended outcomes?
- How have states and other institutions either promoted or hindered the development of new scientific ideas and technologies?

🔑 Key Concepts

KC 1.1: The rediscovery of works from ancient Greece and Rome and observation of the natural world changed many Europeans' view of the world.

KC 2.3: The spread of Scientific Revolution concepts and practices and the Enlightenment's application of these concepts and practices to political, social, and ethical issues led to an increased, but not unchallenged, emphasis on reason in European culture.

KC 3.1: The Industrial Revolution spread from Great Britain to the continent, where the state played a greater role in promoting industry.

KC 3.6: European ideas and culture expressed a tension between objectivity and scientific realism on one hand, and subjectivity and individual expression on the other.

KC 4.3: During the twentieth century, a significant number of diverse intellectual and cultural movements questioned the existence of objective knowledge, the ability of reason to arrive at truth, and the role of religion in determining moral standards.

🔍 Major Topics and Developments

- Development of print technology (15th–16th centuries)

- Advances in means of navigation that supported exploration and colonization (15th–17th centuries)

- Military revolution that promoted centralized state power and national rivalries (15th–17th centuries)

- Scientific Revolution and its application with the Enlightenment (16th–18th centuries)

- First and Second Industrial Revolutions (19th–20th centuries)

- Growing prestige of sciences and social sciences, as well as challenges they pose (19th–20th centuries)

- New communication, transportation, medical, and military technologies supporting imperialism (19th–20th centuries)

- World Wars and technology (20th century)

- Advances and challenges created by medical and other technologies (20th–21st centuries)

- Globalization promoted by communication and transportation technologies (20th–21st centuries)

Learning Objectives (LOs) and Their Use

The AP European History course employs over 100 Learning Objectives (LOs) as statements of what students should know and be able to do. You will find an LO to correspond with each topic in the nine Unit Guides. For studying and review, the LOs can serve as a self-check before a unit test or the AP exam. Further, each exam item will be keyed to one or more LOs. It is suggested that you revisit the LOs periodically—e.g., at the end of a topic or each of the four time periods—to familiarize yourself with the major developments and the conceptual language of the course. Here's an example of a Learning Objective from Unit 1 and the Technological and Scientific Innovation (TSI) theme:

> **Unit 1: Learning Objective E**
> Explain the influence of the printing press on cultural and intellectual developments in modern European history.

Note that the LO is phrased broadly enough to encompass several periods of the course, so that students can consider issues of causation, changes and continuities over time, comparisons across time and geography, and how specific examples illustrate the statement. For this particular LO, a number of effects may come to mind of how the printing press shaped culture and ideas: spread of Renaissance, promotion of vernacular languages, support for ideas of religious reform, and advancement of the Scientific Revolution and Enlightenment. If you engage with these LOs in preparation for the AP exam, you will find them an effective way to cover the chronological and geographical expanse of the course, as well as help you make important connections between periods and between developments during the same period. Because of their sheer number, this review book will not address the LOs in detail, but you can access them at the College Board website for the Course and Exam Description (CED) noted earlier.

A Note on Geography

Before we depart on our journey, it is important to know where we are and where we are going. Some claim that "geography is destiny." Though there is truth in this assertion, it is overstated. As with any geographic region, Europe has been tremendously influenced by its environmental context; economic activities, cultural practices, political forms, and even fashion have all been shaped by geographic and climatic circumstances.

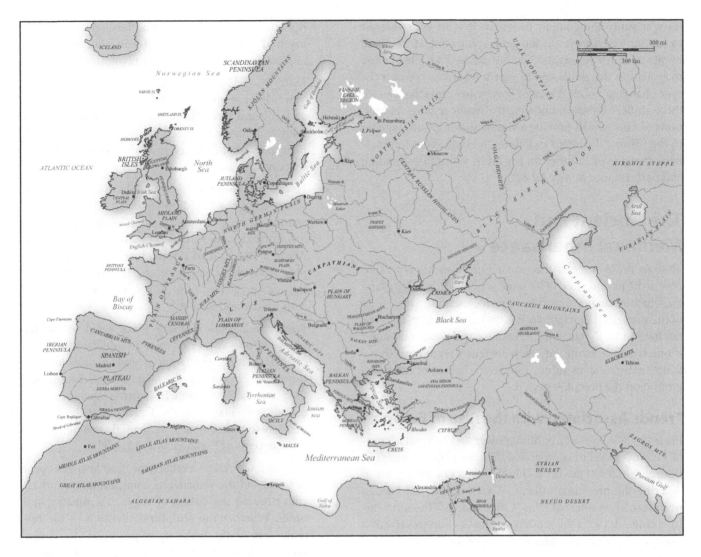

Take note of this map. Several observations come to mind. First, Europe is an oddly shaped peninsula gouged with numerous inland seas, bays, and gulfs; punctuated by islands small and large; narrowing toward the Atlantic and widening into the great plain leading to the vast Eurasian landmass. Second, Europe's location from north to south places it in the temperate climate zone—with wide variations between summer and winter temperatures, though this moderates in proximity to large bodies of water, such as the Atlantic Ocean and Mediterranean Sea. Third, a large variety of navigable rivers, mountain ranges, and plateaus indicate the tremendous diversity of landforms in such a small area (Europe is the second smallest of the seven continents).

What has been the impact of this geographic inheritance? For purposes of your course, two observations are offered. First, a wide variety of economic activities has marked the forward advance of European history. Europe's diverse climate and geography allow it to cultivate almost every important agricultural product—essential cereal grains, livestock, wine—and deploy important natural resources for a wide range of manufacturing and industrial activities—mining, metallurgy, textile production. This geographic inheritance accounts for Europe's economic vitality and its outward reach to control markets and resources abroad, linking geography to the historical developments of exploration and imperialism, the Commercial Revolution, and industrialization.

Second, the European landmass has proved incredibly difficult for one political entity to control. Even the Romans were unable to subjugate all of it, and subsequent conquerors have repeated this failure. As a result, Europe's political and diplomatic history has been defined by a variety of political forms—nation-states, city-states, republics, empires, contested border regions—and multiple centers of power. Because of the inability of one entity—be it the Holy Roman Empire or Napoleonic France—to control the entire region, frequent warfare and shifts in the balance of power define European political and diplomatic history. Though common ground exists among the nations of Europe, until recently sufficient differences in language, culture, and history have prevented a strong enough shared identity to overcome conflicts that too often descended into warfare. Thus, we have a major theme of this course linked to the geographic context—the tension between the identities of the individual nations and the common heritage of Europe.

As you study the content to follow, it is in your interest to keep a vigilant eye on the geographic context for these events and developments. You are advised to refer to the maps within this guide and in your textbook to connect the ever-changing political map of Europe to events that caused these shifts. Moreover, knowing the major regions and nations of Europe will provide a visual cue for grounding you in the historical content to follow. The time spent internalizing the map of Europe will pay off in your understanding and performance on the AP exam.

The Ancient and Medieval Inheritance

Though the Advanced Placement European history exam covers the period after 1450, some general knowledge of the ancient and medieval world will prove useful in your study of the material. For example, it is difficult to understand the fascination of Renaissance humanists with classical values if one has little familiarity with ancient Greece and Rome. With that caveat in mind, this brief chapter offers background on the pre-1450 period.

Trends Associated with the Rise of Europe

Prior to 1300, Europe's political power and cultural accomplishments paled in comparison to other major world civilizations. In 1300 the term "Europe" was not even used to describe the present continent. What we now call Europe was more likely referred to as "Christendom." The term Europe coincides with the modern age just as Europe's rise as a major civilization coincides with modernity.

Heritage of the Ancient World

Greek Civilization The Greeks are often called the founders of Western civilization, with justification. Greek civilization flourished from around 1000 BCE until its conquest by Rome in 146 BCE, and its contributions in philosophy, science, architecture, drama, history, as well as other fields, became the standard and reference point for European civilization for years to come. There are moments and places whose greatness cannot be explained fully by an analysis of historical circumstances. One such place was Athens in the fifth century BCE. The Greek heritage of human accomplishment echoed through the ages and defined excellence in the following areas:

- *Philosophy* – Greek thinkers used reason in asking the most basic questions of nature and humanity, such as "What is the most real?," "What is the good?," "What is a just society?" Philosophers such as Plato and Aristotle established important principles and knowledge that dominated almost all academic fields until the sixteenth century.
- *Politics* – Though the political arena was restricted to free property-owning males, democracy, as well as

the active civic environment of the Greek city-states, inspired imitation among Renaissance humanists and created a model for future revolutionaries.

- *History* – Historians such as Herodotus and Thucydides emphasized the importance of social and political forces in historical causation. Moving away from mythology and divine providence, Greek historians wrote history to edify and warn against human pride and folly.
- *Drama and Poetry* – Literary works in ancient Greece served as mirrors held up to society's faults and the vanities of human nature. The tragedies of Aeschylus, Euripides, and Sophocles and the comedies of Aristophanes influenced later literature in their complex plots, rich characters, and thematic emphases. Europe's great tradition of lyric poetry got its start with Pindar and Sappho.
- *Science and Mathematics* – Once again, Aristotle's ideas—wrong as they often were—defined the fields of physics, astronomy, zoology, and anatomy for centuries, later becoming the target of criticism during the Scientific Revolution. Borrowing much from surrounding civilizations, the Greeks contributed immensely to mathematics, particularly geometry with the theorems of Pythagoras and Euclid.
- *Classical Aesthetics* – Perhaps the most lasting impact of Greek culture remains its emphasis in art and architecture on the virtues of balance, symmetry, and order. Whether the sculptural attention to the human form or the harmony of great civic buildings, how Europeans ordered space and perceived human potential owes much to ancient Greek accomplishments.

Alexander the Great and the Hellenistic Age Like all good things, ancient Greek civilization came to an end. The devastating Peloponnesian War between Athens and Sparta weakened the city-states, opening the way for conquest by the Macedonians from the north. Alexander the Great's armies swept through southeastern Europe, into the Middle East, and eventually halted near India. Alexander died in 323 BCE but not before spreading Greek civilization to the areas he conquered. The subsequent two centuries witnessed the gradual synthesis of Greek ideas with those of surrounding regions. This period is known as the Hellenistic Age.

Roman Civilization As a city, Rome was founded in 753 BCE and graduated into a far-flung empire ruling the entire Mediterranean basin by the second century CE. This outcome was not predetermined, but was aided by luck, circumstance, and sheer determination. Certainly, the Romans deserve recognition for their contributions to many fields and the length of their rule, yet their initial importance lay in spreading Greek ideas to the remainder of Europe following the Roman conquest of the Balkan Peninsula in 146

BCE. With each conquest, Rome successfully integrated new ethnic groups and peoples into its realm, often by extending citizenship and conferring the benefits of Roman civilization upon those lands. While Rome built on Greek learning in many areas, its greatness tends to rest upon its practical accomplishments and enduring legacy.

- *Administration and Law* – As a republic, Rome survived by constantly adapting to shifting circumstances and making use of the patriotism it inspired in its citizens, whether fighting tenaciously in battle or drawing new members into its active political life. Internal social and political conflict, along with the rise of military despots, ultimately undid the republic and led to the creation of the empire. The empire's ability to centralize power and establish a uniform legal code across a vast expanse of territory became the touchstone and goal of many European rulers since the empire's fall in 476 CE in the west (the eastern or Byzantine Empire continued until 1453).

- *Architecture and Infrastructure* – Rome thrived within a distinctly urban culture. Wherever Romans conquered, they brought roads, aqueducts, impressive public buildings, and other amenities previously unknown to their new subjects. Though much of this infrastructure eventually decayed owing to disrepair, even the ruins served as a legacy to be imitated. For example, Renaissance humanists scoured their Italian backyard searching for examples of Roman architecture, baths, and piazzas, not to mention sculptures and literary works for artistic imitation.

- *The* Pax Romana – During its almost half-millennium rule, the Roman Empire generally succeeded in providing a political order that allowed for both an active public life and a thriving intellectual and cultural setting. Certainly the empire experienced turmoil—especially in the third century—due to barbarian invasions, military interference, and demographic decline, but it resiliently rode further on the fumes of its nearly exhausted glory. Even after it fell, many looked to recover the peace and stability of the *Pax Romana*, or Roman peace.

Christianity Though Christianity did not originate there, Europe has traditionally been the heartland of the Christian religion. After the fourth century, when it became the official religion of the Roman Empire, Christianity spread outward from the Mediterranean basin, reaching its final missionary outpost in the Eastern Baltic in the fourteenth century. Christianity's influence extends beyond the religious realm, into politics, ideas, culture, and the arts. Oftentimes, Christian dogma was reconciled and absorbed into pagan customs and beliefs, as can be seen with holiday rituals during Halloween and Christmas. Nonetheless, the implications of Christian theology and practices held profound consequences for European society.

- *The Soul* – Belief in individual immortality and a moral structure that transcended the material world radically altered the perception of the human person. Christianity holds that there is a spiritual reality, the soul, that exists beyond the material world accessible only to the senses.

- *Individual Dignity* – The notion that each individual is "created in the image of God" has often acted as a check on absolutist tendencies in politics and provided a moral basis for law and society.

- *Monotheism* – Drawing from their Jewish roots, the Christian fathers of the early Church maintained a strong belief in one God, while at the same time articulating the doctrine of the Holy Trinity, or the three persons of God (Father, Son, Holy Spirit) who are yet of one substance.

- *St. Augustine (354–430 CE)* – Perhaps the most influential of the early Christian saints, his writings emphasized the predominance of spiritual over temporal authority, the importance of the next world (the City of God vs. the City of Man), and the sovereignty and majesty of God.

- *Caesaropapism* – According to the traditions of the Roman Empire, political and spiritual authority were fused in the same person. While this tradition continued in the Eastern or Byzantine Empire, the two authorities developed separately in Latin Christianity. While this split caused repeated controversies between the Roman Catholic Papacy and the Holy Roman Emperor during the Middle Ages, its positive effect was to carve out a zone between both authorities for political diversity and corporate (meaning "in groups") liberties where neither political nor spiritual power could reach, each being checked by the other.

Heritage of the Medieval World

The Early Middle Ages, 476–ca. 1050 The period following the fall of the Roman Empire is often termed "the Dark Ages." To some extent, this designation is true, as Roman cities became depopulated, roads fell into disrepair, trade dried up, and various barbarian tribes replaced the universal empire with a variety of Germanic kingdoms. In addition, the learning of ancient Greece and Rome was kept alive dimly by the candlelight of monastic scriptoria.

- *Barbarian Invasions* – Due to a traffic jam on the plains of central Asia, barbarian tribes poured into Europe in the waning days of the Roman Empire. Most of these tribes gradually assimilated into the empire, often being deployed for their military skills or to guard distant outposts. What had originally been a strength of the empire—the ability to assimilate various ethnicities—gradually diluted the culture and greatness of Rome. Thus, in 476 a barbarian leader deposed the last emperor in the West.

- *Latin vs. Greek Christianity* – Once the Roman Empire was divided in the fourth century between east and west for administrative purposes, the two drifted further apart culturally and religiously. After the fall of Rome, the Byzantine Empire, centered in Constantinople (today Istanbul) continued the legacy of the empire, but with a distinctly Greek cultural accent. Disputes throughout the medieval period over the authority of the pope, the use of religious icons in church, and other theological controversies led to a formal break between the Latin (Catholic) and Orthodox branches of Christianity that was formalized in 1054, and remains to this day.

- *The Islamic World* – Islam emerged from the desert in the 620s as the fastest growing religion in world history, quickly establishing political and cultural dominance of vast swaths of Asia, North Africa, and southern Europe. Arabs quickly assimilated the intellectual legacy of the Greeks and Roman—keeping alive the learning of Aristotle and others more effectively than Europeans—at the same time making important contributions to mathematics (Arabic numerals, algebra), science (especially in astronomy and medicine), and literature and poetry. Since the early eighth century, Muslims have been a continuous presence in Europe, claiming a common religious heritage with Jews and Christians as "people of the Book," though believing Mohammad and the Koran to be the ultimate fulfillment of God's promise to His people.

- *Germanic Customs* – Unlike the Roman Empire, barbarian culture focused on loyalty to persons instead of institutions. Rather than adhering to abstract legal concepts or ideals, Germanic society revolved around tribal identities, which allowed in many ways for a greater amount of freedom than had existed in the Roman Empire. However, this freedom came at the cost of political unity, economic vitality, and an active civic culture.

- *Monasteries* – Monasteries served as more than houses for religious orders. Beginning in the fifth century, when they adopted the discipline of St. Benedict (ca. 480-543), monasteries retreated from the chaos of political life to concentrate on the life of the spirit and the mind. This meant that monks kept alive ancient Greek and Roman texts, at the same time inventing everything from champagne to pretzels.

- *Charlemagne* – A Frankish king (from the tribe of the Franks, later France), Charlemagne provided a short-lived period of unity and intellectual revival in central Europe. Crowned emperor in 800 by the pope, Charlemagne drove out rival barbarian chieftains and established a seat of government in Aix-La-Chapelle (Aachen) in imitation of the Roman ideal.

Though he could not himself read, Charlemagne led a mini-Renaissance of learning, which faded when his successors fought amongst themselves over the political spoils after his death in 814.

- *Second Wave of Invasions (ninth century)* – Following the rule of Charlemagne, Europe once again was beset by a period of instability and foreign invasion. During the ninth century, tribes from the north, east, and Muslim pirates from the south threatened to overrun the weak kingdoms of the European heartland. As before, the Norse from the Scandinavia and the Magyars from Asia were gradually incorporated into European political culture and converted to Christianity. By 1000, Europe had settled into relative political stability, with the map now filled in with virtually all of the major ethnic groups, though borders would continue to shift and evolve according to war, conquest, and migration.

The High Middle Ages, ca. 1050–1300 As a historical era, the Middle Ages gets a bad rap, whether being spoofed by Monty Python or being associated with terms like "Dark Ages" or "gothic." A more appropriate way is to view this millennium as a gradual synthesis of the major strands of European culture, politics, and society—ancient Greek and Roman, Christianity, and barbarian. In fact, the High Middle Ages was a period of dynamic developments in ideas, economics, technology, politics, and society. Simply because medieval life looks different to our contemporary eyes doesn't mean it was backward or uncivilized. Perhaps the brief review below will convince the skeptic of this notion.

- *Agriculture* – Improvements in agriculture, such as three-crop field rotation, the iron plow, horse collar, and use of windmills, supported an increasing population. More land was brought under cultivation, in places producing a surplus, which helped to stimulate an increase in trade. By 1300, Europe had reached a population peak of 75 million, which represented a doubling from the level of 1000.

- *Feudalism* – Based on the decentralized nature of Germanic political culture and the insecurity of the Early Middle Ages, the system of feudalism emerged during the High Middle Ages. Relationships between lord and vassal were based on specific contractual obligations of loyalty and protection. In return for protection, peasants provided labor and gave loyalty to feudal elites, who controlled peasants and serfs through an intricate set of obligations, fees, rituals, and taxes. As warfare required continuous training and expensive equipment (a result of the invention of the stirrup allowing heavy mounted warriors), only an elite few could engage in the practice. Society became divided, at least in theory, into those who fought (nobles and knights), those who prayed (the clergy), and those who worked (peasants and artisans).

- *Towns and Commerce* – Commercial expansion throughout the High Middle Ages stimulated the growth of towns. Medieval towns were not the teeming urban centers of the industrial era, but did attract skilled labor, ideas, and goods. Towns lay outside the feudal structure and jealously guarded their liberties, which were generally confirmed by charters. Towns often banded together in leagues to protect their independence or promote their commerce, as with the Hanse, the German trading centers in the Baltic. A central institution of most towns was the guild, which controlled the production of goods in a particular craft. Not only did the guild ensure a minimum quality of goods and license its members' skills, it also functioned as a civic institution, reflecting the corporate (small, chartered groups) nature of medieval society. With the continued growth and attraction of cities in western Europe, feudalism, especially serfdom, declined in importance, to be replaced by a more commercial and money-oriented economy.

- *National Monarchies* – The states of the Middle Ages lacked the complexity and administrative tools of more modern forms of government. Nonetheless, kings and queens of this era worked diligently to establish hereditary claims to their thrones. In fact, the beginnings of bureaucracy and representative government can be seen in several nations. First, monarchies established some power to tax their subjects to support the state, though this often required the approval of other bodies. A well-known example demonstrating this trend came when English nobles limited the power of the king in 1215 with the Magna Carta, which eventually led to the formation of the Parliament. Royal councils and representative bodies confirmed limits on the power of monarchs and that traditional liberties must be respected.

- *The Church* – During this period, the Catholic Church reached the height of its political, spiritual, and cultural influence. Throughout the High Middle Ages, the pope and the Holy Roman Emperor continuously vied for power in central Europe, generally over the issue of clerical control, with the result that each checked the power of the other. For a time, popes were successful in establishing their claims to make and unmake kings. The climax of these grand ideals came with the papacy of Innocent III (1198–1216), who attempted to unify the entire Christian world under his authority. At the same time, there was growing criticism of the behavior of the clergy and the lack of regularity in church doctrine and practice. The result was a revival of the monastic ideal (termed the Cluniac movement) and the calling of an exceptional Church council in 1215—the Fourth Lateran—that established new regulations for the clergy and formalized many church doctrines related to the sacraments, which stand to this day.

- *Gender Roles* As with many periods in history, women's roles in the Middle Ages were bound by legal and economic norms. However, medieval women of different classes often found ways to express autonomy, initiative, and talent within these parameters. The nature of medieval warfare often left noblewomen to manage large manors, engage in politics, and organize the defense of castles. Younger noblewomen often joined convents, where they could pursue intellectual and spiritual interests outside the control of men. Women also played major roles in movements of religious change or in so-called heresies. Further, the ideal of courtly love and chivalry placed women at the center of an important cultural tradition. Cities and towns relied on the labor of women in artisan families, often as guild members in food preparation, brewing, and cloth production. Peasant and serf women labored alongside their husbands in mowing hay, tending to vegetable gardens, or in harvesting. Since peasant homes were simple, domestic chores actually played a minor role for women.

- *Universities and Scholasticism* With the rise of towns came a quickening of intellectual life. Informal meetings of students and teachers evolved into the formal founding of the first universities in the early thirteenth century. Universities taught a variety of subjects within their various faculties, but our current separation of spiritual and material subjects did not exist in the medieval world view. In fact, theology stood as the "queen of the sciences," and liberally borrowed from other disciplines to elaborate its truths. The best example of this practice was the creation of Scholasticism. During the thirteenth century, a mini-Renaissance of Aristotle's philosophy swept Europe. Pagan ideas governing logic and the natural world were synthesized into Christian dogma, especially by scholars such as St. Thomas Aquinas, to explain divine truths. This intellectual system dominated universities, though with growing criticism after 1500.

- *The Crusades* The Crusades represent the increasing power of Europe. Due to the expansion of commerce, population, and political organization, Christian Europe was able to go on the offensive against Islamic rule of the Holy Land. The First Crusade was launched in 1095, and subsequent efforts succeeded in establishing kingdoms in Palestine and surrounding areas. However, many of these efforts were driven by prejudice (against Jews, for example) and sheer bloodlust, often producing atrocities and tragic consequences, like the needless sack of Constantinople in 1204 (during the Fourth Crusade). Despite some of the baser motives, the Crusades demonstrated Europe's newfound assertiveness and interest in the outside world, stimulating exploration.

Expanding Europe As of 1300, Europe had become one of several important civilizations on the Eurasian landmass and Africa that came into increasing contact with one another. By this time, Europe stood in a much more advantageous position than it had only a century earlier, able to withstand the onslaught of the Mongols and Ottoman Turks in upcoming centuries. Despite its successes, Europe's technological and cultural accomplishments still paled in comparison to China's, yet in the next 600 years it was Europe that successfully projected its power abroad, not China. Why? Though it invented printing and gunpowder, China did not exploit these technologies in pursuit of global commerce and power. Ironically, Europe's lack of central political power, separation of secular and religious authority, and disorderly conflict among various nations (none of which existed in China) drove technological and scientific innovation, yielding a strange mix of conflict and war along with freedom and dynamism.

Additional Resources

📖 **Jacques Barzun,** *From Dawn to Decadence: 500 Years of Cultural Life, 1500 to the Present* **(2000)** — Filled with fascinating details, this work provides an insightful review of European culture through time.

📖 **Renate Bridenthal, et al.,** *Becoming Visible* **(1998)** — A valuable collection of essays on women's history from ancient times to the present.

📖 **Jared Diamond,** *Guns, Germs, and Steel* **(1997) and** *Collapse* **(2005)** — Drawing from his wide knowledge, the author argues, in the first work, for the importance of environmental factors in explaining the rise of Europe, and in the second, warns of the dangers of civilizational collapse.

📖 **DK and Smithsonian Institution,** *History of the World Map by Map* **(2018)** — A collection of eye-catching maps that visually tell the story of world history.

📖 **Michael Hart,** *The 100: A Ranking of the Most Influential Persons in History,* **2nd ed. (1992)** — This volume is always good for sparking controversy, such as the inclusion of only two women. Many figures covered in the course can be found here.

📖 **Paul Kennedy,** *The Rise and Fall of the Great Powers: Economic Change and Military Conflict from 1500 to 2000* **(1987)** — The author demonstrates the relationship between economic and political power, with cautionary tales from history of imperial collapse.

📖 **William H. McNeill,** *The Rise of the West: A History of the Human Community* **(1991)** — A lengthy work, but each page packs numerous insights into the west and the world.

📖 **Maria Rosa Menocal,** *The Ornament of the World: How Muslims, Jews and Christians Created a Culture of Tolerance in Medieval Spain* **(2003)** — Provides a portrait of Spain prior to the reconquista and charts the relationship there among the Abrahamic religions.

📖 **Geoffrey Parker, ed.,** *Times Atlas of European History* **(1994)** — Clean maps and brief text take the reader through a tour of European history.

📖 **Barbara H. Rosenwein,** *A Short History of the Middle Ages,* **5/e (2018)** — A well-regarded and concise review of an overlooked period in history.

📖 **Jonathan Riley Smith,** *The Crusades: A Short History,* **3/e (2014)** — A good place to start for an understanding of this fascinating and tragic era.

📖 **Peter Stearns and William Leonard Langer, eds.,** *The Encyclopedia of World History: Ancient, Medieval, and Modern, Chronologically Arranged,* **6/e (2001)** — This encyclopedia is a great resource for research.

📖 **Merry E. Wiesner,** *Women and Gender in Early Modern Europe* **(2019)** — This work provides a conceptual introduction to gender and its role in Europe before the French Revolution.

📖 **Carol Strickland and John Boswell,** *The Annotated Mona Lisa: a Crash Course in Art History from Prehistoric to the Present* **(2017)** — The one book you need to study for the art history elements of the course; brief and engaging.

📽 *Civilisations* **(2018)** — A BBC/PBS reboot of a classic video series, the new version focuses more on cultural interaction across the globe. This excellent 9-part series is thematically organized and available through a variety of streaming services.

SECTION II
CONTENT REVIEW

PERIOD ONE
c. 1450 – c. 1648

The chapters in Period 1 will address the following major developments and events:

- Italian and northern Renaissances
- New Monarchs and centralization of power
- Protestant and Catholic Reformations
- Early modern society
- Exploration and colonization
- Religious wars
- Growth of commerce and money economy
- Scientific Revolution

Each chapter will provide a content review and practice questions to test your understanding of the material. At the conclusion of the content chapters, you will be able both to gauge your grasp of the content and practice historical thinking skills in a diagnostic test that will include:

- 30 MC questions
- 2 SAQs
- 1 DBQ
- 1 LEQ (choice of 2)

Each chapter will begin with a brief correlation to the Unit Guides from the Course and Exam Description (CED). Good luck with your review.

❧ CHAPTER 4 ❧

The Renaissance and Reformation

If the High Middle Ages exhibited dynamic growth, then the fourteenth century represented the stick in the spokes of this runaway medieval cart that brought it crashing to the ground. Sometimes, however, tragedy can pave the way for the emergence of new cultural trends. In the wake of social, religious, cultural, and economic crisis, there emerged two defining movements of early modern European history—the Renaissance and Protestant Reformation.

NOTE

The **bolded** terms in this and subsequent chapters indicate required content knowledge from the Course and Exam Unit Guides. Underlined terms denote illustrative content—not required, but examples that can prove useful in explaining and elaborating on Key Concepts.

🔑 **KEY IN** – Chapter 4 addresses all or part of the following topics in the Unit Guides of the CED:

Topic 1.1 Contextualizing Renaissance and Discovery

Topic 1.2 Italian Renaissance

Topic 1.3 Northern Renaissance

Topic 1.4 Printing

Topic 1.5 New Monarchies

Topic 1.11 Causation in the Renaissance and Age of Discovery

Topic 2.1 Contextualizing 16th- and 17th-Century Challenges and Developments

Topic 2.2 Luther and the Protestant Reformation

Topic 2.5 The Catholic Reformation

Topic 2.6 16th-Century Society and Politics

Topic 2.7 Art of the 16th Century: Mannerism and Baroque

Topic 2.8 Causation in the Age of Reformation and the Wars of Religion

The Upheavals of the 14th Century

Europe's peak population in 1300 of 75 million was already pushing up against its natural boundaries when the continent was hit by the Great Famine of 1315–1317 and the cataclysmic Black Death of 1348–1351. The latter represents one of the great natural disasters in world history, costing Europe upwards of 40% of its population. More important than sheer numbers were the psychological and social costs of the disease. Caused by fleas traveling on rats, the bubonic plague spread quickly along trade routes and especially devastated urban areas. No one could explain the cause of the pestilence. Flagellants took the calamity to be God's wrath upon man and whipped themselves in atonement. Many blamed Jews for poisoning wells, which led to a notorious persecution of that minority in Nuremberg. Art reflected the obsession with death; paintings featured skeletons performing the *danse macabre*. The Catholic Church could offer little solace, especially since the disease killed off well over 60% of the top clergy. Perhaps most significantly, the Black Death caused a labor shortage that undermined the feudal structure, as peasants bargained for improved labor conditions, winning lifetime tenures and converting other obligations to cash payments.

Improved peasant conditions did not last long. Governments and nobles reasserted their power throughout the century, which led to the *jacquerie* rebellion in 1358 in France and Wat Tyler's revolt in 1381 in England. Urban revolts also occurred in Florence; each of these revolts was eventually overturned, often with great violence. Of more lasting import was the blow delivered to the feudal system in the west.

National monarchies were young and therefore fragile creations. Dynastic instability (e.g., the inability to produce male heirs) plagued many states throughout the fourteenth century and led most seriously to the Hundred Years War (1337–1453). Really a series of wars, this conflict between France and England over the French throne (and the cloth trade in the Low Countries) also dealt a fatal blow to the medieval idea of warfare. Time and again, English longbowmen demonstrated the power of massed infantry against France's heavily mounted feudal knights. French fortunes revived upon the back of a divinely inspired peasant girl. In 1429, Joan of Arc believed the voice of God called her to break the siege of Orleans. Despite her military successes, Joan was tried for witchcraft and burned at the stake (later made a saint in 1920). Yet the tide had turned, and by 1453, England held only the city of Calais on the continent.

SKILL SET

Though the official course begins in 1450, some basic knowledge of the late Middle Ages will aid in your understanding of the Renaissance and set up a vital and intriguing interpretive issue: To what extent does the Renaissance represent a break from the Middle Ages and a new period in European history?

Each nation then turned inward to resolve pressing political conflicts.

The Catholic Church also stood in the midst of crisis. Since 1307, the papacy had lived in exile in France during the so-called Babylonian Captivity, where its prestige declined in proportion to the increase in its administrative apparatus and material wealth. When an Italian crowd forced the mostly French cardinals to elect one of their own, the church plunged into the Great Schism (1378–1417), with rival French and Italian popes forcing the nations of Europe to choose sides. Advocates of conciliarism attempted to use church councils (unsuccessfully) to solve the crisis *and* to check the power of the papacy. Reformers such as John Wyclif in England and John Hus in Bohemia (part of the Holy Roman Empire) attacked the institutional power and wealth of the church and called for a simpler Christianity. Though Hus was burned at the stake in 1415, his ideas set the stage for the Protestant Reformation of the sixteenth century.

The Setting of the Renaissance

Italy was the first area of Europe to experience the Renaissance. Several reasons account for this early lead.

- *Geographic* – Italy was not only the center of the Mediterranean, which made it a crossroads of trade, it also boasted centers of ancient culture. If artists wished to imitate classical motifs, they need look no further than their Roman backyard. Ideas followed in the wake of trade, particularly as humanists escaped the declining Byzantine Empire, under siege by the Turks (and falling in 1453).

SKILL SET

The question of Italy's head start represents an important early Causation question focused around a nation. It parallels other such issues, such as Britain and industrialization, France and its revolution, and Germany and the Nazis. You may wish to begin your practice for this skill by writing a focused paragraph in response to "Why Italy?" based on the material that follows.

- *Urbanization* – While in most of Europe only 10% of the population lived in cities, up to 25% of Italians partook directly of the civic culture so essential to Renaissance humanism. Cities attracted trade, ideas, and culture—the lifeblood of the Renaissance.

- *Social Factors* – Nobles played a vital role in Italy, just as they did in every European nation, though their attitudes tended to be more oriented to money-making and cultural accomplishments than elsewhere. A common family blending in Italy involved a cash-strapped aristocrat and an up-and-coming wealthy merchant, thus creating a new elite, where wealth and worldly achievement mattered more than merely lineage.

- *Political Variety* – In the fourteenth century, Italy was a collection of small and large city-states. No centralized authority existed to stamp out potentially threatening ideas. If artists or intellectuals found difficulty in one place, they could simply move to another and continue their work. This disunity later became a liability, but at that time, Italy benefited from competing political centers.

With its thriving city-states, Italy imitated the ancient *poleis* of Greece and the Roman Republic. Citizenship and freedom in the ancient world sparked intellectual and cultural life, and the same held true of Renaissance Italy. A major concern of Renaissance thinkers was a life of active civic engagement. The life of the mind (*otium*) must eventually contribute to the bettering of one's city-state (*negotium*). Reflection and action promoted *virtú*, or excellence, in the Renaissance man or woman.

As with today, family functioned as the central social institution of the Italian Renaissance. Renaissance families were patriarchal, placing a great deal of power in the male head of the family, or *patria potesta*. Before a man could achieve legal autonomy, his father officially liberated him before the appropriate authorities. Oftentimes, men were not able to establish an independent existence until their late 20s or early 30s. At the same time, families commonly married off their daughters as early as their mid-teens. Marriages were frequently arranged to the benefit of both families. Economic concerns predominated; compatibility of the couple came second, and often not at all, given the significant age difference between men and women. As a result of this marriage-age gap, Italy experienced predictable side effects. First, prostitution was rampant, and since almost impossible to eliminate, generally tolerated and even regulated by governments. Second, the incidence of rape and sexual violence was high, though lower-class men were punished more severely if their victim was from the upper classes. Finally, spouses often predeceased their partners, who remarried quickly due to the difficulties involved in living an independent existence. This led to remarriage, numerous blended families, and an abundance of stepparents. Though the nuclear family (mother, father, and children) was the norm, Renaissance Italy also depended on African slavery, a result of the labor shortage created by the Black Death. Enslaved persons lived with families and often performed domestic work. Though as much as 10% of Italy's population in 1400 was made up of slaves, the practice *in* Europe declined with the recovery of the population in the fifteenth century.

> **THEME MUSIC**
>
> The Social Organization and Development theme can pose challenges to students. To get a head start, use this and the section below on the social impact of the Reformation to establish the baseline for issues like class, gender, family, child-rearing, and education. Be wary of stereotypes; do not project back on the past your preconceptions for these issues.

Renaissance Humanism and Art

The term "Renaissance" is the creation of the modern Swiss historian Jacob Burckhardt (writing in 1860). Though the average layperson will tend to view the Renaissance, or rebirth of classical culture, as a distinct break from the Middle, or "Dark," Ages, historians often disagree with how useful this term is in describing a specific time period. One of the difficulties is: when do we date the beginning of the Renaissance? **Petrarch** (1304–1374), the father of humanism, already argued for a new age as early as the 1340s. However, this was before the Black Death, so does that mean the Black Death defines the Renaissance? In addition, one of the great painters of the late medieval period, Giotto, influenced later Renaissance painters. So is Giotto a medieval or Renaissance artist? Even if there is much wisdom in viewing the Renaissance as a continuation of medieval trends, there is little doubt that a new self-consciousness regarding human beings and a new self-assertion was evident in Italy by 1350.

As the name suggests, humanists were fascinated by humans and their potential. The fabric of humanism is woven of several important strands.

- *Secularism* – Humanists focused their attention on the here-and-now, and less on the afterworld, as had been the preoccupation during the Middle Ages. Education, self-help manuals, and treatises on civility all reinforced the notion that humans stood to gain rewards—wealth, status, prestige, fame—in the temporal (earthly) world. Even in religious paintings, humans take on increased significance, while painting itself becomes more an exercise to glorify the artist than to glorify God.

> **THEME MUSIC**
>
> Since the Cultural and Intellectual Developments theme deals with the most abstract topics in the course, it is vital that you focus on defining your terms. For this section, it is recommended that you write a historical definition of humanism in a paragraph.

- *Classics* – Ancient Greece and Rome formed the moral center of many humanists' outlook. Collectors of manuscripts, such as Poggio Bracciolini, scoured monasteries, ruins—anywhere—to find evidence of the ancient way of life. For example, the ancient Roman Vitruvius's *On Architecture* provided a guide to the creation of buildings that reflected a coherent system of columns, arches, and pillars. Also, the recovery of the long-lost Hellenistic sculpture *Laocoön* in the early sixteenth century inspired Michelangelo to create his sculptural masterpiece, the *David*. Ancient values and aesthetics, as pre-Christian, told a captivating story with humans at the center, from which humanists took inspiration.

- *Individualism* – By "individualism," humanists meant not a narrow, selfish conception of human actions, but rather that learning and human affairs should concern individual improvement. It was as if humanists had just discovered mankind and could not tear themselves away. This attitude can be seen in the self-consciousness of Petrarch's verse as well as Castiglione's suggestions for achieving fame, wealth, and position.

- *Power* – Amid the inspiring philosophy and mesmerizing art, it is easy to forget that the Renaissance was, at its heart, about human control of the environment. A central humanist aim was to provide society with intellectual tools that could be used to master everything from the globe (cartography), to sound (musical notation), to abstract space (three-dimensional perspective in painting), to business (double-entry book-keeping), and finally politics. It's no coincidence that along with the great works of art came exploration and colonization, the centralization of New Monarchs, and urban planning.

Humanism found many expressions—literature, philosophy, education, politics, and, of course, art. As you review the list of representative figures below, keep in the mind the principles to which they connect above.

Writers and Philosophers

Leonardo Bruni (1369–1444): Bruni studied under Chrysoloras, a Greek scholar who had fled the faltering Byzantine Empire, and translated ancient Greek texts into Latin. In addition, Bruni served Florence in various political capacities and later wrote a Latin history of the city. He is most famous for his admiration of Cicero, the Roman statesman and model of civic virtue.

> **EXAMPLE BASE**
>
> Here you'll find brief explanations of key figures in humanism. However, don't place your focus on rote learning; instead, use 4–5 of these intellectuals or artists to develop your explanation of humanism—in literature, philosophy, history, political theory, and the arts.

Lorenzo Valla (1406–1457): Valla excelled in philology, the study of ancient languages. Even though a member of the clergy, Valla demonstrated through textual analysis that the "Donation of Constantine," which supposedly granted the pope authority over political bodies, was a forgery.

Pico della Mirandola (1463–1494): Under the sponsorship of Cosimo de' Medici, Florence founded the Platonic Academy to revive Plato's philosophy; one of its most famous students, Mirandola promoted the Neoplatonic ideal in his "Oration on the Dignity of Man." Many consider it the classic statement of human potential. Neoplatonism held that humans had once shared a divine nature and though they had freely chosen to enter the material world, they retained a spark of divinity, which could be recaptured through intellectual and spiritual regeneration.

Lorenzo de' Medici (1449–1492): Known as "the Magnificent," Lorenzo ruled Florence during its Golden Age. A strong advocate of **civic humanism** (the ideal of citizen participation in a classically-inspired republic) and a man of diverse interests, Lorenzo is most famous for his patronage of intellectuals and the arts. His untimely death in 1492 led to the invasion of Italy by foreign powers, as well as the decline of Renaissance culture in Florence.

Niccolo Machiavelli (1469–1527): One of the most famous figures of the Renaissance, Machiavelli's claim to fame is *The Prince*. Dedicated to the Medici family, the book serves as a manual for the pragmatic ruler who must appear virtuous, wise, and courageous (like a "lion"), at the same time ready to be ruthless and cunning (like a "fox"). Machiavelli denies the traditional notion that the political realm must uphold the laws of God. Politics follows its own logic in the hard-headed rules of power, or *raison d'etat* (reason of state), which is why *The Prince* is often considered the first modern work of political science. It is important to remember the context for Machiavelli's writing—the invasion of Italy and its subsequent domination by foreign powers. *The Prince*, as well as Machiavelli's other writings endorsing citizen militias and republican government, can be seen collectively as patriotic appeals for a free and united Italy. After being tortured and losing his position in government, Machiavelli tried desperately to win back his influence, with little success. Fairly or unfairly, Machiavelli's name is associated with a brand of amoral politics both practiced and condemned since the sixteenth century.

Petrarch (1304–1374): Often called the "Father of Humanism," Petrarch helped popularize the notion that Italy was entering a new age of learning and individualism, distinct from the "ignorance" he believed characterized the Middle Ages. Petrarch revived a more pure form of Latin and, as such, spent his literary energies composing verse in the language, much of it related to a psychological portrait of humans and the theme of love, wherein he wrote of his beloved Laura.

Baldassare Castiglione (1478–1529): Castiglione first gained fame as a diplomat, but he is most known for his *Book of the Courtier*, a how-to manual on winning fame and influence among the rich and powerful. To gain position and fortune, Castiglione counsels the Renaissance Man to be widely read in the classics, including history, poetry, music, and philosophy, as well as know how to conduct himself in public. The courtier will be skilled in the military arts *and* cultured and polished. In addition, Castiglione advocated education for women, but of a particular kind: a musical instrument, poetry, and literacy. Abstract subjects such as math and science were reserved for men.

Works in Oil, Marble, and Stone

The Renaissance achieved fame for its production of renowned works of art. Several developments mark the upward trend of Renaissance art:

- *Oil-based paints* – Historically, artists had used tempera paints with an egg base, yet with oil-based paints (from the Low Countries), artists could achieve more startling effects with light and shadow by applying layer after thin layer of paint.

- *Perspective* – For centuries, artists had attempted to achieve a realistic effect of three-dimensional space, but their methods tended to be haphazard and approximate. With the rediscovery of theories of optics and perspective geometry, Renaissance painters were able to achieve a strikingly realistic view of a visual plane.

- *Naturalism* – The Renaissance preoccupation with the human body was reflected in its portrayals on canvas and in stone. Painters and sculptors gave increased attention to musculature and movement of the human body. This emphasis is clearly seen in Michelangelo's *Sistine Chapel*, where the master achieves a heroic portrayal of humans, and also in da Vinci's sketches based on anatomical dissections.

- *Subject Matter* – While artists continued to focus on religious paintings, human beings, nature, and classical architecture played a more central role in these works. In addition, artists began to experiment with classical scenes, landscapes, and portraits.

- *Order and Symmetry* – In all three media, Renaissance artists placed great importance on orderly composition. Architects employed proportion in their use of classical motifs such as the column, dome, and arch.

- *Status of the Artist* – Because they were considered craftsmen, most artists of the Middle Ages were anonymous. As patronage by wealthy merchants and the church increased during the Renaissance, the reputation of artists as creative geniuses—people set apart—became the standard.

Donatello (1386–1466): Donatello revived the free-standing sculpture. His depiction of *David* represents the first life-size statue cast in bronze since ancient times. The sculptor imbued his forms with psychological detail and expression, representing Renaissance naturalism.

> ### SKILL SET
>
> Whenever you encounter art in this course, think Contextualization. You may wish to consult one of the websites mentioned in Chapter 1 to view well-known works of architecture, painting, and sculpture. As you consider these images, explain how they reflect the concerns, values, and developments of the period in which they were created.

Masaccio (1401–1428): Masaccio employed perspective geometry for the first time in his *Holy Trinity*, and also achieved a depth of realism and three-dimensional space in a series of frescoes in the Brancacci Chapel, of which the *Expulsion of Adam and Eve from the Garden* is a highlight for depicting the agony and shame of the couple. Unfortunately, this master died young.

Fillipo Brunelleschi (1377–1446): Though an architect, Brunelleschi expressed interest in all the arts, including cast bronze and painting—it was he who helped develop the use of perspective geometry in painting. Brunelleschi's primary achievement by far is the massive dome (*Il Duomo*) he created for the Cathedral of Florence, a feat of artistic vision and engineering.

Leonardo da Vinci (1452–1519): Perhaps the foremost Renaissance Man, da Vinci gained fame for just a few paintings—*Mona Lisa*, *The Last Supper*, *Madonna of the Rocks*. His diverse interests led him into science, engineering, and anatomy. Da Vinci introduced the notion of systematic observation, which he tracked in his notebooks, written backwards to make it difficult for imitators to steal his ideas.

Michelangelo Buonarroti (1475–1564): Bearing a name synonymous with genius, Michelangelo excelled in all the artistic media—sculpture (*David*, *Pieta*), painting (*Sistine Chapel*, *Last Judgment*), and architecture (*St. Peter's Basilica Dome*, *Laurentian Library*). The master's nudes offer a heroic vision of the human form influenced by Neoplatonic philosophy, though his later works express a darker vision. In addition, Michelangelo composed poetry and was working on another Pieta at the age of 88 when he died.

Raphael (1483–1520): The youngest of the great masters and considered a rival of Michelangelo's, Raphael often sought artistic patronage in Rome, where the Renaissance refocused after about 1490. Raphael's *School of Athens* honors ancient learning and his fellow artists, as the Greek philosophers take on the physical appearance of his contemporaries. In addition, Raphael painted numerous portraits of the Madonna, the Mother of Jesus.

Education and the Printing Press

Renaissance humanism spurred education. Humanists founded schools for both boys and girls, though the latter tended to focus more on keeping appearances rather than mastery of abstract subject matter. Latin and Greek were prized by scholars of the fifteenth and sixteenth centuries, yet a truly well-rounded person needed to be conversant in all the liberal arts—grammar, music, arithmetic, geometry, astronomy, rhetoric, and logic—

> ### THEME MUSIC
>
> Reflecting the Technological and Scientific Innovation theme, the printing press can claim to be one of the most important technologies covered in this course. As you read over this and subsequent sections, take note of its effects, keeping in mind that all technologies create both intended and unintended outcomes.

not to mention poetry, horsemanship, and military arts. Renaissance schools provided structure and regular promotion of pupils from one level to the next, and in that sense, have influenced the values and curricula of schools today.

Though the Chinese invented printing, they did not capitalize fully on their early success. Johann Gutenberg and his colleagues perfected the technology of movable type in the 1450s, publishing their famous Gutenberg Bible, of which several dozen still exist. Books continued to be expensive luxury items for the upper classes, but the die had been cast. No longer could church or state exercise a monopoly on education or intellectual life. The **printing press** assisted in spreading the Renaissance and helped to establish standardized texts, as well as promote **vernacular literature** ("in the language of the people," i.e., not Latin). Perhaps printing's most important impact was to secure the success of the Protestant Reformation. Few would deny that the invention of the printing press stands as one of the most, if not *the* most, significant technological developments of the past millennium.

Was There a Renaissance for Women?

Though there were several well-regarded female humanists, women faced significant barriers to their intellectual pursuits. The prevailing notion held that the domestic sphere was the appropriate one for women of wealth. More enlightened humanists favored education for women, but even this never equaled the type of learning available to men. Nonetheless, women often played key political roles, especially when their statesmen-husbands were off at war, and several gained fame for sponsoring the forerunners to the salons of the Enlightenment. By some measures, the status of women declined from the Middle Ages, as they came to be viewed as objects of art or pawns in marriage alliances, a fact accentuated by the gap in average ages between husband and wife. Some famous humanists and early feminists did leave a mark, however:

Christine de Pisan (1364–1431): A French noblewoman, de Pisan is believed to have published one of the first modern statements of feminism, *The City of Ladies*, which defends women's intellectual capabilities against anti-female bias. After her husband's death, de Pisan fought to retain her property and turned to writing to support her family; she may have been the first woman in European history to make a living through her writings.

> ### THEME MUSIC
> Starting now, you should trace this issue of women's participation in various movements of change and the extent to which such involvement altered women's position in society. This question relates both to the SCD theme and the Reasoning Process of CCOT.

Isabella d'Este (1474–1539): Often called the "First Lady of the World," d'Este married into the famous Gonzaga family of Mantua. After her husband departed for war, d'Este conducted diplomacy on his behalf (and sometimes behind his back). She also found time to establish schools for girls, attract humanists to her court, and write hundreds of letters of literary merit.

Laura Cereta (1469–1499): Cereta's life again illustrates the importance of marriage and early mortality. Her husband died after only 18 months of marriage, and rather than enter a convent or remarry, Cereta wrote works advocating equality of opportunity for women. She, too, died young, however.

Renaissance Politics and the New Monarchs

Politics was central to Renaissance views regarding power, status, and values such as civic humanism. As noted previously, Machiavelli's ideas played a major role in introducing a secular conception of politics, and historians such as Francesco Guicciardini emphasized social and political causes, rather than divine providence, in recounting the diplomacy and great events of the day. Given the divided nature of the Italian peninsula, regular diplomacy emerged to secure the balance of power. Ambassadors no longer served Christendom generally, but instead patriotically—and often deviously—represented their city- or nation-state. To ensure that no one power gained dominance, the five major city-states continually jockeyed for position, thus the concept of **balance-of-power** politics emerged, which would come to play a central role in European diplomatic thinking. Perhaps the best example of this attitude is the Peace of Lodi, signed in 1454, which created a fairly stable arrangement that ensured 40 years of peace. Furthermore, the so-called **New Monarchies** aimed to reassert strong dynastic claims with centralizing techniques in response to the disasters of the fourteenth century.

> ### THEME MUSIC
> The following section addresses the States and Other Institutions of Power theme, focusing on the overarching issue of the centralization of power and resistance to it. Take note of the strategies and institutions used by monarchs to overcome provincialism as well as how corporate groups and institutions (nobles, towns, church, e.g.) resisted monarchical forays.

Though it is not necessary to have a detailed knowledge of each city-state, you may find it helpful to link the basics in the chart that follows to KCs 1.2 and 1.5.

City-State	Government	Key Figures	Assessment
Florence	A republic led by members of the guilds, but in reality dominated behind the scenes by the Medici family, which made a fortune in banking.	• Cosimo de' Medici (1389–1464)—Patriarch of the family. Wealthy patron of humanism who helped found the Florentine Platonic Academy. (See Lorenzo, his grandson, on page 62.) • Savanarola (1452–1498)—Preached against the secular focus on art and pagan philosophy, eventually taking over the city, before being burned at the stake.	Florence was the center of banking and textiles on the peninsula, and one of the richest of the city-states. This wealth helped make it the "Queen City of the Renaissance" before the French invasion in 1494. Many of the great names associated with Renaissance culture earned their fame in Florence.
Milan	A military dictatorship ruled by the Visconti family for centuries.	• Francesco Sforza (1401–1466)—Seized control of the city in the 1450s and a good example of how reliance on mercenary soldiers—*condottiere*— undermined Italy's independence.	Of the city-states, Milan was most closely tied to trading interests in central Europe. Strategically located, disputes over its control led to the invasion of foreign armies, and the ultimate end of the Renaissance.
Papal States	Technically ruled as a despotism by the Papacy, it was really an elective monarchy that had difficulty managing the noble factions in its diverse territories.	• Alexander VI (1492–1503)—He represents the height of corruption in the Renaissance Papacy. Used his children to cement marriage alliances and regain power on the peninsula. • Julius II (1503–1513)—Known as the "Warrior Pope," he led armies into battle and also sponsored grand art projects, like the Sistine Chapel.	The period from 1417 to the 1540s is known as the Renaissance Papacy, and it was not a proud moment in the history of the Catholic Church. Popes were deeply involved in politics and seemed to the faithful more focused on luxury, art, and rebuilding Rome, which became the center of the High Renaissance after 1490. Because a line of popes ignored pleas for reform, the problems that would lead to the Protestant Reformation festered.
Venice	An oligarchic republic ruled by wealthy merchant families. Nicknamed the "Serene Republic" for its stability throughout the era.	• Doge—Leader of the Venetian government chosen by <u>wealthy merchants</u>. • Book of Gold—Registry of the leading families in Venice; membership implied full citizenship rights.	The major trading power of the Italian city-states due to its contact with the Byzantine and later the Ottoman Empires. Its arsenal represents one of the first factories in history. Finally, Venetian artists, such as Titian and Bellini, stressed light and color over line and composition.
Naples	A relatively backward feudal monarchy claimed and eventually won by Ferdinand of Aragon.		Though the city of Naples was Europe's largest in 1500, the kingdom participated minimally in the intellectual and artistic Renaissance.

The state as we know it today did not exist in 1500, yet the New Monarchies of this era were laying the foundations for the modern nation. To rebuild after the devastation of the fourteenth and early fifteenth centuries, monarchs engaged in similar policies, while at the same time addressing problems unique to their geographic location with more focused policies. General strategies of centralization comprised the following:

1. *Taxation* – Securing access to revenue, preferably without legislative approval.
2. *Taming the aristocracy* – Monarchs established that they were more than "first among equals" with other aristocrats by forming alliances with the middle class in towns and creating new nobles as officials, called the "<u>nobles of the robe</u>" (because their status came from their official capacities).

3. *Codifying laws and creating courts* – Most nations were still a patchwork of customs, dialects, and legal traditions in 1500, so monarchs attempted to establish royal courts that applied more uniform laws.

4. *Controlling warfare* – Medieval armies were private entities and less than reliable. The New Monarchies worked to make armies and war the prerogative of the state, which made sense given the increasingly complex nature of war.

5. *Early bureaucracy and officials* – Early states lacked the mechanisms to enforce their will, let alone keep track of the affairs of government. To remedy this, monarchs began to use agencies, committees, representative bodies, and councils to assist in implementing royal authority.

6. *Religious control* – The medieval tension between religious and secular authority began to tilt in favor of the latter, even before the Protestant Reformation, as monarchs asserted increased authority over the clergy and the functions of religion within their national boundaries.

Now let's look briefly through the following chart at how these general strategies were applied in specific instances. Throughout this review guide, we will use a straightforward conceptual device to assist you in making sense of the plethora of nations, rulers, and policies: **Challenges** (the issues and problems rulers/nations faced) → **Responses** (policies the rulers/nations enacted to address these issues) → **Results** (the impact these policies had on the nation's strategic position).

Nation	Challenges	Responses	Results
England	Following the Hundred Years' War, England was plunged into the Wars of the Roses, between two factions of nobles. When the war ended in 1485, the Tudors set about rebuilding the power of the state.	• Henry VII (r. 1485–1509) and **Henry VIII** (r. 1509–1547) tamed the nobles, reducing the number of dukes from 9 to 2, and created a new aristocracy • <u>Star Chamber</u>—royal system of courts established outside of parliamentary control • Ended livery and maintenance, the private armies of the nobles • Built England's first state navy • Henry VIII took control of the Catholic Church in England and confiscated its lands	The Tudors established the basis of English political and commercial power. However, Henry VIII's obsession with producing a male heir demonstrated the continuing fragility of royal rule and created a religious issue that would not be easily resolved.
France	France had experienced warfare on its soil for over 100 years, while its eastern neighbor Burgundy aimed to replace French leadership on the continent.	• Louis XI, the "Spider" (r. 1461–1483) added new territory to the royal domain through strategic marriages and by conquering part of Burgundy • Francis I (r. 1515–1547), a Renaissance king, gained control of the French clergy by agreement with the pope (<u>Concordat of Bologna</u>) • Established taxation with the *taille* (direct tax) and *gabelle* (government salt monopoly) • Claimed lands in Italy	France extended its territory, laid a secure foundation for taxes, and created the largest army in Europe. This represents a strong recovery from the Hundred Years' War, but the kingdom continued to face encirclement by the Habsburgs.
Russia	The truncated duchy of Muscovy barely resembled the Russia of today, as it was threatened by powerful neighbors such as the Mongols and Poland.	• Ivan III, the "Great" (r. 1462–1505) drove out the Mongols, claimed Moscow as the "Third Rome" by marrying niece of last Byzantine Emperor, and created the *streltsy*, a military service class • Ivan IV, the "Terrible" (r. 1547–1584)— so nicknamed because of his hatred of the *boyars* (nobles); also continued Russian expansion	Russia emerged as a great power, yet continued to face issues of cultural and technological backwardness. When Ivan IV killed his heir in a fit of rage, Russia fell into civil chaos and foreign invasion for 30 years.

Nation	Challenges	Responses	Results
Spain	Spain did not even exist until the marriage of Ferdinand and Isabella in 1469, and even then, Spain worked to complete the *reconquista* of the Moors and establish a national identity among its diverse kingdoms.	• Isabella of Castile's (r. 1479–1504) and Ferdinand of Aragon's (r. 1479–1516) marriage did not create a fully centralized nation • Made alliances with towns (*hermandades*) to establish law and order • Personally visited each area of the country • Completed *reconquista* • Established strict religious orthodoxy with <u>Spanish Inquisition</u> (from 1478) and expelled Jews in 1492 • Sponsored voyages of exploration • **Charles I** (aka Charles V in the Holy Roman Empire, 1516–1556) inherited diverse lands and became the most powerful monarch in Europe	Spain emerged as the strongest nation in Europe. Access to the wealth of the New World and Charles's inheritance of numerous lands established Spain's Golden Age. However, its crusading mindset, onerous taxes, and persecution of talented minorities set the stage for its subsequent decline.

Northern Renaissance and Christian Humanism

Renaissance culture began in Italy but quickly spread via the new printing press and along trade routes to the rest of Europe. It was particularly strong in France, England, Germany, and the Low Countries (today's Netherlands and Belgium), though almost every nation experienced some manifestation of humanist learning and classical revival.

> **SKILL SET**
>
> When you compare two objects, the process results in an improved grasp of both. For northern and Italian humanism, create a Venn diagram, making sure to note similarities and differences for the same topics (e.g., religion and art).

Though northern humanists employed the same tactics of textual analysis and criticism as their Italian neighbors, their emphasis tended to be on Christian readings, such as the Bible, but also included the writings of the early church fathers (St. Augustine, for example). For this reason, northern humanism is often called **Christian humanism**. In general, Christian humanists criticized many of the Catholic Church's abuses, but wished to maintain the unity of Christianity by reforming from within the Church. Many intelligent observers recognized that the ark of the church was listing badly and desperately needed repairs. The split that occurred in the sixteenth century revolved around this issue—whether the ship could be saved or should simply be abandoned in favor of a more stable vessel. Years before Luther, Christian humanists urged a reform, primarily through education, which would rescue the church from its worldliness and corruption. Though numerous Christian humanists labored to save the church, two clearly stand out for their literary accomplishments and clear teachings.

Before we address Erasmus and Thomas More, we need to paint a picture of late medieval spirituality. Maybe the best word to describe the mood of the fourteenth and fifteenth centuries is "anxiety." Amidst the death and upheaval of the plague, Great Schism, and political breakdown, European Christians became obsessed with securing eternal life. On one hand, this fear fed the mechanical exercises of <u>indulgences</u>, relic veneration, and pilgrimages. Desiring a positive relationship with God, some Christians turned to mysticism—the notion that the believer can bridge the gap between himself and the Almighty through meditation, prayer, and other acts of devotion. A popular book in this regard was Thomas à Kempis's *Imitation of Christ*, which provided daily readings to commune with God through humility and simple piety. In the Low Countries and Germany, an organization of laypersons (i.e., non-clergy) called the Brothers and Sisters of the Common Life ministered to the poor, founded schools for the promotion of virtue, and supported each other in living a Christian life. Religion remained dearly important to many; if it had not, the influence of the Catholic Church might have faded slowly without any disruptive spread of a new and vibrant Protestant theology.

Desiderius Erasmus (1466–1536) became the most famous intellectual of his day, and his name today remains a symbol of tolerance and scholarship. Raised in a monastic environment, he never took vows, claiming he had "a Catholic soul but a Lutheran stomach" (and thus not able to withstand the church's demand for ritual fasting). With humor and style, Erasmus mocked the clergy and its abuses in works such as the *Praise of Folly*, which was eventually placed on the Index of Prohibited Books. Erasmus's primary message, as seen in *Handbook of the Christian Knight* and *On Civility in Children*, lay in the power of education to promote true reverence for God and in living out the good news of the Gospel

(Jesus' teachings). Protected by powerful patrons, Erasmus condemned fanaticism of all kinds, and while his reputation remained undiminished by his death, his voice of moderation had been drowned out by extremists on all sides. He might have opposed the sentiment, but it is often said that "Erasmus laid the egg that Luther hatched."

Perhaps no intellectual better represents the bridging of the medieval and modern worlds than <u>Thomas More</u> (1478–1535). A man of deep piety (More wore a hairshirt—a rough and painful undergarment made of goat's wool–to mortify his flesh throughout much of his life), More played the game of worldly success, but always kept a careful eye on the next world. More's talents brought him to the attention of the monarchy, where he served in Parliament and as the first nonclerical Lord Chancellor (the highest judicial position in England). More's literary fame rests primarily on *Utopia*, a satire of sixteenth-century European society, and vision of a better life based on communal living. A friend of Erasmus, More possessed less of his comrade's moderate tendencies. More *was* willing to die for his beliefs, which occurred when he opposed Henry VIII's takeover of the Catholic Church. More was also willing to kill for them, as he oversaw the burning of several accused heretics as Lord Chancellor. The scholar's last days were spent in the Tower of London, before his beheading in 1535, another victim of the growing rift between religious and political authority.

In art, northern humanism eventually adopted the techniques of Italian painters, including perspective and an emphasis on naturalism. However, northern artists tended to focus more on the theological and emotional content of Christian depictions, instead of classical architecture and wealthy patrons, as was common among Italian artists. In addition, northern painters, such as <u>Pieter Bruegel the Elder</u> (1525–1569), portrayed scenes of **everyday life**, including peasants, agriculture, or the simple customs that tied together small communities.

Causes of the Protestant Reformation

We have already hinted at several causes of the Protestant Reformation—Christian humanism, late medieval spirituality, and the state of the Catholic Church—but now it is time to focus on the last of these. Simply put, the Catholic Church in 1500 confronted a crisis. Desperate to recapture its former glory and influence, the Papacy focused more on artistic patronage and Machiavellian politics than the spiritual state of its flock. Abuses that began during the Babylonian Captivity festered and produced a general cry for reform, a cry generally ignored by corrupt Popes fearful of limits on their power by church councils. These abuses were:

- <u>Simony</u> – The buying and selling of high church offices, which often produced a revenue (annates) for the holder.

- <u>Nepotism</u> – The granting of offices to relatives (e.g., Pope Alexander VI conferred a cardinal's hat upon his 16-year-old son).

- <u>Pluralism</u> – The holding of multiple church offices.

- <u>Absenteeism</u> – The act of not residing in one's spiritual domain because one held multiple positions.

- <u>Indulgences</u> – The most controversial, the belief that a believer could draw on Jesus' and the saints' previous fund of grace to reduce the sinner's or a relative's time in purgatory (that region between heaven and hell reserved for the final "purging" of sinful souls).

It was this last abuse that sparked the Reformation, but prior to this spark, recall that a goodly pile of tinder had been accumulating for generations.

Protestant Reform Movements

Luther and Lutheranism

The Protestant Reformation began with one man's spiritual crisis. This crisis revolved around a nagging but central question in Christianity: "How can I be saved?" It is common to think of Luther as attacking the abuses of the church, but his critique went well beyond that. Luther questioned not only the practices of the church, but condemned it for *teaching* wrongly, calling into question the entire sacramental system of Catholicism as it related to salvation.

In a complex transaction, Pope Leo X (1513–1521) in 1517 allowed the sale of indulgences by the monk Johan Tetzel (a sort of medieval used car salesman) to finance the building of St. Peter's Basilica in Rome. Luther responded almost immediately with the Ninety-Five Theses, wherein he condemned indulgences as twisting the central mystery of Christianity—Jesus' crucifixion as a once-and-for-all sacrifice wiping the human slate clean of sin and death. Previous to the indulgence controversy, Luther had been working out in his reading and lecturing a different conception of salvation. The decisive break became clear to him over the next few years, as Luther published pamphlets elaborating his ideas and denouncing what he considered false teachings. Luther's new theology can be summarized in three Latin phrases:

- *Sola scriptura* – The only authority in Christianity is the Bible. While the Catholic Church had based authority on Scripture *and* the teaching function of the church (the magisterium) in the persons of the bishops, cardinals, and popes, Luther argued that doctrine or practice must be supported by the revealed word of God *alone*.

- *Sola fide* – Salvation comes from faith alone. As Luther put it, "Good works do not make a good man, but a good man does good works." Faith is a free gift of God and cannot be earned through human activity, such as pilgrimages, relic veneration, or indulgences.

- *Sola gratia* – Salvation comes by the free gift of God's grace. Grace is the spiritual quality that gives the sinner merit in the eyes of God. Since humans are incapable of acquiring this merit through their own sinful efforts, it must be God's free gift. In contrast, the Catholic Church held that the primary instruments of grace were the sacraments; in short, that grace was mediated through the clergy.

In some ways, Luther's attack echoed many of the critiques made by Hus and even Erasmus. What made Lutheranism successful was the urgency and passion with which Luther conveyed his message, and more importantly, the power of the printing press. It is hard to imagine the Protestant Reformation's success without the tremendous propaganda instrument of the cheaply printed word. To illustrate, in the first 10 years of the Reformation, one-quarter of the books published in Germany were by Luther. In addition, many of the publications were not designed to appeal to theologians. Songs, sermons, and woodcuts mocking the Pope all appealed to a mass audience. Several of Luther's publications that reveal his new interpretation of Christianity include:

- "On the Freedom of the Christian" (1520) – A short pamphlet in which Luther rejects the notion of free will over salvation. Why, Luther asks, would I want to be in charge of my salvation when God can affect it so much better? The work prompted Erasmus uncharacteristically to reply to Luther by defending free will.

- *On the Babylonian Captivity of the Church* (1520) – This is a longer work, in Latin, for theologians. Here Luther condemned the Catholic conception of the sacraments as holding the faithful "in bondage" to the earthly power of the clergy. In addition, Luther retained only two sacraments—baptism and the Lord's Supper—because these had scriptural justification.

- *An Address to the Nobility of the German Nation* (1520) – Recognizing he needed political support in the Empire, Luther patriotically appealed to the German princes to support his cause and resist Roman taxation and power.

- German translation of the Bible (1530s) – Traditionally, Bible reading had been reserved for theologians or clergymen. By rendering the Bible into his native tongue, Luther made clear that the Bible was to be read by all, including women, and placed it front and center as an act of Christian worship.

It is often said that Luther demonstrated the fire of a theological revolutionary but the caution of a social and political conservative. No doubt, Luther was a complex figure who recognized that his attack on the Catholic Church held the potential to rip the whole of society apart. For Luther, the real church was the spiritual one of the next world; because perfection could not be reached on earth due to the sinful nature of humans, social and political revolution was self-defeating.

Luther's message inspired a host of other reformers, many of whom interpreted it in more radical ways. German firebrands, such as Andreas Carlstadt and Thomas Müntzer, applied Luther's idea of the "priesthood of all believers" more literally, to indicate a move toward social equality. These leaders supported the Peasants' Revolt of 1524–1525, the product of long-standing economic grievances and the new religious ideals. Luther was incensed, denouncing the firebrands and the peasants in his "Against the Murdering and Robbing Horde of Peasants," in which he called for the death of all who challenged legitimate authority and who twisted the true Christian message, which for him, was spiritual not political. Ultimately, the peasants were crushed at the cost of 100,000 lives, and Luther gained a reputation for intolerance that might have spent some steam from his movement in the 1530s. Another reason for Luther's attitude toward social upheaval lies in his need for support among the German princes, the only force standing between him and Charles V, the Holy Roman Emperor, before whom Luther in 1521 stood in defiance at the Diet of Worms. As a result of Luther's attitudes, wherever Lutheranism became the dominant religion (in much of Germany and Scandinavia), the church was placed under the control of the state.

> ### SKILL SET
>
> Consider this classic interpretive question: Was Luther a revolutionary or a conservative? Answering this question requires you to engage in a historical argument using evidence (Argumentation and Claims and Evidence in Sources). Even if you decide not to write out your answer, reflect on what evidence from the preceding discussion might go on each side of the balance sheet.

Through a series of timely marriages and untimely deaths, Charles V (1516–1556) stood in 1519 as the most powerful ruler in Europe, controlling Spain, the Low Countries, the Holy Roman Empire, significant parts of Italy, and the Spanish Empire in the New World. Charles recognized the need for reform in the church and continually pressured the pope to call a general council (unsuccessfully, until 1545). At the same time, Charles believed it his duty to maintain the political unity of Catholicism. Unfortunately for him, Charles's entire reign was spent on horseback attempting to keep his far-flung possessions together in the face of his many enemies:

- *Ottoman Turks* – The Ottomans killed Charles's brother-in-law Louis in battle in 1526, taking Hungary, and moved to besiege Vienna (capital of the Habsburg empire) in 1529.

- *France (Valois)* – Francis I represented Charles's most consistent rival. The perennial goal of France aimed to avoid encirclement by the Habsburgs and prevent the centralization of power in Germany. The Habsburg-Valois Wars (1494–1559) began in Italy but eventually intruded into the outcome of the Reformation in Germany, as Francis, though a Catholic, took the side of the German Protestants.

- *Algerian pirates* – Spain's interests in the Mediterranean were continuously threatened by piracy based in North Africa. Charles launched an expedition in 1541 that temporarily addressed the problem.

- *The Papacy* – Though both Charles and the pope shared an interest in salvaging Catholicism, they differed over tactics and political goals, especially when Charles's troops sacked Rome in 1527, effectively bringing the Renaissance there to an end.

- *German Lutherans* – Due to other preoccupations, Charles was forced to compromise with Lutherans early in his reign. An imperial diet in 1529 at Speyer attempted to impose a religious settlement but failed when Lutherans protested (which accounts for the term "Protestant"). By 1546, Charles was ready to solve the issue through force. The Lutheran princes formed the Schmalkaldic League and were prepared to resist with the aid of outside powers. After an initial victory in 1547 at Mühlberg, Charles was unable to follow up on his success.

To settle the religious conflict in Germany (sometimes termed the "First Thirty Years' War"), Charles agreed in 1555 to the Peace of Augsburg, which employed the compromise formula *cuius region, eius religion* ("his the region, his the religion") to divide the Empire between Lutheran and Catholic areas, as determined by the rulers of those states. It is important to note that this settlement did *not* endorse religious toleration, only to recognize the relatively even balance of religious power in Germany. In addition, Charles V abdicated in 1556, splitting his realm between his brother Ferdinand (as HRE) and his son Philip II, who took everything else.

Calvin's Second Wave

By 1540, the Protestant Reformation already required a boost; **John Calvin** (1509–1564) provided just that. A second-generation reformer, Calvin was born in France and received a strong humanist education at the University of Paris. Unlike Luther, Calvin studied to be a priest but switched to the legal profession, which may account for the strong images in Calvinism of God as the omnipotent sovereign

and law-giver. Calvin set up his reform movement in Switzerland, and after some initial turmoil was recognized as the unquestioned leader of Geneva.

Calvin accepted much of Luther's reformed theology (justification by faith alone, two sacraments) but placed more emphasis on predestination, the notion that God foreknows and fore-judges salvation for each person before birth. Those who had been saved ("the elect") did not suffer from spiritual complacency, as one might expect, but exhibited a zealous determination to create the "Most Holy City on Earth." In *Institutes of the Christian Religion*—published through numerous editions—Calvin synthesized reformed theology and provided a practical program for founding a reformed church. Genevan politics were guided by the Ecclesiastical Ordinances, which divided the church into doctors (who studied scripture), pastors (who preached the word of God), deacons (who administered charity), and elders (who ensured discipline). Elders employed the Consistory to apply "Christian watchfulness" and monitor public morality, such as public drunkenness or gambling. Compared with Luther, Calvin believed the political system must uphold the moral law of a Christian community. Though not a theocracy, church leaders in Geneva played a major role in ensuring public affairs were governed by church teachings.

Calvinism spread quickly among the nobility and the middle class, many of whom likely believed themselves to be among the elect and who resented the privileges of the clergy. To promote the spread of the Reformation, Calvin founded the Genevan Academy in 1559 to train leaders who would sow the seeds of Calvinism in other locales. Its most famous graduate was John Knox (1505–1572), who established Calvinism in Scotland. Taking a cue from their leader and their minority status in most nations, Calvinists represented the forefront of a militant Protestant movement dedicated to battling the still-strong power of Catholicism.

Evangelical Reformers

Some historians divide the Reformation into evangelical (or radical) and magisterial branches. The former refers to the grassroots movement of individual persons, towns, and communities spreading the new reform gospel through preaching, conversion, and town disputations. Some religious reforms, however, were imposed from the top down, by magistrates, princes, and monarchs. We'll discuss the most famous example of this magisterial reform in the next section, but for now, we examine some of the radical reformers.

Ulrich Zwingli (1484–1531) served as a chaplain to the many Swiss mercenaries who were often forced by poor economics to sell their services to a variety of nations. It was in his native Zurich where Zwingli established a reformed movement more radical in style than Luther's. Like Luther, Zwingli accepted two sacraments but disagreed with him over the meaning of the Lord's Supper. While Luther argued that a real presence of Jesus coexisted with the bread and wine (called consubstantiation—"two substances together"), Zwingli held Luther's position to be illogical. Jesus was in heaven at the right hand of the Father and could not be present in body and blood during services; the sacrament was symbolic only. In the context of the mounting power of the emperor, Luther and Zwingli met in an attempt to settle their disagreement. The subsequent Marburg Colloquy failed miserably. With no German allies, Zwingli was killed in 1531 in the Swiss Civil War. Before he died, however, Zwingli had laid the basis for a different style of worship. Followers of Zwingli broke organs, smashed statues, and painted churches white, all in an effort to focus the believer's attention on the Word of God by eliminating perceived distractions.

The first 20 years of the Reformation saw great ferment and experimentation. In many areas, women first accepted the reform message, spreading the gospel and converting their husbands, fathers, and brothers. A famous example was Catherine Zell (1498–1562), who along with her husband Matthias, preached, wrote, and ministered to the poor. One movement most associated with this trend toward equality was Anabaptism. **Anabaptists** believed membership in a Christian community issued from an adult choice, and therefore practiced adult baptism. More importantly, they tended to take the Bible literally when it came to living a life apart from worldly temptations. Because they practiced adult baptism—thereby putting the souls of unbaptized babies in peril—and advocated the total separation of church and state, Anabaptists were hated by Catholics and Protestants alike. However, with a few exceptions, Anabaptists lived in small, peaceful communities and posed little real threat to the state.

Magisterial Reform in England

The most famous example of **magisterial reform** occurred in England. Though Lutheran ideas had gained a few adherents in the kingdom, **Henry VIII** (1509–1547) tolerated no opposition to the Catholic faith, having earned the title "Defender of the Faith" for penning a response to Luther's attack on the sacraments. However, matters of state intervened. Henry had no male heir, which he blamed on his "barren" wife, Catherine of Aragon. Normally Henry's appeal for a divorce would have been granted by Pope Clement VII (1523–1534), but Clement was under the control of Charles V, who happened to be the nephew of Catherine.

> ### THEME MUSIC
> You will notice how a primarily theological movement like the Reformation impinged on questions of state power and national identity. The issue of magisterial, or top-down, religious reform served as a prop to the state (States and Other Institutions of Power) and in some nations, like England, helped to create a national identity (National and European Identity).

After years and numerous appeals, Henry decided in 1533–1534 to act with the support of the Parliament. First, the Parliament declared Henry the head of the new Anglican Church with the Act of Supremacy. Further, the Act of Succession legitimated the offspring (the future Elizabeth I) of Henry and Anne Boleyn, his new wife. With the aid of his principal advisor, Thomas Cromwell, Henry also moved to confiscate the lands of the church. However, Henry held no interest in *religious* reform, pushing parliament to confirm distinctive Catholic practices such as clerical celibacy in the Six Articles. Many English reformers, such as the new Archbishop of Canterbury Thomas Cranmer, wished to take the reform further. They would have to wait until Henry died and his sickly teenage son, Edward VI (1547–1553), succeeded him in 1547.

Under Edward, the reform moved in a Zwinglian direction, with a new Book of Common Prayer and Act of Uniformity providing a simpler interpretation of worship. Edward's early death in 1553 turned England back once again into the Catholic camp, under Mary I (1553–1558), the daughter of the scorned Catherine of Aragon and wife of the Most Holy Catholic Philip II (1556–1598), king of Spain. Mary's persecution of Protestants, memorialized in the famous *Foxe's Book of Martyrs*, and pro-Spanish foreign policy earned her the nickname Bloody Mary and did little in the long run to reestablish Catholicism in England.

It was **Elizabeth I** (1558–1603) who met with the most success in establishing a compromise, the Elizabethan Settlement. Under house arrest for much of her youth, Elizabeth learned the dangers of religious dogmatism. In fact, Elizabeth represented a new type of leader, termed a *politique*, or one who places political unity above conformity to religious dogma. During her reign, Elizabeth entertained many suitors but ultimately adopted the role of national matriarch, never marrying. She refrained from persecuting religious minorities—with the exception of Catholics—and engineered a new Book of Common Prayer, vague enough in its language to satisfy all interpretations. These compromises were cemented in the Thirty-Nine Articles. At the same time, Elizabeth could play the "lion," as she demonstrated by executing her cousin, Mary of Scotland, for plotting against her, and defending England in 1588 against the impending Spanish Armada. By the end of her reign, often called the Golden Age, Elizabeth had established England as the leading Protestant power in Europe.

> ### EXAMPLE BASE
> Many of the examples in this section on the range of Protestant reformers are required knowledge; however, you should take a moment to place them on a continuum of radical to conservative. As you look across the diagram, take note of the diversity of interpretations of religious reform.

Social Impact of the Protestant Reformation

The Protestant Reformation was primarily a religious movement, but it also altered social life. Movements of intellectual or cultural reform often attract those—women, peasants, workers, minorities—who wish to change other features of society. Invariably, these reform movements eventually come to institutionalize new beliefs and practices to head off more wrenching changes. In that sense, the Protestant Reformation can be viewed as a significant shift but also a lost opportunity for many groups. We now look briefly at several affected areas:

- *Family and gender* – As a result of the Protestant Reformation, family was placed at the center of social life. Celibacy was abolished, and many former clergy, like Luther, took spouses and glorified the marital bond as the most natural and God-like. For women, the results were mixed. Though women preached early on and earned limited rights of divorce, as well as education, Luther, Calvin, and other reformers reinforced that women's natural sphere was the domestic. Finally, religious vocations and female religious images were removed from Protestant churches.

- *Education* – There is no doubt that the Protestant Reformation spurred education. With the emphasis on Bible-reading, it was important to ensure literacy for boys *and* girls. Luther's colleague and defender, Philip Melancthon (1497–1560), earned the nickname *Praeceptor Germanie* (Teacher of Germany) for advocating a system of basic schooling called the *Gymnasia*. After the establishment of the Jesuit religious order, Catholic nations also began to place increasing importance on education.

- *Social classes* – Other than the firebrands, few reformers explicitly argued for social equality. However, some historians have argued that a "Protestant work ethic" spurred the development of capitalism, and thus strengthened the middle class. In theory, the emphasis on deferred gratification and building a godly city on earth led to an ethic of **hard work and capital accumulation**. (This interpretation is problematic, but you will probably earn points in an essay for mentioning it.)

- *Religious practices* – For centuries, European religious life had centered around the church calendar, with its saints' feast days, Carnival and Lent, sacraments, and rituals. In many lands, these practices were either abolished or modified. Protestant nations placed more emphasis on Bible-reading and sought to eliminate externals, such as relics, pilgrimages, and festivals. Even many Catholic nations attempted more rigorously to monitor excessive practices and curb long-accepted sins like prostitution, demonstrating the growth of city and **state power to regulate morality**.

Catholic Revival and Reform

Even before 1517, many Catholics recognized the need for religious reform. In fact, reform was already under way if we consider the lay piety movement and the writings of Christian humanists. Under Cardinal Ximenes de Cisneros (1436–1517), Spain had already addressed many clerical abuses and had tightened regulations for the training of priests. However, the institutional church, led by the Papacy throughout the early sixteenth century, "fiddled while Rome burned." Finally, under the pontificate of Paul III (1534–1549), the hierarchical church responded to the challenge of the Protestant Reformation. The Catholic response to the Reformation was multi-pronged and complex. Those actions designed to revive Catholic spirituality are often termed the **Catholic Reformation**, while those designed to halt the spread of the Protestant Reformation are called the Counter-Reformation. Following is a list of the actions, positive and negative, taken by the Catholic Church in response to the Protestant Reformation.

- *New religious orders* – For most Catholics, their connection to the church remained their parish priest. Thus, a major element of reform involved the revival of religious orders and the establishment of new ones. The most important of these was the Society of Jesus or **Jesuits**, founded by Ignatius Loyola (1491–1556) in the 1540s. Like Luther, Loyola underwent a spiritual conversion. After being injured in battle, Loyola practiced rigorous acts of self-discipline and recommitted himself to the mysteries of the church. His important book, *Spiritual Exercises*, contains the famous phrase, "If I see a thing to be white but the institutional church commands it to be black, I will see it as black." Jesuits had no national base, viewing themselves as the "troops of the Pope" and missionaries to those who did not know Christ. Jesuits worked primarily through education and argument, and their efforts paid off by re-Catholicizing large parts of Eastern Europe, including Poland and Hungary after 1560. Other religious orders focused on charitable works and education. Angela Merici (1474–1540) founded the Ursulines to bring education to girls. The Spanish mystic, Teresa of Avila (1515–1582), experienced visions of Jesus and founded the Carmelites, dedicated to a life of contemplation and service. Also, a group of clergy and laypeople formed the Oratory of Divine Love to push for reform in the church and assist one another in leading lives of simple faith. Finally, a new breed of austere and

> **SKILL SET**
>
> Another classic question to consider: Compare and contrast the Protestant and Catholic Reformations on religious doctrines and practices. If you encounter such a question, remember to capture complexity in your interpretation and avoid a one-sided portrayal that may reflect your own sympathies.

hard-working bishops emerged, such as Gian Matteo Giberti (1495–1543) of Verona and Cardinal Charles Borromeo (1538–1584) of Milan.

- *Council of Trent (1545–1563)* – Though tardy and poorly attended, this council finally put the church's house in order. First, the Cardinals (mostly from Italy and Spain) eliminated many church abuses and provided for better education and regulation of priests. Second, the church refused to compromise on religious doctrines, reaffirming distinctive Catholic practices like clerical celibacy, the importance of good works, the authority of the Papacy, and transubstantiation. According to the last, the bread and wine, though retaining the incidents of bread and wine such as taste and texture, are truly transformed into another substance (the body and blood of Jesus) during the Mass.

- *Strengthening the Papacy and Inquisition (1542)* – To better meet the challenge of unorthodox belief, the Papal bureaucracy was centralized and strengthened. A major feature of this revamping was the creation of the Roman Inquisition (not to be confused with the Spanish Inquisition), designed to root out perceived heresies in Italy. In the long run, the Inquisition had a chilling effect on intellectual life, as can be seen by the trial of Galileo in 1633 (see Chapter 6).

- Index of Prohibited Books – Under the conservative pontificate of Pope Paul IV (1555–1559), the church clamped down on any printed materials that threatened to mislead the faithful away from the orthodox interpretations of the magisterium. Though of limited impact in stopping Protestantism, the Index continued until the twentieth century.

- *Baroque art* In an effort to revive Catholic spirituality, the church patronized an artistic movement that emphasized grandeur, illusion, and dramatic religiosity. In music, Palestrina composed numerous masses and sacred pieces geared toward arousing strong religious emotion. Multi-talented artists such as Giovanni Lorenzo Bernini (1598–1680) rebuilt Rome as a showplace of Catholic piety (see Chapter 7 for more on the Baroque).

How successful was the Catholic response? By 1560, the religious divide in Europe was an accomplished fact; in that sense, the Catholic response came too little and too late. On the other hand, some parts of Europe had been re-Catholicized, and the church emerged from its reforms stronger and more militant than in 1500, before the Reformation had begun. One fact is clear: after the completion of the Council of Trent's work in 1564, no religious compromise was possible. With a militant Calvinism and a revived and rearmed Catholic Church, an extended period of religious conflict lay on the horizon.

Additional Resources

🔲 **Roland Bainton, *Here I Stand: A Life of Martin Luther* (1994)** — Considered the classic account of an important figure.

🔲 **Peter Burke, *The Renaissance: Culture and Society in Italy* (1999)** — Explains the concept of the Renaissance and offers a complex account of the term's applicability.

📖 **Alfred W. Crosby, *The Measure of Reality: Quantification and Western Society, 1250–1600* (1997)** — Explores the development of quantitative thinking in the Later Middle Ages and Renaissance. A challenging but fairly brief and interesting read. Highly recommended.

🔲 **T.F. Earle and K.J.P. Lowe, eds., *Black Africans in Renaissance Europe* (2005)** — Essays from historians examining the concept of race and the experiences of Africans in Europe.

📖 **Carlos Eire, *The Reformations: The Early Modern World, 1450–1650* (2018)** — A balanced work that provides a more nuanced and global perspective than many other histories.

🔲 **Elizabeth Lehfeldt, ed., *The Black Death* (2005)** — From the "Problems in Western Civilization" series, this volume offers both primary and secondary sources on a fascinating and relevant topic.

🔲 **Theodore K. Rabb, *Renaissance Lives: Portraits of an Age* (1993)** — Brief and vivid biographies of representative and leading figures.

🔲 **Eugene F. Rice and Anthony Grafton, *The Foundations of Early Modern Europe, 1460–1559* (1993)** — This first volume in the accessible *Norton History of Modern Europe* provides a solid and well-written overview of the period.

🔲 **William H. McNeill, *Plagues and Peoples* (1976)** — Examines the impact of disease in world history.

▦ *Luther* (2003) — This film, produced by the Lutheran Church, provides dramatization of important moments of the Reformation, but omits more controversial features of Luther's life.

▦ *Masters of Illusion* (1991) — Fascinating, brief film illustrating the link between modern movie special effects and Renaissance perspective by a master storyteller, James Burke. Also accessible via https://www.youtube.com/watch?v=Cp5iqYawEw8.

💻 **Metropolitan Museum of Art, https://www.metmuseum.org/toah/** — Explores art by chronology, geography, and theme; a useful resource throughout the course.

CHAPTER TEST

Each chapter will end with 2–3 sets of Multiple-Choice Questions (MCQ) and either a Short-Anwer Question (SAQ) or a Long Essay Question (LEQ) for your practice with content and application of skills. For MCQ answer explanations, see Chapter 18. The SAQ or LEQ will conclude with a sample essay and scoring commentary. You may wish to write the essay first and then compare your answer to the sample. For LEQs, see the rubric on page 5 in Chapter 1.

Multiple-Choice Questions

Questions 1–4 are based on the interpretation below.

"In the Middle Ages … human consciousness … lay dreaming or half-awake beneath a common veil. The veil was woven of faith, illusion, and childish prepossession, through which the world and history were seen clad in strange hues. Man was conscious of himself only as a member of a race, people, party, family, or corporation—only through some general category. In Italy this veil first melted into air; an *objective* treatment and consideration of the State and of all the things of this world became possible.

…[During the Renaissance,] Italy began to swarm with individuality; the ban laid upon human personality was dissolved; and a thousand figures meet us each in its own special shape and dress….The Italians of [this time] knew little of false modesty or of hypocrisy in any shape; not one of them was afraid of singularity, of being and seeming unlike his neighbors."

Jacob Burckhardt, Swiss historian, *The Civilisation of the Renaissance in Italy*, 1860

1. Which of the following features of the Italian Renaissance does Burckhardt endorse most explicitly?
   A. Secularism
   B. Civic humanism
   C. Individualism
   D. Classical revival

2. The Renaissance mindset Burckhardt identifies led most directly in the arts to:
   A. a human-centered naturalism and portrayal of everyday life.
   B. use of distortion, drama, and illusion for state spectacle.
   C. challenging of Church doctrines and ecclesiastical authority.
   D. depictions of scientific inquiry and commercial activities.

3. Writing in 1860, Burckhardt seems most influenced by which of the following ideologies?
   A. Marxism
   B. Positivism
   C. Nationalism
   D. Conservatism

4. Burckhardt seems most concerned that the:
   A. Renaissance compares favorably with other intellectual movements.
   B. Renaissance was caused by a variety of different factors and began in Italy.
   C. humanists of the Renaissance were products of their historical context.
   D. Renaissance represents a transformation and beginning of the modern world.

Questions 5–8 are based on the passage below.

At least twice a year, once in spring and again on the approach of winter, each pastor shall make in his sermons serious admonition to his parishioners that they must be diligent in sending their children to school. And let him stress the great benefit bound to come from this, schools being necessary not only for learning the liberal arts, but also the fear of God, virtue, and discipline. Where the young are neglected and kept out of school, permanent harm, both eternal and temporal, must result, as children grow up without fear and knowledge of God, without discipline, like the dumb beasts of the field, learning nothing about what is needed for their salvation, nor what is useful to them and their neighbors in worldly life.

Wurttemberg (Germany) City Council ordinance, 1559

5. All of the following sixteenth-century developments contributed to the formation of the ordinance above EXCEPT the:
   A. invention of the printing press and advance of literacy.
   B. emphasis in Protestant Christianity on reading the Bible.
   C. ability of the Holy Roman Emperor to centralize power.
   D. movement toward public regulation of morality.

6. Which of the following figures would most likely have agreed with the tone and purpose of the ordinance?
   A. Charles V
   B. John Calvin
   C. Henry VIII
   D. An Anabaptist

7. The purpose of education expressed above differs most strongly from that of the Italian Renaissance in:
   A. focusing primarily on learning for religious purposes.
   B. stressing the application of learning to a public role.
   C. overlooking the role of the liberal arts in forming character.
   D. believing that education should inspire and teach virtue.

8. How would the application of the principles behind education expressed above change most significantly after 1850?
   A. It would no longer address moral concerns.
   B. It would instill patriotism and nationalism.
   C. It would promote revolutionary principles.
   D. It would no longer be supported by the state.

See Chapter 18 for answers and explanations.

Long Essay Question

Directions: Read the prompt below and write your response on a separate sheet of paper. A sample response and commentary are provided on the next page.

Evaluate the extent to which the lives of women changed as a result of the Renaissance and Reformation.

(RP: CCOT)

LEQ Sample Response

Throughout history, women have often been treated less than men. Women were made to be in charge of the domestic sphere and given few chances for education or political power. All of this changed with the Renaissance and Reformation. These were movements that tried to change the way people looked at ideas and religion. Many famous women, like Isabella d'Este and Elizabeth of England, played a major role in these movements. Not all changed for the better, because women were still inferior to men, but they were definitely better off.

The Renaissance was all about humanism, and a big part of that was education. Many intellectuals of this period thought that even women should receive an education. One of these was Castiglione in his *Book of Courtier*. Though this education was not the same as men's, it still was important because before this, women were usually illiterate. Also, there were even some famous women humanists. One of these was Isabella d'Este, a ruler of a city-state on the Italian peninsula. She gathered other thinkers at her court and also wrote treatises about women having more rights. However, women had drawbacks as well. Since men were often much older than women when they were married, they were not always treated well. To escape the control of their husbands, women had affairs and exercised some power "behind the scenes." All in all, women gained an important role in the Renaissance, but this did not always apply to poor women, many of whom turned to prostitution just to survive.

Women also gained some from the Reformation. In fact, many important rulers of this period were women, like Elizabeth and Mary Tudor. These rulers showed that politics was not just for men. Elizabeth may have been the best ruler in England's history. She helped solve the religious conflict left from her father, Henry VIII, and got the Protestants and Catholics back together again. In addition, she was able to fight off the Spanish and their armada in 1588, a great victory that made England the new sea power. Some women even played a role in religious issues, like Catherine Zell. Catherine was an Anabaptist—people who were radical and practiced adult baptism—and preached in churches with her husband. Catholic women even played a role, like Teresa of Avila. She had mystical visions and created a new group of nuns who helped the poor. So, as you can see, women did not just let men control politics and religion. They got involved and proved that they were up to the task.

Women's rights really came later in the twentieth century, when they got the vote, but the Renaissance and Reformation got the ball rolling. Some famous women played major roles in spreading both movements. Of course, not all women gained, especially lower classes, but that doesn't take away from the strides women made. Perhaps if women stand up for their rights, they will continue to gain equality with men.

LEQ Response Analysis

This is a solid essay and one that, with improvements, could earn a top score. First, the student is in control of the question—they address it directly, offer a thesis (if simplified), and provide relevant support. However, the response did not provide sufficient or specific historical background to earn the Contextualization point in the introduction. Second, the essay is balanced, in providing roughly equal treatment of both the Renaissance and Reformation. Third, the response is clearly organized and contains no glaring errors of fact, though some misinterpretations (Elizabeth "got the Protestants and Catholics back together again"). What kept the essay from earning a top score? Though the thesis is evident, it is simplified. In fact, the student often relies on clichés ("get the ball rolling," "up to the task," "got involved") rather than a more specific analysis of how women's status changed or stayed the same (the Targeted RP—Change and Continuity over Time). Finally, though the student addresses Complexity—by carrying the topic forward to a later period—there is not sufficient explanation to earn that point. **Score: 4** (+1 for Thesis, +2 for Use of Evidence, +1 for the Targeted RP (CCOT))

CHAPTER 5

Economic Expansion, Social Change, and Religious Wars, 1550–1650

The European encounter with the Americas, the result of exploration and colonization, changed the world. Not only were Europeans forced to rethink cultural and intellectual assumptions, they gained access to riches, which shifted the balance of political power in Europe, and caused untold destruction to the colonized cultures. The resulting global economy, often termed the Commercial Revolution, altered economic and social structures in Europe. Moreover, this era also saw the effects of the Protestant and Catholic Reformations played out in a century of religious wars, never free from political and economic considerations. A major result of these developments was to shift the locus of European power from the Mediterranean to those nations on the Atlantic.

 KEY IN – Chapter 5 addresses all or part of the following topics in the Unit Guides of the CED:

Topic 1.1   Contextualizing Renaissance and Discovery

Topic 1.6   Technological Advances and the Age of Exploration

Topic 1.7   Rivals on the World Stage

Topic 1.8   Colonial Expansion and the Columbian Exchange

Topic 1.9   The Slave Trade

Topic 1.10   The Commercial Revolution

Topic 1.11   Causation in the Renaissance and Age of Discovery

Topic 2.4   The Wars of Religion

Topic 2.6   16th-Century Society and Politics

Topic 2.8   Causation in the Age of Reformation and the Wars of Religion

Topic 3.6   The Balance of Power

The Opening of the Atlantic

Motives and Means

Europe's outward expansion began in 1095 with the Crusades and continued throughout the Middle Ages, with the *reconquista* in Spain, Marco Polo's journey to China, and the first tentative Portuguese steps to explore the coastline of Africa. What accounts for the burst of exploration in the fifteenth and sixteenth centuries? The standard explanation is "God, gold,

> **THEME MUSIC**
>
> Here we begin our investigation of Interaction of Europe and the World theme (INT). As you study, focus on the motives, means, methods of control, and results of exploration. These issues will recur throughout the course.

and glory," a mantra that captures the missionary impulse, economic incentives, and personal motives of the conquistadores. However, we should not overlook the role that technological developments played, as well as the sponsorship provided by competitive states eager to reap the political advantages of this exploration.

For centuries, Europe's access to the coveted goods of the East was provided by Arab and Ottoman middlemen. Direct control of spices, silks, sugar, porcelain, precious metals, gems, and strategic minerals would reduce costs and ensure a ready supply of profit-making goods. With the growth of towns and commerce in the Middle Ages, merchants and governments were keen on exploiting opportunities to fill their private and state coffers with new-found wealth. And missionaries considered the lands of the East rich ground for spreading the Gospel message. Though many viewed religion as a pretext rather than a motive for exploration, others were genuinely driven by piety, even if it was misplaced. In fact, once the Reformation was under way, religious groups like the Jesuits viewed the new colonies as a proving ground of religious commitment. Motives, then, for exploration were clearly in place; now all that was needed were the means.

The fifteenth century climaxed a long chain of navigational and intellectual advances that supported overseas exploration. Though the Chinese had already made contact with Africa and the Indian Ocean basin in the early fifteenth century, they did not establish permanent outposts. China considered itself culturally and economically superior and thus not desirous of the goods or ideas of neighboring cultures. However, China's ingenuity served Europe well, as its compass and axial rudder allowed Columbus and others the ability to conduct voyages far from their homelands. In addition, the quadrant (and more sophisticated astrolabe) allowed explorers to measure the angle of the Pole Star to determine latitude. New maps, called *portolani*, provided detailed information about headlands and direction, though limited information regarding the open ocean. New ship designs, such as the caravel (a light maneuverable craft) and lateen (or triangular) sail, which allowed a crew to tack against the direction of the wind, made blue-water voyages possible. Finally, perspective geometry and the rediscovery of Ptolemy's *Geographica* (a second-century Greek astronomer) provided for the grid-like structure found on most modern maps, even if Ptolemy had overestimated the size of Asia (a fact that Columbus would use to his advantage).

Not all states were positioned to exploit these technologies. Because Portugal and Spain were the first to establish monarchical control over their diverse realms, they led the way in sponsoring long-distance sea voyages. Setting up and administering colonies on far-flung lands required resources, bureaucracy, and sustained political energy. Though many early explorers hailed from Italy (Columbus, Vespucci, Verrazano, the Cabots), that country sponsored no overseas voyages; it couldn't, being divided and preoccupied with foreign invasion. Also, centralized governments had gained a monopoly on violence and were thus able to employ new techniques and technologies in warfare, such as cannons, steel weapons, and plate armor, which simply overwhelmed colonial opponents.

> ### EXAMPLE BASE
>
> These examples of technology and learning may not be vital *per se*, but try to link them to broader intellectual and cultural developments, such as the Renaissance and subsequent Scientific Revolution, to help provide an explanation for exploration and colonization.

The Development of Colonial Empires

One nation that experienced a substantial economic boost from exploration was Portugal. In retrospect, Portugal's rise is amazing. A nation lacking natural resources with only about one million inhabitants, tucked in the southwestern corner of Europe, Portugal by 1510 had established a worldwide trading empire. Prince Henry (1394–1460), nicknamed "The Navigator," founded a school for seafarers at Sagres, which trained the first generation of sailors who settled the Azores Island chain (a basing area for transatlantic voyages) and explored along the west coast of Africa. Though the Portuguese drained the gold, pepper, and enslaved persons of Africa, they still had not found the coveted sea route to the East. Then in 1498 Vasco da Gama (c. 1469–1524) made it around the Cape of Good Hope and to the riches of India. The single returning ship earned a 1,000% profit for its investors!

Da Gama followed up his success by returning with cannons, which overwhelmed the advanced civilizations of the Indian Ocean basin. By 1510, the Portuguese had established control of several strategic choke points in the East, which allowed them to extract trade concessions and radically reduce the cost of luxury products. Though Portugal lacked the population and resources to maintain extensive settlements, their maritime empire fed Europe's appetite for trade with the East until it was taken over by the Dutch at the end of the sixteenth century.

Right behind the Portuguese came the Spanish. Though Christopher Columbus (1451–1506) completed four voyages to the Americas, he never recognized his miscalculation of the earth's circumference. Subsequent explorers welcomed the prospect of exploiting two previously unknown continents, and in the decades that followed, the Spanish monarchy sponsored expeditions which would lead to the subjugation of an entirely "New World."

Before describing the Spanish empire, let's review the actions of several major figures in the history of exploration, keeping in mind that with this topic, the AP exam will focus less on personalities and more on motives and effects:

- *Hernando Cortez* (1460–1547) – *Conquistador* who overwhelmed the advanced Aztec civilization through use of horses, cannons, and diplomacy. Cortez helped establish the Spanish presence in North America.

- *Ferdinand Magellan* (1480–1521) – Skilled Portuguese seaman who sailed under the flag of Spain. He led his men through the treacherous straits at the tip of South America, now named for him, before perishing in the Philippines. Magellan is credited with the first successful circumnavigation of the earth.

- *St. Francis Xavier* (1506–1552) – Jesuit missionary who used wit and zeal to establish Christianity in India, Indonesia, and Japan.

- *Francisco Pizarro* (c. 1475–1541) – Brutal conqueror of the Incas in the Andes. He was aided by disease, as he and less than 300 men laid claim to South America.

Following Columbus's discovery, the Portuguese and Spanish negotiated the Treaty of Tordesillas (1494), whereby they divided the world in half for purposes of colonization. Eventually Portugal laid claim to Brazil in South America, but the primary force in the Americas proved to be Spain, a presence that had profound consequences for both the colonizer and the colonized.

Soon after the Spanish conquest of the Americas, the exploitation of native peoples began. To provide for the orderly development of the new continents, the Spanish introduced the *encomienda* system. According to this system, settlers were given grants of land and native labor, in return providing for the Christian instruction and protection of their workers. In reality, the indigenous people were brutally exploited in mining and other operations, beginning the rapid decline in their population. The Potosi mine in present-day Bolivia represents a fearful example of how the system quickly went awry. Though the mine became the primary supplier of Spanish silver, this wealth came at the expense of the native civilizations.

The indigenous population found a defender in the Dominican monk Bartolome de las Casas (1484–1566), whose *Brief Account of the Devastation of the Indies* (1542) highlighted the issues of abuse and devastation. De las Casas's account eventually led to the New Laws, which reformed the *encomienda* system. Unfortunately, it was too late; most of the native population had been decimated by neglect and disease. The resulting labor shortage led to another negative legacy from exploration: African slavery. Though the slave trade dated back to the early fifteenth century, it didn't take off until exploitation of the Americas increased demand for menial labor. In all, approximately 12 million Africans suffered the horrors of the deadly <u>Middle Passage</u> across the Atlantic in Portuguese, Spanish, and ultimately Dutch and English ships. Though Africans were able to create new cultures in a new land, the issue of African slavery has left a deep imprint on the history of four continents.

Of all the colonial empires, Spain's operated in the most centralized fashion. Policies were administered directly, if sometimes slowly, by the Council of the Indies, under the control of the Spanish monarchy. Imperial administrators tended to be loyal to Spain rather than to the Spanish Americans they governed. The New World was divided into two viceroyalties—New Mexico and Peru—which were subdivided into captaincies general for ease of administration. To assist and oversee royal governors, *audiencias* served as advisory bodies and courts. To settle in Spanish America, one was required to adhere to the Catholic faith. Over time, remaining native peoples were converted to Catholicism, and the hierarchical structure of the Church was transferred to Spanish America, resulting even today in the largest concentration of Catholics in the world.

Meeting of Two Worlds: Effects

Intellectual and Cultural Impact

A key impact of exploration was the **Columbian Exchange**, the cultural and economic diffusion of practices and goods across the Atlantic. Exploration efforts were richly rewarded with a bounty of new crops and goods from the Americas, such as <u>po</u><u>tatoes</u>, <u>tobacco</u>, <u>tomatoes</u>, cocoa, <u>gold</u> and silver, beans, <u>corn</u>, peanuts, but also possibly <u>syphilis</u>. Many of the crops and animals now considered natural to the Americas, in fact, originated in the Old World: <u>horses</u>, <u>cattle</u>, <u>sheep</u>, <u>pigs</u>, honey bees, rice, <u>wheat</u>, sugar cane, and, most notoriously, diseases. These last, including <u>measles</u>, <u>small</u><u>pox</u>, typhus, and malaria, decimated native peoples, who lacked immunity to such infectious pestilences. Along with abusive treatment, by the end of the sixteenth century the thriving population of the Americas had been reduced by 90%, though historians disagree on the pre-1492 population levels (between 20–70 million).

> **SKILL SET**
>
> The Columbian Exchange offers a rich opportunity for applying HTS. First, you may wish to create a Venn diagram to compare and contrast its effects on both Europe and the Americas. Also, the Exchange sparked changes in the economy, which leads to a CCOT analysis. Finally, to help you develop your Argumentation ability, try writing a brief statement of how 1492 represents a transformative moment in world economic and political history.

Colonization also reoriented Europe's intellectual world. Contact between previously unknown civilizations was bound to prompt all parties to rethink their cultural assumptions. First, Europeans set about creating new maps that more accurately depicted the world in precise, scientific, and abstract space (e.g., with grids and keys). The pioneer in this field was Gerardus Mercator (1512–1594), a Flemish mapmaker who succeeded in mass-producing the first globes and also rendering a three-dimensional space (the earth) on a two-dimensional surface—the still-standard map that continues to bear his name. Also, even though Europeans approached indigenous peoples with little regard for their cultures, some used the encounter to reevaluate and even critique European society. Probably influenced by de las Casas, <u>Michel de Montaigne</u> (1533–1592), a French lawyer and inventor of the essay, introduced a new skeptical attitude toward European customs, even suggesting that native cannibalism was no worse than many of the atrocities of Europe's religious wars. A final legacy of 1492 was the creation of entirely new cultures in the New World from the mixing of the old. From the racial blending of the *mestizos* to the religious practices of voodoo to the Gullah and Creole dialects, and finally to the music of jazz, the Americas continue to bear the legacy of exploration and colonization.

The Commercial Revolution, Phase I

Europe's colonization of the Americas and its creation of maritime empires led to significant changes within Europe. We examine some of the economic and social changes here; in a later chapter, we'll take a turn at the diplomatic and political results.

The economic result of exploration and colonization is termed the **Commercial Revolution**— an acceleration in global trade involving new goods and techniques. Often underestimated as a topic in the course, the Commercial Revolution fed the growth of modern society. Two of these changes were an increase in Europe's population (to about 90 million in 1600, finally surpassing the preplague level) and a steady rise in prices. This latter development promoted a money-oriented economy, which further undermined the feudal system in Western Europe. Though traditionally the **Price Revolution** was attributed to the importation of precious metals from the New World, more recent interpretations have stressed population growth as the source of the inflation. With rising demand chasing a limited supply of goods, prices for scarce products were bid up. Landowners benefited from the inflation, unless they had leased their land via long-term rents, and many turned to the production of cash crops (those for sale, not consump-

> **THEME MUSIC**
>
> This section provides a brief conceptual synopsis of the ECD theme, particularly how Europe moved from a subsistence agriculture system to one based on money and capital. Be careful not to overstate the changes, as much of the traditional economy persisted in regions and localities well into the nineteenth century.

tion). A new class of independent farmers, outside the feudal structure and focused on producing for the market, began to arise. In England, they were called the **gentry** (gentlemen), and they attempted to imitate the lifestyles of the lords and nobles. Like the burghers in towns (bourgeoisie), the gentry were resented by those below and scorned by those above.

Traditionally the **guilds** dominated the production of goods in towns and cities; workers owned the capital *and* performed the labor. With the increase in profit from trade, merchants began to invest their earnings in long-distance business ventures, often ending up in banking like the Medici in Italy or the Fuggers in Germany. Families such as the Fuggers formed close relationships with monarchs, as with Charles V, loaning money for state enterprises such as mining. Eventually larger banks were formed from the resources of numerous investors. One of the more prominent, the Bank of Amsterdam (founded in 1609), funded the commercial dominance of the Netherlands. By this time, bankers ignored the traditional Christian prohibition against usury (the charging of interest on loans); the profits were just too great to ignore.

The separation of capital and labor is a major feature of **capitalism**, and the divergence became more pronounced beginning in the sixteenth and seventeenth centuries. Entrepreneurs began investing in their own manufacturing enterprises. To sidestep the guild structure, they provided (or "put out") the raw materials to rural families eager to supplement their marginal incomes by finishing goods. This was especially pronounced in the textile industries, where the various steps of manufacture—spinning, carding, weaving—were mechanized at different times. The **putting-out system (cottage industry)** signaled the decline of the guild structure and served as an intermediate step toward factory production in the late eighteenth century. Other industries did not fit neatly into the guild structure and also received stimulus from the new capital—printing, bookmaking, mining, shipbuilding, and weapons manufacture.

During the late sixteenth and into the seventeenth centuries, Europeans whetted a strong appetite for luxury and staple items from overseas. As the goods became more common, such as tea and coffee, they gradually established a cultural influence on European styles and diet, often beginning with the aristocracy and seeping down through the bourgeoisie into the lower classes. The New World tomato and potato took a strong hold on European diets, though the latter had to overcome resistance to its appearance and taste. Eventually, however, the potato became the salvation of many nations, especially Russia, Germany, and Ireland, because of its versatility and ease of cultivation. Coffee- and tea-drinking provided opportunities for socializing outside more traditional networks (as in coffeehouses) and also gave workers a jolt of midday energy, particularly when combined with the largest profit-maker of the era—sugar. The sweet tooth of Europeans and the accumulated capital from its trade rested upon the backs of African enslaved persons, forced to work and die in **plantations** throughout the Caribbean.

A status-conscious aristocracy and its middle-class imitators craved symbols of style and status. This meant silks and porcelain from China, calicoes (light, brightly colored cotton cloth) from India, and **spices** from the **East Indies**. Hunger for luxury goods fed the Commercial Revolution; competition among nations encouraged new trading techniques and the search for new goods, carried in the merchant marines of trading powers.

To pool financial resources and share risk, investors created joint-stock companies. Of these, the **Dutch** and **British East India Companies** (both founded in the first decade of the seventeenth century) were the most famous and profitable. Such companies gained monopoly status from government charters and were expected to foster an increase in trade as well as imports of gold and silver. Gradually the Dutch pushed the Portuguese out of the East Indies and, along with England, began to challenge the dominance of the Iberian empires. Colonial competition among the Netherlands, England, France, and Spain accelerated throughout the seventeenth and eighteenth centuries, culminating with a series of decisive commercial wars.

> **EXAMPLE BASE**
>
> These products became key consumer goods, but in some instances, they also changed cultures. For example, the European desire for sugar stimulated the slave trade and plantation economies in the Americas. Coffee and tea led to new venues for public discussion of ideas and culture, which relates to the SOP theme ("other institutions of power").

Global trade on a large scale fed the rise of commercial capitalism in Europe. The credit, financial, and mercantile systems described above defined the nature of capitalism until the rise of mechanized mass production in textiles in the late eighteenth century. In an effort to exploit the potential for wealth, European nations adopted the economic theory of **mercantilism**. This theory—which generally guided the policies of most nations until the *laissez-faire* ideas of Adam Smith—was based on three essential tenets:

- *Scarcity* – The total amount of global resources and wealth are limited. Therefore, any advances by one nation come at the expense of another; trade is a "zero-sum game."

- *Wealth = specie (hard money)* – Mercantilists held that real wealth equaled the amount of gold and silver flowing into a nation. Given this assumption, governments attempted to promote exports through trade monopolies, acquisition of colonies, and subsidies. At the same time these same nations limited imports via tariffs, trade restrictions, and war aimed at an enemy's mercantile potential.

- *Government intervention* – Though governments did not generally own the means of production, they did actively intervene to promote national objectives.

States provided incentives to key industries, sought new colonies, and worked to establish national markets by building roads and canals and abolishing localism. The ultimate goal of these efforts aimed at a favorable balance of trade, i.e., more specie flowing into the nation than flowing out. In the next chapter, we'll examine the mercantilist policies of specific nations.

Changing Social Structures, 1500–1700

Early modern society experienced significant change alongside entrenched stability. Many of the social structures of the period 1500–1700 will seem alien to contemporary students. As you read through this section, try to step outside your assumptions and judgments. Capturing the mentalities of early modern Europeans requires sensitivity to historical context, aided by a vivid imagination. This period serves as a rich area for questions on the AP exam, though it is often overlooked by students. As you study the period, try to establish strong grounding in *specific* developments which influenced the lives of Europeans. When addressing any period, locate it clearly in time and place. Avoid expressions like "throughout history" or "women have always cooked and cleaned," as they reveal an anachronistic ("misplaced") understanding of the past.

Demographic Changes and Social Structures

As noted previously, an increasing population caused a structural change in early modern European society. Until about 1550, this increase helped bring fertile land under cultivation as Europe recovered from the Black Death. After 1550, however, Europe's population began to strain existing resources, resulting in the Price Revolution described earlier. Population continued to increase throughout the rest of the century, but poor weather, war, lack of resources, and periodic famine caused a decline in population throughout the seventeenth century. The discrepancy between population and the resources required to sustain it is termed the "Malthusian trap" after the eighteenth-century British political economist. In fact, some nations, such as Spain, experienced a steep drop in population, which seriously hampered its economy and threatened its great-power status. Though governments did not keep accurate census data until the late eighteenth century, local studies have revealed the serious negative impact of poor economic conditions on daily life,

> **SKILL SET**
>
> Don't overlook the issue of demographics (study of population) throughout the course. A key figure on the topic is Thomas Malthus, who introduced a theory that explained why populations cannot expand progressively in the long term. You are strongly encouraged to trace European population developments throughout the course, especially in explaining the changes and continuities (CCOT) in Europe's interaction with its environment.

as demonstrated by a serious drop in marriages and births during hard times. For the big picture—Europe's population maxed out at 100 million about 1550, dropped to around 80 million by 1650, and had recovered to 100 million again by 1700.

Economic developments altered the class structure. Though the traditional system was not overturned, some changes were evident by 1700. The aristocracy maintained its primary position despite the addition of new blood, that is, members of the middle class who were able to acquire noble status through the purchase of an office, which often became hereditary with a payment of a tax (called the *paulette* in France). Sometimes resented by the older nobles ("nobles of the sword"), these new nobles were termed the "nobles of the robe" and played a more important role as governments expanded their bureaucratic functions.

Below the nobles were the ***bourgeoisie***, or burghers, meaning those who lived in towns. Technically outside the feudal structure, the middle class made their livings in a variety of economic activities. The middle class was by no means a monolithic group. Some owned large tracts of land and lived off of income from rent, others traded goods as merchants, and still others filled out the growing professions, such as physicians, clergy, and attorneys. In addition, towns also thrived on the work of the lower middle class or *petit bourgeoisie*, who labored as shopkeepers, artisans, grocers, and store owners. As the money economy and world trade expanded in the sixteenth and seventeenth centuries, the middle class increased, though they were not yet able to translate these numbers into political power.

Agriculture and the Countryside

The lives of the vast majority of Europeans were dictated by the seasons and the paces of agricultural life. Agriculture was generally practiced in a village setting, with decisions made communally. This **subsistence agricultural system**— growing enough to feed the village with little left over for export—was defined by the **three-field crop rotation** system in the north and the **two-field** system in the south. In these systems, one section of land was left fallow (uncultivated) to allow for replenishment of the soil, limiting full use of resources. Each village included a commons area, used for livestock grazing, wood-gathering, hunting, or eking out a marginal existence for the landless. Throughout the sixteenth century, England began selling off common land for purchase by wealthy landowners. This practice of enclosure had the double effect of creating a new non-aristocratic class of wealthy landowners, the **gentry**, as well as increasing the numbers of landless poor, who either had to contract out their labor or move to the cities. Between these two groups stood the yeomanry, small freeholders who owned their land. As often occurs with economic changes, some took advantage and improved their status while others found their already marginal existence threatened further.

The paths of western and eastern Europe began to diverge further during the seventeenth century. As most of the peasants of western Europe were freed from serfdom and other feudal obligations, those of eastern Europe were drawn more tightly into a highly codified system of laws governing an individual's life. While western peasants continued to owe their lords manorial obligations, such as the payment of taxes, fees for the use of ovens and mills, and the hated labor service (called *corvee* in France, *robot* in the east), they were generally free to leave the land and could call on a set of traditional prerogatives to protect themselves against excessive landlords. Such was not the case in eastern Europe as, for example, **serfdom** became state law in the mid-seventeenth century in Russia. Large manors, often exploiting the labor of up to 100,000 serfs, dominated nations such as Poland and Hungary, where nobles made up 10% of the population, compared to 2%–3% in France or England.

The Life of the Towns

Though only 10%–20% of Europeans lived in towns or cities, urban centers played an economic and a cultural role disproportional to their numbers. Compared with our contemporary individualistic spirit, early modern Europeans were embedded in a web of social relationships—guild, village, neighborhood, church, city, class, family. In fact, popular metaphors for society construed it as a complex organism, with each group playing the appropriate role assigned to it—the Great Chain of Being or the Body Politic. Institutions tended to be **hierarchical** in theory, though traditions and the desire to avoid social conflict often prevented social superiors from becoming arbitrary. In this period, cities attracted from the countryside both landless laborers and those seeking opportunity. By the end of the sixteenth century, most cities could no longer adequately handle the influx of new residents. The working poor comprised the majority of city dwellers and survived by finding odd jobs (e.g., unloading ships, hard manual labor, or domestic service) or by begging.

By 1550, when the resource base showed increasing stress, poverty reached crisis proportions in many European nations. Many of the poor resorted to begging; some even maimed themselves to garner sympathy. Traditional religious and charitable institutions were overwhelmed, so governments began to enact strict regulations that distinguished between the "**deserving**" (disabled, elderly, children) and "undeserving" (able-bodied males) **poor**. England's Poor Law of 1601, for example, provided charitable relief but also seriously punished those who violated its regulations.

Crime often accompanied poverty. Both property and violent crime increased in the period 1500–1700. Because governments lacked modern police forces and prisons, they tended to inflict cruel and often hideous punishments on captured criminals as an example to others. Public executions were common, even for property crimes such as theft.

Not until the eighteenth century did reformers call for the changes in the legal and penal system.

Family and Communal Life

As today, the most basic institution in European life was the family. In western Europe, the **nuclear family** (parents, children, and perhaps an elderly grandparent) predominated. Because taxes in nations like Russia and Hungary were assessed on households, extended families proved more common there. Unlike Renaissance Italy, the average age of marriage for men was mid- to late-20s and early- to mid-20s for women, though these averages increased in hard economic times. Women of the aristocracy tended to marry somewhat earlier and, on average, experienced eight to nine live births, whereas women of the middle and lower classes experienced on average six to seven live births. Part of this disparity can be explained by the use of wet nurses among the upper classes, as breastfeeding tends to dampen fertility. Old age was rare because of high infant mortality and low life expectancy. As a result, remarriage and blended families were common. Despite the stereotype of female labor as primarily domestic, women were, in fact, integral to the family economy. A wife's death often drove a widower to remarry as soon as possible. In artisan households, for example, women supervised the workers, kept the books, and marketed the products.

> **SKILL SET & THEME MUSIC**
>
> From this section it should be apparent how Developments and Processes (DAP) in one theme (ECD) can redefine or create tension in others (SCD). Economic dynamism creates new forms of wealth but can disrupt social traditional communal norms and practices. Practice the skill of Making Connections between themes like the two above for a historical era; good practice for earning the Complexity point on your essays.

By standard interpretation, the concept of childhood did not exist until its invention during the Enlightenment. In fact, evidence indicates that in the early modern period, parents did love their children and considered the loss of a child a tragedy. Nonetheless, children were expected to contribute labor to the family unit—often overseen by the father—and were subjected to corporal punishments for disobedience. Also, keep in mind that society or parents did not provide compulsory schooling or age-appropriate toys, reading materials, or clothing for children. In most nations, children did not earn full legal rights at a specific age, but only when they established their own residences. Female children were expected to bring a dowry into a marriage (land, furniture, personal property, cash), though in Germany, for example, tradition protected a daughter from her father from arbitrarily depriving her of this inheritance.

Early modern leisure differs significantly from our modern diversions. Whereas our forms of amusement tend to be consumptive (shopping, amusement parks, dining, etc.) and in small groups, Europeans of the sixteenth and seventeenth centuries engaged in **communal leisure**. Early-modern rhythms of life were governed by the seasons; periods of extended labor were followed by those of extended celebration. In Catholic nations, the **religious calendar**, with its cycle of saints' feast days and rituals, dictated the pace of work and leisure. Carnival, the period right before Lenten fasting and penance, served as the largest of these festivals. For over a week, villagers and townspeople consumed large amounts of food and alcohol, while playing traditional games and engaging in a higher-than-normal amount of sexual activity. In addition, classes and genders switched roles for the "world turned upside down," which played the important role of letting off discontent in a ritualized way before returning to the normal hierarchy. With the Reformation, many Protestant and even some Catholic areas tried to restrain what they considered the excesses of the practice. Finally, to ensure social conformity, many localities imposed rituals of public humiliation on those who stepped outside of community standards, such as a husband who could not control his wife or a woman who committed adultery. In France, this practice was called _charivari_ and in England, skimmington.

Witchcraft Persecution

A striking phenomenon of early modern Europe was the **persecution of witches**. The height of the scare occurred from 1580–1680, during which approximately 100,000 people, mostly women, were executed for covenanting with the devil. The practice strikes our modern sensibilities as backward and barbaric. However, we should try to understand what beliefs and socioeconomic conditions gave rise to the phenomenon. First, almost all Europeans, even the educated, believed in witches and demons. Increased Bible-reading because of the Protestant Reformation emphasized both the reality of the devil and the supposedly weak and credulous nature of women. Second, the early modern period experienced rapid social and economic change—enclosure, religious wars, poverty, crime, and overpopulation—that tended to undermine or challenge traditional practices. Third, religious passions were inflamed by the Protestant and Catholic Reformations and resulting religious wars, creating suspicion among communities, especially in regions divided by religious belief. Finally, those targeted for accusation tended to exist on the margins of the community—the poor, older women, those living alone—and thus beyond the reach of social norms. Women, in particular, were believed to have special knowledge of and powers over the body (because of their role in childbirth) and often supple-

mented family incomes by preparing traditional cures or potions. In fact, some may have even considered themselves practitioners of white magic (as opposed to "black magic," in league with Satan). With the general acceptance of scientific explanations by elites, the witch trials declined markedly after 1720 and were almost gone by 1750.

The Religious Wars

One of the more complex and challenging topics you will study this year is the religious wars. Amidst the numerous personalities and rapidly changing motives, try to keep your eye on the key issues: the causes, nature, and end results of the wars. Though historians term these "religious" wars, each conflict was also shaped by political and territorial ambitions.

Philip II: Catholic Defender

At the center of the religious conflicts of the second half of the sixteenth century stood Philip II (r. 1556–1598), ruler of Spain and the Low Countries, parts of Italy, and the New World. Like his Habsburg father, Charles I (V as Holy Roman Emperor), Philip saw himself as the political protector of Catholicism in Europe, though Philip lacked Charles's more cosmopolitan background. Philip was rasied as a Spaniard and influenced by that nation's strong Catholic tradition and crusading mentality. El Escorial, Philip's palace on the arid plains outside Madrid, reflected the ruler's personality. Part residence, part monastery and religious retreat, the Escorial formed the central governing point of a huge empire stretching across oceans. Philip insisted on overseeing even the minutest details of government, earning him the nickname the "King of Paper," after his habit of reviewing each document from his diverse realm. Philip's first area of concern was France, even though he did not directly rule that nation.

The French Wars of Religion

France's long series of religious conflicts (1560–1598) grew from religious _and_ political roots. Despite Francis I's (r. 1515–1547) attempts to stamp out the spread of Protestant ideas, Calvinism continued to grow in his kingdom, often indirectly aided by the patronage of his sister, Marguerite of Navarre (1492–1529), a deeply religious woman and author of several controversial stories and religious works. Calvinism found fertile ground among the French aristocracy in particular, perhaps because they already considered themselves "the elect." By 1560, 40% of French nobles embraced the Huguenot faith (as French Calvinists were called), which, because nobles held important positions in the government and military, posed a threat to the Catholic Valois monarchy. These religious causes were exacerbated when the strong French king Henry II (r. 1547–1559) died tragically in a jousting accident. His death plunged France into a civil conflict over control of the throne _and_ over

SKILL SET

You may find the topic of witchcraft fascinating. It is, but make sure to avoid presentism, i.e., judging the past by present standards. Turn the topic into a CAUS question and create a visual to show how and why the phenomenon accelerated (after 1550) and then faded (after 1680). Work toward capturing complexity in your portrayal.

France's religion.

The conflict in France is best viewed as a three-sided struggle. In the middle stood the Catholic Valois family, now led by Henry's widow, the moderate yet cunning Catherine de' Medici (1519–1589). Like the future Henry IV and Elizabeth I of England, Catherine advocated political stability over religious orthodoxy, being known as a *politique*. In addition, Catherine attempted to maintain the throne for her three weak sons—Francis II (r. 1559–1560), Charles IX (r. 1560–1574), and Henry III (r. 1574–1589). Against the Catholic Valois, on one side, stood a faction of Protestant nobles who laid claim to the throne through Henry Bourbon (of Navarre) and wished free worship for those of the Huguenot faith. Also opposed to the Valois and with the backing of the Jesuits, the papacy, and Philip II were the Guise family, or ultra-Catholics. The ultra-Catholics viewed the Valois monarchy as weak in the face of the Protestant threat and wished to restore a more strongly Catholic king.

Religious conflict in France was played out in a series of 13 short wars, with numerous attempts at compromise by Catherine and her sons. One of these attempts at compromise led to one of the worst atrocities during this violent period. In 1572, Henry Bourbon agreed to marry Catherine de' Medici's daughter as a sign of reconciliation. However, during the wedding celebration in Paris, rumors flared that Protestants were plotting to take over the government. What followed was a slaughter of the Protestant nobles, in Paris and throughout France, known as the St. Bartholomew's Day Massacre. In all, approximately 10,000 French Protestants were killed, though Henry Bourbon escaped by converting to Catholicism (a conversion he quickly renounced). The event seemed to show the corruption of the Valois monarchy and deepened resistance to it.

The final stage of France's civil war is called the War of the Three Henrys. In 1588, Henry Guise (leader of the ultra-Catholics) took the city of Paris, threatening the Valois hold on the nation. Henry III, of Valois, felt he had no alternative but to form an alliance against the ultra-Catholics with (Huguenot) Henry Bourbon, whom he promised to make next in line to the throne. On the pretext of compromise, both Henrys invited Guise to the palace and had him assassinated. In reprisal, a fanatical monk killed Henry III in 1589, making Henry Bourbon (IV) ruler of France. However, Henry IV's (r. 1589–1610) way to Paris was barred by Spanish troops, and he would spend the next decade winning control of the nation. To bring peace to the France, Henry converted back to Catholicism (the majority religion of France), supposedly saying "Paris is worth a mass," and then engineered the **Edict of Nantes**, which allowed Huguenots to practice their religion outside Paris and to fortify towns to protect their hard-won liberties. Over the next several years, Henry IV emerged as one of the most beloved monarchs in French history and established a strong Bourbon dynasty, laying the foundations for absolutism.

The Wars of Spain

An important part of Philip's inheritance was Burgundy, the 17 provinces known as the Low Countries, where his father Charles had been raised. Philip was an outsider to those in the Low Countries, who wished to maintain their traditional decentralized political structure and religious freedoms. Philip's policies eventually sparked a revolt, which had at its base religious, political, and economic causes. First, Philip attempted to increase taxes to fund the cost of the Spanish empire, thus alienating many in the middle classes. Next, Philip determined to stamp out heresy by tightening the church structure in the Netherlands (another name for Burgundy) and by employing the Inquisition. Because the 17 provinces stood astride important trade routes and had a tradition of religious tolerance, they attracted many adherents of Calvinism.

> **SKILL SET**
>
> You will notice the complexity of motives, changing courses, and groups/individuals involved in the religious wars. To prevent yourself from bogging down in minutia, focus on a major interpretative question—the relationship between religious and political or economic motives for the wars. Take a position and defend it, using examples from any of the conflicts in this section (CES and ARG).

In response to Philip's tax policy, discontented Burgundians in 1566 directed their ire against the symbols of Catholicism, smashing statues and church decorations, in what were known as the iconoclastic riots. Philip sent the Duke of Alba to the Netherlands to crush the revolt. Alba established the so-called Council of Blood and executed a number of leading Protestant nobles, which only further inflamed the provinces. Soon a leader of the revolt emerged—William "the Silent" (1533–1584–from the House of Orange in Holland), so-called because of his reluctance to discuss his strategies with others. William was aided by the "sea beggars," ships that engaged in acts of piracy against the Spanish. When Spanish troops pillaged the city of Antwerp in 1576 (they had not been paid because Spain lacked funds), all 17 provinces called for the end of Spanish rule in the Netherlands, an event known as the Pacification of Ghent. This action caused Philip to change tactics, and it overshadowed the great Spanish naval victory over Ottoman forces in 1571 at Lepanto, which cleared the western Mediterranean of Islamic power.

Philip appointed his nephew Alexander Farnese (1545–1592), the Duke of Parma and a brilliant military leader, to subdue the Netherlands through reward and punishment. By 1578 Farnese succeeded in prying away the southern ten provinces from the revolt and winning their allegiance to Spain with the Union of Arras. These provinces were populated primarily by the French-speaking Walloons. In response, the seven northern, mostly-Dutch-speaking Flemish provinces formed the Union of Utrecht in 1581 with the intent of separating from Spain. Throughout the conflict, Elizabeth I of England quietly provided the Dutch with financial and naval aid, including attacks on Spanish shipping by the "sea dogs" such as Sir Francis Drake (c. 1540–1596). By 1588, Philip was determined to end English meddling and teach Elizabeth, his one-time sister-in-law who had spurned his offer of marriage, a lesson. Philip's Spanish Armada did not have a chance against the more maneuverable English ships and because his plan for an invasion was too complex. Spain's "confident hope of a miracle" turned into a rout in the "Protestant wind," which signaled the rise of England and the relative decline of Spain as maritime powers, though Philip would raise other armadas and continue the fight.

Though Philip never admitted defeat in the Netherlands, his successor Philip III in 1609 signed a Twelve Years truce with the 7 northern provinces (Union of Utrecht), which all but granted Dutch independence. The southern 10 provinces remained loyal and became known as the Spanish Netherlands. Once the strongest nation in Europe, Spain slowly declined throughout the seventeenth century. Several factors explain Spain's loss of status. First, the Spanish had overextended themselves politically and militarily, taxing their subjects excessively and allowing the nation to fall behind economically. Second, the Iberian crusading mentality led the Spanish to persecute talented minorities, like the *moriscos* (Muslim converts to Catholicism), who were driven out in the early seventeenth century. Finally, internal revolts over high taxes and government centralization, combined with population decline, sapped Spain's internal energy. By the end of the Thirty Years' War, to which we now turn, Spain's *siglo de oro* (Golden Age) was over, an important lesson for nations that believe that power entails invincibility.

The Thirty Years' War, 1618–1648

Prior to the world wars of the twentieth century, the most devastating conflict in European history was the Thirty Years' War. The conflict began as a civil war over religion in Germany but escalated into a continental conflagration involving territorial and political ambitions. Years before war started, German Catholics and Protestants geared up for battle by forming alliances with outside powers. These alliances—the Protestant Union and Catholic League—ensured that when war did come, it would involve the great powers of Europe.

Following the Peace of Augsburg (1555), Germany was divided between Lutheran and Catholic states. However, the treaty did not take into account the fastest growing denomination after 1560—Calvinism. When the ruler of the Palatinate (an elector of the HRE), Frederick V (1610–1623), converted to Calvinism, the delicate religious balance in Germany seemed threatened. It became apparent that neither Protestant nor Catholic leaders had any intention of treating Augsburg as a permanent settlement to Germany's religious division. What complicated matters was the elective nature of the Holy Roman Emperor, nominally the political leader of Catholicism and still a position of importance. According to the Golden Bull of 1356, the emperor was elected by seven states, three of which were controlled by Catholic rulers and three by Protestants. To gain control of the last electoral state (Bohemia), the next Habsburg in line (the traditional imperial ruling house)—Ferdinand II (r. 1619–1637)—promised the Bohemian nobles he would respect their religious liberties if they would elect him the king of Bohemia (whereby he could in turn vote for himself as emperor). After Ferdinand was elected king in 1618, he betrayed his promise to the Bohemian nobles, thus initiating the conflict.

The event that set off the conflict was the so-called Defenestration of Prague (1618), in which Bohemian nobles tossed two imperial officials out of the Prague castle. Following this act of rebellion, the nobles elected Frederick V of Palatine (a Calvinist) as their new king. Subsequent fighting is often divided by historians into four distinct phases, which are outlined below. You are especially encouraged to take note of the shifting motivations and alliances of states.

Phase	Events	Groups/Leaders	Results
Bohemian, 1618–1625	The Protestant forces under Frederick V were defeated soundly at White Mountain. Once Ferdinand II (Habsburg) was elected emperor, he confiscated the lands of the rebellious Bohemian nobles, redistributed them, and then brought the Counter-Reformation to Bohemia.	• Frederick V of Palatine • Ferdinand II (Habsburg, r. 1619–1637) and Holy Roman Emperor	Catholic forces emerged victorious as Bavaria, leader of the Catholic League, took over much of the Electorate Palatine.

Phase	Events	Groups/Leaders	Results
Danish, 1625–1629	Christian IV, the Lutheran king of Denmark, entered the conflict both to support the Protestant cause and to gain territory in the Baltic. Wallenstein defeated Christian, thus giving imperial forces the upper hand.	• Christian IV (r. 1588–1648) of Denmark • Albrecht von Wallenstein (1583–1634)—unpredictable leader of imperial forces who funded his own war machine.	Ferdinand confidently issued the Edict of Restitution (1629), which returned all lands confiscated from the Church since 1517, angering Protestant and Catholic nobles alike who had gained from this confiscation. The Habsburgs appeared on the verge of completing a centuries-old dream of centralizing power in central Europe.
Swedish, 1629–1635	Sweden's king and great military leader, Gustavus Adolphus, entered the conflict to revive the Protestant cause and to secure trade in the Baltic. At Breitenfeld and Lutzen, Gustavus succeeded in defeating the imperial forces and bringing the war to the Catholic south. In an example of the war's horrifying effect, the city of Magdeburg was sacked and burned by imperial forces, killing thousands of civilians.	• <u>Gustavus Adolphus</u> (1611–1632) • <u>Cardinal Richelieu</u> (1585–1642)—advisor under Louis XIII (r. 1610–1643) who brought France into the conflict to reduce the power of the Habsburgs. • Wallenstein was assassinated with the approval of the emperor for negotiating independently with the Swedes.	To end the war, the emperor (now Ferdinand III—r. 1637–1657) revoked the Edict of Restitution and in 1635 signed the Peace of Prague with the other German states. However, the fighting continued and devolved into a continental struggle between the Spanish Habsburgs vs. the Swedes and French (also supported by the Dutch).
Franco-Swedish, 1635–1648	In the most violent phase of the war, Germany became the battleground for the territorial and political ambitions of its neighbors. At the battle of Rocroi (in the Spanish Netherlands) in 1643, the French soundly defeated the Spanish, signaling the rise of the former as the major military power in Europe.	• <u>Philip IV</u> (r. 1621–1665) of Spain—continued to use Spain's dwindling resources to fight against France, despite facing internal <u>rebellions</u> by Portugal (which regained its independence in 1640) and the province of <u>Catalonia</u>.	By the end of the conflict, all sides were exhausted. However, peace negotiations dragged on for years before the war was finally ended in 1648.

The Peace of Westphalia (1648) marks an important turning point in European politics and diplomacy. After this point, the **Holy Roman Empire no longer played a major role** in the affairs of central Europe, though the Austrian Habsburgs turned to the east in subsequent years to revive their imperial fortunes. The treaty formally recognized the independence of Switzerland and the Dutch Republic, as well as reflected a shift in the

---

THEME MUSIC

The Thirty Years' War and its settlement reveal key issues in the SOP and NEI themes—the relationship between church and state as well as religion and national identity, the role of warfare in the expansion of state power, and the shifting balance of power among the nations of Europe. Be prepared to explain briefly each of these relationships.

---

balance of power. Emerging stronger were France, Sweden, Prussia (in Germany), and the Dutch. Losing energy were the Holy Roman Empire and Spain, which now fell into the ranks of the second-tier powers, beset by a declining population and economy.

Historians often view the Westphalia settlement as the "final nail in the coffin of the Middle Ages" because it recognized the sovereignty of each nation over its own religious affairs and ended any hopes of religious unity of Europe. Indeed, the papacy was virtually ignored in the peace negotiations and would play a sharply reduced role in future diplomacy. Though Europe as a whole moved toward a grudging religious tolerance, Germany was decimated. Estimates vary, but Germany's population may have declined by 20%–33%. In areas of heavy fighting, entire towns ceased to exist, and economic life was severely curtailed. Central Europe was left with a power vacuum that would soon be filled by the emergence of two competing German powers—Prussia and Austria—whose fortunes will be traced in Chapter 7.

As a result of the Thirty Years' War, Europe underwent a **military revolution**. Gunpowder and the mounted foot-soldier (pikemen and musketeers) came to play a critical role, with the **infantry** square employing massed volleys (firing at the same time). Tactics became more flexible, with the use of lighter and more mobile cavalry, pioneered by Gustavus Adolphus. In addition, to fund the increasing costs of war and oversee its complexity, governments grew larger and more centralized. Warfare had become the primary function of European states, which often spent up to 80% of their budgets on fielding, training, supplying, and of course, using armies (to meet their political objectives). As we'll see in Chapter 7, this trend caused a further expansion of the state's power in the age of absolutism.

Additional Resources

📖 **Felipe Fernandez-Armesto, *Columbus* (1991)** — An interesting study of a complex figure, includes provocative interpretations.

📖 **Peter Burke, *Popular Culture in Early Modern Europe* (1994)** — A vivid and engaging study of the topic with fascinating examples.

📖 **Carlo Cipolla, *Before the Industrial Revolution: European Society and Economy, 1000–1700* (rev. 1994)** — A wealth of information and data on every major feature of economic activity prior to the eighteenth century.

📖 **Alfred Crosby, *The Columbian Exchange: Biological and Cultural Consequences of 1492* (1972)** — For those of a scientific bent, this book explains how colonization affected the world exchange of plants, animals, and diseases.

📖 **Richard S. Dunn, *The Age of Religious Wars, 1559–1715* (1979)** — Another fine survey from the *Norton History of the Modern World* series.

📖 **J.H. Elliott, *Europe Divided, 1559–1598* (rev. 2000)** — A fast-paced and informative introduction to European politics during the period.

📖 **Peter Laslett, *The World We Have Lost: England Before the Industrial Revolution* (1983)** — A study of family life in England.

📖 **Brian Levack, *The Witch-Hunt in Early Modern Europe* (1987)** — Surveys the many explanations for the phenomenon.

📖 **Steven Ozment, *The Burgermeister's Daughter: Scandal in a Sixteenth-Century German Town* (1997)** — Written like a novel, this book shows how the historian works to recreate the features of everyday life.

📖 **Geoffrey Parker, *Europe in Crisis, 1598–1648* (1979)** — A comprehensive overview of the many complex developments in European politics in this period.

📖 **J.H. Parry, *The Age of Reconnaissance: Discovery, Exploration, and Settlement, 1450–1650* (rev. 1981)** — A brief introduction to the voyages of exploration and their effects.

📖 **Peter N. Stearns, ed., *Encyclopedia of European Social History, 1350–2000* (2000)** — If you can find it at a nearby library, these volumes are a wonderful resource on all areas of social history.

💻 **Graham Darby, "The Thirty Years' War: The Unpredictable Past" (2001) https://sweetchristianapeuro. files.wordpress.com/2017/05/the-thirty-years-war. pdf** — A short article that examines several critical historiographical questions.

💻 **https://www.slavevoyages.org/** — A database of the slave trade, including statistics, essays, and dramatizations.

💻 **https://yaleglobal.yale.edu/globalization-food-plants** — From Yale University, this site examines changes in food regimes as a result of the Columbian Exchange.

CHAPTER TEST

Multiple-Choice Questions

Questions 1–4 are based on the image below.

Theodore De Bry, French engraver and publisher, *Silver mines of Potosi* (Bolivia), 1602

1. The scene above directly resulted from all of the following factors <u>EXCEPT</u>:

    A. the desire of European states to gain direct access to goods and wealth.

    B. European military superiority in the form of steel weapons and cannons.

    C. the spread of classical ideas depicting mythical ancient civilizations.

    D. advances in navigational and cartographic techniques and technologies.

2. The process depicted above most directly affected the European economy in the sixteenth and seventeenth centuries by:

    A. stimulating the growth of a new landed elite, such as the gentry in England. *non-noble, but $*

    B. spurring the development of a money-oriented and commercial economy.

    C. motivating the nobles and states of Eastern Europe to codify serfdom.

    D. reinforcing the importance of hierarchy in determining economic standing.

3. In contrast to the scene depicted in the engraving, the impact of exploration on Africa:

A. led to the establishment of large territorial empires in Africa.

B. promoted the development of indigenous industries in Africa.

C. had minimal effect on Africa's role in the world economy.

D. promoted the African slave trade in support of American plantation economies.

4. A historian studying the topic of exploration would most likely use this source as evidence to make conclusions in which of the following areas?

A. The motivations of Europeans in seeking colonies

B. The impact of exploration on artistic styles

C. The effect of colonization on indigenous peoples

D. The effects of colonization on European rivalries

Questions 5–8 are based on the map below.

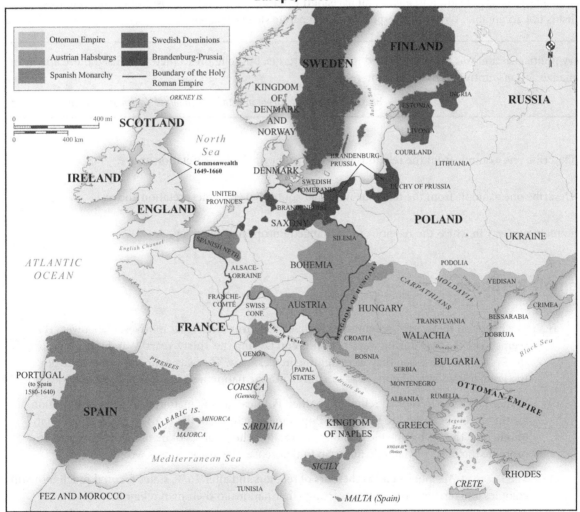

Europe, 1648

Legend:
- Ottoman Empire
- Austrian Habsburgs
- Spanish Monarchy
- Swedish Dominions
- Brandenburg-Prussia
- Boundary of the Holy Roman Empire

5. All of the following developments produced the situation above EXCEPT:

A. competition among nation-states for territory and power.

B. rivalry between England and France over colonies.

C. efforts by the Habsburgs to restore Catholic unity.

D. the pursuit of commercial dominance in the Baltic.

6. The settlement above confirmed which of the following?

A. Spanish control of the Mediterranean

B. State control over internal religious policy

C. The dominance of the Holy Roman Empire

D. Noble control of state and military institutions

7. Which of the following best expresses how the situation depicted on the map represented a transformation in European politics and diplomacy?

?A. Commercial and professional groups solidified their control of the state.

B. Atlantic states were able to focus on the expansion of American empires.

C. With the aid of the Jesuits, the papacy reestablished its diplomatic influence.

D. Religion ceased to be a major source of conflict among European states.

8. The state that experienced the most significant loss of power based on the treaty depicted on the map was:

A. England.
B. France.
C. Spain. —Habsburg
D. Sweden.

See Chapter 18 for answers and explanations.

Short-Answer Question

Directions: Read the excerpt below and answer all parts of the question that follows. Use complete sentences; an outline or bulleted list is not acceptable. Write your responses on a separate sheet of paper.

"Every political action was publicly cloaked in religious terms, but religion seemed to be used more and more to rationalize actions motivated by secular interests."

Hajo Holborn, German-American historian, *A History of Modern Germany: The Reformation*, 1959

1. a) Describe one example from the religious wars that <u>supports</u> the interpretation above.

   b) Describe one example from the religious wars that <u>contradicts</u> the interpretation above.

   c) Explain one way in which the religious wars changed European diplomacy.

SAQ Sample Response

a) The historian thinks that religion was really just a cover for secular motives, like power. This seems to be the case during warfare of this era. During the Thirty Years' War, France supported the Protestant side when they were fighting in Germany. This was done to promote the power of the French state, since France was a mainly Catholic nation helping the opposite religious side.

b) France had its own internal religious conflict. Political factors mattered, like the competition for the throne between the Valois and Bourbon branches. But the war was really about control of religion. That's why outside Catholic groups, like the Jesuits, got involved. They wanted to promote the cause of Catholic unity. So in that sense, the historian was wrong.

c) The Peace of Westphalia ended the wars of religion and after 1650, states focused much more on colonies and territory than on converting other nations to their own religion.

SAQ Response Analysis

This student takes the right approach in getting to their points quickly and also indicating which parts of the question they are addressing. Though brief, each example provides an adequate explanation to earn the point. First, the response correctly, if in simplified fashion, notes French actions during the Thirty Years' War in support of Protestant forces. In Part B, the student correctly points out a religious element to the French civil conflict, a seeming contradiction to Holborn's argument regarding the secular priority of the so-called religious wars. With only one sentence, the student accurately explains how the Peace of Westphalia altered the motivations for warfare in Part C. **Score: 3 points**

❧ CHAPTER 6 ❧

The Scientific View of the World

It would be difficult to overestimate the importance of the Scientific Revolution to the history of humanity. To many historians, the advent of a mathematical, scientific view of the world marks the beginnings of our modern age. For centuries, the achievements of ancient Greece and Rome had established the standard of excellence and reference point for all knowledge. However, during the so-called Age of Genius in the seventeenth century, scientists and philosophers demonstrated that this classical heritage could be surpassed through the application of the scientific method. Scientific thinking has come to infect almost all intellectual disciplines; the result has been not only improvements in technology but the challenging of tradi-

> ## THEME MUSIC
>
> The bulk of this chapter addresses the TSI theme; in fact, the Scientific Revolution establishes one of its central narratives, in that it provides a framework of seemingly objective knowledge that demonstrates the power of scientific thinking to surpass ancient knowledge. The New Science also shaped and redefined other fields of knowledge—such as religion, politics, and the arts—which points to its critical role in the CID theme as well.

tional religious, political, and intellectual perspectives. Modern science represents an intellectual tool of great power, though a power that can also be used to destroy.

 KEY IN – Chapter 6 addresses all or part of the following topics in the Unit Guides of the CED:

Topic 4.1 Contextualizing the Scientific Revolution and the Enlightenment

Topic 4.2 The Scientific Revolution

Topic 4.3 The Enlightenment

Topic 4.7 Causation in the Age of the Scientific Revolution and the Enlightenment

The Old Science

Prior to the sixteenth century, scientific thinking about motion, the cosmos, and the human body was dominated by Aristotle (fourth-century BCE philosopher), Ptolemy (second-century Greek astronomer), and **Galen** (second-century Greek physician). In essence, the worldview of these ancient Greeks was *qualitative*—humans could employ their logical and rational capacities to determine the nature of objects, and from there, describe their behavior. Greek thinking was absorbed into Christianity in the thirteenth century with Scholasticism, which thereafter dominated the investigations of natural philosophy, as science was usually called.

Scholastics dealt first with definitions and general propositions and went on to deduce further structures of knowledge from these, including properties of the natural world.

Systematic observation, **experimentation**, and **mathematics** played a limited role in the Scholastic system. Therefore, the Aristotelian-Ptolemaic view of the cosmos relied on the "logical" view that the earth lay at the center of the universe with the moon, sun, other planets, and stars revolving around it along crystalline spheres in perfect circles. The heavens were made of a separate substance (the quintessence, or fifth substance, to distinguish it from earth, air, fire, and water) and moved in circles, because the sphere represented the perfect geometric shape, reflecting the perfection of the heavens. Earthly objects moved along straight lines and fell toward earth, not because of a mysterious force called gravity, but to be at one with the substance from which they were made. Each object demonstrated properties unique to its nature; thus, heavy objects were believed to fall faster because they contained more matter and thus moved more quickly to their natural resting place. Though the ancient Greek philosophers Pythagoras and Plato did believe mathematical harmonies underlie all of nature, ancient and medieval scientific thought did not contemplate the notion of universal laws that could be expressed through mathematical *equations*.

Ancient cosmology was reflected in views of human anatomy. Galen postulated that the human body contained **four humors**: blood, phlegm, yellow bile, and black bile. Each of these humors was associated with a particular temperament, so individuals dominated by blood, for example, tended to be sanguine, or optimistic and cheerful. Bodily disorders arose from an imbalance of humors. Treatment involved correcting this imbalance through purging (inducing vomiting) and bleeding. Regardless of these treatments' failures, such ideas held sway among physicians for centuries, whose studies revolved more around reading ancient texts than anatomical study or clinical work with patients. Church prohibitions on dissection probably hindered anatomical knowledge in this regard; though Leonardo da Vinci violated this taboo, his detailed sketches of the human body, as well as other amazing diagrams of flying machines, led to few practical consequences, as they were not pursued systematically or taken up by future scientists.

Several factors stimulated the development of new scientific approaches in the sixteenth century: the Renaissance interest in nature, the need for celestial navigation to support exploration, and the Catholic Church's interest in an accurate calendar. Though the old model had worked well for centuries, the discrepancy between its theories and actual observations became more apparent, and could not be explained satisfactorily by continued reference to its assumptions.

Advances in Astronomy and Physics

There are moments when ideas can change the world—literally. Such was the case with **Nicholas Copernicus**'s (1473–1543) *On the Revolutions of the Heavenly Spheres*, published just before the author's death in 1543. A Polish Catholic priest, Copernicus was called on by the church to develop a more accurate calendar. He presented the notion of a heliocentric, or sun-centered, universe as a mathematical supposition. Though Copernicus retained many features of the Ptolemaic cosmology ("model of the universe"), the radical notion that God's special creation—humans and their terrestrial home—were no longer the center of the universe provoked criticism and further astronomical inquiry. The developments that followed in astronomy and physics represent the primary field of advance during the Scientific Revolution; as you review, consider the relationship between new *ideas* and new *methods*.

The work of Copernicus demonstrates how a mathematics-driven astronomy could lead to and support new theories of planetary motion. Copernicanism temporarily stood as a theory without support from observations. Danish astronomer Tycho Brahe (1546–1601) provided these observations, as he spent over 20 years staring at the night sky on the isolated island of Hven off the coast of Denmark—all without the aid of a telescope. In 1577 Brahe charted the path of a comet that seemed to be traveling in an irregular (not circular) path as it passed through the supposed crystalline spheres, something that wasn't supposed to happen under the Ptolemaic system. While Brahe never fully accepted the heliocentric theory, his massive collection of data aided future scientists.

One of history's greatest scientists, Johannes Kepler (1571–1630), put Brahe's data to good use. Formerly Brahe's assistant, Kepler became court astronomer to the Holy Roman Emperor, despite being Lutheran. He used his mathematical genius to make a conceptual leap regarding planetary motion: many of the anomalies in the Copernican system were eliminated if the planets traveled in elliptical (not circular)

> ### SKILL SET
>
> Intellectual frameworks involve an approach or method toward knowledge (epistemology) and a model of the universe (cosmology) to be investigated, which explains the objects and forces that inhabit it and how causation occurs. To reinforce your understanding of the transformation wrought by the new science, consider diagramming the ancient/medieval and modern epistemologies and cosmologies. Use the content in this section to make sure you understand how they compare (COMP) and how they changed during this period (CCOT).

paths. Further, Kepler articulated three laws of planetary motion, all of which could be expressed precisely using equations. For example, Kepler demonstrated that the closer a planet orbited to the sun, the faster it moved, which fit with observations. Nonetheless, not all of Kepler's view would be regarded as scientific today. Something of a religious mystic, Kepler believed that the orbits of the planets expressed a cosmic harmony, which could be heard in the "music of the spheres."

Galileo Galilei (1564–1642) combined interests of wide scope with an ability to attract patronage and attention, not all of which was positive. First, the Italian scientist's correspondence with Kepler demonstrates the emergence of an international scientific community. Second, based on repeated experiments, Galileo devised one of the first mathematical formulas to explain and predict a natural phenomenon, the law of accelerating bodies: 32 ft/sec/sec. Providing **empirical** ("based on the senses") support for the heliocentric theory rep-

> ### EXAMPLE BASE & SKILL SET
>
> Whenever you encounter a series of examples, like the scientists here, it is important that you go beyond rote learning. To sharpen your focus, consider these interpretive questions: How revolutionary was the new science? To what extent did thinkers retain traditional approaches or ideas? Make sure you are able to articulate the Developments and Processes that define the Scientific Revolution.

resents Galileo's most famous contribution to science. In 1609 Galileo created one of the first telescopes and trained it on the heavens. The resulting *Starry Messenger* (1610) depicted the moon with an imperfect and rough surface, sunspots, millions of stars, and moons orbiting Jupiter—all of which contradicted the notion of perfect heavenly bodies, the limited and static size of the universe, and that all bodies rotated around the earth. Despite an agreement with the papacy to teach **heliocentrism** as only a theory, Galileo later published a clear endorsement of it with *Dialogue Concerning the Two Chief World Systems: Ptolemaic and Copernican* (1632), which landed him before the Roman Inquisition in 1633. Galileo remained a Catholic who believed in the unity of truth—scientific and spiritual—and that any conflict between them required a reappraisal of biblical passages in light of new discoveries. In the midst of the Thirty Years' War, the Catholic Church silenced Galileo (placing him under house arrest for the next 9 years) and thereby stifled intellectual life in Italy for the foreseeable future.

Galileo's ideas could not be silenced, and his death in 1642 also marks the birth of the last great thinker of the Scientific Revolution—**Isaac Newton** (1642–1727). One of the eminent geniuses in history, Newton combined profound conceptual insights, precise mathematical expression, and systematic observation. Newton synthesized the work of over a century into a coherent view of the world, based on universal laws, as expressed in his *Principia Mathematica*

(1687); as he later said, "If I have been able to see so far, it is only because I stood on the shoulders of giants." All objects behave similarly, according to Newton, because they obey three laws of motion. What previous astronomers had observed piecemeal and with speculation, Newton synthesized into a cosmic machine, held together with the universal law of gravitation. In addition, to explain infinitesimal changes in motion, Newton invented a new form of mathematics—calculus. With these tools, the universe could now be viewed as a finely calibrated watch that obeyed natural laws with mathematical precision, which allowed it to be explained and controlled by human reason. Though Newton was a deeply religious man who retained the image of God's will behind all, his cosmology helped separate the world of matter from that of spirit, setting the stage for deism in the future (see Chapter 9).

Advances in Anatomy and Medicine

In the same year that Copernicus introduced his heliocentric theory (1543), Flemish anatomist Andreas Vesalius (1514–1564) published the landmark book in his field—*On the Fabric of the Human Body*. Based on dissections and precise drawings, Vesalius contradicted many of Galen's ideas regarding the human body, again by employing direct empirical evidence. Building on this success and working for years in a laboratory, the English physician **William Harvey** (1578–1657) developed the modern cardiopulmonary (heart and lungs) theory of blood flow, with arteries and veins circulating oxygen through human tissue, all pumped by the heart (not the liver, as classical authority held).

Further discoveries in anatomy were greatly assisted by the development of the **microscope**, which became the basis for the investigations of a Dutch nobleman, Anton von Leeuwenhoek (1632–1723). For his discoveries of blood corpuscles, sperm, and bacteria (it was not linked to disease until later), Leeuwenhoek is often given the title, Father of Microbiology. Leeuwenhoek also corresponded with the secretary of the Royal Society of London (see below), Robert Hooke, who had published his own book on the subject, *Micrographia* (1665), and who worked with the chemist Robert Boyle (1627–1692). Boyle's book, *The Sceptical Chemist* (1661), criticized the blending of alchemy (the art of attempting to turn metals into gold) with chemistry, which Boyle believed should involve the scientific investigation of

nature's most basic substances—the elements. In addition, Boyle articulated his famous law whereby the temperature, pressure, and volume of a gas can be related according to a mathematical formula ($PV=nRT$).

Though these developments provided a more modern understanding of the human body and its functions, they did not translate into improved medical care until centuries later. In fact, many physicians continued to receive their training in the traditional classical style—reading Galen and Hippocrates, rather than through experimentation and clinical practice. Hospitals in the seventeenth and eighteenth centuries were as likely to house vagrants as the sick. Given the lack of understanding regarding bacteria and germs, hospitals usually served as venues for the sick to die, not to be cured. Faith healers, midwives, and barber-surgeons, who engaged in the traditional bleeding and purging regimen, continued to provide medical care for the vast majority of Europeans.

The Scientific Method: Bacon and Descartes

Modern scientific thinking was the product of two differing intellectual temperaments—the Englishman **Francis Bacon** (1561–1626) and the Frenchman **René Descartes** (1596–1650). Both shared a disdain for the Scholastic tradition and a skepticism toward knowledge claims that had not been demonstrated through a rigorous system of thought. Bacon, from a noble family and occupying important positions in government, advocated a scientific approach based on **inductive reasoning**. As opposed to the Scholastic tradition of working first with definitions and propositions, Bacon called for systematic investigation and observation of nature (empiricism), as well as experimentation, leading to generalizations about the physical world. In his uncompleted three-volume work, *Instauratio Magna* (the Great Renewal), Bacon called for a new start to human knowledge, for humanity to put aside ancient preconceptions and prejudices and look at nature with fresh eyes. For Bacon, science should be useful to human beings; it should make their lives longer, more secure, and more comfortable. To demonstrate the great potential of science, Bacon published his *New Atlantis* (1627), which portrayed a scientific utopia and prefigured many modern technological developments. Though his ideas proved influential, Bacon himself did not fully appreciate the importance of theory and mathematics in scientific investigation.

A brilliant mathematician, René Descartes initiated the modern turn in philosophy. Descartes deliberately rejected Scholastic notions; his intellectual project subjected every assertion of knowledge to systematic doubt. The goal of his skepticism was not to reject knowledge *per se*, but to build a surer foundation for it. Descartes even doubted that he existed. However, though he could doubt the existence of his body (because his senses often deceived him), Descartes could not doubt the existence of his mind, for in the very process of doubting, he affirmed that he had a mind—"I think; therefore, I am" (*cogito ergo sum*). From this thought experiment, Descartes argued for dualism, the idea that nature is made of two basic substances—an intangible, thinking substance known as mind and a tangible, extended (taking up space) substance known as matter. Descartes also demonstrated the power of mathematics in scientific thinking. With *Discourse on Method* (1637), he argued for a **deductive approach** to knowledge, much like a geometric proof, moving from general principles to more particular cases by steps of reason. With his Cartesian coordinate system (x-, y-, and z-axes), Descartes provided a precise abstract depiction of space useful for engineering, architecture, and the military arts. Some of Descartes' ideas were later proved wrong—he speculated that animals were like machines and felt no pain—and his unorthodox ideas almost landed him in hot water with the Catholic Church. Nonetheless, Descartes stands as one of the great philosophers in history and initiated the separation of matter and spirit that marks the path toward secularism in subsequent centuries.

SKILL SET

All of the natural philosophers (the term "scientist" came into general use during the nineteenth century) of this era expressed religious beliefs and saw their work as partly spiritual, i.e., understanding the "mind of God." However, by establishing a mechanistic view of the universe guided by materialism and mathematics, they set the stage for new religious attitudes, such as deism, agnosticism, and atheism. Take note of how explanations of nature can have an impact on religious belief and the role of religion over time (CCOT).

Women and Science

Women contributed to science and, in turn, were affected by scientific thinking. Given social constraints, it is a wonder that any women were able to contribute to science. Women were excluded from universities, scientific societies, and generally received an inferior education. Opportunities were available, however. In Germany, for example, the craft tradition allowed women to work alongside fathers and husbands; as a result, 15% of German astronomers in the seventeenth and eighteenth centuries were women. One such was Maria Winkelmann (1670–1720), who discovered a comet before her husband and helped to prepare the astronomical calendar for the Berlin Academy of Sciences. Despite these contributions, she was denied admission into the academy. Maria Sybilla Merian (1647–1717) traveled to South America to study insects, and her subsequent text and illustrations, *Metamorphosis of the Insects of Surinam*, became a standard in the field of entomology. Women like Emilie du Chatelet (1706–1749) translated Newton to make his abstract works accessible to a mass audience, while Dorothea Erxleben (1715–1762) became one of the first women to earn a medical degree from a university.

Unfortunately, these women proved to be exceptions. Institutional barriers remained strong, though attitudes served as an even more effective roadblock. Throughout the seventeenth century, philosophers and scientists debated the *querelle de femmes*—the "women question." Ironically, some of science's greatest doubters—Spinoza, for example (see below)—could not extract themselves from long-held prejudices when it came to women. Studies of anatomy suggested that women's smaller skulls and wider hips demonstrated their intellectual inferiority and fitness only for domestic roles. Investigation into human reproduction affirmed the greater importance of males in providing the "life force," with women providing only the matter or location of conception. It was not until 1823 that the ovum was discovered, proving otherwise. Did women, then, experience a Scientific Revolution? On one hand, women did participate in scientific discoveries despite the obstacles, but on the other, "science" was used to corset women even more tightly in limited social and intellectual roles. When it came to women, science in the seventeenth century proved most *un*-revolutionary.

THEME MUSIC

Once again, we see how a movement of cultural and intellectual change (CID and TSI) affected attitudes toward women and their position within society (SCD). Continue to build on this theme as you study.

Religion and Skepticism

Though most scientists of the seventeenth and eighteenth centuries perceived no conflict between scientific inquiry and spirituality, the Scientific Revolution resulted in an increasingly skeptical and secular attitude among European elites. At first, many scientists blended (what would today be considered) superstitious beliefs in **alchemy** and **astrology** with materialist and mathematical perspectives. As time wore on, educated Europeans demanded empirical evidence or conformity with natural laws for claims of knowledge. This new standard is reflected in the decline of **witchcraft persecutions** after about 1650, which no longer received the support of those in positions of power. New standards of evidence eliminating torture and hearsay testimony, especially in England, provided a more scientific basis for legal proceedings. Furthermore, European colonization stimulated travel literature, which in revealing the diversity of human societies and customs suggested the possibility of cultural relativism. Following in the path of the French humanist and skeptic Montaigne (see Chapter 5), Pierre Bayle (1647–1706) examined beliefs from a wide range of human endeavors in his *Historical and Critical Dictionary*, only to conclude that most owed more to human credulity than to rigorous and rational thought. Bayle's work forms a bridge from the Scientific Revolution to the eighteenth-century Enlightenment (see Chapter 9).

Two thinkers stand out in their attempts to create a synthesis of the scientific and the spiritual. Baruch Spinoza (1632–

1677) came from a family of Portuguese Jews forced to immigrate to the Netherlands as a result of the Inquisition. Beginning in the Cartesian tradition of dualism regarding substances, Spinoza came to reject Descartes' understanding of God and substance. For Spinoza, nature in its totality was ultimately one substance: all that we experience is simply a modification of that substance, which is God. We can conceive of this substance with the attribute of extension (taking up space) or of thought (mind), but these attributes are ultimately manifestations of the same substance. Spinoza's substance monism made little sense to the Jewish community from which he was excommunicated, or to orthodox Christians who thought it no better than atheism. Spinoza's rejection of an anthropomorphic God (in the form of humans) led him to a naturalistic view of human affairs and ethics. Even the title of his most famous work, *Ethics, as Determined in a Geometric Manner* (1677), illustrates his rigorous rationalist style. In rejecting miracles, holy books, rituals, dogma, and even free will, Spinoza left human beings primarily with their minds to offer consolation, guidance, and whatever freedom comes from putting oneself in accord with the laws of nature.

Blaise Pascal (1623–1662) was a child prodigy and true mathematical genius. It is said that he independently discovered several theorems of Euclid's geometry at the age of 9. In addition, he later invented the first successful adding machine, developed Pascal's Triangle to show the pattern of ascending exponential functions of algebraic equations, and developed the geometry of solids as well as modern probability theory. After experiencing a profound religious conversion in 1654, Pascal gave up his work in science and mathematics for religion and philosophy. Pascal fell under the influence of the Jansenist movement (see Chapter 6) in France, which rejected the Jesuits' strong view of human freedom. In his famous work the *Pensées* ("Thoughts"), Pascal set out to show the proper relationship between reason and faith. Though scientific discoveries had demonstrated the insignificance of humans in the cosmos, Pascal nonetheless looked at human reason as a distinct capacity in the universe, or as he wrote, "Man is a reed, but he is a thinking reed." When it comes to religious faith, we will always want for evidence and arguments, said Pascal. Therefore, humans can weigh the alternatives—e.g., the promise of eternal reward vs. sacrifice of earthly pleasures—according to Pascal's Wager and gamble on belief, for we have much to gain and little to lose with faith.

A Scientific View of Human Affairs: Law and Political Theory

Scientific thinking inevitably crept into human affairs. If matter followed natural laws, why could human behavior not also be explained according to the same laws? The birth of natural law philosophy and the concept of **natural rights** have grounded much of modern political development toward democracy and equality. Natural law holds that humans can discover what is fair, just, and natural in the political and social realms by consulting reason. Custom, tradition, or the edicts of kings cannot override natural rights, which inhere in human beings because of their unique capacities. For example, the ability of humans to speak, write, and create symbols suggests that they have a natural right to freedoms in these areas. In diplomacy, several seventeenth-century jurists, such as Hugo Grotius in his *Law of War and Peace* (1625) and Samuel Pufendorf in his *Law of Nature and of Nations* (1672), attempted to define rules for commerce and war based on the common good of nations rather than simply the might of the strongest. Even with international organizations like the United Nations today, the world continues to struggle with winning adherence by all nations to a code of international law.

Thomas Hobbes

Natural law can also be used to justify absolutism. A sophisticated and secular justification (compare with Bossuet's divine-right account in Chapter 7) of absolutism comes from Thomas Hobbes (1588–1679). Hobbes wrote his *Leviathan* (1651) amidst the Scientific Revolution and the English Civil War, both of which left their mark on his political philosophy. According to Hobbes, humans are born into a state of nature, in which life is a continual war of "every man against every other man" for gain, glory, and security. If humans are equal, it is only in their ability to destroy one another. Hobbes viewed human society as akin to a closed system of energy, which tends to dissipate (into anarchy) over time. The only solution to this insecurity and chaos is for each individual to leave the state of nature by agreeing to a **social contract** with one another and with the sovereign, who will absorb the wills and force of each member of society into an all-powerful ruler. In the resulting commonwealth, the will of the sovereign (which could be a group of rulers) stands as law. Rebellion is prohibited, as it would only return society to the chaotic state of nature. Hobbes's justification is secular and scientific, and though it would be rejected by many in his native England, his notions of the state of nature and the social contract influenced subsequent thinkers.

John Locke

The most important defense of limited government based on natural law was written by the Englishman **John Locke** (1632–1704) to justify the Glorious Revolution (see Chapter 7). Locke's *Second Treatise on Government* (1689) takes Hobbes and stands him on his head. In Locke's state of nature, man freely enjoys his natural rights of life, liberty, and property. These inalienable rights come *before* the development of human society. Though humans are basically rational, they still conflict in the state of nature over property. Such disputes create insecurity and reduce the enjoyment of one's liberties. Thus, individuals enter into a social contract and leave the state of nature to secure, not surrender, those rights. Governments are limited by their original purpose—arbitrating disputes and providing order and public goods. Should governments become abusive toward these ends, society can invoke the right of rebellion to secure those rights anew. In all, governments are made by people and must display features of the limiting social contract—representation, guarantees of rights, respect of property. Locke's ideas helped promote the unique development of England in this era, though it should *not* be viewed as an endorsement of modern mass democracy.

Like Pierre Bayle, John Locke forms a bridge between the Scientific Revolution of the seventeenth century and the Enlightenment of the eighteenth century. Locke looked at the world from an empirical perspective, yet he believed that Christianity was a reasonable religion. At the same time, he supported religious toleration (except for Catholics and atheists, whom he viewed as a threat to the state) as part of the settlement surrounding the Glorious Revolution. The ideas of Francis Bacon and John Locke form bookends to the seventeenth century regarding the importance of an empirical approach to the world. Locke became the foremost advocate of an empirical approach to knowledge in his philosophical writings. In *Essay Concerning Human Understanding* (1690), Locke rejected Descartes' notion of innate ideas, in favor of the mind as a tabula rasa, or "blank slate." Humans learn primarily from experience, which writes upon their minds and character their personality and knowledge. These ideas held radical implications when it came to education, as Locke argued in *Some Thoughts Concerning Education* (1689); children learn best not from rote memorization but from experience and from "praise and esteem." Locke's wide-ranging interests and writings sparked new thinking in several fields, including child-rearing, education, politics, and philosophy.

Science Applied: Societies and Technology

Governments saw great promise in science. Prestige accrued to nations who sponsored great scientific discoveries, but more importantly, states hoped to exploit theoretical advances for navigational and military purposes. To this end, the first great scientific societies were formed in the 1660s. In England, the privately run Royal Society of London received a government charter in 1662; eventually, Sir Isaac Newton served as its president. Not to be outdone, Louis XIV established, under stricter government super-

> **THEME MUSIC**
>
> Given the competitive environment of the European continent, states will seek advantages in many areas, science being one of them. For the SOP theme, consider the factors that might affect a nation's political position related to science—commerce, navigation, and military weaponry.

vision, the French Academy of Sciences in 1666. Smaller or more regional societies, academies, and universities for the study and perpetuation of science were also founded in the century. These organizations held meetings, published journals, established research projects, and shared their results with scientists across the continent. Even if governments wished to monopolize science for their narrow state interests, it would not have been possible given the modern printing press. An international scientific community seemed necessary to the very nature of modern science; to ensure reliability, experiments had to be repeated, data shared, and theories confirmed.

Science can be of the most abstract nature; at the same time, all humanity shares an interest in its practical results. New scientific equipment and machines—telescopes, microscopes, barometers, globes, marine chronometers, pendulum clocks, improved cannons, early steam engines—all held out the promise of greater human control of the environment. In subsequent centuries, Europeans would exploit these advances to the fullest. The results have been both the greatest period of human technological creativity and the most destructive conflicts in history.

Additional Resources

📖 **Wilbur Applebaum, *The Scientific Revolution and the Foundations of Modern Science* (2005)** — Accessible to high school students, this work comes from the Greenwood Guides to Historic Events.

📖 **Peter Dear, *Revolutionizing the Sciences: European Knowledge and Its Ambitions*, 2/e (2009)** — A brief and accessible overview of the topic.

📖 **James Delburgo & Nicholas Dews, eds., *Science and Empire in the Atlantic World* (2008)** — Essays by various scholars place the New Science in a global context and connect new methods of knowledge to imperial expansion and slavery.

📖 **Steven Shapin, *The Scientific Revolution* (1996)** — An excellent and brief, but challenging, overview of the topic.

📖 **Dava Sobel, *Galileo's Daughter: A Historical Memoir of Science, Faith, and Love* (2000)** — A popular history which shows the trial of Galileo against the backdrop of his relationship with his daughter, a nun.

📺 ***Galileo's Battle for the Heavens*, (2002)** — From PBS, a well-done film reenactment and historical documentary of Galileo's conflict with the Catholic Church over his scientific discoveries.

📺 ***Longitude* (2000)** — This A&E mini-series dramatizes the eighteenth-century contest to develop an accurate marine chronometer while also making a post-1945 thematic connection.

CHAPTER TEST

Multiple-Choice Questions

Questions 1–2 are based on the following passage.

> "But Nature, on the other hand, is inexorable and immutable; she never transgresses the laws imposed upon her, or cares a whit whether her abstruse reasons and methods of operation are understandable to men. For that reason it appears that nothing physical which sense-experience sets before our eyes, or which necessary demonstrations prove to us, ought to be called in question (much less condemned) upon the testimony of biblical passages which may have some different meaning beneath their words. For the Bible is not chained in every expression to conditions as strict as those which govern all physical effects; nor is God any less excellently revealed in Nature's actions than in the sacred statements of the Bible."
>
> Galileo Galilei, Italian mathematician and natural philosopher, "Letter to the Grand Duchess Christina of Tuscany," 1615

1. Based on the passage and your knowledge of the period, Galileo most directly challenged religious authority by:

   A. publishing his findings using the new print technology.

   B. appealing to elites for political support against the Church.

   C. cooperating with scientists from Protestant states.

   D. emphasizing physical observation over biblical authority.

2. In subsequent years, which of the following principles articulated by Galileo would come to dominate elite intellectual life?

   A. There are no inherent conflicts between faith and science.

   B. Classical learning is necessary to support new discoveries.

   C. Nature is guided by universal and mathematical laws.

   D. Appeals to political authority support new ideas.

Questions 3–5 are based on the image below.

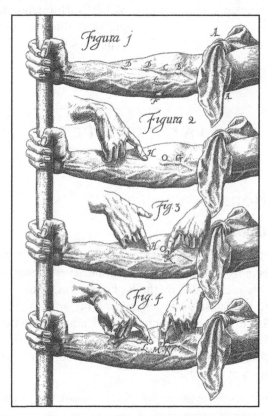

Illustration from medical text, 1628

3. The illustration above reflects all of the following features of the new science EXCEPT:

   A. the importance of observation of the natural world.

   B. the use of experimentation to support explanations.

   C. the persistence of folk traditions about the universe.

   D. the challenge to Galen's humoral theory of the body.

4. Which of the following scientists is most responsible for the ideas represented in the image?

   A. Paracelsus

   B. Andreas Vesalius

   C. Francis Bacon

   D. William Harvey

5. According to nineteenth-century positivism, which of the following attitudes of natural philosophers from the sixteenth and seventeenth centuries would be considered non-scientific?

   A. Belief in a mathematical and mechanical model of the cosmos

   B. Support of alchemy and astrology as predictive systems

   C. Questioning the authority of ancient learning and methods

   D. Patronage of scientific inquiry by state authorities

Questions 6–8 are based on the image below.

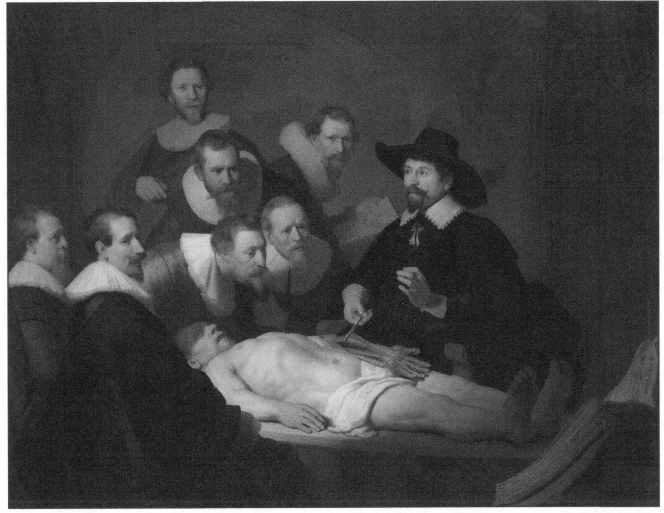

Rembrandt van Rijn, Dutch artist, *The Anatomy Lesson of Dr. Nicolaes Tulp*, 1631

6. Which of the following principles of the new science is depicted in the painting above?

   A. Empiricism

   B. Mathematics

   C. Deductive reasoning

   D. Cosmology

7. All of the following features of Dutch society would have contributed to the development portrayed in the painting EXCEPT:

   A. tolerance toward religious and intellectual dissent.

   B. commercial focus and dominance of merchant elites.

   C. strong central monarchy to patronize science.

   D. trade routes that allowed access to new ideas.

8. An art historian might use the image to support which of the following generalizations about art in the seventeenth century?

   A. "Baroque artists used painting to promote religiosity and state power."

   B. "Art came to reflect a secular outlook of progress and the public good."

   C. "New art movements rejected Renaissance ideas of naturalism and perspective."

   D. "Paintings emphasized Enlightenment ideals of political power and citizenship."

See Chapter 18 for answers and explanations.

Long Essay Question

Directions: Read the prompt below and write your response on a separate sheet of paper. A sample response and commentary are provided on the next page.

Evaluate the most significant impact of the Scientific Revolution on ideas and culture.

(RP: Causation)

LEQ Sample Response

The Scientific Revolution represented a major change in European ideas and culture. Before it occurred, people used the classics and the Bible to understand nature. After scientists like Galileo and Newton, Europeans began to think about natural laws and observations as the focus of understanding. The most important impact of this new approach led people to question authority and change the world through scientific thinking, which later produced the Enlightenment and other revolutions.

Before Copernicus published his heliocentric theory, the understanding of the universe was based on Aristotle and other Greek scholars. Intellectuals at the university would just study ancient texts to understand astronomy or the human body. With heliocentrism, people began to think differently about how the universe was structured. Like that there were no crystal spheres, as Brahe showed by observing a comet. This new thinking challenged authorities like the Church, who put Galileo on trial for teaching the heliocentric theory, which resulted in his execution. But it was impossible to stop the new thinking about science. Other scientists picked up the slack and continued their research. Bacon and Descartes created a new scientific method, with inductive and deductive reasoning, which allowed for proposing and testing hypotheses. All of this new thinking reached a high point with Newton, who broke down everything into natural laws using math (like calculus, which he invented). This accomplishment ("on the shoulders of giants") set the stage for the Enlightenment, which would use science to argue for progress in society.

New scientific ideas also affected culture greatly, as learning became more focused on observation of the world and less on classics and religion. This provided for a new secular focus. New universities and scientific societies were founded that tried to go beyond just lecturing on Ptolemy and Galen and repeating the same old debates. Instead, there was more experimentation and hands-on learning, as you can see in some of the art of this period. One example is the dissection lesson in the Dutch republic painted by Rembrandt; it shows a group of doctors learning about the human body through direct knowledge. Many states saw the importance of science and began to patronize it, like France under Louis XIV and in Britain with the Royal Society. Nations wanted to be more powerful and saw that science could do it. Also with politics, new theories came about from Hobbes and Locke that used the idea of natural laws to understand how governments were formed and should operate. These new theories would affect revolutions later.

The Scientific Revolution is definitely a major event in European history. This development of an objective approach to knowledge, with a reliable method of testing of hypotheses with evidence, undermined the ancient worldview of taking Aristotle and the Church at their word. Enlightenment philosophes publicized this new scientific method and employed it arguing for new ideas in politics, like natural rights and the social contract. Without the new science, it is hard to see how Locke, Rousseau, and others might have developed a new philosophy of politics that eventually led to the French Revolution.

LEQ Response Analysis

In this sample, the student takes a basic approach but one that earns all of the rubric points. The introduction provides just enough background on the old and new scientific methods to earn the Contextualization point. The thesis clearly indicates the most significant effect of "challenging authority," which is also connected to the Enlightenment and political revolutions. Though the subsequent review of examples remains at a fairly basic level and offers up a few minor errors (e.g., Galileo was not executed), the response adequately connects enough evidence to the argument regarding the challenge to authority, earning two Use of Evidence points. Further, an implicit focus on causation throughout earns the first Argument and Reasoning point, while the discussion of the impact of the Scientific Revolution on politics (introducing a new theme) throughout the essay and in the conclusion clinches the Complexity point. **Score: 6** (+1 for Thesis, +1 for Contextualization, +2 for Use of Evidence, +1 for the Targeted RP (CAUS), +1 for Complexity)

PERIOD 1 — DIAGNOSTIC EXAM

Section I, Part A: Multiple-Choice Questions
Time—30 minutes; 30 questions

Directions: Each of the questions or incomplete statements below is followed by four suggested answers or completions. Select the one that is best in each case and then enter the appropriate letter in the corresponding space on the answer sheet. Source materials have been edited for the purpose of this exercise.

Questions 1–4 are based on the map below.

Italian Peninsula, ca. 1454

1. Which of the following features of the Renaissance is reflected in the map above?

   A. The importance of the printing press in spreading a revival of classical culture

   B. The shift during the High Renaissance of cultural influence from Florence to Rome

   C. The importance of city-states, rather than a monarchy, to the growth of humanism

   D. The revival of trade that allowed for wealth to patronize artists and display status

2. All of the following resulted from the situation depicted above EXCEPT that:

   A. theorists like Machiavelli developed secular political justifications for strong rulers.

   B. interstate competition led to the development of the notion of the balance of power.

   C. a lack of unity and rivalry on the peninsula led to foreign invasion and domination.

   D. Italy successfully sponsored voyages of exploration that resulted in a colonial empire.

3. Which of the following political developments contrasts most strongly with the situation depicted on the map?

    A. The rise of a new mercantile elite

    B. The growth of centralized states

    C. Aristocratic efforts to combat centralization

    D. Competition among states for territory

4. When did the situation depicted on the map change most significantly?

    A. 1555

    B. 1648

    C. 1815

    D. 1861

Questions 5–7 are based on the interpretation below.

> "The famous phrase behind the settlement of 1555—*cuius region eius religio* ['his the region, his the religion'] —was a practical commonplace long before anyone put it into words. For this was the age of uniformity, an age which held at all times and everywhere that one political unit could not comprehend within itself two forms of belief or worship.
>
> The tenet rested on a simple fact: as long as membership of a secular polity involved membership of an ecclesiastical organization, religious dissent stood equal to political disaffection and even treason."
>
> G. R. Elton, German-British historian, *The New Cambridge Modern History, Vol. II: The Reformation*, 1958

5. All of the following provide evidence for the interpretation above EXCEPT:

    A. the establishment of the Anglican Church under Henry VIII.

    B. the Spanish monarchy's reliance on the Inquisition.

    C. the establishment of the Index of Prohibited Books.

    D. the independence of the Dutch Republic in revolt against the Habsburgs.

6. Which of the following figures would be most closely associated with the trends identified in the passage?

    A. John Calvin

    B. Desiderius Erasmus

    C. Philip II

    D. Niccolò Machiavelli

7. Which of the following events set the stage for a trend in church-state relations that would run counter to that described in the passage?

    A. The defeat of the Spanish Armada

    B. The Peace of Westphalia

    C. The Elizabethan Settlement in England

    D. The founding of the Jesuit religious order

Questions 8–10 are based on the map below.

Atlantic Trade, 1500–1650

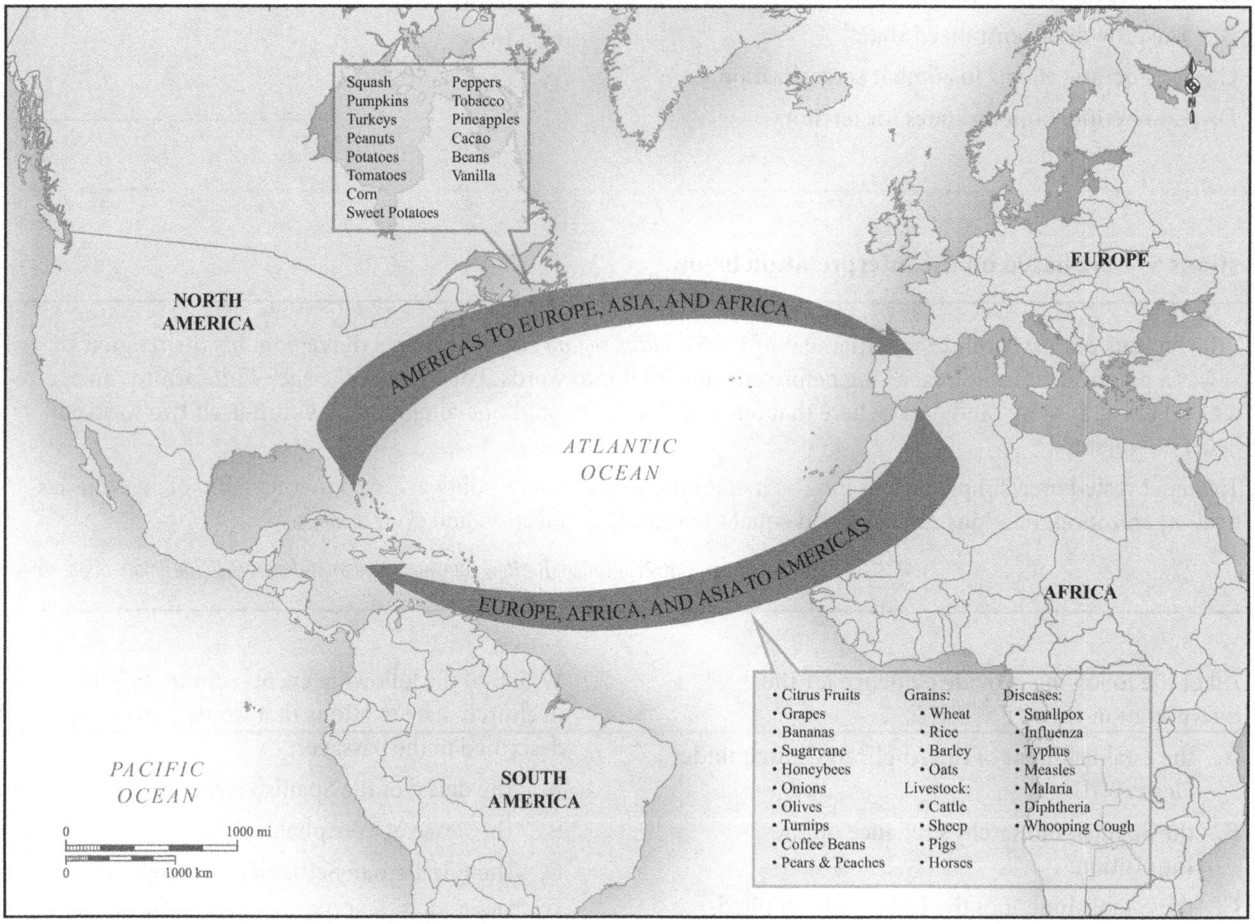

Map showing Atlantic trade flows. Box near North America: Squash, Pumpkins, Turkeys, Peanuts, Potatoes, Tomatoes, Corn, Sweet Potatoes | Peppers, Tobacco, Pineapples, Cacao, Beans, Vanilla. Arrow labeled "AMERICAS TO EUROPE, ASIA, AND AFRICA" and arrow labeled "EUROPE, AFRICA, AND ASIA TO AMERICAS." Labels: NORTH AMERICA, SOUTH AMERICA, EUROPE, AFRICA, ATLANTIC OCEAN, PACIFIC OCEAN. Box near Africa: Citrus Fruits, Grapes, Bananas, Sugarcane, Honeybees, Onions, Olives, Turnips, Coffee Beans, Pears & Peaches; Grains: Wheat, Rice, Barley, Oats; Livestock: Cattle, Sheep, Pigs, Horses; Diseases: Smallpox, Influenza, Typhus, Measles, Malaria, Diphtheria, Whooping Cough. Scale: 1000 mi / 1000 km.

8. The trends depicted in the chart above contributed, during the period 1500–1650, <u>most directly</u> to:

   A. the centralization of power among the new monarchies.

   B. the ascendance of Portuguese naval power in the Indian Ocean.

   C. a shift in power from the Mediterranean to the Atlantic states.

   D. the use of geometric perspective in cartography and painting.

9. Which of the following is the most accurate label for the process depicted on the map?

   A. Mercantilism

   B. Columbian Exchange

   C. Exploration

   D. Commercial Revolution

10. Which of the following historical interpretations is best supported by the map?

   A. "Colonization efforts depended on the ability of Europeans to exploit their advantages in weaponry and political organization to overwhelm non-European cultures."

   B. "Without the Renaissance focus on classical texts, European states would have lacked the intellectual framework to support both the desire to explore and the knowledge necessary to accomplish it."

   C. "European encounters with the Americas shaped the destiny of four continents—the Americas, Europe, Africa—by bringing them into a global trade network, with the opportunities and challenges that followed in their wake."

   D. "Monarchies promoted colonization once they had achieved a sufficient degree of centralization, but in turn, colonization provided the state with new resources and justifications for further expansion of power."

Questions 11–13 are based on the passage below.

"The true method of breaking up the leagues of the Huguenots is to remove the necessity for forming them. This must be done by treating the Huguenots no longer as enemies, but as friends. For, if we examine carefully into the matter, we shall find hitherto they have been dealt with as rebels; and this has compelled them to resort to all means of self-preservation."

Chancellor Michel de l'Hôpital, served 1560–1568 under Catherine de' Medici
during the reigns of her young sons, Francis II and Charles IX

11. As mentioned in the passage, the Huguenots might pose a threat to the French monarchy because:
    A. they could use religious differences to challenge dynastic succession to the throne.
    B. the French monarchs feared intervention by Spain in an effort to combat Calvinism.
    C. they predominated among the commercial classes, threatening the French economy.
    D. France's pursuit of colonies in the Americas could be diverted to internal conflicts.

12. Which of the following would have agreed most with de l'Hôpital's approach to the issue of religious diversity?
    A. Philip II of Spain
    B. The Jesuits
    C. Elizabeth I of England
    D. Ivan IV of Russia

13. Which of the following represents the culmination of de l'Hôpital's policies?
    A. Peace of Augsburg
    B. Edict of Nantes
    C. Twelve Years' Truce
    D. Peace of Westphalia

Questions 14–17 are based on the graph below .

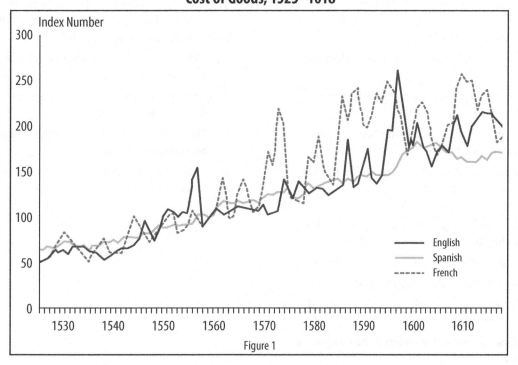

Cost of Goods, 1525–1618

Figure 1

14. The phenomenon depicted in the graph is most accurately identified as:

   A. mercantilism.

   B. enclosure.

   C. the Commercial Revolution.

   D. the Price Revolution.

15. Which of the following best characterizes a major economic and social impact of the phenomenon depicted in the graph?

   A. The movement toward a free peasantry in western Europe

   B. Growth of a new landholding elite engaged in commercial agriculture

   C. A stronger emphasis on hierarchy and inequality in social relations

   D. Delayed marriage and childbearing ("European marriage pattern")

16. Which of the following was the most fundamental cause of the trends depicted in the graph?

   A. Steady population increase in the sixteenth century

   B. Importation of precious metals from the Americas

   C. Noble domination of the lives of the peasantry

   D. State control of financial and banking institutions

17. An economic historian would find which of the following sources most useful in studying the phenomenon depicted in the graph?

   A. Church records of marriages and baptisms

   B. National levels of trade and wages

   C. Data on incidences of crop failures and famines

   D. Charters of national banks and trading companies

Questions 18–20 are based on the interpretation below.

"The popular idea that the craze was medieval is the result of a false prejudice that links everything bad to the clericalism of the so-called 'Dark Ages'. Rather, the witch-craze was a product of the Renaissance and Reformation. Many of the intellectuals of the Renaissance and the leaders of the Reformation were among the most forceful advocates of belief in diabolical witchcraft."

Jeffrey B. Russell, American historian, *A History of Witchcraft: Sorcerers, Heretics, and Pagans*, 1980

18. All of the following features of the Renaissance and Reformation contributed to the development explained above EXCEPT:

   A. Renaissance emphasis on classical values and artistic styles.

   B. Renaissance interest in astrology, alchemy, and magic.

   C. Reformation focus on reading Scripture and biblical authority.

   D. Reformation concern with regulating public morality and behavior.

19. Which of the following was most responsible for the decline of the developments explained above?

   A. Expansion of state control by central governments

   B. Improvements in the economy and weather

   C. New scientific discoveries regarding natural phenomenon

   D. Feminist ideology that ensured the equality of women

20. The historian above would most likely agree with which of the following characterizations of the Renaissance and Reformation?

   A. "Movements that promoted uniformity of thought and political centralization"

   B. "Eras of significant discovery and experimentation in ideas and culture"

   C. "Unfortunate events that might have been avoided with stronger leadership"

   D. "Movements less modern and enlightened than generally believed"

Questions 21–23 are based on the interpretation below.

"In the name of 'science' they [men] gave a supposed physiological basis to the traditional view of women's nature, function, and role. Science affirmed what men had always known, what custom, law, and religion had postulated and justified. With the authority of their 'objective,' 'rational' inquiry they restated ancient premises and arrived at the same traditional conclusions: the innate superiority of the male and the justifiable subordination of the female."

Bonnie S. Anderson and Judith P. Zinsser, American historians, *A History of Their Own*, vol. II, 1988

21. All of the following developments during the period 1450–1700 support the argument of the historians above EXCEPT:

   A. the exclusion of women from universities, guilds, and academies.

   B. women being the primary targets of witchcraft accusations.

   C. the exclusion of women from royal successions and as regents.

   D. the limitation of women's involvement in preaching and the clergy.

22. Beyond the issue of gender, what does the passage suggest about the Scientific Revolution more generally?

   A. It had minimal impact on European society.

   B. States expressed limited interest in it.

   C. It was overshadowed by economic changes.

   D. It was not as revolutionary as commonly believed.

23. Which of the following principles of science would later be employed to justify female <u>equality</u> during and after the nineteenth century?

   A. The importance of empirical observation in asserting knowledge

   B. Universal laws in political theory that supported natural rights

   C. A reliance on efficiency in economics that required female labor

   D. Revolutionary theory in politics used to justify violent change

Questions 24–26 are based on the image below.

Cover illustration from Johannes Kepler, "The Rudolphine Tables," star catalogue and planetary tables (the stone columns on the left and right read "Hipparchus" and "Ptolemy," ancient astronomers), 1627

24. The illustration above could be used to make which of the following conclusions regarding the scientific changes of the sixteenth and seventeenth centuries?

   A. The new science was easily reconciled with folk beliefs in magic.

   B. Direct observation of natural phenomena was considered vital to knowledge.

   C. The ancient inheritance of Greek and Roman classics were no longer useful.

   D. Scientific ideas and religious truths could be blended into a harmonious whole.

25. The ideas presented in the illustration led most directly to which of the following?

   A. Persecution of witches for practicing black magic

   B. Restriction of women from scientific academies

   C. Discovery of the Americas and colonial exploitation

   D. A secular approach to politics and human affairs

26. The ideas depicted in the illustration were embraced most enthusiastically during which of the following eras?

   A. Protestant and Catholic Reformations

   B. Age of Religious Wars

   C. Enlightenment

   D. Age of Revolutions

Questions 27–30 are based on the image below.

Jacques Lagniet, French graphic artist, "The noble is the spider; the peasant is the fly," engraving, ca. 1650

27. The feature of early modern society most directly inferred from the image is the:

    A. dependence of most people on agriculture for their livelihoods.

    B. development of commercial capitalism and resulting inequalities.

    C. persistence of folk beliefs and customs regarding the cosmos.

    D. continuing importance of status and hierarchy in social relations.

28. Which of the following early modern European developments would have posed the most serious challenge to the social and economic realities depicted in the image?

    A. The growth of absolutist political theory and practice

    B. The growth of commerce and emergence of a new economic elite

    C. Religious conflict among rival interpretations of Christianity

    D. A revival of classical literature and languages spread via the printing press

29. How would the situation of the peasant depicted in the image differ most strongly with that of a peasant in Russia?

- **A.** Innovations in banking and finance provided more access to capital.
- **B.** Life revolved around the seasons and a system of three-crop rotation.
- **C.** There was a greater degree of freedom from the land and possible social mobility.
- **D.** Revolts occurred against noble restrictions and abuse of traditional rights.

30. The event that most significantly altered the situation portrayed in the image was the:

- **A.** Protestant Reformation.
- **B.** Scientific Revolution.
- **C.** Enlightenment.
- **D.** French Revolution.

Section I, Part B: Short-Answer Questions

Time—25 minutes; 2 Questions

Directions: Read each question carefully and answer all parts of the question. Use complete sentences; an outline or bulleted list is not acceptable. Sources have been edited for the purposes of this exercise.

"For Machiavelli accepted the political challenge in its entirety; he swept aside every criterion of action not suggested by the concept of *raison d'état**, i.e., by the exact evaluation of the historical moment and the constructive forces which *The Prince* must employ in order to achieve his aim; and he held that the activities of the rulers were limited only by their capacity and energy. Hence, he paved the way for absolute governments, which were completely untrammeled, both in their home and in their foreign policies."

* "the state interest"

Frederico Chabad, Italian historian, *Machiavelli and the Renaissance*, 1960

1. a) Describe one example of a ruler or nation in the period 1450–1600 that supports the interpretation above.

   b) Describe one example of another ruler or nation in the period 1450–1600 that contradicts the interpretation above.

   c) Explain one way in which Machiavelli's ideas represent a feature of the Italian Renaissance.

2. a) Describe one economic or political motive for European exploration and colonization, 1450–1600.

   b) Describe one intellectual or technological innovation that enabled European exploration and colonization, 1450–1600.

   c) Explain one example of how exploration and colonization affected the European balance of power, 1450–1600.

Section II, Part A: Document-Based Question

Total Time—60 minutes; 1 Question

Directions: Question 1 is based on the accompanying documents. It is suggested that you spend about 15 minutes reading the documents and 45 minutes writing your response. The documents have been edited for the purpose of this exercise.

In your response you should do the following:

- Respond to the prompt with a historically defensible thesis or claim that establishes a line of reasoning.
- Describe a broader historical context relevant to the prompt.
- Support an argument in response to the prompt using at least six documents.
- Use at least one additional piece of specific historical evidence (beyond that found in the documents) relevant to an argument about the prompt.
- For at least three documents, explain how or why the document's point of view, purpose, historical situation, and/or audience is relevant to an argument.
- Use evidence to corroborate, qualify, or modify an argument that addresses the prompt.

Question 1   *Evaluate the extent to which the Protestant Reformation changed European society.*

Document 1

Source: The Twelve Articles of the Swabian Peasants, petition, March 1525

The First Article

First, it is our humble petition and desire, as also our will and resolution, that in the future we should have power and authority so that each community should choose and appoint a pastor, and that we should have the right to depose him should he conduct himself improperly. The pastor thus chosen should teach us the Gospel pure and simple, without any addition, doctrine or ordinance of man…

The Third Article

It has been the custom hitherto for men to hold us as their own property, which is pitiable enough, considering that Christ has delivered and redeemed us all, without exception, by the shedding of His precious blood, the lowly as well as the great. Accordingly, it is consistent with Scripture that we should be free and wish to be so. Not that we would wish to be absolutely free and under no authority….We are thus ready to yield obedience according to God's law to our elected and regular authorities in all proper things becoming to a Christian. We, therefore, take it for granted that you will release us from serfdom as true Christians, unless it should be shown us from the Gospel that we are serfs.

Document 2

Source: Martin Luther, religious reformer, *Against the Murderous, Thieving Hordes of Peasant*, pamphlet, 1525

The peasants have taken upon themselves the burden of three terrible sins against God and man; by this they have merited death in body and soul…they have sworn to be true and faithful, submissive and obedient, to their rulers…now deliberately and violently breaking this oath…they are starting a rebellion, and are violently robbing and plundering monasteries and castles which are not theirs…they have doubly deserved death in body and soul as highwaymen and murderers…they cloak this terrible and horrible sin with the gospel…thus they become the worst blasphemers of God and slanderers of his holy name.

Document 3

Source: Ordinances for the Regulation of the Churches Dependent upon Geneva [home of Calvinism], 1547

Concerning the Times of Assembling at Church

That the temples be closed for the rest of the time, in order that no one shall enter therein out of hours, impelled thereto by superstition; and if anyone be found engaged in any special act of devotion therein or nearby he shall be admonished for it: if it be found to be of a superstitious nature for which simple correction is inadequate then he shall he be chastised.

Blasphemy

Whoever shall have blasphemed, swearing by the body or by the blood of our Lord, or in similar manner, he shall be made to kiss the earth for the first offense; for the second to pay 5 sous*, and for the third 6 sous, and for the last offence be put in the pillory for one hour.

Drunkenness

2. That taverns shall be closed during the sermon, under penalty that the tavern-keeper shall pay 3 sous, and whoever may be found therein shall pay the same amount.

3. If anyone be found intoxicated he shall pay for the first offence 3 sous and shall be remanded to the consistory; for the second offence he shall he held to pay the sum of 6 sous, and for the third 10 sous and be put in prison.

Songs and Dances

If anyone sings immoral, dissolute or outrageous songs or dances…he shall be put in prison for three days and then sent to the consistory.

Usury

That no one shall take upon interest or profit more than five per cent, upon penalty of confiscation of the principal and of being condemned to make restitution as the case may demand.

Games

That no one shall play at any dissolute game or at any game whatsoever it may be, neither for gold nor silver nor for any excessive stake, upon penalty of 5 sous and forfeiture of stake played for.

* Swiss currency

Document 4

Source: Argula von Grumbach, Bavarian noblewoman and writer, "Address to the Faculty of the University of Ingolstadt," 1523

…Yes, and Christ himself, he who is the only teacher of us all, was not ashamed to preach to Mary Magdalene, and to the young woman at the well.

I do not flinch from appearing before you, from listening to you, to discussing with you. For by the grace of God I, too, can ask questions, hear answers and read in German….

God grant that I may speak with you in the presence of our three princes and of the whole community. It is my desire to be instructed by everyone…

I have no Latin; but you have German, being born and brought up in this tongue. What I have written to you is no woman's chit-chat, but the word of God; and I (write) as a member of the Christian Church, against which the gates of hell cannot prevail.

Document 5

Source: School Ordinances of Württemberg, Germany, 1559

At least twice a year, each pastor should admonish his parishioners that they be diligent in sending their children to school, not only for learning the liberal arts, but also the fear of God, virtue, and discipline. Otherwise, permanent harm must result, as children grow up without fear and knowledge of God, without discipline, learning nothing about what is needed for their salvation, nor what is useful to them in a worldly life.

Document 6

Source: Johannes Mathesius, Lutheran minister and reformer, *Luther's Table Talk*, "On Marriage," sayings attributed to Martin Luther, 1566

Maternity is a glorious thing, since all mankind have been conceived, born, and nourished of women. All human laws should encourage multiplication of families…

….The state of matrimony is the chief in the world after religion…We ought herein to have more regard to God's command and ordinance, for the sake of generation, and the bringing up of children, than to our untoward humors and [thoughts]; and further, we should consider that it is an [antidote] to sin and unchastity. None, indeed, should be compelled to marry; the matter should be left to each man's conscience, for bride-love may not be forced.

….Men have broad and large chests, and small narrow hips, and more understanding than the women, who have but small and narrow chests, and broad hips, to the end they should remain at home, sit still, keep house, and bear and bring up children.

Document 7

Source: Engraving of Puritan family, England, 1563; Caption: "The whole Psalms [songs of praise in the Bible] in four parts"

Section II, Part B: Long Essay Question

Time—40 minutes; 1 Question

Directions: Choose EITHER Question 2 or Question 3.

In your response, you should do the following:

- Respond to the prompt with a historically defensible thesis or claim that establishes a line of reasoning.
- Describe a broader historical context relevant to the prompt.
- Support an argument in response to the prompt using specific and relevant examples of evidence.
- Use historical reasoning (e.g., comparison, causation, continuity or change over time) to frame or structure an argument that addresses the prompt.
- Use evidence to corroborate, qualify, or modify an argument that addresses the prompt.

Question 2   *Evaluate the most important impact of the Renaissance on European ideas and culture, 1450–1600.*

(RP: Causation)

Question 3   *Evaluate the most important impact of the Thirty Years' War on European religion and diplomacy.*

(RP: Causation)

ANSWERS, EXPLANATIONS, & SAMPLE RESPONSES
for the Diagnostic Exams can be found at
⮞ www.sherpalearning.com/achiever ⮜

The chapters in Period 2 address the following major developments and events:

- Development of absolute monarchies
- Challenges to absolutism, such as republics and constitutional states
- Art movements that reflected absolutism, commerce, and civic ideals
- Commercial Revolution
- Commercial Wars and other conflicts affecting the balance of power
- Enlightened absolutism
- Social and cultural changes, such as the Agricultural Revolution, consumerism, and rise of the middle class
- Enlightenment
- French Revolution and Napoleonic era

Each chapter will provide a content review and practice questions to test your understanding of the material. At the conclusion of the content chapters, you will be able both to gauge your grasp of the content and practice historical thinking skills in a diagnostic test that will include:

- 30 MC questions
- 2 SAQs
- 1 DBQ
- 1 LEQ (choice of 2)

Each chapter will begin with a brief correlation to the Unit Guides from the Course and Exam Description (CED). Good luck with your review.

❧ CHAPTER 7 ❧

Absolutism and the Balance of Power in West and East, 1640–1740

This chapter covers a wide array of nations and rulers. To assist your comprehension, try employing the framework discussed earlier for each nation: **Challenge → Response → Result** . In response to the devastation of the religious wars and the general upheaval in the period 1550–1650, rulers increasingly justified their power based on absolutist or divine-right theories of monarchy. As we'll see in this chapter, not everyone accepted such theoretically expansive powers and thus worked to limit monarchical authority. Rulers also exploited developments in commerce and science to enhance their nations' power. The resulting competition led to nearly continuous warfare in this period over colonies, trade, and territory. To prevent the predominance of any one power (usually France), European

diplomacy relied on the **balance of power**. Both of these trends—development of strong centralized monarchies and balance-of-power diplomacy—played out in eastern and western Europe against the backdrop of various political forms and differing geographic and social imperatives.

SKILL SET

To ensure your focus on the the relevant course themes (SOP, ECD, NEI), think of this unit as an evaluation of how each state in its drive for power addressed: use of resources, religious division, alliance with other states, economic development, administrative control, and military affairs. In other words, try to use the evidence of this chapter (CES) to develop an interpretation on the nature of political power and varying paths to success or failure (ARG).

 KEY IN – Chapter 7 addresses all or part of the following topics in the Unit Guides of the CED:

Topic 2.7 Art of the 16th Century: Mannerism and Baroque Art

Topic 3.1 Contextualizing State-Building

Topic 3.2 The English Civil War and the Glorious Revolution

Topic 3.4 Economic Development and Mercantilism

Topic 3.5 The Dutch Golden Age

Topic 3.6 The Balance of Power

Topic 3.7 Absolutist Approaches to Power

Topic 3.8 Comparison in the Age of Absolutism and Constitutionalism

Topic 4.5 18th-Century Culture and the Arts

Topic 5.2 The Rise of Global Markets

Topic 5.3 Britain's Ascendancy

Political Theories and the Age of Crisis

To understand the drive for centralized power in European states, it is useful to recall the context of the period 1550–1650. Historians often label this era the Age of Crisis, owing to the cumulative effect of the following forces:

- Religious warfare
- Climate change involving poor weather
- Resulting shorter growing seasons, crop failures, and famines
- High taxes
- Internal rebellion
- Witchcraft accusations
- Intellectual changes in explaining natural phenomena (the Scientific Revolution)
- Economic changes: Price Revolution, enclosure, increase in poverty/begging
- Increase in violent and property crimes

Though we prize our liberties today, this fact may be a function of our relative political and social stability. In times of chaos and crisis, people often sacrifice rights in the interests of security and order. Such was the case for advocates of absolutism in the early seventeenth century. To provide for stability, some political theorists developed justifications for the enhanced power of rulers. Not all agreed with absolutist pretensions, and such opponents provided counter-theories justifying *limits* on monarchical power (also see Chapter 6 for Hobbes and Locke).

Given the strong religious beliefs of the period, arguments based on the authority of God carried a natural resonance. Divine-right arguments were new only in the expansive powers with which theorists attempted to imbue them. The most famous advocate of divine-right rule was the French clergyman Bishop Bossuet (1627–1704). Quite simply, kings derive their power from God directly and rule on earth in His stead. Once this view is understood, the resulting magnificent displays of power by Louis XIV and his imitators become clearer as a ruling strategy, as well as the abhorrence with which rebellion and treason were viewed in this era. Some defied the general trend toward absolutism, such as the Huguenots who endorsed resistance by local officials against what was perceived as a repressive monarchy.

The Age of Louis XIV in France

Foundations of French Absolutism: Henry IV and Louis XIII

Absolutism reached its highest expression in France during the reign of **Louis XIV** (r. 1643–1715). The previous two Bourbon monarchs laid the foundations for the sparkling but flawed edifice that was the Age of Louis XIV. Henry IV (r. 1589–1610, the first in the Bourbon line), after bringing the religious conflict to an end with the Edict of Nantes (1598), turned his attention to putting France's financial and economic house in order. Under Henry and his primary advisor, the Duc de Sully, the French state balanced its budget and established a firmer basis for taxation. In addition, Henry promoted economic development through the building of roads and canals, draining swamps, and promoting colonization. His strong rule allowed France to survive his assassination in 1610 and the regency of his wife, Marie de' Medici, on behalf of their son, Louis XIII.

Louis XIII (r. 1610–1643) relied on the advice of his talented and shrewd advisor, Cardinal Richelieu (1585–1642), who increased direct (*taille*) and indirect (*gabelle*—government salt monopoly) taxes. Louis and Richelieu concerned themselves with curbing the power of the nobility. To this effect, Richelieu banned dueling (which suggested violence independent of the state), employed spies to monitor the provincial nobility, and appointed *intendants*, or local officials, whose job it was to be the "eyes and ears of the monarchy." In addition, while allowing Huguenots to maintain their religious practices, Richelieu forced them to relinquish their fortified towns. Though Richelieu was a prince of the Catholic Church, under his guidance France supported the *Protestant* forces during the Thirty Years' War. Like Machiavelli before him, politics for Richelieu embraced *raison d'etat*, or "reason of state," as he expressed it in his *Political Testament*. According to Richelieu, it was in France's interests to limit the growing power of the surrounding Habsburgs (the political leaders of the Catholic cause), regardless of the religious allegiances of Richelieu, or France more generally.

Louis XIV and French Absolutism

When Louis XIV inherited the throne in 1643, France was once again faced with the prospect of a boy king (Louis was 5). Discontent over high taxes and foreign influence in government led to a series of rebellions in Paris and the countryside known as the Fronde (1648–1652). In fact, the young Louis's first memory may have been fleeing from his capital in a carriage surrounded by an angry mob. The event convinced him to build his seat of government in the nearby suburb of Versailles and to establish an iron-fisted rule that could overwhelm any potential future opposition.

Early in Louis's reign, the real ruler of France was Cardinal

> **THEME MUSIC**
>
> The SOP theme in this period revolves around the theory and practice of absolute monarchy, including those in opposition, such as corporate groups, provinces, and religious minorities. Monarchs wished to establish national loyalties, but minority groups often challenged these pretensions and reaffirmed regional or religious identities (reminding us of the NEI theme). As you consider the material here on the French experience, keep an eye forward to explaining the long-term causes of the French Revolution.

Mazarin (1602–1661), who continued many of the policies of his predecessor, Richelieu. Upon Mazarin's death in 1661, Louis at the age of 23 took personal control of government and did not relinquish it until his death in 1715. A major concern for Louis was to overcome the provincialism and feudal remnants of the French state. Seventeenth-century France was divided by linguistic dialects, provincial customs and estates, and by a variety of political bodies that potentially limited monarchical power. One such were the 15 regional *parlements*, or courts, controlled by the nobles, and who by tradition had to register the king's decrees to give them effect. To control these bodies, Louis wielded threats of exile and confiscation of property, or involved nobles in court patronage and intrigue at the glittering palace of Versailles.

The Palace at Versailles

Perhaps no greater symbol of royal absolutism exists than Louis's palace at Versailles. Originally a hunting lodge, Versailles became a seat of government under Louis, as well as a teeming city of patronage-seekers and the backdrop for the drama of Louis's kingship. Looking over the palace itself, with its man-made canal, lush gardens, and grandiose out-buildings, one begins to understand the importance of Louis's expression "I am the state." The palace was constructed over several decades, and though the records were deliberately destroyed, it is estimated that the palace absorbed as much as 60%–80% of the state's revenues during the years of its construction. Versailles was more than a royal residence. Nobles were encouraged to live on the grounds and participate in the pageantry of Louis's rule. Court etiquette and pursuit of royal favor occupied the energies of thousands of the French aristocracy, safely under Louis's gaze and unable to make trouble in the provinces. All of Louis's activities were infused with religious solemnity; nobles competed to participate in the ceremonies of the king's waking, dining, and retiring to bed (*lever*, *dîner*, and *coucher*). French culture and the grandeur of Louis's Versailles became the envy of Europe, as elites across Europe sharpened their French language skills and rulers built their own mini-Versailles.

Economic Policies

Reflecting a continental trend, France practiced mercantilism to enhance its economic position. Under **Jean-Baptiste Colbert** (1619–1683), the minister of finance and Louis's primary advisor, France developed a unified internal market and also expanded its commercial presence around the world. Like many nations, France's economy was limited by internal tariffs; though Colbert did not eliminate these, he did create a free-trade zone, known as the Five Great Farms, to facilitate commerce. In addition, Colbert continued to enhance France's infrastructure with roads, a postal system, and the establishment of manufacturing codes. Industries were organized into corporations, which fell under the guidance of the state, a process that helped the nation earn a

reputation for high-quality luxury goods. To promote commerce, Colbert established the French East India Company (to rival Britain's and the Netherlands') and built a royal navy. High tariffs (taxes on imports) limited foreign goods and, along with the high taxes imposed to finance Louis's many wars, had the effect of increasing the burden on the lower classes (especially peasants) by raising prices and taking much of their hard-earned subsistence. Members of the nobility had negotiated exemptions from many direct taxes over the years, creating a regressive and inefficient system that increased discontent over time.

Religious and Cultural Policies

During Louis's reign, the Jansenist controversy divided those in French intellectual circles. Jansenists opposed the Jesuits' strong version of human free will in favor of a Calvinist predestinationist view of salvation. Perhaps this controversy convinced Louis that he could no longer tolerate "heretical ideas" in an absolutist system that theoretically expressed "one king, one faith, and one law." Louis perceived the very presence of Huguenots in his kingdom as a threat to these theoretical powers, so in 1685 he revoked the Edict of Nantes (known as the Edict of Fontainebleu) and attempted forcibly to convert French Protestants back to Catholicism. Rather than convert, most simply took refuge, along with their property and skills, in those lands that welcomed them, such as the Dutch Republic and Brandenburg-Prussia.

The grandeur of Louis's France was often associated with its artistic and intellectual achievements. In the 1660s, Louis established the French Academy of Arts and the <u>French Academy of Sciences</u>. The former created paintings, sculpture, architecture, music, and drama under clear aesthetic guidelines—artists should glorify Louis, France, and link its greatness with classical subjects and style. Much of this patronage revolved around Versailles, which featured an opera house/theater for playwrights to express their comic or tragic commentaries on classical themes. Under Louis, France achieved a continental reputation for combining the scale of the Baroque (see page 121) with the restraint of the neoclassical. In the area of science, Louis hoped to exploit advances in astronomy, medicine, and navigation to enhance France's prestige as well as its economic and military potential.

The Army

During the seventeenth century, France replaced Spain as the leading military power on the continent and the nation most often threatening the balance of power. Louis XIV tied his and France's greatness to its army. Under the Marquis de Louvois (1641–1691), Louis's minister of

---

THEME MUSIC

The most significant driver for the centralization of power (SOP) was the military imperative. By 1650, most states had brought warfare under central control; however, the expense of war in the form of troops, munitions, and fortresses came to absorb the bulk of the state's budget, often prompting tax revolts and causing shifts in the fortunes of states.

war, France's army became the largest in Europe at 400,000 men. Despite Louvois's skill and the addition of territory on France's eastern border, the wars of Louis XIV (see page 121) drained the treasury and severely taxed the country's manpower and resources.

A Commercial Republic: The Dutch

For all of France's greatness, its small neighbor to the northeast posed a challenge by being different in almost every possible way. The seven northern provinces of the Netherlands (or United Provinces, officially the Dutch Republic after 1648) became Europe's leading commercial power in the first half of the seventeenth century. How did this nation of about one million people with few natural endowments threaten powerful France? First, the Dutch made efficient use of their resources. Land was recovered from the sea by use of dams and dikes and was then organized into *polders* for purposes of diverting water. After 1580, the Dutch moved into Portuguese markets in the East Indies and South America, establishing colonial outposts and reaping huge profits with their joint-stock companies. Second, the Dutch set themselves up as the "middlemen of Europe" by ignoring the prevailing mercantilist philosophy and using their fleet of maneuverable flyboats (or *fluyts*) to trade with all nations and their colonies. It didn't hurt that the Netherlands lay astride important trade routes in the Baltic and Atlantic. Amsterdam served as an *entrepot* city, where ships were efficiently uploaded and offloaded with goods (much like a modern computer file server), as well as the financial center of Europe, what with its Bank of Amsterdam and the Stock Exchange. Merchants played a key role in the Netherlands, and their activities drew investment and trade from all over Europe. Finally, the Netherlands practiced religious toleration, attracting Huguenot refugees from France, Jews, small Protestant denominations, and those fleeing the Inquisition in Spain. These talented minorities lent their business acumen and craftsmanship to the flourishing Dutch economy.

The period from 1550–1650 marked the Dutch Golden Age. Its "embarrassment of riches" fueled an outpouring of cultural activity, which, unlike in France, focused on themes of middle-class domestic life, nature, and science. Talented painters, such as Jan Vermeer (1632–1675), Judith Leyster (1609–1660), Frans Hals (1588–1666), and Rembrandt van Rijn (1606–1669), reflected the Dutch preoccupation with light and shadow, natural landscapes, still lifes, domestic scenes, and group portraits. **René Descartes** (1596–1650) and Baruch Spinoza (1632–1677) found a home for their unorthodox philosophies in the Netherlands when they couldn't elsewhere. Such economic and cultural achievements attracted the envy of the Netherlands' larger neighbors.

Internal strife and external threat posed a problem for the Dutch. In religion, disagreement over the issue of predestination continued to cause conflict within the Dutch Reformed church. Constitutionally, the Netherlands were a loosely connected federation of seven provinces that often jealously guarded their liberties, but in times of war relied on leadership from the House of Orange in Holland (the most important of the 7 provinces). Because of continual threats to their security, the other six provinces elected William of Orange (later king of England) in 1673 the hereditary *stadholder* of the Netherlands, though the House of Orange never succeeded in creating a strong centralized monarchy. Given their inherent limitations, it was probably only a matter of time before the Netherlands were surpassed by its rivals. A major turning point proved to be the Anglo-Dutch Naval Wars, fought in three phases between 1652 and 1674 over the English Navigation Acts (1651, 1660), which attempted to restrict Dutch trade with England's colonies. Though the Dutch survived the onslaught, it seriously undercut their commercial power and set the stage for their conflicts with Louis XIV.

> ### SKILL SET
>
> Rivalries capture our attention, especially when they involve two strikingly different opponents. This is certainly the case with the conflict between the small, commercial Dutch and the opulent, absolutist juggernaut of France under Louis XIV. As you consider the evidence, keep in mind the contrasts (COMP) between these two rivals.

Britain: Civil War and Limited Monarchy

Causes of the Conflict

Like the so-called religious wars, the **English Civil War** was both religious and political in nature. The political component involved conflict over sovereignty (ultimate authority) between the new Stuart line of monarchs and the **English Parliament**. Religiously, Puritans wished to purify the state Anglican Church of what they perceived as the residue of Catholic doctrine and worship, which the Stuarts seemed to endorse. Lasting almost a century (1603–1689), the conflict ultimately laid the foundations for England's unique system of government which combined elements of monarchy, oligarchy ("rule by a few"), and democracy.

Elizabeth I died without an heir, leaving the throne (in 1603) to the son of Mary, Queen of Scots, James I (r. 1603–1625). As a Scottish outsider, James failed to appreciate the important legislative role played by the English Parliament, which James continually lectured on his divine-right powers and foolishly laid out in a book, *The True Law of Free Monarchies* (1598). In addition, James antagonized Puritans with the hierarchical structure he retained for the Anglican Church. To control the clergy and religion in general, James believed such an episcopal ("of bishops") structure was necessary to enforce discipline; hence, his saying, "No bishop, no king." The growing number of Puritans in Parliament preferred a loose church configuration that allowed individual congregations to control local affairs but cooperate through regional governing boards. James's policies fueled anti-Catholic sentiment, which was only heightened when radical Catholics failed in 1605 to blow up the Parliament, an event known as the Gunpowder Plot.

The English Civil War

These issues came to head during the reign of James's son, Charles I (r. 1625–1649). When Charles demanded revenue, Parliament instead issued the Petition of Right (1628), an assertion of its prerogatives regarding taxation and liberties from arbitrary arrest and imprisonment. This latter issue had arisen due to the Stuarts' use of the Star Chamber, a royal court where standard judicial procedures were ignored, in favor of secrecy and arbitrary judgments. Frustrated with Parliament, Charles decided to rule alone from 1629 to 1639, relying on revenues from the royal domain and the use of ship money—in which coastal towns were required to contribute either ships or money for defense. This latter policy had the effect of alienating the growing mercantile elite. Further, Charles's religious policies, guided by Archbishop of Canterbury William Laud (1573–1645), seemed to Puritans little different than Catholicism. Laud attempted to impose uniformity on the realm in 1640 with a new Book of Common Prayer, causing the Scots, who favored a decentralized church structure, to rise in rebellion.

Now Charles had to call the Parliament back into session to defend against a Scottish invasion. Rather than grant Charles his requested taxes, the Parliament once again asserted its liberties and placed two of his top officials on trial for treason. When Charles attempted in 1642 to arrest the parliamentary leaders of the Puritan cause, his action misfired and plunged England into civil war. The war between the forces of the king (Cavaliers) and those of Parliament (Roundheads) resulted in the capture of Charles in 1645. This conflict brought the brilliant and zealous leader of Parliament's New Model Army to the fore—Oliver Cromwell (1599–1658). Not only an outstanding practitioner of the new military revolution, Cromwell was a devout Puritan who believed, along with his men, in religious toleration for all Protestant denominations and a democratic church structure.

Oliver Cromwell and the Protectorate

When Parliament refused to take action against the captured king, Cromwell surrounded the Parliament and drove out its more moderate members. This new Rump Parliament placed the king under arrest and executed him for treason in 1649. Soon Cromwell had disposed of even the Rump Parliament and named himself Lord Protector under the only written constitution in England's history, the Instrument of Government (1653). Eventually Cromwell imposed military rule and pursued vigorous policies aimed at reforming English morals (by banning plays, gambling, and the celebration of Christmas, which smacked of Catholic "idolatry"), promoting English commerce via mercantilism, and violently subduing rebellion in Ireland and Scotland. After Cromwell's death in 1658, the English aristocracy, weary of military rule and Cromwell's Puritanism, agreed to restore the Stuart monarchy.

The Stuart Restoration and Glorious Revolution

With the Restoration of Charles II (r. 1660–1685) as monarch, the same issues of religion and political control quickly reasserted themselves. Though Charles privately inclined toward Catholicism, he hid his sympathies behind a façade of religious tolerance, while appointing Catholics as justices of the peace (local officials). In 1673 Parliament responded with the Test Act, which required all officeholders to take communion in the Church of England. Further, Charles's pro-French foreign policy ran counter to years of English diplomacy. In fact, Charles had in 1670 signed the secret Treaty of Dover with Louis XIV, in which he gained an annual subsidy from the French king while agreeing to reintroduce Catholicism in England at the first opportunity. With these funds, Charles was able to rule without Parliament during the last years of his reign.

The prospect of a permanent Catholic dynasty brought the rule of the Stuarts to an end. Charles's brother, James II (1685–1688), ascended to the throne in 1685, despite the division in Parliament between those who supported his legitimate succession (Tories) and those who opposed him (Whigs). James was an avowed Catholic, which might have been tolerable, until his aging wife in 1688 gave birth to a male heir. Faced with this prospect, Whig members of Parliament invited James's daughter Mary, a Protestant, and her husband, William of Orange, stadtholder of the Netherlands, to invade the nation and claim the throne as co-rulers. The resulting **Glorious Revolution** proved a success, and William III (1689–1702) and Mary II (1688–1694) agreed to parliamentary sovereignty and formalized English liberties with the Bill of Rights (1689). In addition, Parliament passed the Toleration Act (1689), which allowed Protestant dissenters to worship but excluded them from public service, and the Act of Succession (1701), which prohibited the English monarchy from ever being held by a Catholic. Finally, to cement ties formally with Scotland, the English Parliament agreed in 1707 to create the United Kingdom of Great Britain. The Glorious Revolution and these series of acts laid the foundation for Britain's unique but stable government and commercial dominance in the eighteenth century.

> **SKILL SET**
>
> England often seems a genteel and peaceful nation; however, its history involves ongoing conflicts over politics, religion, and ethnicity. Consider this CCOT question: Which of the following dates represents the most significant transformation in English politics: 1534, 1603, 1649, 1689? Be prepared to justify your response (ARG).

Art: From Mannerism to Baroque

Due to foreign invasion and economic decline, the Italian Renaissance style of symmetry, order, and classical themes gave way to one based on complex composition, distortion, and elongated human figures. This late sixteenth-century genre was known as **Mannerism**, meaning those who painted in the manner of the later Michelangelo, such as his *Last Judgment* (completed in 1542). The most famous Mannerist painter, who accomplished his greatest work during the Spanish Golden Age, was El Greco (1541–1614). Known for introducing yellows and grays into the painter's palette, El Greco expressed in his *Burial of Count Orgaz* and *Landscapes of Toledo* a complex psychology which depicted a Spain on the verge of decline. To get an impression of the Mannerist style, you might also view Tintoretto's (1518–1594) version of *The Last Supper* and compare it with da Vinci's. Clearly, Catholic Counter-Reformation mysticism had replaced the classical style and one-point perspective of Leonardo's version.

Mannerism gradually evolved into the **Baroque** style, which dominated art and music from 1600 to about 1730. A major theme of the Baroque is power—reflecting rising absolute monarchs and a reviving Catholic Church, both of whom were the major patrons of Baroque artists. The figure most associated with the rebuilding of Rome in the age of the Counter-Reformation is Gian Lorenzo Bernini (1598–1680), an accomplished painter, sculptor, and architect. Bernini designed the magnificent altar in St. Peter's Basilica, the papal throne, and the welcoming arms of St. Peter's Square outside. In addition, Bernini's version of the *David* demonstrates the Baroque style eloquently: unlike Michelangelo's static psychological portrait, Bernini stimulates the viewer with the action of David flinging his slingshot. Bernini's most famous work—*The Ecstasy of St. Teresa*—combines sculpture and architecture to create a mystical religious vision.

Absolute monarchs needed artists to convey their grandeur. Court painters, such as Velazquez (1599–1660) of Spain, managed to win patronage by not only glorifying monarchy but also creating rich and complex commentaries on their subjects, as with *The Maids of Honor*. Another outstanding painter of the Baroque style who attracted many patrons was Peter Paul Rubens (1577–1640). Rubens was one of the first studio painters, employing a team of assistants to help him complete his many muscular and energetic compositions of both religious scenes, like *The Raising of the Cross*, and the political, such as his *Portrait of Marie de' Medici* (wife of Henry IV of France). In music the compositions of J.S. Bach, Antonio Vivaldi, G.F. Handel, and the operas of Monteverdi expressed the Baroque fascination with ornate, complex structure as well as religious and secular themes of power.

> ### THEME MUSIC
> You may wish to find images of these artworks using an Internet search or by consulting one of the art sites mentioned previously (CID). As always, be prepared to place the art in context (CTX) by explaining the artist's technique and linking its subject matter to the concerns of the period. Baroque is the art of princes and popes, patronage and power. Can you make this conceptual link with a few examples of art?

The Wars of Louis XIV

To understand European diplomacy, you must appreciate the importance of the **balance of power**. Balance-of-power politics developed during the Italian Renaissance but reached its most explicit form during the Age of Louis XIV. Louis's desire to extend France to its "natural frontiers" (the Rhine River) and accrue glory to himself led him into nearly constant warfare during his reign. As Spain continued its decline under the Habsburgs, France rushed in to exploit the vacuum of power in the Western Europe. In each of these wars, Louis animated a coalition of powers against him to prevent his threat to the balance of power, or the dominance of one nation over the rest. As you read over the wars below, focus on how the balance of power operates and shifts with each phase of conflict.

> ### EXAMPLE BASE
> You may be confused by the wars covered in this section. Focus your attention on the nature of war, the rivalries, the changing role of the state, and their effects on the balance of power. Military history on the AP exam tends to revolve around these issues and less on battles and strategy.

The first targets of Louis's ambitions were the Spanish Netherlands and Dutch Republic, the latter whose commercial success he envied. Louis struck in two phases, first in 1667 and again in 1672, now with England as an ally. This Dutch War earned Louis the strategic province of Franche-Comté, or the former Burgundy, which gave France substantial territory on the Swiss border and also outflanked Alsace-Lorraine, his next target. Taking advantage of the growing weakness of the Holy Roman Empire, Louis in 1689 then invaded Alsace-Lorraine. The subsequent Nine Years' War resulted in an anti-French alliance, also known as the League of Augsburg. Now both the stadtholder of the Netherlands and king of England, William III (of Orange) pieced together this coalition to prevent Louis's bid for continental domination. Famines, sieges, and high taxes marked this desultory conflict, which ended in 1697 practically where it started, with Louis gaining only a few towns along his border. Bigger game awaited, as the Spanish monarch, Charles II, continued to decline in health, with no heir to the throne.

European royal houses had waited decades for the death of poor Charles II (r. 1665–1700), the last Habsburg ruler of Spain and sad result of generations of interbreeding between the Spanish and Austrian Habsburg lines. Complicating matters, Louis XIV and the Holy Roman Emperor claimed the throne through family marriages to Charles's sisters. Both contenders signed a treaty in 1700 to partition the Spanish Empire and thus maintain the balance of power. These plans fell to naught when upon his death in 1700,

Charles's will granted all possessions to his nephew, Philip V, the Bourbon grandson of Louis XIV. Louis decided to press his claim to the Spanish throne via his grandson. The resulting War of Spanish Succession (1702–1713) proved to be the most costly, important, and last of Louis's wars for continental domination. France and Spain faced off against England, the Netherlands, the Holy Roman Empire, and a few smaller states. Warfare in the eighteenth century involved measured movements designed to outmaneuver opponents or capture strategic fortresses. The war dragged expensively on, as each nation—large and small—exploited the conflict to meet long-held territorial and political goals.

With the Peace of Utrecht in 1714 the conflict finally came to a close. Louis's grandson, Philip V (r. 1700–1749) became the (first) Bourbon ruler of Spain, but it was a truncated empire that could never be united with its northern Bourbon neighbor of France. To recognize the weaker position of Spain, the 10 southern provinces of the Netherlands were ceded to Austria (now the Austrian Netherlands), as were former Spanish territories in Italy. The big winner of the conflict proved to be England, which gained Gibraltar (former Spanish fortress at the headland of the Mediterranean), new territory in North America, and the privilege of trading with the Spanish Empire, known as the *asiento*. Britain's Protestant succession was also confirmed, and it was poised, with a stable government and enhanced commercial position, to become the leading maritime power in Europe. As we'll see below, other nations either emerged from the conflict with new-found or curtailed power. However, the major consequences of the war and the treaty were to block Louis XIV's last effort to impose French domination on the continent and to confirm the European state system of sovereign nations constantly shifting positions to maintain or create a balance of power. On his deathbed in 1715, Louis told his heir and great-grandson (the future Louis XV) that he feared he "had loved war too much."

Aging Empires in the East

Three aging states dominated central and eastern Europe in the seventeenth century—the Holy Roman Empire, Poland, and the Ottoman Empire. The weakness of these "soft states"— so-called because of their loose organization—allowed for the emergence of a new constellation of powers.

Following the Thirty Years' War (1648), the Holy Roman Empire's status as a loose confederation of over 300 German states was confirmed. The traditional rulers of the empire, the Austrian Habsburgs, turned east over

> ### SKILL SET
> As you may have noticed, some states experienced success and others failure in their attempts to enhance their power and overcome internal divisions and external threats. Be able to place sets of nations side by side (e.g., France and Poland) and explain the reasons for the outcomes (COMP and MAC).

the next century to enhance their power, particularly at the expense of the declining Ottoman Empire. Though Austria was able to gain significant swaths of land in east-central Europe, these conquests continued to bring more non-German minorities (Slavs, Poles, Italians, Romanians, and Ukrainians) into its empire, which later proved a centrifugal force, as nationalism took hold in the nineteenth century.

Poland was the weakest of the European kingdoms. Ironically, Poland had been the largest nation in Europe in 1500. However, throughout the sixteenth century, the powerful nobles of Poland—the *szlachta*, who made up almost 10% of the population—succeeded in limiting the power of the Polish kings. Eventually, the Polish monarchy evolved into an elective position, and one that was fought over by rival European powers who bribed the noble-electors with promises of religious toleration and respect for their "liberties." After 1587, the nation was ruled by only two native-born monarchs. Further, a single noble could effectively block the actions of the Sejm, Poland's representative body, by using the *liberum veto*. Poland's experience ran counter to the broader trend toward absolutism, and unable to establish permanent taxes or a standing army, Poland fell prey to larger rivals. The tragic result of this failure to centralize for the formerly great kingdom was **Poland's Partition** in three phases by 1795.

After the Turks captured Constantinople in 1453, the Ottoman Empire periodically sent shock waves of fear throughout central Europe with an ebb and flow of expansion. In 1529, the Turks had nearly captured Vienna, but eventually fell back into internal turmoil for over a century. Once again in 1683 the Turks besieged the Habsburg capital, which was rescued triumphantly by a multinational Holy League (led by the last great native Polish king, Jan Sobieski) at the **Battle of Vienna**. Never again would the Turks pose a major threat to central Europe. What had once been Ottoman strengths, now decayed; the empire simply did not keep up with the rest of Europe. First, the Turkish rulers, the Sultans, grew corrupt from court intrigue, assassination plots, and sensuous living. Second, the once-great Janissaries, the elite fighters composed of former Christians, became a static force opposed to technological and strategic change. Finally, though the Ottoman rulers tolerated religious minorities (more so than most European nations), the resulting tradition of local rule made it difficult to draw effectively on the resources of the empire's far-flung provinces. Many states, such as France, desired the continued existence of the Ottoman Empire as a counterweight to the Austrian Habsburgs, but only if the Islamic state could be influenced and indirectly controlled from the outside.

Austria Turns East

Once the Austrian Habsburgs held off the Turkish invasion in 1683, they were able to turn the battle back on their long-time enemies. Employing the talents of a castoff from the court of Louis XIV, Eugene of Savoy (1663–1736), the Austrians defeated the Turks, gaining back Hungary and adding Transylvania, as well as territory in the Balkan Peninsula, confirmed by treaty (1699). Austria needed to end the Turkish conflict so as to turn their attention to the impending War of Spanish Succession (see above). Though the Austrians were unable to reunite the two Habsburg branches (Spanish and Austrian) during the conflict, the Peace of Utrecht (1713–1714) granted them territory in the Netherlands and Italy.

The reign of Emperor Charles VI (1711–1740) was dominated by one issue: ensuring the succession of his daughter and heir, Maria Theresa (1740–1780), to the many Habsburg lands. To this effect, Charles negotiated the Pragmatic Sanction with Europe's rulers, whereby they agreed to respect the Habsburg inheritance to a female ruler. Given the circumstances, Austria adjusted effectively after its losses in the Thirty Years' War, but as we'll see in the next chapter, the succession issue would ultimately cost the Habsburgs their dominant position in central Europe.

The Rise of Prussia and Its Army

The rise of Brandenburg-Prussia (later simply Prussia) in the seventeenth century surprised most observers. A scattered nation with a small population (2 million in 1650) and few natural resources, Prussia relied heavily on three factors for its amazing rise to power: (1) skillful and resolute leadership from the Hohenzollern dynasty, (2) efficient use of resources, and, most importantly, (3) an outstanding military tradition. As was often joked, "Prussia is not a state with an army, but an army with a state." For no other nation was the military so closely associated with its power and prestige.

Brandenburg stood in the middle of north-central Germany, of importance only as an Elector of the Holy Roman Emperor. However, in 1618 the Hohenzollerns inherited the Duchy of Prussia, so far east that it was surrounded by Poland. During the Thirty Years' War (1618–1648), Brandenburg experienced widespread devastation, its capital city of Berlin reduced to a village of rubble. Nonetheless, Brandenburg-Prussia gained territory in the west along the Rhine and in Pomerania as a result of the Peace of Westphalia (1648). Frederick William, the "Great Elector" (1640–1688) resolved that his nation would never again be overrun by invading armies.

Frederick William was the first in a line of great Prussian rulers. To gain the support of the Prussian nobility—the Junkers—Frederick William granted them important positions in the army and allowed them almost complete power over their serfs. In exchange, the aristocracy agreed to accept Hohenzollern leadership and an excise tax to fund the activities of the state. With these funds, Frederick William erected the skeleton of the Prussian state. To collect the taxes, Frederick William created the General War Commissariat, which at first provisioned the army but evolved into a state bureaucracy, famous for its punctuality and efficiency. The Hohenzollern rulers generally lived a Spartan existence, allowing most of the state's revenues to flow into the army. Though Frederick William enhanced the army to 40,000 men, his goal was not to use it for conquest, but for security and as the glue that held scattered Prussia together. In addition, Frederick William practiced mercantilism by establishing monopolies, raising tariffs on imported goods, and promoting economic development. When Louis XIV revoked the Edict of Nantes in 1685, the Prussian state welcomed the persecuted Huguenots, eager to cash in on their economic skills.

During the War of Spanish Succession, the Habsburg emperor called on the support of Brandenburg-Prussia to drive out the French from Germany. As a reward for his support, the duke of Brandenburg-Prussia earned himself a new title—king in Prussia. The first great king in Prussia proved to be Frederick William I (1713–1740), not to be confused with Frederick William, the Great Elector. Frederick William's personality and approach to governing were strict, paternalistic, and austere. The ruler could be seen patrolling the streets of his realm with a walking stick, admonishing government officials or wayward citizens. Efficiency and duty took precedence over all else. State funds were used judiciously to augment the size of the army (up to 83,000) and often at the expense of the royal household budget. Frederick William introduced merit to government service, by promoting the middle class, though this practice by no means challenged the primary position of the Junkers or the army. However, Frederick William fought no wars in his reign. This feat he left for the son with whom he never got along, Frederick II.

Peter and the Westernization of Russia

Russia's Unique Position

Much of Russia is *in* Europe, but Russia has not always been *of* Europe. Many of the trends we have addressed thus far—Renaissance, Reformation, Scientific Revolution—did not touch the Russian state or its people. For many in the west, Russia was an enigma, more closely tied to the political and religious traditions of Asia. It is not as difficult, however, to identify the thrust of Russia's experience, as the themes of (1) expansion and (2) relative backwardness define its role in European history.

As we've seen, Russia made strides in establishing a larger and more modern state under both Ivan III and Ivan IV in the sixteenth century. These rulers succeeded in driving the Mongols from much of central Asia, establishing some semblance of an administrative structure and creating a military class (*streltsy*). Unfortunately, Ivan IV killed his heir to the throne in a fit of rage, plunging Russia into a difficult period of internal instability and foreign invasion known as the Time of Troubles (1598–1613). The situation was not resolved until the feudal estates (Zemsky Sobor) elected Michael Romanov (r. 1613–1645) as the tsar of Russia. Romanov rule would last in Russia until the Russian Revolution in 1917 led to the end of the family line.

Russia now gained stability but continued to lag behind Europe. First, it was during the seventeenth century that Russia's oppressive system of **serfdom** was put into legal form. Though other nations in eastern and central Europe practiced serfdom, only in Russia could serfs be bought and sold like chattel. This slave-like existence often provoked massive rebellions, in which discontented serfs often allied with Cossacks (a warrior tribe) in proclaiming the overthrow of landlords and those in authority. Furthermore, Russia's dominant religion was the tradition-bound Orthodox Church, which tended to oppose social and religious changes. When the Russian patriarch Nikon (head of the Russian Orthodox Church) undertook reforms in the Bible and worship, a group called the Old Believers opposed the reforms and threatened to break away from the church. These represent only two issues facing Russia during this period, but they demonstrate well the divide between Russia's people and its government, as well as the conflict between tradition and modernization.

> ## SKILL SET
>
> The skill of CCOT applies especially well to Russian history. Though many rulers have attempted the modernization of Russia, one continuity has been Russia's difficulty in establishing a functioning democracy able to harness the energies of its people, despite the changes in policies and regimes. The vast expanse and ethnic/linguistic diversity of Russia has often meant a top-down government. How does Peter I connect with this issue (MAC)?

The Reforms of Peter the Great

Peter I, the Great (r. 1682–1725) stands as one of the greatest and most fascinating figures in Russian history. On one hand, Peter was attracted by all that was modern—technology, science, industry; on the other, he could be brutal and ruthless in the pursuit of his goals. By the sheer force of his personality and vision, Peter within a generation brought Russia into the European state system and made his nation a great power. Though Peter did succeed in making the rest of Europe take note of Russia's might, his reforms did not seep down to the common person and often created divisions within Russian society.

As a boy in Moscow, Peter enjoyed the company of westerners who lived in the so-called German suburb of the city. Here he learned about engineering and manufacturing. When Peter took the throne, he decided to embark on a Great Embassy (1697–1698) to the west with hundreds of technical advisors. Peter attempted to travel incognito, but it was hard to miss the nearly 7-foot-tall Russian leader as he visited shipyards, manufactories, and colleges. The trip was cut short as Peter faced a rebellion at home by the *streltsy*, who perceived Peter's reforms as a threat to their power. Upon his return, Peter personally interrogated and executed many of the leaders of the rebellion, hanging their bodies on the city gates as a warning to others. With his storehouse of new technical skill, however, Peter helped build Russia's first navy and a more modern army. During his reign, Peter was nearly continuously at war, primarily with the Ottoman Turks and Swedes.

Internally, Peter set out to strengthen the nation as well as reform the habits of his people. Taxes were imposed on a variety of items, including "heads," known as the poll tax. With these funds, Peter would pursue mercantilist policies aimed at making Russia a commercial nation, with its own joint-stock companies, merchant fleet, and monopolies. Peter even employed serf labor in mining, metallurgy, and textile manufacture. Russians also needed to look modern, so Peter banned the wearing of long coats, beards, and the veiling of women. To promote loyalty to the state, Peter required all members of the landowning class to engage in state service. This later evolved into a system of merit, known as the Table of Ranks, whereby subjects could rise in status based on contributions to the state. To make governing the vast Russian expanse more effective, Peter eliminated the feudal organs of self-government and divided the nation into 10 governing units, with a senate of advisers to assist in day-to-day administration. Finally, to resolve the conflict within the Russian Orthodox Church, Peter simply eliminated the position of patriarch and instead placed the church under the control of the state, a power that was exercised through a Holy Synod of bishops.

The Great Northern War

The primary goal of these changes was to gain territory at the expense of Russia's neighbors. At first, Peter directed his attention toward the Black Sea, hoping to gain a port city there. His campaigns failed to achieve much, except to demonstrate the backwardness of the Russian military. However, Peter next directed his attention toward Sweden, whose territory and dominant position in the Baltic he wished to replace. At this time, Sweden was ruled by the militarily talented but unpredictable Charles XII (r. 1697–1718), who was able to defeat a vastly superior Russian force in 1700 at the battle of Narva, which kicked off the Great Northern War (1700–1721). Peter learned from his early mistakes and changed tactics and technology, all while Charles bogged down in Polish politics. Again in 1709, the two armies faced off. This time Peter used the traditional Russian tactic of drawing the enemy into the Russian interior to face its brutal winter. Then at Poltava, Peter struck at Charles's army, crushing it and forcing him into exile in the Ottoman Empire. By the Treaty of Nystad (1721), Russia gained significant territory in the Baltic, which allowed Peter to build a new capital city, St. Petersburg, which represented his "window to the west." Never before had Russian influence extended so far into Europe.

No doubt, Peter accomplished much in his forced modernization of Russia. Prior to his reign, Russia was a large but backward entity relatively unknown to the rest of Europe. When Peter died in 1725, he left Russia a great power of Europe, feared for its sheer size and military potential. Many elites in Russia eagerly adopted Peter's reforms, as they saw in them the potential for individual gain and national power. Nonetheless, most of Peter's reforms came at the expense of the masses—serfs, Old Believers, lower classes. While Russia had adopted a veneer of technological and industrial might, its autocratic (rule by one person) system of government was fastened more tightly on the nation than ever before. In the short run, Russia was now a major power and always a threat to expand; in the long run, these perennial issues of backwardness and autocratic rule contributed to the Russian Revolution in the twentieth century.

Additional Resources

📖 **Peter Burke, *The Fabrication of Louis XIV* (1992)** — Studies the man and myth that was the Sun King.

📖 **Euan Cameron, *Early Modern Europe: An Oxford History* (1999)** — Provides interpretations by leading historians on a variety of relevant topics.

📖 **Christopher Clark, *Iron Kingdom: The Rise and Downfall of Prussia, 1600–1947* (2009)** — Offers a strong analysis of how the small kingdom rose to great power.

📖 **J.H. Elliott, *Imperial Spain*, 1469–1715, 2/e (2002)** — Provides a cautionary tale of Europe's leading power's rise and then its long-term decline.

📖 **Robert K. Massie, *Peter the Great: His Life and World* (1980)** — A fascinating character study, this lengthy book that can be used in sections. Also recommended is the outstanding miniseries based on the book.

📖 **Derek McKay and H.M. Scott, *The Rise of the Great Powers, 1648–1815* (1983)** — A detailed account of how and why the balance of power shifted during this period; useful for research on specific nations.

📺 *Cromwell* (1970) — A fast-paced film portrayal of the English Civil War.

💻 **http://en.chateauversailles.fr/** — The official site of the Versailles Palace (now a national museum).

💻 **http://www.biography.com/people/louis-xiv-9386885/videos/louis-xiv-full-episode-2073406805** — A helpful film biography of Louis XIV.

💻 **https://sourcebooks.fordham.edu/islam/islamsbook.asp** — The Islamic Internet History Sourcebook provides primary sources on a range of topics, including the decline of the Ottoman Empire during this era.

💻 **"What causes economic bubbles?" https://www.youtube.com/watch?v=I5ZR0jMlxX0** — A brief TED-Ed video by Prateek Singh connecting the Dutch Tulipmania speculation to contemporary financial crashes.

CHAPTER TEST

Multiple-Choice Questions

Questions 1–4 are based on the passages below.

Source 1

"[W]ith all humble and due respect to your Majesty our Sovereign Lord and Head...we most truly avouch,

First, That our privileges and liberties are our right and due inheritance, no less than our very lands and goods.

Secondly, That they cannot be withheld from us, denied, or impaired, but with apparent wrong to the whole state of the realm. ...

Fourthly, We avouch also, That our House is a Court of Record, and so ever esteemed."

Form of Apology and Satisfaction, statement of Parliament to James I, 1604

Source 2

"The state of Monarchy is the supremest thing upon earth; for kings are not only God's lieutenants upon earth and sit upon God's throne, but even by God himself they are called gods. There be three principal similitudes that illustrate the state of Monarchy: one taken out of the word of God and the two other out of the grounds of policy and philosophy. In the Scriptures kings are called gods, and so their power after a certain relation compared to the Divine power."

James I, king of England and Scotland, speech to Parliament, 1610

[handwritten: Divine Rights, butting heads w/ Parliament.]

1. Which of the following trends of the seventeenth century do the passages reflect?
   A. Efforts by monarchs to centralize administration and the opposition this created
   B. Use of scientific principles to justify the sovereignty and power of governments
   C. Continuation of traditional beliefs regarding knowledge and the cosmos
   D. Growth of commerce and establishment of mercantilist policies by states

2. The principles stated in Source 1 would be fulfilled with the:
   A. Commercial Revolution.
   B. Glorious Revolution.
   C. Scientific Revolution.
   D. Protestant Reformation.

3. The state that represented the strongest exception to the political ideals articulated in Source 2 was:
   A. Russia.
   B. France.
   C. Poland.
   D. Spain.

4. Which of the following would have most likely agreed with the sentiments expressed in Source 1 and disagreed with those in Source 2?
   A. John Calvin
   B. Thomas Hobbes
   C. John Locke
   D. Louis XIV

[handwritten annotations: Enlightened bc does not like Divine Right. (Leviathan) we are bad people by nature, we need ruler to keep us out.

would have agreed w/ Lord of Flies.

Thomas Hobbes (English) → Not enlightened bc human. Reacting to Civil War. looking at right. Does not believe in Divine Right) government.

John Locke (English) 1st kind of Enlightened writing after Glorious Revolution → people born as clean slate & we are good by nature. justifying G.R. → ∀ = have liberty & property. (Kings job to protect it) Kings job to]

Questions 5–8 are based on the interpretation below.

"[The year 1648] looks like a sensible starting point because it was in that year that the Peace of Westphalia was concluded, bringing to an end a war that had lasted thirty years and had inflicted more devastation on Europe than any previous conflict. Moreover, it settled two major issues, for the independence of the Dutch Republic from Spain was recognized, and the structure of German-speaking Europe was settled for a century and a half. More important still was what lay behind those two settlements: the recognition that [religious] pluralism had come to stay."

Napoleon goes in and turns 300 → N 60. (does not have 60 identities)

Tim Blanning, British historian, *The Pursuit of Glory: Europe 1648–1815*, 2007

5. Which of the following was a political or diplomatic result of the "religious pluralism" cited in Blanning's analysis?

   A. The Ottoman Empire ceased its westward expansion into the heart of Europe.

   B. Dynastic and state interest replaced faith as the main motive for warfare.

   C. Louis XIV of France felt empowered to revoke the Edict of Nantes.

   D. Britain and France engaged in a European and colonial conflict for dominance.

6. The development that fits most closely with Banning's periodization scheme is the:

   A. dominance of centralized nation-states engaged in competition for territory and resources.

   B. movement of the arts from the Baroque style to commercial and Enlightenment themes.

   C. rise of an economy based on commercial agriculture and new methods of finance and trade.

   D. movement toward empirical and rational explanations for natural phenomena.

7. Which of the following most directly affected the German-speaking settlement that Blanning mentions?

   A. Economic and demographic devastation caused by the Thirty Years' War

   B. Incursion of France under Louis XIV into the policies and structure of the Holy Roman Empire

   C. Rise of enlightened absolutism in several central and eastern European states

   D. Emergence of two rival German powers (Austria and Prussia), each checking the advances of the other

   right?

8. The most serious challenge to the political and diplomatic structure described by Blanning proved to be the:

   A. Industrial Revolution and growth of technology.

   B. decline of Spain as a major European power.

   C. rise of the United States as a world power.

   D. French Revolution and Napoleonic wars.

   after French Revolution Industrialism really begins

   w/ nationalism & liberalism.

   See Chapter 18 for answers and explanations.

philosophes = Montesquieu (after Louis 14th death)
· Nobles trying to regain power
· people upset
· took S.R. & wanted
· Checks & balances
· power needs → to many
· Not absolutist
Voltaire = father of Enlight.
· mostly concerned w/ freedoms of people
· antislavery

replaced by Reason & Man

Austria = Maria Theresa & Son Joseph
France: Ferdinand
France = Henry IV (Edict of Nantes)
Louis Napoleon III
H RE Emperor = Charles 5th

= Melinnick.

Short-Answer Question

Directions: Use the images below to answer the question that follows. Answer all parts of the question. Use complete sentences; an outline or bulleted list is not acceptable. Write your responses on a separate sheet of paper. A sample response and commentary are provided.

Detail of gate to Royal Courtyard, with image of Louis XIV, Chateau of Versailles, France, Europe, 1600s

Ferdinand Bol, Dutch painter, *Governors of the Wine Merchant's Guild*. ca.1659

1. a) Describe one way in which the works of art above reflect a <u>political difference</u> between France and the Netherlands in the seventeenth century.

    b) Describe one way in which the works of art above reflect an <u>economic or a social difference</u> between France and the Netherlands in the seventeenth century.

    c) Explain one way in which art (as depicted above) changed *or* remained the same from the Italian Renaissance.

SAQ Sample Response

a) France and the Dutch could not have been more different in the seventeenth century. France was ruled by the Sun King, Louis XIV, who is portrayed in almost god-like fashion on the gate. In fact, this gate led into his extensive palace at Versailles, where he forced his nobles to participate in seeking his patronage. The Dutch, however, were decentralized and controlled by merchants; this helped spread ideas and promote tolerance, but it also made it hard for the Dutch to fight off their more powerful neighbors, like the French.

b) The French were dominated by the aristocracy, who lorded their privileges and tax exemptions over the peasants. It was a very unequal society during this time. On the other hand, the Netherlands was a commercial republic focused on trade and gaining wealth through trade.

c) Renaissance painters glorified the classics in their works and used perspective to provide a realistic view of their subjects. Louis the "sun king" is shown in a classical style, like the ancient sun-god Apollo. One change in art during this period is shown by the Dutch painting. Rather than grandiose scenes of Jesus (by Michelangelo or Raphael), the Dutch art reflected their prosperous middle-class society, as shown by the figures conducting business at the table.

SAQ Response Analysis

Though the response begins with an unnecessary sentence, the remainder succinctly uses specific content references to address each part of the question. For Part A, the student notes the absolutist monarchy of France, as illustrated by Versailles, and contrasts it with the "decentralized" and "tolerant" Dutch Republic. Even with the point already earned, the response adds an effective analysis of how these respective differences affected warfare and diplomacy. The response earns the second point (Part B) in briefly comparing the aristocratic nature of France with the commercial orientation of the Dutch. Once again, in Part C, the student goes beyond the prompt by providing both a similarity between Renaissance and seventeenth-century art (focus on classics for France) and a difference (middle-class scenes for the Dutch). **Score: 3 points**

CHAPTER 8

The Struggle for Wealth and Empire

The eighteenth century marks a watershed in the history of Europe. Many of the developments of previous centuries—the Scientific Revolution, centralized states, commercial advance—reached their full flower during this period. Hope for change and optimism regarding the future took hold, particularly among the upper classes. At the same time, this period was one of immense contradictions: tradition vs. progress, privilege vs. equality, wealth vs. poverty, elite vs. popular culture. In this chapter, we review the social structure of the Old Regime (on the eve of the French Revolution), recount the continuing advance of commerce, and show how competition over wealth and trade led to a major conflict in two phases that altered the European balance of power.

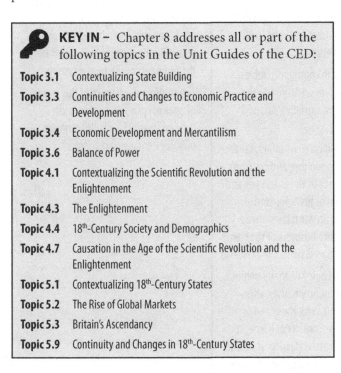

KEY IN – Chapter 8 addresses all or part of the following topics in the Unit Guides of the CED:

Topic 3.1 Contextualizing State Building

Topic 3.3 Continuities and Changes to Economic Practice and Development

Topic 3.4 Economic Development and Mercantilism

Topic 3.6 Balance of Power

Topic 4.1 Contextualizing the Scientific Revolution and the Enlightenment

Topic 4.3 The Enlightenment

Topic 4.4 18th-Century Society and Demographics

Topic 4.7 Causation in the Age of the Scientific Revolution and the Enlightenment

Topic 5.1 Contextualizing 18th-Century States

Topic 5.2 The Rise of Global Markets

Topic 5.3 Britain's Ascendancy

Topic 5.9 Continuity and Changes in 18th-Century States

Social Structure of the Old Regime

Demographic Changes

Prior to the eighteenth century, Europe experienced periods of healthy population growth; inevitably, however, this had been followed by decline. Such declines usually resulted from scarcity of resources, warfare, and disease. This discrepancy between resource needs and resource availability to support an existing population is known as a Malthusian Trap, named for the British political economist, Thomas Malthus (1766–1834). The eighteenth century represented a shift in this trend—though not apparent at the time—in that Europe's population continued a steady and even sig-

nificant growth in following centuries. From 1720, when the growth became evident, until the French Revolution (1789), Europe's population increased from about 120 to 180 million. What factors account for this growth?

- *Diet* – As a result of the Agricultural and Commercial Revolutions (see page 135), Europeans secured access to increased amounts and a <u>wider variety of food supplies</u>. Malnutrition and famine became rarer.

- ***Transportation improvements*** – The building of roads and canals made it easier for national governments to address local shortages of grain and make good on crop failures.

- ***Decline of the plague*** – Despite a few minor outbreaks, the dreaded bubonic plague, which every generation wiped out 10%–15% of the population in certain regions, mysteriously disappeared from the continent.

- *Weather* – Europe's **Little Ice Age** was coming to an end, especially after 1750, which meant a longer growing season and more reliable crops.

- *Medical improvements* – Though Edward Jenner introduced the **smallpox inoculation** in the eighteenth century, medical improvements actually played only a minor role in the population increase. Hospitals, medical training, and the understanding of disease remained woeful.

All of Europe took part in the population growth, but the increase tended to be more gradual in eastern than western Europe, except for Russia, which surpassed France as the most populous European nation around 1780. Urban areas grew the fastest, often straining their still-primitive infrastructure of roads, housing, waste removal, and charitable relief.

THEME MUSIC

An oft-forgotten part of the SCD theme (but also involving TSI) is the so-called "vital revolution," the demographic shift to a society with a stable balance of births and deaths, based on improvements in medicine and hygiene that extend life expectancy and limit infant/child mortality. As you consult this section, consider how the eighteenth century laid the foundations for this trend.

SKILL SET

Over the course of the eighteenth century, economic developments effected changes in the social structure, setting the stage for the French and Industrial Revolutions. As you read through this section, consider the Changes and Continuities Over Time that mark a discrepancy between the traditions of the Old Regime (Three Estates) and those of a more dynamic class structure, linked to the growth of a money economy.

The Class System

In the eighteenth century, European society continued to be divided into estates, or legally defined classes, which determined one's status. Though change was evident with the increasing importance placed on wealth, most nations continued to grant privilege for those who claimed hereditary descent from noble blood. Wealthy merchants and cash-strapped nobles often realized the benefit of blending families, fulfilling the twin purpose of raising the status of the merchants while infusing wealth into a threadbare aristocratic line. The chart below provides you with a snapshot of the class system in the eighteenth century. Keep in mind that this data represents a baseline for comparison's sake to evaluate the social impact of the French Revolution, which began in 1789.

Class	Characteristics	Status/Standard of Living	Developments/Assessment
Nobility	• Lived primarily off of their estates, which varied considerably in size • Pursued mercantile ventures to provide wealth for their ostentatious lifestyles • To be viewed as seeking wealth was considered a characteristic of the "vulgar bourgeoisie" • Often monopolized positions in the military as well as government and judicial offices • Often had more in common with those of the same class in other nations than they did with peasants in their homelands • Often received a classical education, spoke French (the language of philosophy and culture in the eighteenth century), and if male, ventured on a grand tour • A rite of passage, a grand tour allowed male aristocrats to experience European art, ideas, as well as gambling and **prostitution**	• Wealth varied among nobles; it was common for the middle class to exceed the lowliest nobles in means. • Noble status was defined by a set of legal and social privileges—the right to hunt, to be tried in special courts, to hold office, and to claim exemptions from taxes. • Aristocrats enjoyed Europe's best diets, with plenty of meat and wine, fresh fruits, and sweets/nuts. • With advances in commerce, nobles prided themselves on acquiring the newest fashions, carriages, art, and luxury items. • In England, to keep lands intact, families practiced primogeniture and entail, or granting all lands to the eldest son and prohibiting him or his heirs from ever breaking them up. Such laws forced younger sons into business or the clergy and became a hated symbol of privilege. • In imitation of Louis XIV, many nobles built gracious country houses, especially in England. With the grandeur of a palace and the comfort of home, such residences expressed classical style and the need for increased **privacy**. Servants now often lived in separate wings, green spaces established distance between nobles and commoners, and rooms divided public from private functions.	• Aristocrats of the eighteenth century experienced a revival of power following the great age of absolutism. • Remarkably adaptable, nobles used investments and strategic marriages with merchants to meld their noble status with new wealth. • To support a more luxurious lifestyle, nobles tried to wring out of the peasantry whatever taxes, fees, dues, and obligations could be justified from the remnants of the feudal system. • The continued existence of this system of unequal privileges came under increasing attack by Enlightenment philosophes (see next chapter).

Class	Characteristics	Status/Standard of Living	Developments/Assessment
Peasants	• The great majority of Europeans (about 80%-85%) continued to work the land as either peasants or **serfs**. • **Free peasants**, who lived primarily in western and some parts of central Europe, often owned their own land or had the right to work the land of a lord. • **Villages** governed the lives of peasants. Decisions regarding agriculture, local disputes, public order, and religion were made by village leaders according to customs and the needs of the community.	• Standards of living for peasants varied significantly, depending on the degree of freedoms, soil/climate conditions, and strength of the nobility. • Those living east of the Elbe River or in southern Italy and the Iberian peninsula often faced more difficult burdens. • Nobles in eastern Europe and Russia were larger in number and exercised greater power over their peasants and serfs. • Peasant diet was simple and consisted primarily of black breads (which were high in nutrients), gruels, and the occasional meat. New crops such as potatoes and corn provided additional nutrition. Since water was often of unreliable quality, peasants drank diluted beer and wine. • Despite improvements in diet and transportation, peasants still fell prey to famines and diseases (because of greater susceptibility due to malnutrition).	• In some ways, little changed in peasant life from the sixteenth to eighteenth centuries—nobles still held sway, customs dictated everyday life, and fate seemed to rule one's destiny. At the same time, changes were evident. • Peasant life was marginally more secure because of improved diet and better weather. • Discontent over a lingering feudal system often sparked revolts. The most famous of these was the Pugachev Revolt in the 1770s in Russia, the largest peasant uprising in European history. Eventually the revolt was crushed and its leaders executed, but the incident underscored the growing dissatisfaction with the unequal class system.
Towns-people/ Bour-geoisie	• Towns attracted both people and capital. • Cities produced wealth through manufacture and trade. • The middle class often owned land in the countryside, living off rents and dues. • Peasants resented the parasitical role of the towns, which seemed to absorb the wealth of the countryside but provided nothing in return.	• Cities technically existed outside the feudal structure and jealously guarded their liberties. • Standards of living varied widely between the **merchant oligarchs** who dominated political and social life, and the petty bourgeoisie of artisans and shopkeepers, down to the occasional laborers, beggars, and prostitutes. • Wealthy merchants and entrepreneurs imitated the tastes and styles of the nobility, often intermarrying with them or gaining noble status through purchase of an office. • As commerce expanded, cities grew in size and eventually became overwhelmed with the problems of **poverty** and **crime**. Charitable institutions still existed to address needs, but attitudes hardened against professional beggars. Many nations passed laws to house the poor in hospitals or workhouses.	• Cities in the eighteenth century paled in comparison with today's teeming industrial metropolises. Europe's largest city was London with around 1 million people. Many towns had only 10,000 to 50,000 inhabitants. • Towns played an important economic and cultural role, attracting migrants from the countryside, capital from investors, and ideas from all over Europe. • Cities came to realize the inadequacy of their infrastructure of streets, houses, and waste removal in the face of a growing population. • Belief in a "moral economy" led city-dwellers to demand fair prices for bread and grains. • Monarchs tapped into the wealth of towns, especially in western Europe, through taxation and regulation. • To avoid bread riots, governments also stored grain to provide reasonable prices.

Family Life and Child-Rearing

The eighteenth-century European family remained predominantly **nuclear**, with the exception of parts of eastern Europe where the tax system promoted extended families living under one roof. Average ages at first marriage in Europe remained high compared with other civilizations in the eighteenth century—often mid- to late 20s for both men and women—known as the **European marriage pattern**. Couples delayed wedlock until they were able to support themselves economically and provide for children.

Families generally labored together as an economic unit. In agricultural settings, tasks tended to divide based on gender, with men involved in heavier work such as plowing, while women assisted with harvesting, gathering hay, and preparing food. Children were expected to contribute productive labor at an early age. In towns, boys were apprenticed to a local shop or filled any job that augmented the family income. Young women often found themselves in domestic settings as servants and maids, their goal being to earn a sufficient dowry to guarantee a favorable marriage partner. Theoretically, servants were to be treated as members of the family, with the heads of the household responsible for their well-being and moral upbringing. In fact, young women often found themselves subject to verbal abuse and the sexual advances of male family members.

Strong community controls in early modern Europe had ensured that couples avoided having children out of wedlock. As long as the couple was married prior to the birth of the child, social stigma did not attach to premarital sex. However, between 1750 and 1850 a rapid increase of **illegitimacy** occurred. It is unclear what caused this trend. One explanation is that the new opportunities provided by **cottage industry**—making money at home by finishing products—allowed couples to earn income without access to land or regular employment. Additionally, small children could contribute to the family income quickly as part of this system. Furthermore, migration to cities tended to disrupt traditional patterns of arranged marriages and enforcement of marriage promises by men.

The unfortunate consequences of the out-of-wedlock births were the related problems of infanticide and child abandonment. Though Europeans used traditional **birth control** methods to limit population, these techniques proved unreliable (e.g., withdrawal method) and dangerous, as in the case of abortion. Unwanted children were often "accidentally" smothered in bed during the night. Some nations even outlawed the common practice of parents and children sharing a bed to discourage these actions. Given the extremes of poverty and inequality that existed in eighteenth-century cities, it was not surprising that young women felt driven to infanticide. An illustration of this sad practice occurred when the city of Rennes, France opened a storm drain in 1721 only to find the skeletons of 80 infants within. Rather than the extreme measure of infanticide, many couples or mothers abandoned their children on the steps of a church or hospital. Wealthy philanthropists and Catholic religious orders established foundling homes to care for this burgeoning population. However, such homes were often overwhelmed, and the majority of the children under their care died before reaching maturity.

Traditionally, children were viewed as sinful "sprigs of Adam," and parents were warned that "to spare the rod was to spoil the child." The modern expression "rule of thumb," in fact, derives from the limitation on the width of a stick with which a husband was allowed to reprove both children and wife. Children were tightly swaddled to restrict their natural impulsive movements, as parents worked to instill discipline from the earliest ages. Upper-class women relied on wet nurses to provide nutrition for their children, which often meant they went undernourished or neglected.

Such views of children began to change slowly in the eighteenth century. A result of the ideas of John Locke and the educational writings of Jean-Jacques Rousseau (see next chapter), new attitudes began to stress the view of children as innocent creatures who needed tender love and guidance through progressive stages of development. Rousseau and others denounced the practices of wet-nursing and swaddling. Children, they argued, should be insulated from the adult world of vulgarity and cruelty. Among the upper classes, parents began to provide their children with age-appropriate clothing, reading materials, and games. Books and toys were designed to stimulate children's interest and moral development. Simplified scientific ideas found their way into books like Tom Telescope's *Newtonian System of Philosophy*, probably written by John Newbery (1713–1767). Newbery, also famous for *The Pretty Little Pocket Book*, richly illustrated his books to appeal to children's eyes. Along with the jigsaw puzzle, parents lavished children with dolls, *camera obscuras* (a simple machine for projecting images), and tops. New family practices were also reflected in more government attention being given to primary education (see Chapter 9).

> **SKILL SET**
>
> As practice for Argumentation and Claims in Evidence and Sources, consider the following prompt as you read through this section: Evaluate the extent to which child-rearing attitudes and practices changed over the course of the eighteenth century.

The Dynamic Economy of the Eighteenth Century

At the center of the significant social, cultural, and intellectual developments occurring in eighteenth-century Europe stood an expanding and changing economy. More than ever, Europe became enmeshed in a global system of trade; at the

---

[1] Isser Woloch, *Eighteenth-Century Europe: Tradition and Progress*, 1715–1789 (New York: Norton, 1982), p. 162.

same time, the continent reaped the fruits of incremental advances in manufacturing and agriculture. Ultimately, the national pursuit of wealth and empire fueled a series of mid-century wars that altered the European balance of power and set the stage for the French Revolution.

Cottage Industry

For centuries, European manufacturing had taken place in towns under the auspices of the guilds. During the eighteenth century, the system of **cottage industry** expanded, whereby a merchant capitalist paid wages to rural families to finish raw materials. Due to its lack of internal tariffs and weak guild structure, England experienced the most rapid expansion of this **putting-out system**. Though the British Isles later gained the reputation for industrial ingenuity, their manufactures in 1750 were easily surpassed by several other nations. However, England could boast an expanding base of textile production, one of the most basic consumer goods. The many and varied steps of textile production lent themselves to the decentralized nature of cottage industry. Entrepreneurial expansion of manufacturing in the countryside allowed merchants to reinvest profits from trade and later provided sufficient capital for investment in large-scale industrial enterprises. In addition, cottage industry provided rural families the opportunity to supplement a livelihood often threatened by changes in the nature of agriculture.

The Agricultural Revolution

An inefficient agricultural system arrested European population growth. The open three-field system wasted a large proportion of useful land, and primitive techniques offered little margin for error, often plunging regions into famine, as had happened in the 1690s. Much of this insecurity was relieved by the **Agricultural Revolution** of the eighteenth century. The movement began in the Netherlands and England and featured the introduction of new crops and the application of new techniques. Some have labelled these changes in crop and livestock raising "scientific agriculture."

To combat the waste of allowing fields to lie fallow, agricultural reformers like Charles "Turnip" Townsend (1674–1738) supported the use of nitrogen-replenishing crops such as turnips, clover, and alfalfa. Such fodder crops also fed livestock, whose manure was in turn used to further increase the output of fields. One of the more important crops for human use proved to be the potato. Easy to grow, rich in vitamins, and versatile, the crop became a staple of the peasant diet in Ireland, Prussia, and Russia. A large family could subsist on as little as an acre of potatoes.

Increasing production also involved solutions as simple as clearing more land. Using new drainage techniques, such as terracing, the Dutch and English were able to reclaim swamps and bogs. Jethro Tull (1674–1741), another reformer concerned about increasing yields, advocated soil aeration through use of the hoe and by inventing the seed drill, which pushed the seed safely beneath the soil. Tull thus employed Enlightenment reason and empirical study in service of practical solutions. Improvements in livestock, through selective breeding, served as a natural next step. The English government granted awards to those who could produce the fattest and meatiest cattle, providing additional meat for the average person's diet.

Efficiency often requires doing things in a big way, or what is known as economies of scale. In agriculture, this meant that the traditional open-field system of scattered strips of land had to be abandoned. This process had already been underway in England since the sixteenth century with enclosure. Advances in agricultural techniques in the eighteenth century provided an additional spur, as Parliament passed enclosure acts, which allowed wealthy landowners to buy up common land and enclose it within large manors. This destruction of the commons produced an unequal system of landholding in England, with a few large landholders at the top, some independent yeoman and enterprising tenant farmers in the middle, and a mass of landless laborers on the bottom. For this last group, the loss of land rendered them dependent on earning wages, driving them into the newly expanding and industrializing cities as an unskilled labor force.

> ### THEME MUSIC
> The Agricultural Revolution highlights an overarching question for the ECD and TSI themes—how technological advances can benefit overall wealth and those who patronize the new processes (e.g., the gentry), yet at the same time create poverty and inequality for others (e.g., smallholders and peasants in traditional settings).

The Commercial Revolution, Phase II

While the Dutch remained important traders, they had been surpassed by the French and the English, both of whose commerce ballooned in the eighteenth century. Several nations established East India companies, pooling the resources of numerous investors and which exploited the growing European taste for a range of new consumer goods. Triangular trade facilitated the exchange of goods between the continents of Europe, Africa, and the Americas in an Atlantic economy that relied on human trafficking in enslaved persons. Europe's sweet tooth caused untold suffering for Africans forced to work in the horrifying conditions of Caribbean sugar plantation "factories."

Europeans continued to demand spices from the East—cinnamon, nutmeg, cloves, pepper, saffron. The new beverages of coffee and tea appeared on the European menu, making the East Indies, India, and Ceylon focal points for colonial interest, and spawning new venues for conversation (tea- and coffee-houses). These colonial areas were also known for the production of fine cloth and rugs. Light, brightly colored silks, calicoes, muslins, and chintzes poured into the homes of Europe's upper classes, as signs of status and cosmopolitanism. Goods from overseas, as well as porcelain and cloth now produced within Europe, promoted a **consumer revolution** in tastes, as the well-to-do stocked their drawing rooms, boudoirs, and eating areas with genteel finery.

The biggest money-maker of all was <u>sugar</u>. Small sugar islands in the Caribbean easily outpaced the entire North American mainland in value to the British Empire. Throughout the eighteenth century, sugar production skyrocketed. As sugar increased, so did slavery. Over 600,000 enslaved persons were brought from Africa to the island of Jamaica alone from 1700 to 1786. Originally dominated by the Portuguese then the Dutch, the **slave trade** fell into the orbit of English trading interests after the War of Spanish Succession. Because much of the profit from the slave trade and sugar went directly to England's industrial expansion, it would be fair to conclude that British capitalism resulted in part from the enslavement of Africans. What's more, because profits were so easy to come by on these sugar islands, plantation owners inhumanely treated their enslaved persons, causing one of the highest mortality rates in the world.

Global trade produced a myriad of important results. Let's focus on three for right now:

- The profits from commerce promoted the development of a **market economy** based on private capital. Governments became much more dependent on entrepreneurs as a source of taxation and to underwrite state borrowing of funds, through banks and other credit institutions.

- As noted above, the accumulation of wealth by the **middle class (bourgeoisie)** tended to facilitate their merging with the aristocracy, as both gained from intermarriage.

- The potential for great riches led to an intensification of **commercial rivalries**, resulting in war. Conflict over territory in Europe merged with overseas competition for colonies and markets, producing the first world wars in history.

Diplomacy and War

Commercial competition invariably led to war in the eighteenth century. Soon after the Peace of Utrecht (1713–1714), one old rivalry (**Britain vs. France**) reasserted itself while another arose between Prussia and Austria over predominance in German affairs. These two rivalries stood at the center of diplomacy and war in the middle of the century. Spain experienced new life under the Bourbon monarchy of Philip V (r. 1700–1749), and the Netherlands remained important financially, though

---

SKILL SET

Given Great Britain's and France's rivalry for power between 1689–1815 on the European continent and overseas, consider setting up a chart that illustrates the similarities and differences in their respective economic, political, and social systems during this era (COMP and MAC).

---

neither nation was able to exert influence equivalent to that enjoyed before 1715. In the east, Russia demonstrated that its modernization under Peter the Great made it a reckoning force within the system of European diplomacy.

Before moving on to the wars, we take a quick snapshot of Britain and France after 1715. For purposes of the AP exam, this review is helpful in the case of Britain to note how that nation developed a unique constitutional system following the Glorious Revolution, and in the case of France, to lay the foundations for the long-term causes of the French Revolution.

France—Louis XV and the Old Regime

When Louis XV (r. 1715–1774), great-grandson of Louis XIV, ascended to the throne in 1715, he was only 5 years old. For decades, France was ruled by a regency, which was forced to grant concessions to the various *parlements* that Louis XIV had succeeded in taming, representing a theme of French politics leading up to the fateful year of 1789—the emerging political conflict between a supposedly absolutist monarchy and a newly assertive nobility. Making matters worse was the attitude and habits of Louis XV. The king proved lazy and rather than governance preferred the hunt and company of his mistresses, one of whom, Madame de Pompadour, was believed to exercise undue influence in the affairs of government. Such rumors, combined with Louis's weak rule, undermined support for the monarchy.

The landed and commercial classes (they were not always separate) increased their power in France between 1715 and 1789. The government's need to fund the debt left over from its many wars along with the constant desire of investors to profit from the Commercial Revolution led to an unintended crisis in public finance. The monarchy chartered the Mississippi Company (operating in the Americas) in the hopes that its issuance of stocks would underwrite the government's debt, reform the tax system, and make money for its investors. However, speculation in the company stock led to a speculative bubble in 1720, which bankrupted thousands and forced the state to repudiate its debts. Unlike England, France never developed the notion of a public debt funded by banks—the debt was considered the king's *personal* debt—and as a result lagged behind in the development of credit institutions and the ability to borrow money. Not surprisingly, the issues that forced the French monarchy to concede limits on its theoretically absolutist powers in 1789 were government debt and taxation.

Great Britain—the "King in Parliament" and Prime Minister

Following the Glorious Revolution in 1688, Britain developed a unique form of government known as the "king in parliament." In short, English monarchs continued to play an important political role, but worked through Parliament and a Prime Minister to pass legislation and govern. After the last Stuart monarch, Queen Anne (r. 1701–1714), died without an heir, England turned to a related German dynasty—the Hanoverians. Many Tories would have preferred to recall the son (James III) of the last Stuart monarch, who attempted to lead an uprising in 1715 by landing an army on Scotland, as did his son in 1745. However, the Whig influence in government could not countenance another Catholic monarchy, and each of the potential Stuart threats was crushed with wide public support. So despite the unpopularity of the first Hanoverian, George I (r. 1714–1727), who did not speak English, the dynasty was able to establish a functioning government system by relying on a prime minister and the cabinet system.

A major reason for Britain's commercial success in the eighteenth century involved the close relationship between government finance and private enterprise. The Bank of England issued stock to finance government debt and also allowed investors to draw on a larger amount of capital than in other nations. As in France, this system almost led to disaster in 1720 when speculation in the South Sea Company led to a financial crash and major losses for its investors. Unlike France, Britain was able to salvage and further develop its system of public finance.

The man largely responsible for the development of Britain's cabinet system of government was Robert Walpole (tenure, 1721–1743), also considered the first prime minister. Walpole appointed ministers to head up government agencies who also served in the Parliament. Moreover, Walpole carefully selected commercially-oriented Whigs personally loyal to him, creating the notion of the cabinet as a group bound to each other with a common goal. By carefully managing his parliamentary majority through issuance of government stocks, promises of patronage, and the like, Walpole was able to steer legislation through the House of Commons (the more important of the two houses of Parliament). Throughout his tenure, Walpole worked diligently to advance Britain's commercial interests abroad while avoiding war (to keep taxes down), a task he was largely able to accomplish.

Eighteenth-Century Warfare

War in the eighteenth century was waged between highly trained and professional armies for specific strategic objectives. Soldiers were drawn from the underclass and less productive groups in society, perhaps "recruited" after a drunken night in a tavern. Their aristocratic army officers controlled them through harsh discipline. Because conflict proved less destructive to civilians and land than the religious wars of an earlier age, states entered into it more lightly and also withdrew from it more quickly.

> **THEME MUSIC**
>
> As you read this section, keep in mind the strong connection between the SOP and ECD themes. The pursuit of commerce and development of colonies embroiled nations in conflict, stimulated the growth of military states, and altered the balance of power.

Questions of war relied on calculation and strategy. Armies were expensive to maintain, train, and supply, so generals were reluctant to risk them carelessly in battle, often making warfare a game of movement and of securing supply lines. Infantry played the major role in war, with their inaccurate smoothbore muskets and bright uniforms imparting a parade-ground atmosphere to battles. Nonetheless, eighteenth-century warfare was destructive and disruptive; it only seems less so in comparison with the conflagrations of the twentieth century.

The War of Austrian Succession, 1740–1748

The War of Austrian Succession began with a cynical attack by Frederick II "the Great" (r. 1740–1786), king of Prussia, on Austria in defiance of the Pragmatic Sanction. Like a swarm of vultures, other nations (Bavaria, Saxony, Spain) rushed in to claim territorial prizes from the threatened empire. In continuance of their longtime opposition to the Habsburgs, the French joined the assault in alliance with Prussia. To prevent the dismemberment of Austria and maintain the balance of power on the continent, Britain joined the fray on the side of the new Habsburg ruler, Maria Theresa (r. 1740–1780). In this way, the two primary rivalries in European politics merged into a complex conflict, which would be fought in two phases (see Seven Years' War below).

Frederick the Great experienced a difficult youth. More interested in learning French and playing the flute than war, Frederick often feuded with his stern father, Frederick William I (see Chapter 6) who intended to break his son. The young Frederick attempted to escape the kingdom with a friend, whom Frederick William I had executed right before his son's eyes to teach him a harsh lesson. All of Europe expected the new king to drive Prussia into the ground in vengeance against his father. On the contrary, Frederick proved to be one the greatest rulers in German history and a true military genius. The primary target of Frederick's aggression was the resource-rich province of Silesia, which he was able to win and hold until the end of the conflict.

Frederick was almost equally matched by Maria Theresa. In an act of political theater, Maria Theresa held aloft her newborn son (the future Joseph II) before the Hungarian nobles in 1741 to appeal for their support, which they gave in a spasm of chivalric fervor. Though Maria eventually lost Silesia, she did well to hold on to most of her other possessions by treaty (1748), one that reflected an Anglo-French agreement and in which the Habsburg ruler had little say.

Britain and France waged war in several theaters in pursuit of their commercial and colonial objectives. Each side made advances against the other. The British took France's North American fortress and squeezed the Caribbean, while the French grabbed ports in India and held Belgium (long a concern of the British) after a victory in 1745. The antagonists were thus content to return to the situation as it had existed before the war, with the British happy to cede Silesia to Frederick in order to keep Belgium under Austrian rather than French control. Though the map had changed little beyond Silesia, the War of Austrian Succession had highlighted two issues: (1) France sat in an unfavorable strategic position hamstrung between major continental commitments with its large army and a growing commercial empire in need of naval defense, and (2) Austria and Prussia now uneasily co-existed as two relatively even powers in Germany, with the latter immensely enhanced by its capture of Silesia, which had doubled its population to 6 million and strengthened its economic base. Maria Theresa was just as determined to regain the territory.

The Reforms of Maria Theresa and Diplomatic Revolution of 1756

Maria Theresa embarked on a wide-ranging series of reforms after 1748. To reduce inefficiency, Maria Theresa centralized the collection of taxes and combined the chancelleries (administrative offices) of the various territories of her empire. The army was tripled in size, while a military academy and engineering school were also founded. Later in her reign, Maria Theresa promoted primary education in the interests of economic productivity, promoted **smallpox inoculation**, outlawed torture and capital punishment, and eased the burdens of serfdom. Though many of these reforms benefited her subjects, the ruler's primary goal was to strengthen the state so as to recapture Silesia.

In 1756, the great Austrian diplomat and advisor to Maria Theresa, Count von Kaunitz (1711–1794), engineered one of diplomacy's greatest coups. Von Kaunitz convinced France to give up its traditional opposition to the Habsburgs and enter an alliance against Prussia, an alliance that Russia also joined. This Diplomatic Revolution of 1756 forced Britain onto the side of Prussia to prevent another continental disruption to the balance of power (and a threat to Hanover, ancestral home to Britain's monarchy) and helped reignite the worldwide colonial conflict between France and Great Britain. Once again, despite the switch in alliances, the two key rivalries had merged, this time to produce a true world war with profound consequences for three continents.

> **EXAMPLE BASE**
>
> Don't be intimidated by the details in this section. If it helps, consider a focus question: Evaluate the success of states in managing their economic and political resources in pursuit of power and in addressing both internal problems and external challenges.

The Seven Years' War, 1756–1763

The Seven Years' War stands as Frederick II's darkest and finest hour. Though outnumbered by his enemies almost 10 to 1, Frederick fought brilliantly, even when his capital Berlin was burned to the ground and all seemed lost. Britain provided primarily financial support in order to concentrate its energies on the colonial conflict with France. Frederick was aided by the disorganization of his opponents, who never seemed able to coordinate their attacks, and the French lack of enthusiasm for their new Austrian alliance. Despite his sometimes desperate situation and aging seemingly 20 years in 7 years' time, Frederick once again was able to hold onto Silesia by treaty (1763).

Fighting between France and Great Britain proved more decisive. Under the brilliant leadership of William Pitt the Elder (1708–1778), Britain won victories on land and sea in North America, the Caribbean, and in India. France found itself again depleted by fighting major wars on the continent of Europe *and* overseas. France and Britain both used their East India companies to exploit the decaying Mogul Empire in India, enlisting local rulers and warlords in pursuit of their interests. However, with its superior naval forces, Britain emerged victorious on balance, a fact that was reflected in the peace treaty.

By the Treaty of Paris (1763), Great Britain secured sole access to North America east of the Mississippi River and gained the dominant position in India, which became the "crown jewel of the British Empire." France was, however, able to win back its profitable sugar islands in the Caribbean. Though Britain clearly came out the dominant maritime power, French commerce continued to grow after 1763 and may have even outpaced Britain's. The Treaty of Paris set the stage for major developments on three continents. In North America (where the conflict was called the French and Indian War), British colonists were now free of the perennial French threat, while the British were determined to make them pay for the costs of empire, a difference in outlook leading directly to the American Revolution. For Europe, the Seven Years' War confirmed the dualism in Germany of Austria and Prussia, but more importantly, set the stage for the French Revolution by increasing the debt of and criticism against the French monarchy. On the Indian subcontinent, Britain oversaw the further dissolution of the Mogul Empire and established a strong colonial presence that would change both civilizations.

Additional Resources

📖 **M.S. Anderson**, *Europe in the Eighteenth Century, 1715–1783*, **3rd ed. (1987)** — Provides a useful overview of political developments in each country.

📖 **Jeremy Black**, *The Cambridge Illustrated Atlas of Warfare: Renaissance to Revolution, 1492–1792* (1996) — For those students interested in the details of warfare, this book offers excellent maps, concise text, and worldwide coverage.

📖 **Olwen Hufton**, *The Prospect Before Her: A History of Women in Western Europe, 1500–1800* (1996) — A strong history of women, especially the chapters on the eighteenth century.

📖 Steven Mintz, *Sweetness and Power: The Place of Sugar in Modern History* (1985) — A thorough analysis for those interested in Europe's sweet tooth.

📖 Isser Woloch, *Eighteenth-Century Europe: Tradition and Progress, 1715–1798* (1982) — A helpful survey in the *Norton History of Modern Europe* series that skillfully combines political and social history.

💻 https://en.wikipedia.org/wiki/Tulip_mania — Provides a summary of the psychology and financial practices that can produce speculative bubbles, in this case the tulip.

💻 http://www.slavevoyages.org/

💻 http://slaveryimages.org/

💻 https://brycchancarey.com/index.htm — These three sites offer different types of documents and perspectives on slavery and the slave trade.

💻 http://www.representingchildhood.pitt.edu/eighteencent_child.htm — A collection of brief yet scholarly essays on the history of childhood.

CHAPTER TEST

Multiple-Choice Questions

Questions 1–3 are based on the map below.

The Middle Passage

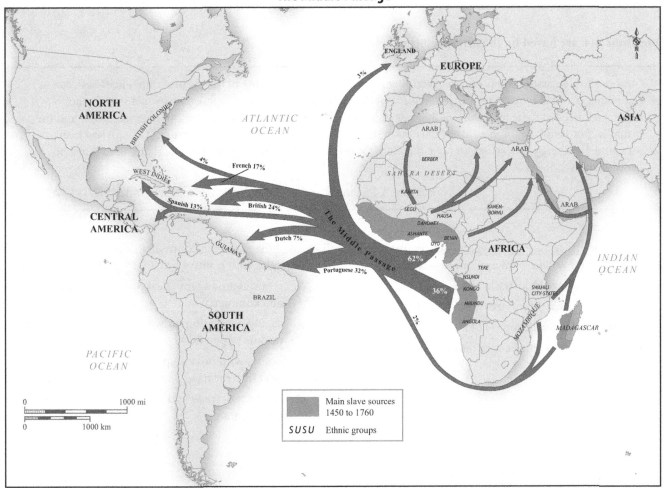

1. All of the following resulted from the trends depicted on the map above during the seventeenth and eighteenth centuries EXCEPT:

   A. European states pursued mercantilist economic policies to exploit colonial resources.

   B. European consumers gained wider access to new goods and venues for purchasing them.

   C. Russia rose as a major power in eastern Europe, gaining territory at the expense of its neighbors.

   D. Colonial rivalries increased among Britain, France, the Netherlands, and Spain.

2. The map above could be used most effectively to support which of the following conclusions?

   A. "European colonial powers employed slave labor in manning their armies and navies."

   B. "European powers effectively controlled the interior of Africa in a race for resources and territory."

   C. "Revolutionary movements in the Americas arose to combat slavery and oppose colonialism."

   D. "European global economic power rested upon a system of transatlantic trade, including slavery."

3. Which of the following represents the most significant change after about 1750 in the situation depicted in the map?

   A. France replaced Britain as the dominant colonial power in the Americas.

   B. Enlightenment anti-slavery movements attacked the slave trade and slavery.

   C. Africa successfully resisted further European incursions into its territory.

   D. The United States replaced Europe as the major colonial power in the Americas.

Questions 4–6 are based on the interpretation below.

> "Across all these assumptions ran an overriding mental conservatism. One of the deepest differences between our own age and the *ancien régime* [old regime] is the pervading conviction of those times that it was innovation which needed to be justified, not the past. A huge inertia generated by usage, tradition, prescription and the brutal fact of simple ignorance, lay heavily upon the institutions of the eighteenth century. As there had been for centuries, there was a self-evident justification for the ways of our fathers, for the forms and laws they had evolved and set down."
>
> John Roberts, British historian, *Revolution and Improvement: The Western World, 1775–1847*, 1976

4. The economic feature of the eighteenth century that best supports Roberts's interpretation was the:

   A. use of cottage industry in rural areas.

   B. reliance on serfdom in eastern Europe.

   C. domination by Europe of global trade.

   D. adoption of scientific agriculture.

5. All of the following contradict Roberts's depiction of the eighteenth century EXCEPT:

   A. rivalries among the great powers over territory and commerce.

   B. steady population growth due to inoculation and decline of plague.

   C. homes with private space and resources dedicated to child-rearing.

   D. freedom of trade and labor from corporate entities and the state.

6. The strongest continuity in the nineteenth century with Roberts's portrayal of the old regime would be the:

   A. mechanization of textiles and other manufactures.

   B. Concert of Europe and influence of Metternich.

   C. positivist approach to social and economic issues.

   D. influence of the middle-class in social and political life.

Questions 7–9 are based on the passage below.

> "It is older than Aristotle, and will be true, when Hobbes is forgot, that man is a sociable creature, and delights in company. Now, [where] shall a person, wearied with hard study, or the laborious turmoils of a tedious day, repair to refresh himself? Or where can young gentlemen, or shop-keepers, more innocently and advantageously spend an hour or two in the evening, than at a coffee-house?....[W]here is there a better library for that study, generally, than here, amongst such a variety of humors, all expressing themselves on divers[e] subjects, according to their respective abilities?
>
> In brief, it is undeniable, that, as you have here the most civil, so it is, generally, the most intelligent society; the frequenting whose converse, and observing their discourses and deportment, cannot but civilize our manners, enlarge our understandings, refine our language, teach us a generous confidence and handsome mode of address…"
>
> "Coffeehouses Vindicated," anonymous pamphlet, England, ca. 1675

7. Which of the following contributed most directly to the rise of the phenomenon described in the passage?

   A. Political challenges to absolutism

   B. The expansion of commerce

   C. Increase in population

   D. Scientific explanations of nature

8. The most important result in the seventeenth and eighteenth centuries of the coffeehouse atmosphere described in the pamphlet was:

   A. the use of government censorship to control ideas.

   B. widespread discussion of the interaction with non-European cultures.

   C. the spread of the New Science and Enlightenment ideas.

   D. the expansion of new methods of finance and trade.

9. All of the following statements are true, but which is best supported by the pamphlet?

   A. "Expansion of overseas commerce and the trade in new goods created a consumer culture in Europe."

   B. "European governments competed globally for control of resources and influence."

   C. "Civic venues emerged to challenge traditional religious views, resulting in deism and skepticism."

   D. "The arts came to reflect a growing bourgeois and commercial society."

See Chapter 18 for answers and explanations.

Long Essay Question

Directions: Read the prompt below and write your response on a separate sheet of paper. A sample response and commentary are provided below.

Evaluate the most significant difference between the periods 1555–1648 and 1650–1763 in European states' motives for warfare.

(RP: Comparison)

LEQ Sample Response

Europe seems always to be at war. This was true during the period 1555–1648 and also 1650–1763. These wars were about gaining land and also for each nation to prove it was the best. Each period involved plenty of bloodshed, but there were some major differences. In the first period, European states fought mostly over religion, while in the second they fought mostly to get territory and promote nationalism.

The period 1555–1648 was a time of religious wars. One of the biggest was the Thirty Years' War in which Protestants battled Catholics to spread their religions. This war was really complicated and also involved nations switching sides to gain territory and status. For example, France fought on the side of the German Protestants to oppose Spain. Speaking of Spain, they were really committed to supporting their cause of Catholicism, since they used the Inquisition to make sure everyone in their empire was Catholic. The war ended with the Peace of Westphalia, and it meant a type of warring that was more focused on the power of monarchs and their lands.

In the second age from 1650–1763, nations fought primarily to gain an edge over others in trade and land. Britain battled France over many places on the globe, and Russia and Prussia fought over the Baltic region. Since religion was no longer of much importance, states focused on their military and economic power. This is nationalism. Each state wanted to be the best, but the warfare led to many ups and downs in the line-up of countries and their power. For example, Austria declined a lot because of its many lost wars and became more of a weak empire. France really advanced in power because of its strong kings, like Louis XIV.

All of this warfare can be compared to wars in the twentieth century. This century was really deadly, with two world wars and genocide. States became really powerful with dictators, like Stalin and Hitler, who controlled everything their people did based on an ideology like fascism or communism. This meant that they could command them to be even more violent than the armies of either one of the early periods. Warfare has been a big part of Europe's diplomatic actions, but even if it has changed in motive, it has always led to widespread death.

LEQ Response Analysis

This response is written in a straightforward manner, and though lacking sophistication, it earns points on the rubric by connecting evidence with its argument. In the introduction, the response did not provide specific or sufficient background on processes or developments to set up the argument, relying primarily on ahistorical generalizations, costing it the Contextualization point. The Thesis was earned by providing a line of reasoning for its statement of the difference between religious and territorial motives, though the point about nationalism during 1650–1763 is out of place. For Use of Evidence, the response is a mixed bag, providing a good discussion of religious motives in the first body paragraph, but relying on overgeneralizations (Austria's decline, France's strong rulers, "wanted to be the best,") and errors (Russia and Prussia fighting, nationalism playing a role) in the second body paragraph. Because of these issues, the response earned only 1 point for Use of Evidence to make an argument. Finally, the response clearly organizes its evidence around the targeted Reasoning Process (Comparison) and provides sufficient connection to a later time period in the conclusion (world wars) to earn the Complexity point. **Score: 4** (+1 for Thesis, +1 for Use of Evidence, +1 for the Targeted RP (COMP), +1 for Complexity)

CHAPTER 9

The Enlightenment and Dynamic 18th Century

The great philosopher Immanuel Kant wrote of the eighteenth-century Enlightenment: "We live in an age of Enlightenment, but not an enlightened age." Kant considered the eighteenth century a time of significant reform and a questioning of established traditions, optimistically pointing toward progress. At the same time, Kant realized how far Europe still had to go toward the ideals of reason, individualism, and secularism—all principles of the Enlightenment. At the same time, Kant did not fully appreciate how much he and other philosophes diverged from their own lofty principles, especially on questions of equality. The Enlightenment, its principles, and its adherents form the central focus of this chapter, but we will also examine cultural and political manifestations of Enlightenment thought. As an intellectual movement, the Enlightenment ranks as one of the most important you will study this year and a frequent subject of AP questions.

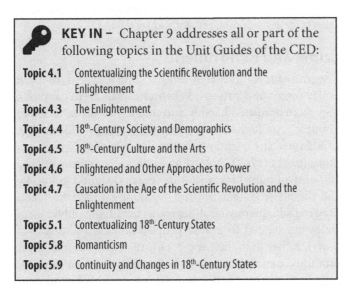

KEY IN − Chapter 9 addresses all or part of the following topics in the Unit Guides of the CED:

Elite and Popular Cultures

Despite differences in station and outlook, peasants and nobles partook of similar cultural experiences in early modern Europe. This changed during the eighteenth-century Enlightenment as elite and popular cultures diverged. Those in the upper classes inhabited a culture of print and ideas, reading the latest novels, periodicals, newspapers, and perhaps philosophical treatises. Congregating in salons, coffeehouses, reading clubs, and libraries, members of the aristocracy and bourgeoisie acquired an appreciation for scientific knowledge and secular learning. Peasants and poor towns-

people, however, moved within an oral culture, with knowledge and stories transmitted through story-telling, legend, or perhaps the symbolic imagery of a religious service. Once again, we are faced with a paradox of the eighteenth century—the Enlightenment gaining a strong cultural foothold, while many if not most Europeans remained relatively untouched by and unaware of it.

The Reading Public

If your life had spanned across eighteenth-century Europe, you would have witnessed a huge increase in the amount of **printed materials** available—newspapers, periodicals, pamphlets, and novels. The phenomenon was both a cause and a result of an increase in the literacy rate, which in turn was supported by improved access to primary education. All classes and groups took part in this increase, though it was strongest among males and the middle classes.

By 1780 most European cities supported publication of at least one daily or weekly newspaper. The phenomenon fed interest and concern regarding public affairs, including government policies, and publishers often catered to specific segments of the population. One of the more notable if short-lived publications was Richard Steele's and Joseph Addison's *Spectator*, which featured articles of public interest and inspired the *Female Spectator*, focusing on domestic topics such as child-rearing and household management. Though books remained expensive, increasing numbers of the upper classes willingly invested resources in their purchase. Popularized scientific accounts, history, and philosophical works all competed for shelf space. These works often reflected a secular focus or took a more critical view of religion. For example, Edward Gibbon's (1737–1794) *Decline and Fall of the Roman Empire*, an immense chronicle of its subject, argued that the adoption of Christianity had sapped the Stoic energy of Rome.

Novels proved to be the biggest sellers. England pioneered the development of these works which featured complex plots, character development, and ultimately, a strong moral message. For example, Samuel Richardson's (1689–1761) *Pamela: or, Virtue Rewarded* recounts the tale of a serving girl who resists the sexual advances of her master, who then comes to understand her worth and eventually proposes marriage to her; thus her chastity is rewarded. Reflecting the eighteenth-century theme of child abandonment, Henry Fielding's *The History of Tom Jones, a Foundling* traces the adventures and ultimate success of the title character, a wily orphan who in traveling around England allows the author to satirize the hypocrisy of the age. Such works illustrated the growth of public sentiment, the belief that open emotional displays equated with sincerity, and that humanitarian impulses elevated society by sustaining reform movements.

Governments did attempt to censor works they deemed threatening to public order or blasphemous to organized religion. Efforts at **censorship** rarely succeeded in the long run, due partly to the decentralized nature of intellectual life in Europe and because states lacked the enthusiasm or manpower to enforce them adequately. To illustrate, the French government at one time or another banned publication of the famous *Encyclopédie* as well as works by Voltaire, yet these works eventually saw the light of day in other nations or the authors went into temporary hiding only to reappear when circumstances had shifted.

Other than the sheer increase in knowledge, why is this increase in reading material important? Two words: **public opinion**. It is hard to imagine the American and French Revolutions occurring without the political energy generated by a reading public which was both informed and concerned about politics.

Education

Even in this age of Enlightenment, education (or lack thereof) reflected social inequality. Secondary schools reinforced the hierarchy of European society and focused on a curriculum of classical languages unlikely to provide practical advantages to an aspiring member of the lower classes. Educational reformers also criticized the stale education of the universities, slow to change in their adherence to Greek and Latin and often ignoring the scientific advances of the previous two centuries. Nonetheless, changes were evident. In Germany, *Realschule* were founded, which focused on practical skills to prepare young men for business. Furthermore, if a modern-minded scholar wished to learn the new science, he could attend one of the following universities: Leiden in the Netherlands, Halle in Germany, or Edinburgh in Scotland.

Art and Music

Though the Baroque style in the arts and music continued well into the eighteenth century, by the 1720s the Rococo style had taken hold, especially in France. Whereas the Baroque expressed power, illusion, and movement—the art of popes and kings—Rococo concentrated on light-hearted and pensive themes of romance and the transitory nature of life. Paintings employed rich creams and golds, subtle curves, and lush settings to portray the graceful material pleasures of the aristocracy.

Nearer the middle of the century, Rococo gave way to another renewal of classical subject matter and motifs. Reflecting the increased attention paid to civic culture in an enlightening age, artists, such as Jacques-Louis David (1748–1825), in their **neo-classical** style drew from stories of ancient Greece and Rome. The David masterpiece *Oath of the Horatii* (1785) recounts the story of three brothers pledging to their father the patriotic sacrifice of their lives. Male figures stand firm and starkly drawn with straight lines and bold colors beneath masculine Doric columns, while emotionally prostrate women await the action in muted colors and passive curves.

With the works of Joseph Haydn (1732–1809) and Wolfgang Amadeus Mozart (1756–1791), we move into the great Age of Classical Music (1750–1820). Composers experimented with full orchestration, writing symphonies of several movements that developed simple themes into complex musical patterns. Operas, like Mozart's *Don Giovanni* or *The Magic Flute*, allowed composers to demonstrate mastery of several artistic forms—drama, music, and set design.

Crime and Punishment

Governments of the eighteenth century lacked modern police forces and prisons. When criminals were captured, they were punished harshly and publicly in order to set an example. An Italian jurist, Cesare Beccaria (1738–1794), condemned the traditional approach in his *On Crimes and Punishments* (1762). According to Beccaria, reason and the certainty of punishment (not its severity) should guide law and the penal system. Torture, breaking on the wheel, and drawing and quartering all served as horrifying public spectacles but tended to arouse people's bloodlust and fear of power, rather than their respect for the law. Beccaria's ideas promoted penal reform and the building of prisons, beginning in the United States, which aimed at rehabilitation of its inmates through structure and discipline. Many enlightened monarchs further reflected humanitarianism by working toward the rational codification of laws to replace the patchwork of local customs and the elimination of torture and even capital punishment (see below).

Medicine

Despite slight improvements, the medical care available to most Europeans remained inadequate and based either on outmoded classical ideas or dubious folk remedies. Life expectancy remained low, even with gradual improvements in urban hygiene and the beginnings of **inoculation**, first developed to address the scourge of smallpox in the 1700s. Most prospective physicians trained at universities that emphasized classical learning and paid little heed to a scientific or clinical approach, an exception being the University of Leiden in the Netherlands, famous as the setting for Rembrandt's paintings of human dissection. To improve standards and training, British physicians formed the first professional group, the Royal College of Physicians, and were followed by surgeons who broke away from barbers to create the Royal College of Surgeons. Professionalization aimed to exclude traditional practitioners, such as midwives and folk healers, as outside the circle of expertise and knowledge of medicine. Though such developments created an improved setting for medical study and practice, the general increase in Europeans' standard of living in this period owed more to improved diet and nutrition than to medicine.

Religious Revival in a Secular Age

Enlightenment philosophes aimed to improve European society through a secular and scientific approach. Many Europeans did not share this goal and adhered to a religious worldview. Strong evidence to counter secularism is offered by several movements of religious revival. **John Wesley**'s (1703–1791) **Methodism** represents the most famous of these movements. Wesley appealed directly to the English lower classes—many of whose lives had been negatively affected by economic changes or alcoholism—with a warm spirituality that emphasized huge open-air meetings highlighted by dramatic stories of conversion. In Germany, Count von Zinzendorf (1700–1760) initiated the Pietist revival within a Lutheran religion that many

> **THEME MUSIC & SKILL SET**
>
> A natural human tendency is to prioritize change over stasis. The Enlightenment—also named the Age of Reason—is one such era. No doubt, secular thinking increased during the eighteenth century, especially among elites. At the same time, religious belief remained strong among the masses; in fact, several revivals of belief occurred in this century, forcing us to balance our understanding of the CID theme and consider Complexity when examining issues of Continuity and Change over Time (CCOT).

perceived as stale and institutional. Revivalism crossed the Atlantic as Wesley's conversion tactics were employed liberally on the American frontier, and German Pietists immigrated to the American colonies to practice their religious faith.

Unlike previous centuries, many enlightened monarchs approached religious matters with skepticism and attempted to create a barrier between private religious belief and public expressions of religion, which were of concern to the state. At the insistence of several governments, the papacy in 1773 banned the Jesuit order, which was perceived as beholden to a foreign power, though it was later reinstated in 1814 following the French Revolution. Furthermore, monarchs began to extend **religious toleration** to minorities. Going furthest in this regard was Joseph II of Austria, whose policies

(Patent of Toleration, 1781 and Edict on Tolerance, 1782) extended tolerance to Protestants and even Jews, allowing the latter to practice their religion freely, though restricting their use of Hebrew and emigration into Austria. The process of emancipation for Jews continued into the French Revolution, allowing them to assimilate more fully into economic and intellectual life. However, it should be noted that Jews continued to be subjected to scorn by Enlightenment thinkers, such as Voltaire, and prejudice by popular opinion.

Popular Culture and Leisure

Literacy increased among all classes in eighteenth-century Europe; however, literate lower class members generally shunned the novels, histories, and treatises of the elites. Many poor townspeople and peasants favored brief, cheaply printed chapbooks, as well as almanacs, both of which carried tales of chivalry and religion, folk wisdom, and information about weather. **Oral culture** remained strong among the illiterate, who often told folk and fairy tales to understand their condition and warn the young about the harsh world outside.

Carnival celebrations punctuated the cycle of seasonal work in early modern Europe. Despite government efforts to curtail them during the Protestant Reformation, many clung to the tradition of concentrated indulgence and riotous behavior that the festival offered. The masses could turn to other amusements even if Carnival was restricted. Drink has always played a major social and dietary role in the lives of Europeans. During the eighteenth century, many in the lower classes turned to stronger (and often cheaper) spirits like gin and whiskey for escape. Taverns in Great Britain advertised "drunk for a penny, dead drunk for two." Alcoholism arose as a major social problem for the first time. For further escape, peasants and poor townspeople turned to the bloodsports of bare-knuckle fisticuffs, cockfighting, and bear-baiting (chaining a bear taken from the woods and siccing ferocious dogs upon it). These popular leisure activities serve to remind us of the growing divergence between popular and elite cultures and that the Enlightenment ethos clearly did not reach all members of society.

Enlightenment Thought

Enlightenment philosophy took its cue from the Scientific Revolution of the sixteenth and seventeenth centuries. Given this, remember the following brief and useful definition of the Enlightenment:

> **An application of the methods and principles of the Scientific Revolution to issues of political, economic, and social reform.**

In other words, Enlightenment thinkers believed that just as laws guided the movements of the planets or workings of the human body, human reason and observation could discover the same laws of human affairs—for example, in law, politics, or even religion. We have already seen how the skeptical mindset liberated by the Scientific Revolution laid the foundations for the eighteenth century. Now we look at the social setting in which this philosophy gained currency.

The Setting of the Enlightenment and the Role of Women

To appreciate the full flavor of the Enlightenment, one needed to live in Paris. Many of the greatest philosophes hailed from France, and French served as the unifying language (*lingua franca*) of intellectual discourse among elites. Scotland, Britain, Germany, and America—all contributed to the Enlightenment, but the movement took its tone and spirit from the salons of Paris. The women who ran the **salons**—known as *salonnières*—attracted philosophers, economists, and writers from all over Europe in an effort to stimulate an ongoing conversation regarding the key issues facing Europe. For 25 years, Madame de Geoffrin (1699–1777) hosted intellectuals, acted as mediator and financial patroness, and invited foreign thinkers and rulers to her famous Parisian salon. Many writers chose the salons of Julie Lespinasse or Suzanne Necker as the settings to introduce newly published works or discuss novel theories.

> ### THEME MUSIC & SKILL SET
> You may have noted throughout this guide the recurring theme (SCD) of women's involvement in various movements of reform, only to be frustrated by lack of change in gender attitudes or practices (CCOT and MAC). Though the evidence of women's advance during the Enlightenment is mixed, one proposition seems undeniable: women gained a language of natural rights that would later bear fruit with feminism.

Women clearly participated in the culture of the Enlightenment. Some women and even a few male philosophes like Condorcet advocated the equality of women. A writer and collaborator in radical political movements, Mary Wollstonecraft (1759–1797), penned the first modern statements of the feminist movement. Wollstonecraft's *Thoughts on the Education of Daughters* took issue with Rousseau's gender-based educational philosophy, arguing that only if women were trained for intelligence and self-reliance could they raise children who exhibited these same characteristics necessary for republican government. Later, during the French Revolution, Wollstonecraft defended the movement for equality with *A Vindication of the Rights of Women* (1792), which held that no legitimate basis, other than physical strength, could be devised to discriminate between men and women. Though these works set the feminist agenda for the next century, women gained few tangible benefits from their participation in a movement that targeted religious superstition and intellectual suppression rather than gender inequality.

For those who could not participate in the salons, other venues provided opportunities for the exchange of new ideas. The middle classes congregated in coffeehouses and reading clubs to discuss the New Science or the latest novel. Though most philosophes boasted aristocratic status, the bourgeoisie often imitated noble fashions and intellectual interests, including Enlightenment philosophy. An additional if more secretive setting for the spread of the Enlightenment were the Masonic (Freemanson) lodges, founded in the early 1700s. Freemasonry attracted many famous intellectuals, including Mozart and some early US presidents, with its tight-knit camaraderie, select membership, and betterment through education and technology.

The Philosophes and Their Ideals

Who were the philosophes? The majority were not, in fact, professional philosophers, though several, like Hume and Kant, were. Most worked as writers, social critics, and publicists for new ideas. Just as an engineer or political leader uses a plan to guide their actions, the philosophes articulated an intellectual project: to subject all of human custom and tradition to a systematic criticism using reason and the methods of science. Promoting revolution was remote from their thinking; progress should occur through gradual acceptance of the Enlightenment message of reform. As you review the important philosophes below, consider how their works reflect the following principles:

- *Reason* – Perhaps the concept most associated with the Enlightenment, belief in human reason's ability to discover the relevant laws of nature and humanity expresses the assumption that the world itself is inherently knowable to the human mind and an optimism in the advance of human understanding.

- *Skepticism* – Not all philosophes demonstrated hostility to organized religion or advocated **atheism**. Most Enlightenment thinkers attacked the perceived dogmatism of organized religion and wanted to quarantine it from public life. Science and rational inquiry should replace theology as the authorities in public affairs. In place of organized religion, many intellectuals adhered to belief in a God based on reason, not revelation. This **deism** portrayed God as a kind of Newtonian clockmaker who designed the world with scientific natural laws and then simply allowed it to function. With this natural religion, the prophets, holy books, dogma, clergy, and rituals of organized religion were considered unnecessary.

- *Equality* – Though many philosophes noted the crushing inequality present in European institutions, few trusted the masses to rule. Belief in the betterment of the lower classes did not necessarily translate into support for democracy.

- *Progress* – A natural byproduct of belief in human reason, the notion of progress lay at the heart of the Enlightenment project. According to the foremost American advocate of the Enlightenment, Benjamin Franklin, the pursuit of knowledge should ultimately yield practical benefits for humankind.

Brief biographical and intellectual sketches of the most important figures of the Enlightenment follow:

Denis Diderot (1713–1784)—Diderot, one of the first outspoken atheists, achieved fame for his editing of the *Encyclopédie*, a 17-volume reference work that ambitiously set out to arrange the sum total of human knowledge alphabetically, without deference to ecclesiastical (religious) or political authority. Many of the articles generated controversy by taking a critical perspective on organized religion or by revealing the trade secrets of the guilds. In addition to print articles, the *Encyclopédie* provided illustrations designed to convey practical knowledge of engineering, the military arts, and manufacturing. Diderot possessed an expansive mind, which led him to write in a variety of genres, including drama, and advocate for humanitarian causes, like education for the deaf, making him a favorite in the salons and at courts like Catherine the Great's of Russia.

> **EXAMPLE BASE**
>
> As you study the figures in this section, focus on connecting each to the principles articulated above and the project of the Enlightenment—to better human affairs through a scientific approach. Also, these thinkers engaged in a debate regarding a new epistemology (method of knowledge) and cosmology (model of the universe). Make sure that you can explain these debates.

David Hume (1711–1776)—A down-to-earth, jovial leader of the Scottish Enlightenment, Hume conveyed a radically empirical approach to human knowledge. According to Hume (see *Enquiry Concerning Human Understanding* [1748]), it was a fallacy of reasoning to say that we experience the "laws of nature" or even that personal identity persists through time. Valid knowledge arises from our *immediate* observations (what Hume called perceptions); the further removed from these we become by forming abstract ideas, the less reliable is our knowledge. Further, in his *Dialogues Concerning Natural Religion* (1779), Hume articulated a skeptical and an agnostic attitude toward miracles and the intelligent design argument for God's existence. Finally, Hume argued that the "oughts" of morality cannot arise from the "is'es" of nature; ethics, then, could only be based on our moral sense, or sentiments (feelings), not our reasoning.

Immanuel Kant (1724–1804)—Kant stands as one of the most brilliant and incomprehensible philosophers of the modern age. Rarely traveling outside his home town of Königsberg, Prussia, Kant never married and dedicated his life to developing a complete system of philosophy. Kant's "Copernican revolution" in philosophy combined the empirical and rationalist traditions into one coherent system of knowledge. Our intuitions about time, space, and causation (rationalism) do provide us with knowledge about what we experience (empiricism), Kant held, but they can never tell us about the "things in themselves," for these lay beyond our experience. Kant's system is called constructivism, because the perceptual "lenses" of our intuitions and categories of understanding construct the world out of our experiences. When it came to ethics, however, Kant rejected Hume's moral-sense ideas in favor of a purely rationalist approach—the ethical act is objectively determined by testing whether it could be applied universally without contradiction.

Baron de Montesquieu (1689–1755)—Montesquieu's experiences as a French Protestant and member of the Bordeaux *parlement* influenced his writings. Keeping with the new travel literature, Montesquieu in 1721 penned the *Persian Letters*, a satirical account of two foreign visitors' adventures through France as they encounter what seem like strange and often ridiculous beliefs and customs. By far, Montesquieu's most important work was *The Spirit of the Laws* (1748). Based on his investigation of history and contemporary states, Montesquieu concluded that geography, climate, and history influenced the forms of government and laws of each nation. Large nations tended toward despotism (like Russia), medium-sized nations toward monarchy (like France), and smaller nations toward republics (like Switzerland). Montesquieu favored a government like Britain's, which incorporated checks and balances to restrain the vices associated with each major political interest: monarchy—tyranny; oligarchy—factionalism; democracy—anarchy.

The Physiocrats and **Adam Smith** (1723–1790)—Adam Smith (Scottish) built off the ideas of the French Physiocrats, both of whom criticized mercantilism for violating the natural laws regarding economics. Whereas mercantilists believed specie (hard money) to be the true source of wealth, the Physiocrats held it to be land, as that resource provided society with its agricultural sustenance and mineral resources. To produce a higher standard of living, Physiocrats argued, one must free land from the inefficient feudal restrictions placed upon it and promote the development of commercial agriculture. It was the Physiocrats who coined the term "laissez faire" ("let it be") to argue against the type of continuous government supervision of the economy associated with mercantilism. Adam Smith agreed with Physiocracy's analysis of mercantilism, but provided a somewhat different analysis of the natural laws of economics in his "bible of capitalism," *Inquiry into Nature and Causes of the Wealth of Nations* (1776). Many of his ideas still guide economic thinking today and can be summarized as follows:

1. Labor is the ultimate source of value, as it is labor that mixes with raw materials to make useful products.

2. Economic activity is too complex to be guided by the blunt instrument of government. The "invisible hand of the marketplace," or the laws of supply and demand (i.e., the **free market**), should determine what is produced, how much is produced, and at what price.

3. Nations should allow the free flow of goods across borders and concentrate on producing those goods for which they possess a comparative advantage (e.g.,

Guatemala produces coffee more efficiently than computers). Mercantilism's assumption of scarcity will be rendered false, as all nations will benefit from this practice of **free trade**, without artificial tariffs that protect inefficient producers and harm consumers.

4. Opposing the traditional guild system, Smith argued for a higher division of labor to produce larger quantities of goods and lower costs. When the production process is broken into its component steps, worker specialization yields greater efficiency.

Voltaire (1694–1778)—The middle-class François-Marie Arouet later took his famous pen name and came to represent the ideals of the Enlightenment. Voltaire's sarcasm, witty style, and commitment to intellectual freedom won him both admiration and resentment. Wide ranging in his interests, Voltaire took aim at religious fanaticism and hypocrisy. During the Calas Affair—when a Protestant father was falsely accused of killing his son to prevent his conversion to Catholicism—Voltaire argued for religious toleration and claimed that revealed religion made people foolish and cruel. His famous battle cry "crush the infamous thing!," indicated his distaste for organized religion. Like many philosophes, Voltaire argued for rational belief in God, or deism. In *Philosophical Letters on the English*, Voltaire expressed his admiration for England's balanced government and relative religious tolerance. Voltaire spent two years at the court of Frederick II of Prussia, with whom he shared a belief in enlightened top-down reform and a distrust of the ignorant masses. In response to what he saw as the the stupidity and shallow optimism of human nature, Voltaire wrote the novelette *Candide*, which recounts the misadventures of a young man who ultimately learns the best we can hope for is "to tend our own garden," or develop our intellectual capacities without interference.

The Later Enlightenment

Some historians believe that after 1760, the Enlightenment entered a new, more radical phase. According to this interpretation, some philosophes grew more insistent and radical in their criticisms of existing society and called for the adoption of an explicitly mechanistic and materialist view of the world. Though he is difficult to categorize, Jean-Jacques Rousseau is often associated with this more radical view of the Enlightenment.

> **THEME MUSIC**
>
> Many of the later Enlightenment figures, especially Rousseau, would come to exercise significant influence on the French revolutionaries, as their critique of the Old Regime and prescription for reform provided an ostensible blueprint for a nation based on reason and equality (SOP).

Jean-Jacques Rousseau (1712–1778)—Unique among the philosophes, Rousseau came from the lower middle class. His life represents a tale of misfortune, as he was a neglected child, lived from job to job, found patronage among older women, and eventually married a local barmaid, with whom he had five children, which he later abandoned. In his many writings, Rousseau developed several themes. Early on, in *Discourses on the Arts and Sciences* and *Discourses on the Origin of Inequality among Men*, Rousseau portrayed civilization as corrupting to humans' natural inclination for mutual association, leading to exploitation and artificial divisions. Rousseau glorified the life of the Noble Savage, exemplified by Native Americans, for whom there was no need for reason, as instinct and emotion more reliably produced happiness. Concerned with the moral dimension of human experience, Rousseau wrote in **The Social Contract** (1762) that the fundamental dilemma of any political system was to find a form of political association in which the General Will of the entire society could be realized through pursuit of the common good. Rousseau left the institutional structure of this republican state ambiguous, for the General Will could not be expressed through representative bodies or legal formalities. With *Émile* (1762) and *La Nouvelle Heloise* (1762), Rousseau completed his presentation of a culture of public sentiment. In the former, Rousseau laid out a new approach to child-rearing and education, with a focus on children's positive experiences rather than rote memorization or a premature focus on reason. Within this system, Rousseau viewed women as naturally fitted for the domestic sphere, in which their duties lie with breast-feeding and nurturing their children. For the latter work, a sentimental novel, Rousseau showed how artificial boundaries between two lovers leads to tragedy. In imitation of Rousseau, many began to weep openly, speak emotionally, and glorify nature. Overall, Rousseau stands as one of the most creative and controversial of the philosophes, but also the first figure of the later Romantic movement.

Though many philosophes wished to retain, with deism, a veneer of spirituality, others were content to push a scientific view of the world to its further limits. Baron d'Holbach (1723–1789) of Germany contributed to the *Encyclopédie* articles attacking Christianity as preventing humanity from reaching its full moral development. In *The System of Nature* (1770), he boldly asserted that all of existence consisted of no more than particles in motion, guided by built-in natural laws. God, souls, angels, and spirits could not exist since they did not possess a material nature. From this, d'Holbach concluded that human behavior itself was subject to the same material forces and was therefore determined (i.e., unfree), even if actions *seemed* the result of free choice. Not just churches, but even thinkers such as Voltaire found d'Holbach's ideas repugnant to the spirit of human progress and improvement characteristic of the Enlightenment.

Marquis de Condorcet (1743–1794), an aristocratic mathematician and political scientist, wrote passionately for equality (including women), justice, constitutional government, and individual liberty. His most famous work, *Progress of the Human Mind* (1795), portrays human civilization as a progressive march toward scientific thinking and freedom and happiness. Condorcet's idealism could not save him from the radicalism of the French Revolution, as he was arrested because of his aristocratic lineage and later died in prison, an example of how the forces unleashed by the Enlightenment could not always be controlled by its creators.

The Limits of the Enlightenment: Race and Inequality

Historical controversy rages over the relationship of the Enlightenment to the issues of race and slavery. On one hand, many Enlightenment philosophes condemned the practice of slavery as a fundamental violation of natural rights and worked toward its abolition. On the other hand, even supposedly skeptical and progressive philosophers promoted an explicitly racial hierarchy of peoples, unable to contemplate the equality of Blacks, Native Americans, and Pacific islanders with whites. Some have argued that these racist views represent basic features of, rather than exceptions to, Enlightenment thinking. Concerned with classifying all of reality, scientists of the eighteenth century investigated and articulated theories of race to explain the differing levels of "civilization" they encountered as Europe expanded its global reach. This was the century during which biologists developed the taxonomy to name species (Carl Linneaus) and postulated that all existing races had originated from a common origin but that some had suffered "degeneracy" (Comte de Buffon). Though some thinkers like Diderot and Montesquieu condemned colonialism based on racial differences, others like David Hume in his "Of National Characters" and Immanuel Kant in his "Lectures on Anthropology," advanced belief in a hierarchy of racial subspecies.

Jews participated in the Enlightenment and were affected by it. Within Judaism itself, there occurred a Jewish Enlightenment (Haskalah) in which Moses Mendelssohn (1729–1786), for example, adopted a more historical and rationalist examination of the Torah (first five books of the Jewish scriptures) and a critical approach toward the Talmud (rabbinic commentaries on the Jewish Law). Mendelssohn's ideas laid the foundations at the beginning of the nineteenth century within his native Germany for the development of Reform Judaism. Despite the movement toward the emancipation of Jews within the political sphere, even skeptical thinkers, such as Voltaire, continued to perpetuate anti-Semitic views. Voltaire portrayed Jews from an "essentialist" perspective, as incapable of adopting fully progressive or enlightened habits due to their "nature." Whether these and the racialist views noted above represent an unfortunate exception to or, instead, define the Enlightenment, this troubling question demonstrates the complexity of how we, even today, evaluate figures from history.

Enlightened Absolutism

Monarchs recognized the potential of Enlightenment methods for the rational ordering of the state. While rulers patronized the Enlightenment and attracted philosophes to their courts, their focus remained on the realities of power. Several rulers in the eighteenth century fit the label **enlightened absolutism**, but the following three stand out:

> ### THEME MUSIC
>
> In Chapter 7, we examined the theory and practice of absolutism (e.g., Louis XIV). As you study this section, please note the way in which enlightened thought both changed and left unchanged the practice of absolute monarchy (SOP). These monarchs embraced the Enlightenment, but as a means to strengthen the state and often sacrificed ideals when it clashed with the realities of power.

Prussia and Frederick II "the Great" (r. 1740–1786)

We have already seen how Frederick established the greatness of Prussia through his military exploits and conquest of Silesia (see chapter 8). A skeptic by nature, Frederick practiced religious toleration, as did his Hohenzollern ancestors, but did not offend the religious sensibilities of his people by ridiculing their faith. Whereas Louis XIV proclaimed "I am the state," Frederick believed himself to be "the first servant of the state." In *Forms of Government* (1781), Frederick specified for each social group its necessary function for the smooth operation of the state machinery. His ideal of efficiency and reason did not produce equality, however. Prussian social classes remained legally defined with little or no social mobility between them. Frederick also reversed many of his father's policies related to merit, once again favoring the Junker nobility above others. In addition, outside of Frederick's own crown lands, serfdom grew worse during his reign. Nonetheless, Frederick achieved a higher degree of centralization, codifying the laws of his diverse lands and enforcing them with Prussia's renowned bureaucracy. Frederick invited Voltaire to his court, but their egos proved too large for close company. Despite such displays of enlightenment and Frederick's early interest in music and philosophy, the aging monarch often cynically put the interests of state above principles, as with his calculated invasion of Silesia in 1740 and the Polish Partition of 1772.

Austria and Joseph II (r. 1780–1790)

Of all rulers, Joseph II most thoroughly believed in and upheld Enlightenment principles during his brief 10-year reign. Building on the reforms of his mother, Maria Theresa, Joseph pursued reform systematically and often recklessly. Genuinely concerned with the plight of the lower classes, Joseph abolished serfdom, granted religious toleration to minorities, granted liberty of the press, and introduced legal equality. Though nominally Catholic, Joseph clashed with the pope and insisted on greater control over the church in Austria. His Edict on Idle Institutions disbanded unproductive monasteries and diverted the funds for the establishment of secular hospitals. Joseph also attempted to promote economic development in his empire by advocating Physiocracy. Despite issuing over 10,000 edicts in his life for the betterment of the people, when Joseph died at 49, many of his reforms were reversed. In his effort to centralize his diverse lands and improve the lives of his people, Joseph offended local traditions and alienated important segments of society, such as the clergy and nobility. No one can doubt Joseph's commitment to the Enlightenment principles, but his fast-paced reform and disregard for opposition ultimately proved too much for many in his empire.

Russia and Catherine II (r. 1762–1796)

Catherine the Great may have been the most famous and admired woman of her era. Between Peter the Great's death in 1725 and Catherine's accession in 1762, Russia had been led by a series of weak and unstable rulers, which allowed the nobility to resurrect their power. In addition, Catherine hailed from Germany and gained power via a palace coup against her weak husband. Despite these obstacles, Catherine exercised strong rule, though she continuously compromised her adherence to Enlightenment principles in favor of practical political realities. The "philosopher on the throne," Catherine attracted Voltaire and Diderot to her court, wrote a famous Instruction to the Legislative Commission (1767) expressing her belief in reason and equality, established schools for girls, and even abolished torture and capital punishment. On the other hand, she gained a reputation for leaving grandiose projects unfinished and acting ruthlessly when it suited her interests. She allowed serfdom to worsen by selling off crown lands, and then brutally crushed the subsequent Pugachev Revolt in the 1770s. At the same time, Catherine liberated the nobles from state service with a Charter of the Nobility (1785) but never followed up with her proposed constitution for all Russia's people. In her greatest accomplishment, Catherine added more territory to Russia than any ruler in its history, both by defeating the weakening Ottoman Empire and by partitioning neighboring Poland out of existence. Reflecting a double standard toward women, Catherine earned a reputation for sexual promiscuity by taking lovers of her advisers and political allies. One of these, Grigori Potemkin, lends his name to the fake villages set up to impress foreign dignitaries with Russia's greatness. Like the Potemkin Villages, Russia appeared immense and powerful to the outside world, but in Catherine's Russia much suffering and unfinished reform hid behind this façade.

The Realities of Enlightened Despotism and the Partitions of Poland

Enlightened despotism allows us to gauge and assess the ideals and realities of the larger movement, which makes it a helpful topic of study for the AP exam. With the problematic exception of Joseph II, enlightened monarchs viewed enlightened ideals primarily as a *tool* to exercise power. When push came to shove, most rulers chose the path of power and compromised on ideals. Even so, enlightened absolutism laid the groundwork for the revolutionary movements of the late eighteenth and early nineteenth centuries. By promoting centralization and calling into question traditional authorities, enlightened monarchs provided an agenda and a method for future changes, even if in the future, these changes occurred by way of revolution. Since the Middle Ages, monarchy had generally acted as a progressive force for change; by 1780, the enlightened despots had taken their reforms about as far as they could without undermining their hereditary dynasties. Not surprisingly, after the French Revolution, monarchies looked backward instead of forward, attempting to avoid change while supporting tradition.

Poland represented an outlier among European monarchies. Its elective monarchy and powerful nobility never allowed the kingdom to achieve centralized institutions like a tax system, bureaucracy, or standing army. As a result, the three great eastern powers—Austria, Prussia, and Russia—took advantage of Poland's internal instability to eliminate its independent existence. While each of the three partitions (in 1772, 1793, and 1795) was prompted by differing circumstances, they ended with the collusion and cynicism of Poland's great power rivals. The **Partitions of Poland** maintained the balance of power in eastern Europe, but at the expense of the old international order, which had often upheld the existence of weaker states like Poland. The enlightened monarchs who helped carve up Poland once again demonstrated how power politics under the guise of enlightened reform held the potential of upsetting the basis for traditional government.

Realizing the Enlightenment in Politics

Reform in Britain

Prior to the great revolution in France (1789), clouds of change wafted across the Atlantic World. We look first at Britain, before traveling to its colonies in America. As part of the humanitarian impulse borne out of the Enlightenment, reformers targeted slavery as one of greatest violations of the principles of equality and freedom. In 1783, the Quakers, who believed all humans possessed an inner light, founded the first abolitionist society in Europe. The **British Abolitionist movement** targeted the slave trade itself for elimination, which achieved success with both Britain's and America's elimination of the practice in 1807.

Within Britain, the system of "rotten boroughs" and patronage came under increasing criticism. Many cities lacked representation, and only the wealthy exercised the vote. Voices for democratic reform rallied around the case of John Wilkes, a radical journalist and member of Parliament who criticized the king's policies. Though the "king's men" excluded Wilkes from Parliament until 1774, his cause animated the crowds of London with cries of "Wilkes and Liberty!" Calls for reform echoed throughout Britain's empire; however, attempts at change in Ireland resulted only in an Act of Union in 1801, which bound it more tightly to Britain. As for India, the rule of the British East India Company grew more centralized under parliamentary supervision. Of these trends toward democratization and centralization, the American colonists took up the first and defied the second.

The Promise of the Enlightenment— The American Revolution

The United States appears on the AP exam only in its relation to European history, which means only sporadically until the First World War. It is not necessary to recount the American Revolution here, but a word is in order to place the Enlightenment in proper context.

First, the American colonists followed events closely in Britain, particularly the Wilkes affair. Such events, as well as the study of British critics of the king-in-parliament system, inspired America in its own rebellion against efforts at centralizing the empire. These protests resulted in American independence and later, the first written constitution in the modern age expressing Enlightenment principles. Enlightenment thinking spanned the Atlantic Ocean, and indeed, several Americans contributed to the movement:

> **THEME MUSIC**
>
> Historians often speak of a transatlantic revolutionary impulse, fed by the winds of the Enlightenment blowing back and forth across the ocean. The American rebellion against Britain inspired the French Revolution, which itself stirred a slave revolt in Saint-Domingue (later Haiti)—all of which drew upon the principles and rhetoric of natural rights and social contract theory from the Enlightenment (INT).

- Benjamin Franklin (1706–1790) – Franklin lived an exceptionally fruitful life, which included the discovery of electricity, several inventions, promoting projects of civic betterment like the postal service, as well as displaying diplomatic acumen as Minister to France. During his term, Franklin wowed Parisians with his humor and intellect, acting as a conduit for the notion that enlightened principles could be realized in a government and an individual.

- Thomas Jefferson (1743–1826) – Jefferson gained fame for crafting the Declaration of Independence, one of the great expressions of Enlightenment thought, justifying natural law, inalienable rights, and the right of revolution. One of the only presidents openly to espouse deism, Jefferson promoted religious toleration and sponsored numerous scientific endeavors. On the other hand, Jefferson's ownership of enslaved persons, and refusal to free them upon his death, demonstrates the limitations to his stated ideals and the anomalies within the Enlightenment more generally.

- Thomas Paine (1737–1809) – Born in Britain, Paine set sail for America in 1774 just in time for the revolution. Paine's *Common Sense* (1776), which criticized monarchy as unnatural, sparked the movement for independence. Later involved in the French Revolution, Paine defended the radical movement for equality and liberty with *The Rights of Man* (1791), as well as deism with *The Age of Reason* (1794).

As we see in the next chapter, the American Revolution inspired belief that Enlightenment principles could be realized politically, and also, indirectly led to revolution in France by bankrupting that nation's treasury through its support for American independence.

Additional Resources

📖 **Robert Darnton,** *The Great Cat Massacre: And Other Episodes in French Cultural History* (1985) — Through several fascinating vignettes, we come to understand how historians recreate the mental worlds of the past.

📖 **Emmanuel Chukwudi Eze,** *Race and the Enlightenment: A Reader* (1997) — A slim volume that examines the philosophes' ideas on race.

📖 **Jostein Gaarder,** *Sophie's World: A Novel About the History of Philosophy* (2007) — Provides an accessible overview of major philosophers set within a compelling story.

📖 **Norman Hampson,** *A Cultural History of the Enlightenment* (1969) — A challenging read, but one that provides strong insight in one focused volume.

📖 **Margaret C. Jacob,** *The Enlightenment: A Brief History with Documents* (2000) — This slim volume in the *Bedford Series in History and Culture* provides primary sources with brief analysis.

📖 **Ellis Markman,** *The Coffee House: A Cultural History* (2004) — Goes beyond the beverage itself to demonstrate the culture created by the space for its consumption.

📖 **Dorinda Outram,** *The Enlightenment* (**New Approaches to European History**), 3/e (2013) — A brief volume that places the Enlightenment in a global context.

📖 **Bonnie Smith,** *Changing Lives: Women in European History Since 1700* (1988) — A good resource that begins with useful chapters on the Enlightenment and French Revolution.

🎞 *Amazing Grace* (2006) — Feature film portraying the inspiring life of William Wilberforce, evangelical Christian, who contributed mightily to the movement toward abolition of slavery and the slave trade.

💻 **https://conversational-leadership.net/coffee-houses/** — Short article and videos on coffeehouse culture and Enlightenment.

CHAPTER TEST

Multiple-Choice Questions

Questions 1–4 are based on the passages below.

Source 1

"Men and women are made for each other, but their mutual dependence differs in degree; man is dependent on woman through his desires; woman is dependent on man through her desires and also through her needs; he could do without her better than she can do without him. She cannot fulfill her purpose in life without his aid, without his goodwill, without his respect….Nature herself has decreed that woman, both for herself and her children, should be at the mercy of man's judgment."

Jean-Jacques Rousseau, French philosopher, *Emile, or On Education*, 1762

Source 2

"If children are to be educated to understand the true principle of patriotism, their mother must be a patriot; and the love of mankind, from which an orderly train of virtues spring, can only be produced by considering the moral and civil interest of mankind; but the education and situation of woman, at present, shuts her out from such investigations….To be a good mother—a woman must have sense, and that independence of mind which few women possess who are taught to depend entirely on their husbands. Meek wives are, in general, foolish mothers…"

Mary Wollstonecraft, British writer and philosopher, *A Vindication of the Rights of Woman*, 1792

1. In <u>Source 1</u>, Rousseau most directly contradicts the principles of the Enlightenment by:
   A. calling into question the notion that the universe follows natural laws.
   B. reinforcing the belief that legitimate governments are based on a social contract.
   C. relying on religious authority to justify adherence to traditional social roles.
   D. not subjecting knowledge claims to methods of skepticism and empiricism.

2. Wollstonecraft's ideas in <u>Source 2</u> best reflect the eighteenth-century cultural trend that:
   A. emphasized the importance of citizenship and political participation.
   B. embraced a religious revival and the renewal of subjective experience.
   C. extolled the value of a comfortable consumer setting for the household.
   D. used travel literature to depict non-Europeans in a primitive manner.

3. The contrasting views in the two sources illustrate which of the following issues during the Enlightenment?
   A. Government use of censorship to halt the spread of radical ideas
   B. Scientific principles challenging religious and state authority
   C. The extent to which equality and rights should apply within society
   D. Whether commercial luxury harmed civic culture and values

4. All of the following represent accurate statements regarding the lives of women in the eighteenth century EXCEPT:
   A. home life was shaped increasingly by concern for privacy, leisure, and consumerism.
   B. the rate of illegitimacy increased, as did use of primitive forms of birth control.
   C. feminists succeeded in establishing property rights and entrance to higher education.
   D. women in cities encountered poverty, prostitution, and increased social controls.

Questions 5–7 are based on the passage below.

> "I believe in one God, and no more; and I hope for happiness beyond this life.
>
> I believe the equality of man, and I believe that religious duties consist in doing justice, loving mercy, and endeavoring to make our fellow-creatures happy.
>
> I do not believe in the creed professed by the Jewish church, by the Roman church, by the Greek church, by the Turkish church, by the Protestant church, nor by any church that I know of. My own mind is my own church.
>
> All national institutions of churches...appear to me no other than human inventions set up to terrify and enslave mankind, and monopolize power and profit.
>
> I do not mean...to condemn those who believe otherwise; they have the same right to their belief as I have to mine. But it is necessary to the happiness of man, that he be mentally faithful to himself. Infidelity does not consist in believing, or in disbelieving; it consists in professing to believe what he does not believe."
>
> Thomas Paine, British political activist and writer, *The Age of Reason*, 1794

5. The beliefs articulated above best reflect which of the following eighteenth-century religious perspectives?

   A. Toleration

   B. Deism

   C. Atheism

   D. Agnosticism

6. The contemporary development that most likely influenced Paine's ideas was the:

   A. rivalry between Britain and France.

   B. establishment of the first factories in Britain.

   C. rule of the enlightened despots.

   D. policies of French revolutionaries.

7. Which of the following is the most accurate comparison between Paine's views and those of Renaissance intellectuals?

   A. Both believed that the state should have no control over religion.

   B. Both emphasized equality, regardless of class, gender, or race.

   C. Unlike Paine, Renaissance intellectuals worked within Christian ideas.

   D. Unlike Paine, Renaissance intellectuals downplayed individualism.

Questions 8–10 are based on the passage below.

> "Never allow yourselves to forget that it is for their own sakes and not for yours that all those wise lawgivers have forced you into your present unnatural and rigid molds. And as evidence of this, I need only produce all our political, civil, and religious institutions. Examine them thoroughly, and either I am very much mistaken or you will find that mankind has been forced to bow, century after century, beneath a mere handful of scoundrels that has conspired, in every age, to impose upon it. Beware of the man who wants to set things in order. Setting things in order always involves acquiring mastery over others—by tying them hand and foot."
>
> Denis Diderot, French philosopher and writer, *Supplement to the Voyage of Bougainville*,
> story in the form of a dialogue between a European traveler and a Pacific islander, 1796

8. The passage best reflects which of the following trends of the eighteenth century?

   A. European commercial expansion creating a global trade network

   B. Political theories that portrayed individuals as driven by self-interest

   C. Empirical methods used to critique traditional institutions and customs

   D. Expansion in goods creating a new consumer culture and civic venues

9. Given the type of publication, Diderot most likely hoped that his story would cause:

   A. a political and social revolution in France, by indicting the old regime.

   B. questioning of social norms, by exposing Europeans to non-European culture.

   C. the end of slavery, by depicting the abuses of the trans-Atlantic slave system.

   D. equality for men and women, by showing the failures of patriarchal politics.

10. Diderot would cite all of the following as sources of the situation he describes EXCEPT:

A. the Catholic Church.

B. the Three Estates structure.

C. persistence of folk beliefs.

D. capitalist economic practices.

See Chapter 18 for answers and explanations.

Short-Answer Question

Directions: Examine the image below and answer all parts of the question that follows. Use complete sentences; an outline or bulleted list is not acceptable. Write your responses on a separate sheet of paper. A sample response and commentary are provided on the next page.

Joseph Wright of Derby, British artist, *An Experiment on a Bird in the Air Pump*, 1768

1. a) Describe one way in which the image illustrates Enlightenment attitudes toward the natural world and/or human reason.

   b) Describe one limitation on the realization of Enlightenment principles that is either depicted in or <u>left out</u> of the image.

   c) Explain how the painting reflects changes in the visual arts in the eighteenth century.

SAQ Sample Response

a) The Enlightenment was also known as the Age of Reason. This is clear in the painting by Wright of Derby. In this work, the figures are viewing an experiment about air pressure, showing the influence of the scientific method. Many of the philosophes supported the idea that science was the best way of understanding nature, because it involved testing of hypothesis, rather than accepting religious dogma.

b) Many women hosted salons and discussed ideas of Enlightenment. However, most of them did not receive rights during the Enlightenment. In the painting, the woman all seem to be taking a passive role or are being protected by others, usually men.

c) During the eighteenth century, the Baroque style was prominent. Baroque artists painted canvases with strong colors and shadowing (as shown here) to convey emotion and power. Also, monarchs patronized Baroque art, so this painting was probably sponsored by the British king to show the power and glory of England.

SAQ Response Analysis

This response starts well enough, with the student using the painting to establish an understanding of the Enlightenment. With the references to experimentation, application of science, and skepticism about religion, the student earns a point in Part A. Additionally, though brief, the response in Part B notes how women's participation in salons did not translate into political rights, as well as notes the passive portrayal in the painting. This earns the point for Part B. However, the response goes off track with the art analysis. Though the Baroque style lingered into the eighteenth century, this painting is more reflective of neoclassical art that promoted a secular and scientific (or perhaps commercial) perspective. Finally, the supposition that the British monarch patronized the art is off base. **Score: 2 points**

⮀ CHAPTER 10 ⮀

The French Revolution and Napoleonic Era, 1789–1815

When asked in the 1950s about the importance of the French Revolution, Chinese revolutionary Zhou Enlai responded, "It's too early to tell." The revolution that gripped France, the European continent, and ultimately the world stands as the crossroads of your course. It is considered the model for all revolutions; it gave us our modern ideologies and our political geography of left and right. Unlike the American Revolution, which today in the United States is considered an accomplished and successful fact, the French public still debates the significance and meaning of this defining event in their nation's existence, not to mention aspiring revolutionaries everywhere. This chapter examines the causes and phases of the revolution and also traces its development through the Napoleonic Era. As you study this complex event, you should focus on the following issues: (1) What interaction of factors brought about the French Revolution? (2) What were the accomplishments of the various phases of the revolution? (3) How and why did the revolution become more violent after 1791? and (4) To what extent did Napoleon uphold the ideals of the French Revolution?

 KEY IN – Chapter 10 addresses all or part of the following topics in the Unit Guides of the CED:

Topic 5.1 Contextualizing 18th-Century States

Topic 5.3 Britain's Ascendancy

Topic 5.4 The French Revolution

Topic 5.5 The French Revolution's Effects

Topic 5.6 Napoleon's Rise, Dominance, and Defeat

Topic 5.8 Romanticism

Topic 5.9 Continuity and Change in 18th-Century States

Causes of the French Revolution

Observers and historians have debated the causes and meaning of the French Revolution since it began. This debate often revolves around: A) which particular factor, or relationship of factors, played the critical role in causing the revolution; *and* B) if we should judge the legacy of the revolution overall as positive or negative. The revolution seized the attention of Europe and the world because France itself was important. After Russia, France was Europe's most populous nation, the center of Enlightenment culture, and, despite the problems of its monarchy, was considered prestigious and stable. For most observers, the revolution came as a surprise, though it could have been foreseen given the constellation of circumstances facing France in the 1780s.

Social Causes: The Three Estates

France in 1788 remained separated into three estates, each with its own legal status and privileges. The First Estate, the clergy, amounted to less than 1% of the population, or about 100,000 clergy of different types. Though the position of the church had declined in previous centuries, it remained a social, cultural, and economic force. The church owned about 10% of the land in France and collected the tithe, a tax that amounted to about 3%–5% of individual income. In an age of increasing secularism, many resented the privileges and high social status

> **SKILL SET**
>
> The historiography of the French Revolution might take a dedicated scholar a lifetime to master (SAS and CES), especially since it grows every year. Though you need not be familiar with particular schools of interpretation for the AP exam, you should appreciate how and why this seminal event provokes such strong historical debate. Further, as you read, consider how you might frame an argument on any of the guiding questions from the introduction above.

of the upper clergy—bishops and cardinals—even if many sympathized with their local priests, known as *curés*.

Nobles comprised roughly 2% of the population, about 400,000 members, though they often differed widely in income, and owned approximately 25% of France's land. Counter to Marxist interpretations, which emphasize the rigidity of the class structure, bourgeois members of the Third Estate could ascend into the Second Estate, often by purchase of a government office. In fact, about 40% of nobles in 1788 had earned their status in the previous 150 years. Aristocratic status depended on **inherited privileges** (e.g., right to hunt on common land, separate courts, right to wear distinctive clothing, etc.) and exemptions from certain taxes. Members of the nobility monopolized positions in government and the military. After the death of Louis XIV in 1715, nobles reasserted their power and as part of a feudal reaction, attempted to support their increasingly extravagant lifestyles by reviving feudal dues and strictly enforcing their collection. Some members of the nobility, particularly the old nobles of the sword, attempted to limit the further entry of the middle classes into their privileged station with the Segur Law (1781), which restricted military positions to those who could trace their noble lineage back at least four generations.

The vast majority of French people (about 24 million) belonged to the Third Estate, obviously not a monolithic group. Members of the Third Estate varied from the wealthiest merchant down to the few serfs or landless laborers still eking out a living from the soil. The bourgeoisie increased in numbers and economic power significantly in the seventeenth and eighteenth centuries with the growth of commerce. In addition to their mercantile and professional interests, the bourgeoisie owned about 25% of the land in France. Many resented the privileges of the aristocracy while at the same time envying noble status and imitating their fashions and interests. The petty bourgeoisie of artisans, shopkeepers, and small business owners felt the pinch of, on one hand, rising prices for goods, while on the other, stagnant wages. These *sans-culottes* ("without breeches" as worn by the well-to-do) favored equality and played a major role in the radicalization of the revolution. Peasants formed the largest social class. Most were small landowners who wished to be free from the plethora of service obligations, taxes, tithes, and feudal dues that could eat away over 50% of their livelihood. Owning about 40% of the land, peasants tended to be conservative in outlook, wishing simply to be free of the feudal system.

France's social inequality is taken to be the most fundamental cause of the revolution. It would be a mistake, however, to portray the revolution as simply a drama of class struggle, with a discontented lower class overthrowing their oppressors. In fact, aristocrats and bourgeoisie often shared similar lifestyles and outlooks. Further, some members of the nobility influenced by the Enlightenment criticized the inequities of the Old Regime and led the initial phases of the revolution. Also, during the radical phase of the revolution, nobles and peasants shared a distaste for the radical policies of Paris. Even with these caveats, the social inequality of the three estates drove the revolution forward and accounts for the depth of its radicalism.

> ### THEME MUSIC
> The causes and events of the French Revolution reveal the tie between economic (ECD) and social changes (SCD). As the mercantile wealth expanded from the Commercial Revolution, there occurred a corresponding increase in the size and importance of the middle class (bourgeoisie). One need not endorse the Marxist view of class struggle (as do some historians) to recognize the ways in which the revolution attacked the privileges and political power of the aristocracy, whose wealth depended on the feudal order.

Political Causes

The conflict between the resurgent nobility and a theoretically absolute monarchy constitutes the fundamental political cause of the revolution. French aristocrats accepted and often admired the monarchy but wished it to evolve along English lines. To limit Bourbon pretensions to absolutism, nobles asserted the powers of the *parlements*, the 15 regional law courts, to check the king's ability to tax and legislate arbitrarily. During the weak reign of Louis XV (r. 1715–1774), some progress was made in this regard. However, near the end of his reign in 1771, Louis reasserted royal power and dissolved the Parlement of Paris. As a gesture of goodwill, the young Louis XVI reconvened the body in 1774. This move only emboldened the nobility in their efforts to move France toward a constitutional monarchy.

Many condemned the capricious nature of the monarchy. Hated symbols of arbitrary government were the *lettres de cachet*, which allowed the king to arrest and imprison any individual without judicial procedures. No doubt the stories of an army of political prisoners rotting in the Bastille proved to be exaggerated, but Enlightenment principles of equality and justice spoke against the practice. Additionally, the personalities of **King Louis XVI** (r. 1774–1793) and his Austrian wife, Marie Antoinette (d. 1793) acted as a magnet for discontent with the regime. By all accounts, Louis was a pious, well-meaning family man. However, he also had difficulty consummating his marriage, which when combined with Marie's promiscuous reputation, earned the couple ridicule and scandal. As events unfolded, it became clear that Louis lacked the energy and purpose to see his nation through its crisis. The king's behavior during key moments of the revolution often escalated conflict and fueled demands by radicals for a republic.

Intellectual Causes

The Enlightenment did not directly cause the French Revolution; however, it ensured that unfocused discontent and class anger crystallized into a more fundamental criticism of the Old Regime. Ideas from Voltaire, Rousseau, Montesquieu, and other philosophes provided systematic tools for the expression of grievances, though most people gravitated more to the salacious underground press with stories of the scandals of the royal couple. Even if readers for high-minded philosophy were lacking, a century of enlightened thought helped create a public concern over political issues, awareness of the larger world, and a strong spirit of criticism.

Economic and Financial Causes

Economic and financial causes for the revolution were distinct but related. France did not fall into revolution because of economic stagnancy; more accurately, the French state and legally defined social system coped poorly with rapid economic change. Between 1714 and 1789, French commerce expanded tenfold, faster than Britain's, and fed the wealth of the nation. However, this wealth was unequally distributed. Though France stood out as one of the wealthiest nations in Europe, it was as if it had one hand tied behind its back.

Due to its semi-feudal nature, the French state never tapped effectively into the nation's wealth. We have already seen how France, unlike Britain, did not develop an extensive credit network. More importantly, France was plagued by an inefficient and regressive tax system. Tax rates varied widely based on geography, the highest class claimed exemptions, and the task of collecting the taxes was franchised out to the Farmers General. This group of wealthy financial families legally skimmed off as much as half of state tax revenue.

Louis XVI realized the dire need for tax reform. The debt of the French monarchy accumulated from numerous wars—most recently the American War for Independence (1778–1783)—threatened to choke the state budget. By 1785, the French treasury was bankrupt, and half of the budget went simply to pay the interest on the debt! Louis attempted several far-reaching efforts at reform but was blocked by restive nobles who insisted on more fundamental changes in the political structure before they would agree to new taxes. If Louis had pursued his plans more consistently or resolutely, he might have staved off disaster. Each time one of his finance ministers encountered opposition, he was dismissed by the king.

Louis began boldly by appointing the noted Physiocrat and economic liberal, Turgot (1774–1776), as Finance Minister. Turgot mercilessly attacked privilege. He proposed converting the *corvée* labor service of the peasantry into a cash payment, eliminated numerous government positions and pensions, attacked government monopolies, slashed spending, advocated free trade, and moved to adopt a single direct tax on land to replace the multitude of confusing indirect taxes. Turgot pursued his plan ambitiously and, as a result, sparked wide opposition. When dismissed by Louis, he was replaced by the talented Swiss Protestant banker, Jacques Necker (1776–1781), whose wife Suzanne hosted a salon. Necker published a complete accounting of the state budget, the *compte rendu*, which revealed the incredible waste therein. Necker's plans for austerity proved too threatening to entrenched interests, so he was dismissed in 1781. This well-respected symbol of reform was recalled by the king during the early phase of the revolution in 1789.

By 1787, the situation in France turned desperate, for two reasons. First, France stood at the verge of bankruptcy, and the efforts at financial reform were stalled by growing opposition across the nation. Second, during the years 1787–1789, which coincided with the early stages of the revolution, France suffered from the last great subsistence crisis of the century. Poor crops led to high bread prices, sending urban crowds into the streets. Louis sat upon an explosive situation, and little seemed left to do but call the Estates General, which Louis did in 1788 after protests spread among the *parlements* to his policies.

The Liberal Phase, 1789–1791

Labeling the first phase of the French Revolution "moderate" or "Liberal" makes sense only if we keep in mind that the violence inherent from the outset paled only in comparison to what came later. From the meeting of the Estates General in 1789 until the onset of war in the spring of 1792, the revolution accomplished a major reordering of French state and society. Unfortunately, ideological divisions and the revolutionaries' inability to address major economic issues increased violence and strengthened the hand of radicals. For ease of study, the following three sections will provide a timeline with commentary.

Prior to the meeting of the Estates General, Louis XVI asked all French people to set down their grievances in notebooks, called the *cahiers de doléances*, most of which expressed moderate demands for tax equality and the gradual abolition of feudalism. The subsequent national election was France's first since 1614, and both the election and grievances helped politicize the entire country with the expectation of change. As the Estates General convened in 1789, immediate disagreements broke out over two issues: (1) whether to double the number of delegates to the Third Estate, seeing as it represented 98% of the nation, and (2) whether the delegates should vote as individuals ("heads") or by orders, with each of the three estates getting one vote. The first issue was easy enough to resolve, but the Third Estate and many liberal nobles, known as the Committee of Thirty, refused to budge on the second. The pamphlet *What Is the Third Estate?* by clergyman Abbé Sieyès (1748–1836) stoked discontent by arguing that the Third Estate was the assembled will of the nation and that the noble caste should simply be abolished.

June 17, 1789 Unable to reach agreement on the issue of voting, the Third Estate declares itself the National Assembly.

June 20, 1789 Finding themselves locked out of their meeting place, the National Assembly adjourns to a nearby tennis court and pledges not to disband until it has written a new constitution for France, an event known as the Tennis Court Oath.

Unsure what to do next, the king begins raising an army, possibly to disperse the National Assembly. In addition, he dismisses Finance Minister Jacques Necker in July, signaling his movement away from reform.

July 14, 1789 Fearing the king's military power, the crowds of Paris march to the Bastille, symbol of royal despotism, but also an armory. After accidentally firing on the crowd, the defenders are captured and many executed by beheading. The fall of the Bastille saves the National Assembly and demonstrates the power of mob violence. Soon after, revolutionaries form the National Guard to protect the revolution, appointing Marquis de Lafayette (1757–1834), called the "hero of two worlds" for this support for the American Revolution, as head.

The king is forced to recognize the National Assembly and orders the other two estates to sit with the new legislative body. However, rumors spread in the countryside regarding events in Paris and of plots to undermine the revolution, leading to attacks on nobles.

June-August 1789 In the Great Fear, peasants attack manorial courts and noble manors, directing anger against feudalism. To reestablish order, the National Assembly on the famous "night of August 4" dismantles the entire feudal system. In one blow, **feudal privileges**, the tithe, noble hunting rights, labor service, and serfdom are all **destroyed**.

August 26, 1789 The National Assembly completes the Declaration of Rights of Man and Citizen, an expression of Enlightenment principles such as legal equality, freedom of religion, judicial rights, and "liberty, property, security, and resistance to oppression."

October 1789 Angry over high bread prices and fearing the king's opposition to the Declaration of Rights of Man (and August 4 decrees), the women of Paris march on Versailles and break into the queen's chamber, killing several guards and forcibly bringing the royal family back to Paris, where they would remain as virtual prisoners of the revolution. The actions of women to protect the revolution are termed the October Days.

By the end of 1789, the revolutionaries succeeded in radically restructuring the French state. One of the more important but underestimated actions the assembly took was the abolition of all feudal institutions, *parlements*, estates, provincial law codes, and tariff and tax bodies, to be replaced by 83 equal departments, subdivided into cantons and communes. As a result, France became a centralized national government based in Paris in a way it never had been under royal absolutism.

November 1789–July 1790 In a fateful move that divided the revolution, the National Assembly attacks the privileged position of the Catholic Church. First, the revolution confiscates the lands owned by the Catholic Church and issues paper currency, *assignats*, based on the value of the land, which results in rapid inflation. Later, the church is brought under control of the state—bishops are to be elected and paid by the state, their numbers reduced to 83, and the pope's influence over the clergy eliminated. In addition, after the pope condemns the revolution, the **Civil Constitution of the Clergy** requires all priests to swear an oath of loyalty to the revolution. About half ultimately swear the oath, while the nonjuring clergy (those who would not swear allegiance) later become a rallying point for counterrevolution.

June 1791 The National Assembly completes the Constitution of 1791, a conservative document that creates a single legislative body with a **constitutional monarchy** possessing only the power to delay legislation. Active citizens are those who own substantial property (about half a million men), while those less well-to-do and women are deemed passive citizens. The document indicates that the revolution still rests in the hands of the wealthy bourgeoisie. Nonetheless, the king, under influence from his wife and *émigrés* who had

escaped the revolution, decides to flee France. His "flight to Varennes" is stopped just short of safety, and the royal family is forcibly returned to the Tuileries Palace in Paris.

July 17, 1791 A crowd gathers in a public park to demand the overthrow of the king and the declaration of a republic. The National Guard under Lafayette disperses the crowd with gunfire, killing 50. This Champs de Mars Massacre radicalizes public opinion and leads to further distrust of the monarchy.

Political culture in France now openly embraces symbols of the revolution—"liberty trees," "liberty caps," *citoyen* and *citoyenne* as forms of address, and the replacement of religious with revolutionary icons. Citizens join in clubs to discuss issues and agitate for change. The **Jacobin Club** grows in influence and later produces many of the most important leaders of the radical phase of the revolution.

By the summer of 1791, the revolution has achieved much. However, its laissez-faire policies have not solved the rapid inflation or government debt. Complicating matters are the behavior of the king and growing divisions over how far the revolution should go. The debate extends across Europe as writers, citizens, and governments choose sides. British conservative Edmund Burke (1729–1797) condemns the radical destruction of France's traditions and predicts in *Reflections on the Revolution in France* (1790) that the revolution will end in military dictatorship. Thomas Paine responds (see Chapter 9) with *The Rights of Man* (1791) in defense of the revolution. *Émigrés* from France heighten tensions by working against the revolution from abroad, a situation that seems ripe for war.

> **THEME MUSIC & EXAMPLE BASE**
>
> Take note in this section on the policies of the revolution how its leaders attempted to create a new source of identity (the nation) to replace the old identities of class, order, and province. In fact, one can argue that the French Revolution represents the true birth of the notion of nationalism, an ideology which will play a vital role in the next two centuries (NEI).

> **SKILL SET**
>
> As subsequent chapters will demonstrate, the French Revolution helped create the political ideologies that dominated debate and fostered action throughout the nineteenth and twentieth centuries. In anticipation of this theme, you may want to compare (COMP and MAC) how a supporter (e.g., a Liberal like Paine, or a nationalist or a socialist) and an opponent (e.g., a Conservative like Burke) of the French Revolution would interpret the causes, key events, and outcomes of this transformative event.

The Radical Phase, 1792–1794

Why did the revolution become more radical after 1792? Several factors present themselves:

- *Economic problems* – Rapid inflation continued and the laissez-faire policies of the revolution angered workers stung by high prices and policies directed against union activity.

- *The royal family* – The king clearly had reservations regarding key events of the revolution, such as the Civil Constitution of the Clergy. His effort to flee the revolution undermined much of his remaining support.

- *Counterrevolution* – By now, several groups actively opposed the revolution—provinces jealous of the power of Paris, nonjuring clergy, *émigrés*, religious peasants—and worked to thwart it.
- *War* – War tends to radicalize politics. When France declared war in the spring of 1792, it strengthened the hands of those who called for an even more violent break with the past.

August 1791 The Austrian emperor (brother of Marie Antoinette), along with the Prussian king, issue the Declaration of Pillnitz, promising to restore order in France if other nations provide support.

This declaration, as well as the actions of the king and *émigrés*, convince the Girondins party (a faction of the Jacobins Club from the provinces) that the only way to save the revolution is to spread it across Europe by force of arms. To the strains of *Le Marseillaise*, the revolutionary anthem, the first citizen-soldiers in modern European history depart for the front.

April 20, 1792 France declares war on Austria. The king supports the declaration because he believes France will *lose*, and thus his power would be restored.

July 25, 1792 With the war going badly for France, Austria and Prussia stand on the verge of invading France. Austria and Prussia issue the Brunswick Manifesto, threatening the revolutionaries with violence if any harm comes to the king and queen. The manifesto produces the exact opposite intended effect by inflaming violence against the monarchy.

By now, the working people of Paris, known as *sans-culottes*, oppose the half-measures of the Girondins and are open to the persuasion of radical leaders. The vehement journalist Jean-Paul Marat (1743–1793) with his *L' Ami du peuple* (*The Friend of the People*) newspaper demands the deaths of traitors and for heads to roll. The skilled politician Georges Danton (1759–1794), works to create a revolutionary government in the capital, the Paris Commune, which would play a major role in forcing moderates to adopt more aggressive measures.

August 10, 1792 In an event known as the "Second French Revolution," an armed mob storms the Tuileries Palace and forces the arrest of the king. The Constitution of 1791 is abrogated and a more radical National Convention is elected to govern France.

September 1792 Fearing that political prisoners will aid the advancing Austrian-Prussian army, revolutionaries break into prisons across France and massacre thousands, many of them innocent bystanders (September Massacres).

September 20–21, 1792 After victory in the battle of Valmy, which stopped the invading armies, the National Convention abolishes the monarchy and declares France a **republic**, with 1792 as Year I of the new era.

January 21, 1793 The king is placed on trial for treason and after being found guilty by the Convention and at the insistence of the Mountain (a faction of the Jacobins), is executed by guillotine. With the execution, France enters the Reign of Terror.

May–June 1793 Under pressure from the *sans-culottes*, the Paris Commune arrests and executes the leaders of the Girondins. The Mountain, under the leadership of the radical **Maximilien Robespierre** (1758–1794), comes to dominate the Convention. The democratic Constitution of 1793, which calls for universal male suffrage, is passed, though is never put into effect because of the crisis situation.

Over the next year, France is ruled by the Committee of Public Safety, a 12-member executive body elected each month by the Convention, which steers France through the Reign of Terror. It is aided by the Committee of General Security, the police arm of the revolution. An entire province, the Vendée, rises in counterrevolution against the centralizing and anti-Catholic policies of Paris. War continues and justifies further radical measures.

Robespierre emerges as the dominant personality. An ambitious lawyer from northern France, Robespierre served in the National Assembly, gaining notoriety with his calls for universal male suffrage and the abolition (ironically) of capital punishment and slavery in the colonies. Obsessed with creating a new political culture, Robespierre argues that virtue must be combined with terror. Even if they condemn his methods, most historians consider Robespierre sincere in his beliefs; indeed, he earns the nickname "The Incorruptible" in his lifetime. As a result of the Mountain's policies, revolutionary tribunals arise across France, executing about 50,000 over the course of the terror, and "representatives on mission" ensure that the policies of Paris are followed outside of the capital. Though members of the clergy and aristocracy represent the largest segment of victims as a percentage of their numbers, in absolute terms peasants and the working class make up 70% of the executions.

> **EXAMPLE BASE**
>
> You will encounter numerous specific content references in this section. To avoid bogging down in detail, consider the following two interpretive questions: 1) To what extent did the revolution fulfill its stated principles of liberty, equality, and fraternity (nationalism)? AND 2) To what extent was the violence of the radical phase necessary to save the revolution during its crisis from 1791–1794?

Many view the Reign of Terror as a period of unnecessary and bloodthirsty excess. Others believe that the radicals enacted many creative reforms that helped see France through its time of crisis.

- ***Mass conscription*** (*Levée en masse*) – All French citizens are required to contribute to the war effort. Never before in European history has a nation marshaled so many citizens in arms, raising an army of over 1 million men, who fight with passion for *liberté, égalité, fratenité*.

- *Law of General Maximum* – Abandoning free-market policies, the Convention establishes maximum prices for key commodities and punishes severely those who break the law. However, this battle against inflation is difficult to enforce.

- *Abolition of slavery* – Ratifying the massive **slave revolt in Saint-Domingue (Haiti)** led by **Toussaint L'Ouverture**, the Convention abolishes slavery in all French colonies (later reinstated by Napoleon in 1802). Napoleon was later unable to subdue the revolt, and Haiti gained its independence in 1804. Despite L'Ouverture's later capture and imprisonment (where he died), Haitian independence represents the first successful slave revolt in modern history, and it indirectly leads Napoleon to sell Louisiana to the new American republic.

- *Revolutionary calendar* – As part of a **de-Christianization** campaign, the Convention devises a new calendar with months and days renamed after weather conditions and agricultural products. Months are divided into 30 days of three *décade*, allowing for only 1 day of rest in 10, rather than 7. The new republican era begins with 1792 as Year I.

- *Cult of the Supreme Being* – De-Christianization leads to the elimination of saints' names on streets and Notre Dame becoming a Temple of Reason. Robespierre opposes these excesses and attempts to create a new deistic civic religion, which culminates with a Festival of the Supreme Being in June 1794.

- *Standardization of weights and measures* – Following a trend of the moderate phase and reflecting Enlightenment rationalism, the Convention promotes use of the metric system and, as above, restructures time along similar principles.

- *Military victories* – With these policies, France turns her fortunes around on the battlefield, invading the Netherlands in June 1794 and creating a sister Batavian Republic to replace the old Dutch provinces.

March 1794 The Committee of Public Safety acts against extremism on the left. Radicals who advocated complete equality and terror known as Hébertists, or *enragés*, are sent to the guillotine.

May 1794 Danton, the popular leader of the Paris Commune and a growing critic of Robespierre, is executed along with his supporters, known as Indulgents.

By the summer of 1794, France seems to have emerged from its crisis. Counterrevolution has been defeated, French armies are advancing on the battlefield, and the worst of the inflation seems to have passed. Despite these successes, the pace of executions quickens in the summer of 1794. When Robespierre announces in the Convention a new law that allows looser standards for proof of treason and a new list of proposed executions, fearful opponents ally against him.

July 27, 1794 The Convention arrests Robespierre and his supporters. After a failed attempt at suicide, Robespierre, along with his associates, is guillotined. This event ends the Reign of Terror.

Thermidor and the Directory, 1795–1799

The period following Robespierre's fall is known as the Thermidorian reaction (Thermidor, or "heat," was the revolutionary month of Robespierre's execution). Revolutionary violence takes a breather as the Terror subsides and extreme policies are reversed. Jacobin Clubs are closed and a "white terror" instigated against former radicals. To provide order while maintaining republicanism, the Convention once again writes up a plan of government, the Constitution of Year III (1795). Though all males can vote, their votes are filtered through well-to-do electors who in turn choose representatives for the two-chamber assembly. For day-to-day governing, this assembly appoints five directors as an executive body. The regime known as the Directory runs France for four years. During this time, aristocratic fashions return as French politics remain divided over the future course of the revolution. These divisions plague the weak Directory, which faces opposition from both the left and the right.

Spring-Summer 1796 Extremists led by Gracchus Babeuf attempt to establish a socialist government with the so-called Conspiracy of Equals, but they are arrested, tried, and executed.

September 4, 1797 After free elections create a majority for royalists, the Directory, assisted by Napoleon Bonaparte (1769–1821), annuls the results and maintains power in the *coup d'état* of Fructidor.

With little popular support, the Directory remains dependent on battlefield victories to maintain itself in power. The situation seems ripe for an ambitious and successful military leader to overthrow the government and restore order.

The Rise of Napoleon

Some have labeled **Napoleon Bonaparte** the first modern man. His rise to power owed nothing to traditional ecclesiastical, aristocratic, or political institutions. Napoleon was self-made and possessed of immense talent and ambition, qualities that account for both his stunning successes and his crushing defeats. Born into a minor Italian noble family on the island of Corsica, which the French had annexed in 1768 (a year before his birth), Napoleon set out to prove he was the equal of every Frenchmen he encountered in his military academy and the army. Napoleon combined a quick mind that excelled in practical subjects, such as engineering, history, law, and administration, with supreme confidence in his talents and destiny.

Napoleon earned his first fame with the Italian campaign. Defying traditional rules of warfare, the general outmaneuvered and outfought the larger Habsburg army, and then proceeded to negotiate with the Austrian emperor on his own terms. The subsequent treaty (1797) established several new Italian republics and spread revolutionary ideas throughout the long-divided peninsula. Napoleon followed up his success with a bold move—the invasion of Egypt in 1798–1799. Though his strategic goals were unclear, Napoleon initially defeated the Ottoman army at the Battle of the Pyramids. However, the British navy cut off Napoleon's supply lines after crushing the French fleet in battle. With bigger stakes in mind, Napoleon abandoned his men in Egypt and found his way back to France, in time to take part in an overthrow of the moribund Directory. Joined by two other conspirators, Napoleon's *coup d'état* of Brumaire succeeded in creating a new government, the Consulate (with three Consuls). Chosen as First Consul, Bonaparte quickly outmaneuvered the other two consuls and in 1801 proclaimed himself First Consul for life. At the age of 32, Bonaparte commanded France and set out to institutionalize the principles of the revolution.

> ### THEME MUSIC
>
> Even when resented by those occupied, Napoleon's invasions exercised a profound impact on conquered nations, often triggering internal reforms or at minimum, debates over revolutionary ideas and modernizing policies. The Egyptian campaign launched Napoleon to power in France, while also stimulating European interest in the Middle East—both strategically and culturally. In addition, the campaign revealed the weakness of the Ottoman Empire (the "sick man of Europe") and stimulated nationalism among the Balkan peoples (SOP and NEI).

Napoleon's Domestic Policies, 1799–1814

Soon after being named First Consul, Napoleon consolidated his power, culminating with his proclamation of the French Empire in 1804 and his crowning as its emperor. It is generally believed that Napoleon promoted equality and nationalism during his rule; however, he implemented his policies from the top down with little democratic input and disregarded individual rights, such as freedom of the press or privacy, whenever it suited his interests. The following provides an idea of the nature of Napoleon's domestic policies in several areas. As you read, consider the extent to which Bonaparte either fulfilled or twisted the ideals of the revolution.

- *Governance and administration* – Keeping with the tradition of the revolution, Napoleon created a constitution for the Consulate and then the Empire. In reality, Napoleon concentrated power in his own hands. Laws were enacted by the Legislative Corps but could not be debated. The body acted in effect as a rubber stamp for the emperor's will. Unlike absolute monarchs, Napoleon succeeded in unifying administration through the creation of a **centralized professional bureaucracy**. Prefects ran each of the 83 departments but reported directly to Paris. To present himself as a man of the people, Napoleon used plebiscites, or referenda, on specific issues, often after the fact, such as whether the people agreed with Napoleon's proclamation of the empire (they did, by a large majority). However, Napoleon would not countenance opposition to his rule. The press was censored, and under the watchful eye of Joseph Fouché (1763–1820), a secret police infiltrated intellectual circles to identify opposition to the regime. Eventually Napoleon became occupied with the trappings of imperial rule, which was reflected in the nation at large with a new Empire Style of architecture and décor.

- *Legal and social policies* – Napoleon announced "careers open to talent" for those like himself who came from middling or lowly station but wished to rise through ability and ambition. Napoleon created a Legion of Honor to recognize the contributions of soldiers who served in the revolutionary wars. It is the **Civil Code** that represented the revolution's ideals of merit and equality and perhaps Napoleon's single most significant accomplishment. Guided by the enlightened impulse toward rational systemization, Napoleon created a single legal code for all of France, as well as the many nations he conquered, which stands to this day. However, the Civil Code reinforced patriarchy in the home and limited the rights of women related to divorce, property, and male infidelity.

- *Economic and financial policies* – To enhance industry, Napoleon modernized the infrastructure of France—building/repairing roads and bridges, beautifying the nation with monuments, and establishing the Bank of France. The bank helped in finally eliminating the budget deficit and modernizing the tax system. Napoleon's efforts at industrial simulation—tariffs, loans, public works—proved less successful, as his failed Continental System (see below) against Great Britain hindered French trade.

- *Educational system* – In an effort to modernize France and promote opportunity, Napoleon established a nationwide system of secondary schools, called the *lycée*, open to all social classes. A national system of technical universities was founded, reflecting the emperor's interest and belief in scientific progress.

- *Religious policies* – Napoleon finally ended the war between the revolution and the Catholic Church in his Concordat of 1801 with Pope Pius VII (r. 1800–1823). By the agreement, the pope regained some control of the French clergy, and Catholicism was recognized as the majority religion of France. However, the Church acknowledged the loss of its properties, and the French government retained a veto power over clerical appointments. Of skeptical mindset himself, Napoleon manipulated popular religious belief to his advantage, proclaiming in Egypt, "I am a Muslim," but also extending religious toleration to those in conquered nations.

Napoleonic Warfare, 1796–1814

Regardless of how Napoleon is viewed politically, he revolutionized the practice of warfare. It will not be necessary for you to grasp the complexities of Napoleonic battles and shifting coalitions, except in general outline, but you should understand the role of warfare in Napoleonic diplomacy and the legacy it left in the nineteenth century.

Though Napoleon met ultimate defeat and blundered strategically, he did not lose a European battle on land until 1813. What accounts for his stunning success?

- *Movement* – Conventional military wisdom emphasized maneuver to conserve manpower and guard supply lines and fortresses. Napoleon turned this wisdom on its head and made the enemy army his target by striking quickly.

- *Defying traditional limits* – Napoleon's armies ignored customs regarding when to fight: Sundays, winter, night—all were fair game. The French army learned to live off the countryside, cut off from supply lines.

- *Offensive* – With no patience for drawn-out campaigns, Napoleon aimed to defeat his opponents in a decisive battle, by concentrating force at the enemy's weakest spot.

- *Propaganda* – Napoleon presented himself as a liberator. He proclaimed republics in conquered nations and ended feudalism for peasants.

- **Citizen armies** – The French Revolution helped establish, and Napoleon advanced, the notion that warfare was an affair for free and equal citizens, not paid mercenaries—an idea that remains to this day.

In the period 1792–1815, France fought a number of different coalitions of nations. Despite the general agreement among rulers that the French Revolution should be quarantined, great power politics continued. Nations pursued traditional territorial and political objectives, even if in a more complex revolutionary environment. Britain most consistently opposed French designs, pursuing its traditional objective of preventing the emergence of a dominant power on the continent and protecting its empire.

France emerged victorious against the first two coalitions, which failed to stop the advance of the French revolution and its expansion into neighboring nations. In 1802, Napoleon negotiated peace with Britain, the final holdout from the Second Coalition. It would not last, as Napoleon's expansionist designs inevitably clashed with British mercantile interests. During the War of the Third Coalition (1805–1807), Napoleon masterfully defeated each of his continental opponents in turn—Austria, Prussia, and Russia—establishing himself as master of the continent. All major continental nations were either annexed to France, allied with it, or a friendly neutral. Napoleon's plans to defeat Britain outright were thwarted at the Battle of Trafalgar (1805), as a Franco-Spanish invasion fleet was destroyed by the British navy under Horatio Nelson.

To subdue Britain, Napoleon forced continental nations to embargo British goods, known as the Continental System. The plan proved difficult to enforce, harmful to continental trading interests (including France), and highly unpopular. By 1810, Russia had withdrawn from the system, compelling Napoleon to launch the fateful Russian campaign. Though many of Napoleon's policies within conquered nations proved popular, his actions also **aroused nationalism**, especially in Germany. These factors, in addition to a decline in Napoleon's tactical skill, led to his final defeat. The Grand Army's retreat from Moscow cost 90% of the men who had set out. Though Napoleon was able to raise another army, he was defeated again in 1814 in Germany (the largest battle prior to the twentieth century) and ultimately at Waterloo in 1815.

Napoleon's Foreign Policies, 1799–1814

In foreign policy, Napoleon pursued two goals: (1) institutionalize the ideals of the Enlightenment and French Revolution in conquered lands and (2) gain territory and influence for the French nation. At first, Napoleon captured the imagination of intellectuals across Europe, such as Beethoven and Goethe, as well as the support of the common people for his abolition of the Old Regime. However, his exploitation of subject lands and ruthless imposition of "French values" alienated a critical mass of nations bent on stopping him. In the last analysis, Napoleon was done in by the same superabundant ego that had led to his amazing rise to power. Again, consider Napoleon's adherence to revolutionary principles as you review the Napoleonic policies below.

- *Reforms* – Napoleon proclaimed the liberation of conquered nations and implemented many of the revolution's policies. To win over peasants, he announced the abolition of feudalism and the Old Regime, including guilds, old town charters, internal tariffs, and local weights and measures. In their place, Napoleon promoted rational government based on enlightened principles of religious toleration, efficient centralized government, and equality under the Napoleonic Code. Among progressives, such policies gained support, at least until opinion against Napoleon turned.

- *Creation of a new diplomatic system* – Napoleon paid

little respect to diplomatic traditions. As he conquered, Napoleon created republics in Italy, the Low Countries, and Switzerland, appointing his relatives to ruling positions (a practice of nepotism seemingly at odds with his ideas of merit). After defeating Austria again in 1806, Napoleon simply abolished the medieval Holy Roman Empire, replacing it with the 35-state Confederation of the Rhine. To gain the support of Polish leaders, Napoleon recreated a smaller version of Poland, the Duchy of Warsaw. Once Napoleon felt secure in his domination of the continent, he attempted to wrap himself with dynastic legitimacy. In 1804, he convinced the pope to attend his coronation as emperor, and when he and his wife Josephine were unable to produce an heir, he married a young Habsburg princess, Marie Louise (which made him by marriage the nephew of the deceased Louis XVI).

- *Continental System* – As noted above, Napoleon attempted to cut the continent off from British trade. This proved difficult because Britain's colonial products could not be easily replaced by consumers. Transportation difficulties and differing tariffs among the member states prevented continental trade from taking up the British slack. Not only did the Continental System fail in its objective, it aroused opposition toward a French-dominated Europe.

- *Peninsular war* – In 1808, Napoleon coerced the Bourbon king of Spain to abdicate and replaced him with his own brother Jerome. The Spanish resented Napoleon's high-handed tactics and religious policies related to Catholicism. With British support, the Spanish bogged the French down in a guerilla war, sapping resources and men.

Coda: Women and the Revolution

Women played a central role in the French Revolution. But did this participation yield tangible results? It was during the moderate phase that women gained the most—the right to divorce, inherit property, and child custody. Also at this time, Olympe de Gouges (1748–1793) published the Declaration of Rights of Women and the Female Citizen to counter the similarly titled document by the National Assembly, but she was guillotined in 1793 for her revolutionary activities. During the radical phase, some women formed the Society for Revolutionary Republican Women, which agitated for equal rights. The club was banned by the Mountain, because they believed it violated Rousseau's ideals regarding women's domestic role. Finally, the Napoleonic Code, often viewed as a blow for equality, generally excluded women from the principle. The code limited female property rights, restricted divorce, and reinforced the sexual double-standard for adultery. Most women who participated in the revolution probably did so on behalf of their class rather than their gender. Nonetheless, it seems that once again a movement promising change and equality left women excluded from the revolutionary application of its principles. Taken together, the Enlightenment and the French Revolution, however, established the agenda for the feminist movement over the next century.

> **SKILL SET**
>
> Though women did not realize the promise of their participation, the French Revolution marks a watershed in the status of women and the feminist movement. To evaluate this claim, you will need to draw upon your understanding of previous movements of change (e.g., Reformation or Scientific Revolution) and anticipate the outcomes for women during the nineteenth century (MAC). You may wish to create a simple timeline or chart that demonstrates these changes and continuities over time (CCOT).

Additional Resources

📖 **David Armitage and Sanjay Subrahmanym, eds.,** *The Age of Revolutions in Global Context, c. 1760–1840* **(2009)** — A brief collection of articles placing revolutions of the era within a broader context.

📖 **Jack Censer and Lynn Hunt,** *Liberty, Equality, and Fraternity* **(2001)** — A wonderful resource for students, this book is concise, focused, and interpretive. Also see the related website: http://chnm.gmu.edu/revolution/.

📖 **William Doyle,** *Origins of the French Revolution* **(1980)** — Provides an account of the events leading up to the revolution, concentrating on the financial crisis and political conflict.

📖 **Francois Furet and Mona Ozouf, eds.,** *A Critical Dictionary of the French Revolution* **(1989)** — For those who need a comprehensive resource for further study and research.

📖 **Georges Lefebvre,** *The Coming of the French Revolution* **(1967)** — This is considered the classic Marxist explanation of the revolution's origins in terms of class struggle.

📖 **R.R. Palmer,** *Twelve Who Ruled: The Year of the Terror in the French Revolution* **(1989)** — Engaging study that examines the personalities of the 12 men on the Committee of Public Safety.

📖 **Andrew Roberts,** *Napoleon: A Life* **(2014)** — The new standard biography of a major figure of the course.

📖 **Alyssa Sepinwall, ed.,** *Haitian History: New Perspectives* **(2013)** — Articles on an often-forgotten revolution, part of the Atlantic wave of upheaval.

📖 **Simon Schama,** *Citizens: A Chronicle of the French Revolution* **(1990)** — Well-written but challenging work focusing on the new civic culture and the use of violence.

📺 *Égalité for All: Toussaint Louverture and the Haitian Revolution* (2009) — An hour-long PBS documentary about the Haitian Revolution and its leader.

📺 *Empires—Napoleon* (2000) — A 4-hour PBS documentary that traces the entire life of Napoleon. Offers a companion website: http://www.pbs.org/empires/napoleon/.

💻 **http://alphahistory.com/frenchrevolution/french-revolution-historiography/** — Explains the evolution of scholarship on and interpretations of the French Revolution. Also, see the home page for other resources on the French Revolution.

CHAPTER TEST

Multiple-Choice Questions

Questions 1–4 are based on the passage below.

> "July 28th, 1789. The Revolution in the French Constitution and Government may now, I think, be looked upon as completed, beyond all fears of any further attempts being made by the Court Party to defeat it. The entrance of the King into Paris was certainly one of the most humiliating steps that could possibly be taken…
>
> There certainly never was an instance of so astonishing a Revolution operated almost without bloodshed, and without the people being led on by any leader, or by any party, but merely by the general diffusion of reason and philosophy. We shall soon be able to form a guess what is the nature of the constitution that is intended to be adopted in France…. From what is known of their ideas and principles it is thought the Executive Power will be left solely to the King, who will be deprived of all share in the Legislative Authority, which will be lodged in the National Assembly, formed into one Body, without distinction of Orders."
>
> Report from the British Ambassador on events in France, 1789

1. The cause of the French Revolution best demonstrated by the report above was the:
   A. financial crisis of the monarchy and inability to resolve its debt.
   B. social divisions among the traditional three estates.
   C. growing criticism of royal absolutism and corruption.
   D. economic crisis caused by rising food prices and famine.

2. The development after July 1789 that most contradicted the ambassador's portrayal of the revolution was the:
   A. abolition of serfdom and feudalism.
   B. confiscation of the lands of the Church.
   C. Declaration of the Rights of Man and Citizen.
   D. execution of Louis XVI and Reign of Terror.

3. The historical situation that most closely parallels the events described above was the:
   A. Protestant attack on the Catholic Church in the sixteenth century.
   B. opposition to Habsburg centralization during the seventeenth century.
   C. unification of Italy and Germany during the nineteenth century.
   D. overthrow of the Russian tsar during the twentieth century.

4. All of the following represent effects of the French Revolution outside of France EXCEPT the:
   A. use of mass citizen armies to conquer lands and impose revolutionary ideals.
   B. emergence of a major slave rebellion in the colony of Saint Domingue.
   C. establishment of a system of stable republics committed to peace.
   D. the creation of an empire under the control of Napoleon Bonaparte.

Questions 5–6 are based on the image below.

Illustration for French revolutionary calendar, 1794

5. The depiction above was likely influenced most strongly by:

   A. the spread of revolutionary ideals by French armies.

   B. Romantic themes in and approaches toward art.

   C. Enlightenment principles of reason and efficiency.

   D. feminist principles of equality and natural rights.

6. Which of the following policies of the French revolutionaries most directly coincides with the visual?

   A. De-Christianization and nationalization of the Catholic Church

   B. Raising of mass citizen armies for total warfare

   C. Overthrow of the monarchy and the execution of Louis XVI

   D. The creation of a government based on popular sovereignty

Questions 7–9 are based on the map below.

Europe, 1810

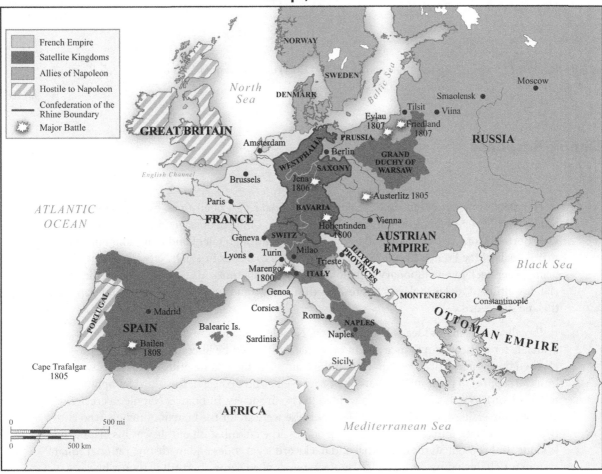

7. The development that contributed most directly to the situation portrayed on the map was:

   A. the mobilization of French women for the revolution under feminist principles.

   B. Britain's extensive empire of colonial possessions and dominance of trade.

   C. the hostility of foreign governments toward the spread of the French Revolution.

   D. France's reliance on mass citizen armies motivated by liberty, equality, and fraternity.

8. The most significant change on the map above from one depicting Europe in 1648 would be the:

   A. dominant position of Russia in eastern Europe.

   B. elimination of the Holy Roman Empire.

   C. unification of Italy and Germany.

   D. state of extended war among the great powers.

9. Which of the following, in the short-term, led to a major diplomatic change that would be reflected on the map?

   A. Nationalist campaigns directed against Napoleon and foreign rule

   B. A revival of the position of the Catholic Church

   C. The expansion of British manufactures and commerce

   D. A civil war in France directed against Napoleon's Empire

See Chapter 18 for answers and explanations.

Long Essay Question

Directions: Read the prompt below and write your response on a separate sheet of paper. A sample response and commentary follow.

Evaluate the extent to which Napoleon Bonaparte (1799–1814) advanced the ideals of the French Revolution.

(RP: CCOT)

LEQ Sample Response

Napoleon Bonaparte was one of the most influential rulers of all-time, not just in France but all over Europe. Napoleon put himself up as a man of the people, and in many ways he was. Born in Corsica, Napoleon had to prove himself through talent and ambition, one of the major goals of the French Revolution. When he came to power in 1799, Napoleon wanted to bring order back to revolutionary principles. Though sometimes his policies seemed dictatorial, his ultimate goal was always to preserve the equality and fraternity for the people, and in this, he succeeded.

Equality was a major idea of the revolution. Napoleon made sure that opportunity was available for all people in France and in other nations. When he liberated a nation, he proclaimed the abolition of feudalism and all the features of the Old Regime. His actions won him the support of great intellectuals like Beethoven (who dedicated the Third Symphony to Napoleon), as well as citizens who wanted to rise in society. In France, Napoleon created schools, universities, and a Legion of Honor. These were all for the benefit of people who contributed to society, unlike the old sponging nobles. The culmination of this was his Napoleonic Code. It threw out all the old feudal and backward legal codes and made one rational equal system for all, including for taxes. If Napoleon overlooked some liberty, it was only because France was in anarchy and someone needed to provide reform and order.

Napoleon protected another great idea of the revolution—nationalism. The reason his soldiers fought so strongly was because they believed they were fighting for their own nation and their equality and liberty. Many countries saw how powerful nationalism could be in their own nations. After Napoleon brought his equal law code and promoted equality, many believed that their nations also could benefit from nationalism. One place where this was especially important was Germany. Many German intellectuals found Napoleon a great figure who showed how a nation could be united, which Germany was not. Philosophers and writers glorified the power of a united state and how old ways must be eliminated. Just because Napoleon promoted the kind of nationalism that led the Germans to get rid of the French does not change the point—Napoleon did promote nationalism!

People who say that Napoleon was a dictator or that he reversed the ideals of the revolution don't understand the situation at the time. France had gone back and forth between monarchy and radicalism and needed a break. Napoleon was that break—someone who took a bunch of lofty ideas and made them into something real. For centuries, monarchs had failed in creating an efficient and centralized state and economy. It was Napoleon who left a legacy of how to create a modern state and win over the people. Napoleon's approach would influence future leaders like Bismarck and Cavour in unifying their nations, as they governed from the top-down but manipulated nationalism and public opinion to secure their power.

LEQ Response Analysis

Clearly our student is an admirer of Napoleon, which for the most part, they use to their advantage. The essay offers a clear thesis, adequate background on Napoleon (Contextualization), strong factual support, and clearly addresses the Targeted RP. On one hand, the student acknowledges the ways in which Napoleon failed to fulfill revolutionary ideas (liberty), but provides an explanation for this anomaly. The body paragraphs focus on the prompt and provide a fairly wide but relevant range of examples. Finally, the conclusion attempts to sew up the Complexity point (which had already been earned by noting counterclaims to the thesis) by connecting Napoleon both to prior monarchs and to subsequent political leaders (Bismarck and Cavour). The essay overlooks obvious counterexamples to his positive portrayal—status of women, conquests, censorship—however, it cannot be denied that the student accomplishes the objective of consistently arguing their point. **Score: 6** (+1 for Thesis, +1 for Contextualization, +2 for Use of Evidence, +1 for the Targeted RP (CCOT), +1 for Complexity)

PERIOD 2 — DIAGNOSTIC EXAM

Section I, Part A: Multiple-Choice Questions

Time—30 minutes; 30 questions

Directions: Each of the questions or incomplete statements below is followed by four suggested answers or completions. Select the one that is best in each case and then enter the appropriate letter in the corresponding space on the answer sheet. Source materials have been edited for the purpose of this exercise.

Questions 1–4 are based on the image below.

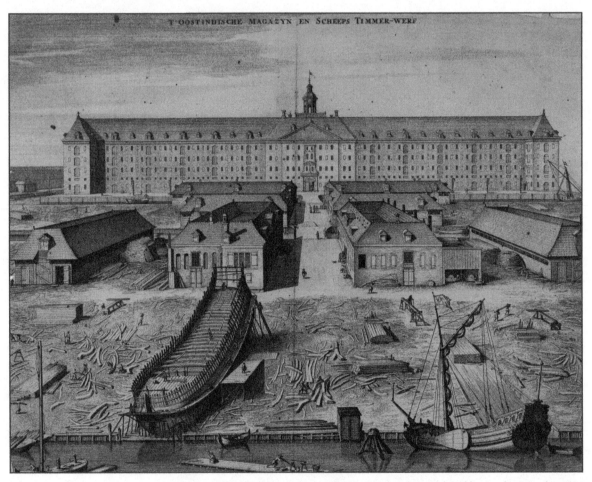

Shipyard of the Dutch East India Company, Amsterdam, by Joseph Mulder, Dutch printmaker, 1726

1. All of the following contributed to the historical situation portrayed above EXCEPT:
   A. the dominance of the Dutch government by merchant elites.
   B. European expansion into the Americas and East Indies.
   C. the end of conflict and warfare among European states.
   D. the development of new tools and techniques of finance.

2. Which of the following nations during this period would be most similar to the depiction of the Dutch above?
   A. Russia
   B. France
   C. Britain
   D. Spain

3. The most significant cultural impact of the processes depicted in the image was:

   A. an increase in the number of printed books and materials.

   B. the growth of a consumer culture in new products and luxuries.

   C. an acceptance of religious toleration and dissenting political views.

   D. the growth of theories of absolutism and divine right monarchy.

4. Which of the following was the most significant change in Europe's interaction with the world as represented by the image?

   A. European commerce facilitated creation of a global economic network.

   B. Travel literature replaced the classics as standard reading material.

   C. Anti-colonial political movements established independence.

   D. The search for raw materials in colonies led to industrialization.

Questions 5–8 are based on the image below. Royalists vs. puritans.

Cromwell after Charels 1
↳ had dictatorship → became stricts. → charels II

"The Royal Oak of Britain," political cartoon, 1649

5. Which of the following was the most direct cause of the situation represented by the cartoon?

   A. The growth of theories that justified absolute monarchy

   B. Conflict over sovereignty between king and Parliament

   C. Expansion of commerce and a rising middle class

   D. Military innovations that emphasized infantrymen

6. The figure to the left of the oak tree would most likely have supported:

   A. a revival of Catholic influence in Britain.

   B. the interests of the landowning class.

   C. patronage of nobles for government offices.

   D. the establishment of a republican government.

7. Which of the following nations in the seventeenth century differed most strongly from the situation depicted in the cartoon?

A. Netherlands

B. Poland *being ÷)*

C. Holy Roman Empire

D. France *(Louis 14)*

8. The most decisive resolution of the issues depicted in the cartoon was the:

A. Glorious Revolution and Bill of Rights.

B. acceptance of the New Science among elites.

C. Treaty of Paris (1763) ending the Seven Years War.

D. revolt of Britain's colonies in North America.

Questions 9–11 are based on the image below.

Joseph II of Austria promotes agricultural reforms by sharing labor with peasants, 1780s

9. A historian would most likely use the depiction above to support which of the following interpretations?

A. "New civic venues, such as coffeehouses and salons, supported the spread of scientific principles to all areas of life."

B. "New World crops, such as the potato, enhanced European diet, standard of living, and life expectancy."

C. "Enlightened despots patronized new intellectual movements in hopes of strengthening their states."

D. "Mercantilist policies concentrated power in the hands of monarchs but generated critiques by free-market thinkers."

10. Which of the following was the most direct social consequence, in Europe as a whole, of the type of policies demonstrated in the visual?

A. The migration of poor and landless peasants to cities

B. A revolution in consumption of luxury goods

C. A more child-centered and private home life

D. The disappearance of epidemic diseases such as the plague

11. Which of the following nations would have been LEAST likely in the eighteenth century to pursue similar policies?

   A. Russia

   B. Prussia

   C. Great Britain

   D. Netherlands

Questions 12–15 are based on the passage below.

> "[P]rejudice transformed itself into superstition; it rooted itself so thoroughly that the crudest people believed themselves capable of penetrating into final causes, as if they had an entire knowledge of them. Thus instead of showing that Nature does nothing in vain, they believed that God & nature thought after the fashion of men. Experience having made known that an infinite number of calamities trouble…life[,] like storms, earthquakes, diseases, hunger, thirst, and they attributed all these evils to celestial anger, they believed the Divinity irritated against the offenses of men, who have not been able to free their brains of such a chimera, nor disabuse themselves of these prejudices by the daily examples which prove to them that goods & evils have in all times been common to the good & the wicked. This error was due to the fact that it was easier for them to remain in their natural ignorance than to abolish a prejudice received for so many centuries & to establish something probable."
>
> Anonymous, *Treatise of the Three Imposters**, pamphlet written ca. 1700
>
> * a reference to Moses, Jesus, and Mohammed

12. Which of the following intellectual developments of the seventeenth and eighteenth centuries most directly influenced the outlook of the author above?

   A. The articulation of new models of politics by theorists like Locke and Rousseau

   B. The embrace of equality by the philosophes of the Enlightenment

   C. The spread of rational and empirical thought that challenged traditional values

   D. The expansion of the number of printed materials and a new literate culture

13. Which of the following developments in early modern Europe would the author most likely have condemned?

   A. The spread of witchcraft accusations and executions

   B. The Protestant Reformation's criticisms of the Catholic Church

   C. Renaissance humanists' glorification of classical values and learning

   D. European exploitation of indigenous peoples in the Americas

14. The figure who would have agreed most with the outlook expressed in the passage is:

   A. Erasmus

   B. Galileo

   C. John Locke

   D. Denis Diderot

15. Which of the following offers the most likely explanation for the author's anonymity?

   A. The author was a woman, and as such, feared that her gender would undermine the document's reception among men.

   B. Since governments attempted to censor ideas perceived as threatening to state and church, the author believed it safest to keep his or her identity hidden.

   C. As commerce and a consumer economy expanded, the author hoped his or her anonymity would raise attention and assist in sales of his publication.

   D. The author was a political revolutionary and hoped to keep his or her identity secret until able to organize a movement opposed to royal absolutism.

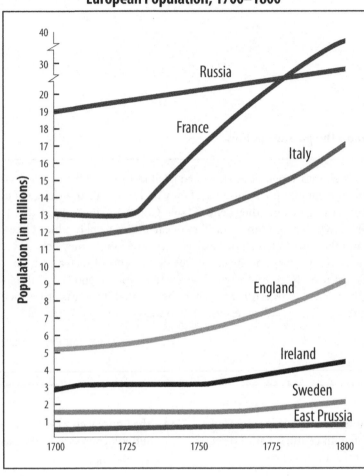

European Population, 1700–1800

16. Which of the following best explains the population trend for the first 25 years depicted?

   A. Loss of life due to constant warfare and civilian casualties

   B. The movement toward a system of commercial agriculture

   C. Upheaval caused by peasant revolts and witchcraft executions

   D. The inability to break out of a limited food supply and scarcity of goods

17. All of the following explain the population trends after 1725 EXCEPT:

   A. increased crop yields due to an agricultural revolution.

   B. the ability of absolute monarchs to provide stability.

   C. the elimination of major epidemic diseases, such as plague and smallpox.

   D. improved food supply due to New World crops, like the potato.

18. The event or development that represents the most significant change in population trends after 1800 was:

   A. the French Revolution.

   B. the Industrial Revolution.

   C. the development of feminism.

   D. imperialism in Africa and Asia.

Questions 19–22 are based on the passage below.

"Several women have complained to us about the revolution. They tell us in many letters that for the last two years it seems that there is but one sex in France. In the primary assemblies, in the sections, in the clubs, etc., there is no longer any discussion of women, as if they no longer existed.

Women have never shown this sustained and strongly pronounced taste for civil and political independence, this ardor to which all cedes, which inspires in men so many great acts, so many heroic actions; that is to say, civil and political liberty is useless to women, and as a result must seem foreign to them...[B]orn to a perpetual dependency from the first instance of their existence to that of their death, they have only been gifted with private virtues; the tumult of camps, the storms of public space, the agitations of the tribunals are not at all suited for the second sex.

Citizenesses! No matter what happens, cultivate in peace and silence your everyday virtues...they are no less precious for being hidden. Woe to you, woe to all of us, if, because of a rivalry harmful to both sexes, you come to see your duties with disgust! ... Leave to us the worries and strains of [what is] outside [the home]; gently reign in the interior of your households."

Louis-Marie Prudhomme, male French newspaper publisher, "On the influence of the revolution on women," *Révolutions of Paris*, February 12, 1791

19. The views above were most likely influenced by:
  A. Louis XIV.
  B. Jean-Jacques Rousseau.
  C. Maximilien Robespierre.
  D. Mary Wollstonecraft.

20. The passage reflects which of the following regarding women and the French Revolution?
  A. Women participated in the revolution through revolts, documents, and petitions.
  B. Women gained legal improvements such as the right to divorce and own property.
  C. Women were denied equality with men according to the Napoleonic Code.
  D. Women supported the war effort on the home front against invading armies.

21. A historian might use the passage as evidence for which continuity with nineteenth-century attitudes toward women?
  A. The fight for women's suffrage
  B. The cult of domesticity
  C. White-collar employment
  D. Universal compulsory education

22. Which of the following expresses a major difference between the experiences of women during the French and Russian Revolutions?
  A. Women gained the right to vote during the Russian Revolution.
  B. Women gained full legal equality during the French Revolution.
  C. Women held positions of policy-making during the Russian Revolution.
  D. Women played a leading role during key events of the French Revolution.

Questions 23–26 are based on the passage below.

> "The plan of this book is fairly simple. We must ask ourselves three questions.
> What is the Third Estate? Everything.
> What has it been until now in the political order? Nothing.
> What does it want to be? Something.
>
> Chapter 1. The Third Estate Is a Complete Nation
>
> …Who is bold enough to maintain that the Third Estate does not contain within itself everything needful to constitute a complete nation? It is like a strong and robust man with one arm still in chains. If the privileged order were removed, the nation would not be something less but something more. What then is the Third Estate? All; but an 'all' that is fettered and oppressed. What would it be without the privileged order? It would be all; but free and flourishing. Nothing will go well without the Third Estate; everything would go considerably better without the two others…"
>
> Emmanuel-Joseph Sieyès, French clergyman and writer, *What Is the Third Estate?*, 1789

23. Which cause of the French Revolution is revealed most directly in Sieyès's pamphlet?

    A. The financial crisis and bankruptcy faced by the state

    B. The inequality and hierarchy that existed within the traditional social order

    C. Growing aristocratic and clerical dissent with absolute monarchy

    D. Economic crises of poor harvests and rising prices

24. The action of the French revolutionaries that would have most affected Sieyès personally was:

    A. the overthrow of the Bastille.

    B. the establishment of a constitutional monarchy.

    C. the nationalization of the Catholic Church.

    D. a declaration of war against foreign enemies.

25. The ideas expressed in the pamphlet affected events overseas by:

    A. inspiring a slave revolt in Saint Domingue (Haiti).

    B. helping the United States establish its independence.

    C. leading to a revolt in the Indian army, the Sepoy Mutiny.

    D. encouraging the development of a French empire in Indochina.

26. During his rule, Napoleon I most directly supported the goals of Sieyès by:

    A. signing a Concordat with the Pope to normalize France's relations with the Church.

    B. opening up careers to individuals of talent from the middle and lower classes.

    C. spreading the French Revolution to other nations through war and conquest.

    D. establishing a secret police and censoring or eliminating newspapers.

Questions 27–30 are based on the image below.

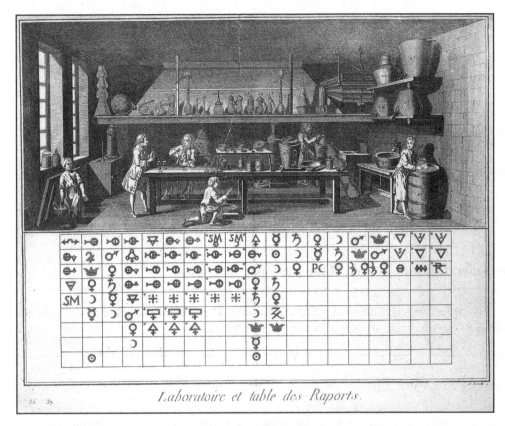

Depiction of chemical laboratory and chemical symbols, *The Encyclopédie*, 1751

27. The feature of eighteenth-century intellectual life best reflected above is the:

    A. popularization and dissemination of the methods of the Scientific Revolution.

    B. promotion of equality and reform among the philosophes.

    C. use of censorship by monarchies to suppress perceived threats to the state.

    D. growth of new public and civic venues based on new consumer products.

28. Which of the following resulted from the publication of works like that shown above?

    A. The exposure of Europeans to non-European cultures

    B. The extension of religious tolerance to minorities

    C. The growth in literacy and spread of public opinion

    D. The spread of artistic movements reflecting middle-class values

29. The processes depicted in the image would lead most directly in the nineteenth century to the:

    A. spread of revolutionary ideologies.

    B. unification of Italy and Germany.

    C. imperial control of Africa and Asia.

    D. growth of industry and technology.

30. Based on the image, historians might label this period the:

    A. Age of Absolutism.

    B. Age of Reason.

    C. Old Regime.

    D. Age of Revolution.

Section I, Part B: Short-Answer Questions

Time—25 minutes; 2 Questions

Directions: Read each question carefully and answer all parts of the question. Use complete sentences; an outline or bulleted list is not acceptable. Sources have been edited for the purposes of this exercise.

1. a) Describe one major innovation that characterized the Agricultural Revolution, 1650–1800.

    b) Explain one example of an economic effect of the Agricultural Revolution, 1650–1800.

    c) Explain one example of a social effect of the Agricultural Revolution, 1650–1800.

Use the passage below to answer all parts of the question that follows.

> "The shifting balance among the European powers from 1650–1763 can be attributed more to the effectiveness of nations' abilities to exploit overseas commerce and less to military power."

2. a) Describe one example that <u>supports</u> the historical interpretation expressed in the passage.

    b) Describe one example that <u>contradicts</u> the historical interpretation expressed in the passage.

    c) Explain one major shift that occurred in the European balance of power due to warfare in the period 1650–1763.

Section II, Part A: Document-Based Question

Total Time—60 minutes; 1 Question

Directions: Question 1 is based on the accompanying documents. It is suggested that you spend about 15 minutes reading the documents and 45 minutes writing your response. The documents have been edited for the purpose of this exercise.

In your response you should do the following:
*   Respond to the prompt with a historically defensible thesis or claim that establishes a line of reasoning.
*   Describe a broader historical context relevant to the prompt.
*   Support an argument in response to the prompt using at least six documents.
*   Use at least one additional piece of specific historical evidence (beyond that found in the documents) relevant to an argument about the prompt.
*   For at least three documents, explain how or why the document's point of view, purpose, historical situation, and/or audience is relevant to an argument.
*   Use evidence to corroborate, qualify, or modify an argument that addresses the prompt.

Question 1 *Evaluate the extent to which the French Revolution was caused and defined in its course, 1789–1794, by class conflict between the bourgeoisie and the nobility and clergy.*

Document 1

Source: "People Under the Old Regime," political cartoon, 1780s

Source: Third Estate of Dourdon, *cahier de doléance* (grievance) in anticipation of Estates General meeting, 1789

[The Third Estate of Dourdon] wishes:

1. That his subjects of the third estate, equal by such status to all other citizens, present themselves before the common father without other distinction which might degrade them.

2. That all the orders, already united by duty and a common desire to contribute equally to the needs of the State, also deliberate in common concerning its needs.

3. That no citizen lose his liberty except according to law; that, consequently, no one be arrested by virtue of special orders, or, if imperative circumstances necessitate such orders, that the prisoner be handed over to the regular courts of justice within forty-eight hours at the latest.

4. That no letters or writings intercepted in the post [mails] be the cause of the detention of any citizen, or be produced in court against him, except in case of conspiracy or undertaking against the State.

5. That the property of all citizens be inviolable, and that no one be required to make sacrifice thereof for the public welfare, except upon assurance of indemnification based upon the statement of freely selected appraisers….

16. That such tax be borne equally, without distinction, by all classes of citizens and by all kinds of property, even feudal and contingent rights.

Document 3

Source: The Women's March to Versailles, illustration, October 1789

Document 4

Source: Abolition of the Feudal System, National Assembly, decree, August 4, 1789

Article I. The National Assembly hereby completely abolishes the feudal system. It decrees that, among the existing rights and dues...all those originating in or representing real or personal serfdom shall be abolished without indemnification.

III. The exclusive right to hunt and to maintain unenclosed warrens is likewise abolished, and every landowner shall have the right to kill, or to have destroyed on his own land, all kinds of game, observing, however, such police regulations as may be established with a view to the safety of the public.

IV. All manorial courts are hereby suppressed without indemnification. But the magistrates of these courts shall continue to perform their functions until such time as the National Assembly shall provide for the establishment of a new judicial system.

V. Tithes of every description, as well as the dues which have been substituted for them, under whatever denomination they are known or collected... are abolished...

VII. The sale of judicial and municipal offices shall be abolished forthwith. Justice shall be dispensed freely. ...

XI. All citizens, without distinction of birth, are eligible to any office or dignity, whether ecclesiastical, civil, or military; and no profession shall imply any derogation.

Document 5

Source: Jacques-Pierre Brissot de Warville, French politician and founder of Society of the Friends of Blacks, "Address to the National Assembly for the Abolition of the Slave Trade," February 5, 1790

Don't let yourself stray from the duty that humanity imposes on you out of fear of some interruption in the economic activity that the Slave Trade brings to France. Did you listen to this fear when, with a bold hand you overturned all the abuses contrary to a free Constitution? These abuses...supported thousands of individuals; the commotion caused by this revolution has made all fortunes uncertain, tightened the availability of capital, suspended practically all [public and private] works. What bad citizen would nonetheless complain of this necessary suspension! It was not however your blood that tyrants spilled; they did not violate the asylum of your home at every instant; they did not unjustly condemn you in order to have the right to sell you; they did not tear you from your homes in order to plunge you into this eternal captivity.

The men, whose cause we defend, do not have... elevated claims, although, citizens of the same Empire & men like us, they have the same rights as us. We do not at all ask that you restore political rights to French Blacks, [those rights] that alone certify & maintain the dignity of man. We do not even ask for their liberty....We ask for...the abolition of the [slave] Trade...

Document 6

Source: Maximilien Robespierre, French politician, Committee of Public Safety, "Report Upon the Principles of Political Morality," February 6, 1794

If virtue be the spring of a popular government in times of peace, the spring of that government during a revolution is virtue combined with terror: virtue, without which terror is destructive; terror, without which virtue is impotent. Terror is only justice prompt, severe and inflexible; it is then an emanation of virtue; it is less a distinct principle than a natural consequence of the general principle of democracy, applied to the most pressing wants of the country.

The protection of government is only due to peaceable citizens; and all citizens in the republic are republicans. The royalists, the conspirators, are strangers, or rather enemies. Is not this dreadful contest, which liberty maintains against tyranny, indivisible? Are not the internal enemies the allies of those in the exterior?

Document 7

Source: Statistics on classes in France and executions during Reign of Terror, 1789–1794

Victims of the Terror, 1793–1794

Class	% of French population	% of victims
Clergy	1.2	7
Nobles	1.6	8
Upper middle class	2	14
Lower middle class	4	10.5
Working class	12	31.5
Peasants	79.2	28
TOTAL	**100%**	**99%***

* 1% of victims were unidentified.

Section II, Part B: Long Essay Question

Time—40 minutes; 1 Question

Directions: Choose EITHER Question 2 or Question 3.

In your response, you should do the following.

- Respond to the prompt with a historically defensible thesis or claim that establishes a line of reasoning.
- Describe a broader historical context relevant to the prompt.
- Support an argument in response to the prompt using specific and relevant examples of evidence.
- Use historical reasoning (e.g., comparison, causation, continuity or change over time) to frame or structure an argument that addresses the prompt.
- Use evidence to corroborate, qualify, or modify an argument that addresses the prompt.

Question 2 *Evaluate the most important difference in how any two nations in the period, 1650–1780, responded to the theory of absolutism.*

(RP: Comparison)

Question 3 *Evaluate the most significant difference between elite and popular culture during the eighteenth century.*

(RP: Comparison)

ANSWERS, EXPLANATIONS, & SAMPLE RESPONSES
for the Diagnostic Exams can be found at
✎ **www.sherpalearning.com/achiever** ✎

The chapters in Period 3 address the following major developments and events:

- Industrial Revolution in Britain and its spread to the continent
- The social and economic impact of industrialization
- Governmental, reformist, and ideological responses to industrialization
- Congress of Vienna, Concert system, and revolutionary responses
- Romanticism and its influences on the arts
- Unification of Italy and Germany and other nation-building efforts
- Second Industrial Revolution and its relation to nationalism and imperialism
- European imperialism into Africa and Asia
- Urban reform and development of a mass society

- Mass politics and pressure groups, including workers, women, and ethnic minorities
- Modernism in the sciences, ideas, and the arts

Each chapter will provide a content review and practice questions to test your understanding of the material. At the conclusion of the content chapters, you will be able both to gauge your grasp of the content and practice historical thinking skills in a diagnostic test that will include:

- 30 MC questions
- 2 SAQs
- 1 DBQ
- 1 LEQ (choice of 2)

Each chapter will begin with a brief correlation to the Unit Guides from the Course and Exam Description (CED). Good luck with your review.

❧ CHAPTER 11 ❧

Industrial Society and the Struggle for Reform, 1815–1850

The Industrial Revolution in economic production and the French Revolution in politics combined to transform much of European life in the nineteenth century. Moving on parallel but often intersecting tracks, these two movements are often termed the Dual Revolution. Many historians consider the revolution in production, transportation, and marketing of goods associated with the Industrial Revolution the single most significant event in human history. In this chapter, we address the growth of industry in Great Britain, its spread to the continent, the effort to restore the Old Order at the Congress of Vienna, the development of political ideologies as a response to the Dual Revolution, and the revolutionary echoes rebounding through the first half of the nineteenth century from the French Revolution, culminating with the revolutions of 1848. This period lays the foundation for modern society, politics, and production, making it a turning point in European history.

 KEY IN – Chapter 11 addresses all or part of the following topics in the Unit Guides of the CED:

Topic 5.7 The Congress of Vienna

Topic 5.8 Romanticism

Topic 6.1 Contextualizing Industrialization and its Origins and Effects

Topic 6.2 The Spread of Industry Throughout Europe

Topic 6.4 Social Effects of Industrialization

Topic 6.5 The Concert of Europe and European Conservatism

Topic 6.6 Reactions and Revolutions

Topic 6.7 Ideologies of Change and Reform Movements

Topic 6.8 19th-Century Social Reform

Topic 6.9 Institutional Responses and Reform

Topic 6.10 Causation in the Age of Industrialization

Topic 7.2 Nationalism

Great Britain's Industrial Experience

Definitions and Great Britain's Advantages

Before exploring the reasons for Britain's industrial lead and dominance, let's define what is involved in the term Industrial Revolution. Each of the following three definitions expresses an essential feature of the process:

1. An assault on the scarcity of the Old Regime, leading to a revolution in access to the means supporting human life.

2. The substitution of mineral and mechanical energy (theoretically inexhaustible) for animal and human energy (which tires or wears out).

3. Rising output *per capita* (per person) at declining unit cost; in other words, each worker produces more goods at a cheaper cost, supporting a rising standard of living.

Europe had enjoyed commercial growth and at times a rising standard of living prior to the Industrial Revolution. Inevitably, these periods of growth ran up against the limits of natural resources or the primitive nature of technology. Britain's accomplishment seemed unique in applying new production techniques and technologies to exploit the full potential of nature's bounty. Owing to the following package of advantages, Great Britain, first among European nations, realized the processes expressed above:

> **SKILL SET**
>
> Here we have a major interpretive question of causation: Why was Great Britain the first nation to experience industrialization? For practice, consider writing a focused introductory paragraph that not only identifies the relevant causal factors, but also takes a position with which another historian might disagree (CAUS and ARG).

- *Geographic advantages* – Britain's unique island status insulated it from continental strife, freeing it from supporting a standing army while at the same time promoting an overseas empire. No place in Britain was more than 70 miles from the ocean. Profits from trade could be reinvested in manufacturing enterprises. In addition, Britain possessed natural resources, such as coal and iron ore, necessary for industry.

- *Economic advantages* – Promotion of the **Agricultural Revolution** allowed for a larger population, and the resulting mobile labor force manned the new factories. Also, no nation could boast a better financial network of <u>banks</u> and credit institutions able to supply entrepreneurs with the capital necessary for industrial enterprises.

- *Political advantages* – Even if many nations mirrored Britain's industrial potential, chances are those groups inclined toward industry exercised little influence over government policy. Not so in Britain. Through Parliament, mercantile and industrial interests enacted laws such as the <u>enclosure acts</u> to promote commercial agriculture and laissez-faire policies to protect <u>property rights</u>. These groups supported development of the British navy and the acquisition of colonies, the source of <u>raw materials</u> and markets for British products.

- *Social advantages* – In traditional European societies, elites frowned upon the pursuit of profit (to be distinguished from the accumulation of wealth) as characteristic of the "vulgar bourgeoisie." In Britain, aristocrats and the middle class instead shared an interest in commerce and profit accumulation. Though Protestant dissenters experienced religious toleration, their exclusion from the paid clergy, the university system, and government positions drove them into commercial and industrial pursuits. Their dissenting academies emphasized practical and technical training, and indeed, many of the early inventors derived from this group.

The Classical Economists

Many of the features outlined above correspond with capitalism, but note that industrial development can occur within a command or socialist economic model. The so-called classical economists articulated the nature of a laissez-faire capitalist economic order, though not always with a positive view of its potential. Of the three figures associated with capitalism, one (Adam Smith, "the father of capitalism") was addressed in chapter 9; now we look at two other important figures:

- <u>Thomas Malthus</u> (1766–1834)—Malthus believed that food supplies, which increase only incrementally, could never keep up with natural population growth, which occurs exponentially. Even today, Malthus's *Essay on Human Population* (1798) represents the classic statement of concern for population growth and the need for its limitation. Malthus was pessimistic about the prospects for birth control and technological advance, though he did underestimate the productive capacity unleashed by both the Agricultural and Industrial Revolutions.

- David Ricardo (1772–1823)—Taking Malthus's ideas regarding population, Ricardo introduced the concept of the Iron Law of Wages. In the short run, Ricardo argued, if the poor gain higher wages, they will simply produce more children, increasing the labor supply and driving down incomes. Thus, in the long run, humanity could not sustain a higher standard of living. Once again, Ricardo miscalculated the potential of new technologies and techniques to generate wealth and the human desire for smaller families within this capitalist, consumerist regime.

Textile Innovations

Textiles led the way during the early Industrial Revolution. The many processes of textile production lent themselves to the development of cottage industry, which took hold in Britain in the eighteenth century. Several basic technological breakthroughs, beginning in the 1730s, paved the way for the mechanization of spinning under one roof, or the first factories. It is important to keep in mind that production processes like the putting-out system and mechanization often complemented one another in industries with multiple steps, such as textile production. Further, mechanization did not penetrate production in other industries for several generations. As you review the **textile innovations** below, focus more on the incremental nature of technological change rather than the names of the inventors.

- Flying shuttle, 1733: John Kay halved the time of the weaving process and allowed a single loom operator to work with wider cloth by creating a shuttle that could be operated with one hand. The invention increased demand for spun yarn.

- Spinning jenny, 1768: Improving on the traditional spinning wheel, James Hargreaves developed the jenny, which enabled operators to spin eight or more threads with additional spindles.

- Water frame, 1771 and "mule," 1780: Richard Arkwright added water power to the principle of the jenny, allowing for the development of factories near rivers, which could harness this natural resource. Samuel Crompton combined the mechanical principles of the jenny and the water frame to create the spinning mule.

- Power loom, 1785: Edmund Cartwright's power loom took several generations to perfect, and when it finally became cost-effective in the 1830s, it quickly drove the many handloom weavers out of business.

By the middle of the nineteenth century, then, the entire textile industry had become mechanized. Demand for raw cotton jumped exponentially, which, along with the new cotton gin (1793), provided a new lease on life for American slavery. Britain thus established dominance in a key consumer item with its cheap, sturdy cotton cloth.

Steam Power, Coal Mining, Iron, and Railroads

These four industries or technologies were closely related. Developments in one tended to feed demand in the others, like a feedback loop. The first steam engines in the early eighteenth century pumped water out of coal mines, but did so inefficiently, using more energy than they produced. James Watt (1736–1819), in partnership with the entrepreneur Matthew Boulton, perfected the steam engine by employing a separate condenser to cool the steam and later added rotary motion, essential to the development of locomotion. Watt's invention provided a much-needed source of power for factories, which could now be located anywhere.

Coal mining expanded significantly in Great Britain in the eighteenth century, driven by the energy needs of the new steam engines and for metallurgical processes. Traditionally, **iron smelting** employed charcoal (fuel produced from burning wood), but this process had depleted English forests. In 1709, Quaker Abraham Darby developed the first blast furnace using coke (a by-product of coal) to heat iron ore, which burned cleaner and allowed for the production of greater amounts of iron. Later in the century, Henry Cort pioneered the puddling and rolling processes that enabled factories to produce higher-quality wrought iron and to shape it more easily for industrial purposes. Soon, all processes were consolidated under one roof, vastly increasing British production of iron in the first half of the nineteenth century. Metallurgy, in turn, required vast amounts of coal, stimulating both industries.

Eighteenth-century Britain witnessed a great age of canal building. Water transportation proved more reliable than roads and cut the costs of bringing goods to market. Many of the first canals were privately funded, earning huge profits for their investors. With the advent of cheaper iron and the power of the steam engine, **railroads** replaced canals as the most efficient form of transportation. At first, railways consisted of horse-drawn wagons over wooden rails, used to transport coal out of mines to foundries. In 1804, Richard Trevithick designed and built the first steam-powered locomotive. Soon after, engineer George Stephenson created a faster engine, The Rocket, which could travel at the (for-the-time) amazing speed of 24 mph! Railroads soon veined across Britain, providing cheaper goods and a new form of reliable passenger transportation. Railroads decreased isolation and allowed for geographic and social mobility, making them one of the most important inventions of the nineteenth century.

The great age of railroad building energized the production of iron, steam engines, and the mining of coal. In addition, machine tools, made of more refined and flexible **steel**, enabled engineers to shape, mold, bore, drill, cut, and saw materials with great precision. Together, these industries formed the spine of the British economy and fed other industrial processes.

The Factory System and Other Industries

History's first industrialists combined the roles of inventor, entrepreneur, and manager. Early businesses grew out of limited partnerships and fed off borrowed funds from Britain's extensive credit network. These industrialists eventually realized the benefits of standardization and specialization by combining industrial processes in one locale—a factory. The first **factories** appeared in textile spinning in the 1780s in the new industrial towns of the north, such as Manchester and Liverpool. Josiah Wedgwood (1730–1795) stands as a fine example of the new entrepreneur who extended the factory principle to new industries. Lacking an academic background in chemistry, Wedgwood nonetheless used trial and error to develop new styles of pottery and porcelain. Wedgwood not only centralized and standardized his industrial processes, he also marketed his products with a keen eye to consumer tastes. His Queens' Ware gained fame throughout Europe for its delicate style and refinement.

Like petroleum later, coal processing led to the development of important by-products. Mauvine, the first synthetic dye, was extracted from coal tar in the middle of the century. Synthetic bleaches and dyes replaced laborious traditional processes and opened up new fashion opportunities. Certain colors, such as purple, had been associated with aristocratic status; with cheap textiles and dyes, fashion became democratized.

By the mid-nineteenth century, Britain had established its industrial preeminence. To celebrate the nation's accomplishments, British leaders organized the first world's fair in 1851 in London called the <u>Crystal Palace Exhibition</u>. Symbols of technology and progress took center stage and beckoned as examples for the continent to imitate.

Industrialization on the Continent

Continental European nations wished to copy Britain's industrial success. Some succeeded; others seemed unable to overcome institutional barriers or <u>limited resources</u>. In some ways, the British lead proved beneficial to others, as its engineers, technicians, and inventors might be enticed by continental powers to share their industrial secrets. Often, however, governments came to adopt a more active role in promoting and overseeing industrial development. Such government intervention stands in contrast to Britain's laissez-faire approach. Let's see how this worked with several brief examples.

> **SKILL SET**
>
> Now that you've considered the reasons for Britain's lead, it is time to set out the similarities and differences with the continental experience with industry. As you read this section, you might create a complex Venn diagram to establish how Britain compares with France, Germany, and the lagging nations (COMP and MAC).

France: A Gradualist Path

Like Britain, France experienced industrialization, but more gradually and with fewer disturbing side effects. As a legacy of the revolution, France continued a tradition of small, family-based agriculture without the destabilizing impact of enclosure and the Agricultural Revolution. Also, France's large internal market and skilled labor force allowed it to focus on higher-end products, such as silks and intricately patterned textiles. Lacking extensive reserves of coal and iron ore, France did not develop Britain's level of heavy industry. As a result, French industrial cities were smaller in number and did not grow as rapidly, avoiding some of the worst effects attending those in Britain. It was not until after 1850 that French finance, railroads, and communications were able to bring about a fuller modernization of attitudes and habits related to production and consumption.

Germany: A Shackled Giant

Remember that there was no such nation as Germany in 1815. "Germany" comprised several dozen states, each with its own tariffs, tax systems, and state priorities. Though Germany boasted an abundant supply of coal and iron ore, a rich agricultural sector, and a strong craft tradition, its disunity hindered its full economic potential. In the 1830s, Prussian economist <u>Friedrich List</u> (1789–1846) argued for the development of a <u>national economic system</u>, beginning with a customs union that would create a free trade zone among the member German states. This Prussian-led *Zollverein* promoted not only economic integration but laid the basis for Germany's later political unity. In addition, List recognized that Britain's hands-off approach would not work in Germany, so he urged government financing of railroads, subsidies for key industries, and protective tariffs. Germany's economic take-off would await political unity in 1871, but it was already establishing strength in key industrial sectors such as iron, coal mining, and chemicals.

The Lagging Lands

While other regions of Europe, such as Belgium and northern Italy, as well as the United States, had built an industrial base by mid-century, many nations languished in the inertia of resource poverty, backward agriculture based on serfdom, and elitist attitudes that discouraged the profit motive. For example, Spain lacked resources necessary for industry and faced geographic obstacles with a barren plain dominating the center of its nation. However, the most important barriers proved to be the continuing influence of aristocratic privilege and religious other-worldliness. After 1848, Russia remained the only major nation relying on serfdom, an enormous waste of labor and land that effectively hindered its economic development and negated its strong resource base. In some cases, underdeveloped nations adopted outward manifestations of industry, such as a show railroad or a model factory, but the essential economic attitudes and the legal and educational infrastructure needed to secure private property or supply technical skills were sadly lacking.

Social Effects of and Responses to Industrialization

The Industrial Revolution profoundly influenced first British and later European society. Problems such as overcrowding, pollution, worker discontent, and inequality compelled governments, reformers, and radicals to devise a range of contending responses to such issues.

> **THEME MUSIC & SKILL SET**
>
> The thematic driver for this section is clearly Economic and Commercial Developments (ECD), but you will notice how wealth and inequality create issues relevant for other themes: 1) class, gender roles, and family (SCD) and 2) government involvement in the economy and reform movements (SOP). You should practice establishing connections across themes, as it can help you earn the Complexity point on the DBQ and LEQ.

Population Increase

Industrialization supported a marked increase in population. From 1750 to 1850, the population of the British Isles rose 200% from 10 to 30 million. What's more, most of this humanity found itself crowded into the new industrial cities of Lancashire and the Midlands, north of London. Manchester came to symbolize the problems of the new industrial city, growing from 20,000 people in 1750 to almost half a million by 1850, making it the second largest city in Britain. Many migrants to the cities were driven by famine in Ireland or landlessness in the countryside. Though many found work in the new cotton mills, urban problems followed closely behind.

Working and Living Conditions

It is easy to dramatize the conditions in the first factories or urban areas, and even though bases exist for these facts, you should incline toward analysis and specifics, not drama, for any essay prompts on the Industrial Revolution. Initial factory conditions were deplorable. Workers were expected to labor up to 14 hours per day with inadequate light and ventilation. Strict rules punished tardiness and fraternization among workers. Owners often preferred **children as laborers** for their small hands able to reach into machinery, as well as women, considered more docile and willing to work for lower wages than men. In coal mines and factories, laborers were exposed to toxic substances and particulates, causing lung and other diseases. Finally, because machines often determined the pace of labor, workers found themselves living by a regimented schedule and subject to fatigue that could be deadly if they should fall into the moving parts of machines.

Living conditions mirrored those in the workplace. Because of their rapid growth, cities found that their infrastructure of streets, housing, and sewage disposal could not keep up with the onslaught of new residents. Cramped housing and diseases, such as cholera, dysentery, and typhoid, reduced life expectancies by half compared with rural areas. Air and water pollution rendered even breathing and drinking dangerous activities. In addition to sanitary and environmental problems, crime, prostitution, alcoholism, and family breakdown defined city life.

As a consequence of the mechanization of labor, the family was transformed from a unit of production to a unit of consumption, i.e., gathering only for activities related to eating and leisure. It is easy to exaggerate how quickly and commonly this occurred; nonetheless, mechanization of labor set the precedent of moving work out of the home, where workers exercised control over the pace and conditions, to a process managed by the owners of capital seeking profit by squeezing out costs through lower wages and sacrificing on basic safety conditions. This separation of labor and capital represents one of the defining features of capitalism, usually to the disadvantage of the worker. Once the British Parliament passed legislation protecting women and children in the 1830s and 1840s, family life was further altered by separating male "productive" work outside the home from female "reproductive" and domestic labor completed in the home.

New Industrial Classes

Industrialization created new classes. At the top, the **industrial middle class** gained wealth and status from the profits of industry. Though they were still few in number, this growing **bourgeoisie** set a social tone of frugality, respectability, and hard work, exemplifying the ideal of social mobility through self-help. The growth of the unskilled working class, or **proletariat**, paralleled that of the industrial middle class. Owning no capital or personal property of which to speak, unskilled workers were forced to sell their labor at a disadvantage, as the supply of workers continued to grow and employers freely dismissed those deemed unproductive or troublesome. Industrial workers remained a relatively small segment of the population in Europe until after the middle of the nineteenth century, and therefore could exercise little influence on politics through union activity or political pressure.

Responses: Reform, Rebellion, and Rejection

It is helpful to think of responses to these industrial problems on a continuum from acceptance of the new industrial system on one side, to complete rejection on the other. We explore this topic further in the section below on "isms," but for now focus on immediate and practical responses to those issues. You may find the following diagram helpful in imagining how these varying responses relate to one another.

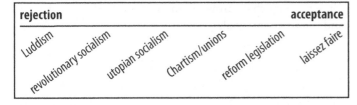

rejection					acceptance
Luddism	revolutionary socialism	utopian socialism	Chartism/unions	reform legislation	laissez faire

We have already examined the laissez-faire (Liberal) approach of the classical economists. Many Liberals ("libertarians" in our current usage) recognized the obvious problems with industrialization but believed that these side effects naturally attended all economic systems. To tamper with the workings of the free market, in their minds, would only create more suffering in the long run. Eventually the problems became too pronounced for any but the most hardened capitalist to ignore. Reformers feared that if nothing were done to ameliorate horrid working and living conditions, moral breakdown or worse, revolution, would occur. In 1832, Parliament appointed the Sadler Commission to investigate child labor in mines and factories. The appalling testimony of workers convinced Parliament to pass the Factory Act of 1833, which provided for inspection of factories, a limitation on hours, and at least 2 hours of education per day for children. Sanitary reformer Edwin Chadwick's (1800–1890) writings highlighted the need for improved sewage and sanitary conditions in the crowded and polluted cities. Soon after, the Parliament again responded with the Public Health Act of 1848, providing for the development of sanitary systems and public health boards to inspect conditions. Further acts are discussed below in the section "Reform in Great Britain."

Despite the first tentative steps toward reform, workers voiced a more fundamental need for change, one that involved greater control over the workplace and political power. It became clear that, as individuals, workers could do little to blunt the capitalist system. To exert collective power, laborers formed unions. Skilled engineers formed a trade union, later called the Amalgamated Society of Engineers in 1851, to bargain for better working conditions and higher wages, much like medieval guilds. The more radical Grand National Consolidated Trade Union, encouraged by the industrialist Robert Owen (see below), attempted to organize all industrial workers for strikes and labor agitation. The British government looked with hostility on efforts at worker organization, passing the Combination Acts in the early nineteenth century to prevent union activity. Many workers favored more direct political activity. The Chartists, named after the founding document of their principles, employed petitions, mass meetings, and agitation to achieve **universal male suffrage** and the payment of salaries to members of Parliament. Chartism became associated with violent disturbances and faded as a movement after 1848, even though many of its goals were later reached.

Since socialism developed into a coherent ideology, it is covered more extensively in the section on "isms." Luddism represented an outright rejection of the principle of mechanization of labor. Named for a mythical figure, Ned Ludd, the supporters of the movement met in secret throughout the early 1810s to plan the destruction of knitting frames and spinning devices they perceived as taking their skilled jobs. Many viewed the perpetuation of an artisanal culture of sturdy skilled craftsmen as preferable to any benefits from industrial efficiency. The British government crushed the movement by exiling or executing those involved. Today, those who oppose technological change are often dubbed by their detractors as Luddites.

The Congress of Vienna and Concert of Europe

The Vienna Settlement, 1814–1815

After the French Revolution and Napoleonic Wars, the great powers of Europe met in Vienna to rebuild a stable diplomatic order. Twenty-five years of violent upheaval and warfare had convinced conservatives of the need to reestablish legitimate governments and create mechanisms to subdue revolutionary movements. Negotiations were interrupted by the escape of Napoleon from Elba and his 100 Days campaign, culminating with his defeat at Waterloo. In general, the victorious powers treated France leniently—though somewhat less so after the 100 Days— so as not to saddle the restored Bourbon monarchy with a harsh treaty. The Congress of Vienna, then, was guided by the following three principles:

> **THEME MUSIC & SKILL SET**
>
> The Vienna settlement and Concert of Europe defined diplomacy in the nineteenth century. To appreciate the diplomatic issues of this period (SOP), you may want to create a balance of sheet of the possible positive and negative assessments of this most important of treaties and efforts at collective security. Also, try drawing some comparisons to other critical moments when the map of Europe was redrawn, such as 1648, 1714, or 1919 (MAC and CCOT).

- *Legitimacy* – Monarchs were restored in those nations that experienced revolutions. This meant the Bourbons back in France (Louis XVIII, brother of the executed king), Spain, and Naples. Though some monarchs conceded constitutions in deference to public opinion, power remained in the hands of conservative interests—"throne, altar, and estate"—that is, monarchy, church, and aristocracy.

- *Compensation* – Nations that lost territory in one area received compensation in another. For example, Austria surrendered possession of the Austrian Netherlands (Belgium) but gained control of several states in northern Italy.

- *Balance of power* – Key to the Congress's deliberations, balance-of-power considerations led to the creation of a series of buffer states to quarantine

France should revolution break out there again. The new Kingdom of the Netherlands combined the former Dutch republic and Austrian Netherlands, Prussia gained extensive territory on the Rhine, and Piedmont-Sardinia in Italy was strengthened on France's southern border.

The following chart provides an overview of the key players and their nations' goals.

Nation	Leader	Goals
Austria	**Klemens von Metternich** (1773–1859)—The dominant personality at the Congress	As the most multi-ethnic of the great powers, Austria wished to repress nationalism and build a system of collective security to maintain the status quo. Owing to Metternich's association with the Congress of Vienna, the period 1815–1848 is sometimes termed the Age of Metternich.
France	Talleyrand (1754–1838)—Wily political survivor who represented revolutionary France, Napoleon, and then the restored Bourbons	France wished to be readmitted into the family of the great powers by demonstrating its return to legitimacy. Talleyrand won over Metternich by exposing the plan of Prussia and Russia to take all of Saxony and Poland without consulting the other powers.
Great Britain	Lord Castlereagh (1769–1822)—Focused on protecting British commercial interests	Britain primarily saw the Congress as as a way to reestablish the balance of power on the continent, its long-time goal. Britain did not wish to be involved in a kind of international police force to crush revolutions.
Prussia	Prince von Hardenberg (1750–1822)—Older leader often outmaneuvered by Metternich	Least influential at the Congress, Prussia generally followed the lead of Austria, the other German power. Prussia also desired to incorporate its long-time enemy, Saxony, into its territory.
Russia	Alexander I (r. 1801–1825)—Began as a reformer, but grew conservative and more religious in response to revolution	The largest of the powers and growing in influence, Russia under the once-Liberal Alexander wanted to control Poland and also gain support for a Holy Alliance of powers committed to stopping "godless" revolution.

The resolutions of the Congress of Vienna reflect the traditional diplomacy of elites redrawing the map of Europe to meet their goals. After almost nine months of deliberations and another war against Napoleon, the great powers finally completed their work in June 1815, with the following decisions:

Territorial adjustments: Some have been addressed above. The Polish-Saxon question almost led to war among the powers, but as a compromise, the Prussians gained 40% of Saxony and the Russian tsar was named King of Poland, though in reality, he ruled Congress Poland directly. To ensure stability in central Europe, a 39-state German Confederation was created with Austria as the dominant power. France relinquished conquests from the revolutionary wars.

Alliances: To ensure peace and stability, the great powers formed the Quadruple Alliance, which became the Quintuple Alliance with the inclusion of France after 1818. In addition, the three conservative central and eastern European powers—Austria, Prussia, and Russia—created the Holy Alliance, envisioned by Alexander I as a brake on revolutionary movements.

Indemnities: After Napoleon's return and the 100 Days, the victorious powers placed some moderate sanctions on France. The nation was required to return the art Napoleon had stolen from conquered lands and had to support an occupation army, which was removed in 1818.

Collective Security: To ensure peace and stability, the great powers agreed to meet periodically to discuss issues of mutual concern, especially related to war and revolution. This **Concert of Europe** provided a degree of informal security in the first half of the nineteenth century; however, Britain disagreed with Metternich's vision of collective security as committing the members to the suppression of revolutionary movements.

The Congress System

Several times after the meeting in Vienna, the great powers invoked the Concert of Europe to address revolutionary situations. The details of these meetings follow:

Congress of Aix-la-Chapelle, 1818: Based on French compliance with the treaty, the army of occupation was removed and France admitted to the Concert of Europe and Quintuple Alliance.

Congress of Troppau, 1820: Revolutionaries in Spain and Naples forced the kings of those nations to admit to constitutional limits on royal power. Metternich perceived the act as the beginning of revolutionary violence and urged the other powers to sign a protocol committed to united action. When France and Britain demurred, Austria (with Prussian and Russian backing) subdued the revolt in Italy.

Congress of Verona, 1822: Two situations preoccupied the great powers—the continuing instability in Spain and Latin American revolts against Spanish control. On the first question, the great powers, excluding Britain, authorized a French army to subdue the threats to the Spanish monarchy and punish the revolutionaries, which was carried out. Britain strongly objected to armed intervention in Latin America, as it wished to exploit the breakup of the Spanish empire to enhance its own trade. More importantly, the United States issued the Monroe Doctrine in 1823 warning against further European colonial ventures in an American sphere of influence.

No congresses met after Verona, demonstrating the differing visions of the Concert of Europe among the Big Five. Even if the great powers failed to create an institutional structure of collective security, a spirit of cooperation lingered until 1848. In assessing the Vienna settlement, some historians point out how its failure to recognize the forces of Liberalism and nationalism led to over 30 years of continuous revolution. On the other hand, the great powers did provide a framework that avoided a general war among all of the great powers for almost a century (until 1914). Regardless of interpretations, clearly the Congress of Vienna fundamentally shaped the political and diplomatic climate for the first half of the nineteenth century.

Restoration and Reaction

What follows is a review-in-brief of domestic developments relating to the post-1815 theme of states restoring traditional governments and attempting to ensure stability. France and other nations that experienced revolutions are covered in the section "Revolutions and Reform."

Great Britain

Conservative Tories controlled British politics after 1815 and were intent on clearing away latent radicalism in the kingdom, often with censorship. Parliament remained unrepresentative, as none of the new industrial towns in the north elected members. Landed interests passed the Corn Laws protecting British grain from competition, but at the same time the policy harmed consumers by raising prices. Democratic movements agitated for political reform; one such peaceful gathering in 1819 in Manchester was met with armed force, killing 11 and wounding hundreds. Opponents of the government derisively dubbed this event the Peterloo Massacre. A gradual loosening of repression in the 1820s paved the way for Liberal reforms in the 1830s.

Germany

The personality of Metternich dominated politics in Germany through the 39-state German Confederation. Idealistic young student nationalists formed the *Burschenschaft* to celebrate liberal German culture and discuss political issues. Viewing these fraternities as a threat, Metternich convinced the Confederation to issue the Carlsbad Decrees (1819), forcing the dissolution of the *Burschenshaft*, censoring the press, and appointing government officials to supervise universities.

Russia

With an inconsequential middle-class and autocratic tradition, Russia proved infertile ground for political Liberalism. Nonetheless, army officers influenced by revolutionary ideologies had formed the Decembrist Society to push for a constitutional government. When Alexander I died in 1825, the <u>Decembrist Revolt</u> agitated for the accession of Constantine, considered a Liberal, rather than his reactionary brother, Nicholas. Nicholas I (r. 1825–1855) crushed the revolt and ruled Russia in succeeding decades. Nicholas took the motto "Autocracy, Orthodoxy, and Nationality" as his policy guide, relying on a secret police, religious uniformity, and imposition of Russian language and culture on ethnic minorities.

The "Isms"

The period 1815–1850 was the Age of Ideologies. In response to the issues raised by the Dual Revolution, many Europeans adhered to a set of ideas that provided both a systematic view of human affairs as well as a blueprint for changing the world. Such ideologies or "isms" influenced how people viewed events as well as motivated them to action.

Conservatism

Conservatism should not be equated with complete rejection of change (such adherents are known as reactionaries). Defying the optimistic views of human rationality associated with the Enlightenment and French Revolution, Conservatives believed that human nature was driven primarily by the passions. Edmund Burke (1729–1797) became a leading advocate for change through adaptation, not violence, with his statements against the events of the French Revolution (see Chapter 10). Humans are capable of reason, he argued, but often employ it as an excuse for self-interested actions. Customs and traditions, which have evolved over time to meet the needs of particular human societies, act as checks on the passions and should not be discarded lightly. Along with Burke, French philosopher Joseph de Maistre (1753–1821) argued that once the revolution in France broke from its traditions of church, monarchy, and nobility, it descended into violent chaos. Burke and de Maistre were not opposed to constitutions *per se*—as Burke supported the American Revolution—only those based on abstract and supposedly universal principles not in keeping with a society's experiences. Conservative philosophy supported the restoration governments of the post-1815 order.

Liberalism

Classical Liberalism of the nineteenth century should be distinguished from the way the term liberal is used today. Based on Enlightenment and revolutionary ideals of reason, progress, and individual rights, Liberalism promoted reform throughout the nineteenth century. Economically, Liberals embraced the **laissez-faire** principles of Adam Smith's capitalism and strong protection of private property. Politically, Liberals favored the social contract theory of limited government advocated by John Locke and the French revolutionaries as the surest guarantee of **religious toleration** and **individual rights**. Many, if not most, Liberals came from the middle class and supported a more representative government and an expansion in suffrage, though only for property holders. British philosopher Jeremy Bentham (1748–1832) articulated the related approach of utilitarianism, wherein "good" was defined as providing pleasure and "evil" as causing pain. Holding that the purpose of government was to promote the "greatest good for the greatest number," Bentham argued for separation of church and state, women's rights, and the end of slavery. Beginning in the utilitarian tradition, John Stuart Mill (1806–1873) later provided in his *On Liberty* (1859) one of the most eloquent defenses of freedom of expression and the dangers of the tyranny of the majority. Mill also collaborated with his wife, Harriet Taylor, and defended the cause of female suffrage in Parliament.

Socialism, Republicanism, and Feminism

Self-proclaimed **radicals** and republicans embraced the "principles of '93" from the French Revolution. Many were drawn from intellectual circles or the working class, and they favored equality and **universal male suffrage**, while opposing the influence of organized religion as well as monarchy and aristocracy. Republicanism shaded off into socialism. **Socialists** criticized the capitalist system as unequal and unjust, wishing to replace it with social and economic planning. One of the first socialists, ironically, was a textile entrepreneur, Robert Owen (1771–1858). Owen built a model factory in New Lanark, Scotland, to better provide for his workers' needs, with high wages, improved conditions, and provision for schools and other amenities. The industrialist also attempted to export his **utopian socialism** to the United States, constructing an experimental but failed colony in Indiana. Most other early socialists were French, reflecting the legacy of the revolution. Henri de Saint-Simon (1760–1825) and Charles Fourier (1772–1837) embraced an ethos of cooperation and shared property to realize human goods, like social and psychological, extending beyond merely economic needs. Additionally, the socialist Louis Blanc's (1811–1882) idea of "national workshops" for the working class played a key role in the revolution in 1848 in France. Despite its creativity, utopian socialism led to few practical successes and gave way after 1850 to the more militant Marxian version of socialism.

Many advocates of women's rights, such as Mary Wollstonecraft and John Stuart Mill, drew from the Enlightenment tradition of individual rights and social equality. Socialists combined their criticism of the class system with that of gender roles. French female socialist Flora Tristan (1803–1844) argued that the oppression of women, whether as factory workers or in domestic roles, sprung from the unequal ownership of property. Numerous famous female writers of the period, such as Jane Austen, George Sand, and Germaine de Staël, once again demonstrated the ability of women to exercise independent and creative voices. By 1850, many **feminists** had established a clear agenda for the movement—obtaining greater access to education along with legal, property, and political rights.

Nationalism

Nationalism proved the most combustible ideology of the nineteenth century, and it is essential to your understanding of political and diplomatic events after 1800. Spread by the example of the French Revolution, nationalism initially focused on cultural revival and celebration of traditions. Long-divided Germany in particular experienced a wave of cultural nationalism fed by the Napoleonic Wars. Johann Gottfried Herder (1744–1803) replaced the political-judicial conception of state with an organic folk-nation best represented by the term *Volksgeist*, or "spirit of the people." Germans celebrated their music and folklore, as with Beethoven's symphonies or the Grimm Brothers' fairy tales. Such cultural nationalism eventually took on political overtones. The German philosopher G.F.W. Hegel (1770–1831) glorified the national state as the march of destiny through history. History itself consisted of a clash of opposing ideas, called the dialectic, which pointed the way to a new synthesis—the idea of German national unity.

Given the atmosphere of repression and reaction during the post-1815 period, many nationalists formed secret societies to promote their agendas of unity. The Italian Giuseppe Mazzini (1805–1872) first joined the secretive Carbonari, who aimed to expel the Habsburgs from the peninsula, before forming Young Italy in 1831. Mazzini worked to foment nationalist uprisings in his native land, while in his writings argued that the overthrow of the Concert of Europe would lead to free, independent states based on linguistic and ethnic identity. States constituted along national lines would eliminate the need for wars and create true brotherhood and peace. Eastern Europe also experienced a revival of national traditions. Intellectuals representing the diverse group of Slavic speakers—Poles, Serbs, Croats, Czechs, Slovaks—looked to common linguistic and cultural traditions and advocated pan-Slavism, or the unity of all Slavs. Pan-Slavism inspired uprisings in the 1815–1850 period, but given the power of the Habsburg and Ottoman Empires over the Slavs, the subsequent failures of these revolutions demonstrated the need for the patronage of an outside power—namely Russia, the protector of the Slavs.

Romanticism

Romanticism was a literary, musical, and artistic movement dominating European culture in the first half of the nineteenth century. Romantics reacted to the Enlightenment's emphasis on reason and science, instead stressing the following:

> **THEME MUSIC & EXAMPLE BASE**
>
> Prior to the nineteenth century, you will have noted the rise of objective thinking toward the natural world (Scientific Revolution, Enlightenment), but with the Romantics, we see one of the first strong reactions to the notion that all knowledge stems from the scientific method. Though not the first to do so, the Romantics embrace the subjectivity of experience in a singular and seductive manner (CID).

- **Emotions** – Taking their cue from Rousseau, Romantics emphasized feeling and passion as the wellspring of knowledge and creativity.

- **Intuition** – Science alone cannot decipher the world; imagination and the "mind's eye" can also reveal its truths.

- **Nature** – Whereas the philosophes studied nature analytically, the Romantics drew inspiration and awe from its mysteries and power.

- **Nationalism** – Romanticism found a natural connection with nationalism; both emphasized change, passion, and connection to the past.

- **Religion (Supernatural)** – Romanticism coincided with a religious revival, particularly in Catholicism. Spirit, mysticism, and emotions were central to both.

- **Individualism** – Romantics celebrated the individual of genius and talent, like a Beethoven or a Napoleon, rather than what was universal in all humans.

With these themes in mind, consider the following topics and individuals.

Literature and History

Lord Byron (1788–1824)—As famous for his scandalous lifestyle as for his narrative poems, Lord Byron died from fever on his way to fight for Greek independence, a cause he supported in his writings.

Thomas Carlyle (1795–1881)—Carlyle pioneered history as the story of great men, as with his famous study of the French Revolution.

François-René de Chateaubriand (1768–1848)—In *The Genius of Christianity*, Chateaubriand glorified the mystical pull of religious faith and its connection with the beauties of nature.

Johann Wolfgang von Goethe (1749–1832)—Goethe's *Sorrows of Young Werther* recounted the tale of a passionate young man who commits suicide over an unrequited love. Along with *Faust*, in which the title character sells his soul to the devil, Goethe's works proved enormously influential in combining a neoclassical style with the Romantic themes of intuition and emotion.

Edgar Allan Poe (1809–1849)—With his short stories, Poe demonstrates the Romantic interest in the occult and macabre.

Mary Shelley (1797–1851)—Daughter of Mary Wollstonecraft, Shelly gained fame with *Frankenstein*, a literary warning about the hubris of modern humans and technology gone awry.

Sir Walter Scott (1771–1832)—Reflecting the Romantic interest in medieval history, Scott's *Ivanhoe* chronicles the conflicts between Norman and Saxon knights in England.

Percy Bysshe Shelley (1792–1822)—Shelley gained fame both from his poetry, as with his tale of rebellion against social conventions in *Prometheus Unbound*, and his lifestyle of free love and vegetarianism. Husband of Mary Shelley.

William Wordsworth (1770–1850)—Wordsworth's poetry glorified nature and suggested that "one impulse from a vernal wood" would teach humans more "than all the sages can."

Architecture and Painting

Eugene Delacroix (1798–1863)—Delacroix is most famous for his large canvases, bold use of color, and exotic themes. His tribute to the French revolutionary tradition, *Liberty Leading the People*, is his most famous work.

Caspar David Friedrich (1774–1840)—Friedrich's paintings gained notoriety for their portrayals of solitary figures confronting the immensity of nature, as with *Wanderer Above the Sea of Fog*.

Théodore Géricault (1791–1824)—His immense canvas, *The Raft of Medusa*, demonstrated the Romantic fascination with nature as well as a critique of a distant and uncaring monarchy. Gericault's portrayals of the insane illustrate the Romantic interest in the exotic and unique.

Houses of Parliament (1830s)—The most famous architectural example of the neo-Gothic revival in Britain.

J.M.W. Turner (1775–1851)—Turner used vivid colors and atmospheric effects to depict the untamed power of nature in his *Rain, Steam, and Speed* and *Slaveship*.

Music

Ludwig von Beethoven (1770–1827)—Beethoven pushed the classical style to its limits with his sophisticated orchestral arrangements. Despite growing deafness, Beethoven helped establish the Romantic movement in music with his nine symphonies.

Hector Berlioz (1803–1869)—Berlioz developed program music in which a drama parallels the motifs of the melody. His famous *Symphonie Fantastique* portrays a drug-induced imagination of a witches' gathering.

Though Romantics occupied themselves primary with cultural expression, many combined their aesthetic vision with political activism. Romantics urged freer lifestyles and political systems, which explains the crossover from Romanticism to nationalism, as well as Liberalism. In fact, many historians term the first half of the nineteenth century, the Age of Romantic Nationalism. As we see below, Romanticism fueled the revolutionary sentiments sweeping across Europe in the period 1815–1850.

Revolutions and Reform

The Restoration political settlement, designed to stop revolution, inadvertently fed the grievances of nationalism and Liberalism in the period 1815–1848. This Age of Revolutions gained fuel from industrial problems and the legacy of unfulfilled promises from the French Revolution. Among the great powers, Great Britain avoided revolutionary outbursts through the enactment of tentative Liberal reforms in this period. Revolutionary turmoil culminated with the revolutions of 1848, one of the more overlooked events in European history.

The Revolutions of 1830–1831

We have already seen how the great powers used the Concert of Europe from 1815 to 1830 to subdue revolutionary movements in Sicily and Spain. However, these successes obscured the underlying force of Liberal and national movements. In 1830, the fever of revolution flared again, as usual beginning with France.

The restored Bourbon kings of France reestablished the power of the Catholic clergy and favored the interests of for-mer aristocrats. When elections repudiated the monarchy's policies, it curtailed voting rights and censored the press. Militant republicans and middle-class moderates joined in overthrowing the king, who quickly abdicated. As a compromise, the throne went to an ostensibly reformist relative of the deposed monarch. The new King Louis Philippe (r. 1830–1848), known as the "bourgeois king," promised to abide by the Constitution of 1814.

Events in France inspired revolts in 1830–1831 in Belgium and Poland. The Belgians never fully accepted their absorption into a Dutch kingdom and, following the French example, declared their independence. Because the great powers agreed to maintain Belgian neutrality, the new nation was permitted to establish a new Belgian kingdom. However, this was not the case with Poland, which also revolted against Russian authority in 1831. With no outside support, the Polish revolt was brutally crushed by Nicholas I, Congress Poland was eliminated, and the territory directly incorporated into Russia.

When the Christian Greeks revolted against their Islamic Turkish rulers in 1821, the event inspired an outpouring of support by European intellectuals, who praised the ancient Greeks as the founders of western civilization. By the 1820s, the great powers had come over to the cause of Greek nationalism, even Metternich. The Turks were defeated and by treaty (1829), a new independent Greek state was created, a rare example of a successful nationalist revolt in this era.

Reform in Great Britain and its Empire

Great Britain avoided revolutionary upheaval because of its ability to adapt to the challenge of Liberalism. To incorporate the new industrial bourgeoisie and provide an orderly process of representation for new cities, Parliament passed the Reform Act of 1832, which doubled the number of males who could vote, but retained a property requirement. Further reforms followed with the abolition of slavery in the British Empire in 1833 and the Poor Law of 1834. In reflecting the Liberal notion of self-help, the latter law actually punished the poor by making relief in government workhouses more unpleasant than any job. One of the more important principles favored by Liberals was free trade, thus their opposition to the protective Corn Laws. In the context of its tardy response to the Irish potato famine, which took a million lives, Parliament in 1846 finally repealed the Corn Laws, initiating a century of British support for free trade. Conservative Tories supported their own notion of reform—through protective legislation. Following the Factory Act of 1833, Tories in Parliament helped pass the Mines Act, banning children and women from mines, and the Ten Hours Act, limiting hours in textile mills. In giving the middle class a stake in society, British reformers hoped to gain their support for compromise over revolution.

The relationship between slavery and industrialization proved complex but undeniable. Britain's economic infrastructure developed within the context of a global trading system reliant on the labor of enslaved persons. Regardless of this national interest, the British government abolished the slave trade in 1807 and slavery itself in British possessions in 1833. The fight for abolition was spearheaded by a small but dedicated group of reformers, notably evangelical Christian William Wilberforce (1759–1833), who at the cost of his physical and mental health led the successful fight within Parliament. Even with the abolition of slavery, Britain's burgeoning textile mills hungered for cotton, a product supplied by the labor of millions of enslaved in the American South. In some measure, Britain's industrial achievements in this era remained entangled in a worldwide economy dependent on the suffering caused by slavery.

The Revolutions of 1848

Revolutions broke out all over Europe in the fateful year 1848. Though few of these revolutions achieved their stated objectives, their consequences proved significant nonethe-less. Three major causes account for the stunning outburst of revolutionary activity: (1) Liberals felt profound frustration at the lack of political change toward constitutional and representative government, (2) nationalists chafed under the 1815 Vienna settlement and its blunt rejection of self-determination for ethnic minorities, and (3) the lives of the working class suffered from poor agricultural productivity (the era was known as the "hungry '40s") and jobs lost to new industrial machinery. The combination of these factors created an explosive compound, and once again the match was lit in France. For an overview of events, see the chart that follows:

SKILL SET
You may note in this section how the unresolved issues of the French Revolution echoed throughout the nineteenth and into the twentieth centuries. Consider the continuities and changes (CCOT) in the issues that prompted revolutions and the rhetoric and strategies employed by revolutionaries to achieve their aims.

Location	"Trigger"	Leaders	Events	Results
France	Discontented over the slow pace of reform and corruption in Louis Philippe's government, Liberals agitate for suffrage expansion. When the government resists (February), Paris rises in revolt.	• Louis Philippe (r. 1830–1848)—king who abdicates under pressure of violence in Paris • Louis Blanc (1811–1882)—socialist advocate of national workshops for workers • **Louis Napoleon** (r. 1848–1870)—nephew of Napoleon I and opponent of monarchy; elected president of the Second Republic in 1848	• Following Louis's abdication, a provisional government is formed, composed of moderate and radical republicans. • To appease the working class of Paris, Blanc's national workshops are formed, but end up as a system of poor relief, not of worker control of industry. • In June, radicals attack the democratically elected Constituent Assembly in hopes of creating a socialist republic. • The June Days see class violence between radical republicans and the army, which results in the deaths of 10,000 radicals and the establishment of a moderate republic. • Louis Napoleon is elected president in December by a wide majority and moves to consolidate power.	France establishes the Second Republic, but only after class warfare reveals the divisions in French society between the middle and working classes. Louis Napoleon exploits fears of further social conflict to establish authoritarian control of the nation.
Prussia	Inspired by the French example, Prussian Liberals in March revolt in Berlin against the Prussian monarch, who had resisted sharing power.	• Frederick William IV (r. 1840–1861)—agrees to the election of a Prussian assembly, but refuses the Frankfurt Liberals' offer of a crown of a united Germany; does grant a conservative constitution to his kingdom in 1850	• Liberals force the election of a Prussian Assembly, which grants autonomy to the Polish minority. • By spring's end, the Prussian army has reestablished control of the nation and reversed the pro-Polish legislation of the Assembly.	Prussian Liberals failed to meet their objectives of political equality and reducing the influence of traditional institutions. However, despite its three-tiered class voting system, the 1850 Constitution provides for representation.

Location	"Trigger"	Leaders	Events	Results
Frankfurt	After the riots in Berlin, Liberals overthrow the traditional political structures of other German states. After elections, delegates meet in Frankfurt to attempt Germany's unification.		• Delegates divide over whether the Austrian empire, with its large non-German population, should be included in a unified Germany. This debate causes a fatal delay while conservatives regather their strength. • By December, the Liberals issue a Declaration of Rights for the German people. • In April 1849, the Frankfurt Assembly completes its constitution and offers the crown to Prussian King Frederick William IV.	By the time German Liberals complete a constitution, their moment has passed. Frederick William IV rejects the "crown from the gutter," and the work of German unification would await the wily diplomacy of a conservative (see next chapter).
Austria	Workers and students rebel in March in Vienna, causing Metternich to flee to Britain.	• **Klemens von Metternich**—conservative Foreign Minister and creator of the Congress System, unable to withstand the revolutions of 1848 • Franz Joseph I (r. 1848–1916)—becomes emperor in December upon his uncle's abdication	• Serfdom is abolished throughout the Austrian empire. • Emperor Franz Joseph agrees to a Constitution in 1849.	After the initial nationalist revolts, the new emperor and army reestablish control and crush further opposition. Franz Joseph rejects the Liberal constitution and works toward centralization of power, though the ethnicities issue would fester.
Prague	Seeing the turmoil in the Austrian Empire, Slavic nationalists meet in Prague to discuss the unification of all Slavs.	• General Windischgrätz (1787–1862)—German army commander who succeeds in dispersing the Prague Assembly	• After initially promising autonomy to Bohemia, whose capital is Prague, the Austrian emperor reverses course and breaks up the Pan-Slav Congress.	Though unsuccessful, Slavic nationalism remains a problem for the Austrian Empire and forms an essential cause of the First World War.
Budapest	Events in Paris inspire the Hungarian Diet in March to proclaim liberty for Magyars (another name for Hungarians).	• Louis Kossuth (1802–1894)—Hungarian Liberal and nationalist who leads the cause of the Magyars	• In the fall of 1848, Hungarian nationalists proclaim a new constitution that promotes the Magyar language but suppresses the rights of Slavic minorities in Hungary. • After the constitution is rejected by the Austrian emperor, Hungary declares complete independence. • Emperor Franz Joseph in 1849 asks Russian leader, Nicholas I, to crush the nationalist movement in Budapest.	The Austrians exploit Slavic fear of Hungarian power to crush the revolt, with Russian support. However, Magyars remain the most restive of the ethnic minorities in the empire.

Location	"Trigger"	Leaders	Events	Results
Italy	After the March Days in Vienna, several Italian states rise in revolt against Austrian rule.	• Charles Albert (r. 1831–1849)—king of Piedmont-Sardinia who urges the Italian states to resist Austrian rule • Pope Pius IX (r. 1846–1878)—begins as a reformer, but when expelled from Rome by revolutionary forces, turns against modernism • **Giuseppe Garibaldi** (1807–1882)—Italian nationalist military leader who helps establish the Roman Republic	• Charles Albert of Piedmont-Sardinia grants a constitution to his people and declares war on Austria to gain territory in Italy. • Numerous other Italian states rise in revolt against Austrian rule. • When the pope is expelled from Rome, Mazzini proclaims it a Roman Republic. • Austrian authorities agree to abolish serfdom in Italian Habsburg lands, hoping to win over peasants. • The Austrian army defeats Charles Albert and restores authority in the other Italian states. • To curry favor with Catholics, Louis Napoleon in 1849 sends French troops into Rome to restore Pope Pius IX.	Italians experience few specific victories in 1848, other than the abolition of serfdom in some states and a constitution for Piedmont. However, the revolutions set the stage for Italian unification under Piedmont-Sardinia later and its opposition by the papacy.

What began with heady enthusiasm and high hopes ended with bitter disappointment and violent suppression. In general, the Liberal and nationalist revolutions of 1848 failed to achieve their objectives, and for this three key factors are responsible: (1) Though revolutionaries boasted lofty rhetoric and inspiring visions, they lacked the institutional power of conservative forces, such as armies and bureaucracies, (2) conservatives successfully exploited middle-class fears of radical revolution after the June Days in Paris, and (3) rulers pitted ethnic minorities against one another to divide and conquer and reestablish authority. Despite these failures, the revolutions of 1848 may be the most underestimated event in European history. The revolutions set the stage for the rise of socialism and a growing division between the middle and working class. In addition, the Romantic age of revolution seemed dead and, philosophically, many intellectuals turned to a more hard-headed realist and materialist vision of the world. Most importantly, conservatives learned the lesson that they could no longer ignore nationalism, so if they wished to stay in power, they had to appeal to public opinion and sponsor movements of national unity from the top down. It is to this topic that the next chapter is devoted.

SKILL SET

One wag argued that the revolutions of 1848 were "a turning point at which history failed to turn." It will be useful to take this notion and turn it into a Change and Continuity over Time (CCOT) question, identifying the ways in which this statement is true or false by tabulating the evidence, particularly in subsequent decades. The short answer is that they helped establish the modern world. How and why?

Additional Resources

📖 **Robert C. Allen,** *The British Industrial Revolution in Global Perspective* **(2009)** — As the title suggests, this text seeks to explain "why Britain?," rather than other advanced areas of the world.

📖 **Benedict Anderson,** *Imagined Communities: Reflections on the Origin and Spread of Nationalism,* **rev. ed. (2006)** — An influential perspective on the meaning of nationalism.

📖 **Timothy Blanning,** *The Romantic Revolution* **(2010)** — A concise and insightful interpretation of a cultural movement and its impact.

📖 **Emma Griffin,** *A Short History of the British Industrial Revolution* **(2010)** — A fast-paced overview makes this a useful resource for students.

📖 **Eric J. Hobsbawm,** *The Age of Revolution: Europe, 1789–1848* **(1996)** — Challenging, but packed with insights, this volume is authored by a famous Marxist historian.

📖 **Adam Hochschild,** *Bury the Chains* **(2006)** — A master storyteller recounts the campaign to end the slave trade.

📖 **Henry Kissinger,** *Diplomacy* **(1995)** — By the former Secretary of State, this book offers chapters on the Vienna settlement and beyond.

📖 Arno Mayer, *The Persistence of the Old Regime: Europe to the Great War* (2010) — An updated version of a classic study that challenges the notion of pervasive modernization in the nineteenth century.

📖 Paul W. Schroeder, *The Transformation of European Politics, 1763–1848* (1994) — An encyclopedic analysis of the changes brought to diplomacy by an era of revolutions.

📖 Philip A.M. Taylor, *The Industrial Revolution in Britain: Triumph or Disaster?* (1969) — From the Problems in European Civilization Series, this volume provides both primary and secondary readings.

💻 https://eh.net/encyclopedia/irelands-great-famine/ — A brief article providing a lucid account of the Irish Potato Famine of the 1840s.

💻 https://www.iep.utm.edu/ — The Internet Encyclopedia of Philosophy provides articles on the "isms," a topic that in my experience poses great difficulty for students; a helpful resource.

💻 http://spartacus-educational.com/IndustrialRevolution.htm — This site addresses many issues related to the Industrial Revolution with primary and secondary sources.

💻 http://www.victorianweb.org/technology/index.html — This site focuses on the technology of industrialization.

CHAPTER TEST

Multiple-Choice Questions

Questions 1–3 are based on the passage below.

> "These, then, are the laws by which wages are regulated, and by which the happiness of far the greatest part of every community is governed. Like all other contracts, wages should be left to the fair and free competition of the market, and should never be controlled by the interference of the legislature.
>
> The clear and direct tendency of the poor laws is in direct opposition to these obvious principles: it is not, as the legislature benevolently intended, to amend the condition of the poor, but to deteriorate the condition of both poor and rich; instead of making the poor rich, they are calculated to make the rich poor; and whilst the present laws are in force, it is quite in the natural order of things that the fund for the maintenance of the poor should progressively increase till it has absorbed all the net revenue of the country...."
>
> David Ricardo, British political economist, *On the Principles of Political Economy and Taxation*, 1817

1. The argument above reflects the influence of:
   A. the principles of the radical phase of the French Revolution.
   B. Conservative political thought opposing new economic ideas.
   C. Romantic conceptions of an emotional connection to the nation.
   D. Liberal, laissez-faire economic theories articulated by Adam Smith.

2. In the second half of the nineteenth century, the ideas in the passage would be embraced by the political philosophy of:
   A. Social Darwinism.
   B. anarchism.
   C. feminism.
   D. Marxism.

3. The experiences of continental European nations in relation to the economy differed most markedly from the ideas in the passage by:
   A. actively sponsoring industry and economic growth.
   B. more slowly developing workers' movements and unions.
   C. denying reforms intended to address industrial problems.
   D. lacking access to natural resources such as coal and iron ore.

Questions 4–7 are based on the passage below.

> "Young Italy is a brotherhood of Italians who believe in a law of progress and duty, and are convinced that Italy is destined to become one nation, convinced also that she possesses sufficient strength within herself to become one, and that the ill success of her former efforts is to be attributed not to the weakness, but to the misdirection, of the revolutionary elements within her—that the secret force lies in constancy and unity of effort. They join this association with the firm intention of consecrating both thought and action to the great aim of reconstituting Italy as one independent sovereign nation of free men and equals…"
>
> Giuseppe Mazzini, Italian politician and activist, "Instruction to Members of Young Italy," 1831

4. The ideas above were most likely a response to:
    A. the abolition of feudalism.
    B. Napoleon's declaration of the empire.
    C. the Congress of Vienna.
    D. the Crimean War.

5. Which of the following political ideologies does the passage best reflect?
    A. Liberalism
    B. Romanticism
    C. Socialism
    D. Nationalism

6. The fulfillment of the ideas in the passage above occurred:
    A. during the revolutions of 1848.
    B. with Cavour's policies of *Realpolitik*.
    C. with the conquest of Libya.
    D. after the Treaty of Versailles ended World War I.

7. Which of the following figures would have <u>disagreed</u> most strongly with the passage?
    A. Napoleon
    B. Metternich
    C. Garibaldi
    D. Bismarck

Questions 8–9 are based on the image below.

John Martin, British painter, *The Bard*, depicting England's conquest of Wales, 1817

8. The painting above reflects all of the following principles of Romanticism EXCEPT:

   A. interest in national histories.

   B. the mystery and awe of nature.

   C. skepticism regarding science.

   D. fascination with the unique individual.

9. Romanticism, as depicted in the painting, anticipated the general trends in ideas and culture of the:

   A. realistic depiction of social problems caused by industry.

   B. subjective nature of experience and knowledge.

   C. questioning of representation and beauty in the arts.

   D. growth of positivism, the effort to make all knowledge scientific.

See Chapter 18 for answers and explanations.

Short-Answer Question

1. a) Describe one <u>similarity</u> between Great Britain and continental European nations in their industrialization.

    b) Describe one <u>difference</u> between Great Britain and continental European nations in their industrialization.

    c) Explain one way in which industrialization changed the relationship of the government to the economy in the nineteenth century.

SAQ Sample Response

a) Great Britain took the lead in industrialization with mechanical developments in textiles and mining. However, industry soon spread to the other nations. One development that promoted industry in Britain and on the continent was the railroad. The new steam rail system helped bring products to market and lowered costs, prompting factories.

b) While Britain raced ahead in the nineteenth century with technology, Russia was mired in backwardness. One reason for this difference were their agricultural systems: while Britain adopted scientific approaches and enclosure, Russia relied on the inefficient system of serfdom. Britain could feed an expanding urban population, but Russia couldn't.

c) Industry created many problems, like pollution and overcrowded cities. At first, Britain ignored these issues, but they just got worse. Many laws were eventually passed, like the Factory Act of 1833, which regulated conditions and provided education to children. Basically, the complete free-market capitalist system had to be rethought to help deal with these issues.

SAQ Sample Response Analysis

This student knows their topic. For Part A, the response clearly identifies a similarity between Britain and the continent as a whole—the importance of transportation systems in creating an industrial market, while at the same time showing a recognition of its relationship to other industries. The student chooses a nation (Russia) to emphasize contrasts, pointing out the differences between Britain's Agricultural Revolution and Russia's reliance on serfdom. Finally, the student correctly notes how states, like Britain, adopted regulations to oversee the workings of the free market. An effective and focused response. Score: **3 Points**

CHAPTER 12

Realism, Nationalism, and Imperialism, 1850–1914

Though dispiriting in result, the revolutions of 1848 vaulted Europe into a new era. Intellectually, the Romantic temperament faded, as artists, scientists, and politicians adopted a hard-headed mindset of **realism** and **materialism**. Military power, industry, organization, electricity, commodities—these products of modern life replaced the imaginary, spiritual, emotional, idealistic, and rhetorical values of Romanticism. This chapter reviews the post-1848 realist and materialist ethos in the arts and ideas, its application in national unification projects, in the continuing progress of technological and industrial change, and, ultimately, how these trends were deployed in Europe's domination of Asia and Africa through imperialism. The events in this chapter culminate centuries-long developments and represent the zenith of European power in world history.

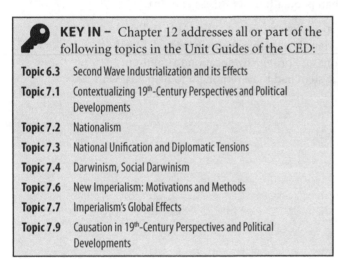

KEY IN – Chapter 12 addresses all or part of the following topics in the Unit Guides of the CED:

Topic 6.3 Second Wave Industrialization and its Effects

Topic 7.1 Contextualizing 19th-Century Perspectives and Political Developments

Topic 7.2 Nationalism

Topic 7.3 National Unification and Diplomatic Tensions

Topic 7.4 Darwinism, Social Darwinism

Topic 7.6 New Imperialism: Motivations and Methods

Topic 7.7 Imperialism's Global Effects

Topic 7.9 Causation in 19th-Century Perspectives and Political Developments

Realism and Materialism

If the Romantics presented a world of possibilities through the imagination, then the realists refocused their attention on the world as it really was, warts and all. For writers and artists of the second half of the nineteenth century, industry and technology dominated the lives of Europeans.

Art and Literature

After 1850, writers turned from Romantic themes to the lives of those directly affected by a changing material reality. Characters in realist novels struggled to understand and cope with the impersonal forces of economic and social change. British author Charles Dickens (1812–1870) populated his novels with compelling characters thrown into a world of sooty cities, cruel orphanages, and corrupt business

practices. Stories such as *Hard Times* and *Oliver Twist* revealed the underside of Britain's rapid industrialization and the crushing inequality attending material progress. Realist writers abandoned the conventions of Romantic rhetoric in favor of an unsentimental, precise style, as in Gustave Flaubert's (1821–1880) *Madame Bovary*. The title character becomes disillusioned with her mundane middle-class life and marriage, engages in several adulterous affairs, and ultimately commits suicide.

Realist artists turned their canvases into windows on the lives of the downtrodden. French painters led the way in revealing the difficult circumstances of landless peasants and exhausted factory workers. Jean-François Millet (1814–1875) highlighted in paintings such as *The Sower* and *The Gleaners* the backbreaking labor of culling enough from the earth to eke out survival. His paintings were echoed by those of Gustave Courbet (1819–1877), whose *Stonebreakers* eloquently captured the brutal work of two manual laborers crushing stones for gravel. We focus on the physical posture of the workers rather than their faces, which are covered in shadows. As photography developed throughout the century, an additional medium became available to depict difficult social problems.

Positivism

As the influence of organized religion declined in Europe, many substituted it with belief in the potential of science. The power of scientific thought seemed validated by its production of immense material benefits through industry and technology. French philosopher Auguste Comte (1798–1857) captured this faith with the theory of **positivism**. Comte believed that history had progressed through three stages—the theological, metaphysical (or philosophical), and the scientific. The great revolutions of 1789–1848 faltered, according to Comte, because of their adherence to overly abstract principles. Progress must rely on a hard-nosed and empirical investigation of reality, avoiding wishful thinking and unsupported generalizations. Comte categorized all the sciences and argued for a science of society (sociology), which would become a new secular religion.

> **THEME MUSIC**
>
> Positivism marks the culmination of the authority of science and belief in objective knowledge (CID), representing a continuity with the Scientific Revolution and Enlightenment (TSI). However, positivism goes beyond a particular epistemology (method of knowledge) to take up a philosophical or cosmological position—that only objects verifiable by the senses can exist.

Marxism

Karl Marx (1818–1883) claimed the mantle of a "**scientific socialism**" and turned his political philosophy into one of the most influential movements in history. From a middle-class family, Marx studied philosophy and law in college and eventually fell in with German radicals. Working for a series of left-wing publications, Marx hailed the revolutions of 1848 as the beginning of the socialist age. Marx's lifelong collaborator, <u>Friedrich Engels</u> (1820–1895), was the son of a German textile owner who rebelled against his inheritance and had published *The Condition of the Working Class in England* (1844) to highlight the inequalities generated by capitalism. Together the two produced the famous pamphlet, *The Communist Manifesto* (1848), urging the working class to unite and throw off their chains of oppression. Though the revolutions of 1848 failed, the manifesto established the outlines of Marxian socialism and a program of nationalization of property, universal suffrage, and the redistribution of income. As the collaborators helped establish the First International in 1864 to promote a union of working-class parties, Marx labored at his masterwork of political economy, *Capital*, later finished by Engels in the 1880s. Marx and Engels wove together three diverse strands into their comprehensive critique of capitalism: German philosophy, British industrialism, and French radicalism. Marxian socialism rests upon the following pillars:

- *Alienation of labor* – In his early writings, Marx blamed the increasing division of labor (i.e., specialization) for alienating (or creating a feeling of separation of) the worker from his product, his labor, himself, and his fellow man, who exploits him.

- *Labor theory of value* – Borrowing from the British classical economists, Marx held that the value of a product equaled the amount of labor that went into producing it. Therefore, the difference between the worker's wages and the ultimate price of the products—what the factory owner calls profit—robs the worker of his uncompensated "surplus labor."

- *Dialectical materialism* – Marx took Hegel's historical notion that the clashing of opposing forces produces change (thesis → antithesis → synthesis) and applied it to clashing systems of production. Whereas Hegel emphasized a dialectic of ideas, Marx held that antagonistic *material* forces produced change, called economic determinism. Marxism, therefore, offered a complete view of history, in keeping with German philosophy.

- *Class struggle* – Each economic system is associated with a dominant class that owns the means of production. In feudalism, for example, the aristocracy owns the essential resource (land) and exercises power based on this ownership. The **bourgeoisie** who own capital (factories, banks, etc.) represent the most pro-

ductive class in history, but their exploitation of the propertyless unskilled workers who are forced to sell their labor, the **proletariat**, inevitably produces the system opposing capitalism—socialism. As workers increase in number, they will develop **class identity** (consciousness) and eventually unite to overthrow those who oppress them.

- *Revolution* – Marx condemned early utopian socialists and the anarchists of eastern and southern Europe for what he considered unrealistic schemes. Successful revolution by the oppressed proletariat would only result from organization, agitation, and planning, not by separate communes and assassinations. Though Marx hoped for a worldwide movement of the working class, he believed it possible, if unlikely, that the proletarian rule might succeed through democratic means in some nations.

Marxism exercised wide influence among all working-class movements, both revolutionary and democratic. Even those who rejected Marx's critique of capitalism had to confront his powerful ideology of change. Many have claimed that the appeal of Marxism lies in its similarity to an organized religion, though Marx rejected religion as the "opiate of the masses." Marxism offers its adherents quasi-religious symbols: prophets (Marx and Engels), holy books (Marx's writings), a chosen race (proletariat), and an end of the world (history's culmination with **communism**, where the state "withers away"). Marxism would finally gain power in the twentieth century, though some claim that these national experiments represent a distortion of Marx's doctrine, suggesting that there may be "as many Marxisms as there are Marxists."

> ### SKILL SET
>
> This section distills and addresses orthodox Marxism; however, the theory has been altered and fitted to many contexts—including the most backward of the industrial powers (during the Russian Revolution) and used by anti-colonial powers to establish economic independence and promote global equality (CCOT).

National Unification

It seems as if each century produces an event that transforms the diplomatic landscape. In the nineteenth century, the unifications of Italy and Germany altered the entire framework of European diplomacy. European political structures proved unable to incorporate the emergence of these two new powers, leading to the most destructive wars in history in the twentieth century. Italy and Germany had been divided for centuries. What allowed for their unifications in the middle of the nineteenth century? Once again, we must look to the failed outcomes of the revolutions of 1848.

The Crimean War, 1853–1856

Revolutions in 1848 undermined the Concert of Europe—the agreement of the great powers to resolve issues collectively—and paved the way for the mid-century **Crimean War**. Eminently avoidable and poorly fought, the Crimean War ultimately proved of great importance for subsequent diplomacy.

For centuries after its last foray in 1683 into central Europe, the Ottoman Empire slowly receded in power. The empire found itself prey to continual attacks by a Russian nation intent on gaining a warm-weather seaport. Only the intervention of Britain, which opposed Russian expansionism into the Mediterranean, kept the "Sick Man of Europe" on life support. When Napoleon III of France in 1853 wrung concessions from the Ottoman sultan to protect Christian minorities within the empire, the Russians demanded the same treatment. Fearing the further growth of Russian power, the French and British stiffened the sultan's resistance to Russian intrusion. When war ensued, the Russian navy shattered the archaic Ottoman fleet in the Black Sea and moved into two Turkish-held provinces (current-day Romania). France and Britain demanded that the Russians evacuate the provinces or face war. Even though Russia complied, the two western powers declared war anyway, due to strong anti-Russian sentiment in their nations. Austria attempted to use the situation to its own benefit. Russia had aided Austria in 1849 by crushing the Hungarian revolt. Instead of repaying the favor, Austria exploited Russia's predicament by moving into the recently evacuated provinces. Isolated, Russia attempted to defend itself against the combined weight of France, Russia, and the Italian kingdom of Piedmont-Sardinia.

The Crimean War represents the initial industrialized conflict, with the first use of trenches, telegraphs, and railways. Nonetheless, poor communication, strategic errors, and disease cost an inordinate number of lives. The struggle's only hero was Florence Nightingale (1820–1910), who helped establish the nursing profession and demonstrated the ability of women to take on productive public roles. By 1855, the new Russian tsar, Alexander II, realized that the war had unveiled Russia's technological and economic backwardness. With the Treaty of Paris (1856), Russia agreed to demilitarize the Black Sea and halt its expansion into the Balkans.

Though the war was over, the issues raised by it were not. By forever destroying the Concert of Europe, the Crimean War encouraged states to pursue national interests with little regard for the effects on the international order. Napoleon III considered the war a great victory and was falsely convinced of France's strength and prominence. Britain felt disappointed at the cost and outcome of the war and fell into "splendid isolation" for half a century, standing aside while Italy and Germany unified. With its overly subtle diplomacy, Austria had isolated itself, a fatal error as it would face two wars in the next 10 years. Before the ink was dry on the treaty, Russia was determined to reform internally and continue its expansion at the first opportunity. Finally, by its involvement, little Piedmont-Sardinia won itself a great power patron in its drive for unification.

The Unification of Italy

Background and Romantic Nationalism

The Italian peninsula had been divided since the fall of the Roman Empire. Though Italy pioneered the Renaissance, its diverse city-states lost their independence as a result of foreign invasion. Since the sixteenth century, foreign powers had dominated politics in Italy. The nationalism of the French Revolution and the policies of Napoleon revived dreams of a united Italy. The Congress of Vienna's restoration of traditional rule frustrated these aspirations. Despite failure to expel foreign rule in the revolutionary period 1815–1848, Italian nationalists could now look to leadership from Piedmont-Sardinia and exploit the increasingly tenuous position of Austria, the foreign power blocking unification.

> **SKILL SET**
>
> To ensure your understanding of the new politics of realism (*Realpolitik*, DAP), compare and contrast (COMP and MAC) the tactics used by Cavour and Bismarck, respectively, to unify Italy and Germany.

Many Italian nationalists preferred the creation of a united republic, which would require a takeover of the Papal States. Following the Congress of Vienna, the resurgence of Italian nationalism was fueled by two republican advocates: Giuseppe Mazzini (see Chapter 11) and **Giuseppe Garibaldi**, the charismatic leader of the Red Shirts. Both represented the spirit of romantic nationalism. Much of the practical work for Italian unity, however, was accomplished by a bookish and wily moderate, **Camillo Benso di Cavour (1810–1861)**.

The Role of Piedmont-Sardinia and Cavour

Because of Piedmont-Sardinia's anti-Austrian role in the revolutions of 1848, many Italian nationalists looked to it for leadership. In 1848–1849, the king granted a constitution and attempted to unite the other Italian states in a war of liberation against Austria. Owing to his failure, the king abdicated in 1849, turning over power to his son Victor Emmanuel II (r. 1849–1878). In 1852, the new king appointed Cavour as prime minister. Cavour supported Liberal ideas and had urged the unification of Italy in his newspaper, *Il Risorgimento*; further, he understood practical affairs, having made a fortune in agriculture and business. As prime minister, Cavour looked to modernize the Piedmontese state—updating the tax and budget system, building railroads, pursuing free trade, limiting the power of the Catholic Church, and building a small but strong army. Though Cavour was willing to use Romantic ideals to his advantage, he favored a realistic (*Realpolitik*) approach to Italian unity—and this required a foreign ally.

With the Treaty of Plombières (1858), Cavour persuaded Napoleon III of France to ally with Piedmont-Sardinia in a joint attack on Austria. By the agreement, Piedmont would gain the Italian states of Lombardy and Venetia, while Napoleon would reconfirm French leadership of nationalism and exercise influence in Italy. In the ensuing war, Piedmont and France defeated the Austrian army, setting off revolutions in the northern Italian states. Fearing that the situation was spinning out of control, Napoleon III signed a separate agreement with Austria, leaving Cavour high and dry. However, the northern Italian states in 1860 voted via plebiscites (elections related to issues, not candidates) to join the Piedmontese state, which Napoleon acknowledged in exchange for Nice and Savoy from Piedmont.

Cavour now urged Garibaldi to take advantage of the revolutionary situation brewing in the Kingdom of the Two Sicilies, the backward Bourbon monarchy controlling the southern half of the peninsula. With just over a thousand of his Red Shirts, Garibaldi rallied the countryside to his cause and moved up the peninsula. Once again, concerns over the position of the papacy complicated matters. Cavour did not wish to involve French troops guarding Rome in the situation, so he and Victor Emmanuel met Garibaldi south of Rome and urged him to relinquish his conquest to Piedmont-Sardinia. Though a republican, Garibaldi consented, and plebiscites confirmed the unification of the northern and southern halves of the peninsula. In March 1861, the new Italian kingdom was proclaimed, with Victor Emmanuel as its first monarch. Two months later, Cavour died, one might say from complications of nation-birth. Thus, it has been said that the new Italian kingdom represented the "passion of Mazzini, the audacity of Garibaldi, and the cunning of Cavour."

Italy completed its unification by gaining Venetia in 1866 and Rome (excluding the Vatican) in 1870 when Prussia, with whom Italy was allied, defeated Austria and then France in war. Though united, Italy experienced significant problems—opposition by the papacy to the new Italian state, economic underdevelopment, a corrupt political system known as *trasformismo* (the bribing of political opponents), and the wide cultural and economic differences between northern and southern Italy. Because it came so late to national unity, Italy often compensated by aggressively seeking colonies and attempting to regain "unredeemed" Italian-speaking territories.

The Unification of Germany

Background: German Dualism

Like Italy, Germany's limbs had lain severed in central Europe for centuries. Conflicts between the Holy Roman Emperor and papacy in the Middle Ages stymied either from unifying Germany. Due to its elective nature, the emperor never became a strong absolutist ruler like the kings of France. Religious conflict in the sixteenth and seventeenth centuries splintered German politics, formalized with the Westphalia settlement in 1648. In the nineteenth century, the dualism of two German powers—Austria and Prussia—effectively checked either from consolidating the smaller German states into one nation unified around German language and ethnicity. When Liberals failed in 1848 at Frankfurt to unify Germany, it opened the door for a different path to the same objective.

Prussia's great military tradition had decayed since the time of Frederick the Great (d. 1786). The kingdom entered the French revolutionary wars late (1807) and then was defeated decisively by Napoleon. Moreover, Austria under Metternich dominated German politics after the Congress of Vienna, leaving Prussia to play second fiddle. When William I (r. 1861–1888) inherited the Prussian throne from his faltering brother, he set out to reestablish Prussia's power.

With his first act, William introduced long-overdue reforms in the army. At the advice of his generals, William called for the expansion of the army, regular conscription (the draft), the creation of a General Staff (to devise war plans), and the introduction of modern rifled weapons, such as the breech-loading needle gun. According to the Prussian Constitution of 1850, representatives to the Reichstag (lower house of the parliament) were apportioned by a unique three-tiered voting system, designed to favor the traditional Prussian nobility (the Junkers). However, as Germany industrialized, the power of the middle-class Liberal Party grew in Prussia. Liberals in the Reichstag resented the conservative influence of the army as well as the Junker class who dominated it and opposed the king's reforms. Neither king nor Reichstag would budge, plunging Prussia into a constitutional crisis.

The Work of Bismarck

To solve the crisis, William turned in 1862 to **Otto von Bismarck** (1815–1898), appointing him Chancellor. Bismarck hailed from the Junker class, but surpassed that often provincial and mediocre group with his intelligence and ambitions. A romantic turned conservative, Bismarck gained wide diplomatic experience representing Prussia to France, Russia, and the German Confederation. In his political approach, Bismarck played the consummate game of *Realpolitik*. Bismarck possessed no predetermined plan for the unification of Germany; rather, he took advantage of opportunities presented to him. To deal with the political crisis in Prussia, Bismarck turned the tables on the Liberals in the Reichstag, claiming that they held no constitutional power to block needed reforms. He appealed to Prussian patriotism, arguing that the other German states did not look to Prussia's liberalism—that was the mistake of 1848—but to its "iron and blood." When the Reichstag

> ### SKILL SET & THEME MUSIC
>
> Certainly the unification of Germany represents one of the critical moments of the course (CCOT), and it may be useful for you to identify its effects. As the Prime Minister of Britain noted at the time: "There is not a diplomatic tradition which has not been swept away. You have a new world, new influences at work, new and unknown objects and dangers with which to cope….The balance of power has been entirely destroyed." Consider how subsequent political and diplomatic events were shaped by the creation of this new restless empire (SOP & NEI).

continued to refuse taxes to implement the army reforms, Bismarck simply instructed the bureaucracy to collect the taxes anyway.

To unify Germany, Bismarck waged three separate wars. His opponent in each war found itself diplomatically isolated and maneuvered into appearing as the aggressor. When the Poles revolted against Russian authority in 1863, almost every great power expressed support for their national aspirations, but gave no tangible assistance. Bismarck calculated that he needed the future friendship of great-power Russia, so he supported their crushing of the Polish revolt. In 1864, Denmark formally incorporated the mainly German-speaking provinces of Schleswig and Holstein (which it had occupied since 1848) into the Danish kingdom, violating an international treaty. Nationalism flared in Germany. Rather than working through the German Confederation as Austria preferred, Bismarck suggested a joint approach by the two leading powers. Austria relented, and the two powers easily defeated their enemy in the Danish War, occupying the two provinces of Schleswig and Holstein.

The joint occupation of the two provinces offered ample opportunity for conflict between the two German powers. The dispute festered, as Bismarck intended, and eventually Austria turned to the German Confederation for relief. Citing a violation of the occupation agreement, Prussia went to war against Austria. Before entering the conflict, Bismarck ensured Austria's isolation—Russia was favorable after Bismarck's support for the Polish revolt; Napoleon was bought off with vague promises of French expansion; Italy hoped to gain Venetia from Austria; and Britain maintained its splendid isolation. In the ensuing Austro-Prussian War (or Seven Weeks' War) of 1866, Prussia's superior railroads, staff organization, and needle gun overwhelmed the Austrians. Despite the designs of William I, Bismarck treated Austria leniently; they lost only Venetia and, more importantly, were forced to bow out of German affairs. Prussia annexed the states of north Germany, and in 1867 Bismarck created the North German Confederation, insisting that its Reichstag be elected by universal male suffrage. What's more, the Reichstag hailed Bismarck's achievement by retroactively approving the illegally collected taxes with the Indemnity Bill of 1866.

The mostly Catholic German states stood outside this union. Anticipating future conflict with France, Bismarck convinced these states to join in an alliance with the North German Confederation should war break out with France. When the Spanish throne became vacant in 1870, Bismarck had his pretext. The Spanish nobles offered the throne to a Hohenzollern relative of William's, an offer that Bismarck pressed the candidate to accept. Not wishing to be surrounded by Hohenzollerns, the French vehemently objected. William I relented and encouraged his cousin to drop the offer. Now Napoleon III of France overplayed his hand and demanded an apology from William via the French ambassador. Bismarck edited an account of the meeting, known as the Ems Dispatch, to make it seem as if the king had insulted the French ambassador. Napoleon took the bait and declared war. Once again, Bismarck's opponent was isolated; the French were easily defeated in the Franco-Prussian War and embarrassingly, Napoleon himself was captured at Sedan. The resulting treaty imposed a 5-billion franc indemnity on the French, and, more importantly, they lost Alsace-Lorraine, which became a source of enmity between the two nations throughout the twentieth century. In January 1871, Bismarck's work was complete with the proclamation of the German Empire with William I as Kaiser.

Though Bismarck helped engineer a federal constitution that respected the traditions of the other German states and allowed elements of democracy, power was still exercised in an authoritarian fashion. Government ministers reported to the Kaiser, not the Reichstag, and Bismarck effectively concentrated key positions in his own hands (Chancellor, Prussian Minister of State, Foreign Minister), which allowed him to exploit democratic mechanisms to ensure his domination of policy. This new German empire immediately upset the balance of power in Europe. Its economic and military potential threatened to dwarf its neighbors. Even though Bismarck worked to maintain peace in Europe after 1871, some historians believe that he laid the foundation for the militarism and state glorification that gave rise to the Nazis in the twentieth century.

Other Nation-Building Efforts

Italy and Germany represent the most salient examples of nationalism's power to unify states. However, already territorially unified states, such as France and Russia, worked toward greater internal cohesion through reform. The following states demonstrate three different models of reform.

France: Napoleon III and the Second Empire

After being elected president of the Second Republic, Louis Napoleon quickly consolidated his power. Presenting himself as a man of the people, he dissolved the legislature over the issue of universal male suffrage. In a *coup d'etat* in 1851, Napoleon rescinded the 1848 republican constitution. With popular approval through a plebiscite, Napoleon in 1852 proclaimed the Second Empire with himself as Emperor Napoleon III. Though Napoleon's foreign adventures proved disastrous—loss of control over Italian and German unification, a failed effort to create an empire in Mexico—he did modernize France internally.

Working through a professional and centrally controlled bureaucracy, Napoleon focused on France's economic development. He established a national bank, built railways, promoted French industry, and in his most celebrated reform, rebuilt the city of Paris. Napoleon hired the talents of the architect and engineer <u>Baron von Haussmann</u> (1809–1891), who tore down old city walls and housing, constructed a modern sanitary system, built grand boulevards, and adorned it all with a feast of opera houses, theaters, and shopping centers. As Napoleon said, "I found Paris stinking, and left it smelling sweet." Due to increasing criticism, Napoleon after 1860 allowed more legislative input, relaxed press censorship, and pursued a policy of free trade with Great Britain. But such reforms could not rescue Napoleon from his foreign policy failures, and in 1870, the emperor himself was captured by the Prussian army (see above) and the empire ended. Workers in the shiny new Paris refused to surrender, however, and established a revolutionary Paris Commune, which harkened back to the principles of 1793 with its socialist program. Eventually, a popularly elected Constituent Assembly crushed the Paris Commune and established the Third Republic. Another French republic started off with the taint of class violence and military failure.

Russia: Alexander II's Modernization

The Crimean War demonstrated Russia's weakness *vis-à-vis* the other great powers. Recognizing the backwardness of his nation, <u>Alexander II</u> (r. 1855–1881) embarked on a series of top-down reforms that proved ultimately too little too late to save the Romanov dynasty. Fearing violent peasant upheaval, Alexander **abolished serfdom** in 1861. By terms of the liberation, peasants continued to live on the village *mirs* until they paid for the land they received. Russian agriculture continued to suffer from land shortages and rural overpopulation into the twentieth century. In addition, Alexander introduced equality into the legal system, abolished corporal and capital punishment, created local assemblies known as *zemstvos*, and reformed the army. These wide-ranging reforms did not heal the growing rift in Russian society between those who emphasized Russia's unique traditions (called Slavophiles) and those who believed Russia must become more modern (Westernizers). Led by discontented intellectuals, such as Alexander Herzen and <u>Mikhail Bakunin</u> (1814–1876), **anarchism** gained support in the context of an autocratic and archaic Russia. Eventually, an anarchist-inspired movement known as the People's Will succeeded in 1881 in assassinating Alexander after numerous failed attempts.

Austria-Hungary: The Dual Monarchy

The tattered Austrian empire was, until the First World War, ruled by Franz Joseph I (r. 1848–1916), a leader not known for his decisive actions or ambitious projects. Franz Joseph attempted to hold together his diverse realm through the bureaucracy, the army, and loyalty to the Habsburg dynasty. Following the revolutions of 1848, Austria focused on internal development, building railroads and promoting industry, as well as centralization around the German language. These policies further alienated the Slavic and Magyar ethnic minorities. Following losses in the Italian and German wars of unification, Franz Joseph allowed the creation of the **Dual Monarchy** in 1867. This new **Austro-Hungarian** monarchy allowed autonomy for the Magyars but maintained unity through common ministries of finance, foreign affairs, and war. However, neither of these kingdoms was democratic. In fact, the Hungarians pursued Magyarization in their part of the empire, suppressing Slavic languages and culture. Not until 1907 did Austria grant universal male suffrage and even then, the imperial Reichsrat so often descended into ethnic conflict that Franz Joseph was forced to rule by decree. Austria-Hungary's ethnic problems laid the powder trail that ignited into the First World War.

The Second Industrial Revolution

Historians point to the year 1850 as roughly dividing the initial phase of industrialization from a new one characterized by a larger scale of industrial enterprises, a further geographic expansion of industry, and a much closer relationship between theoretical science and its application in technology. We call this new phase the Second Industrial Revolution.

New Technologies and Methods

The period 1875–1910 represents arguably the greatest concentration of technological advance—including our own age—in the history of the human race. Steam engines now powered larger factories, as mechanized production became the predominant form of manufacture. American Henry Ford pioneered a new form of **mass production**, the assembly line, which allowed for increased economies of scale (i.e., reduced costs at high levels of production) and cheaper products. With the <u>Bessemer process</u>, steel replaced iron as the essential metal in construction, railways, and for military use. Reinforced concrete and steel girders allowed for the development of skyscrapers, adding a new visual element to modern cities.

Theoretical advances in chemistry boosted the chemical industry. Germany quickly became the dominant producer of chemicals, which had numerous industrial, pharmaceutical, and military uses. Europeans harnessed the power of **electricity** to light cities, power <u>streetcars</u>, and provide for a seemingly inexhaustible source of energy. After its discovery in 1859, petroleum grew into a mineral resource vital to the needs of the new <u>internal combustion engines</u> and to nation-states dependent on its potential power. This catalog only scratches the surface; <u>refrigeration</u>, photography, elevators, kitchen appliances, motion pictures, synthetic fabrics, TNT, x-rays, and many others could also be included.

Transportation and Communication

Technological advances revolutionized transportation and communications. Steamships allowed for faster ocean journeys and wider geographic mobility, establishing an essential means for European control of distant empires. The completion of the Suez (1869) and Panama Canals (1914) reduced transoceanic travel times even further. Invented in 1903, airplanes would not alter passenger travel for several generations, but yielded immediate military applications. New power sources also allowed for the development of trolleys and subways, and by extension, the creation of suburbs and the further separation of home and work.

The technology of human communication had not changed much since the invention of the printing press in the 1450s. The late nineteenth century witnessed a series of inventions that made the world smaller and allowed European power a truly global reach. A transatlantic telegraph cable was laid in the 1870s to create the first instantaneous communication across continents; the invention of the telephone was not far behind. To facilitate railway schedules, standardized time zones were introduced in the 1880s. Marconi's discovery of radio waves translated in the early twentieth century into a means for states to coordinate military power and control public opinion.

Business Cycles and Managing Markets

Despite the great wealth generated by this technological dynamo, the European economy suffered from boom-bust cycles during the period 1873–1896. Overproduction and unpredictable commodity prices routinely plunged Europe into recession, creating fear for governments of worker unrest and corporate bankruptcies. To manage the market, businesses became more organized. The **modern corporation**, with its complex administrative structures, accounting procedures, and stocks, dates from the late nineteenth century. Some industries informally collaborated in cartels to control the production and thus the prices of their manufactures. Banks pooled investment resources in consortia to control interest rates. These **monopolies** represented an attempt by companies to control an unpredictable market. Though governments continued to rely on market mechanisms and the gold standard to ensure stable currencies, many states began to move away from free trade toward **protective tariffs** to shield domestic industries.

Technological advances translated into new goods. Former luxuries now became necessities. To reach consumers, corporations began to exploit communication advances for marketing purposes. Advertising in billboards, newspapers, and catalogs opened a new world of **consumerism** to European citizens. With its modernization, Paris sponsored the first **department store**, Bon Marché, in the 1870s. An increasingly sophisticated economy opened new employment opportunities in so-called white collar areas, such as retail, marketing, communications, and services.

> **THEME MUSIC & SKILL SET**
>
> The Second Industrial Revolution reveals the tension inherent in the Technological and Scientific Innovation theme, as it provided immense wealth to industrialists and European powers, while at the same time left other groups (unskilled laborers, poor peasants, colonial areas) with inequality and dependence. Consider exploring this disparity in an essay response to nail down your Complexity point.

The Balance of Power and Global Integration

New developments in industry shifted the balance of economic power worldwide. Within Europe, Germany by 1900 surpassed Britain in steel, iron, coal mining, and chemical production. The United States arose as a competitor outside Europe, besting Britain and Germany both in steel and coal production, also by 1900. European capital, however, commanded the world. With huge profits and sophisticated banking and investment methods, European corporations and governments came to dominate the functioning of the world economy. Imperial powers like Britain, France, and Germany invested in Asian, African, and Latin American ventures, influencing those regions' economic decisions, if not controlling them outright. By 1914, economic activity had become truly global, with developments in one area of the world rippling throughout.

Imperialism

European influence on global markets was nothing new in the nineteenth century. However, the period 1763–1871 saw a net decline in European colonial control, with American independence and Europe's preoccupation with revolutionary movements and internal development. Following the unification campaigns of Italy and Germany, as well as other internal nation-building programs, Europe's aspirations for national greatness moved beyond the continent. With the advance of technology and organization stemming from the Second Industrial Revolution, European powers as of 1870 possessed both the means and motives for further penetration of the global market. Compared with earlier colonization, what distinguished European imperialism in the period 1871–1914 was more direct control of foreign territory and greater emphasis placed on colonies' internal infrastructure development.

Motives and Means

Motives for European imperialism can be divided into three basic categories—economic, political, and cultural. As you might expect, Marxist historians stress economic motives stemming from the expansion of capitalism. However, other historians contend that the pursuit of even financially valueless colonies demonstrates the power of national prestige as a driving force, or that the cultural "civilizing mission" acted as more than a cynical pretext, but as a genuine idealistic impulse.

- *Economic motives* – As nations industrialized, they needed access to **raw materials**, particularly with the sophisticated industries of the Second Industrial Revolution. Rubber, oil, bauxite, copper, diamonds—all could be found in great supply in Asia, Africa, and Latin America. With European rivalries heating up, great powers feared dependence on potential enemies for strategic resources; colonies opened the door for self-sufficiency. With the problem of overproduction, nations also desired colonies as **markets** for finished products and outlets for investment of profits. However, most of the imperialist powers' capital went into more established industrialized areas, such as the United States or other European nations.

- *Political motives* – Imperialist powers coveted strategic locations. Great Britain bought up shares in the Suez Canal Company and eventually formed a protectorate (a nominally independent state indirectly controlled by another state) over Egypt in 1882 because of the geopolitical value of the Suez as a "lifeline to the British Empire." When the United States became an imperial power in 1898 after the Spanish-American War, it looked at the Philippines and Pacific islands as important coaling stations and military bases. At great cost, nations like Italy pursued colonies primarily as a claim to status as one of the great powers. After 1871, the European powers carved up Africa with a **nationalistic fervor** driven by public opinion. In Germany, Bismarck disdained colonies in Africa but pursued them anyway to appease public opinion; colonies are "for elections," he said. Finally, many feared that the mushrooming European population (from 260 million in 1850 to 450 million in 1914) would lead to political discontent. Colonies might act as an outlet for surplus population; indeed, 30-50 million immigrants left Europe in this period, but most went to the United States, the Americas, or Australia.

- *Cultural motives* – Missionaries arrived first in Africa. The famous David Livingstone traveled to the "Dark Continent" as a medical missionary and was followed by British middle-class Victorians who believed it their duty to civilize those they encountered. This paternalistic European attitude found expression in Rudyard Kipling's (1865–1936) famous poem "The White Man's Burden," which some view as an endorsement of the civilizing mission, whereas others view it as a satire of these very same attitudes. By the 1870s, the influence of Charles Darwin's ideas (see next chapter) had seeped into the consciousness of writers, businessmen, and political leaders. Many viewed history as an ongoing struggle among races for resources and territory. According to **Social Darwinism**, war elevated the nation by calling for self-sacrifice and establishing the proper hierarchy among the victors and the defeated. Europeans often took their easy subjugation of technologically less advanced peoples as a moral endorsement of their imperial ambitions.

How was it possible for the small continent of Europe to control, directly or indirectly, almost two-thirds of the world's population by 1914? First, European control arose directly from the technological advances of the Second Industrial Revolution. Steam power, telegraphs, **medical advances** (e.g., the discovery of quinine to treat malaria), and railroads allowed for global trade and communication as well as penetration of the interior of Africa and Asia. Second, with the industrialization of war, Europeans gained an overwhelming military superiority. The Asian civilizations of India and China, not to mention the tribal societies of Africa, had no answer for high-powered artillery, armored battleships, and machine guns. Finally, the complex and highly organized nature of modern corporate capitalism sustained a long-term presence in colonies and provided for the systematic exploitation of resources.

The Partition of Africa

As of 1870, Europe had colonized little of Africa; most inland areas, away from the coasts, were unknown. The pursuit of African colonies got under way with the founding of the International Congo Association in 1878 by King Leopold II (r. 1865–1909) of Belgium. Private bankers financed Leopold's venture, which was an entirely personal rather than a national concern. To manage the possible exploitation of Africa, Bismarck in 1884–1885 called the Berlin Conference among the great powers. The imperial powers agreed to create the Congo Free State as Leopold's personal fiefdom and devised procedures for the orderly establishment of colonies. Leopold's rule proved to be one of the harshest in Africa, as he ignored the prohibition on slavery, plundered the nation of rubber and ivory, all while the Congolese population was decimated by disease and overwork. According to some estimates, the death toll reaches 10 million.

The Berlin Conference produced the opposite of the intended effect. By simply establishing coastal control, European nations could claim huge swaths of Africa's interior by drawing lines on a map, usually with no regard for linguistic or tribal divisions. Imperialists exploited Africans' lack of experience with European legal and economic concepts, as tribal leaders often unknowingly signed away trade and resource concessions. By 1900, all except Liberia and Ethiopia had fallen under direct European rule.

> **THEME MUSIC**
>
> From the beginning of the course (1450), Europe had pushed to expand its influence across the globe. The drive for resources and power stimulated exploration in the fifteenth and sixteenth centuries, created the Columbian Exchange and Commercial Revolution, and here culminates with the establishment of a European-dominated global economy via imperialism (INT).

Africa, 1914

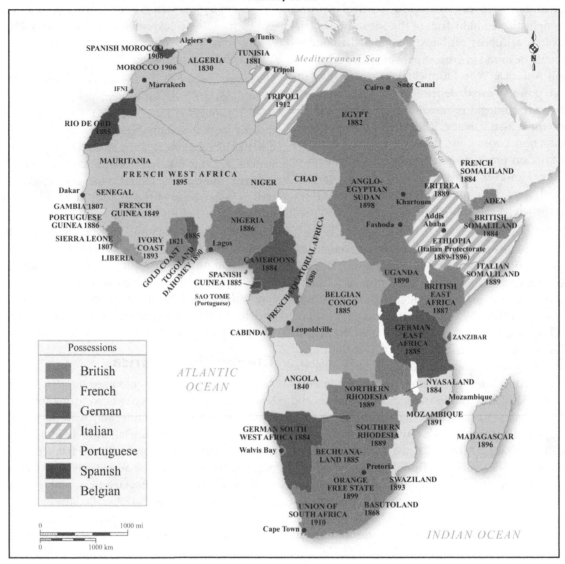

To understand the nature of African imperialism, we briefly examine the British example. Fearing the spread of independence movements, colonial secretary Joseph Chamberlain (1836–1914) proposed a tariff union between Britain and its colonies, thereby binding the colonies together in a system of imperial preferences. Gradually these dominions (self-governing areas such as Canada) would achieve complete self-rule but maintain strong economic ties with the mother country. Chamberlain's idea would later bear fruit with the commonwealth system following World War I. However, African imperialism seemed to belong more to adventurers like Cecil Rhodes (1853–1902) rather than statesmen like Chamberlain. Britain had already established in 1815 control of the Cape of Good Hope on the southern end of Africa, dispossessing the Dutch settlers who trekked overland to create the Orange Free State and Transvaal. When Rhodes was made prime minister of this Cape Colony, he dreamed of establishing a Cape-to-Cairo connection to cement Britain's dominance of Africa and the exploitation of his dia-

mond interests. Rhodes went too far by trying to provoke war with the two Dutch republics and was forced to resign.

Imperial pursuits in Africa demonstrated the potential for conflict involving the great powers. To secure control of Egypt, Britain extended its power into Sudan. This intrusion brought resistance by Islamic troops, and the retaliatory expedition in 1898 at Omdurman demonstrated the lethal advantage of machine guns and artillery over muskets and spears, as the British lost only 48 men to 10,000 for the Sudanese. After their victory, British troops almost fell into conflict with the French, who controlled much of north and west Africa, at Fashoda. Cooler heads prevailed, and war was avoided. Such was not the case with the Dutch Boers. Rhodes's policies eventually embroiled Britain in the costly Boer War (1899–1902), in which Britain's use of concentration camps and scorched-earth policies led to international condemnation. The potential for further conflict in Africa shook Britain out of its isolation as it went shopping for allies.

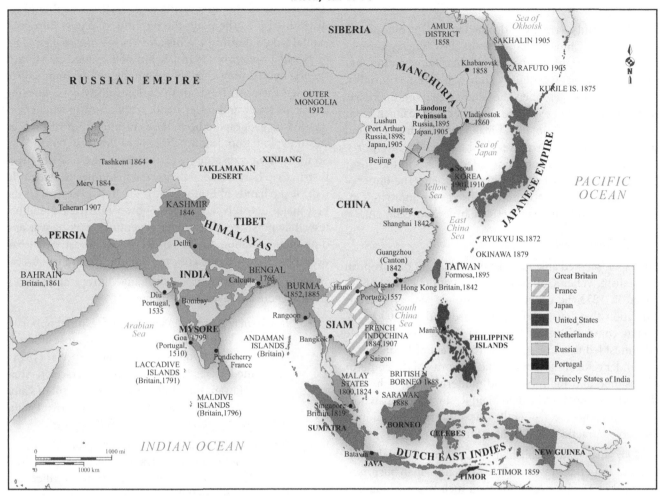

Imperialism in Asia—Three Examples

The British in India

Compared to their policies in Africa, European powers employed indirect control in Asia. Because civilizations like India and China already possessed complex political and social hierarchies, European imperialists preferred to "plug in" to the existing power structure to establish control. In India, Britain had exploited that country's political divisions to gain local allies and establish indirect control through the British East India Company. In 1857, soldiers (called sepoys) in the Indian army revolted against Britain's insensitivity toward Hindus and Muslims. Britain subdued the Sepoy Mutiny with great brutality, dissolved the East India Company, and established direct rule, with Queen Victoria (1837–1901) proclaimed Empress of India.

Though India possessed an indigienous manufacturing base, Britain turned the country into a raw materials producer. At the same time, Britain attempted to "modernize" India's infrastructure by building railroads, instructing the population in English, and educating elites at British universities so they might become effective civil servants. Ironically, many such students imbibed western ideas of nationalism and equality, tools that would be used by the likes of Mahatma Gandhi (1869–1948) and Jawaharlal Nehru (1889–1964) to establish Indian independence later.

Intrusion into China

China disdained contact with foreigners and generally dismissed them as uncivilized. However, the weakness of the Qing Dynasty (1644–1911) allowed westerners to exploit China's growing disintegration to their advantage. Though Europeans coveted Chinese goods, the only commodity Europeans seemed able to sell in China was opium. When the Chinese government attempted to stop the import of the noxious substance, the British responded with overwhelming military force. After several such Opium Wars at mid-century, Britain and France had imposed upon China trading and other concessions. By the Treaty of Nanjing

> **EXAMPLE BASE**
>
> Though you have choices, the Unit Guides require that you understand how colonial areas responded to and resisted European imperialism. As you read through this section, consider the range of responses, perhaps making a visual organizer to show similarities and differences, or provide a brief assessment of the effectiveness of these responses (ARG).

(1842), China surrendered Hong Kong and was forced to create free trade treaty ports.

Soon Russia and Germany had joined in carving out spheres of influence in China. Even worse for the Chinese, Europeans were subject only to the laws of their home nation, not to those of China, an indignity known as extraterritoriality. In an attempt to keep open the Chinese market, the newly imperial United States secured agreement to the Open Door Policy, an effort to maintain China's territorial integrity and the free access of each power to the others' treaty ports. Anger against foreign control resulted in 1900 in the Boxer Rebellion, led by a secretive Chinese society. The imperial nations crushed the revolt and imposed even more indemnities and controls on the faltering Chinese government.

Japan's Meiji Restoration

Only Japan seemed able to resist the onslaught of European imperialism. When Commodore Perry of the United States arrived in 1853, he encountered a united and prosperous civilization that had been virtually isolated for 300 years. Foreign contact brought down the Tokugawa Shogunate and almost led to a Chinese-style treatment of Japan. However, under reforming samurai, the authority of the emperor was restored and the most rapid modernization in history followed. During the so-called Meiji Restoration, Japan borrowed from the West liberally—its industrial techniques, educational practices, and military arts.

By 1890, Japan had established itself as an industrial, military, and imperial power in its own right. Japan surprised the world in 1894 by defeating the much larger China and establishing dominance over the Korean peninsula. In a sign of Japan's new-found prestige, Britain allied with this emerging Asian power in 1902. Conflict with Russia over resources in Manchuria soon led to the Russo-Japanese War of 1904–1905. Japan shocked the world by defeating the Russians on land and sea, destroying the Russian fleet at Tsushima Strait. The outcome represented the first time in modern history that an Asian power had defeated a European power in war. Profound consequences issued from the Russo-Japanese War: first, Russia turned back toward expansion in the Balkans, setting the stage for the First World War; second, Russia's weak showing led to the **Revolution of 1905**, a warm-up for the great Russian Revolution of 1917; and finally, Japan had demonstrated to the rest of the world that Europeans could be defeated by turning their own weapons against them.

Critics and Consequences

Though many Europeans saw great glory in imperialism, some condemned it. Two of the most famous critiques came from J.A. Hobson, a British economist, and the great Russian revolutionary, **V.I. Lenin** (1870–1924). Hobson argued that European imperialism was driven by the accumulation of capital, which in turn required overseas investment and markets. If corporations would simply invest in workers' wages and if governments taxed excess wealth and redistributed it to the poor, the impulse to export European capital would diminish. In his *Imperialism, the Highest Stage of World Capitalism* (1916), Lenin contributed to Marxist theory by claiming that the phenomenon of imperialism revealed the crisis inherent in capitalism. By concentrating power in fewer and fewer hands, capitalism inevitably expanded its geographic boundaries in pursuit of further areas of exploitation, leading directly to the First World War. Some historians dispute these assertions; the case of Italy is instructive. Italy desperately pursued colonies in Africa. In fact, at the hands of Ethiopia in 1896, Italy experienced the first major defeat by a European power in Africa. Nonetheless, Italy persisted in its imperial ventures, risking war and diplomatic isolation, to gain in 1911 Libya, a vast expanse of desert hardly worth the cost in men, money, and resources.

How did European imperialism change Europe and the world? There are several arguments:

- *Rise of new powers* – As a result of colonial opportunities, the United States and Japan both rose as imperial powers. After the Spanish-American War (1898), the United States acquired its first overseas possessions—Hawaii, the Philippines, and control of Cuba and the Panama Canal. The rise of these two Pacific powers would lead to conflict in World War II.

- *Intensification of European rivalries* – The First World War did not begin in Africa or Asia, but seeds of war were planted in colonies. To illustrate, conflicts between Russia and Britain over Persia and between Germany and France in the Moroccan Crises (1905, 1911) helped cement the mutually antagonistic alliance systems that escalated into World War I.

- *Decolonization and dependency* – Europe's hold on its colonies weakened after World War I and was severed after World War II. Today, no European nation possesses a colonial empire, yet issues of colonial dependence and resentment toward former European (and American) dominance show up in the form of terrorism, tribal conflicts, and persistent economic underdevelopment.

Imperialism reveals a domestic connection as well. Colonial ventures acted as a laboratory for some to test the ideas of Darwinism and eugenics (the pseudoscience of studying racial characteristics), as well as new industrial and military technologies. The overseas drive for colonies reveals the intense domestic pressures operating at home—social, intellectual, and political. In the next chapter, we turn to these issues.

Additional Resources

C.A. Bayley, *The Birth of the Modern World, 1780–1914: Global Connections and Comparisons* (2004) — Discusses imperialism and nationalism within a broader global context of modernization.

Gordon Craig, *Germany, 1866–1945* (1980) — The interested student will find a strong narrative of German unification.

T.S. Hamerow, *Otto von Bismarck: A Historical Assessment* (rev. 1993) — This volume provides various interpretations on a key figure of the period.

Eric Hobsbawn, *The Age of Empire, 1875–1914* (1989) — An insightful account of the period from a famous Marxist historian.

Adam Hochschild, *King Leopold's Ghost: A Story of Greed, Terror, and Heroism in Colonial Africa* (1998) — A gripping account of one of the worst experiences under imperial rule.

Thomas Pakenham, *The Scramble for Africa* (1992) — A strong narrative account of the partitioning of Africa.

Norman Rich, *Great Power Diplomacy, 1814–1914* (1991) — A survey of European diplomacy in an important era.

Congo: White King, Red Rubber, Black Death (2004) — A powerful documentary on Leopold II's brutal exploitation of the Congo.

https://faculty.wcas.northwestern.edu/~jmokyr/castronovo.pdf — A brief conceptual explanation of the defining features of the Second Industrial Revolution by a noted economic historian.

http://people.umass.edu/hist101/imperialism%20documents%202008.pdf — This site provides a variety of sources on the motives for imperialism.

CHAPTER TEST

Multiple-Choice Questions

Questions 1–4 are based on the map below.

European Railroads, 1870 and 1914

1. The map best supports which of the following conclusions about the European economy?

   A. Governments played a more important role on the continent than in Britain in promoting industry.

   B. Mechanization and the factory system became the predominant modes of production by 1914.

   C. German industrialization experienced a significant stimulus with its unification in 1871.

   D. Transportation developments like railroads helped create more fully integrated national and international economies.

2. The most direct result of the trends shown in the map was the:

   A. growth of a new consumer economy.

   B. development of rival alliance blocs.

   C. creation of the feminist movement.

   D. expansion of leisure time and activities.

3. The differences shown on the map between western and eastern Europe can be explained by:

   A. the prevalence of volatile business cycles in western Europe.

   B. better access to natural resources in western European states.

   C. the dominance of agricultural elites in eastern Europe.

   D. the control over eastern European states by Russia.

4. Which of the following technologies or processes would be most comparable in its effects to those depicted on the map?

   A. The printing press during the Renaissance

   B. Advances in navigation during exploration

   C. Military weapons and tactics in the seventeenth century

   D. Astronomical discoveries of the Scientific Revolution

Questions 5–8 are based on the interpretation below.

"But the crux of the global economic situation was that a number of developed economies simultaneously felt the same need for new markets. If they were sufficiently strong their ideal was 'the open door' on the markets of the underdeveloped world; but if not strong enough, they hoped to carve out for themselves territories which, by virtue of ownership, would give national business a monopoly position or at least a substantial advantage. Partition of the unoccupied parts of the Third World was the logical consequence."

Eric Hobsbawm, British historian, *The Age of Empire, 1875–1914*, 1987

5. The development in the period 1850–1914 that relates most directly to the interpretation above was:

   A. the development of Racial Darwinism.

   B. nationalist competition among states.

   C. the unification of Italy and Germany.

   D. the Second Industrial Revolution.

6. How did Europe's interaction with the world, as presented by Hobsbawm, differ most significantly from Europe's interaction with the world during the period 1450–1600?

   A. The reliance on notions of European cultural superiority

   B. Imbalances of technology between Europeans and non-Europeans

   C. The economic demands produced by an industrializing economy

   D. Widespread conversion of non-Europeans to Christianity

7. Which of the following ideologies most likely influenced the historian's interpretation of the motivations for European imperialism?

   A. Positivism

   B. Marxism

   C. Nationalism

   D. Darwinism

8. The historian could use all of the following as evidence to support his interpretation EXCEPT:

   A. the persistence of backward agricultural practices in areas of Europe.

   B. transportation advances such as railroads and steamships.

   C. reliance on monopolies by governments and corporations.

   D. volatile business cycles of boom and bust in Europe.

See Chapter 18 for answers and explanations.

Long Essay Question

Directions: Read the prompt below and write your response on a separate sheet of paper. A sample response and commentary are provided on the next page.

Evaluate the most significant difference in the effects of nationalism on any two European nations in the period 1850–1914.

(RP: Comparison)

LEQ Sample Response

Following the Napoleonic Wars, there was a rise in nationalism in Europe. The French were proud to be French and fight for liberty, equality, and fraternity, while other nations were similarly proud not to be French. These national identities were passed through generations and could not be squandered by the Congress of Vienna, which hoped to maintain a conservative balance of power in Europe. The Revolutions of 1848, though suppressed, laid further groundwork for the rise in nationalism across Europe. Still, the rise in nationalism changed the balance of power in Europe, for the benefit of Germany and the detriment of Austria-Hungary.

Germany, prior to 1871, was a collection of fiefdoms that were influenced both by Austria and Prussia and shared a common heritage, culture, and language. However, many of these territories and Prussia sought a united German state that had been desired for centuries. Otto von Bismarck helped with this endeavor using nationalism. Bismarck managed to build a strong military for Prussia and integrate the rest of the future German state in conflicts against France, Denmark, and Austria, thus feeding and capitalizing on nationalism. Additionally, due to Germany's subjects that desired further national prestige, Bismarck was pushed to pursue colonies in Africa. Thus, nationalism in Germany helped unite the country into one of the great powers of the time, with great technological innovation, economic prosperity, and colonialism resulting from the unification, benefiting the people.

However, in Austria, nationalism had a very different effect. Since the revolutions of 1848, Magyars and Slavs had fought against the Austrian elite. By mid-century, the Magyars had been given local autonomy and Budapest, in modern-day Hungary, became a joint capital of the empire. Still, Franz Joseph made German the official language of the Austrian bureaucracy to emphasize the power of the Austrians in the empire. However, the Magyars and Austrians weren't the only groups that had wanted representation in Austria. Underneath the Magyars and Austrians were the Slavs, in groups like the Serbians, Croats, and Czechs. The Slavs similarly wanted representation and autonomy in Austria-Hungary, but the non-Slavic groups, that is, the Austrians and Magyars, opposed them. Thus, nationalism among Slavic groups posed a grave threat to the Austrian Empire as it had in 1848. As a result, Austria fell behind its former role as leader of Europe, was unable to stop Germany and Italy from unifying and failed to gain any new colonies. Nationalism in Austria, specifically among the Slavic people, had weakened the nation.

The period leading up to WWI was a turbulent time in European politics. Each country was striving to be as powerful and prosperous as possible and national and cultural identities were a major part of conflicts. In the case of Germany, nationalism and cultural similarities helped unify the nation in 1871 and made Germany possibly the strongest nation in Europe. In Austria-Hungary, on the other side of the spectrum, faced many obstacles to its growth and power due to the Slavic peoples' nationalism within its borders. Connecting to National and European identity (NEI), nationalism would play a major role in the First World War. Germany's unity and strength would make it a difficult opponent for Britain and France while Austria's oppression of the Slavs would spark the conflict and end its empire. Germany was similarly strong in its economy thanks to nationalism and unification, while Austria fell behind in industry and remained more agricultural. Ultimately, nationalism remained and still remains an important part of European politics, playing a role in everything from the world wars to Brexit.

LEQ Response Analysis

This is a strong essay. In the introduction, the response earned the Contextualization point for its concise background on the French Revolution, Congress of Vienna, and revolutions of 1848. In addition, the essay takes a position and provides a clear line of reasoning (nationalism was to the "betterment of Germany" and "detriment of Austria") to earn the Thesis point. With its multiple examples for both nations clearly applied to its argument (Bismarck's wars, colonies in Africa, Dual Monarchy, Slavic discontent), the essay easily earns both points for its Use of Evidence. An AP reader would appreciate the student's ability to use evidence clearly to frame an argument focused on the HTS of Comparison, drawing effective contrasts between the two nations selected. Finally, the conclusion brought home the Complexity point by extending its analysis into how nationalism in both nations helped bring about the First World War. While the explicit connection to the NEI theme is appreciated, this does not in itself earn any points, as that theme is already the focus on the question. **Score: 6** (+1 for Thesis, +1 for Contextualization, +2 for Use of Evidence, +1 for the Targeted RP (CCOT), +1 for Complexity)

∾ CHAPTER 13 ∾

The Challenges of Modern Europe, 1850–1914

By 1914, Europe had reached the zenith of its power and influence in the world. Many observers hailed this era of technological advance, scientific discovery, democratic reform, and creativity in the arts as *la belle époque*, the golden age. Optimists proclaimed a coming utopia in which problems would be solved by application of the scientific method and tapping the dynamism of Europe's industrial and political structures. Concurrent with Europe's greatest accomplishments, modern trends toward mass politics, mass society, and mass production threatened to overwhelm classical Liberal ideas of individualism and rationality. Outsiders demanded inclusion in the political process and often used violence to liberate themselves from traditional restrictions. Intellectual currents glorified struggle, the irrational, and violence. Art moved from the objective portrayal of reality to subjective emotional states and abstraction. Amid the power and prosperity, many sensed an impending explosion of either revolution or war. This fear provides a contrasting pessimistic perspective on this era of plenty— the *fin de siècle*, or the end of an era.

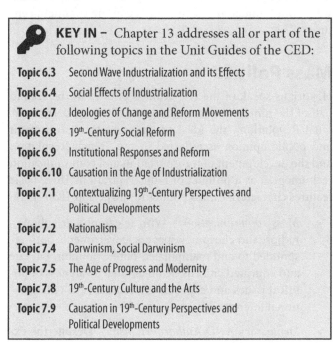

KEY IN – Chapter 13 addresses all or part of the following topics in the Unit Guides of the CED:

Topic 6.3 Second Wave Industrialization and its Effects

Topic 6.4 Social Effects of Industrialization

Topic 6.7 Ideologies of Change and Reform Movements

Topic 6.8 19ᵗʰ-Century Social Reform

Topic 6.9 Institutional Responses and Reform

Topic 6.10 Causation in the Age of Industrialization

Topic 7.1 Contextualizing 19ᵗʰ-Century Perspectives and Political Developments

Topic 7.2 Nationalism

Topic 7.4 Darwinism, Social Darwinism

Topic 7.5 The Age of Progress and Modernity

Topic 7.8 19ᵗʰ-Century Culture and the Arts

Topic 7.9 Causation in 19ᵗʰ-Century Perspectives and Political Developments

Mass Society

Demographic Trends

From 1850 to 1914, industrialization and improved public health and medicine supported a rapidly expanding European population. During the period, Europe's population soared by 75% from 260 to 450 million. This increase was fueled by a drop in the death rate, not a rise in the birth rate. Europe began to adopt the modern population trend of smaller family sizes with an increasing life expectancy. In addition to the rising population, more people congregated in industrial cities. By the end of the period, Great Britain housed more than 50% its population in urban areas. Cities ballooned in size, taxing infrastructure and causing a myriad of problems for governments to address. This new urban context formed the breeding ground for a culture of mass leisure and mass politics.

Medicine

The late nineteenth and early twentieth centuries represent the heroic age of medicine. Central to this breakthrough was the discovery of bacteria and the germ theory of disease. Louis Pasteur (1822–1895) demonstrated that microorganisms caused disease and, further, devised a method for killing them in liquids, called pasteurization. To combat infectious diseases, Pasteur advanced the field of vaccination, developing a rabies vaccine, and helped to create modern immunology. Using Pasteur's ideas, Joseph Lister (1827–1912) developed the first antiseptic treatment for wounds and for use by physicians before surgery. Surgery itself became safer with the development of anesthetics by American William T.G. Morton, who pioneered the use of ether. Improved clinical training allowed for the furtherance of such discoveries. In the United States, Johns Hopkins University was incorporated in Baltimore along the German university model, with a focus on research; its medical program and associated hospital set the standard for a new scientific and clinical approach to medicine. Governments recognized the importance of **public health** in an urban setting, wishing to avoid infectious disease outbreaks and potential unrest among the working classes. The British government, for example, tracked the spread of disease, established public health boards, sponsored vaccinations, and introduced modern sewage and sanitation.

> **THEME MUSIC & SKILL SET**
>
> Modern societies produce a particular demographic profile. As technology improves (TSI), wealth increases (ECD), and state power penetrates more areas of life (SOP), populations evolve toward smaller family size with increased life expectancy. These trends over time (CCOT) can alter the relationship between the individual and society (SCD); for example, with family life geared toward consumption (rather than production) and high expectations for state involvement in social life (e.g., universal schooling and regulation of business).

Urban Reform and Mass Leisure

By 1870, most governments recognized the need for reform in crowded, industrial cities. In the late nineteenth and early twentieth centuries, states began to address pollution, working and living conditions, and transportation needs. Moreover, urban planners advocated for development of public parks, architectural attractions, and cultural amenities. We have already addressed how Baron von Haussmann (1809–1891) helped rebuild Paris with its grand boulevards, opera houses, theaters, shopping areas, and modern sewage and sanitation, to make it the cultural center of France and a venue for **consumerism**. In the process, many workers and poorer residents lost their housing to the new grandiose buildings. This Haussmannization was completed in other European major cities, notably in Vienna with its Ringstrasse, a famous boulevard circling the city and an attraction with its architecture, coffeehouses, and shopping. New technological developments, such as **electricity**, provided cleaner power sources and allowed for the construction of subways and streetcars. Social reformers addressed the need for public housing for the poorer classes, and though states responded slowly, they did provide stronger regulation and higher minimum standards. Governments also encouraged municipal and private charitable efforts. In Britain, Octavia Hill symbolized a new public spirit by championing local associations in providing social housing for the poor.

An increase in **leisure time** corresponded with urban reform. With the recognition of unions and protective legislation by governments, workers began to see improved wages and shorter working hours. Many reformers were concerned about the lower classes using this time for excessive drinking, crime, or revolutionary agitation. Cities established organized leisure pursuits to meet this need, such as dance halls, amusement parks, and sporting contests. With their competitive ethos, team spirit, and regimentation, sports teams paralleled military discipline. Rules for soccer, tennis, cricket, and others were formalized in this period to allow for orderly play and avert violence. Nationalists created gymnastics associations to promote discipline and physical fitness. The ideas of Racial Darwinism influenced notions of national health and spurred the physical fitness craze. Not surprisingly, the competitive nations of Europe established the modern Olympiad, first held in 1896 in Athens.

Education and Literacy

Literacy rates increased markedly in the period 1850–1914, with some states in western Europe achieving nearly universal literacy. Governments came to view **state-supported compulsory education** as essential to their national interests. Educated citizens could handle the more complex demands of an industrial and increasingly service-oriented economy. Under the Liberal administration of William Gladstone, the Parliament passed the Education Act of 1870, establishing the basis for elementary education in Britain.

For nations like Germany, the traditional *Gymnasia* and *Realschule* systems were expanded and extended to all classes. Literate citizens could discuss politics and read dissenting opinions; however, governments increasingly exploited nationalism and xenophobia for purposes of national unity.

Family and Childhood

In Britain, Queen Victoria (1837–1901) modeled domestic propriety; this so-called Victorian ideal reflected distinct gender roles for men and women. Males were to dominate the rough-and-tumble public sphere of business, politics, and war, while women managed the domestic sphere. In this model, the home was viewed as a refuge from the harsh world outside and women its moral guardians. Isabella Beeton published her *Book of Household Management* (1859) to introduce women to domestic engineering, reflecting this "**cult of domesticity**."

With the decline in birth rates, European families invested more resources in the upbringing of their children. Enlightenment attitudes of childhood as a distinct phase of development seeped slowly down to all classes. New attitudes were reflected in governmental legislation restricting child labor and providing for **compulsory schooling**. Reformers and educators created special games, toys, books, clothing, and activities for children. Reflecting the trend toward **mass leisure** and physical fitness, the Boy Scouts and Girl Scouts were both founded in the first decade of the twentieth century.

Mass Politics

Historians speak of the rise of mass politics in the second half of the nineteenth century. Mass politics arose from the Dual Revolution—the ideal of representative government and public opinion as reflected in the French Revolution and the development of transportation and communication technologies, as a product of industrialization. Three basic features characterize mass politics in the period 1850–1914:

- *Mass communication* – With telegraphs, telephones, radios, and cheap newspapers, governments both responded to and manipulated public opinion. Literate and educated citizens demonstrated awareness of political issues and expected governments to reflect national interests.

- *Democracy AND Authoritarianism* – Despite the expansion of democratic forms such as elections, representation, and constitutions, authoritarian structures (ruling dynasties, bureaucracies, the military) continued to play the decisive policy-making role in most states.

- *Increase in conflict* – Public opinion also sharpened ethnic and class conflict. Outsiders, such as women, workers, and ethnic/religious minorities, demanded inclusion in the political process while demagogues (those who appeal to prejudice and fear) fanned popular hatreds like **anti-Semitism** and extreme nationalism.

Liberal Accomplishments and Challenges

The nineteenth century marked the high tide of classical Liberalism. By 1880, Liberals had accomplished many of the items on their economic, social, political, and religious agenda. Symbols of the Liberal achievement include:

- Constitutional government
- Representative assemblies
- Free trade
- Expansion of suffrage (the vote)
- Guarantees of rights (though not always observed)
- Middle-class influence in government
- Spread of education and literacy
- Weakening of established churches
- Self-determination for nations (though not for all)

Most of the above catalog reflects the Liberal concern for individual rights, representative government, economic freedom, and the expansion of opportunity. Despite these significant outward achievements, classical Liberalism was already weakening by 1880. Mass politics mobilized citizens in large groups and allowed authoritarian leaders to manipulate public sentiment; individual and minority rights were often threatened by this trend. With an increasingly complex industrial economy, it became impossible to sustain a laissez-faire approach toward the negative effects of industrialization—urban blight, crime, poor working conditions, and boom-and-bust cycles. Already by 1880, many governments had abandoned free trade in favor of protecting domestic markets. Many Liberal parties had by 1900 surrendered the notion of pure capitalism in favor of extending social welfare benefits to those in need. Finally, rising nationalism, imperial conflicts, and the militarization of society strengthened the hand of authoritarian interests, who seemed ready to subvert Liberal ideas and institutions in times of crisis or emergency.

> **THEME MUSIC**
>
> You may be familiar with political labels like "liberal" and "conservative," but note that the usage of these labels has mutated over time. Classical liberals (of the nineteenth century) are closer to present-day libertarians. With the expansion of industry and cities, most liberal parties adopted a social welfare approach around the turn of the twentieth century to promote equality through state action. This shift reflects a new conception of the state's power (SOP) and of how progress can be accomplished through science and technology (TSI), rather than the "hands-off" view prior to 1870.

France and the Tensions of the Third Republic

Ideological conflicts have marked French politics since 1789, and the Third Republic (1870–1940) proved no exception. You may recall the poor start to the Third Republic—class conflict followed loss in the Franco-Prussian War and the end of the Second Empire. Moderate republicans crushed the revolutionary Paris Commune and either shot or exiled 30,000 of its participants. By 1878 and after exploiting divisions within the royalist camp, moderates had succeeded in establishing the basis for a parliamentary democracy. Nonetheless, important groups, like the Catholic Church and monarchists, never reconciled themselves to the existence of republican government, which they associated with the worst excesses of the French Revolution.

The Dreyfus Affair, a highly-publicized scandal, revealed the divisions within the Third Republic. In 1894, a French military court found Captain Alfred Dreyfus, a Jewish officer, guilty of treason on thin evidence. Despite indications Dreyfus was an innocent victim of anti-Semitism, he was sent to Devil's Island, and the army refused to reopen the case. Republicans and even foreign governments rallied to Dreyfus's cause, which became the legal case of its day. French author Emile Zola (1840–1902) condemned authoritarian institutions in his pamphlet *J'Accuse* (*I Accuse*) and made the issue a test of republican strength in France. Eventually the government pardoned Dreyfus, but the fallout grew. Republicans conducted an anticlerical campaign culminating in the complete separation of church and state in 1905 and the secularization of education by the state.

Parliamentary Democracy in Britain

Britain's Victorian Age projected an image of prosperity and imperial grandeur, all while evolving toward genuine parliamentary democracy. Unlike the continent, reform in Britain was driven by the competing visions of two mass political parties—the Conservatives and the Liberals—and was implemented locally rather than by a centralized bureaucracy. Parliament passed further reform bills in 1867 and 1884, expanding the vote to almost all adult males. The brilliant though occasionally arrogant William Gladstone (1809–1898) led the Liberal reform effort, geared toward expanding opportunity and lifting religious and political restrictions on citizens. Under Gladstone's first prime ministry, the Parliament enacted universal schooling, the secret ballot, and legalized unions; introduced civil service exams; and lifted religious requirements for universities. Conservatives under Benjamin Disraeli (1804–1881) pursued a more interventionist philosophy, passing legislation to protect workers from the worst effects of industrialization and to regulate public housing and sanitation.

By 1900, the Liberal party had abandoned its laissez-faire economic approach, and in an effort to combat support for the new Labour Party (see page 221), moved toward the development of a **social welfare state**. Between 1906 and 1916, the Liberal Party initiated a wide-ranging system of sickness, accident, old-age, and unemployment insurance (National Insurance Act—1911). To conciliate labor, restrictions on strikes and unions were lifted. To pay for these programs, the Parliament passed progressive income and inheritance taxes. When the House of Lords attempted to block this agenda, its veto power was removed with the Parliament Act of 1911. Despite these reforms, workers continued to agitate for improved working conditions, initiating a wave of strikes in 1911 and 1912. Moreover, women's groups, called suffragettes (see below) pushed for the vote, using militant tactics to gain publicity for their cause and provoking embarrassing conflicts with police and government. Britain's most difficult issue, however, continued to be the situation in Ireland. Though Gladstone had disestablished the Anglican Church in Ireland and assisted tenant farmers there, the Catholic Irish demanded home rule. The Home Rule issue split the Liberal Party and was not granted until 1914, but implementation was delayed until 1922 because of the outbreak of the First World War. Though one of splendor, the Victorian Age also witnessed Germany and the United States surpass Britain in industrial production and the increased tensions of mass parliamentary democracy.

Germany's Growing Pains

After its unification, German industrial, political, and military power soared. However, this rapid development placed great strains on an authoritarian political system struggling to incorporate democratic principles. One figure dominated German imperial politics until 1890—**Chancellor Otto von Bismarck** (1815–1890). Bismarck successfully manipulated democratic politics and the party system in the Reichstag to enact his policies. First, Bismarck allied himself with the Liberal Party, who supported his attack on the Catholic Church in Germany. The *Kulturkampf* (struggle for culture) arose from the complex situation surrounding Italian unification. Pope Pius IX (r. 1846–1878) had lost control of the Papal States during this process. In response, the pope condemned modern ideas such as religious toleration, nationalism, and Liberalism, in his *Syllabus of Errors* (1864), and in 1870 called the First Vatican Council to enunciate the doctrine of papal infallibility (the acceptance of papal decrees on doctrine without question). To counter these moves, Bismarck pushed through the Reichstag laws restricting the powers of the clergy, expelled the Jesuits, and jailed a number of bishops. When the campaign proved un-

> **EXAMPLE BASE**
>
> This section on mass politics offers numerous specific examples. As you read over each nation, focus on how it illustrates the features and tensions that define mass politics. Consider similarities between states and unique features within each nation. Also, these conflicts will influence decision-making and strategic concerns as each nation enters the First World War (1914).

successful, and after Pius died in 1878, Bismarck abandoned it and formed an alliance with the Catholic Center Party.

Bismarck now moved to restrict the power of the Social Democratic Party (SPD). Though Marxist in theory, the SPD in reality functioned as a moderate socialist party interested in obtaining benefits for the working class through the exercise of political power. Using several assassination attempts against Kaiser William I (r. 1861–1888) as pretext, Bismarck won approval for Anti-socialist Laws, which restricted the ability of the SPD to meet and publish its newspaper. To win workers over to "state socialism," Bismarck initiated a social welfare program—the first in Europe—of old age, accident, unemployment, and health benefits. Despite these efforts, support for the SPD continued to grow. To appease extreme nationalists like the Pan-German League and industrialists, Bismarck moved further away from Liberalism in the 1880s with protective tariffs and the pursuit of colonies in Africa. When the young, erratic, and ambitious Kaiser William II (r. 1888–1918) ascended to the throne after his grandfather's and father's sudden death, he soon dismissed Bismarck and embarked on a more conciliatory policy toward the SPD at home and a more aggressive foreign policy abroad. With immense potential power, emerging conflicts at home, and an insecure ruler, Germany was poised for entrance into the First World War.

Austria-Hungary: Ethnic Tensions

Austria-Hungary continued to experience ethnic tensions after the creation of the Dual Monarchy in 1867. Within Hungary, large landholders continued to dominate, and the Magyars imposed their language and culture on the many Slavic minorities in their half of the empire. To manage the political situation in Austria, the government expanded voting rights and tried to win over the Czechs, Slovaks, and Poles by including them in the Imperial Parliament (Reichsrat) and appealing to their loyalty toward the Habsburg emperor. German nationalists resented these policies, and the resulting tensions often led to the breakdown of parliamentary function. Anti-Semitism emerged as a political force in Austrian politics with the rise of the Christian Social Party. From 1897 to 1910 (when Hitler lived in the city), Karl Lueger (1844–1910) served as mayor of Vienna and pursued policies of restriction and exclusion against Jews. On the eve of the First World War, the Habsburg Empire was fracturing along nationalist and ethnic lines.

Other Areas and Developments

As noted in the previous chapter, Italy faced a rocky road after unification. Liberal parties in the parliament engaged in the suspect practice of *trasformismo*, whereby political leaders attempted to keep out extremist nationalists on the right and socialists on the left by use of bribery and personal alliances. As a result, Italy did not develop political parties around consistent ideas or programs but along shifting personal relationships. To illustrate, the leader most associated with the practice of *trasformismo*, Giovanni Giolitti, served as prime minister five different times between 1892 and 1922. Economically, northern Italy industrialized while the south remained mired in poverty and illiteracy. Irrational anti-parliamentary ideologies and an active anarchist movement also plagued Italian political life.

Spain lingered on the periphery of European events in the nineteenth century. Despite its constitutional monarchy and parliamentary democracy, Spain continued to be dominated by conservative interests, such as large landowners and the Catholic Church. Spain's defeat in the Spanish-American War (1898) led to loss of its empire and calls for social reform, urged by a group of intellectuals known as the Generation of 1898. Like other less-developed nations, Spain encountered anarchist violence. In 1909, anarchists in Barcelona resisted government efforts to call up army reserves, leading to an armed clash. Because of its preoccupation with internal divisions, Spain did not enter either of the world wars in the twentieth century.

Parliamentary democracy had taken root in most European nations by 1914. All but Romania and Hungary allowed universal male suffrage prior to the First World War. Political parties developed modern techniques of electioneering, communication, and institutional organization. In short, political life in many ways was more institutionalized and democratic than ever before. However, many still felt excluded from the political process and agitated for change, often straining the new foundations of democratic government.

Outsiders in Mass Politics

Workers and Socialist Variants

By the late nineteenth century, workers leveraged their growing numbers into political influence. Early unions faced the difficulties of small numbers and government opposition. By the 1870s and 1880s, most states had recognized the rights of unions to bargain collectively for better wages and working conditions. Many **trade unions** supported this "bread-and-butter" approach of concentrating energies on practical improvements. Workers suffered from the boom-and-bust cycles of the period 1873–1896 and used strikes to achieve their demands. Strikes became more violent and persistent in many nations on the eve of the First World War.

With the expansion of suffrage, the working classes also created political movements to agitate for change. One of the more successful efforts occurred in Germany with the Social Democratic Party (SPD), founded in the 1870s by moderate socialists. Though officially adhering to the Marxist doctrine of class warfare, the SPD in reality operated as a mass-based political party dedicated to winning seats in the German Reichstag. Despite Bismarck's efforts to eliminate the party, the SPD grew into the largest party in the Reichstag by 1912. Other socialist parties were founded in France,

Italy, and Russia in the late nineteenth century. To organize for the coming socialist revolution, the leaders of these parties formed the Second International in 1889, which eventually broke up amidst the nationalism unleashed by the First World War. British labor leaders and intellectuals, such as H.G. Wells (1866–1946) and George Bernard Shaw (1856–1950), advanced a more moderate, or Fabian, socialist movement. In 1900, Scottish worker James Kier Hardie (1856–1915) helped organize the movement into the Labour Party, which won 29 seats in 1906 and eventually became Britain's second political party, replacing the Liberals.

By 1900, it was clear to many socialists that the Marxist prediction of impending revolution was in the distance. In addition, many believed that participation in democratic processes, rather than violence, might better secure workers' rights. These insights led to the development of Revisionism, or the brand of socialism represented by most western and central European socialist parties. In Germany, the primary voice of this evolutionary path was Eduard Bernstein (1850–1932), and in France, Jean Jaurès (1859–1914). Militant socialists condemned Revisionists as "sell-outs" to capitalism and worked to expel them from the International.

In less-developed nations where workers were smaller in numbers, revolutionary movements focused more on violent tactics or mass political agitation. French workers boasted a strong tradition of militant action stemming from the French revolution. Influenced by the ideas of French philosopher Georges Sorel (1847–1922), anarcho-syndicalists worked to create a single industrial union aimed at shutting down the nation through the General Strike, an act that gained the force of mythological proportions. Pure **anarchism** arose out of Russia's weak social institutions and tradition of democracy. Mikhail Bakunin (1814–1876) opposed all governmental systems as a corruption of human freedom and a tool of the privileged classes. Anarchists believed that assassination ("the Act") would sever the head (the leader) from the body (the state), thus opening the way for voluntary and mutual associations of free individuals. Despite thousands of assassinations across Russia and of other European leaders, anarchism seemed only to deepen government repression in the face of such terrorism.

The "New Woman" and Feminism

During this period, feminists articulated a clear agenda for change and achieved some significant economic and political gains. Economic developments during the Second Industrial Revolution allowed women to establish a measure of autonomy. White-collar jobs in new economic sectors—telephone operators, clerks, nurses, teachers—provided many women with income and better working conditions. However, many working-class women found themselves strapped with the dual responsibility of raising children at home while aiding the family income through the assembly of simple items, known as "sweating." The measure of autonomy gained from these jobs led many women, particularly those in the middle class, to demand economic and legal reforms.

The first area women targeted for reform was the legal system. In some western nations between 1850 and 1914, women won the right to control property, divorce, and gain custody of their children. Most states, however, prohibited the publication and distribution of information regarding birth control. Believing female control of reproduction a vital element of the feminist program, Annie Besant of Britain (1847–1933) and Margaret Sanger of the United States (1879–1966) both championed the cause of birth control in the face of obscenity laws. Reflecting the double standard regarding sex, the British Parliament in the 1860s passed the Contagious Diseases Acts, which required prostitutes to submit to tests for venereal disease and be confined to prison hospitals if found to be infected. Due to the unyielding efforts of reformer Josephine Butler (1828–1906), Parliament repealed the laws in 1886.

> **THEME MUSIC**
>
> Another expression for those addressed in this section on political outsiders is "the Other" (SCD). Otherness is created by cultures as they establish values and norms regarding behavior. For example, a male-dominated culture defines women in reference and opposition to masculine traits of dominance, rationality, and leadership. Of course, similar strategies can be used on any minority groups to normalize their exclusion from decision-making and equality—for example, Jews, unskilled laborers, or ethnic minorities.

Some women viewed suffrage as the logical culmination of women's advance toward equality. Suffragettes, as they were called, established a transatlantic movement to agitate for the right to vote. These suffragettes were led in Britain by the Pankhurst family—Emmeline (1858–1928) and her daughters Christabel and Sylvia (1882–1960). The Pankhursts' organization, the Women's Social and Political Union (WSPU), participated in militant actions to achieve the vote—throwing eggs at public officials, arson, chaining themselves to public buildings, engaging in hunger strikes, and in the case of Emily Davison, throwing herself in front of the king's horse at a racing event. Government officials even attempted to force-feed the imprisoned suffragettes. Eventually, many nations in western and northern Europe granted women the vote immediately after the First World War, a recognition of their contributions to that conflict.

The independent figures highlighted above earned the designation of New Women. Though many, if not most, women accepted as natural the dependent and domestic role prescribed by tradition, the New Women articulated and lived an autonomous existence. They were not confined to an explicitly feminist agenda. Italian education reformer Maria Montessori (1870–1952) pioneered a child-centered elementary curriculum. Florence Nightingale (1820–1910) and others founded the modern nursing profession. British-born Elizabeth Blackwell (1821–1910) became the first woman in the United States to earn an M.D. degree and established a hospital for the poor in 1857. Literature also reflected themes of independent women. In Henrik Ibsen's play *A Doll's House*, his character Nora Helmer eventually leaves her traditional marriage and children to establish her own personhood; the play provoked controversy for its scathing critique of the sexual double standard inherent in the Victorian ideal.

Jews, Anti-Semitism, and Zionism

With the Enlightenment and French Revolution, many governments liberated Jews from their segregated existence in ghettos and from legal restrictions. Throughout the nineteenth century, this emancipation led to the assimilation of Jews into business, medicine, law, and academia. Prominent Jewish intellectuals, such as Marx, Freud, and Einstein, not only contributed significantly to developments in the period but also seemed to provoke a backlash of **anti-Semitism**. Anti-Semitism was nothing new to Europe and had traditionally been based on religious discrimination. In the late nineteenth century, anti-Semitism took on a new racial tone, indirectly influenced by Charles Darwin's ideas of struggle among species. Mass politics fed the creation of popular anti-Semitic political movements, which were especially strong in central Europe. In response to anti-Semitism, some prominent Jews called for the creation of a Jewish homeland. Appalled by the Dreyfus Affair in France, Austrian journalist Theodor Herzl (1860–1904) founded **Zionism** in the 1890s, which resulted in the immigration of thousands of Jews to Palestine, then controlled by the Ottoman Empire. Some nations, such as Russia, organized persecutions against Jews, called pogroms, to divert popular energies away from potential anti-state activities. Despite the assimilation of millions of Jews into European cultural and economic life, they remained a vulnerable religious and ethnic minority. It is not difficult to see the outlines of the future Holocaust already taking shape in the nineteenth century.

Modern Ideas

As an intellectual framework, modernism was born in the period 1850–1914. In philosophy, the sciences, and the social sciences, thinkers fulfilled the Enlightenment project of using reason to discover the laws of nature in various fields. However, many cherished Enlightenment notions were called into question by the emerging trends of **irrationality**, subjectivity, randomness, and **struggle**.

New Ideas in Science

Darwinian Evolution

Theories of evolution predated the nineteenth century. Previous versions explained evolution by the inheritance of acquired characteristics. After studying the diversity of finches on the Galapagos Islands, **Charles Darwin** (1809–1882) concluded that the species he observed descended from a common ancestor. Knowing his theory would be controversial, Darwin waited 25 years to work out the details before writing *On the Origin of Species* (1859), one of the most influential scientific works ever published. Darwin borrowed from Malthus's population theories to argue that species are locked in a constant struggle for resources and survival. Through random variations (what we would call mutations, but Darwin did not understand the mechanism that produced them), some individuals gained a survival advantage in a local environment. If an evolutionary change was adaptive, the mutation would spread within a species population through reproduction, eventually producing new species. What Darwin called natural selection, and others later termed "survival of the fittest," suggested that biological development occurred *randomly*, not through design or purpose. All of nature seemed in chaotic flux, with no role for the permanent and the good, as defined in theological terms.

Darwin's theory caused an immediate uproar and was condemned by religious figures, particularly those committed to biblical literalism. Not only did Darwin reject the hand of God in creation, his theory suggested that the earth was millions, not thousands, of years old. Geological developments in the nineteenth century lent credence to Darwin's rejection of a "young earth." Scientists and intellectuals, such as T.H. Huxley (1825–9184), known as "Darwin's Bulldog," rushed to Darwin's defense. Austrian monk Gregor Mendel (1822–1884) later provided additional support for natural selection by articulating the gene theory of reproduction. With *The Descent of Man* (1871), Darwin applied his theory to the evolution of the human race from earlier primate species, once again undermining humanity's special place in the universe. Though some counseled dialogue between religion and science, partisans on both sides drew the cultural lines sharply between "atheistic science" and "superstitious religion."

The New Physics

Newtonian physics ruled science for two centuries. In addition to providing accurate explanations of natural phenomena, Newtonian mechanics offered an appealing vision of the cosmos as orderly and predictable. Quantum mechanics and relativity theory undermined this confidence. Accepted theory held that the atom was the simplest, indestructible particle, the fundamental building block of reality. Accumulating scientific evidence proved this atomic theory incorrect. Marie Curie (1867–1934) demonstrated how atoms emitted radioactive energy as they disintegrated. British scientists J.J. Thomson and Ernest Rutherford elaborated a more complex view of the atom as made up mostly of empty space and comprising subatomic particles. Such discoveries provided practical applications, as with William Rönt-

gen's (1845–1923) discovery of the x-ray and its ability to see within the human body.

German physicist Max Planck (1858–1947) in 1900 articulated **quantum theory**. According to Planck, particles do not emit or absorb energy in constant streams but in packets of energy. Further, experiments demonstrated how light acted sometimes as a particle and sometimes as a wave, depending on the circumstances of observation. More jarring to the Newtonian view, it was demonstrated that the behavior of many particles could only be expressed by probability, not with objective certainty.

It took the great physicist **Albert Einstein** (1879–1955) to transform our commonsense assumptions regarding time and space. Through a series of scholarly articles, Einstein argued that absolute time and space do not exist, but rather are relative to the observer and their status of motion. For example, Einstein showed how for objects that traveled at or near the speed of light, time slows down relative to a stationary observer. To our three-dimensional universe, Einstein's **relativity theory** thus added another dimension—space-time. In the presence of a massive object, such as the sun, space and time *both* curve, as was confirmed from observations of a solar eclipse in 1919. In addition, Einstein expressed how matter and energy were interconvertible in the famous formula, $e = mc^2$. This discovery suggested how the destruction of an atom might potentially liberate massive amounts of energy and wreak destruction.

Advance of the Social Sciences

As European civilization became more complex, the social sciences offered further explanations for human behavior. Many of the social sciences were born during the Enlightenment but reached their modern expression during this period. Psychology, political science, anthropology, criminology, and sociology each demonstrated how human behavior issued from impersonal economic, political, and social forces. And many of these theories radically altered Europeans' conception of human nature.

Freudian Psychology and the Irrational

Enlightenment philosophes glorified human reason. **Sigmund Freud** (1856–1939), in contrast, revealed the instinctual and unconscious nature of human behavior. Based on his systematic clinical studies, Freud developed the theory and practice of psychoanalysis, wherein the therapist attempts to unlock the hidden desires, fears, and memories of the patient causing his mental illness. Freud divided the psyche into the id (the

SKILL SET
The period 1850–1914 represents one of most significant in the course. As you consider the methods and content of modernism in ideas, you may want to formulate an argument (ARG and CES) for how and why this era represents a watershed (CCOT) in the history of Europe, as well as compare it to previous eras of intellectual change (MAC).

pleasure principle), the ego (reason), and superego (conscience), and claimed that unresolved conflicts among these parts created neuroses. Unpleasant or painful memories might be buried in the **subconscious**, though such memories could be explored through hypnosis and analysis of the patient's dreams, a conclusion articulated in *The Interpretation of Dreams* (1900). Perhaps most controversially, Freud claimed that sexual feelings occurred early in life, with children developing through a series of stages, each marked by a conflict, such as the hidden desire to replace the parent of the same sex in the eyes of the parent of opposite sex (the Oedipal or Electra complex). Freud's ideas gained increasing currency during the twentieth century and added a new psychological vocabulary to everyday experiences.

Sociology

Freud's work showed that human actions often resulted from factors other than free choice. His work found support in further studies. Russian psychologist Ivan Pavlov (1849–1936) famously demonstrated how he could condition dogs to salivate automatically at a particular signal, and suggested that human behavior could also be controlled through the appropriate stimuli. Criminologists gathered statistics and performed studies to show that criminal behavior might result from genetic inheritance rather than deliberate choice, a conclusion subversive to the cherished notion of free will. Sociologists such as Max Weber (1864–1920) and Emile Durkheim explored the influences of impersonal bureaucratic structures and crowd mentalities on the individual. In Weber's study, he determined that only a charismatic individual could overcome the inertia of large institutions.

Social scientists borrowed the methods and ideas of science. Many recognized the power of Darwinian theory to explain cultural and historical evolution. British sociologist Herbert Spencer (1820–1903) applied Darwin's ideas to society with **Social Darwinism**. Spencer argued that inequalities and divisions with classes or races arose from the same process of natural selection applied to human affairs. Public aid and charity for the destitute would only weaken the genetic pool and cause more suffering in the long run; it was Spencer who coined the phrase "survival of the fittest." Nationalists distorted Darwinian science to advance their ideas of racial inferiority, producing justification for European imperialism of Africa and Asia. Francis Galton, a half-cousin of Darwin's, developed the pseudoscience of race, known as eugenics, in a misguided attempt to better the human race through "selective breeding." In the context of competitive nation-states, Darwin's ideas eventually found their way into justifications for war as a natural mechanism to separate the fit from the unfit.

Philosophy: A Flight to the Irrational

Philosophy had long upheld reason, but in the late nineteenth century, the most influential philosophers showed the power of irrationality. French thinker Henri Bergson (1859–

1941) introduced his theory of vitalism, which declared the impossibility of dividing nature into analyzable units or discrete parts, as premised in the scientific method. According to Bergson, irreducible vital forces pervaded the natural world, suggesting that human behavior was driven by the same forces and therefore not capable of being reduced to any set of explanatory factors. Beginning with the provocative assertion "God is dead," German philosopher Friedrich Nietzsche (1844–1900) embraced the chaos and flux inherent in nature. Ideas did not actually represent reality, which was inaccessible to human reason. Human systems of thought and morality instead represented a "will to power" and should be deployed by individuals to "self-overcome." Nietzsche also recognized that human nature encompassed both the rational and the instinctual. Christianity twisted human nature by teaching people to suppress their natural tendencies toward domination and self-assertion. Morality, for Nietzsche, was personal and beyond common conceptions of good and evil. Ultimately, Nietzsche called on the best Europeans—not the "herdlike masses"—to create a new, more honest system of values and to make of their lives a "work of art."

Religion: The Challenge of Modernism

Modern ideas produced a crisis for Protestant and Catholic Christianity. As is clear from the above descriptions, scientific and philosophical works stressed secular if not openly anti-Christian approaches to knowledge. Even within religious communities, some scholars attempted to update religious beliefs in light of modern techniques of understanding. French historian Ernst Renan (1823–1892) in his *Life of Jesus* explained the origins of Christianity as if Jesus were merely human and a result of historical, not providential, forces. Being more committed to the Bible as the source of authority, Protestants found it difficult to shield members from such ideas. As a result, Protestant denominations began to split between modernists and fundamentalists, as church attendance declined or merely expressed adherence to cultural customs.

The long and conservative pontificate of Pope Pius IX (r. 1846–1878) represented the high tide of the Catholic Church's negative reaction to modernism and the perceived new **relativism in values**. His successor, Leo XIII (r. 1878–1903), attempted to tone down antimodern attacks and advance the cause of social justice. Leo ended the prohibition of Catholics' participation in Italian politics and formulated a social doctrine that combined a belief in private property with a concern for poverty and inequality. In the encyclical *Rerum Novarum* ("of modern things"), Leo suggested that much of socialism reflected Christian teachings, but he firmly rejected Marxist ideology as materialist and antireligious. Perhaps with the Galileo incident firmly in mind, the church refrained from issuing any condemnations of Darwinian theory, adopting a wait-and-see attitude. Catholic Church attendance remained fairly stable through the period, but the church's full reconciliation with modern trends would not occur until the second half of the twentieth century.

The Avant-Garde in the Arts

A diversity of cutting-edge artistic movements marked the period 1850–1914. Artists placed a premium on experimentation and self-expression within the media of paint, architecture, print, and music. It is helpful to consider art as a reflection on the economic, political, and social context in which it was created. As you review below, keep in mind the dominant themes of industrialization, nationalism, mass politics, and imperialism.

Painting: Beyond Representation

Photography altered the purpose of the artist. By 1860, the technology of picture-taking was perfected, and photography emerged as both an artistic medium and a means of photojournalism. Danish-American Jacob Riis (1849–1914) used his camera to document the underworld of New York City's slums and back alleys in his book *How the Other Half Lives*. While photography provided new tools to journalists, it undermined a traditional purpose of painting, to represent life and nature, as the camera could accomplish this more directly.

Impressionism

The first major artistic trend following the invention of photography was **Impressionism**. A self-named movement, Impressionism attempted to capture how the eye really sees, with off-center positioning, visible brushstrokes, fleeting glimpses of street scenes, and exploration of light and shadow. Claude Monet (1840–1926) named the French-centered movement and became famous for his many depictions of water lilies, haystacks, and Notre Dame Cathedral at different times of day or seasons. For good depictions of the Impressionist interest in middle-class scenes of urban life and its interest in glimpses of reality, see Renoir's (1841–1919) *Dance at Le Moulin de la Galette* or *Luncheon of the Boating Party*. In Edgar Degas's (1834–1917) paintings of ballet studios, we appreciate the Impressionist experimentation with perspective and off-centered framing. Demonstrating the international flavor of the movement, American Mary Cassatt (1844–1926) exhibited her works of domestic scenes, such as a mother bathing her child, with her European compatriots in Impressionism.

Postimpressionism

Postimpressionists moved away from the Impressionist fascination with light and shadow. More interested in form and structure, major post-impressionist painters included Vincent Van Gogh (1853–1890), Paul Cézanne (1839–1906), Paul Gauguin (1848–1903), and Georges Seurat (1859–1891). Though Van Gogh sold only one painting in his lifetime, his paintings today reap tens of millions of dollars at auction. Expressing his inner psychological torment, Van Gogh painted with swirling brushstrokes and, showing the influence of Japanese woodblock prints, distorted perspective and a strong palette of yellows. Van Gogh's unique style is best seen in *Starry Night* and *The Night Café*. His suicide in 1890 seemed to capture the archetype of the tortured artist. Cézanne incorporated a geometric approach in his paintings, and with his still lifes, how depth and the passage of time can be captured if we look at an object with a binocular vision, first with one eye and then the other. Frustrated by what he considered the overly artificial nature of European painting, Paul Gauguin traveled to Tahiti and developed a primitive style of bulky figures and simple lines reminiscent of the artistic styles of the Pacific. Georges Seurat created a related movement named pointillism, after the small dots of color, which when combined, form a clear picture of shadow and light. Seurat's *Sunday Afternoon on the Island of La Grande Jatte* provides a view of the individualistic and small-group leisure in the modern city.

Expressionism

Near the turn of the century, artistic experimentation accelerated. A group of French painters known as the Fauves, or "wild beasts," emphasized strong fields of color and simple lines to prioritize expression over detail. When Henri Matisse (1869–1954) received criticism for his work *Green Stripe*, a portrait of his wife with a green stripe down the middle of her face, he replied, "I have not made a woman, I have painted a painting." Like the later **expressionists**, Matisse demonstrated that the key task of the modern artist was not to represent reality but to convey an emotional stance. To appreciate the intensity of expressionist distortion and use of color to capture the angst and alienation of modern Europe, one must view Norwegian Edvard Munch's (1863–1944) *The Scream*, in which a ghostly figure's silent scream wafts into an ominous red sky. Painting gradually moved toward abstraction, as with the Russian Wassily Kandinsky's (1866–1944) canvases exploding with color, designed to convey musical compositions in visual form—a genre known as abstract expressionism.

Cubism and Futurism

Prior to the First World War, the movements of **Cubism** and futurism most directly show the influence of technology on artistic representation. Founded by Georges Braque and Pablo Picasso (1881–1973), Cubism broke apart scenes into analyzable parts and reassembled them in unique ways to provide the viewer with simultaneous multiple perspectives. In this way, Cubists employed the revolutionary insights of Einstein's theory of relativity to art. One of the first paintings in the Cubist style was Picasso's *Les Demoiselles d'Avignon*

(1907), which stirred controversy for its unconventional depiction of female beauty by portraying a group of prostitutes with African and Oceanic masks for faces. Picasso painted in many styles, creating one of the most prolific and influential oeuvre of works by any artist. The Italian futurists F.T. Marinetti and Umberto Boccioni (1882–1916) glorified speed and technology in art as a means to achieve political change. Not content with artistic creation alone, the futurists published manifestoes calling for the abolition of traditional aesthetics (such as nudes, religion, and historical paintings) in favor of automobiles, airplanes, and industrial plants. Many of Boccioni's works, like *Dynamism of a Cyclist*, actually portray *motion* as their subject. Futurism fizzled out in the technological nightmare that was World War I.

Modern Architecture

Modern buildings express the ideal that "form follows function." Instead of employing ornamentation or classical motifs, modern architects allow the functional requirements of a building to determine its shape and visual logic. The first modern architects were American and used the new building materials of concrete, reinforced steel, and glass. Louis Sullivan (1856–1924) created the first skyscrapers and designed buildings with simple, clean lines and few decorative elements. Frank Lloyd Wright (1867–1959) strove to create a new aesthetic for single-family homes, replacing "Victorian monstrosities" with buildings that employ horizontal lines and earth tones, called the Prairie Style. After the First World War, **modernism** emerged as the dominant architectural style.

Literary Trends

Like art, literature reflected the larger social and intellectual context of the time. Darwin's ideas influenced the literary movement of Naturalism. French author Émile Zola (1840–1902) wrote a series of novels portraying the destructive influence of heredity on the lives of his characters, as they seemed unable to determine their actions freely. Zola's frank depiction of sex, alcoholism, and violence brought him condemnation from traditionalists. This period also represents the great age of Russian literary genius, best shown in the works of Leo Tolstoy (1828–1910) and Fyodor Dostoevsky (1821–1881), both of whom explored the themes of suffering and spirituality. Tolstoy's *War and Peace* presents the reader with a tapestry of events and characters designed to show how social and economic forces override the designs of great men. In *Crime and Punishment*, Dostoevsky explored the moral dilemma of whether good ends justify evil acts. Dostoevsky's lifelong theme of the individual struggling to find meaning in a world of suffering and alienation helped lay the foundations for existential philosophy in the twentieth century.

Music: Romanticism and Nationalism

Romanticism did not die in music after 1848. Many composers worked to explore founding myths and create national styles. The most influential of these figures was the German Richard Wagner (1813–1883), who used his music to express a vision of a revolutionary and nationalist Germany. Wagner envisioned music as a *Gesamtkunstwerk*, or "total work of art," combining all artistic genres and capable of transforming national culture. Wagner synthesized music and drama through the use of leitmotifs—musical themes that coincided with particular characters or plot lines. The *Ring Cycle*, a series of four operas spanning 16 hours, represents the culmination of Wagner's grandiose vision and is one of the most ambitious pieces of music ever written. Russian Igor Stravinsky (1882–1971) also explored national themes in his *The Rite of Spring*. When the ballet was first performed in 1913 in Paris, its theme of pagan Russian rituals, dissonant primitive music, and unorthodox dance maneuvers caused a riot in the theater.

Postscript—The Road to World War I

The riot following the performance of *The Rite of Spring* demonstrates the divided legacy of modernism. On one hand, advances in industry, technology, ideas, and the arts demonstrate the intense dynamism of modern European civilization. On the other hand, the themes of revolutionary liberation, racial and national struggle, and the glorification of the irrational reveal the destructive potential of Europe's modern achievements. These two themes would merge tragically in the First World War.

Additional Resources

📙 **Jacques Barzun, *Darwin, Marx, Wagner: Critique of a Heritage* (rev. 1981)** — The author explores how each of the figures undermined classical Liberalism.

📙 **Stephanie Coontz, *Marriage, a History: From Obedience to Intimacy or How Love Conquered Marriage* (2005)** — An entertaining analysis with interesting anecdotes on an overlooked topic.

📙 **Stephen Kern, *The Culture of Time and Space* (1983)** — This challenging but worthwhile book explores how technology altered conceptions of time and space.

📙 **Stephen J. Lee, *Imperial Germany, 1871–1918* (1999)** — A slim interpretive volume with documents, from Routledge's Questions and Analysis in History series.

📙 **Karen Offen, *European Feminisms, 1700–1950: A Political History* (2000)** — Provides broad historical background on the development of the feminist movement.

📖 **Antoine Prost, ed., *A History of Private Life: Riddles of Identity in Modern Times*. vol. 5 (1998)** — Part of a thorough series examining how individuals and families lived amidst broader historical changes.

📖 **Carl E. Schorske, *Fin-de-Siècle Vienna: Politics and Culture* (1981)** — In a series of essays, the author paints a fascinating portrait of a city on the precipice of its last imperial days.

📖 **Barbara Tuchman, *The Proud Tower: A Portrait of Europe Before the War, 1890–1914* (1996)** — A popular historian examines the unsettled nature of European culture and politics amidst prosperity through a series of vignettes.

📖 **Robert Wohl, *The Generation of 1914* (1981)** — This book examines the experiences of the generation that came of age right before the First World War.

💻 **www.artchive.com/** — A helpful supplement to this text; you can search by artist or movement.

💻 **http://users.clas.ufl.edu/ufhatch/pages/02-TeachingResources/readingwriting/darwin/05-DARWIN-PAGE.html** — This site provides links to resources on Charles Darwin and related topics.

💻 **https://sourcebooks.fordham.edu/science/sciencesbook.asp#New%20Science:%20Darwin,%20Freud,%20Einstein** — From the Internet History of Science Sourcebook, this page is an excellent clearinghouse for documents on the intellectual life of this important period.

💻 **https://spartacus-educational.com/WomensHistoryIndex.htm** — This comprehensive site provides biographies of key figures in women's suffrage, women's organizations, and feminist tactics and campaigns.

CHAPTER TEST

Multiple-Choice Questions

Questions 1–3 are based on the interpretation below.

> "In the advanced countries of western Europe during the 1870s, when liberalism was at its zenith…liberal governments, abandoning the liberal opposition to the power of the state and seeing the state as the most effective means of securing the liberal conception of freedom in changed circumstances, accepted the early steps toward the inevitable extension of the functions of government and the use of unprecedented state compulsion on individuals for social ends…"
>
> F.H. Hinsley, British historian, "Introduction," *New Cambridge Modern History*, vol. XI, 1962

1. All of the following developments in the nineteenth century help explain the trend in Liberalism described by the Hinsley EXCEPT:

   A. volatile business cycles associated with the Second Industrial Revolution.

   B. communication and transportation technologies that led to a more complex economy.

   C. the emergence of new consumer goods and an increase in leisure time.

   D. growth of urban areas and issues of economic and social equality.

2. The reference to "the liberal conception of freedom" involved which of the following principles?

   A. A government based on popular sovereignty

   B. The sharing of property for the common good

   C. Glorification of the state based on common ethnicity

   D. Distrust of reforms based on the perfectibility of humans

3. Which of the following events resulted in the most serious challenge to liberalism as outlined by Hinsley?

   A. The pursuit of colonies in Africa and Asia

   B. The experience of total war during World War I

   C. The granting of equal political rights to women

   D. Scientific theories such as relativity and natural selection

Questions 4–6 are based on the passage below.

"It is interesting to contemplate an entangled bank, clothed with many plants of many kinds, with birds singing on the bushes, with various insects flitting about, and with worms crawling through the damp earth, and to reflect that these elaborately constructed forms…have all been produced by laws acting around us. These laws… being Growth with Reproduction…Variability from the indirect and direct action of the external conditions of life, and from use and disuse; a Ratio of Increase so high as to lead to a Struggle for Life, and as a consequence to Natural Selection, entailing Divergence of Character and the Extinction of less-improved forms. Thus, from the war of nature…the production of the higher animals, directly follows. There is grandeur in this view of life, with its several powers, having been originally breathed into a few forms or into one; and that, whilst this planet has gone cycling on according to the fixed law of gravity, from so simple a beginning endless forms most beautiful and most wonderful have been, and are being, evolved."

Charles Darwin, British biologist and naturalist, *On the Origin of Species*, 1859

4. In the passage, Darwin draws most directly on the Enlightenment principle of the:

   A. equivalence of humans with other forms of animal life.

   B. emphasis on struggle for life and change through random forces.

   C. glorification of nature and as a source of emotional inspiration.

   D. idea that physical phenomena proceed according to natural laws.

5. All of the following resulted, either directly or indirectly, from the ideas above EXCEPT:

   A. Europeans justified imperial conquests through theories of racial superiority.

   B. art moved away from representation toward abstraction and subjectivity.

   C. political theorists glorified warfare as a means of improving humanity.

   D. traditional religious and ethical views were called into question.

6. The passage by Darwin reflects a broader intellectual trend after 1848 in its:

   A. focus on themes of realism and materialism in science and the arts.

   B. relativism in values and loss of confidence in the idea of objective knowledge.

   C. romantic emphasis on intuition and the subjectivity of experience.

   D. revival of classical forms and themes of ancient history and culture.

Bon Marché Department Store, Paris, late 1800s

7. The illustration could be used as evidence for all of the following nineteenth-century developments EXCEPT:

   A. the realization of feminist goals of economic rights and acceptance of public roles.

   B. the growth of consumerism as a result of the Second Industrial Revolution.

   C. urban reforms that provided amenities such as electricity and leisure pursuits.

   D. an increase in wealth due to efficiencies of production and transportation systems.

8. In what way does the image demonstrate a key difference between nineteenth-century economic activities with those of the early modern period (1500–1700)?

   A. An interest in luxury items, such as imported cloth and spices

   B. Urban markets as a venue for the display and purchase of goods

   C. Mass production of goods and mass marketing techniques

   D. The role played by the bourgeoisie in trade and industry

9. Which of the following characterizations is best supported by the image?

   A. Age of Nationalism

   B. Age of Industry

   C. Age of Mass Politics

   D. Age of Empire

See Chapter 18 for answers and explanations.

Short-Answer Question

Pablo Picasso, Spanish painter, *Les Demoiselles d'Avignon*, 1907

1. a) Describe one way in which the painting reflects a modern approach toward art.

   b) Describe one major difference between the painting above and another specific artwork and artistic style prior to 1850.

   c) Explain how the painting reflects the general intellectual and cultural climate in Europe, 1850–1914.

SAQ Sample Response

> Modern art was all about challenging the viewer, and that is certainly what Picasso does in this painting. We see a group of nude women—probably prostitutes—and they are not portrayed like in classical scenes, either beautiful or like Greek goddesses. These women are given a Cubist look, where perspective has been destroyed and then put back together. Picasso's painting reflects the intellectual and cultural mood of the period 1850–1914. Intellectuals and artists began to question objective knowledge and the idea of progress through technology. For example, in his theories of psychoanalysis, Sigmund Freud emphasized how humans were motivated by instincts and irrational impulses—for sex, power, and even death. His ideas influenced politics and even art, as with surrealist paintings that showed dream-like states.

SAQ Sample Response Analysis

It is clear that this student knows the period and the specific content of the question; however, they did not earn all the possible points. First, the response adequately explains the features of modern art ("challenging the viewer," "Cubist," "perspective destroyed," "surrealism"), which earns the point for Part A. Although the student notes a contrast with earlier works of art, they do not cite or fully develop a contrast with a specific work of art, costing the point for Part B. However, they recover strongly to explain the general intellectual climate of the period 1850–1914 with an application of Freud's ideas to the period. This analysis earns the point for Part C. Once again, you are encouraged to label each part of your SAQ response, both to remind yourself to answer all parts of the prompt and to show the reader that you have done so. Score: **2 points**

PERIOD 3 — DIAGNOSTIC EXAM

Section 1, Part A: Multiple-Choice Questions

Time—30 minutes; 30 questions

Directions: Each of the following questions or incomplete statements below is followed by four suggested answers or completions. Select the one that is best in each case and then enter the appropriate letter in the corresponding space on the answer sheet. Source materials have been edited for the purpose of this exercise.

Questions 1-3 are based on the interpretation below.

"In these areas [of industry] there were not enough openings for female wage employment and, in consequence, many women were forced into the almost totally new situation of full-time housewife. However, as more and more traditional tasks were taken over by the application of factory production, the home increasingly became confined to consumption. Only then did the distinction between male productive work outside the home and female consumption-oriented work inside the home become common among the working class."

Michael Anderson, British historian, "The Family and Industrialization in Western Europe," 1978

1. The historical interpretation above most closely parallels which of the following effects of industrialization on society?

   A. A rising standard of living due to higher wages and access to consumer goods

   B. The growth of leisure time as a result of state regulation of industry

   C. The decline of economic motivations for marriage in favor of compatibility

   D. Gendered roles of work and the growth of a cult of domesticity for women

2. The passage reflects the significant shift in family life from a preindustrial to an industrial economy and society in highlighting the:

   A. movement of family life away from working as a unit.

   B. growth of female and child labor outside the home.

   C. regimentation of work based on factory rather than domestic manufacture.

   D. ability of rural families to supplement income through cottage industry.

3. What factor might have limited the development of these trends for Eastern Europe?

   A. Domination by absolute monarchies

   B. Multi-ethnic conflicts within empires

   C. Reliance on serfdom and subsistence agriculture

   D. Lack of legal and political rights for women

Questions 4–6 are based on the map below.

Europe, 1815

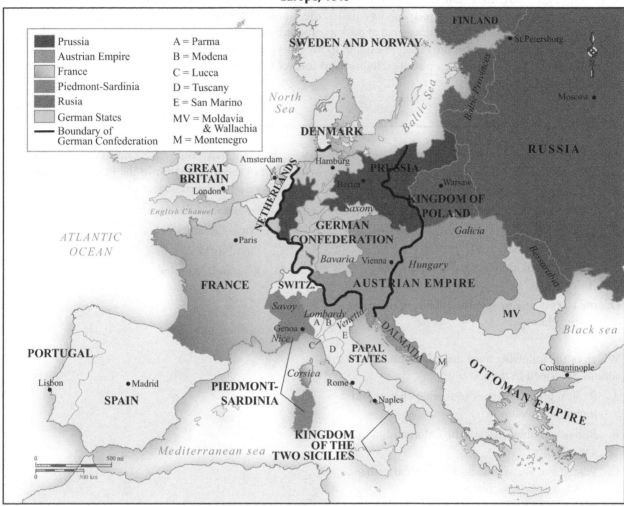

4. The decisions reflected in the map coincide most closely with:

   A. a desire to suppress further radicalism following the French Revolution and Napoleonic Wars.

   B. a consensus that diplomacy should be guided by pacifism and international institutions.

   C. the continued dominance of the Habsburg dynasty over central Europe.

   D. the widely held belief in the need for Italian and German unification.

5. Which of the following resulted most directly from the diplomatic decisions depicted on the map?

   A. A general acceptance of Conservative principles in politics and society

   B. The gradual decline of nationalism within and among polities

   C. Continued efforts by revolutionaries to overthrow the established order

   D. A formal agreement among the Great Powers to suppress revolutions

6. The most significant transformation of the diplomatic situation depicted on the map came with:

   A. the revolutions of 1848.

   B. the Crimean War.

   C. the unifications of Germany and Italy.

   D. imperial ventures in Africa and Asia.

Questions 7–9 are based on the passage below.

> "5 March. A great day. The emancipation manifesto! I received a copy around noon. I cannot express my joy at reading this precious act which scarcely has its equal in the thousand-year history of the Russian people. I read it aloud to my wife, my children and a friend of ours in my study, under Alexander II's portrait, as we gazed at it with deep reverence and gratitude. I tried to explain to my ten-year-old son as simply as possible the essence of the manifesto and bid him to keep inscribed in his heart forever the date of March 5 and the name of Alexander II, the Liberator."
>
> Aleksandr Nikitenko, former serf, *The Diary of a Russian Censor*, 1893

7. The actions described in the account above were likely in response to all of the following EXCEPT:

   A. Russia's technological and economic backwardness.

   B. the poor showing of Russian forces in the Crimean War.

   C. fear of a revolution by serfs and peasants "from below."

   D. the tsar's desire to appeal to public opinion in western Europe.

8. Which of the following most directly resulted from the actions described in the account?

   A. Radical groups demanded further change and fomented revolution.

   B. Russia was able to defeat the Ottoman Empire and gain territory.

   C. France and Russia concluded a military alliance directed against Germany.

   D. Russia experienced widespread industrialization and modernization.

9. The event that would have caused the most decisive shift in the attitude toward the Russian monarchy, as expressed in the passage, would be the:

   A. Congress of Berlin (1878).

   B. Triple Entente.

   C. First World War.

   D. Russian Revolution.

Questions 10–12 are based on the charts below.

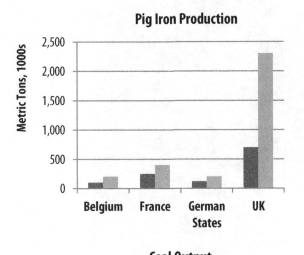

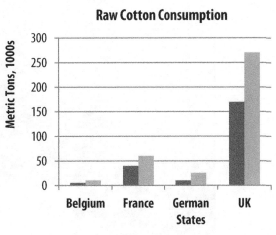

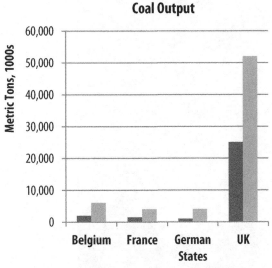

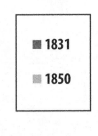

10. All of the following explain the data for Britain (UK) in relation to the other nations EXCEPT:

   A. Britain's parliament allowed participation of industrial and commercial interests.

   B. Britain's lead in banking and finance provided the capital for industrial investment.

   C. Britain's national army allowed it to conquer and exploit continental resources.

   D. Britain's education system and culture promoted scientific and technical innovation.

11. Which of the following dates represents the most significant shift in Germany's industrialization?

   A. 1815

   B. 1848

   C. 1871

   D. 1914

12. The trends shown in the data during the second half of the nineteenth century would foster European imperialism in Africa and Asia primarily by:

   A. promoting national rivalries and rival alliances.

   B. requiring raw materials and markets for products.

   C. supporting ideologies of racial and cultural superiority.

   D. spurring interest in non-European artistic movements.

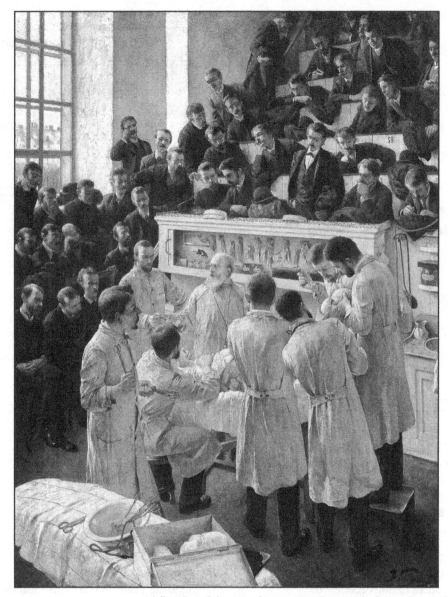

Adalbert Franz Seligmann, German artist, *Operation by German Surgeon Theodor Billroth*, 1890

13. The image best reflects which of the following intellectual trends of the period?

   A. Marxism

   B. Social Darwinism

   C. Positivism

   D. Romanticism

14. The medical practices depicted in the painting had the result of:

   A. facilitating European control of Africa and Asia.

   B. eliminating class conflict in European cities.

   C. confirming state control of scientific discoveries.

   D. promoting cultural exchange across national borders.

15. A historian might use the image to support most directly which of the following regarding life in the late nineteenth century?

   A. The assimilation of women into scientific and professional life

   B. The rising standard of living and improved infrastructure of cities

   C. The growth of private reform movements addressing needs of the poor

   D. The shift of Liberalism from laissez-faire to intervention in the economy

Questions 16–18 are based on the passage below.

"Nothing confirms me more in this conception than the anxiety with which some persons seek to maintain certain statements in *Capital*,* which are falsified by facts. It is just some of the more deeply devoted followers of Marx who have not been able to separate themselves from the dialectical form of the work—that is the scaffolding alluded to—who do this. At least, that is only how I can explain the words of a man, otherwise so amenable to facts as Kautsky,** who, when I observed in Stuttgart that the number of wealthy people for many years had increased, not decreased, answered: 'If that were true then the date of our victory would not only be very long postponed, but we should never attain our goal. If it be capitalists who increase and not those with no possessions, then we are going ever further from our goal the more evolution progresses, theft capitalism grows stronger, not socialism.'"

* Karl Marx's and Friedrich Engel's work of socialist political economy

** Karl Kautsky was a German socialist and supporter of orthodox Marxism

Eduard Bernstein, German socialist, *Evolutionary Socialism*, 1899

16. Which of the following developments of the nineteenth century provides the strongest explanation for Bernstein's perspective on Marxian socialism?

    A. European states were able to divert working-class agitation through imperialism.

    B. The Second Industrial Revolution produced volatile business cycles and unemployment.

    C. Governments enacted reforms to improve urban life and working conditions.

    D. Feminists agitated for and won economic, legal, and political rights.

17. Which of the following facts about Bernstein, all true, would be most helpful to a historian in interpreting the passage?

    A. Bernstein spent years in exile in Switzerland after the passage of Chancellor Otto von Bismarck's Anti-Socialist legislation in Germany.

    B. As a delegate of the German parliament, Bernstein came to oppose the First World War and helped establish the Independent German Socialist Democratic Party to do so.

    C. Bernstein was strongly criticized by other German socialists for a lack of militancy and opposing revolutionary action against the state.

    D. As a Jew, Bernstein first supported assimilation for Jews but became more sympathetic to Zionism near the end of his life.

18. Bernstein's writing could best be used as evidence for the late-nineteenth-century development of:

    A. the spread of industrialization from Britain to the continent.

    B. an emergence of class identities and movements to support them.

    C. the shift in Liberalism from laissez-faire to government intervention.

    D. *Realpolitik* policies of nationalism and manipulation of public opinion.

Questions 19–21 are based on the map below.

Jewish Migration, 1870–1914

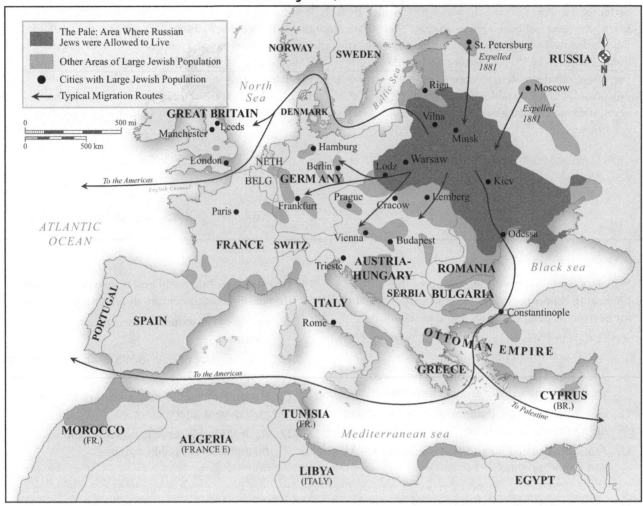

19. All of the following developments led to the phenomenon depicted above EXCEPT:

    A. the growth of political anti-Semitism and persecution of Jews.

    B. volatile business cycles that produced periods of unemployment.

    C. refugee programs that encouraged Jews to settle open lands.

    D. the opportunity of Jews to assimilate into economic and cultural life.

20. Jews responded to the situation portrayed on the map by:

    A. joining anarchist movements and assassinating leaders.

    B. advocating for a Jewish homeland with Zionism.

    C. promoting public education to expand tolerance.

    D. converting to Christianity in large numbers.

21. Which of the following nations was the most inhospitable place for Jews during this period?

    A. England

    B. Germany

    C. France

    D. Russia

Questions 22–26 are based on the passage below.

"Scarcely a century ago the traditional policy of European states and the rivalries of sovereigns were the principal factors that shaped events. The opinion of the masses scarcely counted, and most frequently indeed did not count at all. Today it is the traditions…and the tendencies and rivalries of rulers which do not count; while, on the contrary, the voice of the masses has become preponderant.

We see, then, that the disappearance of the conscious personality [in crowds], the predominance of the unconscious personality, the turning by means of suggestion and contagion of feelings and ideas in an identical direction, the tendency to immediately transform the suggested ideas into acts; these, we see, are the principal characteristics of the individual forming part of a crowd. He is no longer himself, but has become an automaton who has ceased to be guided by his will.

Moreover, by the mere fact that he forms part of an organized crowd, a man descends several rungs in the ladder of civilization. Isolated, he may be a cultivated individual; in a crowd, he is a barbarian—that is, a creature acting by instinct."

Gustave Le Bon, French sociologist and psychologist, *The Crowd: A Study of the Popular Mind*, 1895

22. The passage most strongly indicates the intellectual influence of:
    A. quantum physics.
    B. realism.
    C. Romanticism.
    D. the irrational.

23. Which of the following European leaders would have corresponded most closely in governing approach with Le Bon's characterization in the first two sentences of the passage?
    A. Metternich
    B. Napoleon I
    C. Bismarck
    D. Queen Victoria

24. A historian might use this passage to support which of the following conclusions?
    A. "Europe at the turn of the twentieth century stood on the verge of a popular revolution."
    B. "The pursuit of colonies caused European states to ignore internal political problems."
    C. "Leaders manipulated popular opinion but only at the cost of a destabilized polity."
    D. "Intellectuals helped create an atmosphere of crisis through their publications."

25. Which of Le Bon's contemporaries would have most likely agreed with his analysis?
    A. Charles Darwin
    B. Karl Marx
    C. Sigmund Freud
    D. Albert Einstein

26. The last two paragraphs anticipate which subsequent development?
    A. The further pursuit of colonies before the First World War
    B. The advance of extremist movements before and during the Second World War
    C. The growth of social welfare benefits following the Second World War
    D. Feminist agitation for equal rights around the time of the First World War

Questions 27–30 are based on the passages below.

Source 1

"The 'Scramble for Africa' by the nations of Europe—an incident without parallel in the history of the world—was due to the growing commercial rivalry, which brought home to civilized nations the vital necessity of securing the only remaining fields for industrial enterprise and expansion…It is in order to foster the growth of the trade of this country, and to find an outlet for our manufactures and our surplus energy, that our far-seeing statesmen and our commercial men advocate colonial expansion….

…In Africa, moreover, there is among the people a natural inclination to submit to a higher authority. That intense detestation of control which animates our Teutonic races does not exist among the tribes of Africa…."

Sir Frederick Lugard, British soldier, explorer, and colonial administrator, *The Rise of Our East African Empire*, 1893

Source 2

"Take up the White Man's burden—
Send forth the best ye breed—
Go, bind your sons to exile
To serve your captives' need;
To wait, in heavy harness,
On fluttered folk and wild—
Your new-caught sullen peoples,
Half devil and half child….

Take up the White Man's burden—
The savage wars of peace—
Fill full the mouth of Famine,
And hid the sickness cease;
And when your goal is nearest
(The end for others sought)
Watch sloth and heathen folly
Bring all your hope to nought."

Rudyard Kipling, British writer, "The White Man's Burden," 1899

27. The sources reveal all of the following motives and justifications for imperialism EXCEPT:
    A. national rivalries among the great powers for colonies and prestige.
    B. the search for vital resources and markets for industrial products.
    C. the development of advanced weaponry, communications, and transportation.
    D. an ideology of cultural and racial superiority in relation to those colonized.

28. Which of the following occurred as a result of the policies advocated in the sources?
    A. Imperial rivalries created diplomatic tensions among the great powers
    B. Movements of social change took root within nations promoting imperialism
    C. Nationalists in Italy and Germany succeeded in unifying their nations
    D. Intellectuals and artists began to embrace subjective views of reality

29. The peoples of Africa and Asia responded to the attitudes expressed in the sources by:
    A. adopting ideas of Social Darwinism.
    B. establishing nationalist movements.
    C. developing superior military technology.
    D. rejecting European methods of manufacture.

30. A historian might use the sources as evidence for which of the following intellectual developments of the late nineteenth century?
    A. Freudian preoccupation with the irrational
    B. Marxist notions of class struggle in history
    C. Realist and materialist themes in literature
    D. Emphasis in philosophy on struggle and conflict

Section I, Part B: Short-Answer Questions

Time—25 minutes; 2 Questions

Directions: Read each question carefully and answer all parts of the question. Use complete sentences; an outline or bulleted list is not acceptable.

"The Silent Highwayman," political cartoon, *Punch*, British satirical magazine, 1858

1. a) Using the cartoon above and your knowledge of European history, describe one specific problem created by industrialization in the nineteenth century.

    b) Describe one <u>specific</u> response in the nineteenth century to the problem identified in <u>Part A</u>.

    c) Explain how the intended audience, purpose, or historical situation may have influenced the point of view of the cartoon.

2. a) Describe one factor that promoted European imperialism in the period 1871–1914.

    b) Explain one example of an economic or a political effect on Europe of imperialism in Africa and Asia in the period 1871–1914.

    c) Explain one example of how Africans or Asians responded to European imperialism in the period 1871–1914.

Section II, Part A: Document-Based Question

Total Time—60 minutes; 1 Question

Directions: Question 1 is based on the accompanying documents. It is suggested that you spend about 15 minutes reading the documents and 45 minutes writing your response. The documents have been edited for the purpose of this exercise.

In your response you should do the following:

- Respond to the prompt with a historically defensible thesis or claim that establishes a line of reasoning.
- Describe a broader historical context relevant to the prompt.
- Support an argument in response to the prompt using at least six documents.
- Use at least one additional piece of specific historical evidence (beyond that found in the documents) relevant to an argument about the prompt.
- For at least three documents, explain how or why the document's point of view, purpose, historical situation, and/ or audience is relevant to an argument.
- Use evidence to corroborate, qualify, or modify an argument that addresses the prompt.

Question 1   *Evaluate the extent to which European women achieved equality in the period, 1840–1913.*

Document 1

Source: Elizabeth Poole Sanford, middle-class British writer, *Woman in Her Social and Domestic Character*, 1842

There is, indeed, something unfeminine in independence. It is contrary to nature, and therefore it offends. We do not like to see a woman affecting tremors, but still less do we like to see her acting the amazon.* A really sensible woman feels her dependence. She does what she can, but she is conscious of inferiority, and therefore grateful for support. She knows that she is the weaker vessel, and that as such she should receive honor. In this view, her weakness is an attraction, not a blemish.

* The Amazons were a mythical race of female warriors

Document 2

Source: Jules Michelet, French nationalist historian, *Love*, marriage manual addressed to men, 1860

It is the paradise of marriage that the man shall work for the woman; that he alone shall support her, take pleasure in enduring fatigue for her sake, and spare her the hardships of labor, and rude contact with the world.

He returns home in the evenings, harassed, suffering from toil, mental and bodily, from the weariness of worldly things, from the baseness of men. But in his reception at home there is such an infinite kindness, a calm so intense, that he hardly believes in the cruel realities he has gone through all the day.

This is woman's mission (more important than generation even), to renew the heart of man. Protected and nourished by the man, she in turn nourishes him with love.

…Man's business is to earn money, hers to spend it: that is to say, to regulate the household expenditures, better than man would.

Document 3

Source: Jenny P. d'Hericourt, French feminist and writer, *A Woman's Philosophy of Woman, or Woman Affranchised: An Answer to Michelet*, 1860

Take care, gentlemen! Our rights have the same foundation as yours: in denying the former, you deny the latter in principle.

…Do you know why, in 1848, so many women, especially among the people, declared themselves for the Revolution? It was because they hoped that this Revolution would be more consistent with respect to them than the former had been.

When, in their senseless arrogance and lack of intelligence, the representatives not only forbid them to assemble, but *drove* them from the assemblies of men, the women abandoned the Revolution by detaching their husbands and sons from it, and you know what ensued.

Do you comprehend at last?

I will tell you truly; all your struggles are in vain, if woman does not go with you.

Document 4

Source: John Stuart Mill, British Liberal philosopher and politician, *The Subjection of Women*, 1869

The principle which regulates the existing social relations between the two sexes—the legal subordination of one sex to the other—is wrong in itself, and now one of the chief hindrances to human improvement; and that it ought to be replaced by a principle of perfect equality, admitting no power or privilege on the one side, nor disability on the other.

…All women are brought up from the very earliest years in the belief that their ideal of character is the very opposite to that of men; not self-will, and government by self-control, but submission, and yielding to the control of others…

For what is the peculiar character of the modern world—the difference which chiefly distinguishes modern institutions, modern social ideas, modern life itself, from those of times long past? It is, that human beings are no longer born to their place in life, and chained down by an inexorable bond to the place they are born to, but are free to employ their faculties, and such favorable chances as offer, to achieve the lot which may appear to them most desirable.

Document 5

Source: Friedrich Engels, German journalist and socialist, *The Origin of the Family, Private Property and the State*, 1884

The legal inequality of the two partners, bequeathed to us from earlier social conditions, is not the cause but the effect of the economic oppression of the woman….Not until the coming of modern large-scale industry was the road to social production opened to her again—and then only to the proletarian wife. But it was opened in such a manner that, if she carries out her duties in the private service of her family, she remains excluded from public production and unable to earn; and if she wants to take part in public production and earn independently, she cannot carry out family duties. And the wife's position in the factory is the position of women in all branches of business, right up to medicine and the law. The modern individual family is founded on the open or concealed domestic slavery of the wife, and modern society is a mass composed of these individual families as its molecules.

Document 6

Source: French telephone exchange, Illustration from French newspaper *Le Petit Journal*, April 17, 1904

LES DEMOISELLES DU TÉLÉPHONE
Aspect d'un bureau téléphonique parisien

Document 7

Source: Suffragettes chained to the railings at 10 Downing Street (Prime Minister's residence), *Illustrated London News*, May 24, 1913

Section II, Part B: Long Essay Question

Time—40 minutes; 1 Question

Directions: Choose EITHER Question 2 or Question 3.

In your response, you should do the following.

- Respond to the prompt with a historically defensible thesis or claim that establishes a line of reasoning.
- Describe a broader historical context relevant to the prompt.
- Support an argument in response to the prompt using specific and relevant examples of evidence.
- Use historical reasoning (e.g., comparison, causation, continuity or change over time) to frame or structure an argument that addresses the prompt.
- Use evidence to corroborate, qualify, or modify an argument that addresses the prompt.

Question 2 *Evaluate the extent to which the responses to industrialization changed in the period 1815–1914.*

(RP: CCOT)

Question 3 *Evaluate the extent to which European ideas and culture moved toward belief in reason and progress in the period 1815–1914.*

(RP: CCOT)

ANSWERS, EXPLANATIONS, & SAMPLE RESPONSES
for the Diagnostic Exams can be found at
~ **www.sherpalearning.com/achiever** ~

The chapters in Period 4 will address the following major developments and events:

- The causes, nature, and course of World War I
- The debate over the Treaty of Versailles settlement and its immediate aftermath
- Causes and course of the Russian and Bolshevik Revolutions, including establishment of the Soviet Union
- Causes, effects, and responses to the Great Depression, including extremist movements
- Rise of totalitarian governments in fascist Italy, Nazi Germany, and the Soviet Union under Stalin
- Trends in elite and high culture in the interwar period
- Failed attempts to appease fascist powers and the causes of World War II
- The experience of total war from 1939–1945, including mobilization of home fronts and genocide
- Causes, course, and effects of the Cold War, 1943–1991
- Development and fall of the Soviet Union after 1945 and its relationship to Eastern Europe
- Decolonization and international conflicts since the collapse of communism

- Western European recovery and policies of economic and political unity
- Social and economic developments in post-1945 Europe, including growth of the welfare state, demographics, and feminism
- Advance of medical and industrial technologies and their environmental impact
- Developments in ideas, culture, and religion within the framework of modernism and postmodernism

Each chapter will provide a content review and practice questions to test your understanding of the material. At the conclusions of the content chapters, you will be able both to gauge your grasp of the content and practice historical thinking skills in a diagnostic test that will include:

- 30 MC questions
- 2 SAQs
- 1 DBQ
- 1 LEQ (choice of 2)

Each chapter will begin with a brief correlation to the Unit Guides from the Course and Exam Description (CED). Good luck with your review.

∾ CHAPTER 14 ∾

The First World War and Russian Revolution

The First World War and Russian Revolution represent the defining events of the twentieth century. For decades, intellectuals and political leaders had predicted the coming of a great war, but few expected the devastation and disillusionment that broke upon Europe in 1914. This chapter examines the complex causes of World War I—one of the most analyzed events in European history—the course and nature of the war, how various nations organized for the first total war, and how the war ended in revolution and a controversial peace settlement at Versailles. It also explores the fall of the Romanov Dynasty in Russia—a consequence of the country's poorly organized involvement in World War I

and a growing discontent with the tsarist rule. By 1921, the Bolsheviks (later Communist Party) defeated their foes in a civil war, purging enemies of the state in the Red Terror and securing control of the new Soviet Union (USSR), Europe's first socialist government. The existence of the Soviet Union coincides directly with the twentieth century that helped create it, a century that began in violence and revolution.

The Causes of the First World War

Who or *what* caused the First World War is a hotly debated historical issue. Long-term diplomatic and political clashes building up for over a century were ignited by the assassination of the heir to the Austro-Hungarian throne, Archduke Franz Ferdinand. As you review below, consider how long-term and short-term factors interacted to produce the conflict.

MAIMIN'

Students often find mnemonic devices helpful in recalling content. The standard for World War I's causes is **MAIN**. However, this formula tends to overlook the importance of internal and intellectual causes, which are harder to identify precisely but important nonetheless. Therefore, we will use **MAIMIN'**. The following provides a bird's-eye view of these causes.

Militarism and **Military Plans**—After the wars of unification in the mid-nineteenth century, armies exploded in size and firepower, driven by mass production and the dynamic Second Industrial Revolution. These technological and industrial advances rendered warfare even more efficient and deadly. Never before or since have greater percentages of populations served in their nations' military. Conscription (the draft) and regular military training militarized society by creating **mass citizen armies**. Government leaders associated national great-

> **SKILL SET**
>
> Historians have debated the question of causation (CAUS) for the First World War since it began, a common reaction to a devastating event brought about by a seemingly minor loss (the assassination of Franz Ferdinand). The issue makes for an ideal historiographical question and one that requires you to make an argument (ARG) by considering the range of evidence (CES) from both long- and short-term factors. As you read this section, consider these interpretive questions: 1) Which causal factor played the most critical role?, 2) Could the conflict have been avoided? If so, how?, and 3) How should we apportion national responsibility bringing about the conflict?

ness with a strong military, and many adopted military dress in public ceremonies. In preparation for the upcoming conflict, nations expanded their armaments and navies.

Germany's desire to build a world-class fleet of battleships antagonized Great Britain and created an enemy out of a potential ally. Kaiser Wilhelm II's (r. 1888–1918) reading of American Admiral A.T. Mahan's *The Influence of Sea Power on History* (1890) convinced him that if Germany desired a "place in the sun," it must develop a commercial empire akin to Britain's. Compounding the Kaiser's erratic and bombastic personality, this threat to British naval dominance represented the first of many actions by Germany upsetting the balance of power after 1890. As often occurs in history, the Great War was preceded by arms and naval races.

Upon the completion of the Franco-Russian alliance in 1894, Germany began work on the Schlieffen Plan, designed to fight a two-front war against Russia (to the east) and France (to the west). Germany's was only the most famous of such plans; each nation developed complex blueprints involving railroad timetables, troop movements, and battle strategies that often significantly affected *political* decisions. These plans limited, or were perceived to limit, the options open to policy makers and, in most cases, escalated regional clashes into a world war. For example, when Germany began mobilizing troops in 1914 in accordance with the Schlieffen Plan, all hopes of political negotiations to prevent war were lost.

Alliance System—After Germany's unification in 1871, Chancellor Otto von Bismarck worked to maintain the balance of power and prevent war through a complex system of interlocking alliances. As Bismarck put it, Germany was a "satisfied giant" that desired no additional territory. He believed a war among the great powers would be a disaster for Germany. Bismarck aimed to stay allied with three of the five great powers in order to isolate a French nation bent on avenging the loss of Alsace-Lorraine. To achieve this purpose, Bismarck attempted to mediate the potential for dispute in the Balkans by forming the Three Emperors' League in 1873 between Germany, Austria, and Russia. This agreement proved difficult to maintain, so Bismarck formed a strong mutual defense treaty with Austria (Austro-German Alliance) in 1879 and supplemented this with the Triple Alliance with Italy and Austria in 1882. When Russia refused to revive the alliance with both Germany and Austria, Bismarck convinced the Russians to sign the Reinsurance Treaty in 1887 with Germany alone. Moreover, Bismarck maintained friendly relations with Great Britain and even avoided antagonizing France. Within the Bismarckian alliance structure, no great power could count on the support of any other should it initiate aggressive war, and might in fact trigger a hostile alliance against it.

Kaiser Wilhelm dismissed Bismarck in 1890 and quickly undid his alliance system. Wilhelm allowed the Reinsurance Treaty with Russia to lapse, counting on his personal relationship with the Russian tsar (they were cousins), which freed Russia to complete the Franco-Russian alliance in 1894. As it industrialized and pursued colonies more vigorously, Germany's potential military and economic might sparked concern among the other great powers. Wilhelm's efforts to match Britain's navy, and his militant personal style, drove France and Britain together with the Entente Cordiale (friendly understanding) in 1904. Soon after, in 1907, Russia, smarting from its military debacle against Japan, agreed with Britain to the Anglo-Russian Entente to compromise their contending interests in central Asia. This series of loose agreements among Britain, France, and Russia came to be known as the Triple Entente, which now opposed the Triple Alliance. Within a generation, Wilhelm had destroyed Bismarck's alliance system and caused Germany's encirclement. As of 1907, two mutually antagonistic alliances faced off, with the potential of a minor conflict between Austria and Russia dragging the whole of Europe into war. The alliance system thus acted as a chain of causation leading to an all-out war once the first trap was sprung.

Imperialism—World War I did not begin over colonial issues; however, conflicts among imperial powers increased tension and hardened the emerging alliance structure. Italy's pursuit of colonies in North Africa brought it into conflict with France and led in 1882 to its joining the Triple Alliance. To test the new alliance between France and Britain (Triple Entente), Wilhelm provoked the Moroccan Crises of 1905 and 1911, disputes over French control of the North African region. His aggressive actions produced the opposite of the intended effect, as the two Atlantic nations drew closer in their joint military plans. In addition, Britain's isolation during the Boer War (1899–1902) led it to approach Japan, France, and Russia in the next decade to ensure its security vis-à-vis an expansive Germany. Finally, Italy's attack on the crumbling Ottoman Empire in pursuit of the North African colony of Libya (1911) triggered a series of crises in the Balkans culminating in the First World War.

Mass Politics—By 1914, many European states faced significant internal problems—strikes, ethnic violence, extremist groups, and political outsiders demanding rights. To sustain internal unity, governments promoted imperialism and fanned nationalist sentiments. As leaders contemplated the momentous decision for war in July 1914, they may have viewed the crisis as an opportunity to solve domestic issues. When war broke out, citizens celebrated in European capitals, and political dissenters called for an end to internal disputes. Kaiser Wilhelm announced a *Burgfrieden*, or "castle peace," for the duration of the war, while in Britain, female suffrage and Irish home rule were tabled. Socialist parties, which wished to unite workers of all nations, generally supported the call to arms, in spite of their Marxist ideology. Mass politics had worked only too well in promoting popular nationalist sentiment in favor of war.

Intellectual Context—Many observers of the European scene sensed that a major war loomed on the horizon. It had been 40 years since the Franco-Prussian War, and with the advent of Darwinism and irrationality in philosophy, some glorified war as a natural product of human advancement—how it called upon patriotism and sacrifice and separated the weak from the strong nations. For example, German writer Friedrich von Bernhardi, in *The Next War* (1912), welcomed the prospect of demonstrating Germany's national greatness and predicted that technological advances would render warfare violent yet decisive. Europeans' faith in technological and scientific solutions to problems and belief in the productivity of warfare seem naïve today only because of the results of the war they produced.

Nationalism—**Nationalism** caused the First World War in two ways: (1) by making it difficult for nations to compromise what they perceived as their national honor and (2) by feeding the ethnic tensions in the Balkans that drew Austria and Russia into conflict there.

European Diplomacy, 1871–1914

By destroying the Concert of Europe, the Crimean War not only opened the way for the unification of Italy and Germany, it effectively destroyed an international mechanism for containing conflict. Germany's defeat of France in the last of its unification wars established the perennial rivalry at the base of the First World War. With this unstable diplomatic situation and intense national rivalries, all that was needed was a *casus belli* (cause of war). This proved to be the volatile situation in the Balkan Peninsula, involving Austria, Russia, and the Ottoman Empire.

> **THEME MUSIC**
>
> Much of this chapter addresses the SOP and NEI themes, particularly the structure of diplomatic rivalries, balance of power, and the state's control over the economy and society. In many ways, World War I formed a turning point in politics and diplomacy. It laid the groundwork for totalitarian movements of subsequent decades, planted the seeds of the Second World War, and set the stage for the superpower rivalry between the US and USSR.

Like Russia, the Ottoman Empire realized its backwardness during the Crimean War. However, efforts by reformers, known as Young Turks, to introduce national citizenship, abolish religious hierarchies, and establish legal equality only provoked a conservative backlash. The Sick Man of Europe seemed unable to stem the disintegration of its multi-ethnic realm, which drew in Russia as the protector of its brother Slavs and in its perennial drive to gain territory at the Ottomans' expense. The ensuing Russo-Turkish War (1877–1878) produced a clear victory for Russia but one that threatened the balance of power in the region and Britain's control of the Suez Canal. To prevent further conflict, Bismarck acted as an "honest broker" in hosting the Congress of Berlin (1878) to resolve the controversy. The

Congress reduced Russia's territorial gains and allowed Austria to occupy (but not annex) Bosnia-Herzegovina, coveted by nationalistic Serbs. Most viewed the Congress of Berlin as a defeat for Russia. The subsequent anti-German feeling in Russia led Bismarck to conclude an Austro-German alliance in 1879; however, Germany and Russia eventually reestablished friendly diplomatic relations with the Reinsurance Treaty. Nonetheless, the conflict revealed the explosive potential of the Balkans.

As the twentieth century began, tensions spiked in the Balkan region. In a rare sign of cooperation, Austria and Russia in 1908 concluded a secret agreement at the expense of an Ottoman Empire once again undergoing internal instability. In exchange for allowing Russia to take the strategic Dardanelles straits (from the Black to Mediterranean Seas), Austria was to annex Bosnia-Herzegovina, which it already occupied. Fearing the dismemberment of the Ottoman Empire, the other great powers blocked Russia's advance into the Mediterranean. Meanwhile, Austria grabbed Bosnia anyway, demonstrating the power of coercion over diplomacy. Russia stood humiliated, while its smaller neighbor Serbia grew incensed, viewing Bosnia's Slavic population as rightfully belonging to a future greater Serbia. Soon after, Serbian pan-Slavists formed the terrorist Black Hand, bent on expelling Austrian influence from the Balkans.

Like a flock of vultures, the smaller Balkan nations circled the carcass of the dying Ottoman Empire. After Italy's defeat of the Turks in 1911, the smaller nations formed the Balkan League (Serbia, Bulgaria, Greece, and Montenegro) and attacked the Ottomans in the First Balkan War (1912–1913). Following the Balkan League's victory, Serbia stood poised to gain access to the Adriatic Sea. At the London Conference, Austria, Italy, and Germany forced upon Serbia and its protector Russia the creation of an independent Albania, designed specifically to block Serbian access to the sea. Once again, Russia had been forced to back down in its own backyard. When the victors could not agree on how to divide the conquered territory of Macedonia, Bulgaria (created in 1878 at the Congress of Berlin) faced off against the other Balkan nations and the Ottomans in the Second Balkan War (1913). Bulgaria was easily defeated. The two conflicts heightened the animosity between Serbia and Austria, convinced Russia of the need to save face in the next crisis, and set the stage for the ultimate conflict.

The July Crisis of 1914

Archduke Franz Ferdinand (1863–1914), the heir to the Austrian throne, visited the capital of Bosnia (Sarajevo) with the intention of building support for his solution to the ethnic problems in the Balkans—a Triple Monarchy. Franz Ferdinand hoped to appease the Slavic minorities in the region by granting them autonomy *within* the Habsburg Empire (like the Magyars); however, the Black Hand feared the plan would undermine its goal of establishing a unified independent Serbian kingdom. To stop Ferdinand's plan and punish Austria, the Black Hand trained a group of young assassins to kill the Archduke and his wife, Sophie. On June 28, 1914, the 19-year-old Gavrilo Princip fulfilled his mission, plunging Europe into crisis.

Austria believed that the Serbian government had instigated the assassination, and a month later issued it a harsh ultimatum. Kaiser Wilhelm of Germany gave his only reliable ally a "blank check" to settle its ethnic issue permanently, emboldening Austria to take a hard line and risk war with Serbia's ally, Russia. Fearing Germany's military plans, France in turn stood firm behind its ally Russia. Meanwhile, Britain refused to signal its intentions clearly, trying in vain to mediate the dispute. When Serbia rejected one point of Austria's ultimatum, Austria declared war against it, an action that prompted Russia's declaration of war against Austria. Russia's war plan presumed a war against *both* Germany and Austria, forcing Tsar Nicholas to mobilize his army on both nations' borders. Despite a last-minute flurry of telegrams between cousins "Willy and Nicky," Germany declared war on Russia, triggering the trap of the alliance system. France quickly joined the conflict, and because Germany's Schlieffen Plan had violated Belgian neutrality, Britain too declared war on Germany. Europe was now engulfed in the war for which many had planned, but of a nature that few expected.

Fighting on the Fronts

Europe did not get the war it expected. What was supposed to be over by Christmas turned to stalemate by the end of 1914. Though the war eventually involved the nations of six continents, the hinge turned on the Western Front. It is most important for you to understand the nature of the war and its phases; do not be overly concerned with battles.

The Nature of the War

Military tactics often lag a generation behind technologies. The First World War illustrates this adage in bold type. Generals of the day learned the Napoleonic tactics of rapid movement and the massed infantry assault. Military theorists assumed that the new technologies of airplanes, high-powered artillery, and machine guns would favor the traditional offensive by overwhelming a static opponent with massive firepower. The reverse turned out to be the case, as these weapons and technologies proved advantageous to entrenched defensive positions. In all, almost 10 million soldiers were killed during the First World War, largely the result of an inability to conceive of new tactics in dealing with defensive weapons.

Once the Western Front settled down to a stalemate, each side entrenched positions and fortified them with barbed wire. In between stood "no-man's land," an expanse denuded of trees, houses, and crops. Generals attempted to soften up enemy positions with artillery bombardments, often lasting days, as a prelude to "over the top," where infantry ran exposed through no-man's land in a vain effort to overwhelm the enemy trench. Though trenches had been used during the Crimean War and the U.S Civil War, the Great War (what WWI was called at the time) combatants relied on them extensively. **Trench warfare** emerged as a dehumanizing and absurd symbol of the futility of the First World War. Many other important technological breakthroughs occurred or were first used in World War I, but none exercised the decisive impact as hoped and only increased the body count: <u>tanks</u>, <u>airplanes</u>, flamethrowers, <u>submarines (U-boats)</u>, high-powered artillery, grenades, <u>poison gas</u>, <u>barbed wire</u>, zeppelins, and aerial bombardment.

The War of Illusions: 1914

Germany gambled that its Schlieffen Plan would defeat France before Russia could mobilize. The plan called for a huge right flanking maneuver in August 1914 through Belgium to hit Paris from the rear and trap the French army at Alsace-Lorraine. Violation of Belgium neutrality brought Britain in the war on the side of the Entente, and moreover, Belgium put up unexpected resistance to German forces. This resistance led to the first atrocities of the war against Belgian civilians, providing the Allies with an important propaganda weapon against Germany.

As the German advance toward Paris stalled, the French regrouped and hit the German flank at the Marne River. The Miracle of the Marne halted the German offensive. After each side unsuccessfully tried to outflank the other by racing to the English Channel, the Western Front had settled down by Christmas to a stalemate, with a string of trenches from the English Channel to the Swiss frontier—300 miles in length. On the more open and less populated Eastern Front, the Germans met with more success by taking an entire Russian army at Tannenberg. This battle was the prelude to the generally poor performance of the Russian army, whose men were captured in much larger numbers than any combatant nation.

Stalemate: 1915

To break out of the stalemate, the Central Powers (Austria-Hungary, Germany) and the Allied forces (Russia, France, Britain, Belgium) expanded the war by bidding for new allies. To recapture its lost territories, Turkey joined the Central Powers in November of 1914. The Allies, meanwhile, bribed Italy, via the Treaty of London, with the promise of Austrian territory to join the war against the Central Powers. From 1915 to 1917, Bulgaria, Romania, and Greece all entered the conflict to achieve territorial objectives left over from the pre-1914 Balkan conflicts.

Each side engaged in probing offensives aimed at finding the enemy weak spot. To knock out the Turks and secure Europe's "soft underbelly," the British in April 1915 launched the poorly planned Gallipoli campaign, an amphibious assault designed to capture Constantinople and the Dardanelles. British forces found themselves pinned down on a narrow ridge and after months of futile assaults withdrew in early 1916.

Germany and Great Britain both attempted to blockade the other and starve it into submission. The German navy's reliance on the submarine made blockades dangerous—the U-boat had to either surface to inspect enemy ships, making it vulnerable to enemy fire, or gamble and destroy the potential enemy craft. This problem almost brought the United States into the conflict when a German U-boat sank the British liner *Lusitania* off the coast of Ireland, killing 1,200, including 128 Americans. President Wilson was able to maintain US neutrality while extracting a promise from the German government to avoid unrestricted submarine warfare. However, US exports and loans to Britain and France skyrocketed as aid and trade to Germany fizzled.

Slaughter: 1916–1917

By 1916, the effects of total war were exhausting all nations involved in the conflict. To break the deadlock, Germany rolled the dice on another bold plan. In February 1916, Commander Erich von Falkenhayn launched a massive surprise attack at the key position of Verdun in the French line. Though the attack met with initial success, the Germans were unable to maintain their momentum. They did

> ### EXAMPLE BASE
> Few of the specifics in this section constitute required knowledge; however, you can deploy examples from the fighting to examine how military stalemate and technology affected mobilization, home front issues, and the relationship between governments and science.

not call off the battle, however, until January 1917, making Verdun the longest battle of the war and one of the deadliest in history. In all, the French and German armies combined experienced 750,000 casualties.

To take the pressure off the French, the British launched the Somme offensive in July. The battle proved a disaster for the British army, which lost 30,000 dead in the first 3 hours of the attack, known as the bloodiest day in British military history. In addition, the Russian command surprised the Austrian army with the Brusilov Offensive, driving their enemy back hundreds of miles before the Germans stabilized their collapsing ally. One success for the Central Powers was their victory over Serbia; this country was knocked completely out of the war, losing a greater percentage of its population than any other warring nation.

In one of the ironies of the war, the large battleships that had provoked such animosity between Britain and Germany generally stayed in port, with leaders fearful of destroying such large investments. The only major naval engagement of the war occurred in 1916 off the coast of Denmark at Jutland. Both sides were bloodied but survived, and the German battleships returned to port. After the armistice, the

Germans scuttled (sank) their expensive fleet rather than allow it to fall into enemy hands.

Exhaustion and Revolution: 1917–1918

In 1917, the Allied forces lost a key nation: Russia. At the same time, they gained perhaps an even greater force: the United States. Russia's deteriorating economic and political situation resulted in the fall of the Romanov Dynasty, and in late 1917 the newly empowered Bolsheviks pulled Russia out of the war. Germany once again rolled the dice to end the war, betting that unrestricted submarine warfare around the British Isles, in violation of an earlier pledge, could knock Britain and France out of the conflict before the United States could effectively mobilize. They were wrong. The announcement of Germany's U-boat campaign, combined with the Zimmerman Telegram—in which the German ambassador promised Mexico the recovery of lands lost to the United States if it entered the war—drew the United States into the war in April 1917. Contrary to German plans, American involvement proved decisive.

By mid-1917, it looked as if the Central Powers might prevail. Austrian and German forces routed the Italian army at Caporetto, forcing the diversion of French and British forces into the difficult Alpine fighting to prop up their ally. In Belgium, British, ANZAC (Australian and New Zealand Army Corps), and Canadian forces worked to retake the town of Passchendaele. In the subsequent battle, thousands drowned in muddy shell holes, a morbid symbol of the futility of warfare. By March 1918, the Germans imposed on the Bolsheviks the draconian Treaty of Brest-Litovsk, costing Russia significant territory and resources.

In Germany's final gamble of the war, its High Command launched one last major offensive in spring 1918 on the Western Front. Despite initial gains, which brought the Germans to within 30 miles of Paris, American troops began to inject fresh manpower and morale into the Allied cause. American and French counter-offensives pushed the German lines back by early fall 1918. By this time, ethnic minorities were establishing independence from the Austrian Empire, while Germany confronted a revolutionary situation at home from an exhausted populace. Though few troops stood on German soil, the German High Command asked for an armistice on November 11, 1918. The Armistice ended fighting on the battlefield, yet Europe faced a revolutionary situation in which a return to the prewar world would prove impossible.

Organizing for Total War

The Great War involved full mobilization of each nation's resources and populations. Despite their modern industrial, military, and bureaucratic structures and techniques, all nations found the burdens of fighting the war an enormous strain, often fueling a revolutionary situation.

Government and Economy

Pressures of total war forced the abandonment of laissez-faire practices. Governments moved quickly to oversee wartime production to ensure an adequate supply of matériel. To appreciate the demands of the Great War, you may consider that at the battle of Verdun more projectiles were dropped than in all previous warfare in human history combined! Many combatant nations managed production via bureaucratic centralization—that is, running the war effort as one large industry. In Germany, industrialist Walter Rathenau (1867–1922) helped Germany deal with severe shortages and maintain adequate supplies by overseeing production in the War Ministry. When Britain experienced a shortage of shells in 1915, future Prime Minister David Lloyd George (1863–1945) was made Minister of Munitions to prevent further shortfalls. These policies benefited larger corporations and labor unions, as governments found it more efficient to award government contracts to and oversee large enterprises.

To pay for the war, governments used three options: raise taxes, depreciate currencies, and borrow money. Raising taxes could only go so far; as the war dragged on, governments grew fearful of placing additional demands on an already strained populace. By the end of the conflict, France and Britain had borrowed significant amounts from the United States, making it a creditor for the first time in its history. All nations appealed to their citizens' patriotic duty to purchase war bonds. In all, the war cost the nations involved over $350 billion. Inflation worked as a hidden tax and resulted in currency depreciation, a situation that rendered a return to prewar economic stability impossible when the conflict finally ended.

Nationalist Unrest and Agitation

Almost every nation experienced internal ethnic conflicts, which their enemies attempted to exploit to strategic advantage. For example, the German government gave aid to Irish rebels revolting for independence from the British in the Easter Rising of 1916. Though British men and resources were diverted, the attempt failed. Not to be outdone, the Allies promoted the creation of independence committees for various minorities within the Austro-Hungarian empire, especially for the Poles and Czechs, an effort that yielded the dissolution of the empire by 1918. Most famously, the British sent Colonel T.E. Lawrence ("of Arabia," 1888–1935) to promote the cause of <u>Arab nationalism within the Ottoman Empire</u>. Though these efforts did not play a decisive role in the outcome of the war, they did set up future conflicts in the **Middle East**, often over the new strategic resource of oil.

The Home Fronts

The First World War culminated the trend in mass politics of the previous half-century. Governments called on citizens to sacrifice for the war effort by enlisting, buying war bonds, and rationing. Rationing went furthest in Germany. By 1916, the Kaiser had turned the government over to the famous generals Erich Ludendorff (1865–1937) and Paul von Hindenburg (1847–1934), who quietly established a military dictatorship, part of which involved allotting families ration books for a particular number of calories per day. By the end of the war, many Germans agonized over eating "sawdust bread" and a scarcity of essential fats and oils.

Because of the manpower shortage, many women entered the workforce outside the home for the first time. In Britain, industrialists employed women in the production of TNT and shells. Neglect of safety conditions led tragically to the poisoning and infertility of thousands of female laborers. These "women with yellow hands" demonstrated the potential public role of women and helped to earn them the vote in many nations after the war ended. The Provisional Government of Russia even formed a military unit, the Women's Battalion of Death, which saw action at the front and in defense of the state. Among other groups, skilled workers gained the most, as they won wage increases and recognition of union collaboration in production. Nonetheless, strikes did occur. Governments often responded with the promise of improved conditions *and* the threat of violence if strikes continued. By the end of the war, union discontent broke out into open rebellion, helping to bring down teetering governments in the Fall of 1918. On the other hand, small business owners, those in traditional crafts, and the lower middle-class often found themselves struggling with competition from large businesses favored by government officials.

Freedom is often the first casualty of war. Though states worked to build positive support for their war efforts, they were also quick to crush dissent. Early in the war, the British Parliament passed the Defense of the Realm Act (DORA), which in addition to regimenting the lives of British citizens, censored the press and allowed the government to requisition war supplies from private citizens. All nations, including the United States, established stricter laws against treasonous activities and dissent against the government. Germany used spies to infiltrate radical unions, while many governments simply jailed the most outspoken opponents of the war effort.

Propaganda and Genocide

Propaganda came of age during the First World War. To motivate citizens, governments employed both positive patriotic appeals with national symbols as well as negative attacks on the en-

---

SKILL SET

World War I elevated mass politics to a new level with its need for mobilization. Governments employed propaganda to motivate citizens both to sacrifice and to view enemies as less than human. Using the firstworldwar.com site (metioned in the Additional Resources), peruse some of the propaganda posters from various nations and place them in historical context, considering how and why they might have motivated combatants and citizens (CTX and SES).

---

emy, portraying the war as a battle over civilization against a brutal and inhuman foe. Demonizing the enemy seemed like a logical climax of mass political pressures building for decades—anti-Semitism, xenophobia, extreme nationalism, and glorification of struggle. A tragic culmination of this trend was the first genocide of the twentieth century. In 1915, the Ottoman government feared that its Armenian Christian minority might aid the Russian war effort. Several hundred leaders of the Armenian community were executed, while thousands of Armenians were deported to camps with inadequate facilities, where between 500,000 and 1.5 million died from neglect, disease, and starvation. Even today, the Turkish government rejects the notion of an Armenian Genocide, though most independent scholars classify the event as such.

Hard Landings: The Treaty of Versailles and Revolutionary Instability

The Treaty of Versailles ending the First World War represents one of the most significant diplomatic events you will study this year and is essential to your understanding of the twentieth century. The Versailles settlement is often compared with the Congress of Vienna in 1814–1815 regarding their respective mechanisms for collective security and the success of their decisions. Though the Allies negotiated treaties with each of the Central Powers, the settlement with Germany proved most decisive for future events.

Revolutionary Fallout

When the Allied victors met starting in January 1919 in the Palace of Versailles, they found it nearly impossible to put Humpty Dumpty back together again. Revolutionary violence led to the toppling of four empires—Austro-Hungarian, German, Ottoman, and Russian. What kind of governments and states would replace these traditional diplomatic entities remained an open question. Allied leaders were prepared to confirm the **creation of new states** out of the former Habsburg Empire (Austria, Hungary, Czechoslovakia, Poland, Yugoslavia, and the Baltic states of Lithuania, Latvia, and Estonia) and promote democratic governments there and in Germany. To consider the armistice and treaties a return to peace would ignore the waves of ethnic violence and civil wars that beset Eastern Europe. Pogroms against Jews broke out in Ukraine (killing 100,000) even as the new Polish and Bolshevik states clashed to expand their territories. Vicious ethnic campaigns marked the Greco-Turkish War (1919–1922), during which Turkey's Mustafa Kemal (1881–1938) succeeded in being the only defeated Central Power to reject a dictated peace settlement; nonetheless, his nation-building ended with the forcible transfer of 1.5 million ethnic Greeks and 500,000 ethnic Turks across borders to achieve religious homogeneity. In addition, Hungary and

Bulgaria were riven by ideological conflict between communists and reactionaries, leading to extended periods of government instability. Space here is too limited for detailed coverage of the full scope of such violence, which was often followed by famine and impoverishment. Much, though not all, of this revolutionary unrest was fed by the existence of a new socialist government in the east, the Soviet Union.

Differing Goals for and Visions of the Peace

President Woodrow Wilson (1856–1923), the first American president to travel abroad, set foot on European soil a hero. He authored the renowned Fourteen Points, his idealistic vision for reconstructing Europe and "making the world safe for democracy." He also declared that WWI should be the "war to end all wars." Wilson dreamed of a new diplomatic order guided by open diplomacy, freedom of the seas, arms reduction, **national self-determination**, and collective security. Representatives from African and Asian colonies attended the negotiations in hopes of gaining autonomy, only to be thwarted as former German and Ottoman colonies were granted to Britain and France under **mandates**, handing them control until such colonies were prepared for self-governance. Collective security was to be achieved by the creation of an international governing body to mediate disputes—the **League of Nations**. Wilson recognized that Germany must be punished but hoped that drastic action might be avoided to build a more secure foundation for democratic governments after the war.

French Premier George Clemenceau (1841–1929), nicknamed "the Tiger," considered Wilson's vision naive and concentrated on security for France by emasculating Germany's military and economic potential. British Prime Minister David Lloyd George stood somewhere in between Wilson and Clemenceau (famously remarking, "I had God on one side and the devil on the other") in wanting to punish Germany but not utterly destroy it. And though Prime Minister Vittorio Orlando (1860–1952) represented Italy in negotiations, he eventually walked out in protest over his nation's lack of territorial spoils. Importantly, Russia sat out the negotiations, as the new Bolshevik leader Lenin denounced the gathering as a capitalist plot. The Allies rejected German participation and maintained the naval blockade against it until June 1919 when Germany signed the treaty; in all, some historians estimate that 750,000 Germans died of starvation during and after World War I. Given these circumstances, it is not surprising that the treaty pleased no nation.

A Divided Settlement

After months of negotiations, the reluctant German delegates signed the Versailles settlement in the palace's famous Hall of Mirrors on June 28, 1919 (5 years to the day from the start of the war). By most accounts, the treaty represented a harsh peace:

- *Territorial Losses* – Germany lost 13% of its territory and 12% of its population. The important Saar industrial region was placed under League of Nations control until 1935. East Prussia was cut off from the rest of Germany to provide the new Polish state with access to the sea. Finally, German surrendered its overseas colonies.

- *Demilitarization* – The German army was reduced to 100,000 men; the nation's naval fleet was severely curtailed (including the banning of U-boats); and its air force was eliminated. Fearing further German aggression, the French insisted on the demilitarization of the Rhineland, adjacent to France.

- *War Guilt* – In the most controversial provision of the treaty, Germany was forced to accept full responsibility for the war via Article 231.

- *Reparations* – Based on the War Guilt clause, the Allies in 1921 set a reparations amount for the German government of 132 billion marks (some $33 billion), a figure most German observers considered exorbitant.

- *League of Nations* – To promote collective security, the Allies agreed to Wilson's idea of a League of Nations. However, because the US Senate refused to ratify the treaty, the United States never joined, and the new Soviet Union and Germany were initially excluded.

> **SKILL SET**
>
> The Treaty of Versailles's Article 231, which assessed full responsibility for the war to Germany, represents the first official interpretation of the war's origins (SAS and CES) and of great political consequence, since it was used to justify the victors' actions against the defeated. To sharpen your skill of Comparison (COMP), make a balance sheet of pros and cons for the Congress of Vienna and the Treaty of Versailles. Which was more successful in addressing its respective situation and promoting collective security?

Consequences and Conflicts

Few were fully satisfied with the Treaty of Versailles, but none less so than Germany. Germany's new postwar government, the **Weimar Republic**, started off with two strikes against it, being saddled with what most Germans perceived as a dictated peace. Discontent over the treaty was fed by extremists groups like the Nazis and played a major role in bringing down Germany's short-lived experiment with democracy. Almost immediately, observers condemned the economic arrangements of the treaty. Economist John Maynard Keynes (1883–1946) attended the negotiations on behalf of Britain and afterward predicted in his *Economic Consequences of the Peace* (1919) the ruination of the world economy, which was not long in coming. Overall, the inability of the victors to employ a consistent diplomatic approach torpedoed their efforts at establishing a stable balance of power, but perhaps the complexity of the issues and intensity of the conflicts might have doomed any settlement. Certainly a major reason for the treaty's failure proved to be the subsequent isolation of both the United States and the Soviet Union. America's unwillingness to guarantee French security after 1920 and the fear of Soviet communism opened the way for a revival of German power. Without a full commitment to collective security and the League of Nations, Europe in the next two decades drifted toward an even more destructive war.

The Russian Revolution: Importance and Causes

Like the First World War that sparked it, the Russian Revolution helped define the political and ideological issues of the twentieth century. Historians often compare it with the earlier French Revolution. Both revolutions proceeded through several phases, appealed to those outside their borders, and cleaved philosophical divisions throughout the world. One difference, however, was that France stood as Europe's leading nation in 1789 when its revolution began, whereas Russia lagged behind in 1914. Russia's revolution did prove more immediately successful, though, as the Bolsheviks were able to secure power and held it for three-quarters of a century. In France, the Old Regime returned to control in 1814, just 25 years after the struggle began. Without the Russian Revolution, the history of the twentieth century—including the Second World War, the Cold War, decolonization, and the nuclear arms race—would be a different story.

Long-Term Causes, 1861–1905

Throughout its history, Russia faced two perennial and irresolvable problems: (1) its technological and economic backwardness vis-à-vis the other European powers and (2) its inability to develop a form of government that successfully harnessed the will of its people. The Russian Revolution can be viewed as a drastic solution to these problems.

Following Alexander II's (r. 1855–1881) reforms, Russia seemed to be moving in the right direction. However, each top-down move by the government engendered a new set of problems. Following the abolition of serfdom, former serfs were forced to continue living on the *mirs* (rural communities practicing subsistence agriculture) until they had paid for their lands. Moreover, large landholders (the gentry) garnered most of the best lands for themselves, sticking former serfs with the rest. Rural overcrowding and a shortage of land led to continual unrest in the countryside, which served as a magnet for revolutionary groups.

Russian intellectuals were divided between those who lauded the unique features of Russia's Slavic culture (called Slavophiles) and those who believed the nation needed to become more like the West to survive (Westernizers). As Russia industrialized after 1880 under the leadership of Finance Minister Sergei Witte (1849–1915), these divisions

deepened. Many of the worst problems of industrialization previously experienced by western European nations seemed accentuated within Russia's undemocratic political system. Moreover, the rapid pace of advance proved problematic. Industry and the attendant urban problems of overcrowding, pollution, and poor working/living conditions were concentrated in two cities—Moscow and St. Petersburg. Russian manufacturing enterprises tended to be large, making it easy for workers to organize politically. As such, cities and factories emerged as centers of proletarian unrest and revolution in subsequent decades.

Reform ironically fueled the growth of revolution. Among the Slavophiles, an anarchist movement known as the People's Will succeeded in assassinating Alexander II in 1881, causing a brutal suppression of revolutionary groups by his successor, the reactionary Alexander III (r. 1881–1894). Anarchists succeeded, moreover, in assassinating thousands of Russian officials between 1870 and 1914. Less violent but also radical were the Social Revolutionaries, who favored a socialism led by the peasants that stressed Russia's rural tradition. Westernizers were divided between the Constitutional Democrats (Cadets), who favored the development of a capitalist economy and a parliamentary democracy like Britain's, and the Social Democrats, a Marxist party founded in 1898 in Swiss exile. Even within the Social Democrats, divisions emerged; the Mensheviks wished to establish a mass-based political party like the SPD in Germany, while the **Bolsheviks** claimed that only a conspiratorial group of professional agitators could survive in Russia's autocratic political climate.

Revolution of 1905

The divisions in Russian society burst to the fore under the ongoing pressure of the country's repeated military defeats. Russia's poor showing in the Russo-Japanese War (1904–1905) produced economic crisis and a breakdown of the nation's infrastructure. Revolutionary groups looked to exploit the situation to foment change. Strikes broke out in the major cities; the small number of university students rallied; and a group of peaceful protestors marched on the tsar's Winter Palace to request reform. Troops, though unprovoked, fired on the crowd, killing hundreds, in an event known as Bloody Sunday. To calm the furor that followed, Tsar Nicholas II (r. 1894–1917) issued the October Manifesto promising the creation of a legislative assembly, known as the Duma, and further reforms. For the moment, these actions appeased the reform parties.

Any moderate efforts toward the evolution of a constitutional monarchy were undermined by the actions of Nicholas II. Much like Louis XVI, Nicholas seemed like a well-meaning and religious family man who, while espousing divine right rule, proved incapable of upholding what this ideal entailed. Nicholas's prime minister, Peter Stolypin (1862–1911), offered the last chance to pull Russia through its difficult transition. Stolypin introduced a series of far-reaching reforms in the decade before WWI, designed to move Russia toward a functioning parliamentary democracy and a modern economic system. Peasants were finally allowed to sell their land shares to the *mir* and move to cities; property rights were advanced; and the provincial zemstvos (government councils) were strengthened. Unfortunately, Nicholas thwarted Stolypin's attempts to work with the Duma in creating parliamentary coalitions, exercising his royal prerogative to suspend the legislature whenever its policies annoyed him. Upon Stolypin's assassination in 1911, Russia's chance for a peaceful transition to modernity died with him.

The March Revolution and Provisional Government

World War I served as the proverbial straw that broke the camel's back of the Romanov Dynasty. Russia did not fare well in the conflict, experiencing a lack of supplies, poor morale among troops, and numerous casualties. Once again, war had exposed Russia's economic and technological weakness in comparison with the western European powers. As political divisions deepened, Tsar Nicholas II in 1915 dissolved the Duma. Following failures at the front, Nicholas took personal control of the troops, a task for which he was woefully unprepared. Many soldiers were sent into battle with inadequate clothing and weapons. Meanwhile, public opinion turned against the monarchy, as it became increasingly viewed as distant and corrupt. Discontent toward the royal family centered on the mysterious figure of Rasputin (1869–1916), a dissolute monk who exercised sway over the tsarina (tsar's wife) because of his supposed ability to cure her son, Alexis, of hemophilia. Nobles at the court decided to end Rasputin's corrupting influence by assassinating him in December 1916.

Only a crisis was needed to topple the tsarist regime. On March 8, 1917, International Women's Day, a food riot broke out over the high cost of bread in an event eerily similar to the women's march on Versailles during the French Revolution. Revolutionary agitators pushed the crowd toward a political insurrection. When local troops refused to fire on the crowd, the Romanov Dynasty collapsed like a house of cards. Two new governments came to the fore as a result of the March Revolution. First, the **Provisional Government** replaced the deposed tsar with a coalition of constitutional democrats and moderate socialists. Second, more radical groups formed councils of workers, sailors, and soldiers known as **soviets**, the most important of which was the Petrograd Soviet (the city of St. Petersburg had been changed to Petrograd because it sounded less German). The Petrograd Soviet played much the same role as the Paris Commune during the French Revolution, pushing the government further to the left.

The Provisional Government opted to continue the war effort and honor its treaty commitments. Meanwhile, peasants seized land from the gentry, and discipline among troops dissolved. The Petrograd Soviet aided the latter development by passing Army Order No. 1, which provided for democratically elected committees to run the army, causing the breakdown of all discipline. In April 1917, the German army sent Lenin through their lines in a sealed train to Petrograd in hopes that

---
SKILL SET

You should be able to establish many parallels, as well as differences, between the French and Russian Revolution—causes, phases, role of women, ideology, nature of revolutionary regimes, warfare, etc. The better you understand the reasons for the similarities and differences (COMP), the more you will appreciate the changes and continuities in politics in these differing settings (CCOT).
---

he would undermine the Provisional Government. He did not disappoint. Bolshevik leaders were blamed in July for trying to overthrow the Provisional Government, now led by the young and charismatic moderate socialist Alexander Kerensky (1881–1970). The effort failed, and top Bolsheviks were arrested. Lenin fled to Finland. Just one month later, Kerensky faced an attempted coup from the right led by conservative general Lavr Kornilov (1870–1918). To defeat the coup, Kerensky released Bolshevik leaders to aid in the defense of the government, clearly a sign of weakness.

The Bolshevik Revolution

The Role of Lenin

V.I. Lenin (1870–1924) provided the intellectual and organizational energy behind the Russian Revolution. From a prosperous middle-class family, Lenin became radicalized when his brother was executed for indirect involvement in an assassination attempt against Tsar Alexander III. Unable to find work and arrested for his revolutionary affiliations, Lenin sought exile in Switzerland, where he joined the Social Democratic Party and urged a hard line against capitalism. Lenin's writings, such as the *April Theses* issued upon his arrival in 1917 in Russia, accommodated Marxism to the experience of Russia. His contributions to socialist ideology include:

- *Imperialism* – As noted in Chapter 12, Lenin incorporated the phenomenon of imperialism into Marx's critique of capitalism. Lenin claimed that imperialism represented the highest stage of capitalism's concentration of power into fewer and fewer hands and signaled an imminent crisis. World War I represented the climax of that crisis.

- *Vanguard Party* – Lenin insisted, in contrast to the Mensheviks, that only a small group of professional revolutionary conspirators could operate successfully in Russia's undemocratic political climate.

- *"Weakest link in the chain"* – Orthodox Marxism held that the revolution would occur first in the most developed capitalist nation, such as Britain or Germany. Lenin countered that because capitalism operated as a worldwide system, revolutionaries should concentrate on the weakest link—Russia—to destabilize the entire chain of capitalism.

- *Telescoping* – Many Russian socialists cooperated with the Provisional Government, believing Russia was unready to enter into a socialist phase of development before its complete industrialization. Lenin rejected this notion and claimed that the moment was ripe for revolution. He further claimed that Russia's rapid industrialization could occur under the dictatorship of the proletariat.

- *Revolutionary tactics* – To stir the masses, Lenin and the Bolsheviks focused on simple slogans and uncompromising opposition to the Provisional Government. "Peace, bread, and land" and "All power to the soviets!" marked the thrust of the Bolshevik message.

Bolshevik Consolidation of Power

By November 1917, Lenin judged that the hour for action had arrived. Troops in Petrograd voted to support the Bolshevik-controlled soviets. The Bolsheviks easily seized key communication, transportation, and power facilities, while the Provisional Government fled for lack of support. Lenin and the Bolsheviks timed their takeover to coincide with the Congress of Soviets, which elected Lenin the head of the Council of People's Commissars, an executive body. Bolshevik leaders quickly moved to consolidate their power by confirming peasant seizures of land and worker control of factories. More importantly, the Bolsheviks in January 1918 disbanded the recently elected Constituent Assembly, which had produced majorities for the Social Revolutionaries and Mensheviks. This action plunged Russia into civil war. Claiming to speak on behalf of the proletariat, the Bolsheviks (now the Communist Party) proclaimed a dictatorship in their name.

The Treaty of Brest-Litovsk

Now preoccupied with a civil war, Lenin desperately needed to end Russia's involvement in the First World War. In March 1918, the Bolsheviks signed the harsh Treaty of Brest-Litovsk with Germany. By the agreement, Russia recognized the independence of the Baltic provinces, Poland, and Ukraine. In the process, the Bolsheviks lost the most densely populated regions of their nation, important mineral resources, and some of Russia's best farmland. Bolshevik leaders gambled that Russia would regain these lands amid the inevitable socialist revolution accompanying the collapse of the war effort all around.

Russian Civil War, 1918–1922

To fight the civil war, the Bolsheviks formed the Red Army. Led by the brilliant organizer and former head of the Petrograd Soviet, Leon Trotsky (1879–1940), the army faced a motley collection of former tsarists, Cadets, Mensheviks, and Social Revolutionaries known as the White Army. Organizing the war effort was accomplished through war communism. The Bolsheviks nationalized key industries, allowing workers to run factories but dealing harshly with peasants who hoarded grain and refused to surrender their crops and livestock for the Reds' worthless paper money. Bolshevik policies, exacerbated by economic problems, produced class warfare, especially between wealthy peasants on one side and landless laborers and urban dwellers on the other. Complicating the situation, Allied governments landed armies under American, Japanese, and Czech control to aid the Whites and attempt futilely to bring Russia back into World War I.

Despite being outnumbered, the Bolsheviks prevailed. Several factors account for this. First, the Bolsheviks were united in a common vision, in contrast with their enemies who could only agree that they hated the Bolsheviks. Second, intervention by foreign powers allowed the Bolsheviks to paint their opponents as traitors. Third, efforts by the White Army were hindered by exterior lines of communication, making it difficult for them to coordinate their attacks and allowing the Bolsheviks to travel on the inside of the circle they controlled to meet any incursion. Finally, the Bolsheviks simply exhibited a more ruthless willingness than their opponents to maintain their newly won power. Soon after their revolution, the Bolsheviks formed a secret police to infiltrate and eliminate centers of opposition.

Though the situation remained fluid, by 1922 the Bolsheviks had secured control of the nation. In fact, the Red Army recaptured some of the lands lost in the Treaty of Brest-Litovsk and from ethnic minorities that had declared independence since 1918. Once the Bolsheviks had secured power, they engaged in a Red Terror designed to eliminate class enemies. Under the influence of the Cheka (security police), thousands of former bourgeoisie, gentry, and White Army collaborators were shot summarily without trial. The Bolsheviks were determined not to repeat the "mistakes" of French revolutionaries, who allowed supporters of the Old Regime to survive or escape. Estimates run to over 2 million for those killed by the Bolsheviks; no Russian after 1922 would openly call for a return to traditional or even antisocialist government.

The Union of Soviet Socialist Republics (USSR)

By 1922, the Bolsheviks felt secure enough in their power to create the **Union of Soviet Socialist Republics (USSR)**, also known as the **Soviet Union**. Eventually the new nation consisted of 15 such republics. It is important to remember that only about 50% of the citizens in this new USSR claimed Russian ethnicity and language. In that sense, the USSR acquired an international character. During the 1920s, many communists outside Russia continued to hold out hope for the imminent overthrow of capitalism. To this purpose, the Bolsheviks in 1919 created the Third International of communist parties, or Comintern, to replace the Second International, which had divided over entry into the First World War. Supposedly an alliance of socialist parties, in actuality, the Comintern represented a Soviet effort to control the international communist movement.

Party-State Structure

The political structure of the Soviet Union reflected a unique party-state dualism. For each function of government, there existed both a party and a state organ. Because the party acted as the driving force of the revolution and direct representative of the proletariat, it played the primary policy-making role. State organs essentially worked to carry out policies. Constitutions were created in 1924 and 1936 to outline the complex workings of a strongly centralized government. Elections featured only one party, the CPSU (Communist Party of the Soviet Union), and authority worked according to the principle of democratic centralism, a core principle of Lenin's political philosophy. Elections and discussion flowed upward to the top, where decisions were made and adhered to by all party members. At the top of this centralized structure stood the Central Committee, made up of several hundred top CPSU officials. Within the Central Committee, a Politburo (policy bureau) of a dozen individuals dominated the decision-making process. Once Stalin came to power, the position of General Secretary took on the important role in maintaining strict discipline, selecting members to key positions, and managing decision-making.

The Nationalities Issue

For centuries, the Russian tsars had unsuccessfully attempted to Russify the 50 different ethnic groups of their empire, in which over a hundred languages were spoken. To address the nationalities issues, the Bolsheviks adopted a federal structure of government whereby the various republics, and less important autonomous regions, could theoretically secede. In fact, the dominance of the Communist Party, many of whose officials were appointed by Russian leaders of the CPSU, prevented any movement away from the Soviet Union's centralized structure. However, the minority issue never died, and under Mikhail Gorbachev's rule (1985–1991) once again came to the fore in the form of national independence movements, leading to the disintegration of the Soviet empire.

The New Economic Policy (NEP)

As a result of the ravages of the First World War, civil war, and resulting famine, the Soviet economy stood at only 13% of its prewar productivity. To jump-start production, Lenin introduced the **New Economic Policy (NEP)** in 1921, a strategic retreat from communism and compromise with capitalism. Under the NEP, peasants were allowed to sell their grain themselves, and middlemen in towns and cities began exchanging goods for profit. A new class of wealthy peasants, called **kulaks**, arose in the countryside, often resented by landless laborers. Though the NEP did help to revive production, the Soviet economy by 1928 had just returned to its prewar level. Moreover, the policy provoked a split in the Politburo between those who favored continuing the NEP and those who wished to move further toward communism.

Social and Cultural Changes

The 1920s were a decade of experimentation in the Soviet Union. Legal changes provided women with a measure of equality—the vote in 1918, the right to divorce, and access to birth control and abortion. Such reforms did not always translate into immediate changes in the daily lives of women, especially as families struggled to rebuild after a disastrous decade of violence. One of the more prominent women involved in the building of a socialist society was Alexandra Kollontai (1872–1952), appointed People's Commissar for Social Welfare. Kollontai helped found Zhenotdel, a women's bureau designed to fight illiteracy and educate women about the new marriage laws. Sparking controversy, Kollontai argued that as a natural instinct, sexuality should be freed from oppressive traditions like traditional marriage, which mainly harm women. As for children, the Soviet Union created the Communist Youth League, or Komsomol, to promote socialist values and promote membership in the CPSU.

Artists and intellectuals eagerly assisted in the government's efforts to promote socialism. The great filmmaker Sergei Eisenstein pioneered new techniques of portraying action and political themes. Soviet leaders sponsored Eisenstein's famous film about the revolution, *Potemkin* (1925), critically acclaimed by film critics for its innovations. Radical artists blended the style of futurist art with a socialist message. Eventually, Stalin ended this period of experimenta-

> ### THEME MUSIC
> The Russian Revolution initially promoted women's rights (e.g., granting suffrage); however, the end of social experimentation after 1928 coincided with a harsher time for women. Take note of how revolution and total war in the first half of the twentieth century altered attitudes and practices toward women and other social groups (SCD), such as workers, peasants, and ethnic minorities (e.g., Jews).

tion, enforcing a cultural orthodoxy of socialist realism in the arts, celebrating factories and tractors, and reversing many of the provisions regarding women's equality.

Stalin versus Trotsky

Soon after the Russian Civil War, Lenin fell ill from a series of strokes. Behind the scenes, General Secretary **Josef Stalin** (1879–1953) and Leon Trotsky—a true intellectual force in socialism and the organizer of the Red Army—battled for control of the party. Trotsky condemned the NEP as a sellout to capitalism, calling for "permanent revolution" and protesting the bureaucratization of the communist party. Stalin proved the more organized and ruthless combatant. By controlling patronage in the CPSU and by wrapping himself in the mantle of Lenin, Stalin engineered Trotsky's dismissal from the party and then his exile. By 1928, Stalin had secured his absolute hold on power and moved to implement his plans to modernize the Soviet Union.

Results of WWI and the Russian Revolution

It would be difficult to overestimate the combined impact of the First World War and Russian Revolution on European and world history. In 1914, Europe stood at its zenith of power. Less than a decade later, total war and revolution had altered the global order. First, violent and extreme forces liberated by war and revolution would bear full fruit with the totalitarian movements of the 1920s and 1930s. Second, laissez-faire ideas regarding the economy were abandoned under pressure of the war effort, and the Versailles settlement laid the seeds for the Great Depression. Third, World War I and the Russian Revolution both radically altered diplomatic structures and destroyed the balance of power. Fourth, prewar cultural trends toward irrationality and alienation gained currency from a decade of upheaval, and dominated ideas during the interwar period. Though the Treaty of Versailles attempted to remake a stable world order, the task proved too much given the extreme circumstances facing Europe (and the world) in 1919. The twentieth century achieved its violent birth amid the chaos of the First World War and Russian Revolution.

Additional Resources

📖 Christopher Clark, *The Sleepwalkers: How Europe Went to War in 1914* (2014) — One of the more provocative books to emerge in the centennial year of WWI's onset.

📖 Sheila Fitzpatrick, *The Russian Revolution, 1917–1932*, 3/e (2003) — A concise and somewhat sympathetic analysis of the founding of the Soviet Union.

📖 Paul Fussell, *The Great War and Modern Memory* (2013) — One of the great nonfiction books, this volume explores how British writers interpreted their war experiences.

📖 Robert Gerwarth, *The Vanquished: Why the First World War Failed to End* (2017) — Upsets the western-centric bias of WWI by recounting the harrowing ethnic and revolutionary violence unleashed in central and eastern Europe after the war ended.

📖 Susan Grayzel, *Women and the First World War* (2002) — This brief volume provides a geographic scope of its topic along with useful sources and supplements.

📖 Margaret Macmillan, *Paris 1919: Six Months that Changed the World* (2003) — Provides strong global context for and evaluation of the most important treaty of the twentieth century.

📖 G.J. Meyer, *A World Undone: The Story of the Great War, 1914 to 1918* (2007) — Lengthy, but a pleasure to read, with vivid writing and engaging character profiles.

📖 John Mosier, *The Myth of the Great War: A New Military History of World War I* (2002) — The author argues that the German army fought most effectively, with only the United States saving the Allies. For military history aficionados.

📖 Theodore H. von Laue, *Why Lenin? Why Stalin? Why Gorbachev?: The Rise and Fall of the Soviet System*, 3/e (1998) — The author analyzes the continuities and difficulties of Russian history.

📖 Richard Pipes, *The Russian Revolution* (1990) **and** *Russia Under the Bolshevik Regime* (1994) — In these volumes, a former US diplomat provides an insightful but a critical view of the revolution.

📖 Erich Maria Remarque, *All Quiet on the Western Front* (1929) — This is the classic antiwar novel.

📖 Jay Winter, *The Experience of World War I* (1989) — Combining a wealth of text, special features, and maps, this coffee-table book presents the war from the perspectives of politicians, generals, soldiers, and civilians.

🎞 *The Great War and the Shaping of the Twentieth Century* (1998) — An outstanding BBC/PBS documentary focusing on the psychological impact of the Great War. Search online for various streaming options.

💻 http://www.firstworldwar.com/ — This excellent site offers interpretive essays, primary sources, and thousands of visuals.

💻 https://encyclopedia.1914–1918-online.net/home/ — An international encyclopedia offering feature articles and a variety of sources and maps.

CHAPTER TEST

Multiple-Choice Questions

Questions 1–4 are based on the map below.

Southeastern Europe, 1914

1. The map above depicts which of the following causes of the First World War?

   A. The increase in armaments and influence of military plans

   B. The growth of mass politics and power of nationalism

   C. Tensions in the Balkans that drew in the great powers

   D. Policies of *Realpolitik* that led to the emergence of new powers

2. The map reflects which of the following diplomatic issues of the period, 1850–1914?

   A. The unifications of Italy and Germany

   B. The competition for colonies

   C. Nationalist tensions within the Austrian Empire

   D. The decline of the Ottoman Empire

3. Contrasting the situation depicted in the map with the diplomacy of Europe in 1815, all of the following express major <u>differences</u> between the two situations EXCEPT the:

   A. Concert of Europe provided a mechanism for the great powers to avoid war.

   B. nationalist impulses created tensions and caused revolutionary upheaval.

   C. alliance system made it difficult for European powers to compromise in 1914.

   D. industrialization of warfare created potential for more destructive conflicts.

4. The event that caused the most significant change in the system of European alliances before 1914 was the:

   A. dismissal of Bismarck as German Chancellor in 1890.

   B. Berlin Conference over African imperialism, 1884–1885.

   C. British effort to subdue the Boer revolt, 1899–1902.

   D. defeat of Russia in the Russo-Japanese War, 1904–1905.

Questions 5–6 are based on the poem below.

"Does it matter?—losing your legs? …
For people will always be kind,
And you need not show that you mind
When the others come in after hunting
To gobble their muffins and eggs.
Does it matter?—losing your sight? …
There's such splendid work for the blind;
And people will always be kind,
As you sit on the terrace remembering
And turning your face to the light.
Do they matter?—those dreams from the pit? …
You can drink and forget and be glad,
And people won't say that you're mad;
For they'll know you've fought for your country
And no one will worry a bit."

Siegfried Sassoon, British WWI soldier and poet, "Does It Matter?," 1918

5. The poem above reflects most strongly how the First World War led to the:

   A. creation of a disillusioned and cynical lost generation.

   B. fall of traditional empires and creation of new republics.

   C. movement toward subjectivity and experimentation in the arts.

   D. economic problems of hyperinflation and high unemployment.

6. The style of the poem was most likely influenced by the:

   A. Renaissance emphasis on classics.

   B. Reformation concern with morality.

   C. Romantic preference for subjectivity.

   D. realist preference for truthful descriptions.

Questions 7–9 are based on the poster below.

Caption: "On the ruins of capitalism, let us walk towards fraternity:
farmers and workers are walking towards the peoples from all over the world"

Bolshevik propaganda poster, 1920

7. The poster reveals how the Russian Revolution was caused by:

   A. the incompetence of the tsarist government.

   B. discontent created by social inequality.

   C. incomplete industrialization and economic development.

   D. conflict among various revolutionary groups.

8. Given the historical context, the poster above was likely intended to:

   A. defeat the German army during World War I.

   B. overthrow the Provisional Government.

   C. collectivize Russian agriculture.

   D. help the Bolsheviks win the Russian civil war.

9. In <u>contradiction to the message of the poster</u>, the Soviet Union under Lenin in 1921:

   A. requisitioned grain and supplies from the peasants.

   B. adopted centralized planning to promote industrialization.

   C. adopted limited free-market ideas in the New Economic Policy.

   D. liquidated the wealthy kulak peasant class in the Ukraine.

See Chapter 18 for answers and explanations.

Long Essay Question

Directions: Read the prompt below and write your response on a separate sheet of paper. A sample response and commentary are included below.

Evaluate the most important cause of the First World War.

(RP: Causation)

LEQ Sample Response

After a long build-up of tensions, World War I was caused by the assassination of Franz Ferdinand, who was heir to the Austro-Hungarian empire. This produced a crisis that could not be resolved before all the great powers went to war. Many would argue that the "Great War" was caused by nationalism in the Balkans, but it was the alliance system that turned a regional dispute into a worldwide disaster.

The Balkans is a complex region of Europe, with many different ethnic groups and languages. Slavic languages and peoples dominate the region and had been ruled for centuries by the crumbling Ottoman Empire. As the Sick Man of Europe faded like an old photograph, the Slavic Russians moved in to lead the Slavic peoples there and seek their warm-weather port. However, the Austro-Hungarians controlled many of the Slavs and did not want them to establish strong independent nations, because then their Slavic groups, especially the Serbs, would want to join with them. This was shown in 1878, when a war in the region led to the creation of a few new states but also Austria's control of Bosnia, which the Serbs thought should be theirs. Later on, these new Balkan states attempted to gain more territory in the two Balkan Wars, which almost led to war when Austria and Germany stood firm in blocking Serbia's access to the sea.

This Balkan nationalism posed a big problem, but it would not have mattered that much without the alliance system. Without the two opposed alliances, the crises in the Balkans probably would have stayed between Austria and Russia. When Bismarck ran Germany, he focused on keeping the balance of power and isolating France. His alliance system was really complex, but that meant there weren't just two armed camps ready to defend their allies. However, when

Kaiser Wilhelm got rid of Bismarck in 1890, he decided to get Germany's "place in the sun" by building up the navy and getting colonies. His actions alienated Russia and Britain, who both joined with France in an alliance. Though Germany was allied with Italy, their only true ally was Austria. This meant that Germany depended on a weak nation with lots of nationalism problems. Germany was surrounded and feared losing its only ally, so when Austria took a hard line against Serbia in 1914, the Kaiser issued the "blank check." When Russia defended Serbia, this drew in Germany, France, and eventually Britain.

The situation of World War I can be compared to the French Revolution. Both events produced a great deal of violence and led to monumental changes afterwards. We are still living with these issues, as war and violence continue to play a large role in world politics.

LEQ Response Analysis

Here we have a strong yet incomplete essay, and one that demonstrates that content knowledge needs to be supplemented by awareness of the LEQ rubric. Though the response easily earns the Thesis point with a complex argument noting the tension between two causes, it did not provide enough specific background for the Contextualization point in the introduction. The student clearly conveys strong content knowledge, and more to the point, uses it effectively to analyze the causes of the First World War, earning both Use of Evidence points. Moreover, the response clearly earns the first Analysis and Reasoning point by employing causation to structure an argument (rather than merely narrating events). Even though the strategy in the conclusion fails to earn Complexity since it lacks explanation, the response had already established a complex argument throughout the essay by playing two possible causal factors off one another. With a clearer understanding of the rubric, this would have earned a top mark. **Score: 5** (+1 for Thesis, +2 for Use of Evidence, +1 for the Targeted RP (CAUS), +1 for Complexity)

❧ CHAPTER 15 ❧

Democracy, Totalitarianism, and the Second World War, 1919–1945

Europe struggled mightily to re-establish peace after the First World War. Though the continent had never before boasted so many democratic governments, in the next two decades, most of these new democracies crumbled under the onslaught of the Great Depression and the rise of totalitarian ideologies, such as fascism and communism. Nineteenth-century intellectual trends alongside the extreme circumstances of the First World War combined to produce the totalitarian movements. Dictators exploited new technologies of mass communication to mobilize their populations. At the same time, themes of alienation and disillusionment permeated high culture. Ultimately, Europe's inability to deal with the dual crises of economic depression and extreme political movements culminated in the most destructive conflict in history—the Second World War.

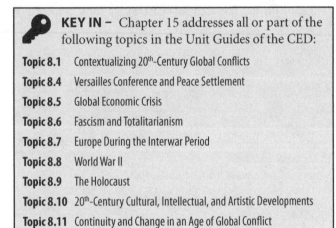

KEY IN – Chapter 15 addresses all or part of the following topics in the Unit Guides of the CED:

Topic 8.1 Contextualizing 20th-Century Global Conflicts

Topic 8.4 Versailles Conference and Peace Settlement

Topic 8.5 Global Economic Crisis

Topic 8.6 Fascism and Totalitarianism

Topic 8.7 Europe During the Interwar Period

Topic 8.8 World War II

Topic 8.9 The Holocaust

Topic 8.10 20th-Century Cultural, Intellectual, and Artistic Developments

Topic 8.11 Continuity and Change in an Age of Global Conflict

An Uncertain Peace: Enforcing the Treaty of Versailles

After the First World War, France attempted to enforce the Versailles settlement vigorously. This proved difficult without the active support of Great Britain and the United States—both isolationist in sentiment—and due to the Bolshevik Revolution, which eliminated Russia as a counterweight to a revived Germany. Many in Europe preferred to rely on the new **League of Nations** to ensure collective security. The League unfortunately lacked enforcement mechanisms as well as the membership of Germany, the Soviet Union, and the United States. For security, France turned to the less satisfactory alternative of allying with those new eastern European democracies sandwiched between Bolshevik Russia and a vengeful Germany. France's Little Entente with Yugoslavia, Czechoslovakia, and Romania proved no

substitute for France's recent WWI allies in balancing Germany. In 1922, when Germany agreed in the Rapallo Pact with the Soviet Union to supply it with manufactures and engage in joint military maneuvers, it signaled the potential danger to France's security system and to the position of the new eastern European democracies.

The Advance of Democracy in Eastern Europe

Europe enjoyed a general but short-lived trend toward democracy after the First World War. Women earned the right to vote in many nations, labor unions gained power, and governments enacted social legislation to benefit their citizens. An entire new region experienced democracy for the first time. In eastern Europe, the new nations of Czechoslovakia, Yugoslavia, Austria, Hungary, Poland, and the Baltic states emerged out of the former empires. Other than Czechoslovakia, none of these

<table>
<tr><td>

SKILL SET

It is easy to overlook the nations of eastern Europe. This section provides an important reminder to evaluate the political, diplomatic, and economic trends of the era against the experience of the new states created after the Versailles settlement. As you read, it is recommended that you think in terms of the changes and continuities (CCOT) in the situation of these nations from 1815 to 1945.
</td></tr>
</table>

new nations claimed a democratic tradition. Though these new states were formed around the notion of national self-determination, each confronted an ethnic minority problem (e.g., the presence of millions of ethnic Hungarians in Romanian Transylvania). More ominously, millions of ethnic Germans lived in Czechoslovakia and Poland.

Of greater concern to the new democracies, conservative interests opposed them as illegitimate, while extreme socialists worked toward their overthrow. The specter of Bolshevism hung over eastern Europe, as in 1919 when radical leader Béla Kun attempted to establish a Soviet regime in Hungary, before his ouster in 1920. Even the great social change in the region—land reform—failed to solve the problem of underdevelopment. The new democracies lacked the integrated economies they had experienced as part of former empires. Though peasants were confirmed in ownership of their small farms, the development of a middle class—the traditional basis for parliamentary democracy—lagged far behind western Europe. Other than Czechoslovakia, the new eastern European democracies proved to be thin reeds and toppled easily with the crisis of depression and the threat of dictatorship.

Germany's Failed Experiment with Democracy: The Weimar Republic

Germany's Weimar Republic began with two strikes against it. Born amidst the turmoil accompanying the end of the First World War, the republic faced a myriad of economic and political problems. Many influential Germans, particularly military officials, judges, and civil servants, opposed the new government as a weak substitute for imperial Germany. Extremists on both the left and the right attempted to overthrow the government in its first years of existence.

Two parties helped establish the republic and draw up its constitution—the Social Democratic Party (left-center) and the Catholic Center Party (right-center). The former had all but abandoned its Marxist rhetoric and seemed more concerned with advancing Germany's welfare system; both wished to avoid communist and rightist takeovers. In 1919, a Soviet-inspired communist movement, known as the Spartacists and led by Rosa Luxembourg and Karl Liebknecht, attempted an overthrow of the Berlin city government but were captured and executed by the *Freikorps*, a right-wing paramilitary group. Then in 1920, the *Freikorps* itself attempted a *coup d'etat* against Weimar known as the Kapp putsch. Only the intervention of the working class saved the republic from an early death. Political violence punctuated the short history of Weimar, as when Foreign Minister Walter Rathenau was assassinated in 1922 by two conservative army officers.

According to the Weimar constitution, delegates to the Reichstag (the popular branch of the parliament) were chosen by proportional representation, meaning that if a party received 10% of the vote, it would earn approximately 10% of the seats in the Reichstag. Though this allowed for a diversity of views, the system also made it difficult to establish stable majority governments and easier for extreme views to gain a political voice. Also, in times of "imminent danger," the president of the republic could suspend parliament and rule by decree. This so-called suicide clause (Article 48) provided a pretext for those who wished to undermine democratic rule.

Perhaps most damaging to Weimar was its association with the Versailles settlement. Even left-of-center Germans viewed the treaty as a *Diktat*, or dictated peace. Demagogues like Hitler perpetuated the myth that the German army stood on the verge of victory in 1918 when it was "stabbed in the back" by the "Jews, socialists, communists, and democrats" bent on establishing republican government at any price. No matter how untrue and unfair this charge, it allowed right-wing groups to scapegoat the Weimar Republic for Germany's problems. When this catalogue is added to the economic problems of reparations, hyperinflation, and the Great Depression, Weimar's failure is not difficult to understand.

Reparations, the Ruhr, and Hyperinflation

In 1923 the Weimar Republic fell behind on its reparations payments. In response, the French and Belgians invaded the industrial Ruhr Valley to extract the payments in the form of coal and steel. The result benefited neither France nor Germany. Weimar leaders encouraged workers to engage in a campaign of passive resistance and refuse to operate the factories and mines. This action required the Weimar Republic to pay the workers' benefits and wages in ever-increasing amounts of paper money. By November 1923, the German mark had plummeted to catastrophic levels. At the worst of this hyperinflation, $1 equaled 4 trillion marks! Overnight, middle-class savings, pensions, insurance policies, and interest income all become worthless. Confidence in the Weimar Republic plunged, emboldening **Adolf Hitler** (1889–1945) and his Nazi party to attempt to overthrow the Bavarian government with the Beer Hall putsch (1923). Though the coup failed, Hitler received only a 5-year sentence from a justice system always more lenient on right-wing than left-wing violence (of which he only served 264 days). While in prison, Hitler wrote his political testament, *Mein Kampf* (1924), which outlined his racial ideas and goals for Germany.

Great Britain and the United States criticized France for its provocative gesture. To defuse the situation, the US intervened economically. Because America's former allies claimed that they could not pay back loans to the United States without German reparations, the US extended loans to Germany and rescheduled the reparations payments in exchange for a French withdrawal of the Ruhr. Funds from this Dawes Plan aided a short-lived economic revival in Germany, while a new spirit of cooperation emerged from the French and Germans. However, the French learned an important lesson; its vigorous action brought down the government and earned it the criticism of allies fearful of another war.

The Spirit of Locarno

The period 1924–1929 produced optimistic hopes of peace and prosperity. Moderate leaders emerged in the principal nations who were dedicated to resolving disputes through negotiation and diplomacy, most importantly Gustav Stresemann (1878–1929) of Germany and Aristide Briand (1862–1932) of France. In 1925, these two leaders engineered the Locarno Pact, which contemporaries considered the true end to the First World War. Germany recognized its west-

> **THEME MUSIC & SKILL SET**
>
> In this section, we address the factors explaining the failure of democratic governments, especially the Weimar Republic, whose failure held profound consequences for Europe's future. Americans may take for granted how natural democracy seems, but if you consult the SOP theme, you'll realize the struggles many states have experienced along the road to or even away from democracy. When finished with the chapter, consider writing a focused paragraph explaining how and why democracy faltered during the interwar period (ARG and CES).

ern borders as permanent (accepting the loss of Alsace-Lorraine) and agreed to revise its eastern borders with Poland and Czechoslovakia only by common agreement. As a result, Germany was allowed to enter the League of Nations in 1926. The "spirit of Locarno" culminated with the Kellogg-Briand Pact of 1928, by which the 65 signatory nations condemned war as an instrument of international politics.

Like the Kellogg-Briand Pact, the League of Nations lacked the means to enforce its decisions. When Japan invaded Manchuria in 1931 and Italy invaded Ethiopia in 1935, the League made rhetorical protests and contemplated sanctions, but took few concrete actions to punish the aggressors. Such diplomacy left underlying issues unresolved and lulled some nations into adopting isolationist policies in deference to the League. In 1930, France began work on a set of defensive fortifications along the German border known as the Maginot Line, a term that symbolizes a false notion of security behind an imaginary strong frontier.

The Great Depression

Causes

The First World War and Treaty of Versailles sowed the seeds of the Great Depression. Before 1914, economic activity had become increasingly global, meaning that disturbance in one region transmitted quickly to other regions. During the brief period of international stability, 1924–1929, the world economy was marked by prosperity, especially in new sectors such as automobiles, household appliances, and communications. This prosperity proved shallow, however, and was hindered by the following factors:

- *Strong inflationary pressures* – During the First World War, governments engaged in rationing and borrowed money at record rates. In addition, most states depreciated their currencies in an effort to reduce their debt. Inflation complicated the return to a peacetime economy and wreaked havoc on the world system of stable currencies existing before 1914.

- ***Disrupted trade patterns*** – While Europe fought World War I, competitors moved into its global markets. For example, India developed its own textile industry and showed less interest in British imports following the war. North America and Australia established themselves as major exporters of grain. When the war ended, European nations found it difficult to reestablish former trade patterns.

- *Agricultural depression* – A glut of grain worldwide drove down prices and left many farmers bankrupt or destitute.

- ***Economic nationalism*** – To protect fragile domestic markets and head off unrest, most states enacted high tariff barriers. The United States, in particular, refused to replace Great Britain as financial world leader; rather than lower tariffs to allow Germany to accumulate capital from trade and thus pay off reparations, the United States enacted some of its highest barriers ever.

- ***Reparations*** – The cycle of world capital flowed from the United States to Germany, then from Germany to France and Britain, and finally back to the United States. This unnatural arrangement disrupted investment, while making world economic activity unusually **reliant on American financial conditions**.

- *Credit financing* – The advent of the installment plan allowed consumers to defer payment on purchases. In addition, those who invested in the ballooning American stock market purchased their shares "on margin," by borrowing up to 90% of the stock's value. Any small economic downturn threatened to burst this speculative bubble.

When the United States **stock market crashed** in October 1929, it triggered the components of the above trap into place, causing a downward economic spiral.

Effects

Europe had experienced economic cycles throughout its history, but nothing compared with the Great Depression of the 1930s for length and depth of contraction. Stock values plunged from 1929 to 1932 as businesses cut back production and laid off workers. Investment and world trade plummeted. Unemployment reached shocking proportions, strengthening those parties who promised extreme solutions to problems. Germany and the Unites States were hardest hit; as many as 35% of workers were idled in both nations. Due to the unstable credit situation, the stock market crash rippled throughout the financial world, causing global bank failures. In 1931 the failure of the leading Vienna bank, the *Creditanstalt*, dominoed further financial collapses.

Most nations experienced a drain on their treasuries to meet debt obligations. Currency values depreciated even further, wrecking the stable gold-backed system dating from the mid-nineteenth century. Investors lost confidence in the British pound, causing a massive sell-off. Long the world financial leader, Great Britain was forced off the gold standard in 1931, followed soon after by the United States and the rest of the industrialized world. In many cases, trade reverted to bilateral agreements and even barter, wherein one nation would exchange goods directly with another. Such arrangements hindered world trade and made it difficult for nations to obtain necessary products and to earn income from exports.

THEME MUSIC
The Great Depression revealed the fragility of the post-WWI settlement. Also, the Depression represents a critical moment in the ECD theme, in that it changed the relationship between the government and economy and laid the foundations for the modern welfare state.

Democratic Responses

The Great Depression created a crisis for democratic governments. Economy orthodoxy seemed impotent in addressing the downward spiral. According to Liberal economic theory, in times of depression states should pursue austerity much like individual families: cut the budget and raise taxes. However, these policies failed to stimulate production and increased the misery of the unemployed. British economist John Maynard Keynes (1883–1946) introduced an alternate approach to economic stimulation in his *General Theory of Employment, Interest, and Money* (1936). Contrary to accepted wisdom, Keynes argued that governments needed to "prime the pump" through deficit financing, by cutting taxes and spending on government programs to aid the needy. Though few nations consistently followed such policies before the Second World War, Keynesian economics emerged as the new orthodoxy after 1945. On the AP exam, questions tend to focus on the general structure of the economy during this period; however, the following brief review of responses by the democratic states illustrates the depth of the crisis:

Great Britain: Of all the industrial nations, Great Britain relied most on trade. The First World War and Great Depression both struck blows against Britain's dominant position. Welfare legislation enacted before the war had eased some of the burden on the unemployed. Despite the negative economic conditions, workers were reluctant to surrender gains made in wartime. Conflicts between labor and industry led in 1926 to a General Strike, which was eventually suppressed by government intervention. Politically, the Labour Party replaced the Liberal Party and, after gaining power in 1924 and again in 1929, aimed to extend the rights of workers. In 1931, former Labour Prime Minister Ramsay MacDonald (1866–1937) joined with Conservatives in a National Government that attempted to reduce the budget deficit through traditional retrenchment. To address imperial issues, Britain granted autonomy to Egypt and the Irish Free State in 1922, and in 1931 formalized relations with former colonies such as Canada, Australia, New Zealand, and South Africa by granting dominion status. The combined problems of economic stagnation, diminished world status, and political tensions placed Britain in a weakened position to confront Nazi aggression.

France: France escaped some of the worst effects of the Great Depression. Less dependent on trade than Britain, France was not as hard hit by the world downturn. In addition, the nation succeeded in stabilizing the franc at a fraction of its prewar level, making French exports cheaper on the world market. Amid the growth of right-wing and fascist groups, a coalition of left-wing parties, called the Popular Front, held power briefly from 1936 to 1938 and enacted a series of significant reforms—the 40-hour workweek, paid vacations, and stronger collective bargaining rights for unions. Socialist Prime Minister Léon Blum's (1872–1950) government eventually fell victim to heightening ideological tensions, particularly after the outbreak of the Spanish Civil War. However, France preserved its republican government for the time being and enacted legislation that still benefits French workers today.

United States: Under President Franklin Roosevelt (1882–1945), the United States initiated a wide-ranging but somewhat haphazard program of relief, recovery, and reform. The New Deal began with a flurry of legislation in 1933 providing subsidies for farmers, public works jobs through the Civilian Conservation Corps (CCC), and market regulation by the National Recovery Administration (NRA). Congress created numerous "alphabet" agencies to regulate the stock market and the banking industry, provide jobs, and address environmental issues. Later, Roosevelt turned to reform. The Social Security Act (1935), for example, provided unemployment, disability, and old-age insurance. Though these acts provided relief, unemployment spiked again in 1937–1938. It would take the Second World War for the United States to recover fully from the Great Depression.

Scandinavia: The Scandinavian nations of Norway, Sweden, and Denmark demonstrated how governments could effectively combine elements of socialism and democracy. These states enacted the most wide-ranging social welfare programs to curb the worst effects of the Great Depression. Additionally, Scandinavian nations most eagerly embraced creative and Keynesian approaches, such as producers' cooperatives to regulate the price of agricultural products and state ownership of key industries.

Totalitarianism

Totalitarianism represents a political phenomenon of the interwar period, yet it also claims roots in the pre-1914 period. Mass politics and intellectual trends after 1870 fueled the development of irrational ideologies. You may recall the growth of political anti-Semitism, anarchism's glorification of violence, and the rabid nationalism associated with imperialism. In addition, Darwinian evolution emphasized the importance of struggle, a notion taken up by racists and extremists to justify domination of the "weaker." During the First World War, states grew significantly in their powers of regimentation and mobilization, employing propaganda to control public opinion. Communication advances in the interwar period, such as radio and motion pictures, provided additional means for controlling the populace.

Dictatorship was not new to Europe, so how can we distinguish totalitarianism from the absolutism of the seventeenth and eighteenth centuries? Absolute monarchs like Louis XIV derived their legitimacy from traditional dynastic and aristocratic institutions, and they extended their power to those areas deemed essential to the state's interest, such as trade, taxes, and religion. Even then, geographic and customary obstacles hindered centralization. Totalitarian dictators exploited mass media to mobilize the public to fanatical support of the movement, not merely passive obedience, as absolute monarchs had accepted. Twentieth-century dictators aimed at total control of society; any independent civic or social life must be subordinated to the party, movement, and leader. Modern communications allowed for such control but also increased the potential for catastrophic violence, as would be clear during the Second World War.

Fascism on the March

Fascist Ideology

The traumas of the interwar era provided fertile ground for the European and even world phenomenon of fascism. For many, fascism provided a third way between faltering Liberal democracies and revolutionary, class-based Marxism. With its origins in nineteenth-century irrational ideologies but feeding on the unstable conditions of the 1920s and 1930s, fascism posed a genuine threat to supplant democracy as the wave of the future. Before turning to the Italian variant of fascism, the following list may prove helpful in understanding the nature of fascist ideology:

- **Militarism** – Fascists extolled war as the proving ground of national identity and for sorting out the hierarchy of nations.

- *Glorification of the state* – Not only was the state seen as all-powerful, it also represented the culminating force in historical evolution.

- *Führer principle* – German for "leader," the Führer principle stated that the voice of the people reached its highest expression not in assemblies or representation, but in a single **charismatic leader**—for example, Mussolini or Hitler.

- **Anti-democracy** – Fascists scorned the weakness of democratic mechanisms of government and argued that the national spirit cannot be expressed through such institutions.

- **Anti-communism** – Though communists and fascists shared many tactics, fascists condemned class warfare and upheld the centrality of racial and national identity, in contrast to communists who condemned racism and nationalism.

> ### SKILL SET & THEME MUSIC
>
> Totalitarian governments represent, on one hand, the culmination of the trend toward mass politics since the French Revolution, and on the other, a unique manifestation of the extreme conditions existing during the interwar period (SOP). The entire twentieth century might be viewed as a three-sided struggle among Liberal democracy, communism, and fascism—each representing a specific conception of legitimate government and manner of expressing popular will. If you consider the historical context (CTX), perhaps you can explain how and why totalitarian governments differed from absolute monarchies of the seventeenth and eighteenth centuries (COMP and CCOT).

- *One-party rule* – In fascist states, democratic mechanisms such as elections, multiparty systems, and the free press were suppressed.

The Rise of Fascism in Italy

Italy came out of the First World War as a victor, but in name only. Right-wing nationalists condemned the Versailles settlement for depriving Italians of "unredeemed" lands from Austria and the new nation of Yugoslavia. To make matters worse, the Italian economy suffered under the weight of unemployment, inflation, and high budget deficits. Workers engaged in numerous strikes, often fanned by extremist groups hoping to institute a socialist state. Already low before the war, respect for Italy's parliamentary democracy sank further.

Into this atmosphere strode **Benito Mussolini** (1883–1945) and his fascists (after the Latin *fasces*, or bundle of sticks carried by ancient Roman officials to symbolize state power). Named for a Mexican revolutionary, Mussolini began as a left-wing journalist but moved rightward with the outbreak of World War I. Influenced by the writings of Sorel and Nietzsche regarding the irrational, Mussolini glorified the state and violence as a means of combating Italy's perceived enemies. To gain power, Mussolini relied on the paramilitary *squadristi* (or Blackshirts), to intimidate political opponents and subvert the parliamentary order. Though the Fascist movement won only a small percentage of parliamentary seats in the 1921 election, Mussolini continued to gain adherents, who ironically saw him as a champion of law and order against the threat from the left. By 1922, Mussolini decided the moment had arrived for his movement to seize power. In October of that year, thousands of fascists converged on the capital to intimidate the king into appointing Mussolini as head of government. The so-called March on Rome convinced Victor Emmanuel III to name Mussolini as premier.

The Italian Fascist State under Mussolini

Mussolini moved quickly to exploit the emergency powers he was granted to cement his hold on the government. To ensure a functioning majority, the parliament passed an amendment that granted two-thirds of the seats to the party gaining the most votes in elections. With help from this law and the tactics of the *squadristi*, the fascists in 1924 gained control of the parliament. Soon after the election, a respected Socialist deputy, Giacomo Matteotti, was assassinated by fascist thugs for exposing corruption and violence within the government. Public outrage demanded the resignation of Mussolini, who, cynically, manipulated the incident toward consolidating his hold on power.

By 1926, fascism had censored the press, eliminated all opposition parties, and employed a secret police, the OVRA, to ferret out dissent. In keeping with fascist ideology, Mussolini condemned laissez-faire capitalism, democracy, and

Marxist appeals to class. National solidarity and glory, symbolized by Mussolini himself (called *Il Duce*—the leader), replaced a pluralistic society. In economic affairs, Mussolini introduced corporatism, in which the economy was run as 22 separate corporations, with representatives from business, fascist-organized labor unions, and the state. State interest dictated actual policy and production priorities, though private property and profit were allowed.

In social and cultural life, the fascists worked to orient the lives of Italians around the state. To end the conflict with the Catholic Church dating from 1870, Mussolini signed the Lateran Accord in 1929, which recognized the sovereignty of the church over the Vatican in exchange for the papacy's promise not to interfere with the functions of the state. To address Italy's declining birthrate, Mussolini provided incentives for larger families, gave awards for fertile mothers, and created holidays to honor motherhood. In a fascist state, women were clearly to play the domestic role of rearing strong children for the state. A healthy race demanded a regimen of physical fitness. Schools required calisthenics, and the government sponsored recreational and outdoor activities through the state-sponsored *Dopolavoro*.

The fascist corporate state never fully solved the Great Depression. Mussolini turned to a program of public works to provide jobs—swamps were cleared, roads built, and self-sufficiency in wheat and power was attempted. Though it was said that Mussolini "made the trains run on time," he was forced increasingly after 1935 to engage in imperialist adventures to revive support for his flagging movement. Despite fascist efforts, Italy was never able to realize the totalitarian state to the degree of Nazi Germany or Stalinist Soviet Union.

Nazi Germany

Hitler and the Rise to Power

Perhaps no political movement in history is associated more with a single person than Nazism and Adolf Hitler. Hitler came from a lower-middle-class Austrian family of unremarkable circumstances. The young Hitler moved to Vienna to pursue his artistic aspirations. After failing entrance to the Viennese art academy, Hitler survived by selling watercolors and postcards. While in Vienna, Hitler absorbed the anti-Semitism of its mayor, Karl Lueger, and grew to hate the "mongrel" Habsburg Empire with its ethnic diversity and aristocratic airs. To avoid being drafted into the Austrian army at the outset of World War I, Hitler crossed the border into Bavaria and enlisted in the German army. The young corporal served with distinction at the front as a message runner, and ended the war in a hospital, the victim of a poison gas attack, when he heard the news of the armistice. Hitler believed his war experience to be the the most significant of his life and joined a military-style political group in 1920 known as the National Socialist German Workers'

Party (NSDAP), later known as National Socialists, or simply **Nazis**. The ragtag group of political misfits soon recognized the spellbinding quality of Hitler's oratory and made him their leader.

After the failed Beer Hall putsch of 1923, Hitler and the Nazis focused on a legality strategy of exploiting parliamentary politics to create a mass movement capable of taking power when democracy collapsed. The Nazi message was simple: Weimar represented rule by the worst—democrats, socialists, Jews—and Germany needed a strong national state based on race. As Hitler laid it out in *Mein Kampf*, Germany required *Lebensraum* (living space) in the east, as part of a new European order constructed around a racial hierarchy. At every opportunity, Hitler blamed Germany's problems on the Treaty of Versailles and pledged to restore German honor. Members of the S.A. (Brownshirts or Stormtroopers) provoked street fights with rival political groups, yet received lenient treatment from sympathetic officials and judges. Initially, the Nazis pitched their message to workers but gained little support, earning less than 3% of the vote in 1928. Two developments caused a turnaround in Nazi fortunes: (1) the Great Depression and (2) a switch in Nazi tactics to appeal to the middle class.

The Nazis used modern electoral tactics to gain support. Nazi party leaders gave speeches tailored to specific audiences and portrayed themselves as the party of the young and dynamic. Hitler made effective use of modern technologies, as with the Hitler over Germany campaign, in which he visited 50 cities in 15 days via airplane. By 1932, the Nazi vote total had increased to 37%, winning 230 seats in the Reichstag and making it the largest party. As early as 1930, the Weimar Republic survived on life support, with the chancellor ruling by decree. Some old-line conservatives believed Hitler represented the best hope to defeat communism and restore order in Germany. Intriguers behind President Hindenburg convinced the aged and perhaps senile leader to appoint Hitler chancellor in January 1933. It was believed that Hitler could be controlled by other members of the cabinet, certainly one of the most egregious miscalculations in political history.

> **EXAMPLE BASE**
>
> Among the specific examples in this section, try to deploy them toward explaining the nature and manner of totalitarianism and to test whether these regimes actually realized the degree of control claimed by the theory (CES).

The Nazi Total State

It did not take long for Hitler to consolidate his power. Soon after his appointment, the parliament building caught fire. The Nazis blamed the Reichstag fire on the Communist Party, which they banned as illegal, and arrested its leaders. In an atmosphere of manufactured crisis, the Nazis rammed through the Reichstag an amendment allowing Hitler to rule by decree for five years. This Enabling Act essentially made Hitler a dictator, and it was followed by the 1933 Civil Service Act, requiring all government employees to swear a personal oath of loyalty to the Führer.

In 1934, Hitler removed the last obstacles to his power. First, all parties but National Socialism were declared illegal. All federal governments, such as Bavaria or Saxony, were eliminated in favor of a unitary state. To win over the army high command, Hitler agreed in June 1934 to purge the leadership of the S.A., grown to 500,000 men and perceived as a threat to the army's monopoly of military force. With Hitler in power, the S.A. was no longer deemed necessary, and its leader, Ernst Röhm (1887–1934), represented one of the last potential challenges to Hitler's unquestioned leadership of the party. On the night of June 30, 1934, top leaders of the Brownshirts, in addition to numerous other political opponents, were summarily executed in what became known as the Blood Purge. When President Hindenburg died 2 months later, Hitler assumed the position of president.

Nazi rule wielded terror as an elemental weapon. Internally, a secret police, the Gestapo, arrested real and imagined opponents, interning thousands to a constellation of concentration camps. Following the S.A. purge, the S.S. (*Schutzstaffel*) emerged as the primary perpetrators of terror, eventually absorbing control of the Gestapo, running the death camps, and forming the leading edge of a new Aryan racial elite. Another ingredient of the total state involved coordinating all independent social and civic organizations—charities, youth groups, unions—into Nazi organizations. Though only one-tenth of Germans belonged to the Nazi Party, all social activity was to be geared around the state and its goals. The Nazi Party also promoted loyalty through **propaganda**, such as the annual Nuremberg rallies, a spectacle of pageantry and regimentation captured effectively in the film *Triumph of the Will*.

To solve Germany's economic problems, the Nazis attempted to spend Germany out of the Depression with public works projects and rearmament. By 1936, the Nazis had developed a Four-Year Plan to promote the goal of self-sufficiency (autarky) in strategic commodities such as fuels and rubber. Hitler won over industrialists with the promise of government contracts for rearmament and eliminating the perceived socialist threat. In addition, the independent labor unions of the Social Democratic Party were replaced by the National Labor Front, a state-run union requiring each worker in good standing to carry a booklet in order to procure a job. With projects like the Autobahn, many Germans credited Hitler with getting Germany back to work, even if his pump-priming did not represent a long-term solution to Germany's problems.

Nazi racial policy touched all areas of life. Boys were enrolled in the Hitler Youth and girls in the League of German Maidens to reinforce traditional gender roles and build a strong racial stock. Women were expected to fulfill the domestic duties of "church, kitchen, and children," while their public and economic roles were limited by the state. Anti-Semitic policies reflected the Nazi racial vision. At first, Jews were excluded from the civil service and army. To codify the position of Jews in Germany, the Nazis passed the Nuremberg Laws of 1935, which defined who was a Jew, stripped Jews of citizenship, and prohibited sexual relations between Aryans and Jews. Many Jews preferred to remain in Germany, hoping to ride out the Nazi tide. However, Nazi policies turned violent with the *Kristallnacht* (Night of Broken Glass) of November 1938, in which synagogues were burned, businesses destroyed, and hundreds of Jews killed or arrested. To further the goal of racial purity, the Nazis also engaged in campaigns of sterilization for the mentally unfit and euthanasia for the terminally ill, insane, and physically deformed. This so-called T-4 program killed approximately 200,000 German citizens between 1939 and 1941 before protests by religious groups slowed and eventually halted it. For the attentive, the genocidal program laid out in *Mein Kampf* was apparent *before* the onset of World War II.

The Soviet Union under Stalin, 1928–1939

In the 10-year period 1928–1938, the Soviet Union under Stalin experienced one of the most rapid modernizations in history. After expelling Trotsky, Stalin ended the **New Economic Policy** (NEP; see chapter 14) and began building "socialism in one country." It was clear by 1928 that world revolution was not imminent, and Stalin, wishing to push forward the Soviet Union's industrialization as rapidly as possible, appropriated Trotsky's ideas regarding strong central planning to accomplish it. As Stalin saw it, "We are fifty or a hundred years behind the advanced countries. We must make good this distance in ten years. Either we do it, or we shall be crushed."

To move forward, Stalin instituted the first of several Five-Year Plans in 1928. Its goals were to build a strong base of heavy industry, aim for self-sufficiency, and create a modern infrastructure of electricity, roads, and factories. Overseeing intricate details of production and resource allocation was Gosplan, a central government agency staffed by thousands of party bureaucrats. Because the Bolsheviks had repudiated tsarist debt and could thus not draw on foreign capital, funds for industrialization had to come from the agricultural sector. During the NEP, a class of wealthy peasants arose, who accumulated land and often hired labor among the landless. These **kulaks** were resented by many among the poor. To absorb the excess capital of the kulaks, Stalin forced them and all peasants onto collective farms. The kulaks resisted the forced collectivization of agriculture, often by destroying crops and slaughtering livestock. By 1932 almost all peasants lived on collective farms, but the cost proved high— millions of kulaks were killed for resisting collectivization, and millions more died in the **famine** that ensued in Russia and Ukraine from the disruption in agriculture.

By some measures, the Five-Year Plans proved remarkably successful. The Soviet Union avoided the economic contraction of the Great Depression and soon became the world's largest producer of tractors and railway locomotives. Overall, only the United States and Germany surpassed the Soviet Union in productive capacity. Soviet authorities extolled socialist heroes like the miner Alexey Stakhanov, who exceeded his quota for coal by 1300%. However, many Soviet manufactures were of poor quality, and consumer goods lagged far behind. Indeed, the exponential growth in the Soviet economy is explained partly by its start from such a low level.

Stalin imposed a rigid totalitarian system on the Soviet Union. Independent political parties, labor unions, and free expression were eliminated. Government controlled cultural life—art, literature, film—for **propaganda** purposes. The cultural experimentation of the 1920s came to a harsh end; socialist realism, glorifying factories and workers, became the accepted standard. Huge posters of Stalin adorned factories and street corners as part of a cult of personality. To rid himself of real or potential enemies, Stalin initiated the Great Purges. Aimed at the Old Bolsheviks, the purges ultimately eliminated "leftists" who supported Trotsky, now in exile in Mexico, and "rightists" charged with supporting capitalism. During the Great Terror, from 1934 to 1938, it is estimated that almost 4 million people were charged with crimes against the state, and close to 800,000 were executed. Though Soviet citizens experienced an improved basic standard of living, it was earned at a high cost. Ethnic minorities and perceived opponents, for example, filled Siberian gulags, or hard-labor camps. Women, also, found that many of the reproductive rights gained in the 1920s were reversed as part of a campaign to increase the birth rate, forcing them to do double-duty with factory work and family chores. Regimentation of Soviet social life came as the by-product of its astounding economic successes.

The Culture of the Interwar Period

Cultural developments from 1918 to 1939 reflected two distinct trends: (1) the disillusioning effects of the First World War in high culture and (2) the further development of a truly mass culture based on new communications technologies. We address both of these areas in turn.

Experimentation and Alienation in High Culture

The writers, artists, and intellectuals who came of age during the First World War became known as the **Lost Generation**. The experience of war reinforced the prewar trends of **irrationality**, **subjectivity**, and alienation. German historian Oswald Spengler (1880–1936) reflected this sense of pessimism in his book *The Decline of the West*, which argued that Europe's golden age was nearing its end due to a tendency toward self-destructive acts and was fated for eclipse by other civilizations. Writers of fiction worked in similar themes. Franz Kafka (1883–1924) described characters caught up in an incomprehensible world with no capacity to alter their fates. In one of the great anti-war novels, Erich Maria Remarque's (1898–1970) *All Quiet on the Western Front* matter-of-factly depicted how war destroys innocence and meaning. T.S. Eliot's epic poem "The Waste Land" (1922) captured a similar sense of **cynicism** and the absurdity of human existence.

Many writers experimented with stream-of-consciousness styles and unstructured works to convey the subjective nature of experience. Marcel Proust's *Remembrance of Things Past* explores the narrator's memories of childhood experiences amid a half-waking state. James Joyce's *Ulysses* stands as the masterwork of modernist literature, examining one day in the life of Dublin resident Stephen Dedalus through mental associations and word play. Virginia Woolf experimented with similar techniques but combined them with feminist themes. Expatriates (those who live outside their culture or nation) from the United States—Ernest Hemingway, F. Scott Fitzgerald, and Gertrude Stein—worked in similar styles and themes while demonstrating the growing influence of American culture as well as the profound sense of alienation in the western world as a whole.

> **SKILL SET**
>
> As during the Enlightenment, elite and popular culture diverged strongly in the interwar period. Identify the themes and focus for both high and popular culture (COMP) and be prepared to explain how each reveals the mood and developments of the 1920s and 1930s (DAP and CTX).

Modern art branched out into diverse realms during the twentieth century. Weimar Germany, and Berlin in particular, became a center of experimentation in the arts; in painting, German artists such as George Grosz and Hannah Hoch employed expressionist and Dadaist techniques to critique the perceived weakness and corruption of Weimar. An anti-art movement, Dadaism used artistic media to convey the absurdity of life. Examples include collages of disconnected images or distorted caricatures. Abstraction reduces reality down to its essentials—line, shape, and color. In the massive mural *Guernica* (1937), Pablo Picasso depicts the horror of a fascist atrocity during the Spanish Civil War through the spare use of symbols and Cubist multiple perspectives. Furthermore, Freud's ideas regarding the unconscious influenced painting through the artistic movement of surrealism. Spanish surrealist Salvador Dali (1904–1989) gained fame for his bizarre juxtaposition of objects and dreamy landscapes, as in his ubiquitous *The Persistence of Memory* (1931). In architecture, modernists from the German Bauhaus school worked with concrete, steel, and glass to design straightforward "boxes with windows." When the Nazis took power in 1933, they condemned the works of such architects and other artists as degenerate and drove them out of the country.

The sciences and the social sciences confirmed prewar trends toward the irrational and the uncertain. In *Civilization and Its Discontents* (1931), **Sigmund Freud** argued that aggressive human drives inevitably culminate in violence and war, an observation given credence by the First World War. Building on Freud's ideas, Swiss psychiatrist Carl Jung (1875–1961) developed the notion of the collective unconscious, the part of a person's psyche common to all human beings and made up of archetypes, basic character patterns comprising all human experience. Physicists continued to explore the structure of the subatomic world and time. Werner Heisenberg (1901–1976) demonstrated with his **uncertainty principle** how a subject could not observe *both* the position and momentum of a particle, as the act of observation itself alters the behavior of what is observed. Heisenberg's theory supported the quantum notion of probabilities over objectively determined realities.

Mass Culture and Leisure

The experience of shared suffering during World War I provoked a shift in public morals. During the Roaring Twenties, displays of sexuality grew more blatant, women smoked in public, and dance halls gained popularity. Fashion challenged traditional gender roles, as women wore less defining and more revealing clothing. In many European states, laws against the distribution of birth control were abandoned. Germany's Cabaret culture featured sultry jazz music along with frank themes of sexuality. African-American Josephine Baker took Europe by storm with exotic and erotic dance routines. These developments divided Europeans between those who celebrated the new openness as part of a general democratization and those who condemned it as a decadent feature of post-WWI society.

During the prosperous 1920s, many businesses developed installment plans and allowed buying on credit. Advertising, often using celebrities and sports figures, fed a new **consumerism** in household appliances, beauty aids, and automobiles. Governments openly encouraged the purchase of radios and attendance at motion pictures. New communication technologies offered opportunities to shape public opinion and promote propaganda. Nazi Germany ensured that all citizens owned a radio so as to hear Hitler's speeches. Minister of Propaganda Joseph Goebbels (1897–1945) elevated visual spectacle to new heights in Nazi films and festivals. Democratic states also recognized the potential of mass communication; in 1927, the British Broadcasting Corporation (BBC) was chartered. Ironically, filmmakers like Charlie Chaplin with *Modern Times* (1936) and Fritz Lang with *Metropolis* (1927) used the medium to critique the modern obsession with technology.

With increased leisure time, Europeans participated in more air travel and tourism. Totalitarian states encouraged such activities around state-run agencies, such as *Kraft durch Freude* (Strength through Joy) in Nazi Germany, which sponsored camping, hiking, and boating trips. In tune with racial ideologies and eugenics, governments promoted a "cult of the body" through organized sports, such as gymnastics, soccer, and track and field. Nazi Germany hosted the 1936 Berlin Olympics as a showplace for the superiority of the Aryan race. Though Germany did win the most medals, African-American track star Jesse Owens stole the show with four gold medals.

The Road to the Second World War, 1933–1939: Appeasement

Though historians still debate the causes of the First World War, those of World War II lack controversy—the ambitions of Nazi Germany to overturn the Versailles settlement. Every year after taking power until the commencement of hostilities in 1939, Adolf Hitler provoked an international crisis related to his goals of creating a New European Order around race. Hitler sought first to regain those lands lost at Versailles; second, to subdue France and bring Britain to friendly terms; third, to turn east and conquer Slavic Europe and use it as a vast granary and slave labor force; and finally, in the process, to eliminate "culture destroyers" such as Jews and Gypsies. That Hitler almost accomplished these goals demonstrates the fragility of the post-WWI diplomatic order.

To avoid another war, the western democracies engaged in **appeasement**, or an attempt to meet Hitler's demands through diplomacy. Today, the term suggests cowardice and folly, but at the time was driven by several concerns: (1) lack of military preparedness due to budget constraints created by the Great Depression, (2) fear of Soviet communism, and (3) the genuine feeling that the horrors of Verdun and the Somme must not be repeated. The following chronology serves to demonstrate the evolution of Hitler's goals and tactics, as well as the application and eventual abandonment of appeasement. Without the active diplomatic support of the Soviet Union (due to its exclusion) and the United States (due to its **isolation**), the faltering system of collective security failed to deter Hitler and Mussolini, not to mention the Japanese. What follows is a timeline of events leading up to the Second World War:

1931: In pursuit of natural resources, Japan invades China's Manchuria province. Rhetorical denunciations by the League of Nations provoke Japan's withdrawal from that body.

1933: Hitler withdraws Germany from the League of Nations and Geneva disarmament conference, primarily to consolidate domestic support for his regime.

1935: Hitler openly repudiates the Versailles provisions related to demilitarization. Great Britain rewards Germany's rearmament with a naval agreement, allowing Hitler to build up his navy.

To avenge Italy's defeat in 1896, Mussolini invades Ethiopia without provocation. In a failure of collective security, Britain and France's half-hearted economic sanctions and military actions fail to prevent Italy's conquest of Ethiopia.

1936: Rejecting Versailles and the Locarno Pact, Hitler boldly remilitarizes the Rhineland. France and Britain do nothing in response, convincing Hitler of their weakness.

Since 1931, Spain had been ruled by a republic. The republican government moved against the entrenched power of the Catholic Church and large landowners. Elections in 1936 lead to the creation of a Popular Front of leftist parties aimed against monarchists, clerical supporters, and army officers. Military officers, led by **General Francisco Franco** (1892–1975) and aided by the fascist Falange movement, attempt to overthrow the republic, plunging the nation into a vicious civil war between Nationalists and Loyalists. The **Spanish Civil War** (1936–1939) becomes a test of rival ideological forces—fascism vs. communism—and a warm-up for World War II. Other than a few idealists from the democracies, the only nation willing to commit significant resources for the anti-fascist battle is the Soviet Union. Fascist forces launch aerial bombardments aimed at civilians in Madrid, Barcelona, and Guernica, a preview of the horrors to come. By 1939, Franco gains control of the nation, but only at the cost of 600,000 lives—Spain's deadliest conflict.

In the wake of the Spanish Civil War, Hitler signs the Rome-Berlin Axis with Mussolini and the Anti-Comintern Pact with Japan.

1937: In a secret meeting with his military advisors, Hitler outlines his future plans for the absorption of Austria, Czechoslovakia, and Poland into the German Reich. Those opposing Hitler's plans are replaced with Nazi yes-men.

Japan launches an all-out invasion of China proper, leading to its control of China's coastal cities. Though Chinese troops move inland to continue the fight, Japanese forces capture Nanking, in the process indiscriminately killing 250,000 civilians and raping thousands of women in an atrocity known as the Nanjing Massacre.

1938: With Mussolini's approval, Hitler marches into his native Austria, directly incorporating it into the German Reich. In a subsequent plebiscite, the Austrian people overwhelmingly approve the annexation (*Anschluss*).

Hitler demands incorporation of 3 million Germans of the Czech Sudetenland. Czechoslovakia represents the most democratic, industrial, and strategically vital nation of Eastern Europe. Tied to France through the Little Entente and with strong defenses, Czechoslovakia represents an ideal place to confront Hitler's aggression. Nonetheless, British Prime Minister Neville Chamberlain (1869–1940) urges compromise at a four-power meeting (Britain, France, Germany, Italy). The western democracies exclude the Soviet Union and Czechoslovakia itself at the Munich Conference, which signs over the Sudetenland to Germany. Upon arriving back in Britain, Chamberlain proclaims he has achieved "peace in our time."

1939: Quickly violating the Munich Agreement in the following spring, Hitler marches into Moravia and Bohemia, creating a Czech protectorate, while making Slovakia a puppet government. In addition, Mussolini moves into Albania to establish a foothold for his *mare nostrum* ("our sea") project of controlling the Mediterranean. These actions cause a decisive shift in public opinion against appeasement within the west; however, France and Britain prove unable to win over a suspicious Soviet Union into a joint alliance against Nazi Germany.

Shocking the world, Hitler and Stalin in late August conclude the Nazi-Soviet Non-Aggression Pact, giving Hitler a free hand for his next project—an invasion of Poland to regain the Danzig corridor, which cuts off East Prussia from Germany proper. A secret protocol provides for the division of Poland, the Baltic States, and Finland between the supposedly bitter ideological enemies. A week later, Hitler invades Poland to begin World War II.

World War II, 1939–1945

The Second World War stands as the most destructive conflict in history, killing an estimated 60–80 million people. It involved the nations of six continents and decisively altered Europe's position in the world. As with any war, new technologies—radar, rockets, jet airplanes, atomic weapons—played a major role. Never before had the line between soldier and civilian been so blurred, with civilians and entire ethnic groups targeted for extermination.

> **SKILL SET**
>
> Total war's effects extend beyond the death toll and material destruction. As you read this section, apply selected examples to this prompt: "Evaluate the extent to which the Second World War transformed the government's relation to the economy, society, and science." In addressing this question, you will draw on the ARG, CES, and CCOT skills.

The following chart should provide a general understanding of the nature and course of the conflict:

Phases of the Conflict

Phase	Goals and Strategy	Actions and Results	Assessment
Blitzkrieg, 1939–1941	In the early phase of the war, Hitler takes the initiative and attacks Poland. The following spring, the Nazis move against Norway, the Low Countries, and France. In its first defeat, Germany is unable to bring Britain to its knees. Without directly entering the conflict, President Franklin Roosevelt of the United States provides aid to Great Britain with the Lend-Lease Act and signs the Atlantic Charter with Winston Churchill (British PM),outlining Anglo-American war aims. By the end of 1941, Japan's attack on the United States and Hitler's invasion of its former ally, the USSR cements the Grand Alliance against the Rome-Tokyo-Berlin Axis powers.	• With armored divisions and aerial bombers, Hitler's ***blitzkrieg*** ("lightning war") defeats Poland in a matter of weeks. • Soviet troops move into the Baltic states, eastern Poland, and attack Finland. • In the spring of 1940, Hitler secures his northern flank vis-à-vis Britain and supplies of iron ore by taking Norway. The Nazis next defeat the Low Countries and France. German forces occupy the northern two-thirds of France, allowing the creation of the collaborationist Vichy government in the south. Free French forces under Charles DeGaulle (1890–1970) continue resistance from abroad. • Under the strong leadership of Prime Minister Winston Churchill (1874–1965), Britain defeats Germany in the Battle of Britain. The German *Luftwaffe* loses twice the planes of the Royal Air Force (RAF). Bombing of cities by the Nazis only hardens British resistance. • Mussolini's attempted invasion in 1941 of Greece falters, drawing German forces into the Balkans. • In the largest land battle in history, Hitler invades the Soviet Union in June 1941, capturing huge swaths of territory before stalling in front of Moscow in December. • The Japanese capture French colonies in Indochina, prompting the United States to cut off oil and scrap metal shipments. In retaliation, the Japanese launch the surprise attack on Pearl Harbor, drawing America into the war.	By the end of 1941, Hitler still holds the initiative. Nazi Germany continues to dominate Europe and works (unsuccessfully) toward a joint strategy with Japan to link forces in Central Asia. Churchill and Roosevelt agree to concentrate on the war in Europe, with the Pacific theater taking a back seat. Hitler's invasion of the USSR takes Stalin by surprise and also ignites the systematic **genocide** of Slavs, Roma, and Jews.

Phase	Goals and Strategy	Actions and Results	Assessment
The Turning of the Tide, 1942–1944	Hitler divides his armies into three groups in the Soviet Union—aimed at Leningrad (formerly St. Petersburg), Moscow, and the Caucasus oil fields. The Japanese attack on Pearl Harbor is followed by the expansion of its empire throughout the Pacific, which reaches its height in Spring 1942. Italian and then German armies attack British forces in North Africa, threatening the Suez Canal. In a series of counterattacks, the Allies defeat the Axis in North Africa, the Soviet Union, and in the Pacific.	• Soviet forces regroup and capture an entire German army in February 1943 at Stalingrad. At the subsequent tank Battle of Kursk, the Soviet Union decisively turns the tide and begins an inexorable advance toward Germany. • The German-Italian advance toward the Suez Canal in North Africa is stopped in July 1942 at El Alamein. An Anglo-American invasion pushes German forces under Erwin Rommel out of North Africa. • Anglo-American forces launch an invasion of Sicily and move slowly up the peninsula of Italy. Mussolini is captured by Allied forces in 1943 but rescued by German paratroopers. The Allied drive up the peninsula stalls outside Rome as German forces take up the fight. • The American naval victory at Midway deals a decisive blow to Japan's surface fleet. At Guadalcanal, the US amphibious invasion blunts Japan's threat to Australia.	By 1943, the tide turns against the Axis powers. In late 1943, the Big Three (Churchill, Roosevelt, and Stalin) meet at the Tehran Conference and agree on the unconditional surrender of the Axis powers, while the Anglo-Americans agree to open a second front in France. Before launching an amphibious assault, the Anglo-American allies must secure control of the seas from German submarines, accomplished by early 1944. In the Pacific, American forces begin the strategy of "island hopping" to establish bases of operations directly against the Japanese home islands.
Endgame, 1944–1945	Anglo-American forces establish a second front in France and, along with the advance of Soviet forces, move toward the German homeland. Soviet forces divert into the Balkans to ensure Soviet control of Eastern Europe following the war. US forces close in on the Japanese home islands. Following fierce fighting, the Pacific war ends with the dropping of two atomic bombs on Hiroshima and Nagasaki.	• At the D-Day invasion of Normandy (June 1944), the United States and Britain establish a beachhead in France, which leads to the liberation of Paris by August. • Soviet forces advance toward but pause outside Warsaw in September 1944 to allow the Nazis to destroy the western-backed Polish Home Army during its effort to liberate the city, a bloody precursor to Cold War conflicts over Eastern Europe. • In the Pacific, US forces retake the Philippines, capture Iwo Jima and Okinawa after fierce fighting, and begin aerial bombing of Tokyo. • Widespread targeting of German cities begins, exemplified by the fire-bombing of Dresden in February 1945. • A last-ditch German advance in Belgium (Battle of the Bulge) is turned back, and Anglo-American and Soviet forces end the war in Germany in May 1945. • After the dropping of the atomic bombs, Japan sues for peace in September 1945.	The combined manpower and economic potential of the Allied powers wields a decisive influence on the course of the war. In addition, strategic errors by the Axis powers as well as the unification of numerous groups opposed to the brutal rule of the Nazis eventually works in the Allies' favor. America's use of the first atomic weapons ends the Second World War but also marks the beginning of the **Nuclear Age** and the Cold War.

Mobilization of the Home Fronts

The Second World War required an even higher level of mobilization and sacrifice among civilians than did the First World War. Many governments centralized production, instituted rationing programs, and called on all citizens to contribute to the war effort in some way. The following are several examples of such mobilization:

Germany – Despite the perception of Nazi efficiency and invincibility, Germany did not mobilize effectively for wartime production. Hitler was reluctant to employ women in the workforce or call on German citizens to sacrifice consumer goods, recognizing the collapse of the war effort in 1917–1918. Nazi Germany relied extensively on slave labor from conquered and occupied territories for armaments production. It was not until 1942 that Hitler appointed a young architect, Albert Speer (1905–1981), to centralize production as Minister of Armaments. Only in 1944, when the war was nearing its end, did Germany move toward full mobilization, closing down popular amusements and rationing goods. German women never did enter the workforce in large numbers.

Soviet Union – For the Soviet Union, the conflict was known as the Great Patriotic War, a fight for its very survival. Over 20 million Soviet citizens perished in the war, by far the most of any combatant. Once the Nazis had captured some of the best agricultural lands and threatened key industrial cities, the Soviets moved entire factories inland, which commenced production before the walls went up. Stalin promoted super-centralization of the economy around the war effort and reduced the already paltry production of consumer goods, allowing the USSR to win the "battle of the machines." The city of Leningrad endured a 900-day siege, its residents often surviving on rodents; spring thaws revealed thousands of corpses in the streets. Women also served in the armed forces, unique among the combatants, as with the famous Night Witches fighter pilots protecting Stalingrad.

Great Britain – Great Britain effectively centralized its economy for wartime production. Almost every able-bodied adult assisted the war effort—women went into armament production and older citizens joined the Home Guard. The government created ministries to oversee and distribute fuel, food, and war supplies. In addition, citizens were encouraged to develop self-sufficiency in food production, as with Dig for Victory gardens. Citizens received ration books with coupons and received only those goods assigned to them. The shared sacrifice of rationing continued until after the war, ending only in 1951.

United States – President Roosevelt urged the United States to become the "arsenal of democracy" for the Allied powers. On one hand, no nation was producing more tanks, planes, and ships by the end of the conflict. However, the United States never entered a complete wartime production footing. Though rationing was practiced, it did not reach the levels of European control, particularly with fuel consumption. After Pearl Harbor, thousands of Japanese citizens of the US on the west coast were forced into internment camps for fear of their conspiring with the Japanese Empire.

Collaboration and Resistance

Europeans of occupied nations faced stark choices—collaborate or resist. A major reason for Nazi success militarily and with genocide involved the active cooperation or apathetic acceptance of many in occupied lands. Conservatives in many nations welcomed the Nazi takeover as a solution to indigenous political problems. To assist in ruling occupied lands, Nazi Germany created puppet governments. In Norway, Vadkun Quisling lent his name, "quisling," to those who betray their nation by assisting a foreign power's conquest. Though nominally independent, the Vichy regime in France cooperated with Nazi authorities, assisting in the Nazi Final Solution (see below). Reprisals against thousands of French collaborators followed right after the armies of liberation. In the complex Balkans, the Ustasha, a nationalist and Catholic government of Croatia, assisted the Nazis in taking reprisals against Orthodox Serbs.

Anti-Nazi movements gained momentum as the tide of war turned. Resistance groups engaged in acts of sabotage and assassination, hindered production, rescued ethnic minorities, and spread anti-Nazi or nationalist propaganda. Strongly organized movements arose in France under Charles DeGaulle and in Yugoslavia under Joseph Broz Tito (1892–1980). Due to the latter's efforts, Yugoslavia became the only nation in Eastern Europe that did not require the aid of the Soviet army to liberate itself from Nazi rule. The Polish council, Żegota, saved hundreds of Jews in Poland, while Denmark was able to engineer the rescue of almost all 8,000 of its Jewish population. Within Germany, a group of idealistic university students, named the White Rose, distributed pamphlets against the Nazis before being caught and executed. Conservative army officers attempted but failed to assassinate Hitler in July 1944, leading to the execution of thousands.

The Holocaust

Soon after taking power, the Nazis established a network of concentration camps to punish political prisoners and other undesirables. From that point, Nazi policy moved step by step, from exclusion to concentration to extermination, or the Final Solution—the elimination of all of Europe's Jews, as well as **Roma**, Slavic intellectuals, Russian prisoners of war, Jehovah's Witnesses, and **homosexuals**. Mass killing began with the Nazi invasion of the Soviet Union in 1941; mobile killings squads, known as *Einsatzgruppen*, machine-gunned thousands and buried them in mass graves.

In January 1942, top Nazi officials met at the Wannsee Conference. Led by Reinhard Heydrich (1904–1942), the head of the S.S. security office, the meeting decided on the implementation of the Final Solution to the "Jewish problem." The Nazis erected a system of <u>death camps</u> in Poland—<u>Auschwitz</u>, Treblinka, and others—designed to kill thousands per day in gas chambers, their bodies destroyed in crematoria. Even as the war turned against the Nazis on the battlefield, Hitler continued to pour resources into this race war, stepping up the extermination as Allied armies approached. Only the participation of thousands of people, including those in the occupied nations, made such a massive and systematic process possible. By the end of the war, 6 million Jews had been killed (the **Holocaust**), along with another 5 million from the above categories, in the Nazi genocide.

Results of the Second World War

By 1945, much of Europe lay in ruins; some cities, like Warsaw, experienced complete devastation. The Second World War represents the lowest point for European civilization. Some of the results can be measured in numbers; others would become clear only in subsequent years.

- 60–80 million dead, mostly civilians
- Widespread destruction of infrastructure
- 30–50 million displaced persons (DPs) wandering the continent
- Europe's hold on its colonies nearly broken
- Traditional values questioned in postwar Europe
- Economic activity brought to a standstill
- Conditions laid for the Cold War

All analyses aside, the Second World War stands as the single largest event in the history of the human race.

Additional Readings

📖 **Anne Applebaum, *Gulag: A History* (2004)** — An in-depth study of the background and development of the gulag system and police terror in the Soviet Union.

📖 **Judith Tydor Baumel and Walter Laqueur, *The Holocaust Encyclopedia* (2001)** — A comprehensive and well-written resource chronicling the horrors of the holocaust.

📖 **Hannah Arendt, *The Origins of Totalitarianism* (rev. 1966)** — Explores the meaning of a major political development in the twentieth century; by a well-known political philosopher.

📖 **Christopher Browning, *Ordinary Men: Reserve Police Battalion 101 and the Final Solution in Poland* (2001)** — Debunks many myths about those who perpetrated genocide.

📖 **Peter Gay, *Weimar Culture: The Outsider as Insider* (rev. 2001)** — A noted historian examines cultural experimentation amid a fractured political climate.

📖 **Benjamin Carter Hett, *The Death of Democracy: Hitler's Rise to Power and the Downfall of the Weimar Republic* (2019)** — Written amidst the rise of populist authoritarianism worldwide, the author shows how democracy can die a slow death before many realize it's gone.

📖 **John Keegan, *The Times Atlas of the Second World War* (1989)** — An impressive collection of detailed maps of every theater of war, supplemented with text and analysis by a leading military historian.

📖 **Ian Kershaw, *To Hell and Back: Europe 1914–1950* (2016)** — Another strong installment by a noted historian in *The Penguin History of Europe* series.

📖 **Mark Mazower, *Dark Continent: Europe's Twentieth Century* (1999)** — Portrays the era as a violent clash between democracy, fascism, and communism.

📖 **Ron Rosenbaum, *Explaining Hitler: The Search for the Origins of His Evil* (1999)** — A psychologist pursues various theories regarding Hitler to reflect on the nature of human evil.

📖 **Timothy Snyder, *Bloodlands: Europe Between Hitler and Stalin* (2010)** — An important and sobering examination of the power of states and ideology to instigate the slaughter of millions.

📖 **Gerhard Weinberg, *A World at Arms: A Global History of World War II* (rev. 2005)** — The most comprehensive and riveting account of the war, strictly for military history buffs.

💻 **https://spartacus-educational.com/Germany.htm** — Spartacus site on the Weimar Republic and Nazi Germany.

💻 **https://www.ushmm.org/** — The official site of the United States Holocaust Museum in Washington, D.C.; features a searchable encyclopedia.

💻 **http://www.fallen.io/ww2/** — A fascinating video providing a statistical sense of WWII within the context of world history.

CHAPTER TEST

Multiple-Choice Questions

Questions 1–4 are based on the passage below.

> "Men are proud of those achievements [in science and technology], and have a right to be. But they seem to have observed that this newly-won power over space and time, this subjugation of the forces of nature, which is the fulfillment of a longing that goes back thousands of years, has not increased the amount of pleasurable satisfaction which they may expect from life and has not made them feel happier. From the recognition of this fact we ought to be content to conclude that power over nature is not the only precondition of human happiness, just as it is not the only goal of cultural endeavor..."
>
> Sigmund Freud, Austrian psychologist and neurologist, *Civilization and its Discontents*, 1930

1. Freud's analysis best reflects the trend during the interwar period of:
   A. high unemployment brought about by the Great Depression.
   B. failure of the League of Nations to provide collective security.
   C. loss of confidence in human reason and the role of science.
   D. the threat of violent revolution from the communist Soviet Union.

2. Freud's perspective was most likely a reaction to:
   A. Darwin's theory of natural selection.
   B. devastation and death caused by World War I.
   C. the rise of the Nazi party in Germany.
   D. women's entrance into the workforce.

3. All of the following interwar cultural developments support Freud's perspective EXCEPT:
   A. the challenge to Newtonian physics from quantum and relativity theories.
   B. literature that emphasized the subconscious and addressed controversy.
   C. art that satirized western values and emphasized subjective experience.
   D. mass production that created a consumer culture in domestic comforts.

4. The most accurate characterization of a historical era supported by the passage is the:
   A. Clash of Ideologies.
   B. Age of Anxiety.
   C. Great Depression.
   D. Age of Totalitarianism.

Questions 5–7 are based on the photograph below.

German children stacking paper money, 1923

5. The situation depicted in the photograph was most directly caused by:

   A. the rise of fascist political movements.

   B. reparations imposed on Germany at Versailles.

   C. tariff and trade policies of the United States.

   D. loss of German territory and colonies.

6. The situation depicted in the photograph led to:

   A. the rise of extremist movements and ultimate failure of the Weimar Republic.

   B. a treaty between Germany and the Soviet Union to oppose western democracies.

   C. new artistic movements that satirized western values and standards of beauty.

   D. entrance of large numbers of women in the workforce to supplement family income.

7. This situation would likely have been avoided after the Second World War through all of the following EXCEPT:

   A. American financial aid and leadership.

   B. continental economic and political integration.

   C. extension of widespread social welfare benefits.

   D. adoption of a centralized command economy.

Questions 8–10 are based on the passage below.

"THE HIGH CONTRACTING PARTIES,

In order to promote international cooperation and to achieve international peace and security

by the acceptance of obligations not to resort to war,

by the prescription of open, just and honorable relations between nations,

by the firm establishment of the understandings of international law as the actual rule of conduct among Governments, and

by the maintenance of justice and a scrupulous respect for all treaty obligations in the dealings of organized peoples with one another,

Agree to this Covenant of the League of Nations.

ARTICLE 10.

The Members of the League undertake to respect and preserve as against external aggression the territorial integrity and existing political independence of all Members of the League. In case of any such aggression or in case of any threat or danger of such aggression the Council shall advise upon the means by which this obligation shall be fulfilled."

Charter of the League of Nations, 1919

8. The charter most directly reflects the influence of:
   A. the conflicting goals of the victors at Versailles.
   B. the idealistic vision of American President Wilson.
   C. French aims to punish and disarm Germany.
   D. fear of Soviet communism spreading across Europe.

9. Which of the following most affected the success of the goals indicated by the charter?
   A. The onset of the Great Depression and widespread unemployment
   B. A loss of confidence in western values and aesthetic standards
   C. Weakness of the new democracies in central and eastern Europe
   D. Lack of participation of major powers such as the United States

10. The action in the 1930s that most directly undermined Article 10 of the charter was:
   A. agreeing to the rearmament of Nazi Germany and fascist Italy.
   B. allowing fascist powers to absorb territory from League members.
   C. excluding the Soviet Union from membership in the League until 1934.
   D. depending on American capital for the functioning of the European economy.

See Chapter 18 for answers and explanations.

Short-Answer Question

Directions: Answer all parts of the question below. Use complete sentences; an outline or bulleted list is not acceptable. Write your responses on a separate sheet of paper. A sample response and commentary are provided below.

1. a) Describe one way in which the use of state power by absolute monarchies in the seventeenth and eighteenth centuries differed from that of the totalitarian regimes in the twentieth century.

b) Describe one specific historical development that explains the difference you noted in <u>Part A</u>.

c) Explain one limitation on <u>any one</u> of the following regimes in its ability to realize the theory of totalitarianism:
- Fascist Italy (1922–1943)
- Nazi Germany (1933–1945)
- Soviet Union under Stalin (1928–1953)

SAQ Sample Response

There were many differences between the absolute monarchies of the seventeenth and eighteenth centuries and the totalitarian dictators of the twentieth century. Louis XIV was an absolute monarch, and he tried to control religion in France by taking away the right of Huguenots to worship in their Protestant ways. However, totalitarian dictators didn't really care about religion and made no policies related to it. Many of the differences between these two eras can be explained by the growth of nationalism. Mussolini of Italy wasn't really a strong dictator; certainly not as much as Hitler and Stalin. Though he tried to increase his population through incentives and to enforce a reproductive role for women, the population didn't actually increase and it also created opposition to Mussolini.

SAQ Response Analysis

Unfortunately, this response offers underdeveloped analysis along with some errors. The student did not earn the point for Part A, as the statement regarding religious policies is incorrect. Both Hitler and Mussolini attempted to replace loyalty to religion with loyalty to the state or party. Also, each fascist regime signed agreements with the Catholic Church. Further, the ideology of the Soviet Union was officially atheistic and openly hostile to organized religion, viewed as a prop of the tsarist system. The student correctly identifies for Part B a key factor (nationalism) to explain the difference between states in the two eras, but provided no explanation, missing that point. In Part C, the student earns a point for the correct explanation of the failure of Mussolini's population policy. Short-answer responses may be brief, as is this one, but this attempt would benefit from further explanation, as well as indicating which parts of the prompt are being addressed. **Score: 1**

CHAPTER 16

The Cold War and European Recovery

Looking across Europe in 1945, one saw a civilization in ruins. Europeans suffered through one of the coldest winters on record in 1945–1946; Germans called this grim time their *Stunde Null*, or zero hour. Destruction and devastation created a power vacuum in Europe, into which rushed the new contending superpowers of the United States and the Soviet Union. Due to fundamental economic and political differences and a cycle of action-and-reaction, by 1947 the two superpowers were locked in a Cold War that divided Western from Eastern Europe. Competition between the superpowers decisively shaped the contrasting development of the two regions: the West toward economic recovery and integration, and the East under Soviet domination and ultimately rebellion. In the final analysis, Europe rose like a phoenix from the ashes after 1945, but its recovery has been marked by fits and starts, successes and failures. By 1991, a new era opened with the fall of communism and the collapse of the Soviet Union—an opportunity for the continent to work toward a European identity that combined East and West.

 KEY IN – Chapter 16 addresses all or part of the following topics in the Unit Guides of the CED:

The Cold War, 1943–1991

Origins of the Conflict

The Grand Alliance between the Anglo-American powers and the Soviet Union had always been a shotgun marriage; it was a relationship based on a battle against a common enemy—the Nazis. Since the Bolshevik Revolution, mutual suspicion had strained relations between the new Soviet Union and the west: (1) the Allies sent assistance to the White Army during the Russian Civil War; (2) the United States did not recognize the Soviet Union until 1933; (3) the western democracies excluded the Soviet Union from interwar diplomacy while appeasing Hitler; and (4) Stalin and Hitler joined in dividing Poland to initiate the Second World War.

During World War II, the so-called Big Three (Stalin, Churchill, Roosevelt) met several times to forge common policies; these meetings also revealed strains in the alliance. In February 1945 at Yalta, just months from victory, the Big Three convened to address the layout of postwar Europe. Soviet armies stood within 40 miles of Berlin and dominated most of eastern Europe. This reality determined much of the Anglo-American posture toward Stalin, though Roosevelt tended to see himself as the mediator between the more *Realpolitik*-oriented Churchill and Stalin. The parties agreed to the Declaration on Liberated Europe, which promised national self-determination and free elections in Eastern Europe. Stalin was especially concerned with controlling postwar Poland, which was moved 300 miles west at the expense of Germany and to the benefit of the Soviet Union. As for Germany, the three leaders agreed it must be disarmed and denazified, though they differed over Stalin's proposal for its complete dismemberment and the extraction of $20 billion in reparations. Finally, the Big Three agreed to create the **United Nations** in hopes of resolving future security issues. Despite the agreements, it soon became clear that the Anglo-Americans and Soviets interpreted these decisions differently, particularly free elections. Later critics viewed Roosevelt's position as a sell-out of Eastern Europe in order to gain Soviet support for the continuing war against Japan.

When the Allies next met at Potsdam in July 1945, the war in Europe had ended. In the interim, Roosevelt had died and his successor, Harry Truman (1884–1972), harbored suspicion of Stalin's intentions. Also, during the conference, Labour leader Clement Attlee was voted into office as prime minister, replacing Churchill. The Allies agreed to hold war crimes trials of the top Nazi leaders at Nuremberg, divide Germany into four occupation zones, and provide reparations for the rebuilding of the Soviet Union. However, disagreements between the United States and Soviet Union deepened over Poland and other Eastern European states. When the United States abruptly ended aid to the Soviet Union (but not Great Britain) in spring 1945 and developed its monopoly on atomic weapons, Soviet suspicions of American intentions mounted. By 1947, a series of disagreements led to a fracturing of the wartime alliance and open if often restrained conflict between the former allies.

Nature of the Conflict

The Cold War played out as a complex, multi-pronged worldwide competition between the superpowers, United States vs. Soviet Union.

Political: The United States and Soviet Union vied to spread their respective political influence throughout the world. Beginning in Europe, the Cold War soon spread to Asia, and eventually to the Middle East, Latin America, and Africa. In some cases, direct control was exercised, as with the Soviet sphere of influence in Eastern Europe; in others, indirect economic control, as with US policy in Latin America, proved sufficient to maintain bloc cohesion. The system of Liberal democracy and free markets became known as the First World, the Soviet system of planned economies and one-party rule as the Second World, and those nonaligned nations refusing to choose sides as the Third World, a term often used to signify less-developed nations. Both sides developed alliances to maintain collective security in their blocs. In response to the Berlin Crisis of 1948–1949, the United States entered into its first peacetime alliance, the **North Atlantic Treaty Organization (NATO)**, later followed by CENTO in the Middle East and SEATO in Southeast Asia. When the West rearmed Germany in 1955, the Soviets responded with the **Warsaw Pact** to defend the Eastern Bloc.

With its expressed goal of spreading world revolution, the Soviet Union created fear among the western capitalist and democratic nations. During the late 1940s and early 1950s, President Truman relied on the expertise of former diplomat and historian George Kennan (1904–2005) to develop the strategy of containment. Containment employed a variety of techniques—war, diplomacy, aid, intelligence, funding rebel groups—to halt the spread of communism around the world. To support its new international presence, the US Congress passed the National Security Act (1947), which created the National Security Council (NSC, also with a National Security Advisor), the Central Intelligence Agency (CIA), the National Security Agency (NSA), and reorganized the Department of Defense. Numerous novels and films have since reflected the cloak-and-dagger spy battles between the CIA and Soviet KGB to gain the upper hand.

Military: Nuclear weapons technology fostered an **arms race** between the two superpowers. The Soviet Union exploded its first atomic weapon in 1949, and both nations developed the hydrogen bomb after 1952. Under the leadership of Nikita Khrushchev in 1957, the Soviet Union launched its first satellite—*Sputnik*—bringing the arms race to outer space. Fearing a so-called missile gap, the United States hurriedly worked to develop rocket technology, culminating with Intercontinental Ballistic Missiles (ICBMs) capable of reaching the Soviet Union from silos in America or Europe. By the 1970s, both sides combined deployed about 25,000 long-range nuclear weapons. Moreover, each side developed nuclear submarines with the capacity to fire nuclear missiles from the depths of the ocean, forming a nuclear triad—on land, in the air, and under the sea.

An ironic consequence of the Nuclear Age was the doctrine of Mutual Assured Destruction (MAD): both sides were deterred from launching a first strike as it was sure to incur unacceptable casualties from the opponent's missiles in response. Therefore, "missiles that kill people" kept the peace by precluding a nuclear strike, but "missiles that kill other missiles" (Anti-Ballistic Missiles—ABMs) threatened to upset the nuclear balance by providing an incentive to launch a first strike; as a result, the superpowers banned such weapons in a 1972 agreement. During the height of the Cold War, the Soviet Union may have spent as much as 25%–30% of its gross domestic product on military hardware, a massive commitment of resources for a modern society and a tremendous drain on its economy.

Economic: Perhaps never in history had one nation so dominated the world economy as did the United States at the end of the Second World War. Fully 80% of the world's trade passed through American hands, and 50% of the world's productive capacity was American. The United States thus stood in the unique position of helping to rebuild the world economy, which it wished to do by promoting free markets and access to American goods. To pursue this goal, the United States extended aid to Europe in the form of the **Marshall Plan** (1947). The Soviet Union prohibited its Eastern European satellites from accepting such aid, viewing the plan as a capitalist plot aimed at the Soviet sphere. In response, the Soviet Union organized the Eastern Bloc around the rival **Council for Mutual Economic Assistance (COMECON)**, an effort to create a specialization of production among its satellites.

As the Cold War expanded, the United States often exploited the power of its multinational corporations to control the economies of underdeveloped nations, particularly in Latin America. For example, when a socialist government was elected to power in 1954 in Guatemala with the intention of nationalizing US fruit companies (which dominated that nation's banana industry), the US government engineered a CIA-backed coup deposing the government. Many such underdeveloped nations and former colonies sympathized with the Soviet critique of capitalism and adopted state planning to promote internal development and gain control of resources vis-à-vis the former colonial powers of the West. Both superpowers often extended aid in strategic regions with the goal of gaining allies.

> ### SKILL SET
>
> To focus your analysis in this section, consider the following two interpretive questions: 1) Did the Cold War arise due to fundamental differences between the superpowers or from miscommunication and miscalculation? AND 2) Which of the superpowers was more responsible for beginning and continuing the Cold War? Both topics are the source of historical discussion; take a position on both as practice for making and developing arguments (ARG and CES).

Ideological: At its heart, the Cold War represented a battle over rival and antagonistic ideologies. Each side aimed to win hearts and minds with propaganda. In 1946, Winston Churchill fired the first salvo in the war with a speech in Fulton, Missouri, when he announced that an **Iron Curtain** had descended across the continent of Europe, dividing the free peoples of the West from the oppressed peoples of the East. The United States established the Voice of America and Radio Free Europe to broadcast messages from "free and prosperous citizens" across the Iron Curtain. Internally, the United States in the 1950s plunged into a Red Scare, or McCarthyism (named after Wisconsin Senator Joseph McCarthy), aimed at real and imaginary communist enemies in the upper reaches of government and in Hollywood.

Though Soviet propaganda tended to be more heavy-handed, it also aimed to control public opinion within its bloc. In 1948 the Communist Information Bureau (Cominform) was created to replace the old Comintern suspended during World War II. The notion that each side struggled for a cherished way of life—the future of civilization itself—added intensity to the Cold War not fully captured by traditional conceptions of geopolitical maneuvering.

> **THEME MUSIC**
>
> The Cold War played out on a global scale. As such, it facilitated decolonization and forced world conflicts into an artificial bi-polar divide between capitalism vs. command economy, and liberal democracy vs. communism. Europe's relationship to the rest of the world was redefined as it sat uneasily between the two superpowers (INT).

Chronological Development of the Cold War

This section is designed to suggest the scope and duration of the Cold War. It is divided chronologically into phases, with brief explanations of the main areas of conflict. Consider it a supplement to the conceptual overview discussed above.

Beginnings, 1945–1953

The Cold War began with mutual suspicions over the status of Germany, control of Eastern Europe, nuclear weapons, and eventually the spread of rivalry into Asia.

1945: Germany is divided into four zones of occupation—British, American, Soviet, and French. Additionally, the city of Berlin (entirely within the Soviet zone) is divided into four occupation zones. Germany, and more specifically Berlin, become the epicenter of the emerging Cold War.

The United States explodes atomic bombs over Hiroshima and Nagasaki in Japan, ending the Pacific War, but also initiating the **Nuclear Age**.

Soviet troops occupy all of the nations of Eastern Europe except Albania and Yugoslavia. At first, coalition governments of socialist/communist parties rule along with democratic and/or free market parties.

1946: Winston Churchill delivers his **Iron Curtain** speech, warning of Soviet domination of Eastern Europe.

1947: The United States extends Marshall Plan aid to the nations of Europe, funneled through the Office of European Economic Cooperation (OEEC) rather than to each nation individually.

Fearing the spread of communism in Greece and Turkey, President Truman offers financial assistance to any nation facing "insurgencies by armed minorities." Along with the Marshall Plan, this Truman Doctrine establishes the early outlines of a new interventionist approach by the United States in European affairs.

In most Eastern European nations, Western-backed parties are pushed out of power, while in Italy, elections vault the pro-US Christian Democrats to leadership while limiting the influence of the usually strong Socialist and Communist parties.

1948: Concerned over economic conditions in Germany and Soviet reparations policies, the United States, Britain, and France merge their three German zones and introduce a new *Deutschmark* currency. In response, the Soviet Union imposes the Berlin Blockade, cutting the western part of the city off from rail and auto traffic, threatening to starve it out. Rather than confront the Soviets directly, President Truman initiates the Berlin Airlift, an almost year-long mission designed to supply the basic needs of West Berliners.

Non-communists are kicked out of the Czechoslovakian government in a coup. The leader of the noncommunists, Jan Masyrk, is later found dead outside his window, either by suicide or murder.

1949: Stalin ends the Berlin Blockade, and the division of Germany becomes formal with the creation of West Germany and East Germany. Under American leadership, Western Europe forms a mutual defense system known as NATO to defend against future Soviet provocations.

Communists under Mao Zedong (1890–1976) gain control of the Chinese mainland, driving the Nationalists onto the island of Taiwan. In addition, the Soviet Union explodes its first atomic bomb. These two events spur the Red Scare in the United States.

1950: Communist North Korea invades the Western-backed government of South Korea. Taking advantage of the Soviet boycott of the Security Council, President Truman builds a UN coalition to combat the invasion and signify the American commitment to the policy of containment. The Korean War drags on for 3 years and involves fighting between the United States and China.

1953: Joseph Stalin's death opens a new era in Cold War diplomacy. The Korean War ends with the division of North Korea and South Korea at the 38th parallel.

Coexistence and Confrontation, 1953–1970

This period begins with an effort at peaceful coexistence, but rivalries reheat over Berlin, control of the vital Middle East, and Soviet intrusion into America's perceived sphere of influence in Latin America, which almost brings the superpowers to nuclear war in 1962.

1954: Vietnamese resistance fighters under Communist leader <u>Ho Chi Minh</u> (1890–1969) defeat French colonial forces at Dien Bien Phu, leading to Vietnam's division along the 17th parallel between communist North Vietnam and Western-backed South Vietnam.

The United States supports a coup against socialist Guatemalan leader Jacobo Arbenz Guzman to prevent the nationalization of land owned by US fruit companies.

1955: NATO agrees to rearm West Germany, leading to the Soviet creation of the **Warsaw Pact** alliance in Eastern Europe.

Secretary of State John Foster Dulles announces the American policy of massive retaliation, threatening an all-out nuclear attack in response to Communist aggression anywhere in the world.

A summit in Geneva, Switzerland, between President Dwight Eisenhower (1890–1969) and Khrushchev leads to the evacuation of forces from Austria and its neutralization.

1956: Soviet leader **Nikita Khrushchev** (1894–1971) gives a secret speech at the 20th Party Congress of the Communist Party of the Soviet Union condemning the excesses of the Stalin period and signals his goal of **de-Stalinization**. Khrushchev also suggests the possibility of peaceful coexistence between the capitalist West and communism.

Taking their cue from Khrushchev, the leadership of the Polish and Hungarian Communist Parties begins a liberalization of economic and intellectual life. The Hungarian revolt goes too far for Khrushchev and is crushed by Soviet forces.

1957: Soviet leaders announce the launching of the first satellite into outer space—*Sputnik*. The United States follows with the creation of the National Aeronautics and Space Agency (NASA), launching the beginning of the space race.

1959: Leftist forces under Fidel Castro (1926–2016) overthrow the US-backed government of Cuba. Castro nationalizes the sugar industry, seizes American assets, and establishes strong ties with the Soviet Union.

1960: Soviet forces shoot down a U-2 spy plane over Russian territory, forcing the United States to recant previous statements denying such flights. The incident forces the cancellation of a planned superpower summit.

1961: A US-backed invasion of Cuba by exiled Cubans ends disastrously with the capture of such forces at the Bay of Pigs.

Another crisis over control of the city of Berlin leads to the building of the Berlin Wall by East Berlin to prevent its citizens from escaping to the West.

1962: Soviet plans to install nuclear missiles in Cuba lead to a 2-week crisis, pushing the world to the brink of nuclear war. The Cuban Missile Crisis ends when President John F. Kennedy (1917–1963) assures Khrushchev that the United States will not invade Cuba in exchange for the removal of the missiles.

1963: The superpowers agree to the creation of a Hot Line establishing direct contact in times of crisis. In addition, the two sides, along with Great Britain, agree to the Limited Nuclear Test Ban Treaty, prohibiting the testing of nuclear weapons in the atmosphere, in outer space, or under water.

1964: America's commitment to fighting in <u>Vietnam</u> (between the communist North and US-backed South) deepens with the Gulf of Tonkin Resolution, allowing President Lyndon Johnson (1908–1973) greater latitude to involve American forces.

1967: Israel preemptively attacks its Arab neighbors and seizes the West Bank, Sinai Peninsula, and Golan Heights. In this Six-Day War, the United States backs Israel while the Soviets support Arab forces.

1968: Soviet forces crush the Czechoslovakian reform movement, known as the Prague Spring, and announce the Brezhnev Doctrine, whereby a perceived threat to socialism in one nation is taken as a threat to socialism everywhere.

Détente, 1970–1978

A French term, détente means an easing of tensions. During the decade, the superpowers work to normalize relations between their two rival blocs and to accept the permanent existence of the opposing side.

1970: The Treaty of Moscow between West Germany and the Soviet Union establishes diplomatic relations between the two nations and formalizes the split between East and West Germany. Soon after, both nations are admitted to the United Nations.

1972: Soviet and American negotiators agree to the first limitations on nuclear weapons, the Strategic Arms Limitation Talks (SALT I), which also recognizes the nuclear parity that exists between the superpowers. In addition, both sides agree to an Anti-Ballistic Missile (ABM) Treaty to reduce the possibility of a first-strike launch.

President Richard Nixon (1913–1994) becomes the first US president to visit the People's Republic (Communist) of

> ### EXAMPLE BASE & SKILL SET
>
> Use the examples in this section as evidence in pursuit of the interpretative questions posed above in the previous Skill Set. Only those in bold are required knowledge; however, the illustrative examples may serve as a fodder for your conclusions (ARG and CES).

China, which leads to formal diplomatic relations later in the decade.

1973: The United States removes its last significant military units from fighting in Vietnam. In 1975, North Vietnam captures Saigon, the South Vietnamese capital, ending the war with Vietnam's unification under communism.

The Yom Kippur War between Israel (backed by the West) and its Arab neighbors (backed by the Soviet Union) once again almost brings the two superpowers to blows.

1975: Signed by all nations of Europe, including the United States, Canada, and USSR, the Helsinki Accords bring a formal end to the Second World War by acknowledging existing national boundaries. In addition, human rights provisions open the door for dissent within the Soviet Union and in the Eastern European satellites. The agreement represents the height of détente.

Revival and End, 1979–1991

The period of détente ends with a series of actions by both the United States and Soviet Union that increase Cold War tensions. However, Mikhail Gorbachev's accession to leadership of the Soviet Union helps bring an end to the Cold War by the late 1980s.

1979: To prop up a communist regime on its border, the Soviet Union invades Afghanistan, bogging it down in a Vietnam-style quagmire until 1988. In response, the US Senate refuses to ratify the SALT II agreement to limit nuclear weapons, and President Jimmy Carter (1924–) reduces grain shipments to the Soviet Union and boycotts the 1980 Olympics in Moscow. Further, the United States provides aid to Afghan freedom fighters known as the *mujahadeen*.

1983: President Ronald Reagan (1911–2004) denounces the Soviet Union as an "evil empire" and pledges to install intermediate range nuclear weapons in Europe. World concerns grow over the proliferation of nuclear weapons and the dangers of nuclear power.

A Korean commercial jet strays into Soviet airspace and is shot down by Soviet forces, killing all 269 people aboard.

1985: Mikhail Gorbachev (1931–) becomes the new Soviet leader and works toward an internal reform of the Soviet system that necessitates a reduction in Cold War tensions.

1987: After several inconclusive superpower summits, Reagan and Gorbachev agree to the Intermediate-Range Nuclear Force (INF) Treaty, which eliminates an entire class of weapons on European soil.

1988: Gorbachev withdraws the final Soviet troops from Afghanistan.

Reagan and Gorbachev sign the Strategic Arms Reduction Treaty (START), which reduces the number of long-range missiles on both sides.

1989: Communist governments in Eastern Europe collapse as Gorbachev refuses to mobilize Soviet troops to defeat the peoples' revolutions. **The Fall of Communism** results in the end of Germany's division (by 1990) and the movement toward democracy and free markets in the former Soviet satellites.

1991: After a failed coup by communist hardliners fails, the **Soviet Union collapses** into its member national republics. Soviet President Mikhail Gorbachev resigns with the official end of the USSR.

International Conflicts since 1990

With the end of the Cold War, the existential threat of widespread nuclear war seemed to abate; however, because the bi-polar nature of Cold War diplomacy tended to repress nationalist and religious conflicts in both Europe and globally, these have risen to the fore since the collapse of communism.

The first opportunity to test the post-Cold War diplomatic order was the Gulf War. In 1990, Iraqi forces under the command of leader Saddam Hussein (1937–2006) invaded Kuwait, claiming it as a historic province of Iraq. Ironically, the United States lent support to Hussein during the brutal Iran-Iraq War (1980–1988), which followed Iran's Islamic revolution (against the US-backed government of the Shah) and subsequent hostage crisis of US embassy personnel. President George H.W. Bush (1924–2018) pledged that the aggressive action would not stand and secured agreement from both the Soviet Union and China on the UN Security Council for a multinational force to liberate Kuwait. With minimal casualties, the US Desert Storm Operation of 1991 defeated Iraqi forces in Kuwait but left Saddam Hussein in power.

Following the Second World War, the United States became more deeply involved in the Middle East, driven to secure strategic oil supplies and support its Israeli ally. The presence of American military bases and troops in many undemocratic Middle Eastern nations, as well as US support for Israel, inspired terrorist incidents beginning in the 1970s, such as the Palestinian Liberation Organization's (PLO) killing of the Israeli Olympic team in 1972 in Munich and the hijacking of western airliners. Such terrorist incidents caused concern for the US government but posed no direct threat to the United States itself.

America's sense of invulnerability shattered when al-Qaeda—a terrorist group supported by the radical Islamist Taliban regime in Afghanistan—hijacked commercial jets and crashed them into the World Trade Center in New York City and the Pentagon in Washington, D.C., on September 11, 2001, causing the deaths of 3,000 people. In response, President George W. Bush (1946–) pledged a war on terror. With broad international support, American forces successfully deposed the Taliban regime in Afghanistan, and eventually captured or killed many top leaders of al-Qaeda, including Osama bin Laden in 2011. However, the Bush administration's subsequent War in Iraq (2003), based on the presumption of Saddam Hussein's possession of weapons of mass destruction, won only limited support among its European allies and caused a rift in the alliance. Though President Barack Obama (1961–) moved to bring both wars to a close, the Middle East has continued to draw the attention of the Western alliance, whether through encouragment of the Arab Spring (2011) or combatting the efforts of the Islamic State of Syria (ISIS) to establish an Islamist caliphate in the region and support terrorist attacks on European and American soil.

The Soviet Union: From Superpower to Collapse

Cold War Repression under Stalin

Stalin reaffirmed his dictatorship in the Soviet Union during and especially after World War II. Rigid controls over economic, intellectual, and cultural life resulted in millions of people being sent to forced labor camps (gulags) for deviations from the official line. During Stalin's final years, the KGB (secret police) increased in power; right before Stalin's death, official anti-Semitism led to fabricated charges against a group of Jewish doctors accused of poisoning Kremlin officials. Fortunately for the accused, Stalin died before a new round of executions and imprisonment could commence in the so-called doctor's plot.

Khrushchev's Abortive Reforms

After a short period of collective leadership in the USSR, **Nikita Khrushchev** emerged as the Secretary General of the Communist Party of the Soviet Union (CPSU). Khrushchev secured his leadership by distancing himself from his predecessor, initiating a campaign of **de-Stalinization** with the 1956 speech noted above. Soviet intellectual life thawed, as writers were encouraged to air excesses of the Stalinist period. One example is Alexander Solzhenitsyn's grim depiction of the gulag system, *One Day in the Life of Ivan Denisovich* (1962). Khrushchev dramatically stated his goal of surpassing the US economy by 1980 with the phrase "We will bury you." Despite Soviet space successes like *Sputnik*, Khrushchev's decentralization of the economy and focus on consumer goods fell far short of overtaking the US economy. More importantly, Khrushchev failed to fix the woeful productivity of Soviet collective farms; his so-called virgin lands project of opening Soviet Central Asian areas to cultivation did little to address the bureaucratic structure of Soviet agriculture. Khrushchev found his way blocked by party bureaucrats, known as *apparatchiki*, who feared the effect of his reforms on their power. Along with his provocative foreign policy failures over Cuba, Berlin, and the break with Communist China, Khrushchev's incomplete reforms led to his downfall in 1964.

Nuclear Parity and Domestic Drift: Brezhnev

Soviet life in the era of Leonid Brezhnev (1907–1982) reminds one of the Potemkin villages in the era of Catherine the Great (see chapter 9)—a glittering façade of power to the outside world that hides the rot within. Party leaders specifically selected Brezhnev for his status quo credentials; his goal was "no experimentation," that is, to maintain the influence of the army, *apparatchiki*, and state-owned industrial enterprises. Brezhnev did preside over an important diplomatic achievement—nuclear parity with the United States by the 1972 SALT agreement. In addition, Soviet leaders could boast a formidable space program, thriving scientific communities, and Olympic athletic successes. With the Brezhnev Doctrine (see page 287), the Soviet Union stood poised to maintain its sphere of influence on its borders without American interference. However, these successes could not compensate for the staggering Soviet economy. Successive Five-Year Plans barely met established quotas and hid the fact that in an emerging digital age, the nation continued to focus on production in heavy industry—tractors, steel, construction equipment. Economic life drifted amid a lack of consumer goods and poor productivity. Many workers failed to show up for work (absenteeism), and alcoholism became rife. Important indicators of social health, such as infant mortality, suicide, and life expectancy, experienced troubling reversals.

Gorbachev: *Perestroika* and *Glasnost*

Soviet leadership in the late 1970s and early 1980s resembled a geriatric ward. Following Brezhnev, two aged leaders maintained the status quo. When Mikhail Gorbachev was chosen General Secretary of the CPSU in 1985, he came as a breath of fresh air to the Soviet Union. At 54, he was the youngest member of the Politburo. Gorbachev recognized the problems within both the Soviet economy and social life; he hoped to save the Soviet system by creating "socialism with a human face." The centerpiece of the Gorbachev's reform movement was *perestroika*, or restructuring, of the centrally planned Soviet economy. Gorbachev wanted to produce more consumer goods and to decentralize control of the inefficient state-owned enterprises. The new Soviet leader underestimated the entrenched power of Soviet bureaucrats and soon added another fundamental principle to his reform—*glasnost*, or openness. Soviet citizens were encouraged to discuss openly the failures of the past; an underground press, *samizdat*, came out into the open, and

> ### SKILL SET
>
> Mikhail Gorbachev represents one of the most significant figures of the latter part of your course. By the end of his political career, Gorbachev drew more respect from outside than inside the (former) Soviet Union. As a way to consider the long- and short-term problems of the USSR, take a position on this question (ARG and CES): To what extent was Mikhail Gorbachev responsible for the collapse of the Soviet Union?

Gorbachev allowed Soviet Jews to emigrate and promoted religious freedom. A nuclear disaster at Chernobyl in 1986 actually strengthened Gorbachev's hand by demonstrating the vital need for Soviet modernization and reform.

By 1988, Gorbachev found himself in an increasingly difficult position, pinched between hard-line defenders of the old system and advocates of free-market capitalism. Agriculture presents a good example of the Soviet leader's dilemma. Gorbachev allowed small farmers to lease plots from the government collectives, but the state remained the sole owner of the land. As a result, commercial agriculture never developed, and productivity remained low. Politically, Gorbachev moved power from the party over to state institutions, as with the creation of a Congress of People's Deputies, which then elected him president. Dramatic by any standard, these reforms nonetheless proved inadequate either to save the old system or create a new one. Ironically, as approval for these measures plummeted in the Soviet Union, Gorbachev's reputation and celebrity in the West skyrocketed as the liberator of Eastern Europe and a hero for helping end the Cold War.

Reformers and defenders of the old system both began to lose faith in Gorbachev. Many reformers turned to the newly elected maverick president of the Russian republic—Boris Yeltsin (1931–2007)—who had been expelled from the CPSU by Gorbachev in 1987. More importantly, *perestroika* and *glasnost* had inadvertently sparked independence movements by the many ethnic minorities within the Soviet empire, particularly among the Baltic republics. Gorbachev see-sawed between threats of force and conciliation to prevent the break-up of the USSR. However, the Soviet leader was able to hammer out a union treaty with the 15 republics (except for the Baltic States and Georgia) for greater autonomy within the USSR to take effect in August 1991. Before the treaty could be implemented, communist hard-liners attempted to overthrow Gorbachev. The August 1991 coup failed miserably due to lack of planning, popular resistance, and the opposition of Yeltsin. Gorbachev returned to power, but not for long; Yeltsin outlawed the Communist Party in Russia, and the Soviet Union was voted out of existence by the federation council of the various republics. The entity that had coincided with and helped define the turbulent twentieth century no longer existed.

Russia since 1991

Russia's history since 1991 has been a troubled one. Following the collapse of the USSR in 1991, 12 republics agreed to form the loose Commonwealth of Independent States (CIS). Like Gorbachev, Yeltsin veered back and forth with reforms. Pushing for a strong presidential republic, Yeltsin in the spring of 1993 dissolved the Duma (legislature) and called for new elections. Hard-liners in the Duma refused to leave the building, leading to a violent clash that left 100 dead. Though Yeltsin won the battle and his new constitu-

tion took effect, public support for reform flagged, as shown by the return of Communists and Soviet nationalists to the new Duma. In addition, Yeltsin after 1994 bogged the now-decrepit Russian army down in an ethnic conflict with separatist Chechnya, a small Islamic enclave. The conflict involved atrocities on both sides, but Russia was able to restore nominal control of the breakaway republic.

Before his resignation in 1999, Yeltsin sponsored the rise of his handpicked successor as president, Vladimir Putin (1952–). Putin has worked to advance Russia's independent position in world affairs, promote economic development, and centralize state authority. Putin's presidency has been marked by an increase in state control of the media and repression of internal opponents of his regime. However, Putin retains high approval ratings internally for restoring Russian power, as with his annexation of Crimea (from Ukraine) in 2014, hosting the Sochi Olympics (also in 2014), and countering US diplomacy in the Middle East and elsewhere. These renewed tensions have led some to characterize Putin's presidency as fomenting a new cold war between Russia and the western alliance. Indeed, evidence suggests that Putin has promoted populist authoritarianism throughout Europe—often with the implied threat of cutting off Russia's supply of natural gas—and influenced US political disunity to his advantage through social media bots and computer hacking.

Eastern Europe: In the Soviet Shadow

Stalinization

After suffering two invasions by Germany within 30 years, and in keeping with its perennial expansion, Russia under Stalin was determined to create a buffer zone to its west. Disagreements over the fate of Eastern Europe helped precipitate the Cold War between the superpowers. By 1948, all but Albania and Yugoslavia lay firmly within the Soviet sphere of influence. To combat the Marshall Plan, the Soviet Union developed its own framework for integration in the East known as COMECON. Communism and socialism in Eastern Europe found wide appeal after the war even without Soviet pressure. However, Stalin wanted to assure himself of pro-Soviet communist regimes on his western border, so he forced purge trials of any independent-minded, homegrown leftists. Therefore, the Soviet Union imposed Stalinist regimes on the **Eastern European satellites**, a trend that involved the following to greater or lesser degrees:

- *One-party police states* – Once the Cold War broke open, all political parties but the Communist Party and its direct allies were banned. Eastern European states closely controlled speech, culture, and religious expression.

- *Planned economies* – The Soviet model of centralized control by party bureaucrats was exported to Eastern Europe. Moreover, the USSR assigned specific economic roles to the various nations, with, for example, East Germany focusing on heavy industry, Romania on oil production, and Bulgaria on agricultural products.

- *Collectivization of agriculture* – During the interwar period, most Eastern European states redistributed land to peasants in small plots. The Soviet Union now reversed this trend by requiring its satellites to collectivize agriculture and establish communal farms; in the more western-oriented nations such as Poland and Hungary, some private farmland was allowed.

These policies fomented discontent among key segments of the populations of Eastern Europe—small farmers, the middle class, nationalists, and intellectuals. However, the ever-present fear of Stalinist repression kept a tight seal on such discontent.

De-Stalinization, Revolt, and the Brezhnev Doctrine

Stalin's death in 1953 prompted revolts and hopes for change. East Berliners toppled statues of Stalin, but their revolt was quickly suppressed. A more momentous push for change came with Khrushchev's official policy of **de-Stalinization** in 1956. Several Eastern European states took the Soviet policy as their cue to liberalize their own economic and political systems.

Communist leaders in Poland and Hungary wished to establish a system more in keeping with national traditions. Polish party officials turned to reformer Wladyslaw Gomulka (1905–1982), who halted collectivization of agriculture, relaxed control over the economy, and improved relations with Poland's strong Catholic Church. The Soviet Politburo warned Polish leaders that their reform had gone too far, but Gomulka stayed in power by promising allegiance to the Warsaw Pact and because the Soviets faced an even thornier issue in Hungary.

Events in Poland sparked protests in Hungary. The Communist Party replaced hard-line leaders with former Prime Minister Imre Nagy (1896–1958), who had previously been expelled from the party for "deviation." Nagy freed political prisoners and worked toward liberalizing Hungary's political and economic systems. When Nagy announced Hungary's withdrawal from the Warsaw Pact and called on the world to recognize his nation's neutrality, the Soviets forced the Hungarian Communist Party to depose Nagy and appoint János Kádár (1912–1989) as the new leader. Soviet tanks now rolled in and crushed the uprising, at the cost of about 100,000 lives. Over 200,000 Hungarians fled the country, and Nagy himself was captured and hanged. The message was clear: reform must not threaten the Soviet sphere of influence.

Despite the failed promise of de-Stalinization and the imposition of even harsher Soviet controls after 1956, many Eastern European satellites continued to desire greater autonomy. As part of a worldwide youth protest movement, Czechoslovakia attempted to liberalize its communist system during the Prague Spring of 1968. Reformers within the Communist Party replaced its Stalinist leaders with the Slovak reformer Alexander Dubček (1921–1992). Dubček encouraged a new spirit of openness and promised the relaxing of political controls, all in an effort to create a humane socialism. Though Dubček reassured Soviet leaders of his nation's commitment to the Warsaw Pact, he ultimately could not control the euphoria of the Czechoslovakian reform movement nor assuage the concerns of surrounding Warsaw Pact leaders, who feared the spread of reform to their own nations. In August 1968, Soviet troops ended the reform, and its leaders declared in the Brezhnev Doctrine that deviations from the socialist line would not be tolerated. As with Hungary, the United States tacitly accepted the Soviet action.

The Fall of Communism, 1989–1990

The collapse of communism during 1989–1990 represents one of the most momentous and surprising events of the twentieth century. Reasons for the collapse divide into (1) propellant forces *toward* change and (2) the *lack* of restraining forces *against* it. By the 1980s, the economies of the Eastern European states were losing ground to more technologically dynamic Western Europe. Also, high oil prices and inefficient state-owned enterprises contributed to huge government debts. Politically, the desire for national autonomy, religious freedom, and political rights percolated under the surface of passive obedience. Given these conditions, the presence of the Soviet army *and* the satellites' agreement to maintain their borders vis-à-vis one another (to prevent refugees from escaping) acted as the only checks on a revolutionary situation. When these props were removed by Gorbachev and some members of the Warsaw Pact, the Berlin Wall came tumbling down.

With this general context in mind, we survey developments in the major Eastern European nations leading to the collapse of communism:

Poland: Gomulka began as a reformer, but price increases by the government in 1970 caused his ouster. His replacement, Edward Gierek, embarked on economic reforms, but borrowing from the West forced upon the nation an austerity program. Once again, price increases in 1980 led to discontent and strikes by workers. Uniquely in a Communist nation, workers founded an *independent* labor union called Solidarity, led by the militant shipyard worker Lech Walesa (1943–), which soon boasted a membership of 10 million. Emboldened by the Catholic Church and a newly elected Polish pope, John Paul II (r. 1978–2005), workers demonstrated for free elections and a share in government power.

Fearing Soviet intervention, the new Communist leader General Wojciech Jaruzelski (1923–2014) declared martial law in 1981. Walesa was arrested and Solidarity driven underground. When Gorbachev embarked on his *perestroika* reforms, pressure grew on the satellites to liberalize. By 1989, Solidarity had convinced the government to allow <u>free elections</u>, which resulted in a universal repudiation of Communist rule, as Solidarity won all but one seat in the legislature. The following year, Nobel Peace Prize winner Walesa was elected president in a stunning reversal of fortunes.

Hungary: Following the Soviet crushing of the Hungarian revolt, Jánós Kádar maintained strong political control while allowing a more decentralized economy. By the 1980s, like the other satellites, Hungary experienced economic stagnation and rising debt. Communist party leaders quietly pushed Kádar out of power in 1988 and soon opened the door to a social democratic economy and multiparty elections. In an act of reconciliation with its past, Hungary rehabilitated Nagy and the other leaders of the revolt and provided a burial with honors for those who had been killed. More important for future events, Hungary removed the barbed wire "iron curtain" around its borders, triggering a flood of refugees from nearby East Germany.

East Germany: Since 1961, the aged and increasingly out-of-touch Erich Honecker (1912–1994) strictly ruled East Germany with the aid of the state police, the Stasi. East Germany possessed the strongest economy in Eastern Europe; however, East Germany's leaders always felt insecure in the presence of their larger and more dynamic sister (West Germany), an insecurity that accounts for the Berlin Wall. When Hungary opened its borders, the action prompted a flood of East German refugees fleeing west. When Gorbachev visited East Germany in 1989 to celebrate its 40th anniversary, he inadvertently sparked mass demonstrations demanding reform and open travel. Though Honecker contemplated military repression using the Stasi, the Communist Politburo removed him and opened travel through the Berlin Wall. Soon after, a euphoric populace destroyed the hated symbol, and the Communists were kicked out of power. Momentum became unstoppable toward the **unification of Germany**. With the approval of the four WWII Allied powers, including the Soviet Union, Germany was reunified in October 1990.

SKILL SET

Since Europe was officially divided into East and West during the Cold War, the question of comparisons naturally arise. As you read through the material on each bloc, make a diagram in which you note differences AND similarities (for LEQs, you can use the "opposing" reasoning process for your Complexity point) in economics, society, politics, and diplomacy. Can you devise a focused argument for this prompt?

Czechoslovakia: Events in Eastern Europe began to resemble the proverbial snowball rolling downhill. Inspired by the revolts in Poland, Hungary, and East Germany, mass demonstrations broke out in autumn 1989 in the capital city of Prague. A group of intellectuals, Charter '77, led by the jailed playwright Vaclav Havel (1936–2011), became a rallying point against the Stalinist regime. By this point, Communist leaders had lost both their nerve and remaining moral authority; within weeks, the Communist monopoly on power evaporated, to be replaced by free elections, a free press, and the emergence of Havel as the president of Czechoslovakia. Observers dubbed the nonviolent change the Velvet Revolution. Because of its democratic past, the nation moved quickly toward a multiparty political system and a free-market economy. In the aftermath, Slovakia pressed for independence, accomplished through the so-called Velvet Divorce that created the **Czech Republic and Slovakia** in 1993.

Romania: Since 1965, the iron-fisted Nicolae Ceausescu (1918–1989) had ruled Romania. Ceausescu justified his regime by striking an independent pose in foreign policy—opposing the Soviet invasion of Czechoslovakia in 1968 and building friendly ties with Western nations. Through rigid one-person rule, Ceausescu wished to force Romania into the modern industrial age; however, Ceausescu compromised his nation's standard of living to pay off foreign debt and support his family's extravagant lifestyle. Ceausescu brutally crushed any opposition with his Securitate police. Encouraged by the revolts across Eastern Europe, protests erupted in the city of Timisoara, which the Securitate smashed at the cost of hundreds of lives. Violent street battles broke out among the regular army, which now supported the revolutionaries, and the Securitate. Ceausescu's forces collapsed and the dictator, along with his wife, were captured and executed on Christmas Day 1989. The National Salvation Front reform movement emerged to oversee the nation's difficult transition to democracy and capitalism.

Following the Velvet Revolution, new president Havel proclaimed, "Czechoslovakia is reentering Europe." In that spirit, many of the former Soviet satellites have rejoined the West by entering NATO and the European Union (EU); for some nations, such as Romania, Bulgaria, and Albania, the evolution toward parliamentary democracy and free markets has proven more painful but continues today.

Yugoslavia: The Balkans Again

The most violent break from communism occurred in multiethnic Yugoslavia. A diverse collection of Slavic ethnic groups, Yugoslavia was always an artificial state. Though Croats and Serbs speak the same language, the former historically were tied more to the West religiously (Catholicism) and politically, whereas the latter were oriented more toward Russia and Orthodox Christianity. The Nazi invasion of 1941 led to the creation of a Croat fascist movement, the

Ustashe, which committed atrocities against Serbs. Communist resistance leader Marshal Tito liberated his nation from the Nazis while also resisting Soviet domination. To maintain control of Yugoslavia, Tito experimented with a decentralized though socialist economic system and a federation of ethnic states, kept tightly together by the authority of the Communist Party. Tito's joke about the nation he ruled became prescient in the 1990s: "I am the leader of one country which has two alphabets, three languages, four religions, five nationalities, six republics, surrounded by seven neighbours, in which live eight ethnic minorities."

Following Tito's death in 1980, ethnic tensions reemerged and burst into the open with the events of 1989–1991. The Western-oriented republics—Croatia, Slovenia, and Bosnia—voted in 1991 for independence. However, significant minorities of Serbs lived in each of these regions, prompting a series of violent wars between 1991 and 1999. Led by the Serb nationalist Slobodan Milosevic (1941–2006), Yugoslavia (now simply Serbia and Montenegro) attacked Bosnia in an effort to secure Serbian enclaves; in the process, Serbian troops used **ethnic cleansing** campaigns against <u>Bosnian Muslims</u> involving mass killing, rape, and the destruction of homes. Croatian armies responded with their own atrocities against Serb civilians. Europe stood appalled and impotent at the sight of ethnic conflict thought to be a relic of the WWII era. Finally in 1995, NATO and the United States engineered a cease-fire, and with the Dayton Peace Accord, the parties agreed to the partition of Bosnia, enforced by UN peacekeepers. Now Milosevic turned to the historically important province of Kosovo, populated primarily by ethnic <u>Albanians known as Kosovars</u>. To halt another ethnic cleansing campaign, US President Bill Clinton (1946–) sponsored a NATO bombing operation that once again ended the killing with the placement of peacekeepers. By 2001, Milosevic had been voted out of office and placed on trial at The Hague, Netherlands, for crimes against humanity; however, he died in 2006 before his trial was completed.

Western Europe: Pulling Back and Together

In 1945 Western Europe lay in ruins. By the mid-1950s, however, it had experienced a remarkable recovery. How? First, the nations of Western Europe pulled back from their imperial commitments, either surrendering or losing their colonies, thus freeing themselves from the expense of defending empires. Second, the two world wars threw an icy bucket of water in the face of extreme nationalism. After 1945, the peoples of Western Europe, prompted by the United States, worked toward economic and political unity. The Atlantic alliance (NATO) provided collective security while economic unity produced a stunning turnaround.

Recovery and Reconstruction

Following the Second World War, Western Europe faced immense devastation. Important industrial areas had been bombed to oblivion, infrastructure lay in ruins, and regular economic structures such as currencies and trade had collapsed. Complicating recovery was the issue of displaced persons (DPs)—the 30–50 million refugees seeking relatives and shelter, and the ethnic minorities (mostly Germans) forcibly removed in the redrawing of postwar boundaries. What's more, harsh winters and poor harvests from 1945 to 1947 increased fears of the spread of communism.

With its dominant economy and readiness to enter decisively into European affairs, the United States offered **Marshall Plan** aid (totaling $12 billion) to the nations of Europe. American leaders insisted that such aid be funneled through the Organization for European Economic Co-operation (OEEC) to promote unity—both for efficiency's sake and to create bloc solidarity as the Cold War heated up.

> **THEME MUSIC**
>
> Western Europe's unexpectedly rapid recovery from the destruction of World War II has been termed an "economic miracle." Though this economic dynamo powered new forms of prosperity, it also raised continuing issues of inequality and, for the first time, the potential for environmental devastation (ECD and TSI).

Learning lessons from the post-WWI settlement, industrial nations began creating international economic institutions even before the Second World War ended. The Allied nations in 1944 adopted the Bretton Woods system, which included an <u>International Monetary Fund (IMF)</u> for currency stabilization. Currencies were to be backed by gold and exchange rates fixed to ensure stability. Based on the strength of the US economy, the dollar evolved into an unofficial reserve currency, at least until 1971 when President Nixon was forced to abandon the gold standard due to inflation, returning the industrial world to a system of floating currencies. In addition, the <u>International Bank of Reconstruction and Development (World Bank)</u> provided loans for the modernization of infrastructure (e.g., dams, roads, and sewers). To avoid the economic nationalism of the interwar period, Western nations embraced free trade. The informal <u>General Agreement on Trade and Tariffs (GATT)</u> worked toward the reduction and elimination of trade barriers and eventually gave way to the more formal <u>World Trade Organization (WTO)</u> in 1997. In all, these institutions performed admirably in regulating the world economy and promoting growth, though they came under increasing criticism from opponents of economic globalization in the 1990s.

Western European governments accepted the need for state management of a capitalist economy. <u>Keynesian economics</u> emerged as the reigning theory; states employed tax and budget policies to promote growth and cushion recessions. In Britain, the new Labour government signaled its commitment to full employment and the **social welfare state** by following the recommendations of the wartime Beveridge

Report (1942). Some European states nationalized key industries, such as utilities and transport, to ensure the public welfare, but these new mixed economies (free markets *and* government regulation) did not approach the rigid controls of the Soviet-style system. European growth continued throughout the 1960s but stalled with the oil shock of the 1970s and 1980s. Stagflation (inflation *and* unemployment) forced a reappraisal of Keynesian theory and a move to reduce the welfare state and government regulation in favor of supply-side economics.

Decolonization

World War I shook Europe's control of its colonies, and World War II fractured it. By 1945, most European nations no longer possessed the means or the inclination to continue as colonial powers. Also, the dominant member of the Western alliance, the United States, generally opposed Europe's continued control of colonial empires. Nonetheless, the road to independence proved rocky in many cases, both for the mother country and the colony. On the AP exam, if you encounter this topic, it may be couched in a comparative framework. What follows are three approaches to **decolonization**.

Great Britain: The new Labour government lacked enthusiasm for the British Empire. After the First World War, Britain ruled several areas of the world under **mandates**, a system of tutelage (protection and guidance) leading to independence. After World War II, Britain adopted a strategy of "partition and depart" for its colonies and mandates, encouraging the contending groups to sort out the political settlement. In the case of Palestine, a proposed partition in 1947 led to the founding of the state of Israel in 1948 and the first of several wars between Arabs and Israelis. Both Hindus and Muslims had for decades urged Britain to leave India, led by Gandhi's campaign of nonviolent resistance (Indian National Congress). Britain's partition of the subcontinent in 1947 left Muslim East and West Pakistan divided between India; this geographic anomaly, along with dispute over the border region of Kashmir, has fed a succession of conflicts between Muslim Pakistan and mainly Hindu India, both now nuclear powers.

In Africa, the push for independence accelerated after 1960 and is demonstrated by the increase in UN membership from the 51 original members to almost 200 today. Britain faced its most difficult situation in Egypt. After overthrowing the British-backed government in 1952, Egyptian leader Gamal Abdul-Nasser (1918–1970) announced the nationalization of the Suez Canal, sparking an invasion by British, French, and Israeli forces. The Suez Crisis of 1956 ended when the United States and Soviet Union denounced the invasion and forced its withdrawal. This defeat is usually taken to signify the end of Britain's status as a major world power. Britain's retreat from direct colonial control continued throughout the 1950s and 1960s in Asia as well, though many former colonies retained political and economic contacts with Britain through the commonwealth system.

Low Countries: During the Second World War, Japan "liberated" many Asian colonies of the European powers, including the Dutch East Indies. Even before the war, an Indonesian Nationalist Party under Sukarno (1901–1970) agitated for autonomy. After the expulsion of Japanese forces in 1945, Sukarno's movement actively sought independence. Attempts to subdue the revolt failed, and the Netherlands withdrew from the archipelago and refocused on European issues. After 1949, Indonesia faced a number of difficult transitional issues, such as a communist threat, government corruption, and political violence over East Timor (a Christian enclave among a Muslim majority). However, Indonesia has haltingly moved toward democracy and become a major economic and political power in Asia.

Belgium planned to grant independence to its African colony, Congo, over a 30-year period following World War II. Faced with increasing pressures, Belgium changed its position and pulled out in 1960. Chaos ensued, due to separatist movements, rival political factions, and army mutinies. With UN support, Belgian forces returned in 1961 to restore order, but a leftist rebellion continued. Eventually, the Congo was ruled as a brutal and corrupt dictatorship by Mobuto Sese Seko. Because of Congo's vast but untapped resources, its political problems spilled over into neighboring Burundi and Rwanda. The latter nation descended into ethnic violence in 1994 between rival tribes (Hutus and Tutsis); after several of its peacekeepers were killed, Belgium pulled out of the country as genocide took almost 1 million lives. Many criticized western imperialism both for seeding ethnic conflict with its initial heedless division of Africa and then for acting weakly and tardily in not trying to prevent it.

France: To reestablish prestige after its poor showing in the Second World War, France was determined to hold onto its colonial empire. It soon faced a nationalist and communist insurgency in Indochina from the Viet Minh, led by Ho Chi Minh. The conflict represents an appropriate example of how communism and anticolonialism often became fused in the context of the Cold War. As noted above, the French were forced to withdraw in 1954, only to have the United States take up the battle in its own war in Vietnam. An even more agonizing colonial war for France occurred in Algeria. Unlike Indochina, a substantial portion of the Algerian population were French settlers (*colons*), and the postwar French government resolved to defend their interests. A militant nationalist group, the National Liberation Front (FLN), waged an almost 8-year war for independence against the French, with atrocities on both sides. The war produced a crisis for the French government, eventually bringing down the Fourth French Republic and leading to the reemergence of Charles DeGaulle. President DeGaulle ended the war in 1962, despite opposition from the army, and granted Algerian independence.

As these examples demonstrate, European nations came to realize the inevitability of independence at different times and with varying approaches, some of which proved violent. Before refocusing on Europe, you should keep in mind that Europe's involvement with its former colonies did not end with independence—issues of terrorism, peacekeeping, **migrant workers**, and colonial dependence continued.

Western European Unity and Economic Integration

Putting aside the narrow nationalism that had brought them low, Western and Central Europeans moved incrementally in the postwar period toward economic and political integration. Key to this unity was the partnership between France and West Germany. In 1952, two practical men of business and politics, both from Alsace-Lorraine—Jean Monnet (1888–1979) and Robert Schuman (1886–1963)—proposed the **European Coal and Steel Community (ECSC)**, involving Belgium, the Netherlands, and Luxembourg (Benelux nations), France, Italy, and Germany. These nations (Inner Six) eliminated tariff barriers and placed coal and steel production under a High Authority. Within 5 years, production had doubled. Flush with success, the Inner Six in 1957 agreed to the Treaty of Rome, creating the **European Economic Community (EEC)** or **Common Market**, which worked toward the abolition of trade barriers, the free flow of capital, and common economic policies. In addition, the six agreed to coordinate their nonmilitary atomic research and development under the European Atomic Community (Euratom).

At first, Great Britain stood aside from the Common Market, owing to its special relationship with the United States and its commonwealth. Later in the 1960s when the British changed their attitude, DeGaulle of France vetoed their entry for fear Britain's overseas commitments would dilute European unity. Eventually, the British joined the EEC in 1973, along with Denmark and Ireland. During the 1980s and 1990s, more nations on the Mediterranean and in Eastern Europe—with the fall of communism—joined the growing community. After the passing of the oil shock of the 1970s, the European Community moved toward a stronger integration. In 1991, the member states signed the Maastricht Treaty aimed at creating a single Europe. This new **European Union (EU)** was governed by an elected European Parliament and a centralized decision-making European Commission of civil servants and administrators. Recent

THEME MUSIC & SKILL SET

Decolonization fittingly culminates the theme of Europe's interaction with the world (INT), including the indirect effects of immigration and terrorism. Consider what impact decolonization has had both upon Europe and the world (CAUS). For the perspective of a French anti-colonial, consult *The Wretched of the Earth* by Frantz Fanon (1925–1961), a black Caribbean psychiatrist and political philosopher who challenged both colonial policies and western ideas of race: https://iep.utm.edu/fanon/.

expansion has increased the number of EU members to 27. More importantly, 12 EU members in 2000 (now 19) adopted the new **euro** currency to replace their national currencies. Some have criticized the distant and bureaucratic nature of the EU—and indeed the movement toward a truly United States of Europe has moved in fits and starts and may never realize its initial dream. Nonetheless, progress since the late 1940s has resulted in a economic bloc of over 500 million people, which accounts for about 12% of the world's trade. During the global financial crisis of 2007–2009, many of the weaker EU nations (such as Portugal, Spain, Greece, Ireland, and Cyprus) experienced severe budget shortfalls that required bailout packages from the stronger states (e.g., Germany), as well as unpopular austerity measures. Though the situation has been stabilized for now, the crisis has once again demonstrated the difficulties of coordinating such a diverse economic entity and continued popular discontent with the distant power of EU bureaucrats and bankers. The 2016 vote in the UK for Brexit shocked the European Union and served as a reminder that many nationalists oppose the project of surrendering autonomy to the idea of a United States of Europe.

EXAMPLE BASE

Many observers prematurely predicted the end of nationalism or other ideological conflicts with the fall of communism. You are encouraged to identify and explain several instances of how nationalist and separatist movements have continued to trouble policymakers and citizens on the European continent.

Western European National Politics

Though the themes of Western Europe as a region take precedence, you will find it useful to draw from specific nations in applying your understanding of broader themes. To keep this material to a manageable size, consult the following chart:

Nation	Issues	Leaders/Groups	Events	Analysis
Great Britain	Since 1945, Britain has faced an older and less advanced economic infrastructure than the other Western European nations. In addition, it has battled high unemployment and its adjustment to a second-tier power.	• The Labour and Conservative Parties have alternated control of the government, with Labour working toward the expansion of the welfare state. • Margaret Thatcher (1925–2013)—Ideological ally of President Reagan, Thatcher curbed the size of the welfare system, denationalized industries, attacked the power of labor unions, and reasserted British power abroad. • Tony Blair (1953–)— Labour Prime Minister from 1997–2007, Blair appealed more to the middle class, promoted economic growth, and supported US efforts against terrorism.	• The "Troubles" in Northern Ireland between the Catholic Irish Republic Army (IRA) and Protestants led to continued violence, though a peace agreement has largely held since 1998. • In 1982 Thatcher aroused British nationalism with the Falklands War against Argentina over control of an island chain off of South America. • In 1973, Britain joined the Common Market but not the euro, and recently (2016) voted to leave the EU ("Brexit") in protest against the effects of globalization. • Britain has "devolved" political decision-making to its various nations, such as Scotland and Wales.	Britain continues to face decaying industrial cities and lower economic productivity, while trying to retain a British identity that unites its several nations.
France	The postwar Fourth Republic (1945–1958) struggled with the legacy of collaboration during the Vichy regime and political instability yet enacted important reform legislation. With the Fifth Republic's (1958–) strong presidency under DeGaulle, France left the NATO military alliance and pursued a more independent line in foreign affairs, known as Gaullism.	• Charles DeGaulle (1890–1970)—DeGaulle supported European integration but an independent foreign policy vis-à-vis the United States. • Francois Mitterand (1916–1996)—Socialist president from 1981 to 1995, Mitterand at first expanded the welfare state but was forced to retrench and cohabit with conservative prime ministers. • Jean Monnet (1888–1979)— architect of European unity	• In 1961, France pulled out of the NATO military alliance (remaining in the political alliance). • France developed independent nuclear weapons. • **Student revolts** in 1968 led to violence in Paris and almost brought down the DeGaulle government. • Colonial conflicts in Indochina and Algeria caused internal political conflict and changes.	France benefited from its involvement in the EU and partnership with Germany. French assertions of political and diplomatic power have not always coincided with its economic power, which is second in Europe to Germany's.

Nation	Issues	Leaders/Groups	Events	Analysis
(West) Germany	West Germany (Germany after its reunification in 1990)—has worked to demonstrate its allegiance to democracy and the Western alliance by distancing itself from the Nazi past. It has played a crucial role as the banker of the EU.	• Konrad Adenauer (1876–1967)—Known as the founding Chancellor, he led the Christian Democratic Party (CDs), a right-center party favoring laissez-faire economics and close ties to the US. • Ludwig Erhard (1897–1977)—economic minister and brains behind Germany's economic miracle • Willy Brandt (1913–1992)—Socialist chancellor whose *Ostpolik* ("opening to the East") normalized relations between East Germany and the Soviet Union.	• In 1955, Germany rearmed and joined NATO. • Germany joined the UN in the 1970s as part of détente. • **German reunification** came soon after the collapse of the Berlin Wall in 1989. • Chancellor Angela Merkel (1954–) has reaffirmed Germany's commitment to the EU by engineering a bailout during the euro crisis and to its global openness by accepting more refugees from the Syrian civil war than any other European state.	Germany seems firmly established as a democracy and committed member of the Atlantic Alliance. Reunification has cost trillions of marks and the eastern part still suffers from higher unemployment and environmental problems. Germany's economic power makes it the strongest member of the EU.
Italy	Following World War II, Italy abolished the monarchy and worked toward economic modernization. Leftist parties proved resilient, and Italy's parliamentary system has produced more than 60 different governments since 1945.	• Alcide de Gaspari (1881–1954)—Christian Democratic prime minister who helped establish Italy's new parliamentary system and membership in the Atlantic alliance. • Socialists finally gained power in 1983 but their policies differed little in practice from the Christian Democrats.	• In 1946, Italians by a small majority voted to abolish the monarchy due to its involvement with fascism. • Eurocommunism, centered in Italy, rejected ties to the Soviet Union and the more radical features of Marxism-Leninism. • In 1993, Italy restructured its system of proportional representation, which has allowed for longer-lived governments and more stability.	Italy recovered economically after the war, but was hard hit by the oil shock. It continues to deal with the lack of development in the south and corruption in government.

Additional Resources

📖 Timothy Garton Ash, *In Europe's Name: Germany and the Divided Continent* (1993) — The author examines the roots of German reunification.

📖 Timothy Garton Ash, *The Magic Lantern: The Revolution of '89 Witnessed in Warsaw, Budapest, Berlin, and Prague* (1993) — A gripping journalistic account of the fall of communism.

📖 John Lewis Gaddis, *The Cold War: A New History* (2005) — A noted diplomatic historian incorporates the latest interpretations of the conflict.

📖 Eric Hobsbawm, *The Age of Extremes: A History of the World, 1914–1991* (1996) — The conclusion of Hobsbawm's series introduces the idea of the "short twentieth century."

📖 Samuel Huntington, *The Clash of Civilizations and the Remaking of the World Order* (1996) — The author argues controversially that the post-Cold War world has been defined by rising conflicts over culture and religion.

📖 Tony Judt, *Postwar: A History of Europe Since 1945* (2006) — A strong resource and the best single-volume history of the period.

📖 Ian Kershaw, *The Global Age: Europe 1950–2017* (2020) — The concluding volume of the comprehensive *The Penguin History of Europe* series.

📖 Paul Kennedy, *The Rise and Fall of the Great Powers: Economic Change and Military Conflict, 1500–2000* (1989) — With broad historical perspective, the author examines the importance of economic productivity and "imperial overreach" in the rise and decline of great powers.

📖 David Remnick, *Lenin's Tomb: The Last Days of the Soviet Empire* (1994) — A journalist's account of the fall of the Soviet empire.

📖 Todd Shepard, *Voices of Decolonization: A Brief History of with Documents* (2014) — A brief volume in *The Bedford Series in History & Culture* that provides analysis and sources.

📖 Laura Silber and Alan Little, *Yugoslavia: Death of a Nation* (1997) — A clearly written story of a nation's collapse into ethnic conflict.

📖 John O'Sullivan, *The President, the Pope, and the Prime Minister: Three Who Changed the World* (2008) — Argues for the primacy of its three figures in the collapse of communism.

📖 Lawrence Wright, *The Looming Tower: Al-Qaeda and the Road to 9/11* (2006) — Provides background on events and intelligence failures leading up to 9/11. Also see the 10-episode mini-series based on the book that first aired on Hulu in 2018.

📺 *Cold War* (1998) — An ambitious 24-part CNN series with analysis and interviews from many of the policymakers and participants.

💻 https://www.nobelprize.org/prizes/peace/1990/gorbachev/biographical/ — Biographical information related to Mikhail Gorbachev, including primary sources.

💻 http://www.johndclare.net/cold_warA1.htm — A compilation of resources and perspectives on the Cold War

💻 http://chnm.gmu.edu/1989/ — Materials and lessons focused on the collapse of communism in Eastern Europe

CHAPTER TEST

Multiple-Choice Questions

Questions 1–5 are based on the passage below.

> "In an ironic sense Karl Marx was right. We are witnessing today a great revolutionary crisis, a crisis where the demands of the economic order are conflicting directly with those of the political order. But the crisis is happening not in the free, non-Marxist West, but in the home of Marxist-Leninism, the Soviet Union. It is the Soviet Union that runs against the tide of history by denying human freedom and human dignity to its citizens. It also is in deep economic difficulty…. Over-centralized, with little or no incentives, year after year the Soviet system pours its best resource into the making of instruments of destruction. The constant shrinkage of economic growth combined with the growth of military production is putting a heavy strain on the Soviet people. What we see here is a political structure that no longer corresponds to its economic base, a society where productive forces are hampered by political ones."
>
> US President Ronald Reagan, address to the British Parliament, June 8, 1982

1. The speech suggests all of the following features of the Cold War EXCEPT:
   A. American economic and military influence over Western Europe.
   B. an arms race between the superpowers with the threat of nuclear war.
   C. covert actions and limited "hot wars" globally to secure power and influence.
   D. the division of Europe into rival blocs, known as the Iron Curtain.

2. Which of the following Soviet leaders would have most likely agreed with Reagan's analysis of the Soviet Union's situation?
   A. Lenin
   B. Stalin
   C. Khrushchev
   D. Gorbachev

3. Which of the following directly resulted from the situation Reagan outlines?
   A. A new period of cooperation between the US and the Soviet Union
   B. The fall of the Berlin Wall and reunification of Germany
   C. The collapse of the communist system and break-up of the Soviet Union
   D. A renewal of nationalism in the Balkans and wars of ethnic cleansing

4. As suggested by Reagan's speech, US policy toward Europe after World War II differed most strongly from US policy toward Europe after World War I in that the US:
   A. guaranteed Western European security through the NATO alliance.
   B. joined the United Nations and other international organizations.
   C. promoted its economic interests through trade and financial policies.
   D. President visited Europe and engaged in direct diplomacy.

5. Which of the following facts—all of which are true— would most seriously limit the source above as a credible account of the Soviet system?
   A. President Reagan and British Prime Minister Margaret Thatcher were not only allies, but friends, and offered support to one another's policies.
   B. President Reagan had never visited the Soviet Union and thus did not possess any first-hand experience with their economic or political system.
   C. President Reagan and his Republican Party faced difficult congressional elections in autumn 1982, and he wished to present himself as a strong world leader.
   D. President Reagan had throughout his career strongly opposed communism, and in the following year called the Soviet Union the "evil empire."

Questions 6–9 are based on the passage below.

"At that time I acted for Germany as the German Chancellor, but also a firm believer in Europe. Because I believe in Europe, I proposed that my parliament, the German Bundestag, take unusual and previously unimagined routes in order to help Greece and thus to ensure the stability of the eurozone as a whole. I was motivated to do so by the European project. This is the only reason why I decided to implement a short-term solution for the rescue package as well as ambitious reforms and strict austerity programmes for Greece and other countries. I faced severe criticism for this: For some it was too slow, for others too fast. But I believe it was the right thing, on the one hand, to insist that countries which caused such a crisis will have to take action themselves in the future and, on the other hand, to make clear that we bear a shared European responsibility."

Angela Merkel, German Chancellor, speech to students at the College of Europe in Bruges, Belgium, November 2, 2010

6. The post-World War II trend in European politics most strongly reflected above is the:
   A. end of the Cold War between the superpowers.
   B. commitment of the United States to European security.
   C. recovery of Germany from the devastation of the war.
   D. movement toward continental cooperation and unity.

7. All of the following institutions would be consistent with Merkel's perspective EXCEPT the:
   A. European Coal and Steel Community (ECSC).
   B. North Atlantic Treaty Organization (NATO).
   C. Council for Mutual Economic Assistance (COMECON).
   D. European Community (EC) and European Union (EU).

8. The most significant change in German politics after 1950 was:
   A. its admission into NATO in 1955.
   B. the building of the Berlin Wall in 1961.
   C. the election of SPD Chancellor Willy Brandt in 1969.
   D. the reunification of West and East Germany in 1990.

9. Which of the following post-World War II trends has worked most strongly against Merkel's vision?
   A. The independence of African and Asian colonies
   B. The revival of nationalist and separatist movements
   C. The collapse of communism in Eastern Europe
   D. The establishment of the UN and other international organizations

See Chapter 18 for answers and explanations.

Long Essay Question

Directions: Read the prompt below and write your response on a separate sheet of paper. A sample response and commentary are provided on the next page.

Evaluate the most significant difference between the impact of the Cold War on Western Europe with the impact of the Cold War on Eastern Europe.

(RP: Comparison)

LEQ Sample Response

The Cold War had a big impact on Europe after WWII. However, different parts of Europe were affected differently. Western Europe really gained a lot from being allied with the United States, but the East was dominated by the Soviet Union. In this essay, I will discuss the different policies of the superpowers and how the Cold War created blocs of countries that opposed each other over the Iron Curtain.

Western Europe was in shambles in 1945. At first, the United States did not know what to do about the situation. Soon conflict with the Soviet Union broke out over Berlin and free elections in Eastern Europe. To oppose communism, the United States tried to help rebuild Europe; American leaders knew that communism might spread if conditions continued to be bad. So the United States provided Marshall Plan aid and helped unify the West. NATO was created and West Germany was admitted into it. This alliance tried to defend against the spread of communism. Also, Western Europe began to pool their resources together. They created the Coal and Steel Society and eventually the Treaty of Rome to knock down tariff barriers. These two organizations promoted an "economic miracle" and helped Europe get back on its feet. Some leaders, like DeGaulle of France, did not like US domination of Europe but most in the West realized that they needed an American ally to fight the Soviet threat.

The Soviet Union wanted to dominate Eastern Europe, because the Soviets were all about world domination. It was part of their communist philosophy. Soviet-type governments were imposed on their satellites, called this because they revolved around the Soviet Union. Oppression reigned in the East and all the bad features of communism were imposed on these nations—gulags, press censorship, and rigid economies. Some states rebelled against the Soviet Union like Hungary, because of their domination. This did not help the unity of the East because it was unity imposed by the Soviet Union. This is shown later when the nations of Eastern Europe revolted against the USSR with the fall of the Berlin Wall in the late 1980s.

Western European nations like France and Germany experienced growth in their economies from 1945–1960 and banded together to oppose communism. NATO protected them against the Soviet Union. On the other hand, the East was dominated by the Soviet menace. Nations had to toe the Soviet line or face invasion. So in the long run, the West was positively unified but the East was negatively unified, which was a major difference. This division was similar to what happened in Europe during the religious wars, especially after the Peace of Westphalia, when countries supported either the Protestant or Catholic Church. Eventually the religions decided to "coexist peacefully;" however, with the superpowers, one of them no longer exists.

LEQ Response Analysis

The student addresses the question, but might do so more explicitly. Major contrasts between the two blocs are provided, often with a negative portrayal of the Soviet Union. Certainly there is evidence to support this view, but the response grows repetitious in its assertions by the end of the essay. Despite a weak introduction—inadequate thesis and minimal historical context—the student does provide two cogent body paragraphs. Though the response could be more explicit in connecting the examples to the most significant difference between the two regions, it does clearly address the Targeted RP (Comparison). If the student did not provide a line of reasoning for the Thesis in the introduction, the first several sentences of the conclusion make up for this lapse. However, the explanation for Complexity by comparing the Cold War to the religious wars falls short. **Score: 4** (+1 for Thesis, + 2 for Use of Evidence, +1 for the Targeted RP (COMP))

CHAPTER 17

Contemporary European Society and Culture

Wars reorder the balance of power and diplomatic structures, but they can also produce major changes in society and culture. This truism applies to the period following World War II. Pent-up demand for products and the need for material reconstruction fed an **economic miracle**, especially in Western Europe. Prosperity, in turn, promoted population increase, consumerism, and technological advance. Most governments committed themselves to a more active role in economic regulation and ensuring a social welfare system. Renewed prosperity and the specter of the Cold War also worked a downside. Numerous groups of outsiders—students, feminists, environmentalists, terrorists—offered various critiques of European society in the years after 1945. Culturally, experimentation flourished in the postwar intellectual climate but also revealed divisions between traditionalists and modernists, and even postmodernists. Following World War II, Europe's problems are increasingly seen in a global context.

 KEY IN – Chapter 17 addresses all or part of the following topics in the Unit Guides of the CED:

Topic 8.11 Continuity and Changes in an Age of Global Conflict

Topic 9.1 Contextualizing Cold War and Contemporary Europe

Topic 9.2 Rebuilding Europe

Topic 9.5 Postwar Nationalism, Ethnic Conflict, and Atrocities

Topic 9.6 Contemporary Western Democracies

Topic 9.8 20th-Century Feminism

Topic 9.11 Migration and Immigration

Topic 9.12 Technology

Topic 9.13 Globalization

Topic 9.14 20th- and 21st-Century Culture, Arts, and Demographic Trends

Topic 9.15 Continuity and Changes in the 20th and 21st Centuries

The Economic Miracle and its Consequences

Europe's remarkable recovery from the destruction of the Second World War produced a higher standard of living and increased life expectancy, as well as negative side effects. In this section, we examine the social changes provoked by the changing European economy and the advance of technology.

The Baby Boom and After

The Great Depression and World War II dampened European birth rates. After 1945, the western world underwent a steady increase in the birth rate, known as the **Baby Boom**. Governments encouraged the trend in an effort to replace population loss from war and also to allay a labor shortage. State policies of pronatalism subsidized additional births, infant nutrition, and day care. Also aided by an influx of immigrants, Europe's population increased by 25% between 1945 and 1970. With the onset of artificial means of contraception, particularly the birth control pill, birth rates trended downward after the mid-1960s. The Baby Boomers born in this interval and who grew up amidst prosperity and **consumerism** benefited from the increased standard of living but also came to criticize it, along with their parents' values.

Since the 1970s, and especially since 1990, the population of many European nations has stagnated. In some states, like Italy and much of Eastern Europe, populations have already begun to decline. This trend affects politics for two reasons. Government provision for generous retirement benefits must be funded by taxes from the young. When these programs were first implemented, 20 workers supported the benefits of one retiree. That ratio has decreased to between 3–5 workers per retiree, creating a potential entitlements time bomb in the next few decades. Europe's prosperity also attracts immigrants from Asia, the Middle East, and elsewhere. Greater ethnic diversity has increased social tension and led to the growth of nationalist and **anti-immigrant political movements**. With the decline in religious observance among European Christians, some estimate that Muslims will outnumber Christians during the twenty-first century. It is likely that this demographic shift will be accompanied by increased conflict, as witnessed by recent violence over publication of cartoons satirizing the Prophet Muhammad (Denmark, 2006; France, 2011 and 2015) and the assassination of Theo Van Gogh in 2004 in response to his (Dutch) film critical of Islam. Such tensions have arisen not merely due to conflicting religious loyalties but more fundamentally over the status of religion in state and society, the growing divide between secularism and religiosity.

THEME MUSIC
We live in an age of globalization (INT), with the fluid transmission of goods, information, and people across borders and regions. As such, events in the non-European world exercise growing influence on the continent. A recent global trend affecting Europe has been the refugee crisis, with victims of war and state collapse from the Middle East (and other regions) seeking refuge in Europe. Such large population movements rarely occur without conflict, as is apparent in Europe today.

Growth of and Challenge to the Welfare State

Western and Eastern governments both significantly expanded **welfare benefits** (known as **"cradle-to-grave"**) following World War II. In Eastern Europe, this trend coincided with the establishment of Marxist governments dedicated to social equality and providing the basics for all citizens. In the West, the adoption of social welfare was driven by the dominance of <u>Keynesian economic theory</u> and fears about socialist exploitation of class conflict. Western nations provided old-age pensions, unemployment, and disability insurance; subsidized or socialized medical care; and redistributed income through progressive taxation. For the most part, this social safety net proved popular, though it came under increasing criticism during the stagnant 1970s and 1980s.

The late 1970s and early 1980s witnessed a resurgence of conservative political parties in several nations, such as Great Britain and the United States. Leaders like <u>British Prime Minister Margaret Thatcher</u> and President Ronald Reagan identified an over-regulated economy and a bloated government bureaucracy as the key causes of the high inflation and unemployment of the period. Even Socialist Francois Mitterand of France was forced to abandon the more ambitious elements of his social reform program by the mid-1980s due to budget deficits and stagnating productivity. Supply-side economists argued that reduced taxes, regulation, and government spending on the welfare state would stimulate economic productivity and liberate entrepreneurship. Supply-side policies did produce growth in the 1980s and early 1990s, but leftist parties believed the costs proved too high in the form of poverty, inequality, and the decline of organized labor.

Consumerism and Its Critics

Postwar prosperity brought a flood of new consumer goods. Pent-up demand from two decades of retrenchment during the Depression and WWII burst open with a spree of kitchen appliances, television sets, automobiles, and clothing fashions. **Mass marketing** techniques grew in sophistication, employing TV spots and computer technology to sell the good life. Images of blue jeans and Coca-Cola were beamed across the Iron Curtain to demonstrate the superior abundance of Western society. Marketers often employed sexuality to sell products, a fact condemned both by religious conservatives and some feminists who decried the objectification of women. The Western economies (including the United States) began a shift away from traditional heavy industry toward services and information processing. While this postindustrial economy created new opportunities and wealth, it also gutted jobs from older industrial areas, such as the Midland cities of Britain—Leeds, Liverpool, Manchester, and Sheffield.

Many across the political spectrum—from traditionalists to socialists—found the new consumerism both shallow and extravagant. Environmentalists objected to the waste of non-renewable resources and levels of pollution. Socialists found confirmation for theories of Marxist alienation in Western society's high levels of crime, suicide, and social dislocation. British economist E.F. Schumacher (1911–1977) argued for balancing society's need for efficiency and productive centralization with humanistic values of community and the dignity of labor. In his famous work *Small Is Beautiful* (1973), Schumacher argued for **sustainable development** that would take into account the needs of future generations and the impact of production on the health of the planet.

Technological Advances

Continued scientific progress marked the postwar era. Major advances in medicine and medical care almost doubled life expectancy during the twentieth century. Antibiotics cured formerly deadly infectious diseases. Medical personnel first used penicillin widely during the Second World War to fight infections following surgeries and amputations. In addition, vaccines also helped curtail a number of other dreaded diseases; Jonas Salk in 1955 pioneered an easily administered vaccine against polio. Safe and effective surgery, including organ transplantation, became common after the 1970s. Due to worldwide public health efforts, often

> ### THEME MUSIC & SKILL SET
>
> There is a tendency in our digital age of wonders to lionize new technologies for expanding our speed and scope of access to information and goods. It is vital when addressing Technological and Scientific Innovation (TSI) that you evaluate the tensions inherent within the theme between efficiency and humanity, speed and stress, production and sustainability. As you consider the evidence in this chapter, be prepared to make an argument that captures these tensions in a coherent argument (ARG and CES).

sponsored by the United Nations, smallpox was eradicated by the 1970s. However, the threat of global pandemics, such as AIDS (acquired immunodeficiency syndrome), avian flu, and most recently, COVID-19, have intensified with the further development of global trade and travel.

Much scientific research in the postwar period has been funded by governments. With the onset of the Cold War, both superpowers invested huge resources in gaining a technological edge over the other—in rocket technology, nuclear power, and the space race. The space race produced the first moon landing by America's Apollo program in 1969. Not all applauded these advances. In his farewell address, President Eisenhower warned of the political dominance of a "military-industrial complex," comprising large, bureaucratic militaries, arms manufacturers, and corporations, all of whom held an interest in the continuation of the arms race or even war. A new class of technocrats—engineers, managers, scientists—seemed to wield authority out of proportion to their numbers and outside democratic political processes.

Moreover, many European nations adopted **nuclear power** as a beneficial side effect of the Cold War nuclear arms race. Currently, France supplies more than 75% of its energy needs via nuclear power. Opponents feared that reliance on nuclear power would lead to environmental problems, such as waste disposal and nuclear meltdowns, as occurred at Chernobyl in 1986 and almost occurred at Three Mile Island, Pennsylvania, in 1979.

Critics and Outsiders in European Society

Despite renewed economic prosperity, many Europeans either felt overlooked or alienated by postwar society. These groups offered critiques of consumerism, conformity, and inequality that often crossed the political spectrum.

Youth Revolts and the Generation Gap

The postwar Baby Boom generation was the first to attend college in large numbers. However, universities became a victim of their success in attracting students. Classes tended to be large and impersonal, and the professors distant. Students criticized living conditions in the dorms and demanded the addition of more up-to-date and relevant courses and programs in psychology, sociology, and women's studies. Youth criticisms were not unique to Europe; the years 1967–1968 witnessed worldwide protests against repression and bureaucratization. European protests began in Italy and Germany before spreading to France; these **revolts of '68** evolved into the most fundamental critique of postwar society and nearly brought down President DeGaulle's government.

French students criticized DeGaulle as an elderly and distant figure, more interested in foreign affairs than domestic reform. In addition, many students and those sympathetic to leftist ideologies, such as Maoism and Trotskyism, opposed America's involvement in Vietnam and other Cold War colonial conflicts. Many students were attracted to the New Left critiques of neo-Marxist thinkers like Herbert Marcuse (1898–1979), whose *One-Dimensional Man* (1964) condemned both the bureaucratic centralism of Soviet ideology and the rampant consumerism of Western society in favor of a culture of protest and rebellion.

In May 1968, the University of Paris exploded with student unrest. Students seized control of campus buildings and battled police, demanding improved conditions but also a more open and less bureaucratic society. Workers initially supported the students with a nationwide general strike. When it looked as if DeGaulle's government would collapse, he defused the situation by co-opting the workers with wage increases and by assuring the support of the army for his government. Now isolated, the students eventually settled for concessions such as input into university governance and relief of overcrowding. Though the students' more ideological demands were not met, their actions highlighted growing divisions within European society.

Young people often clash with elders as they establish autonomy. However, some have referred to a "generation gap" to describe the widely divergent experiences of parents who grew up in the Great Depression and World War II with their children who experienced Cold War pessimism and economic prosperity. Youth culture embraced themes of rebellion, symbolized by the slogan "sex, drugs, and rock 'n roll." Postwar European governments **decriminalized gay and lesbian relationships** and abortion, and made birth control widely available. The resulting sexual revolution sought to separate sexual expression from family and commitment. Many young people embraced premarital sex and open sexuality as acts of rebellion against a society they perceived as rigid and conventional. During the 1960s, the recreational use of drugs such as marijuana and LSD spread as a way to explore new states of consciousness. Postwar music also expressed themes of rebellion. The Beatles' long hair, irreverent attitudes, and drug references introduced a generation to rock 'n roll music. American protest music from Bob Dylan and Janis Joplin linked social consciousness with popular culture. Fittingly, the children of the Boomers launched their own musical rebellion in the 1980s with punk and alternative.

Feminism

Militant feminism began as a transatlantic movement and coincided with the push for civil rights in the United States during the 1960s. Now that women had gained the vote in almost all European nations after World War II, this Second Wave Feminism turned toward economic and cultural criticism. Women's liberation was inspired by several key publications. First, French philosopher Simone de Beauvoir (1908–1986), in *The Second Sex* (1949), demonstrated how gender functioned as a social construction of expectations and attitudes rather than a biological category. Throughout history, de Beauvior argued, women have been treated as "the Other," that is, a deviance from the "default" male gender, rather than beings in their own right. American Betty Friedan's *The Feminine Mystique* (1963) encouraged women to battle blatant and subtle oppression that limited women's entrance into leadership positions in academia, business, and government.

Indeed, women in Eastern and Western Europe entered the workforce in larger percentages than ever before. Moreover, many women attained **high political office** during the postwar era. Scandinavian legislatures today claim close to 50% of seats held by women. Several famous women were elected for the first time in modern history as heads of government or state, such as Margaret Thatcher in Britain, Angela Merkel in Germany, Golda Meir in Israel, and Indira Gandhi in India. Feminists believed that reproductive rights, such as access to birth control and legalized abortion, were essential to this progress. Worldwide, Europe led the way for the liberation of women, and European feminists have proven instrumental in pushing the United Nations to develop programs for female literacy, contraception, and universal rights in those developing regions where women often suffer the brunt of oppression and poverty.

Environmentalism

Postwar economic growth created a host of environmental problems, such as pollution, acid rain, and global climate change. American zoologist Rachel Carson (1907–1964) spawned the global environmental movement with her investigation of the effects of pesticides on the food chain in *Silent Spring* (1962). Environmental groups sprung up in response and agitated for ecological protections, the more radical of which demanded a complete reassessment of the nature of global, consumerist capitalism. The fall of communist states in Eastern Europe revealed that socialist economies could despoil the environment as much as capitalist ones; in fact, much of the cost of German reunification has involved bringing the former East Germany up to similar ecological standards as the rest of Germany. In the 1980s **Green parties** sprung up in Central Europe, advocating for sustainable development and supporting other leftist causes, such as social justice and pacifism. Germany's Green Party has proved most successful, having served in coalition with the Social Democratic Party from 1998 to 2005. Environmentalists often combined forces tactically and philosophically with feminists and the antinuclear movement in the 1980s and 1990s.

> **THEME MUSIC & EXAMPLE BASE**
>
> For the examples in this section, consider how they help flesh out your understanding of the Social Organization and Development (SCD) theme. After 1945, the lives of individuals were shaped by forces—economic, environmental, technological—often beyond their direct control. You will notice that to address issues of concern, individuals will form groups, such as reform movements or political parties, as was the case with feminists, environmentalists, and youth.

Most industrialized nations now support at least some of the environmental agenda. In 1992, 178 nations sent representatives to the first Earth Summit, held in Rio de Janeiro to address concerns over global warming. Science has confirmed that human use of chemicals and burning of fossil fuels (anthropogenic climate change) has reduced the ozone layer and increased global temperatures. To address the issue further, 150 nations in 1997 signed the Kyoto Protocol to halve greenhouse gases by 2010, and 196 nations in 2016 agreed in Paris to limit global temperature increases to 2 degrees Celsius. However, one of the largest producers of such gases, the United States, declined to ratify Kyoto and has seesawed in its support for the Paris Agreement. Another issue of concern for the environmental movement has been world population growth. At the beginning of the twentieth century, the Earth's population stood at 1.7 billion; as of today, it is approaching 8 billion. Much of this growth has occurred in the developing world, often complicating global problems of poverty, illiteracy, and lack of infrastructure. Controversy over measures to address this issue, such as promotion of birth control, often provokes controversy among differing cultural and religious traditions.

Guest Workers and Immigration

During the economic boom times of the 1950s and 1960s, Europe allayed its labor shortage by enticing immigrants from Southern Europe, Africa, and the Middle East. As with the United States today, these *Gastarbeiter* (as they are called in Germany) often performed jobs that local populations were reluctant or unwilling to assume. Moreover, governments often refused to extend citizenship or state benefits to these workers. When the European economy slowed in the 1970s and 1980s, local populations urged the **migrant workers** to leave. When the fall of the Berlin Wall led to increased unemployment in the former East Germany, anti-immigrant parties and neo-Nazi groups urged their expulsion, or worse, attacked ethnic enclaves. In France, Jean-Marie Le Pen's National Front Party called for an end to immigration and supported economic nationalism; Le Pen polled enough votes in the 2002 presidential election to force a run-off before losing. An heir to the pan-German nationalist parties of the nineteenth century, the anti-immigrant Austria Freedom Party won almost 27% of the 1999 legislative vote, before falling back in subsequent elections. Issues of immigration and refugees (from the Middle East) highlight the growing diversity of European culture in an age of global capitalism and the challenges of successfully integrating new groups and redefining what it means to be European.

Domestic Terrorism

Indigenous European terrorist movements took root in the 1970s and divided basically into two types of groups: leftists and separatists. Leftist groups arose out of the violent youth movement of the late 1960s, especially among those influenced by Maoist and Trotskyite ideologies. The Red Brigade used armed violence to force (unsuccessfully) Italy's withdrawal from the Western alliance. Most famously, it kidnapped and assassinated Prime Minister Aldo Moro in 1978; its influence has declined since the late 1980s. Germany's Baader-Meinhof Gang also employed assassinations and kidnappings of public and business officials, most famously in the so-called German Autumn of 1977. Since the collapse of communism, the influence of the group has decreased.

Ethnic **separatist movements** in Northern Ireland and Spain have used tactics similar to leftist groups. The Troubles in British-ruled Northern Ireland began in 1968–1969 with communal clashes between Protestants wishing to remain in the United Kingdom and Catholics wishing to unite with the Republic of Ireland. The Irish Republican Army (IRA) campaigned against the British presence with car bombs, assassinations, and hunger strikes. Not until 1998 did the two sides work out a power-sharing agreement; in late 2005, the IRA announced that it had abandoned all of its weapons. Similarly in Spain, the ETA has agitated with assassinations and bombings for a separate socialist government representing the Basque people, the oldest ethnic group in Europe and one of the few not speaking an Indo-European language.

Intellectual and Cultural Trends

The experience of two world wars has fomented experimentation in the arts and reevaluation in the realms of philosophy and religion.

Modernism and Postmodernism

We often use the term "modern" simply to mean contemporary. Modernism, however, is associated with the Enlightenment project, that is, the effort to discover the laws of nature and of human society, and thereby reach objective knowledge of the world. Once humans possess objective knowledge, they can harness nature for their flourishing and achieve progress. These notions define developments in ideas, economics, politics, and culture from the eighteenth into the twentieth centuries. The wrenching experiences of the two world wars and disgust over the crimes of absolutist ideologies like Nazism and communism have produced a movement in opposition to modern assumptions of objective knowledge, a movement known as **postmodernism**.

> ### SKILL SET
> From the rubble of 1945, many Europeans reevaluated their civilization. As a focal point, consider the following interpretative question: To what extent and in what ways does the Second World War represent a transformation in European intellectual and cultural life? To practice the skill of Change and Continuity over Time (CCOT), try writing a focused thesis paragraph in response (ARG).

Postmodernism's roots lay in the nineteenth-century ideas of Friedrich Nietzsche and Danish philosopher Søren Kierkegaard (1813–1855), both of whom emphasized the lack of objective values in the world and the importance of **subjective experience**. In the postwar intellectual world, postmodernism has exercised a significant influence on literary criticism, philosophy, the writing of history, architecture, and film. Postmodernists aim to deconstruct texts—fiction and nonfiction—to find the underlying sociopolitical structure of gender, class, and race embedded in the authors' works. All ideas carry the baggage of their creator's biases and drive for power. As Thomas Kuhn (1922–1996) argued in his *The Structure of Scientific Revolutions* (1962), not even science possesses objective authority, instead representing a series of paradigm shifts that deal only with fact and theory, not truth. Postmodernists express interest in how knowledge is constructed rather than its correspondence with Truth, since the latter does not exist. In art, postmodernists employ irony and satire and promiscuously blend traditional and modern styles.

Existentialism

Existentialism dominated the postwar intellectual world. The philosophy arises out of humanity's modern predicament—our feeling of angst amid a world of dizzying economic and technological change, the decline of traditional religious values, and the horrors revealed of humanity during the twentieth century. Most but not all existentialists began with Nietzsche's premise "God is dead." If this is so, then man must "create himself." As a movement, existentialism took hold among French intellectuals wrestling with the agonizing issues of resistance or collaboration during the Nazi occupation of France. Jean-Paul Sartre (1905–1980) was captured by the German army during World War II and later founded an underground resistance movement. Sartre argued that for humans, "existence precedes essence," meaning that we "turn up on the scene" without choosing to exist; because we have no creator, our essence must be defined by our own choices and values. As is demonstrated in Albert Camus's (1913–1960) novels *The Stranger* (1942) and *The Plague* (1947), humans must face the absurdity of existence by making life-defining choices utterly alone and with incomplete knowledge of their surroundings. Human experience is thus subjective, and because no objective values exist for us to draw on, we must accept our radical human freedom and act with authenticity—without self-deception and by accepting responsibility for our choices. Existentialism significantly influenced the arts (see below), and with its emphasis on subjectivity and criticism of modern society, it helped lay the foundations for postmodernist thought.

Art, Theater, and Music

Signifying the increasingly important role of the United States in European affairs, the center of the Western art world shifted to New York City following World War II. Two styles dominated art in the contemporary era: abstract expressionism and pop art. In abstract expressionism, the artist does not portray anything, but instead uses the canvas and paint to express an emotional attitude or mood. American painter Jackson Pollock (1912–1956) popularized the style with his drip technique of pouring and splashing paint on immense canvases lying on the floor. Pop art is associated with both the rise of consumerism in the postwar Western world and also the irony and satire of postmodernism. Artists such as Americans Andy Warhol (1928–1987) and Roy Lichtenstein (1923–1997) employed advertising, celebrities, and comic books in their art to comment ironically on the artificiality of consumer capitalism. When contemplating Warhol's Campbell's soup cans or Lichtenstein's comic strips, the line between advertising and artistic creativity becomes blurred.

The ideas of existentialist Albert Camus directly influenced the so-called Theater of the Absurd. Whereas traditional drama concentrates on the development of plot and character, absurdist drama provokes the question, "What is happening now?" Along with the characters, the audience attempts to ascertain the significance of what is occurring on stage. Perhaps the most famous absurdist drama is Irish playwright Samuel Beckett's *Waiting for Godot* (1954), in which two tramps arrive on stage and discuss waiting for a figure named Godot; Godot never shows, but the audience is never told why this person is important. In Tom Stoppard's *Rosencrantz and Guildenstern Are Dead* (1967), two characters from Shakespeare's *Hamlet* discuss their upcoming fate but seem unable to prevent their untimely deaths—a play within a play.

While popular music incorporated rebellion and consumerism, composers of avant-garde (cutting edge) music experimented with serialism. Serialist composer Arnold Schoenberg (1874–1951) employed a 12-note scale and used mathematical series of tone rows to create a more abstract sound than standard tonal and melodic music. Pioneering American composer John Cage (1912–1992) experimented with chance music, where elements of a composition occur randomly. Most famously, Cage "played" his composition "4'33"" in concert, a piece consisting of not a single note; Cage simply timed the composition and then closed the piano cover. In conclusion, perhaps many of these works strike the reader as far-fetched, ridiculous, or nonsensical; with postwar culture, it may very well be that the point is that there is no point.

Religion in the Modern World

As noted, religious belief in Europe declined markedly in the postwar period. Nonetheless, religious developments continued to play a role in European culture after 1945. For the Catholic Church, the most important development has been the ecumenical movement, or the effort to reach out and establish common ground with other, particularly Christian, religions. Since the Council of Trent (1545–1563), the church had generally been on the defensive against modern ideas and culture. When Pope John XXIII (r. 1958–1963) called the **Second Vatican Council** (1962–1965), it signaled the willingness of the Church to update doctrine and practice more in keeping with modern developments. John opened dialogues with different faiths and called on wealthy nations to support social justice and work toward human rights. His successor, Paul VI (1963–1978), contin-

> **THEME MUSIC**
>
> How relevant is organized religion in an age of technological and intellectual pluralism? There are no easy answers to this question. Before responding, draw on what you've learned from the role of religion throughout the relevant themes of the course—in shaping views of the world (CID), influencing political life (SOP), and affecting belief and practice (SCD).

ued the work of Vatican II but sparked controversy with his encyclical *Humanae Vitae* (1968), which condemned artificial means of birth control.

Paul's death in 1978 opened the door for a historic change in the church, the election of the first non-Italian pope since 1522 and the first Slavic pope ever. John Paul II (1978–2005), often considered the first postmodern pope, lived under both Nazi and Soviet oppression in his native Poland. Many commentators consider this experience to have shaped the John Paul's concern with what he later called the twentieth century's "culture of death." As pope, John Paul supported the anti-Soviet Solidarity movement in Poland and worked toward the end of communist oppression in Eastern Europe but also condemned the nuclear arms race and the excesses of consumer capitalism. John Paul's long reign also witnessed his many efforts to reconcile the Catholic Church with its past, apologizing for the Crusades, Galileo's persecution, and the failures of the Catholic Church during the Holocaust. Though progressive on economic issues, John Paul adhered to a conservative line on church dogma, upholding bans on contraception, female and married priests, and abortion. His supporters saw him as providing a brake on the hasty changes made at Vatican II, while his detractors grew concerned with a renewed hierarchical stance. Though it will likely take decades, if at all, for radical changes to occur in Catholic doctrine, Pope Francis (2013–) has worked to humanize the Church further, with a humble style and a more accepting rhetorical stance toward divisive issues. However, the unfolding sexual abuse scandal among the clergy has undermined efforts to rejuvenate the Church and led to declining membership and mass attendance.

Most European Protestant denominations have reconciled themselves to modern biblical scholarship and have adapted their faiths in keeping with modern science. Nonetheless, Protestant theologians like the Swiss Karl Barth (1886–1986) took reformed Christianity back to its roots in biblical revelation. Barth held that divine revelation stood on its own feet, without the possibility of being judged by human reason. The European Protestant experience since 1945 has differed markedly from that of the United States. Evangelical Christianity along with a renewed fundamentalism has experienced widespread growth in America, trends that have not generally touched Europe. In addition, formerly communist Eastern Europe suffered under religious persecution, which effectively killed religious belief in several nations. This unchurched Europe often conflicts with the United States when it comes to issues like Darwinian evolution and foreign policy.

Globalization

Since the beginning of this course, Europe's place in the world has been a recurring theme. More than ever, the issues confronting Europe today reflect those facing the world. With global communication developments, such as cell phones, the Internet, and social media, it is no longer possible for one region of the world to wall itself off from the rest. Recognition of past mistakes in this regard is already apparent with postwar efforts to build a common European identity through economic and political integration. In some ways, Europe has renewed its power and prestige after the horrors of the twentieth century, yet it continues to struggle with its role and place in the world, as seen in the belated response to the Balkan conflicts of the 1990s, recent struggles over the euro currency and EU, and conflicts with shifting religious diversity. As confirmed by history since 1945, many Europeans seem to recognize that their continent functions increasingly within a global context.

Additional Resources

📖 **Karen Armstrong,** *The Battle for God* **(2001)** — A comparative and critical analysis of the growth of fundamentalism among the monotheistic faiths.

📖 **Sarah Bakewell,** *At the Existentialist Café: Freedom, Being, and Apricot Cocktails with Jean-Paul Sartre, Simone de Beauvoir, Albert Camus, Martin Heidegger, Maurice Merleau-Ponty and Others* **(2016)** — Explores the meaning and context of those who made a new philosophy.

📖 **Albert Camus,** *The Stranger* **(1942) and** *The Plague* **(1947)** — These two well-known novels convey the existentialist ethos well and raise profound questions about the human condition.

📖 **Thomas Friedman,** *The World is Flat: A Brief History of the Twenty-First Century* **(2007)** — The author examines the process of global economic and technological change.

📖 **Steven R.C. Hicks,** *Explaining Postmodernism: Skepticism and Socialism from Rousseau to Foucault* **(2011)** — Introduces a recent and complex movement by examining its historical roots.

📖 **Tony Judt,** *Postwar: A History of Europe since 1945* **(2005)** — A well-received history that offers powerful insights and the author's unique voice.

📖 **Mark Kurlansky,** *1968: The Year That Rocked the World* **(2005)** — An interesting analysis of the personalities involved in a year of upheaval.

💻 **https://www.wilsoncenter.org/** — A major international program that offers sources and seminars on a range of topics for global history.

💻 **www.art-for-a-change.com/Paris/paris.html** — This site provides text and posters of the student revolts in 1968 Paris.

💻 **https://www.youtube.com/watch?v=PUwmA3Q0_OE** — ["Human Population Through Time"] Brief yet sobering statistics on the growth of world population over time in the context of global events. Highly recommended.

CHAPTER TEST

Multiple-Choice Questions

Questions 1–4 are based on the chart below.

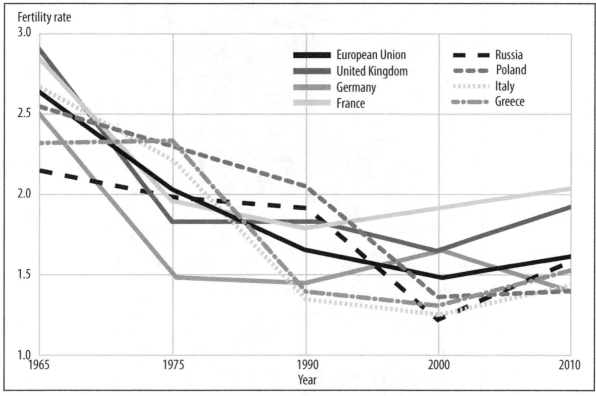

Fertility Rates in Europe, 1965–2010

1. The fertility rates at the beginning date of the chart are explained by all of the following EXCEPT:
   - **A.** government policies to increase birthrates.
   - **B.** economic recovery and a rising standard of living.
   - **C.** improved political stability after the world wars.
   - **D.** the threat of Soviet communism and nuclear war.

2. Fertility levels after 1965 reflect the trend of:
   - **A.** the growth of gay and lesbian rights.
   - **B.** a youth culture emphasizing rebellion.
   - **C.** advances in artificial birth control.
   - **D.** immigration of workers from outside Europe.

3. The fertility trends after about 1975 have prompted debates over:
   - **A.** whether women should have the right to vote.
   - **B.** the benefits of European economic unity.
   - **C.** the role of technology in European society.
   - **D.** the economic feasibility of the welfare state.

4. A feminist would most likely use the data to support which of the following conclusions?
   - **A.** "New conceptions of marriage and motherhood have freed women from a solely domestic role."
   - **B.** "High fertility rates cause significant problems of environmental degradation and resource overuse."
   - **C.** "Emigration from overseas should be curtailed to provide European women with greater job opportunities."
   - **D.** "Western European nations have provided higher status and greater rights to women than those in Eastern Europe."

Questions 5–8 are based on the image below.

Advertisement for Belling Electric Cooker, Britain, 1954

5. The image above most strongly reflects the postwar economic trend of:

   A. continental integration.

   B. feminism.

   C. consumerism.

   D. American aid.

6. The image coincides with which of the following postwar trends?

   A. Competition from the Soviet economic bloc

   B. Economic recovery and a rising standard of living

   C. Existentialism's focus on freedom and individualism

   D. Concern with technology's destructive potential

7. A European historian would mostly likely use this ad as evidence of:

   A. the growing cultural influence of the United States.

   B. a general decline in the belief in progress.

   C. attitudes toward gender and family.

   D. the effectiveness of social welfare policies.

8. The postwar development represented by the image would have received the strongest criticism after 1970 from:

   A. the Green Party.

   B. guest workers.

   C. national separatists.

   D. postmodernists.

See Chapter 18 for answers and explanations.

Short-Answer Question

Directions: Read the excerpt below and answer all parts of the question that follows. Use complete sentences; an outline or bulleted list is not acceptable. Write your responses on a separate sheet of paper. A sample response and commentary are provided below.

"The general policy of the twentieth century was to try to make the most of resources, make Nature perform to the utmost, and hope for the best.

With our new powers we banished some historical constraints on health and population, food production, energy use, and consumption generally. Few who know anything about life with these constraints regret their passing. But in banishing them we invited other constraints in the form of the planet's capacity to absorb wastes, by-products, and impacts of our actions. These latter constraints had pinched in the past, but only locally. By the end of the twentieth century they seemed to restrict our options globally. Our negotiations with these constraints will shape the future as our struggles against them shaped the past."

J.R. McNeill, American historian, *Something New Under the Sun: An Environmental History of the Twentieth-Century World*, 2000

---

1. a) Describe one example that supports McNeill's depiction of European economic and social life <u>before</u> the twentieth century.

    b) Describe one issue or example after 1945 that supports McNeill's perspective on the environment.

    c) Explain one way in which the historical situation of the passage and/or author may either limit or add to the credibility of its/his claims.

SAQ Sample Response

    a) Before the twentieth century, most Europeans struggled to put food on the table and therefore, as the historian says, could not overcome the natural obstacles to achieving prosperity. There was famine and lack of transportation for much of this period and it was only in the modern age when new technologies made lives more bearable for most people.

    b) Today we have many problems with how we deal with nature, just as the historian says. There's an island of plastic floating in the Pacific Ocean the size of Texas, and our earth is really suffering from so many people and how we use products. So the historian is correct in explaining how all of these advances can also create big problems that we will have to deal with.

    c) The historian is American, and since the United States is one of the largest consumers of goods and energy, he would be concerned with what our nation is doing to the earth. Also, the US has not always followed along with the world in enforcing climate restrictions. He would want to bring these issues to light in his book on the environment, making it credible.

SAQ Response Analysis

Here is an example of mistakenly substituting current events for a substantive historical response. The student did not earn credit for either Part A or Part B, as the references in both are too generalized and do not suggest adequate content knowledge. The anecdote regarding plastic in the Pacific Ocean tantalizes, but it is not connected specifically to an environmental issue post-1945, nor does it evince a clear enough understanding of McNeill's interpretation of resource constraints. However, the response did earn a point for its explanation of how the situation of the historian (American and responding to specific US actions on the environment) might enhance the credibility and immediacy of his analysis. Please take note: make sure your SAQ responses include specific examples and provide context that shows your familiarity with the course. **Score: 1 point**

PERIOD 4 — DIAGNOSTIC EXAM

Section I, Part A: Multiple-Choice Questions

Time—30 minutes; 30 questions

Directions: Each of the questions or incomplete statements below is followed by four suggested answers or completions. Select the one that is best in each case and then enter the appropriate letter in the corresponding space on the answer sheet. Source materials have been edited for the purpose of this exercise.

Questions 1–3 are based on the passage below.

> "[Women] have no past, no history, no religion of their own; and they have no such solidarity of work and interest as that of the proletariat…They live dispersed among the males, attached through residence, housework, economic condition, and social standing to certain men—fathers and husbands—more firmly than they are to other women….
>
> Now, what peculiarly signalizes the situation of woman is that she—a free and autonomous being like all human creatures—nevertheless finds herself living in a world where men compel her to assume the status of the Other. They propose to stabilize her as object….The drama of woman lies in this conflict between the fundamental aspirations of every subject (ego)—who always regards the self as the essential—and the compulsion of a situation in which she is the inessential."
>
> Simone de Beauvoir, French philosopher and writer, *The Second Sex*, 1949

1. Which of the following post-1945 trends related to women does the passage above reflect most strongly?

   A. A significant increase in the birth rate (Baby Boom) promoted by many governments

   B. Growth of feminist critiques of social inequality and of traditional values

   C. The greater involvement of women in legislative bodies and leadership positions

   D. Oppression of and unequal burdens placed upon working-class women in the Soviet Union

2. The passage above most closely parallels which of the following post-1945 developments?

   A. Gay and lesbian pursuit of civil rights and legal benefits

   B. Reform within the Catholic Church that redefined doctrine and practice

   C. Medical technologies that extended life but provoked moral questions

   D. The expansion of social welfare programs and higher taxes

3. With which of the following developments or principles from the nineteenth century would de Beauvoir have most <u>disagreed</u>?

   A. The development of companionate marriage

   B. Increase in family leisure time and space

   C. Laws improving the lives of the working class

   D. The bourgeois focus on the cult of domesticity

4. The passage could be used as evidence for all of the following postwar intellectual developments EXCEPT:

   A. postmodernism.

   B. existentialism.

   C. Futurism.

   D. feminism.

Full-sized mural reproduction of *Guernica*, by Pablo Picasso, Spanish painter, 1937

5. The painting illustrates the twentieth-century cultural trend of:

    A. exploring subconscious and subjective states.

    B. questioning the validity of objective knowledge.

    C. accelerating global communications through new technologies.

    D. attacking traditional aesthetic standards to address controversial issues.

6. A historian might use Picasso's depiction as evidence of:

    A. the mixed responses of Christian churches to totalitarianism.

    B. the destructive potential of new technologies in warfare.

    C. agitation against immigrants by nationalist political groups.

    D. the influence of existentialism on popular culture.

7. The post-1945 development that would have provided the strongest confirmation of Picasso's message in the painting was:

    A. the development and use of nuclear weapons.

    B. the collapse of communism in Eastern Europe.

    C. feminist demands for social and political equality.

    D. expansion of consumerism and environmental problems.

Translation: "Deposit your gold for France. Gold fights for victory."

French poster, 1915

8. The poster reflects the pre-1914 trend of:
   A. mechanization of production through the factory system.
   B. state appeals to nationalism through mass communications.
   C. volatile business cycles that led to government intervention in the economy.
   D. Bismarck's creation of an alliance system to isolate France.

9. To advance its message, the poster draws from the pre-1914 period by appealing to the:
   A. German wars of unification.
   B. Congress of Vienna.
   C. French Revolution.
   D. Second Industrial Revolution.

10. Which of the following is the most accurate statement regarding the impact of total war on European society (1914–1918)?
   A. Women entered the workforce in large numbers and gained the right to vote.
   B. The creation of the League of Nations provided for renewed stability and peace.
   C. The pre-war belief in progress was reaffirmed by the defeat of the Central Powers.
   D. Traditional elites continued in power and suppressed revolutionary movements.

Questions 11–13 are based on the passage below.

"Fascism combats the whole complex system of democratic ideology; and repudiates it…Fascism denies that the majority, by the simple fact that it is a majority, can direct human society…and it affirms the immutable, beneficial, and fruitful inequality of mankind, which can never be permanently leveled through the mere operation of a mechanical process such as universal suffrage….

For if the nineteenth century was the century of individualism (Liberalism always signifying individualism) it may be expected that this will be the century of collectivism, and hence the century of the State….

For Fascism, the growth of empire, that is to say the expansion of the nation, is an essential manifestation of vitality, and its opposite, a sign of decadence. Peoples that are rising, or rising again after a period of decadence, are always imperialist: any renunciation is a sign of decay and of death."

Benito Mussolini, Italian dictator, "The Political and Social Doctrine of Fascism," 1935

11. The pre-1914 cultural trend that most influenced Mussolini's view was:

   A. the movement away from representation in the arts.

   B. the embrace of struggle and irrationality in philosophy.

   C. the undermining of classical physics by relativity theory.

   D. a consumer culture that emphasized leisure and status.

12. All of the following developments in the post-1914 period contributed to Mussolini's ideas EXCEPT:

   A. resentment over the Versailles settlement.

   B. the threat of a communist revolution.

   C. the civil war in Spain won by Franco.

   D. economic instability and stagnancy.

13. The western democracies responded to the goals articulated in the last paragraph by:

   A. appeasing fascist aggression.

   B. reviving the League of Nations.

   C. forming an alliance with the Soviet Union.

   D. pursuing policies of economic nationalism.

Questions 14–17 are based on the passage below.

"We are now engaged in a gigantic and exciting task of achieving rapid and large scale economic development of our country. Such development, in an ancient and underdeveloped country such as India, is only possible with purposive planning. True to our democratic principles and traditions, we seek, in free discussion and consultation as well as in implementation, the enthusiasm and the willing and active cooperation of our people. We completed our first Five Year Plan 8 months ago, and now we have begun on a more ambitious scale our second Five Year Plan, which seeks a planned development in agriculture and industry, town and country, and between factory and small-scale and cottage production. I speak of India because it is my country and I have some right to speak for her. But many other countries in Asia tell the same story, for Asia today is resurgent, and these countries which long lay under foreign yoke have won back their independence and are fired by a new spirit and strive toward new ideals. To them, as to us, independence is as vital as the breath they take to sustain life, and colonialism, in any form, or anywhere, is abhorrent…"

Jawaharlal Nehru, Indian Prime Minister, speech in Washington, D.C., December 1956

14. All of the following likely influenced the tone and content of Nehru's speech EXCEPT:

    A. nationalist movements in opposition to imperial control.

    B. Cold War conflicts between the United States and Soviet Union.

    C. creation of international organizations like the United Nations.

    D. immigration from the Middle East and Asia into Europe.

15. Which of the following is most responsible for the situation and attitude that Nehru expresses in his speech?

    A. The Great Depression

    B. World War I and World War II

    C. Europe's postwar economic recovery

    D. The rise of existential and postmodern philosophy

16. Which of the following facts about Nehru, all true, would be most useful to a historian in analyzing Nehru's speech?

    A. Nehru attended Trinity College in Britain studying economics, law, and politics.

    B. Nehru supported the Allied effort during World War II, with political conditions.

    C. Nehru studied several religions but wished India to adopt a secular constitution.

    D. Nehru promoted education as Prime Minister, including founding universities.

17. The content and circumstances of the speech reveal an interaction with Europe most similar to the:

    A. conquest of the Aztecs by the Spanish.

    B. founding of the Dutch East India Company.

    C. slave revolt in French Saint Domingue.

    D. mandate system set up by the League of Nations.

Questions 18–21 are based on the passage below.

"To the editor of 'The Times':

Even we, the adherents of the parties of the Extreme Left, and hitherto ardent anti-militarists and pacifists, even we believe in the necessity of this war. This war is a war to protect justice and civilization…

The German peril, the curse which has hung over the whole world for so many decades, will be crushed, and crushed so that it will never again become a danger to the peace of the world…

To Russia this war will bring regeneration….

All the parties without any exceptions have supported the Government without even waiting for it to make any definite announcement about these crying needs. This is the measure of the belief of the people in the inevitableness of liberal reforms. The Government unfortunately still seems irresolute, and has up till now only done the minimum to justify the popular belief in it, but we are convinced that circumstances will develop in such a way that the Government will not be able to delay for long that which has become for Russia a historical necessity. And the sooner this happens, the better."

V. Bourtzeff, Russian socialist, letter to the *London Times* about six weeks after the outbreak of war in 1914

18. The letter above reveals which of the following causes of the First World War?

    A. The complex alliance system that drew in all the great powers to the conflict

    B. The ability of governments to promote and manipulate nationalism

    C. Competition for colonies in Africa and Asia that heightened tensions

    D. Growth in arms production and influence of military plans on policy-making

19. The situation described above caused the tsarist government to:

    A. complete an alliance with France and Britain.

    B. conclude a separate peace with Germany.

    C. enact reforms such as the abolition of serfdom.

    D. collapse under the strain of total war.

20. The letter reflects all of the following political trends of the period 1850–1914 EXCEPT the:

A. growth of working-class parties and movements, along with industrialization.

B. development of mass politics based on wider participation and new technologies.

C. persistence of traditional elites in power and pressure by outsiders for reforms.

D. growth of private and religious organizations designed to uplift the poor.

21. Which of the following dates represents the most distinct break in Russian history?

A. 1861

B. 1905

C. 1917

D. 1945

Questions 22–24 are based on the photograph below.

Workers, soldiers, and onlookers gather on both sides as the Berlin Wall is constructed, 1961

22. The best explanation for the situation depicted above is:

    A. the desire to punish Germany following the Second World War.

    B. fundamental differences between liberal democracy and communism.

    C. the policies of *perestroika* and *glasnost* of Soviet leader Mikhail Gorbachev.

    D. development of nuclear weapons that posed a threat of annihilation.

23. Which of the following represents the most significant change in the situation depicted?

    A. European nations relinquished their colonies in Africa and Asia

    B. The United States extended aid to Europe through the Marshall Plan

    C. Policies of economic and political integration such as the European Union

    D. The collapse of communism and the end of Soviet control of Eastern Europe

24. The most similar situation in Germany to that shown above was the:

    A. Thirty Years' War and Peace of Westphalia.

    B. wars of liberation against Napoleon.

    C. nationalist policies of Otto von Bismarck.

    D. "blank check" given to Austria by Kaiser Wilhelm.

Questions 25–27 are based on the passage below.

"It is an extraordinary fact that the fundamental economic problems of a Europe starving and disintegrating before their eyes, was the one question in which it was impossible to arouse the interest of the Four.* Reparation was their main excursion into the economic field, and they settled it…from every point of view except that of the economic future of the States whose destiny they were handling….Europe consists of the densest aggregation of population in the history of the world…In relation to other continents Europe is not self-sufficient; in particular it cannot feed itself. Internally the population is not evenly distributed, but much of it is crowded into a relatively small number of dense industrial centers. This population secured for itself a livelihood before the war, without much margin of surplus, by means of a delicate and immensely complicated organization, of which the foundations were supported by coal, iron, transport, and an unbroken supply of imported food and raw materials from other continents."

* the leaders of the victorious Allied powers

John Maynard Keynes, British economist, *The Economic Consequences of the Peace*, 1920

25. All of the following developments brought about the situation that Keynes describes EXCEPT the:

    A. First and Second Industrial Revolutions.

    B. disruptions caused by World War I.

    C. Treaty of Versailles settlement.

    D. rise of the Nazis in Germany.

26. Democratic governments in the interwar period (1918–1939) responded to the economic issues that Keynes outlines by:

    A. establishing mandates over colonies of the Central Powers.

    B. unsuccessfully trying new economic theories and political alliances.

    C. opposing the spread of Soviet communism across Europe.

    D. establishing a system of collective security under the League of Nations.

27. Which of the following distinguishes the interwar economic situation (1918–1939) from previous eras of economic and financial crisis in European history?

   A. Rivalries among nations and political ideologies

   B. Use of tariffs to protect domestic industries

   C. Reliance on capital and leadership from the United States

   D. Issues of national debt and payment of reparations

Questions 28–30 are based on the passage below.

"In this respect [popular violence] the Russian Revolution resembled, however vaguely, the French Revolution: propelled by domestic discontent it aimed at some form of democratic government. Yet that revolution was quickly overtaken by an altogether different one: The revolution of forcible reculturation carried out from above by a small minority, the Communist party, determined to revive the collapsed Russian empire in superior form. Both society and government had to undergo a drastic process of catching up to the social, economic, and political efficiency of Russia's more powerful rivals, the victors in World War I and ever more prominently the United States."

Theodore H. von Laue, German-American historian, *Why Lenin? Why Stalin? Why Gorbachev?*, 1993

28. Which of the following in Russian history would von Laue most likely cite in support of his interpretation regarding "reculturation"?

   A. The policies of Peter the Great

   B. The partitions of Poland

   C. Napoleon's invasion of Russia

   D. Russia's involvement in World War I

29. All of the following actions of the Bolsheviks support the interpretation EXCEPT:

   A. the establishment of control by the soviets.

   B. the Red Army's actions in the Civil War.

   C. Lenin's New Economic Policy (NEP).

   D. Stalin's Five-Year Plans and purges.

30. Mikhail Gorbachev (1985–1991) attempted to address the problems of the Soviet Union (Russia) that von Laue discusses by:

   A. eliminating the exclusive control of the Communist Party.

   B. restructuring the economy away from top-down control.

   C. allowing autonomy for ethnic minority populations.

   D. refusing to maintain Soviet control of Eastern Europe.

Section I, Part B: Short-Answer Questions

Time—25 minutes; 2 Questions

Directions: Read each question carefully and answer all parts of the question. Use complete sentences; an outline or bulleted list is not acceptable. Sources have been edited for the purposes of this exercise.

> "We think of what has disappeared, we are almost destroyed by what has been destroyed; we do not know what will be born, and we fear the future, not without reason. We hope vaguely, we dread precisely; our fears are infinitely more precise than our hopes; we confess that the charm of life is behind us, abundance is behind us, but doubt and disorder are in us and with us. There is no thinking man, however shrewd or learned he may be, who can hope to dominate this anxiety, to escape from this impression of darkness, to measure the probable duration of this period when the virtual relations of humanity are disturbed profoundly."
>
> Paul Valéry, French poet, writer, and philosopher, "On the European Mind," 1922

1. a) Describe one specific way in which the attitude expressed above differs from the cultural climate in Europe prior to 1914.

    b) Describe one example from intellectual or cultural life in the period 1918–1939 that exemplifies the attitude expressed in the passage.

    c) Explain one impact of the attitude expressed in the passage on political or diplomatic events in the period 1918–1939.

> "Europe's recovery was a 'miracle'. 'Post-national' Europe had learned the bitter lessons of recent history. An irenic, pacific continent had risen, 'Phoenix-like', from the ashes of its murderous—suicidal—past."
>
> Tony Judt, British-American historian, *Postwar: A History of Europe Since 1945*, 2005

2. a) Describe one economic factor that contributed to the situation discussed by the historian above.

    b) Describe one political factor that contributed to the situation discussed by the historian above.

    c) Explain one example in the period after 1945 that would contradict the historian's interpretation.

Section II, Part A: Document-Based Question

Total Time—60 minutes; 1 Question

Directions: Question 1 is based on the accompanying documents. It is suggested that you spend about 15 minutes reading the documents and 45 minutes writing your response. The documents have been edited for the purpose of this exercise.

In your response you should do the following:

- Respond to the prompt with a historically defensible thesis or claim that establishes a line of reasoning.
- Describe a broader historical context relevant to the prompt.
- Support an argument in response to the prompt using at least six documents.
- Use at least one additional piece of specific historical evidence (beyond that found in the documents) relevant to an argument about the prompt.
- For at least three documents, explain how or why the document's point of view, purpose, historical situation, and/or audience is relevant to an argument.
- Use evidence to corroborate, qualify, or modify an argument that addresses the prompt.

Question 1   *Evaluate whether scientific and technological developments in the period 1890–1990 promoted optimism and progress in Europe.*

Document 1

Source: Alfred Michelson, Polish-Jewish-American physicist, dedication of Ryerson Physical Laboratory, University of Chicago, 1894

While it is never safe to affirm that the future of Physical Science has no marvels in store even more astonishing than those of the past, it seems probable that most of the grand underlying principles have been firmly established and that further advances are to be sought chiefly in the rigorous application of these principles to all the phenomena which come under our notice....The more important fundamental laws and facts of physical science have all been discovered, and these are so firmly established that the possibility of their ever being supplanted in consequence of new discoveries is exceedingly remote.

Document 2

Source: Siegfried Sassoon, British World War I poet, "Counter-Attack," 1918

…Things seemed all right at first. We held their line,
With bombers posted, Lewis [machine] guns well placed,
And clink of shovels deepening the shallow trench.
The place was rotten with dead; green clumsy legs
High-booted, sprawled and groveled along the saps…

…And then, of course, they started with five-nines*
Traversing, sure as fate, and never a dud.
Mute in the clamor of shells he watched them burst
Spouting dark earth and wire with gusts from hell,
While posturing giants dissolved in drifts of smoke.
He crouched and flinched, dizzy with galloping fear,
Sick for escape,—loathing the strangled horror
And butchered, frantic gestures of the dead…

…Then the haze lifted. Bombing on the right
Down the old sap: machine-guns on the left;
And stumbling figures looming out in front.
'O Christ, they're coming at us!' Bullets spat,
And he remembered his rifle…rapid fire…
And started blazing wildly…then a bang….
Lost in a blurred confusion of yells and groans…
Down, and down, and down, he sank and drowned,
Bleeding to death. The counter-attack had failed.

* German artillery shells

Document 3

Source: Joseph Stalin, General Secretary of the Communist Party and Soviet leader, speech to the Communist Party of the Soviet Union, November 1928

We have assumed power in a country whose technical equipment is terribly backward…[W]e have around us a number of capitalist countries whose industrial technique is far more developed and up-to-date than that of our country. Look at the capitalist countries and you will see that their technology is not only advancing, but advancing by leaps and bounds, outstripping the old forms of industrial technique….Do you think that we can achieve the final victory of socialism in our country so long as this contradiction exists? What has to be done to end this contradiction? To end it, we must overtake and outstrip the advanced technology of the developed capitalist countries. We have overtaken and outstripped the advanced capitalist countries in the sense of establishing a new political system, the Soviet system. That is good. But it is not enough. In order to secure the final victory of socialism in our country, we must also overtake and outstrip these countries technically and economically. Either we do this, or we shall be forced to the wall.

Document 4

Source: Advertisement in the *Good Housekeeping Cookbook*, British Edition, 1948

Document 5

Source: Robert Schuman, French Foreign Minister, declaration proposing creation of the European Coal and Steel Community, May 9, 1950

The pooling of coal and steel production should immediately provide for the setting up of common foundations for economic development as a first step in the federation of Europe....The setting up of this powerful productive unit, open to all countries willing to take part and bound ultimately to provide all the member countries with the basic elements of industrial production on the same terms, will lay a true foundation for their economic unification…

This production will be offered to the world as a whole without distinction or exception, with the aim of contributing to raising living standards and to promoting peaceful achievements.

To achieve these objectives, starting from the very different conditions in which the production of member countries is at present situated, it is proposed that certain transitional measures should be instituted, such as the application of a production and investment plan, the establishment of compensating machinery for equating prices, and the creation of a restructuring fund to facilitate the rationalization of production.

Document 6

Source: Anti-nuclear march led by British philosopher Bertrand Russell (center), alongside his wife, Edith, London, February 1961

Document 7

Source: Petra Kelly, German Green Party politician, environmentalist, and feminist, *Fighting for Hope*, 1984

We are often told, that the experts and the big firms do not know how to deal with the problems which threaten worldwide disaster, 'that all the facts are not in', that more research must be done, and more reports written. This is simply an excuse for endlessly putting off action. We already know enough to begin to deal with all our major problems: nuclear war, over-population, pollution, hunger, the desolation of the planet, the inequality among peoples. The present crisis is a crisis not of information, but of policy. We cannot cope with all the problems that threaten us, while maximizing profits.

Section II, Part B: Long Essay Question

Time—40 minutes; 1 Question

Directions: Choose EITHER Question 2 or Question 3.

In your response, you should do the following:

- Respond to the prompt with a historically defensible thesis or claim that establishes a line of reasoning.
- Describe a broader historical context relevant to the prompt.
- Support an argument in response to the prompt using specific and relevant examples of evidence.
- Use historical reasoning (e.g., comparison, causation, continuity or change over time) to frame or structure an argument that addresses the prompt.
- Use evidence to corroborate, qualify, or modify an argument that addresses the prompt.

Question 2   *Evaluate the extent to which the Russian Revolution transformed European diplomacy and politics.*

(RP: CCOT)

Question 3   *Evaluate the extent to which the Second World War transformed European culture and society.*

(RP: CCOT)

ANSWERS, EXPLANATIONS, & SAMPLE RESPONSES
for the Diagnostic Exams can be found at
ܦ www.sherpalearning.com/achiever ܦ

CHAPTER 18

Multiple-Choice Answers

Chapter 4

1. **Answer: C. HTS: CTX & CES; Theme: CID; KC 1.1.** All of the terms listed apply to the Renaissance. This reminds you that stimulus-based questions will often present several appealing choices. In the last paragraph, Burckhardt explicitly calls out individualism (C) and presents this value as characterizing the break between the attitude of the Renaissance and the Middle Ages, which according to Burckhardt, promoted identity based almost exclusively within groups, such as classes or church. Choices A, B, and D can only be inferred from the passage.

2. **Answer: A. HTS: CAUS; Theme: CID; KC 1.1.** These choices reflect accurate features of art prior to the French Revolution. Only A expresses an attitude of the Renaissance (both northern and Italian) toward art. In addition, A connects most explicitly to the theme of individualism tested in Question 1. Choice B reflects features of the Baroque, while D captures Dutch art. Choice C represents an overstatement about art during this period.

3. **Answer: B. HTS: SAS & MAC; Theme: CID; KC 3.6.** As you try these questions, you will encounter several like this—requiring knowledge of topics you may not have covered. I've included them here-and-there to give you practice with cross-chronological thinking and to sharpen your powers of inference. Again, all the choices express intellectual movements during Burckhardt's life, yet B connects most strongly to the origins of modernism that the author seeks to find in the Renaissance (note the word "objective"). A is incorrect since there are no references to class conflict. C and D would seem to be excluded by the references to individualism and the challenge presented to the status quo in the Renaissance.

4. **Answer: D. HTS: CES & ARG; Theme: CID; KC 1.1.** B is not addressed within the content of the passage, and though Burckhardt presents the Renaissance favorably, his purpose goes beyond merely applauding it (A). Certainly C is true, but historical figures will always reflect their historical context, a trivial point. Burckhardt seeks primarily to find within the Renaissance those features that came to dominate the modern ethos—individualism, secularism, and rationalism (D).

5. **Answer: C. HTS: CAUS; Themes: SCD & CID; KCs 1.1 & 1.5.** Since this is an EXCEPT question, we are seeking the one cause that does not apply. The printing press (A) facilitated the spread of literacy and promoted the Protestant focus on reading the Bible (B). The tone clearly indicates the importance placed upon the role of forming morality through education, not to mention that the source comes from a municipal government (D). C is the correct answer, both because of its inapplicability to the stem and also

since the emperor failed to centralize power during this period.

6. **Answer: B. HTS: COMP & MAC; Themes: SCD & CID; KC 1.2.** Each of the figures relates to issues of religious reform during the sixteenth century; however, it was Calvin who most strongly promoted education. Not only did Geneva create its own academy for training pastors, but like most mainstream reformers, Calvin placed strong emphasis on biblical reading and seeking knowledge as a way of glorifying God. As rulers, Charles (A) and Henry (C) focused on other issues, and Anabaptists (D) concentrated more on living simply in small Christian communities.

7. **Answer: A. HTS: DAP & COMP; Themes: SCD & CID; KCs 1.1 & 1.2.** One of the key differences between the Italian and northern Renaissances (and Reformation) was the former's emphasis on secular values. Both pursued education and revived classical texts, but as can be seen from the ordinance, northern religious reformers saw education primarily in religious terms. The other choices (B-D) express attitudes of both movements.

8. **Answer: B. HTS: CCOT & MAC; Themes: SCD & SOP; KC 3.3.** Here again you are asked to apply your understanding of a topic (education) across a time period. After around 1850, most governments legislated universal education for all citizens, in part to support the skills necessary to sustain a more complex economy but also to inculcate national loyalties (B). D is the opposite of this idea, and governments would certainly not wish to promote violence against the state (C). In both periods, education addressed moral concerns, such as formation of character and promoting group affiliation—to regions, religion, or the state (A).

Chapter 5

1. **Answer: C. HTS: CAUS; Theme: INT; KC 1.3.** The scene depicted is the largest mining operation in the Americas, established by the Spanish with the enslaved labor of indigenous peoples. The question aims at explaining how it is that Spain (and other European states) were able to establish such domination. Since this is an EXCEPT question, you should look for the one factor that does not apply. Though C may have happened, the depiction of mythological civilizations did not motivate states directly to seek colonies, nor did it provide the means to do so. Choices A, B, and D played key roles in sustaining European exploration and colonization.

2. **Answer: B. HTS: CCOT & CAUS; Theme: ECD; KC 1.4.** The mining operation extracted precious metals and injected these into the European economy. This fact, in addition to the trade in goods from colonies, stimulated the

development of new financial and banking practices (B). The influence of precious metals *indirectly* influenced the growth of landed elites (A), and affected serfdom even less so (C). Though hierarchy continued to guide social relations, the new money economy tended to undermine this principle (D).

3. **Answer: D. HTS: COMP; Themes: INT & ECD; KCs 1.3 & 2.2.** In this question, you compare the effects of exploration on the Americas and Africa. The main impact on Africa, which also affected the Americas, was the trade in enslaved persons, most of whom ended up working on plantations producing sugar, cotton, indigo, tobacco, etc. Large territorial empires did not occur until the nineteenth century (A). Indigenous industries would have been hindered not promoted by European colonization, so B is incorrect. As with all regions, the further integration of the global economy (C) affected Africa, as we see with the slave trade.

4. **Answer: C. HTS: SAS & CES; Theme: INT; KC 1.3.** Here you are asked to think like a historian. Each of the choices reflects possible uses of the document, but to settle on the key, make sure you look again at the depiction. It shows brutal labor and reveals the poor conditions of the indigenous peoples (C). We can infer European motivations from the activities and manner of the work, but other sources would work better to reveal these facts (A). Since this does not seem like a work of fine art, we can exclude B. Of course, exploration affected European rivalries, but these issues are not raised by the image (D).

5. **Answer: B. HTS: CAUS; Themes: SOP & NEI; KCs 1.2 & 1.5.** You are asked here about the causes of the Thirty Years' War, the settlement of which is shown on the map. A, C, and D all express major causes and motivations of the powers involved. Though England and Britain had by this time established colonies outside Europe, their long competition for overseas dominance did not begin until after 1650 and did not influence the course of the Thirty Years' War.

6. **Answer: B. HTS: CAUS & CCOT; Themes: SOP & NEI; KCs 1.2 & 1.5.** By 1648, Spain had begun its decline, so we can exclude A. Westphalia confirmed the decline of the Holy Roman Empire, the opposite of C. With the military revolution that helped define the conflict, the state gained greater control over warfare, eliminating D. We are left with the major impact of the peace—the establishment of state sovereignty over religious matters and the end of religion as a key motive for warfare (B).

7. **Answer: D. HTS: CCOT; Theme: SOP; KCs 1.2 & 1.5.** The Peace of Westphalia confirmed state control of religion, removing it as a source of conflict between states (D). Since the aristocracy continued to dominate political offices, we can exclude A. Choice B did occur, but the Thirty Years' War did not involve the issue of colonies. The papacy, in fact, declined in political influence, excluding C.

8. **Answer: C. HTS: CAUS; Theme: SOP; KCs 1.2 & 1.5.** The states mentioned in Choices A, B, and D either gained from the treaty (e.g., Sweden, with lands in the Baltic) or experienced no reduction in their diplomatic situation. Spain, however, failed to maintain itself as the political leader of Catholicism and, in attempting to do so, futilely expended much of its wealth. Along with population decline and cultural stagnation, the Thirty Years' War pushed Spain outside the ranks of the great powers of Europe (C).

Chapter 6

1. **Answer: D. HTS: DAP & CTX; Themes: TSI & CID; KC 1.1.** Galileo engaged in all the activities indicated by these choices, as evidenced by appealing to his patron's wife in this letter (B). And though he stirred controversy with his written works (A) and helped create an international dialogue with other scientists such as Kepler (C), it was his questioning of biblical and church authority in the context of the Counter-Reformation and later Thirty Years' War that brought him before the Roman Inquisition (D).

2. **Answer: C. HTS: CCOT; Themes: TSI & CID; KC 2.3.** Answer A is clearly incorrect, since Galileo's trial reflects conflicts between religion and science, not to mention later such conflict during the French Revolution and with Darwin's theories. Galileo, in fact, took scientific ideas beyond ancient thinkers, eliminating B. Though states patronized science, scientists did not generally appeal to their authority to bolster their ideas. We are left with C; the Scientific Revolution led directly to a mechanistic worldview based on the invocation of natural laws and application of mathematics. This approach would sustain the eighteenth-century Enlightenment.

3. **Answer: C. HTS: CTX & DAP; Theme: TSI; KC 1.1.** As an EXCEPT question, you are seeking the one choice that does not apply. The visual demonstrates a use of empiricism to make conclusions about blood flow. A, B, and D all represent important features of the new science and which are explicitly or implicitly demonstrated in the visual. Though C is true, folk traditions are not portrayed in the visual and were not considered a defining feature of the new science.

4. **Answer: D. HTS: CTX & CAUS; Theme: TSI; KC 1.1.** This is a straightforward factual question, inferred from the visual. William Harvey discovered the modern theory of blood flow, through a system of arteries and veins (and later capillaries). Paracelsus (A) formed a bridge between Galenic and modern anatomy but worked more by trial and error. Vesalius (B) also contributed to anatomical discoveries but not specifically with blood flow. Bacon (C) helped establish the scientific method but was not known for specific discoveries related to anatomy.

5. **Answer: B. HTS: COMP & MAC; Themes: TSI & CID; KCs 1.1 & 3.6.** Here you are asked to project the methods and ideas of the Scientific Revolution forward. Between nineteenth-century positivism and the new science of the

sixteenth and seventeenth centuries, there are many similarities. These include A, C, and D. However, by the completion of Newtonian cosmology (around 1690), most scientists had moved beyond their fascination with alchemy and astrology as part of the project of explaining nature.

6. **Answer: A. HTS: DAP & CTX; Theme: TSI; KC 1.1.** In the painting, we see a physician demonstrating the features of human anatomy through direct observation. An interested group of spectators stand around, rapt by the exhibition. This scene reveals the importance of empiricism (A) to the new science. Of course, mathematics was also a key feature (B), but not shown in the painting. One might make deductions from these observations, but this process is not revealed directly in the visual (C). Finally, no particular model of the universe is depicted, eliminating D.

7. **Answer: C. HTS: CAUS; Themes: CID, ECD, & SOP; KCs 1.1 & 2.2.** This question asks you to connect intellectual and cultural developments with the features of Dutch society and politics. The Netherlands was generally considered the most tolerant area of Europe (A) and oriented toward trade and commerce (B and D). However, the Netherlands was a decentralized oligarchic republic dominated by the wealthy merchants. It was not controlled by a strong, central monarchy (C).

8. **Answer: B. HTS: CTX & CES; Theme: CID; KCs 1.1 & 2.3.** All of the statements accurately express purposes of art; however, the Enlightenment did not occur during the seventeenth century, eliminating D. Though the painting arguably employs Baroque style, it certainly does not advance a religious or political outlook (A). C can be excluded since the painting does employ perspective and, because of its scientific subject matter, embraces a natural style. That leaves us with B, which does accurately express an artistic trend that is shown in the painting—the idea of advancing our understanding of the human body to address illness and promote medicine.

Chapter 7

1. **Answer: A. HTS: CTX & DAP; Theme: SOP; KCs 1.5 & 2.1.** Each statement is accurate in itself; however, the two passages illustrate the conflict between the English Parliament and the Stuart monarchs (James I) over political sovereignty. Neither employs scientific language to justify its position (eliminating B); instead the Parliament calls on tradition while James invokes God. Neither passage relates to beliefs about the cosmos (C) or the issue of commerce (D). A is the only choice that captures the notion of conflict and conveys the debate over absolutism.

2. **Answer: B. HTS: CCOT; Theme: SOP; KCs 1.5 & 2.1.** The Parliament achieved its recognition of sovereignty by English monarchs with the Glorious Revolution in 1689 (B). Of course, England participated in the Commercial and Scientific Revolutions (A and C), as well as the Protestant Reformation (D); however, the stated goals in Source 1 were primarily political (with religious issues as a complicating factor), making B the best choice.

3. **Answer: C. HTS: COMP & MAC; Theme: SOP; KC 2.1.** In Source 2 James argues for an absolutist divine-right monarchy, most akin to what Louis XIV aimed for in France (B). However, this question asks for the exception to the ideal. Since Russia was an autocracy, it is also eliminated (A). Though Spain declined in this period, its monarchs maintained strong political and religious power (D). Poland, however, struggled during this period with an elective monarchy and was ultimately partitioned out of existence by 1795, demonstrating its weakness (C).

4. **Answer: C. HTS: MAC & CES; Themes: SOP & CID; KCs 2.1 & 2.3.** John Locke supported the Glorious Revolution with his *Two Treatises on Government* and provided a theoretical foundation for limited government and the social contract, ideals that later influenced political revolutions (C). Since Calvinism tended to be a minority religion, it did express some anti-monarchical strains, but without the theoretical foundations of Locke and not in the appropriate historical context (A). B can be eliminated, since Hobbes provided a secular defense of absolutism in opposition to Locke's later ideas. D can be safely eliminated, as Louis represents the strongest strain of absolutist thinking, more in line with Source 2.

5. **Answer: B. HTS: CES & CAUS; Theme: SOP; KCs 1.2, 1.5, & 2.1.** Blanning's interpretation focuses on the results of the Peace of Westphalia, which provided for religious diversity within the Holy Roman Empire. Now that states came to control religion, warfare shifted toward secular concerns, as noted in B. A, C, and D are accurate statements; however, A and D have little to do with religion directly, while C violated the principle of pluralism.

6. **Answer: A. HTS: CCOT & CES; Theme: SOP; KCs 1.2, 1.5, & 2.1.** Blanning argues for the significance of 1648 as a watershed in politics and diplomacy. One such justification for this claim is given in A, since states turned to commercial and territorial (not religious) rivalries on the heels of the Commercial Revolution. The year 1648 does not weigh substantially on the arts (since the Baroque style bridges the date—B), nor does it for commerce and finance (since these trends evolved over time—C) or for the Scientific Revolution (which began with Copernicus in 1543 and ended with Newton in 1687—D).

7. **Answer: D. HTS: CAUS & CCOT; Themes: SOP & NEI; KC 2.1.** This is a difficult question, as it asks you to project forward from 1648 and anticipate the structure of diplomacy in central Europe. From the Thirty Years' War there emerged two strong German powers—the Austrian Empire and Brandenburg-Prussia, each of which prevented the other from unifying the German-speaking peoples (until diplomacy changed in the nineteenth century) giving D as the key. A is true but did not directly affect the settlement and pattern of diplomacy. B and C are also true in their periods; however, they represented developments complicating the essential division of Germany and did not change that division directly.

8. **Answer: D. HTS: CAUS & CCOT; Themes: SOP & NEI; KC 2.1.** B was already in process and did not directly affect German politics. The United States did not substantially affect European diplomacy until World War I (eliminating C). Industrialization eventually altered the balance of power in central Europe, but only after Germany had been unified (in 1871, A). It was the spread of revolutionary ideas and upheaval to the traditional state system (D) that opened the door to new patterns of diplomacy and allowed Prussia after 1850 to defeat Austria and unify the other German-speaking states.

Chapter 8

1. **Answer: C. HTS: CAUS; Themes: SOP & ECD; KCs 2.1 & 2.2.** The map displays the economic role of the slave trade, connecting this practice to the development of a European-dominated global economy. Except for C (the key), all of the choices did result directly or indirectly from the slave trade. To manage their trade and exploit colonies, most states practiced mercantilist policies, such as France under Colbert (A). This competition led to rivalries and commercial wars (D), as well as put new goods (such as sugar) in the homes of Europeans, stimulating a consumer culture. However, Russia did not participate in the Atlantic trade and was primarily a territorial power (C).

2. **Answer: D. HTS: SAS & CES; Themes: ECD & SOP; KCs 2.1 & 2.2.** Enslaved labor was not widely employed in military and naval operations, excluding A. European powers did not come to control the interior of Africa until after 1871 (B). Though C is true, the map does not support any conclusions regarding anti-slavery ideals directly and such a development would follow in subsequent decades. This leaves D as the key, which ties the question back to a major theme of the course and close to the wording of KC 2.2 itself.

3. **Answer: B. HTS: CCOT; Themes: ECD & CID; KCs 2.2 & 2.3.** This CCOT question asks you to project beyond the map data and consider how the issue of slavery and the slave trade changed after the middle of the eighteenth century. You may recall that the eighteenth century was, in part, defined by the Enlightenment, which critiqued inequality in institutions, including slavery (B). A is incorrect, as Great Britain came to dominate the Americas (due to the Seven Years War). European powers continued to intrude into Africa, at least along the coasts and in North Africa (C). Though the US did emerge as a major power and considered the Americas as its sphere of influence, it did not generally become a formal colonial power until later (D).

4. **Answer: B. HTS: CTX & CES; Theme: ECD; KCs 1.5 & 2.2.** Roberts portrays the eighteenth-century old regime as lacking in innovation and oriented toward the preservation of traditional norms. This coincides with the prevalence of serfdom in eastern Europe (B). The areas suggested by A, C, and D represent innovations in the economy, all of which increased productivity and challenged the control of traditional groups (e.g., guilds, nobles) over production.

5. **Answer: A. HTS: DAP & CES; Themes: SOP, ECD, & SCD; KCs 2.1, 2.2, & 2.4.** Here you are asked to consider evidence that runs counter to the historical interpretation. Since Roberts argues for the static nature of the old regime, your job is to find the one that supports it (since this is an EXCEPT question). Rivalries among the great powers of Europe were nothing new to the eighteenth century, making A the answer. Each of the choices represented by B, C, and D express major new developments in the areas of demographics, social life, and economic organization.

6. **Answer: B. HTS: CCOT & MAC; Themes: SOP & NEI; KC 3.4.** Since Roberts argues for the inherent conservatism of the eighteenth century, we need to find the expression of conservatism in the nineteenth century. The answer is B: through the Concert of Europe, Metternich (of Austria) attempted to suppress the revolutionary fallout from the French Revolution. Mechanization of textiles replaced the old system of guild production, making it an innovation (A). Positivism developed after 1840 with the success of science and technology in seeming to provide new means to address human problems (C). Along with the growth of commerce, and especially industry in the nineteenth century, the middle class grew in influence, which fed the revolutionary ideologies of the period (D). Thus, B-D represent key changes defining the nineteenth century, counter to the view of Roberts regarding the eighteenth century.

7. **Answer: B. HTS: CAUS; Themes: ECD & SCD; KCs 2.2 & 2.4.** Once again, each of the choices represents an accurate statement of eighteenth-century trends. The passage connects a cultural venue (coffeehouses) with a new product from overseas expansion, reflecting the development of a new consumer culture (B). Though A may have occurred as a result of the phenomenon, it is not directly addressed in the passage. Population did increase (C) in the eighteenth century; this, however, was more the result not the cause of the introduction of new goods into Europe. Patrons of coffeehouses certainly discussed new ideas (D), as the passage implies, but a better explanation relates to how coffeehouses helped spread such ideas rather than the reverse.

8. **Answer: C. HTS: CAUS; Themes: ECD & CID; KCs 2.2, 2.3, & 2.4.** This question effectively reverses the Causation issue of the previous question. Governments practiced censorship, but the practice predated the development of coffeehouses (and in most states proved ineffective—A). B also occurred, but this result did not prove as consequential as the application of scientific ideas to society—i.e., the Enlightenment (C). As for D, this was more the cause than the result of the coffeehouse (and related development of civil society) captured by the passage.

9. **Answer: A. HTS: SAS & CES; Theme: ECD; KC 2.2.** Let's again remember to focus on connecting your content knowledge to what is indicated by the passage. European governments did compete for global control of resources, but the passage does not address that point (B). Contro-

versial new religious views did emerge from new civic venues (such as coffeehouses and salons), but the text does not address that point (C). The same can be said for D—true as well, but not addressed by the passage. A is the correct answer, as the pamphlet addresses a new venue and atmosphere created by a new product (A).

Chapter 9

1. **Answer: D. HTS: CTX & CES; Themes: CID & SCD; KC 2.3.** In this passage, Rousseau reinforces his gendered perspective on social roles and intellectual capacities. Rousseau embraced the idea of natural laws, which he seems to believe in the passage apply here to the roles of men and women, though mistakenly (A). Rousseau endorsed and articulated the idea of a social contract in his other work of that title, eliminating B. Though he supports traditional social roles, Rousseau's argument does not depend on religious authority (C). This leaves D as the answer, and indeed, Rousseau seems to take it for granted, without data or evidence, that his gendered perspective is a fact of nature, not in keeping with Enlightenment epistemology.

2. **Answer: B. HTS: CTX; Theme: CID; KC 2.3.** Wollstonecraft justifies female equality in society and through education, specifically in this passage for the purpose of raising children capable of citizenship, making A the key. Choices B–D do not appear in the passage, as Wollstonecraft makes no mention of religion, commerce, or non-European peoples.

3. **Answer: C. HTS: COMP; Themes: CID & SCD; KCs 2.3 & 2.4.** It is clear that Rousseau and Wollstonecraft differ sharply over the extent to which the Enlightenment principles of equality and natural rights apply to women, making C the answer. Neither mentions censorship (A), the relationship between science and religion (B), or the role of commercial luxury in questions of citizenship (D), excluding these as options.

4. **Answer: C. HTS: CTX & CCOT; Theme: SCD; KCs 2.3 & 2.4.** This question in the set does not require the stimuli. Statements A, B, and D express important features of social life affecting women. Feminists drew on the language of natural rights to argue for female equality (e.g., Mary Wollstonecraft), but the statement is overstated and premature. Women did not gain the rights listed until the middle of the nineteenth century at the earliest (C).

5. **Answer: B. HTS: CTX; Theme: CID; KC 2.3.** In the text, Paine endorses a view of the Supreme Being commensurate with scientific and secular attitudes toward nature, a position known as deism (B). Though Paine would also have embraced toleration (A), this principle is not the focus of the text. Paine clearly expresses a belief in a Supreme Being, eliminating C and D.

6. **Answer: D. HTS: CAUS & SAS; Themes: CID & SOP; KCs 2.1 & 2.3.** Here is where a sensitivity to historical context can assist your ability to infer correct answers. This passage was published during the de-Christianization campaign of the French Revolution, possibly in support of the secular policies of that regime (D). Paine explicitly rejected monarchy in other writings, eliminating C. Though Paine hailed from Britain, the passage does not address its rivalry with France (A). Paine focuses on systems of belief, not the material conditions of factories, excluding B.

7. **Answer: C. HTS: COMP & MAC; Theme: CID; KCs 1.1 & 2.3.** A is false, as Renaissance intellectuals did not argue for separation between church and state, merely a more secular outlook on life. Paine endorsed equality, but B overstates the Renaissance attitude, which tended to accept some hierarchies as natural. Both Paine (as shown in the passage) and Renaissance humanists strongly endorsed individualism (D). Despite their purported secularism, Renaissance humanists accepted the authority of the church and did not reject Christianity as a belief system.

8. **Answer: C. HTS: DAP & CTX; Themes: CID & INT; KC 2.3.** Though the passage by Diderot relies on travel and interaction with non-Europeans, no references are made to commercial expansion or a consumer culture, eliminating A and D. Diderot criticizes arbitrary government, but does not do so using natural law or social contract theory, excluding B. The passage references the "examination of institutions," reflecting the empirical approach toward addressing social and political issues in the interests of reform, giving C as the key.

9. **Answer: B. HTS: SAS & CES; Themes: CID & INT; KC 2.3.** Eighteenth-century travel literature spurred the questioning of European norms and customs by way of comparison. In this dialogue, Diderot hopes to show the absurdity of European political traditions by questioning their adoption by peoples who already seem to live in equality and peace, giving B as the key. Despite Diderot's political criticism, he makes no revolutionary appeals (A), nor does he address the question of women (D). Though Diderot criticized the trans-Atlantic slave trade, this book is set in the Pacific and does not address slavery *per se* (C).

10. **Answer: D. HTS: CES & MAC; Themes: ECD & SCD; KCs 2.2, 2.3, & 2.4.** Diderot vocally criticized the Catholic Church (A), "superstition," or folk beliefs (C), and entrenched inequality, as with the legally defined Three Estates in France (B), thus eliminating these choices for this EXCEPT question. The only trend of the era that Diderot did not explicitly condemn—and that was endorsed and articulated by his fellow philosophe, Adam Smith—was the development of a free-market, rather than mercantilist, economy, making D the key.

Chapter 10

1. **Answer: C. HTS: CAUS & CTX; Theme: SOP; KC 2.1.** All of the choices represent causes of the French Revolution; however, the passage makes no reference to economic or financial issues, excluding A and D. In addition, although the last line refers to the elimination of "Orders" in the new National Assembly (B), the primary thrust of

the passage centers around discontent with the monarchy and the desire by revolutionaries to strip the king of his powers and force upon him a constitutional form of government, making C the correct choice.

2. **Answer: D. HTS: CCOT & CES; Themes: SOP & SCD; KC 2.1.** The British ambassador presents the revolution in its early stages as a bloodless constitutional change. Even so, many of the early events of the revolution involved outright violence or conflict, including A and B. *The Declaration of the Rights of Man* would fit directly in with the passage, as it marks another legal change from above (C). However, the execution of Louis and subsequent Reign of Terror clearly do not fit the portrayal of a relatively smooth transition to a new regime (D).

3. **Answer: D. HTS: COMP & MAC; Theme: SOP; KCs 2.1 & 4.2.** You are asked here to make a historical comparison across time periods. The French Revolution most closely parallels the Russian Revolution (D), in that both involved a fundamental political reordering against a perceived inept and corrupt monarchy fueled by a combination of economic grievances and new political ideologies (Enlightenment and socialism). The Protestant Reformation caused political changes but was primarily religious in character (A), and opposition to the Habsburgs occurred within the basic structure of early modern dynastic politics (B). Finally, choice C (national unification) expresses an almost-opposite outcome—a political revolution that created unity under a stronger monarchy.

4. **Answer: C. HTS: CAUS & CCOT; Themes: SOP & INT; KC 2.1.** The stimulus should remind you that the world took note of the French Revolution; thus, the stem asks you in turn to gauge the effects of the revolution outside Europe. The French employed mass citizen armies effectively to spread the ideals of the revolution (A), through which Napoleon also created an empire that dominated Europe for a decade (D). In addition, the revolution led to the abolition of slavery in French colonies and a revolt in Saint Domingue (Haiti)—B. This leaves C as the only false outcome (remember, this is an EXCEPT question). Though Napoleon did impose such republics, they did not prove long-lived and certainly not committed to peace, since warfare defined the continent from 1792–1815.

5. **Answer: C. HTS: CTX & CAUS; Themes: CID & SOP; KCs 2.1 & 2.3.** This image was used by radical revolutionaries to promote the new calendar, which replaced the "religious" Gregorian calendar. These policies formed part of a de-Christianization campaign based on the Enlightenment trend toward rationalizing law and weights and measures (C). If anything, the style of art is neoclassical, not Romantic (B). Though the figure is a woman, it is not aimed at women's rights, which were not advanced during the radical phase; instead, the figure is more akin to a goddess of liberty/reason (D). Of course, French armies spread the ideals of the revolution, but this image does not touch on that issue (A).

6. **Answer: A; HTS: CTX & CES; Themes: SOP & CID; KC 2.1.** As noted above, the calendar (among other reforms during the radical phase) coincided with the general effort to expunge the features of the Old Regime believed to be "superstitious and fanatical," particularly religion (A). Each of the other developments occurred during the French Revolution; however, they are not addressed by the image. Once again, the visual does not touch on military affairs (B), nor does it deal with the execution of the king (C). A government based on popular sovereignty preceded the calendar and occurred with the early actions by the National Assembly (D).

7. **Answer: D. HTS: CTX & CAUS; Themes: SOP & NEI; KC 2.1.** The map portrays the height of Napoleon's empire, a feat that was accomplished primarily by force of French arms, relying on mass citizen armies (D). With the *levee en masse*, women were mobilized for the war effort, but not to promote feminist ideals (A). Britain, of course, possessed an extensive empire, but because of this fact, it tended to act as the most consistent opponent of Napoleon, which would not have aided his conquests (B). Finally, the hostility of foreign governments resulted from, but did not cause, the situation on the map (C).

8. **Answer: B. HTS: COMP & CCOT; Themes: SOP & NEI: KCs 1.5 & 2.1.** Russia's dominance in the east predates the map (A), and even though Russia had grown much since 1648 (making this an appealing distractor), it had been the largest power in the east since the sixteenth century. C did not occur until later in the nineteenth century, and both periods witnessed extended war among the great powers (e.g., Thirty Years' War), eliminating D. That leaves B, and indeed, the Holy Roman Empire had dominated central Europe since the Middle Ages until Napoleon abolished it in 1806.

9. **Answer: A. HTS: CAUS; Themes: SOP & NEI; KC 2.1.** C occurred but not specifically in relation to the diplomatic situation depicted, rather due to internal British policies and circumstances. The Catholic Church never did regain the power it had lost during the early modern movements of reform, including the French Revolution (B). Despite serious blunders, Napoleon did not provoke a civil war *within* France related to his rule. However, the great powers of Europe eventually felt emboldened by Napoleon's errors to wage campaigns of nationalist liberation, defeating him for good at Waterloo (A).

Chapter 11

1. **Answer: D. HTS: CTX; Themes: ECD & SOP; KCs: 2.3, 3.1, & 3.3.** In the passage, Ricardo (one of the classical economists) argues for the unfettered operation of a free-market economy, echoing the principles first articulated by Adam Smith and associated with Liberalism (D). During the radical phase of the French Revolution, its leaders attempted to regulate prices—not what Ricardo advocates (A). The laissez-faire approach presented in the passage was associated with Liberalism, not Conservatism during

the first half of the nineteenth century (B). Finally, Ricardo does not address the typical concerns of the Romantics, many of whom were skeptical of industrialization (C).

2. **Answer: A. HTS: CCOT & CES; Themes: CID & SOP; KCs 3.1 & 3.6.** It is clear that Ricardo does not endorse Marxism (D), since this passage argues for a free-market economy. Also, there is no mention or implication of feminism (C). Though Ricardo calls for a limited government, it is a government nonetheless, excluding anarchism (B). This leaves us with Social Darwinism, and indeed, supporters of this application of Darwin's ideas argued for a "survival-of-the-fittest" philosophy toward the economy.

3. **Answer: A. HTS: COMP & MAC; Themes: ECD & SOP; KC 3.1.** Ricardo's passage tends to parallel the British government's approach toward industrialization—providing a framework of property rights and the economic infrastructure, and then allowing market forces to work. Playing catch-up with Britain, continental states relied much more on government subsidies and protective tariffs to support industry (A). The growth of unions coincided with the pace of industrialization, and thus, continental nations paralleled Britain; in fact, the German SPD became Europe's strongest socialist movement (B). All states were eventually forced to address the problems of industry, eliminating C. Some nations did lack natural resources (e.g., Spain); however, many like Germany and Belgium drew effectively on their resource base (D).

4. **Answer: C. HTS: CTX & SAS; Themes: SOP & NEI; KCs 3.3 & 3.4.** Mazzini writes from a strong nationalist perspective, within a nation lacking unity (Italy). The reason for Italy's lack of unity relates to decisions made at Vienna (C). Napoleon's invasion of Italy and proclamation of a republic (1796–1797) stimulated nationalist sentiment, but Mazzini's writing is too removed in time for this to be the key (B). Napoleon also abolished feudalism in most parts of Italy, but again, the passage does not address this issue (A). Finally, the Crimean War (1853–1856) had not yet occurred (D).

5. **Answer: D. HTS: CTX; Theme: NEI; KC 3.3.** Though Mazzini expressed both Liberal (A) and Romantic (B) tendencies, his writing here focuses on the bonds of nationhood and the need to create a nation (D). Mazzini believed in political equality, but the text does not support any notions of collective ownership of property or redistribution of income, as in socialism (C).

6. **Answer: B. HTS: CCOT; Themes: SOP & NEI; KC 3.4.** Attempts at Italian unity (A) failed during the revolutions of 1848; however, it was the work of Cavour (Prime Minister of Piedmont-Sardinia) that established the new Italian kingdom in 1861 (B). Both C and D occurred after Italy became unified, though they do relate to Italian nationalism.

7. **Answer: B. HTS: SAS & CES; Themes: NEI & SOP; KCs 3.3 & 3.4.** Napoleon, Garibaldi, and Bismarck were all nationalists of one variety or another (A, C, and D), even if

Bismarck achieved nationalism from the top-down rather than the bottom-up. However, Metternich attempted through the Concert of Europe to blunt nationalism, a predictable tactic by the minister of a multi-ethnic empire (B).

8. **Answer: C. HTS: CTX & CES; Theme: CID; KC 3.6.** In this painting a solitary figure stands atop a mountain in defiance of those below. Romantics embraced a revival of national histories (A), and this scene harkens back to founding stories from the Middle Ages. The painting also reveals Romantic mysticism toward nature (B) and the importance of the unique individual (D). Though Romantics critiqued the Enlightenment overemphasis on reason, this work does not comment on that feature of the movement (C).

9. **Answer: B. HTS: CCOT & MAC; Theme: CID; KCs 3.6 & 4.3.** Choice A is incorrect, as the attitude described is associated with realism, a reaction to Romanticism. Though Romantics established the notion of artists as critics of society, they continued to employ representational images and convey beauty, excluding C. D is incorrect, as Romanticism often criticized the attitude that only science yields knowledge. Choice B is a rephrasing of KC 3.6, which reminds you that a familiarity with the KCs and Unit Guides will serve you well on the MC questions.

Chapter 12

1. **Answer: D. HTS: CTX & CES; Themes: ECD & INT; KC 3.1.** The map shows the expansion of European railways over a span of about 40 years. Of course, several economic processes during this period (Second Industrial Revolution) relate to transportation developments. A is true, but the map does not provide any inferences about government involvement in the economy. Mechanization did become the predominant form of manufacturing; however, that process was separate from transportation developments (B). Germany's unification did stimulate its industrialization, yet the map does not address that issue (C). The option most directly related to the map remains the integration of the European and world economy, since these would depend on the cost-effective ability to reach (far-flung) markets (D).

2. **Answer: A. HTS: CAUS; Theme: ECD; KCs 3.1 & 3.2.** Choices B, C, and D all occurred during this period; however, they were only affected indirectly, if at all, by the growth of railroads. However, railroads reduced the cost of products and enabled a wider geographic scope to purchase goods, including those that had once been expensive luxuries, but now became accessible to the middle- and even working-classes (A).

3. **Answer: C. HTS: COMP; Themes: ECD & SOP; KC 3.1.** It is true that Europe experienced volatile business cycles during this era, but these were not unique to western Europe and did not impede industrialization overall (A). Resource access relates to industrial development; however, even states in eastern Europe with the resources

to industrialize often failed to do so because of poor government policy (B), which suggests the answer of C: most polities in eastern Europe were dominated by aristocrats tied up in traditional landholding and thus averse to promoting industry. Though Russia often influenced eastern European diplomacy, it too suffered from many of the same drawbacks as those smaller nations, which were controlled by the technologically stagnant Ottoman Empire (D).

4. **Answer: B. HTS: COMP & MAC; Theme: ECD; KC 1.3.** The map depicts an economic and transportation development and suggests its effects on the development of a larger and more integrated market. The choice most related to this trend in a different period is B, as advances in navigation helped to create a more global economy. The printing press spread ideas, but relates less to economic integration (A). Choices C and D occurred and significantly affected warfare and diplomacy, on one hand, and ideas on the other—both of which were not connected to the economy.

5. **Answer: D. HTS: CTX & CES; Themes: ECD & INT; KCs 3.1 & 3.5.** The passage focuses on the economic imperatives driving imperialism, suggesting the answer is D. Choice A does not relate to the passage, even if Social Darwinism did facilitate imperialism. Though the passage touches on the behavior of nations, Hobsbawm's interpretive focus is on economic motivations, excluding B and C.

6. **Answer: C. HTS: COMP & CCOT; Themes: ECD & INT; KCs 1.3, 3.1, & 3.5.** This question asks you to consider the similarities and differences between the era of exploration (fifteenth and sixteenth centuries) and imperialism (nineteenth and twentieth centuries). In both instances, Europe's relation to the non-European world was shaped by notions of superiority (A), technological imbalance (B), and conversions to Christianity (D). The main difference between the two periods relates to the development of an industrial economy in the latter period, which both drove and allowed for widespread European control of overseas territories.

7. **Answer: B. HTS: SAS & CES; Themes: INT & CID; KCs 3.5 & 3.6.** Any of the options could relate to the time period described in the passage, but the stem directs your attention to the *historian's* philosophical commitments. Given his emphasis on the driving force of capitalism and industry in promoting imperialism, Choice B emerges as the most fitting choice. Hobsbawm does not glorify science *per se* (A), nor does he endorse nationalism (C) or Darwinism (D).

8. **Answer: A. HTS: CES; Themes: ECD & INT; KCs 3.1 & 3.5.** Choices B, C, and D all describe features of the Second Industrial Revolution and thus relate to the economic analysis provided by Hobsbawm. However, backward agricultural practices were both diminishing around the turn of the twentieth century and certainly did not promote imperialism, since those areas relying on traditional agriculture tended to be more isolated from the world economy and in nations less likely to pursue overseas colonies.

Chapter 13

1. **Answer: C. HTS: CES, CCOT, & CAUS; Themes: ECD & SOP; KCs 3.1, 3.2, & 3.3.** The passage explains the shift in classical liberalism from laissez-faire individualism to government intervention in order to promote equality. In the choices you are presented with four economic developments, all of which represent accurate statements about the late nineteenth century. A, B, and D posed new social and political problems for governments that required some degree of regulation or policy initiative. However, the growth of consumer goods and leisure time (C) did not in themselves require government action, as they tended to be ancillary to the more fundamental changes in the structure of the economy.

2. **Answer: A. HTS: CTX & DAP; Themes: SOP & CID; KC: 3.3.** Liberal political theory emphasized that legitimate governments are based on the will of the people, as with the American and French Revolutions (A). The sharing of property (B) characterizes socialism and would undermine the Liberal notion of the free market. C better expresses a principle of nationalism, and the skepticism regarding the perfectibility of human nature relates more closely to conservatism (D).

3. **Answer: B. HTS: CAUS & CCOT; Themes: SOP & NEI; KCs 4.1 & 4.2.** Given that the passage focuses on the shift toward intervention, you should look for the choice that most strongly promoted it. The demands of total war (B) forced governments to expand their powers significantly and establish new precedents for state power in many areas. A is more the result than the cause of government expansion, as imperialism required a high degree of state power. Women did gain new rights during this era (C); however, these would represent more of a fulfillment of classical Liberalism's notion of natural rights. Though new scientific theories posed cultural challenges, they did not directly affect the issue of state intervention (D).

4. **Answer: D. HTS: MAC & CAUS; Themes: TSI & CID; KCs 2.3 & 3.6.** Enlightenment philosophes interpreted nature primarily through the operation of natural laws, as does Darwin in this passage (D). Darwin does endorse A and B, yet these do not express principles of the Enlightenment, which promoted the uniqueness of human reason and the assumption of rationality in human relations. The glorification of nature as a source of emotion represents more of a Romantic attitude and less an enlightened one (C).

5. **Answer: B. HTS: CAUS; Themes: TSI, SOP, & CID; KCs 3.3, 3.5, & 3.6.** This EXCEPT question asks you to identify the least connected outcome of Darwinism. The theory of natural selection certainly raised religious and ethical controversies (D). Also, many theorists applied the theory to political, social, and military affairs, as is indicated accurately in Choices A and C. One area that saw limited direct impact of Darwinism was in the arts, or at least it was not directly responsible for the shift away from representation and toward abstraction (B).

6. **Answer: A. HTS: CTX, DAP, & CCOT; Themes: TSI & CID; KCs 3.3 & 3.6.** The failure of romantic revolution in 1848 caused political and intellectual figures to adopt a more hard-headed and realistic attitude toward an industrializing Europe, making A the key. B is true, but this trend stems more from other ideas in the sciences and social sciences (such as Freud), not to mention that Darwin endorses objective knowledge based on the scientific method in the passage. Though there is a poetry to the excerpt, Darwin does not endorse a primarily emotional attitude toward nature, as would the Romantics (C). Finally, there is no reference here to classical or ancient themes, excluding D.

7. **Answer: A. HTS: CES & CTX; Theme: ECD; KCs 3.1 & 3.2.** The image depicts one of the new urban amenities of reformed cities—a department store (C). Further, the scene provides the viewer with a testament to the new consumerism with its conspicuous displays of goods for purchase (B). This abundance of goods at relatively low prices can be attributed to advances in production and transportation (D). Though women are portrayed in the image, they are presented in the traditional role as purchasers of household goods and not holders of new rights or independent actors, making A the false choice (or key) for the EXCEPT question.

8. **Answer: C. HTS: COMP & CCOT; Theme: ECD; KCs 1.5, 2.2, & 3.1.** This question asks you to compare two eras in their economic patterns, aiming for the area of difference. Both the early modern and industrial eras emphasized luxury goods (A), urban markets (B), and the key role played by the middle-class in commerce (D). However, the early modern period relied for production on guilds and craftsmen for production, as opposed to the ability of an industrial economy to mass-produce goods at lower prices, making them more available to a wider public (as shown in the department store), indicating C as the key.

9. **Answer: B. HTS: CCOT; Theme: ECD; KCs 3.1 & 3.2.** All of the labels given might accurately characterize the period 1850–1914. However, the image relates primarily to the advances produced by industrial production (B) and only indirectly, if at all, to nationalism (A), mass politics (C), or the pursuit of colonies (D)—all of which would be related only indirectly to the scene depicted.

Chapter 14

1. **Answer: C. HTS: CAUS; Themes: SOP & NEI; KCs 3.4 & 4.1.** The map shows the Balkan peninsula prior to WWI. Even if you didn't recall the two Balkan Wars (1912–1913), you should be prompted by the map to note the smaller Balkan nations, especially Serbia, adjacent to Austria-Hungary and Russia. It was tensions here that drew in Austria and Russia and then sprung the trap of the alliance system (C). Choices A, B, and D all express causes of WWI, but these are not portrayed on the map.

2. **Answer: D. HTS: CTX & SAS; Themes: SOP & NEI; KCs 3.4 & 4.1.** As the Ottoman Empire declined, the Slavic minorities worked toward independence, often aided by the Slavic power of Russia. This deterioration of a major empire created instability in the region (D). The map does not portray Germany (A) nor colonies (B). Though Austria-Hungary appears, the map does not break down the ethnic composition of that empire, eliminating C.

3. **Answer: B. HTS: COMP, MAC, & CCOT; Themes: SOP & NEI; KCs 3.4 & 4.1.** This is a challenging question, as it asks you to make a comparison across eras and select the one false difference. It is true that in 1815 the Concert of Europe provided a means for the great powers to address security issues, while no such mechanism existed in 1914 (A). Whereas in 1815 there existed a consensus among the great powers, pre-1914 diplomacy struggled to reconcile the interests of two rival alliance blocs (Triple Alliance vs. Triple Entente)—C. Finally, warfare had been altered in the century between 1815 and 1914 due to industrialization of weapons as would be revealed in WWI (D). This leaves B as the correct answer, and indeed, both eras involved nationalist conflicts that threatened revolution and forced the great powers to act.

4. **Answer: A. HTS: CCOT & CAUS; Theme: SOP; KCs 3.4 & 4.1.** Through Bismarck's alliance system (1871–1890), Europe avoided major wars among the great powers. However, with Bismarck's dismissal by Wilhelm II, Germany moved toward a more assertive international posture, which led to a more rigid system of alliances and a series of conflicts (A). The Berlin Conference did stimulate African imperialism, but the resulting conflicts among the great powers did not cause actual warfare (B). Britain was criticized for its actions in the Boer War (C), and as a result, shopped for allies, but again, this action was not as critical as A. Finally, Russia's defeat by Japan shocked it into reconciling with Britain, yet this was still not as critical as Germany's action leading up to 1914 (D).

5. **Answer: A. HTS: DAP, CTX, & CAUS; Themes: CID & SCD; KCs 4.3 & 4.4.** Hopefully you noted the tone of sarcasm in the poem, representing the disillusionment many experienced with the First World War, producing a cynical "lost generation" (A). The poem does not address politics *per se*, eliminating B. Though there are references to the economic struggles of the soldier, the poem conveys more about the psychology of the veteran rather than an analysis of economic matters (D). C does express a trend in the arts (making it an appealing choice); however, this poem does not reveal this trend as directly as Choice A.

6. **Answer: D. HTS: CAUS & CTX; Theme: CID; KCs 3.6 & 4.3.** The writer tackles a difficult topic through vivid description and irony (the supposedly wonderful opportunities that exist for wounded soldiers returning home), which is expressive of a realist approach to literature, as in the writings of Dickens and Zola (D). There are no classical references here (A), nor does the text promote Christian morality (B). One might argue that the passage conveys subjectivity, but it certainly does not employ the typical Romantic subjects, such as nature (C).

7. **Answer: B. HTS: CTX & CAUS; Themes: ECD & SOP; KCs 3.4 & 4.2.** The poster requires you to make inferences. Given the depictions of peasants and working classes, you would correctly conclude that the message relates to how the revolution would overthrow the inequality of the tsarist government (B); however, there are no specific critiques given of government itself, eliminating A. Choice C does express a cause of the Russian Revolution, but this issue of economic development does not appear as directly as does the key. By 1920, the Bolsheviks were eliminating other revolutionary parties in the Russian Civil War and certainly wouldn't be keen to remind Russians of that in their propaganda (D).

8. **Answer: D. HTS: SAS & CTX; Themes: SOP & ECD; KC 4.2.** In 1920 Russia was entrenched in a deadly civil war. Choice A can be eliminated, as World War I had already ended; further, by 1918 Germany had imposed the harsh Brest-Litovsk Treaty on Russia. The Provisional Government had also been overthrown by 1920 (B), and C would occur only later under Stalin (C). This leaves us with Choice D, and we may surmise that the poster was designed to motivate the Russian people to support its agenda of "peace, bread, and land" during the Civil War.

9. **Answer: C. HTS: SAS, CES, & CCOT; Themes: ECD & OS; KC 4.2.** To stimulate the dead-in-the-water Russian economy, Lenin compromised with capitalism by enacting the New Economic Policy (NEP), which allowed for limited free market activity (C). These policies caused a rift in the Politburo between "leftists" (led by Trotsky) and "rightists" (led by Bukharin). Stalin later eliminated both groups and adopted B and D as policies in his drive for modernization, which could be interpreted as attacks on capitalism. Choice A occurred during the Russian Civil War, but one might argue that such shared sacrifice is in keeping with the spirit of the poster.

Chapter 15

1. **Answer: C. HTS: CTX & DAP; Theme: CID; KC 4.3.** Freud calls into question the power of science and its technological fruits to resolve the fundamental condition of humanity. His writings reflect the disillusionment of the interwar era on notions of progress (C). A, B, and D express problems of the interwar period of a political or economic nature, but they do not relate to the crux of Freud's argument.

2. **Answer: B. HTS: CAUS; Theme: CID; KC 4.3.** World War I caused profound disillusionment in western civilization, reversing the course of technological and material progress prior to 1914 (B). Darwin's theory certainly raised questions about the human condition; however, it was remote in time (1859) from Freud's concerns. The Nazi party had not yet risen to power when Freud wrote this passage, eliminating C. Women did enter the workforce during the war, but this does not seem to touch on Freud's points (D).

3. **Answer: D. HTS: SAS & CES; Themes: CID & ECD; KCs 4.3 & 4.4.** Since Freud critiques the notion of progress (and this is an EXCEPT question), we are looking for an example that represents progress. A, B, and C express themes of disillusionment in high culture, or that questioned objective knowledge. D represents a significant improvement in the ability of economies to raise the standard of living through mass production, not fitting with Freud's point.

4. **Answer: B. HTS: CCOT & CES; Theme: CID; KC 4.3.** Some historians refer to the interwar period as the Age of Anxiety (B), which also fits well given Freud's field of psychiatry. Each of the other labels (A, C, and D) also fits the interwar period; however, they do not touch on the main point of Freud's writing (and its title): the doubt seeping into the project of western civilization.

5. **Answer: B. HTS: CAUS; Themes: ECD & SOP; KCs 4.1 & 4.2.** The picture shows the absurd effects of the hyperinflation that broke upon Germany in the early 1920s. Along with poor policies, this situation was caused most directly by the imposition of reparations from the Versailles settlement (B). Fascism had not yet gained a foothold in Germany, and in any case, fascism *resulted* from such economic problems. The trade policies of the US exacerbated the situation (C), but such policies played a more central role in bringing on the Depression. Germany did lose territory and colonies under Versailles (D), which created resentment, but these decisions bear only indirectly on the economic situation portrayed here.

6. **Answer: A. HTS: CAUS; Themes: SOP, NEI, & ECD; KCs 4.1 & 4.2.** The inability of democracies like the Weimar Republic to address economic crises led directly to support for fascist and communist parties (A). Germany and the Soviet Union did sign the Rapallo Pact in 1922, but this preceded the hyperinflation (B). There was no relation between the hyperinflation and artistic movements (C) or women entering the workforce (D).

7. **Answer: D. HTS: CCOT, MAC, & COMP; Themes: ECD, SOP, & NEI; KC 4.2.** Learning the lessons of the past, governments in both Western and Eastern Europe after 1945 instituted strong welfare programs (C). In addition, the United States (in a policy reversal from after WWI) extended significant aid to Western Europe (A) and encouraged successful policies of integration (B). This leaves us with the outlier (D) and in fact, this statement applies only to Eastern Europe, whose policies of central control provided for less prosperity than obtained in Western Europe.

8. **Answer: B. HTS: CTX, DAP, & CAUS; Themes: SOP & NEI; KC 4.1.** President Wilson championed the League of Nations as a means to prevent further security breakdowns and wars, one of his justifications for US entrance into the conflict (B). Versailles was beset by conflicting goals among the victors (A), French desires for vengeance (C), and fear of Soviet Communism (D)—a reason this nation was excluded—but these issues are not reflected in the League charter itself.

9. **Answer: D. HTS: CAUS; Themes: SOP & NEI; KC 4.1.** Each of the choices represents problems of the interwar period. This section of the League charter deals primarily with collective security, a goal that was seriously compromised by the non-adherence or exclusion of the United States, Germany, and the Soviet Union (D). The Great Depression fomented the rise of extremist groups (A), but this did not bear directly on the weakened structure of the League. The loss of confidence in western values may have contributed to lack of confidence in the League (B), but this did not bear as directly on its failure as D. Certainly the weak new democracies in central and eastern Europe created challenges for a reconstruction of the balance of power (C), but this issue only accentuated but did not cause the failure of the charter.

10. **Answer: B. HTS: CES & CCOT: Themes: SOP & NEI; KC 4.1.** In some ways, the League seemed to participate in its own death, primarily by undermining the security mechanism of Article 10 with the appeasement of the fascist powers (B). Though the decision to allow Germany and Italy to rearm contributed to the failure of security, it was not in itself the failure described in Article 10 (A). Choice C does not apply, since the appeasement of fascism occurred after the admission of the USSR. Dependence on US capital relates more directly to economic issues and the onset of the Depression and less to collective security (D).

Chapter 16

1. **Answer: C. HTS: DAP & CTX; Themes: SOP, INT, & ECD; KC 4.1.** Reagan explicitly addresses the Cold War division of Europe into blocs, excluding D. Also, he implies the drain of the arms race on the Soviet Union (B). Further, the very fact that Reagan appears before the British Parliament suggests the influence exercised by the US during the Cold War (A). This leaves C, and covert actions and "hot wars" (e.g., Korea) did feature as part of the Cold War, but these are not covered by the speech.

2. **Answer: D. HTS: SAS & CES; Themes: SOP & ECD; KCs 4.1 & 4.2.** Reagan notes the difficulties present in a Soviet economy geared toward production of heavy industry and weapons, sacrificing consumer goods. Khrushchev (C) attempted some reforms, but these did not extend as far as Gorbachev's policies of *perestroika* and *glasnost* (D). Lenin (A) and Stalin (B) established the command economy of the Soviet Union that Reagan critiques.

3. **Answer: C. HTS: CAUS; Theme: SOP; KC 4.1.** The passage suggests the problems associated with the communist system, particularly with production of goods. In fact, Reagan presented his speech as Cold War tensions revived, eliminating A. Choice B relates to the prompt, but more indirectly, since it addresses Germany and not the Soviet Union. The better choice is C, which did occur from 1989–1991, for many of the reasons that Reagan identifies in the speech. Balkan nationalism revived after communism's collapse, but this phenomenon is not the purpose of the address to Parliament (D).

4. **Answer: A. HTS: COMP, MAC, & CCOT; Themes: SOP & INT; KC 4.1.** This question asks you to consider the shift in US foreign policy following each world war. Both Wilson and (here) Reagan visited Europe to engage in diplomacy, even if Wilson's vision for the League of Nations fell short (D). In both cases, the US pursued its economic interests in relation to Europe, even if in a more enlightened way after WWII with the Marshall Plan (C). Both A and B state differences between each era; however, choice A relates directly to American involvement with Europe (i.e., NATO), whereas the US might have joined the UN without becoming a guarantor of European security.

5. **Answer: D. HTS: SAS & CES; Themes: SOP & INT; KC 4.1.** This MC set ends with what is known as a "skills only" question, since it asks you to think like a historian. All of the choices could limit the credibility of the speech's claims; however, the focus of the address is a particular interpretation of the Soviet system, which should incline you to the key (D). Reagan and Thatcher cooperated on many policies, but the president does not address Anglo-American relations (A). It is true that Reagan had, at that time, never visited the Soviet Union, but it is possible he may have obtained useful information from advisers or US intelligence (B). C is an appealing choice, but unless we knew more about the US electorate at this time, it would be difficult to judge how Reagan's portrayal would resonate with it.

6. **Answer: D. HTS: CTX & DAP; Themes: SOP & ECD; KCs 4.1 & 4.2.** Merkel recommits Germany to the notion of a single Europe economically and politically in this address (D). By 2010, the Cold War was well over, but the passage does not relate to this development, nor does it consider the US role in Europe (B). Of course, Merkel's position is predicated on C, but Germany's recovery was well established by 2010; in fact, it forms the basis of Merkel's leadership on the euro crisis, as referenced in the passage. However, her focus remains on the "Europe project," not the particular situation of Germany.

7. **Answer: C. HTS: SAS & CES; Themes: SOP & ECD; KCs 4.1 & 4.2.** Choices A, B, and D all represent transnational economic, political, or military organizations aimed at Western European security and cooperation during the Cold War. COMECON united the Eastern bloc under Soviet influence, making it the outlier here (C).

8. **Answer: D. HTS: CCOT; Theme: SOP; KC 4.1.** This question does not require the stimulus directly. Each of these choices expresses a key date in German politics; however, the defining fact of German politics after WWII was its division into East and West, which was overcome with its reunification in 1990 (D), following the fall of the Berlin Wall. A and B reflect this division, and though Brandt's Chancellorship did help ease tensions between the two Germanies, it did not change the official divide between them (C).

9. **Answer: B. HTS: CES & COMP; Theme: SOP; KC 4.1.** Merkel focuses on the common heritage of Europe and the importance of unity. A prerequisite for this unity may have been decolonization (A), eliminating this choice. Choice C facilitated Merkel's vision, as it opened the door for former Eastern bloc nations to join the EU and euro. Choice D (international institutions) also meshes with Merkel's ideas, though on a broader and more global scale. This leaves B, and indeed, such conflicts as the Balkan Wars, the Basque separatist campaign, or the Troubles in Northern Ireland reveal the continuing power of nationalism in the postwar period (B).

Chapter 17

1. **Answer: D. HTS: CAUS; Themes: SCD, ECD, & SOP; KC 4.4.** The beginning date of the chart depicts the end of the Baby Boom, marked by increased birth rates from 1945–1965, often promoted by government pronatalist policies (A). Pent-up demand for products after two world wars and the Great Depression led to increased prosperity and confidence in the future (B), boosting births. Despite the Cold War, Europe generally enjoyed political stability and the absence of military destruction (C), which also promoted fertility. This leaves D, and although such threats (communism and nuclear war) existed, they exercised little if any causal influence on birth rates.

2. **Answer: C. HTS: CAUS & CTX; Themes: TSI & SCD; KCs 4.3 & 4.4.** Here we are looking for the choice that best explains the decline in birth rates. Advances in artificial birth control (e.g., the pill) largely explain this decline (C). Though A, B, and D occurred (in fact, immigrant fertility rates were higher than established residents), they do not explain how and why birth rates continued to decline during this period.

3. **Answer: D. HTS: CCOT & CAUS; Themes: SCD, ECD, & SOP; KCs 4.2 & 4.4.** Women already exercised the vote in most European states before the dates in the chart (A), eliminating that option. European unity has been debated, but not in the context of fertility rates, but rather with respect to nationalism (B). Many technological developments, including birth control, have prompted debates in European cultural life; at this point, however, artificial birth control has won general acceptance, except from the hierarchy of the Catholic Church (C). With an expanding welfare state, many of the benefits go to the elderly (pensions, sickness, disability); in an age of declining population growth, fewer young tax-paying workers will support a larger, aging population—meaning either benefit cuts or higher taxes (D).

4. **Answer: A. HTS: SES & CES; Theme: SCD; KC 4.4.** In this question, you are asked to take the perspective of a feminist, who in the postwar era worked to provide women with improved opportunities for education and public life. Access to such opportunities required greater control of fertility, to free women from exclusively reproductive and domestic roles (A). The negative effects of high birth-

rates may be true, but the data actually show a decline in birth rates after 1965 (B). Overseas emigration occurred, but it had a minimal effect on the opportunities of existing populations in Europe (C). It is also true that Western European nations provided a higher standard of living than their Eastern European counterparts, but this fact is not derivable from the chart itself (D).

5. **Answer: C. HTS: CTX & DAP; Theme: ECD; KCs 4.2 & 4.4.** Pent-up demand from the sacrifices of two world wars and the Great Depression led to an expansion in production and consumption of new products. such as the appliance depicted here (C) along with cars, new foods, and leisure pursuits. Though continental integration indirectly aided this process, it cannot be inferred from the ad (A). The same is true for D. Given that the ad portrays women in a domestic role, B seems out of place.

6. **Answer: B. HTS: CTX & DAP; Theme: ECD; KC 4.2.** Each of the choices provides an accurate development of the era, but B links most closely with the image, since it showcases a new consumer item. Though competition with the Soviet Union may have aided the West's economic miracle, it did so only indirectly (A). Existentialists generally derided consumerism as conformist and inauthentic, running counter to the portrayal of it here as liberating (C). Finally, D seems out of place, as the ad presents appliances in a positive light. with no suggestion of consumerism's destructive potential.

7. **Answer: C. HTS: CES; Theme: SCD; KC 4.4.** Several of the choices pose an attractive possibility, so we must consider which is most directly illustrated. The answer is C, since the ad portrays a traditional domestic role for women during the Baby Boom (when many governments promoted the birth rate). Though the cultural influence of US culture expanded post-1945, this ad seems to be for a British product and British consumers, eliminating A. It certainly does not suggest a general decline in the belief in progress; instead it portrays progress as arising from improved use of technology, dropping out B. Welfare systems did expand after World War II, but the ad provides the historian with a glimpse into the operation of a free-market system (D).

8. **Answer: A. HTS: CCOT & COMP; Themes: ECD & SOP; KC 4.4.** The Green Party reacted strongly to the type of consumerism promoted in the ad, believing that it produced waste and environmental destruction (A). Having come to Europe primarily for economic reasons, migrant workers focused their attention on building a new life and gaining citizenship rights (B). National separatists focused on issues of identity and political influence, far removed from domestic concerns of the ad (C). Postmodernists, such as pop artists, often employed advertising to comment ironically on culture, providing a more ambivalent attitude toward such advertising (D).

SECTION III
PRACTICE EXAMS

PRACTICE EXAM 1

Section I, Part A: Multiple-Choice Questions
Time—55 minutes; 55 questions

Directions: Each of the questions or incomplete statements below is followed by four suggested answers or completions. Select the one that is best in each case. Source materials have been edited for the purpose of this exercise.

Questions 1–3 are based on the passage below.

> "And first, where I affirm the empire of a woman to be a thing repugnant to nature, I mean not only that God, by the order of his creation, has spoiled [deprived] woman of authority and dominion, but also that man has seen, proved, and pronounced just causes why it should be. Man, I say, in many other cases, does in this behalf see very clearly. For the causes are so manifest, that they cannot be hid. For who can deny but it is repugnant to nature, that the blind shall be appointed to lead and conduct such as do see? That the weak, the sick, and impotent persons shall nourish and keep the whole and strong? And finally, that the foolish, mad, and frenetic shall govern the discreet, and give counsel to such as be sober of mind? And such be all women, compared unto man in bearing of authority. For their sight in civil regiment is but blindness; their strength, weakness; their counsel, foolishness; and judgment, frenzy, if it be rightly considered."
>
> John Knox, Scottish minister and theologian, *The First Blast of the Trumpet Against the Monstrous Regiment of Women*, 1558

1. Knox's views on women were most likely prompted by which of the following?
   - **A.** The prevalence of women involved in spreading Renaissance humanism
   - **B.** Reformation reforms that initiated debates over women's nature and roles
   - **C.** Weakness among the new monarchies in addressing religious dissent
   - **D.** Economic changes that enhanced the status of women within households

2. Which of the following was most important in allowing views such as Knox's to gain an audience?
   - **A.** Stability provided by increased state control over religion and administration
   - **B.** An expanding consumer economy fed by exploration and colonization
   - **C.** The invention and expansion of the printing press and printed materials
   - **D.** Scientific discoveries that allowed for increased control of nature

3. For a historian researching the lives of ordinary women in the sixteenth century, which of the following sources would be most useful?
   - **A.** Statistics on rates of marriage and childbirth
   - **B.** Laws enacted by female monarchs
   - **C.** Paintings of well-known female intellectuals
   - **D.** Diagrams of female anatomy by scientists

Questions 4–6 are based on the chart below.

Estimated Relative Temperature Variations, 1000CE–2000CE

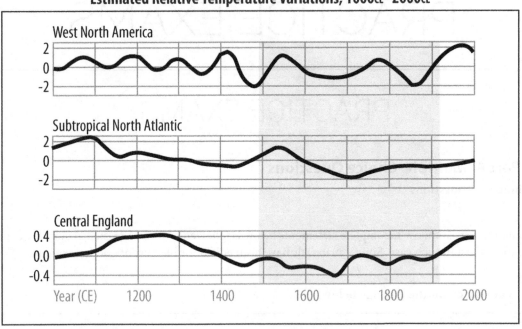

4. The graph depicts the early modern phenomenon of the:

    A. Price Revolution.

    B. Age of Crisis.

    C. Little Ice Age.

    D. Black Death.

5. Which of the following resulted from the trends depicted in the graph?

    A. Europeans delayed marriage and childbirth, restraining population growth.

    B. Landowners enclosed common lands and increased agricultural productivity.

    C. Cities and states began to regulate morality and restrict traditional freedoms.

    D. Serfdom was codified into law in much of eastern and central Europe.

6. In the period after 1945, a similar issue to that depicted above was:

    A. the development of ideas that challenged objective knowledge and reason.

    B. the increase in immigrants from the Middle East and Asia.

    C. the Cold War division between Eastern and Western Europe.

    D. the impact of consumerism and burning of fossil fuels.

Questions 7–10 are based on the passage below.

> "There are two means by which states are maintained in their weal and greatness—reward and penalty: the one for the good, the other for the bad. And, if the distribution of these two be faulty, nothing else is to be expected than the inevitable ruin of the state....
>
> Now, if there is any means to appease the wrath of God, to gain his blessing, to strike awe into some by the punishment of others, to preserve some from being infected by others, to diminish the number of evil-doers, to make secure the life of the well-disposed, and to punish the most detestable crimes of which the human mind can conceive, it is to punish with the utmost rigor the witches....
>
> Now, it is not within the power of princes to pardon a crime which the law of God punishes with the penalty of death—such as are the crimes of witches. Moreover, princes do gravely insult God in pardoning such horrible crimes committed directly against his majesty, seeing that the pettiest prince avenges with death insults against himself. Those too who let the witches escape, or who do not punish them with the utmost rigor, may rest assured that they will be abandoned by God to the mercy of the witches. And the country which shall tolerate this will be scourged with pestilences, famines, and wars; and those which shall take vengeance on the witches will be blessed by him and will make his anger to cease."
>
> Jean Bodin, French jurist and political theorist, *On the Demon-Mania of Witches*, 1580

7. Which of the following political trends is most strongly reflected in the passage?

   A. The expansion in power of commercial and professional groups in government

   B. Noble challenges to royal power based on the defense of traditional privileges

   C. Development of a new competitive state system based on sovereign nations

   D. Growth of monarchical power and theories justifying centralization

8. All of the following contributed to the trend discussed in the final paragraph EXCEPT:

   A. persistence of folk ideas regarding natural events.

   B. negative gender stereotypes regarding women.

   C. humanist literature emphasizing individualism.

   D. poor economic conditions and social breakdown.

9. The attitudes expressed in the final paragraph had changed among elites:

   A. as they adopted the New Science.

   B. with the onset of the French Revolution.

   C. as they sponsored industrialization.

   D. with the growth of positivism.

10. The passage <u>differs</u> most strongly from political writings in the eighteenth century in that the latter:

   A. did not concern themselves with strong state power.

   B. relied on natural law principles to justify authority.

   C. did not seek to identify or punish perceived outsiders.

   D. emphasized the importance of central legal codes.

Questions 11–14 are based on the poem below.

> "I own I am shock'd at the purchase of slaves,
> And fear those who buy them and sell them are knaves;
> What I hear of their hardships, their tortures, and groans
> Is almost enough to draw pity from stones.
> I pity them greatly, but I must be mum,
> For how could we do without sugar and rum?
> Especially sugar, so needful we see?
> What? give up our desserts, our coffee, and tea!
> Besides, if we do, the French, Dutch, and Danes,
> Will heartily thank us, no doubt, for our pains;
> If we do not buy the poor creatures, they will,
> And tortures and groans will be multiplied still."
>
> William Cowper, English poet and evangelical Christian, *Pity for Poor Africans*, 1788

11. Which of the following nations initiated the practice referenced by the poet?

    A. Spain

    B. Portugal

    C. England

    D. Netherlands

12. The development in the Americas that coincided with the practice referenced by the poet was the:

    A. destruction of indigenous cultures.

    B. conversion of indigenous peoples to Christianity.

    C. development of plantation economies.

    D. rivalry among colonial powers.

13. The practice referenced in the passage led to the:

    A. widespread colonization of Africa.

    B. growth of a consumer culture in Europe.

    C. development of new political theories.

    D. decline in political power of the nobility.

14. Which of the following movements stimulated opposition to the practice referenced by the poet?

    A. Protestant Reformation

    B. Scientific Revolution

    C. Enlightenment

    D. Industrial Revolution

Questions 15–18 are based on the passage below.

> "That the only purpose for which power can be rightfully exercised over any member of a civilized community, against his will, is to prevent harm to others. His own good, either physical or moral, is not a sufficient warrant. He cannot rightfully be compelled to do or forbear because it will be better for him to do so, because it will make him happier, because, in the opinions of others, to do so would be wise, or even right. These are good reasons for remonstrating with him, or reasoning with him, or persuading him, or entreating him, but not for compelling him, or visiting him with any evil, in case he do otherwise. To justify that, the conduct from which it is desired to deter him must be calculated to produce evil to someone else. The only part of the conduct of any one, for which he is amenable to society, is that which concerns others. In the part which merely concerns himself, his independence is, of right, absolute. Over himself, over his own body and mind, the individual is sovereign."
>
> John Stuart Mill, British philosopher, *On Liberty*, 1859

15. All of the following developments most likely influenced Mill's ideas EXCEPT the:
    A. Enlightenment.
    B. French Revolution.
    C. Concert of Europe.
    D. rise of mass political parties.

16. Which of the following nineteenth-century political ideologies does the passage reflect?
    A. Romanticism
    B. Liberalism
    C. republicanism
    D. nationalism

17. The ideological position expressed by Mill had been changed most by the end of the nineteenth century by the:
    A. need for government intervention due to problems of industrialization.
    B. pursuit of colonies and resources in Africa and Asia.
    C. shifting balance of power due to the unifications of Italy and Germany.
    D. rise of a feminist movement demanding equal economic and political rights.

18. Which of the following figures would have agreed most strongly with the ideas above?
    A. René Descartes
    B. John Locke
    C. Jean-Jacques Rousseau
    D. Maximilien Robespierre

Questions 19–22 are based on the two passages below.

Source 1

"One way of life is based upon the will of the majority, and is distinguished by free institutions, representative government, free elections, guarantees of individual liberty, freedom of speech and religion, and freedom from political oppression.

The second way of life is based upon the will of a minority forcibly imposed upon the majority. It relies upon terror and oppression, a controlled press and radio; fixed elections, and the suppression of personal freedoms.

I believe that it must be the policy of the United States to support free peoples who are resisting attempted subjugation by armed minorities or by outside pressures."

President Harry Truman, speech to United States Congress, 1947

Source 2

"The U.S.A. decided to take advantage of the economic and political difficulties in the other leading capitalist countries and bring them under its sway. Under the pretext of economic aid the U.S.A. began to infiltrate into their economy and interfere in their internal affairs. Such big capitalist countries as Japan, West Germany, Italy, France and Britain all became dependent on the U.S.A. to a greater or lesser degree."

Boris Ponomaryov, Soviet politician and historian, *History of the Communist Party of the Soviet Union*, official publication of the Soviet government, 1960

19. The two sources above reveal which of the following causes of the Cold War?

   A. Military confrontation and the race to develop nuclear weaponry

   B. Competition over strategically and economically valuable areas of the world

   C. Fundamental differences over economics, ideology, and politics

   D. Failure of the United Nations to moderate conflict in the postwar period

20. All of the following resulted from the US policies referenced in both sources EXCEPT:

   A. a higher degree of economic, political, and military coordination in Western Europe.

   B. an economic recovery that increased the standard of living and consumerism.

   C. an increased reliance of Western Europe on US military and economic power.

   D. expansion of cradle-to-grave welfare programs and accompanying higher taxes.

21. The Soviet Union responded to the American policies addressed in the sources by:

   A. imposing central planning and specialized production in Eastern Europe.

   B. reforming the communist system through *perestroika* and *glasnost*.

   C. promoting de-Stalinization and peaceful coexistence with the West.

   D. crushing revolts in Eastern Europe through the Brezhnev Doctrine.

22. Which of the following is the strongest limitation for a historian using either of the sources as a basis for attributing responsibility for the Cold War?

   A. Source 1 is drawn from a speech, attempting to persuade for political purposes.

   B. Source 1 does not refer to specific geographic areas or indicate monetary amounts.

   C. Source 2 is from an official government publication under a regime lacking a free press.

   D. Source 2 does not explain the background or motivations of its author.

Questions 23–27 are based on the passage below.

"In the year 5280* (1519), our lord, the Emperor Charles, was crowned king. I came to him and to his servants to plead for our people and our inheritance. We…obtained comprehensive privileges for all of Germany. Notwithstanding this, in the same year, charters were issued authorizing the expulsion of [the Jews] from Rosheim and from the Vogtei of Kaysersberg. With the help of God, blessed be He, I interceded with the King, and succeeded in having the expulsion from the Vogtei of Kaysersberg cancelled altogether, with the annulment of that particular charter of expulsion. However, the charter to Rosheim was not rescinded, [nor was that city's decision to expel the Jews]. By dint of supreme efforts we succeeded time after time, with great difficulty, in obtaining yet another postponement. To this day we still do not know [how matters will turn out], and we can but place our trust in our Father in Heaven. He will redeem us and save us from [our] assailants. May it be His will. Amen."

* according to the Jewish calendar

Josel von Rosheim, Jewish rabbi and merchant, memoirs, 1540s

23. The text reflects the situation of the Holy Roman Empire in the sixteenth century by:
    A. exhibiting the ability of Charles V to draw on the wealth of his Spanish Empire.
    B. demonstrating the spread of the ideals of Christian humanism to Germany.
    C. showing the inability of the Holy Roman Empire to centralize like other new monarchies.
    D. illustrating the rise of new commercial and professional elites to challenge the nobility.

24. Religious reform in the sixteenth century likely affected the status of Jews in Germany by:
    A. providing wealth from the confiscation of church lands.
    B. allowing them the option to convert to Protestantism.
    C. preventing them from emigrating to areas of religious diversity.
    D. posing a threat due to heightened concerns for religious orthodoxy.

25. The most significant change in the issues faced by Jews in the text came with the:
    A. Commercial Revolution.
    B. Enlightenment.
    C. Industrial Revolution.
    D. world wars of the twentieth century.

26. Which of the following subsequent developments worsened the situation faced by Jews in the text?
    A. Darwin's theory of natural selection
    B. Voltaire's criticism of organized religion
    C. Rousseau's notion of the noble savage
    D. Marx's emphasis on class struggle

27. All of the following groups faced similar situations in early modern Europe EXCEPT:
    A. women accused of witchcraft.
    B. nobles exiled for opposing absolutism.
    C. Africans taken for the slave trade.
    D. peasants executed for revolting.

Questions 28–31 are based on the interpretation below.

> "[Napoleon] Bonaparte belongs to the Revolution, surely, in matters that seemed irreversible at the time—civil equality, the destruction of feudalism, the ruin of the privileged position of the Catholic Church. As for the rest, the enjoyment of liberties, the form of political institutions, there had been since 1789 so much instability, so many contradictions between grand principles and the practice of governments, so much persistent uncertainty on the outcome of the war and the unity of the nation, that the field lay open for a strong man who, on condition of preserving the essential conquests of the Revolution, would do something new in the matter of government and refuse to be embarrassed by scruples. By anchoring France securely to the shores that the Constituent Assembly had been unwilling to leave, Bonaparte accomplished somewhat late in the day that 'revolution from above' of which the old monarchy had been incapable."
>
> Louis Bergeron, French historian, *France Under Napoleon*, 1981

28. Which of the following labels would the historian most likely apply to Napoleon?
    A. New monarch
    B. Divine-right ruler
    C. Enlightened absolutist
    D. Totalitarian dictator

29. Which of the following best accounts for the situation in France prior to Napoleon, as outlined by the historian?
    A. The meeting of the Estates-General
    B. The abolition of serfdom and feudalism
    C. The Declaration of Rights of Man and Citizen
    D. The threat of invasion and counterrevolution

30. Napoleon responded to the historical situation he inherited, as described by the historian, by:
    A. curtailing rights behind a façade of democracy.
    B. extending citizenship to women.
    C. provoking nationalist responses in other nations.
    D. reaffirming popular revolutionary violence.

31. All of the following leaders imitated many of Napoleon's political strategies EXCEPT:
    A. Cavour.
    B. Metternich.
    C. Napoleon III.
    D. Bismarck.

Questions 32–35 are based on the image below.

Jean-Honoré Fragonard, French artist, *The Visit to the Nursery*, 1775

32. The scene reflects all of the following economic and social features of the eighteenth century EXCEPT:

    A. the nuclear family as the predominant social and economic unit.

    B. the development of privacy within the family home.

    C. a rise in the rate of births that occurred out of wedlock.

    D. a consumer revolution with more resources dedicated to child-rearing.

33. The thinkers most responsible for the attitude toward children shown above were:

    A. Voltaire and Diderot.

    B. Locke and Rousseau.

    C. Smith and Quesnay.

    D. Montesquieu and Beccaria.

34. Which of the following developments of the nineteenth century would confirm the attitudes expressed in the painting?

    A. The development of political ideologies that challenged the status quo

    B. The mechanization of production that increased the standard of living

    C. Growth of private reform movements to aid the poor and disadvantaged

    D. Restrictions on child labor and provision for universal compulsory education

35. A historian might use the painting as evidence for which feature of the Enlightenment?

    A. Social reforms based on empirical and rational principles

    B. Expansion of printed materials and increase in literacy

    C. Development of public venues, like salons, to spread ideas

    D. Skeptical approaches toward traditional religious beliefs

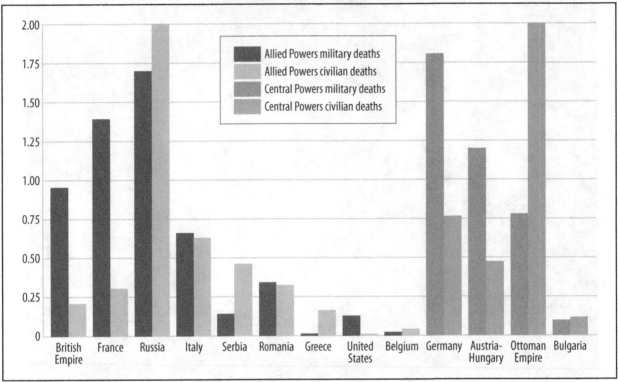

World War I Fatalities (in millions)

36. Which of the following best explains the overall pattern for the data above?

   A. New technologies overwhelmed traditional military strategies.

   B. Widespread fighting disrupted trade and led to famine.

   C. The strain of total war led to insurrection and revolution.

   D. Military stalemate led to widening of the war to a global conflict.

37. All of the following resulted from the data depicted above EXCEPT:

   A. women entered the industrial workforce in large numbers.

   B. a disillusioned and cynical "lost generation" was created.

   C. peace movements were successful in reestablishing stability.

   D. the hold on power of traditional elites was destroyed.

Questions 38–40 are based on the poster below.

Caption: "At the end of the Plan, the basis of collectivization must be completed."

Soviet poster, 1932

38. The poster reflects Stalin's goal of:

   A. establishing his control of the Bolsheviks.

   B. rapidly modernizing the Soviet economy.

   C. promoting revolution through the Comintern.

   D. embracing Lenin's New Economic Policy.

39. A major result of pursuing the initiatives depicted above was:

   A. the liquidation of the kulak class.

   B. closer relations with western Europe.

   C. Soviet admission to the League of Nations.

   D. new rights and status for Soviet women.

40. The most significant change after 1945 in the initiatives depicted in the poster came through the policies of:

   A. Lenin.

   B. Khrushchev.

   C. Brezhnev.

   D. Gorbachev.

Questions 41–44 are based on the passage below.

"Up to the year 1856, the year before the outbreak, there had been for a whole century a continuous, aggressive advance of the British power, till it completed the ring fence of the empire…some provinces being brought under its direct administration and others being left as feudatory or vassal states under their native rulers. At the start the old Mogul dominion had been in a hopeless state of decay…and some of the native principalities had gladly turned for safety to the shelter of English protection and supremacy.

….The benefits of civilized rule, of the Pax Britannica, were felt only skin-deep, and the old fierce instincts, the outcome of centuries of strife and oppression, were still in the ascendant. The memory of injuries was still keen and vivid, the newer cases helping to recall the old ones, and to reopen sores that might otherwise have been getting healed; so that, briefly, the mood and temper which prevailed were those of a conquered people who had wrongs and humiliations to remember, and were chafing at having to endure the sway of aliens in race and creed."

P.R. Innes, British colonial officer, "Review of the English progress in India from 1757 to 1857," 1885.

41. The beginning of the process that Innes describes stemmed from Britain's rivalry with:

   A. the Netherlands.

   B. France.

   C. Germany.

   D. Russia.

42. What does Innes likely mean by the "benefits of civilized rule"?

   A. Communication and transportation technologies, like railroads

   B. Medical technologies that allowed European states to conquer empires

   C. Advanced weaponry that overpowered colonized nations

   D. New artistic styles that provided realistic depictions of nature

43. Which of the following provided the most decisive shift in the relationship explained by Innes?

   A. Boer War

   B. Russo-Japanese War

   C. Founding of League of Nations

   D. Second World War

44. Colonized peoples responded to the situation outlined above in all of the following ways EXCEPT by:

   A. modernizing their economies and societies.

   B. refusing to join the United Nations after 1945.

   C. establishing national resistance movements.

   D. emigrating to Europe in search of new opportunities.

Questions 45–47 are based on the passages below.

Source 1

"The map of Europe will be redrawn. The countries of the peoples, defined by the vote of free men, will arise upon the ruins of the countries of kings and privileged castes, and between these countries harmony and fraternity will exist. And the common work of Humanity, of general amelioration, and the gradual discovery and application of its Law of life, being distributed according to local and general capacities, will be wrought out in peaceful and progressive development and advance."

Giuseppe Mazzini, Italian politician and journalist, *The Duties of Man*, ca. 1820s–1830s

Source 2

"Germany is not looking to Prussia's liberalism, but to its power; Bavaria, Württemberg, Baden may indulge liberalism, and yet no one will assign them Prussia's role; Prussia has to coalesce and concentrate its power for the opportune moment, which has already been missed several times; Prussia's borders…are not favorable for a healthy, vital state; it is not by speeches and majority resolutions that the great questions of the time are decided—that was the big mistake of 1848 and 1849—but by iron and blood."

Otto von Bismarck, Prussian Chancellor, Speech to the Prussian Reichstag, 1862

45. Which of the following situations do both sources reference which hindered the unification of their respective nations?

   A. Revolutions of 1848

   B. Growth of industry

   C. Congress of Vienna

   D. Pursuit of colonies

46. The historical development that best explains the differences in the tone and goals of the sources was the:

   A. adoption of nationalism by conservative politicians.

   B. spread of the Romantic movement in the arts.

   C. growth of the labor movement and socialism.

   D. situation created by the Crimean War.

47. Which of the following developments most directly contributed to the achievement of the goals of both sources?

   A. Growth of factories and transportation systems

   B. Breakdown of the Concert of Europe

   C. Creation of the Dual Monarchy in Austria

   D. Nationalist tensions in the Balkans

Questions 48–51 are based on the image below.

The Bauhaus Building at Dessau, designed by Walter Gropius, German architect, 1926

48. The building above reflects which of the following cultural trends?

    A. Irrationality and the notion that struggle leads to progress

    B. New theories in the sciences that undermined Newtonian physics

    C. Growth of spaces dedicated to consumerism and mass leisure

    D. A modernist focus on the abstract and efficient use of space

49. Which of the following economic trends most directly enabled such buildings?

    A. Production of materials like steel during the Second Industrial Revolution

    B. The expansion of European states into African and Asian markets

    C. A move toward protective tariffs to shield domestic production from competition

    D. Improvement in working conditions and wages for unskilled laborers

50. The building contrasts most strongly with one built during the sixteenth through early nineteenth centuries in its:

    A. emphasis on natural light.

    B. explicitly economic focus.

    C. lack of ornamentation.

    D. solitary geographic location.

51. Which of the following events created the most decisive shift in cultural attitudes in the half-century around when this building was created?

    A. Scramble for Africa

    B. First World War

    C. Great Depression

    D. Second World War

Questions 52–53 are based on the passage below.

> "The strongest nation has always been conquering the weaker; sometimes even subduing it, but always prevailing over it. Every intellectual gain, so to speak, that a nation possessed was in the earliest times made use of—was invested and taken out—in war; all else perished. Each nation tried constantly to be the stronger, and so made or copied the best weapons, by conscious and unconscious imitation each nation formed a type of character suitable to war and conquest. Conquest improved mankind by the intermixture of strengths; the armed truce, which was then called peace, improved them by the competition of training and the consequent creation of new power."
>
> Walter Bagehot, British journalist and businessman, *Physics and Politics*, 1872

52. Bagehot's ideas were most directly influenced by the:
    A. development of workers' movements and socialism.
    B. ideas of natural selection developed by Charles Darwin.
    C. pursuit of colonies and resources in Africa and Asia.
    D. growth of populations and influence of mass politics.

53. Which of the following led to the strongest criticism of ideas like Bagehot's?
    A. Growth of the feminist movement
    B. Freud's theories of the unconscious
    C. Effects of World War I and World War II
    D. Abandonment of laissez-faire economics

Questions 54–55 are based on the image below.

French Women's World Cup Soccer Team, 2015

54. The photograph above reflects most directly the post-1945 trend of:

   A. the spread of new technologies that promoted globalization.

   B. immigration into Europe from the Middle East, Africa, and Asia.

   C. the rise of nationalism following the collapse of communism.

   D. an "economic miracle" that increased the standard of living.

55. Independence in the post-1945 period for many of the peoples represented above was delayed for which of the following reasons?

   A. Cold War geopolitical competition between the superpowers

   B. Use of nationalist and separatist violence alienated potential supporters

   C. A loss of faith in progress and the ability of science to solve problems

   D. Military technologies that allowed for genocide and the threat of nuclear war

Section I, Part B: Short-Answer Questions

Time—40 minutes; 3 Questions

Directions: There are four short-answer questions on the exam. Answer Question 1 *and* Question 2, and then choose to answer *either* Question 3 *or* Question 4. Note that the short-answer questions do not require you to develop and support a thesis statement. Use complete sentences; an outline or bulleted list is not acceptable.

Use the image below to answer all parts of the question that follows.

Sébastien Leclerc, French artist, *Louis XIV Visiting the French Academy of Sciences*, 1671

1. a) Describe one way in which the image above conveys the principles of the Scientific Revolution.

    b) Describe one example that conveys the relationship between science and politics during the seventeenth century.

    c) Explain one way in which the artist's identity or his historical situation may have influenced the subject and portrayal of the painting.

Use the interpretation below to answer all parts of the question that follows.

> "What no one understood, at the beginning of 1989, was that the Soviet Union, its empire, its ideology—and therefore the Cold War itself—was a sand pile ready to slide. All it took to make that happen were a few more grains of sand. The people who dropped them were not in charge of superpowers or movements or religions: they were ordinary people with simple priorities who saw, seized, and sometimes stumbled into opportunities. In doing so, they caused a collapse no one could stop. Their 'leaders' had little choice but to follow.
>
> One particular leader, however, did so in a distinctive way. He ensured that the great 1989 revolution was the first one ever in which almost no blood was shed…People did die, but in remarkably small numbers for the size and significance of what was happening. In both its ends and its means, then, this revolution became a triumph of hope. It did so chiefly because Mikhail Gorbachev chose not to act, but rather to be acted upon."
>
> John Lewis Gaddis, American historian, *The Cold War: A New History*, 2005

2. a) Describe one specific example that helped bring about the situation described in the first paragraph.

   b) Describe one policy that would support the historian's interpretation in the second paragraph.

   c) Explain one way in which the identity and/or historical situation of the author may have influenced his perspective in the passage.

Answer all parts of *either* Question 3 *or* Question 4.

3. a) Describe one example of how the Catholic Church pursued religious and/or institutional reform in the sixteenth century.

   b) Describe one example of how the Catholic Church responded to the challenge of the Protestant Reformation in the sixteenth century.

   c) Explain one religious or political result of these reforms and responses in the period 1500–1650.

4. • French Revolution (1789)

   • Napoleon takes power (1799)

   • Congress of Vienna (1815)

   • Revolutions of 1848

   a) Select one of the dates above and describe one example of how it represents the most significant shift in European politics or diplomacy.

   b) Select another one of the dates above and describe one example that <u>limits it</u> from being as significant a shift in European politics or diplomacy.

   c) Explain one social or economic <u>continuity</u> during the nineteenth century that persisted during these political changes.

Section II, Part A: Document-Based Question

Total Time—60 minutes; 1 Question

Directions: Question 1 is based on the accompanying documents. It is suggested that you spend about 15 minutes reading the documents and 45 minutes writing your response. The documents have been edited for the purpose of this exercise.

In your response you should do the following:

- Respond to the prompt with a historically defensible thesis or claim that establishes a line of reasoning.
- Describe a broader historical context relevant to the prompt.
- Support an argument in response to the prompt using at least six documents.
- Use at least one additional piece of specific historical evidence (beyond that found in the documents) relevant to an argument about the prompt.
- For at least three documents, explain how or why the document's point of view, purpose, historical situation, and/or audience is relevant to an argument.
- Use evidence to corroborate, qualify, or modify an argument that addresses the prompt.

Question 1   *Evaluate whether the First World War was caused primarily by political miscalculations or by the build-up of tensions over decades.*

Document 1

Source: Benjamin Disraeli, British Prime Minister and Conservative Party leader, speech to House of Commons upon the declaration of the unified German Empire, February 9, 1871

There is not a diplomatic tradition which has not been swept away. You have a new world, new influences at work, new and unknown objects and dangers with which to cope, at present involved in that obscurity incident to novelty in such affairs. We used to have discussions in this House about the balance of power. Lord Palmerston*, eminently a practical man, trimmed the ship of State and shaped its policy with a view to preserve an equilibrium in Europe....But what has really come to pass? The balance of power has been entirely destroyed, and the country which suffers most, and feels the effects of this great change most, is England.

* former Prime Minister of Great Britain

Document 2

Source: Friedrich Engels, socialist revolutionary and political theorist, 1887

[There will be a] world war of never before seen intensity, if the system of mutual outbidding in armament, carried to the extreme, finally bears its natural fruits…eight to ten million soldiers will slaughter each other and strip Europe bare as no swarm of locusts has ever done before. The devastations of the Thirty Years' War condensed into three or four years and spread all over the continent: famine, epidemics, general barbarization of armies and masses, provoked by sheer desperation; utter chaos in our trade, industry and commerce, ending in general bankruptcy; collapse of the old states and their traditional wisdom in such a way that the crowns will roll in the gutter by the dozens and there will be nobody to pick them up; absolute impossibility to foresee how all this will end and who will be victors in that struggle; only one result was absolutely certain: general exhaustion and the creation of circumstances for the final victory of the working class.

Document 3

Source: John Tenniel, political cartoonist, "Dropping the Pilot" (depicting Kaiser William's dismissal of Chancellor Bismarck), *Punch*, British periodical, 1890

Document 4

Source: The Franco-Russian Alliance Military Convention, August 18, 1892

France and Russia, being animated by a common desire to preserve peace, and having no other object than to meet the necessities of a defensive war, provoked by an attack of the forces of the Triple Alliance against either of them, have agreed upon the following provisions:

1. If France is attacked by Germany, or by Italy supported by Germany, Russia shall employ all her available forces to attack Germany. If Russia is attacked by Germany, or by Austria supported by Germany, France shall employ all her available forces to attack Germany.

2. In case the forces of the Triple Alliance, or of any one of the Powers belonging to it, should be mobilized, France and Russia, at the first news of this event and without previous agreement being necessary, shall mobilize immediately and simultaneously the whole of their forces, and shall transport them as far as possible to their frontiers.

3. These forces shall engage to the full with such speed that Germany will have to fight simultaneously on the East and on the West.

7. All the clauses enumerated above shall be kept absolutely secret.

Document 5

Source: Kaiser William II, German Emperor, speech before the North German Regatta [boat-racing] Association, 1901

In spite of the fact that we have no such fleet as we should have, we have conquered for ourselves a place in the sun. It will now be my task to see to it that this place in the sun shall remain our undisputed possession, in order that the sun's rays may fall fruitfully upon our activity and trade in foreign parts, that our industry and agriculture may develop within the state and our sailing sports upon the water, for our future lies upon the water. The more Germans go out upon the waters, whether it be in races or regattas, whether it be in journeys across the ocean, or in the service of the battle flag, so much the better it will be for us.

Document 6

Source: Oath and Constitution of the Black Hand (Union or Death), secretive Serbian organization opposed to Austro-Hungarian control of the Balkans, 1911

Oath sworn by all members of the Black Hand group

I, in joining the organization 'Union or Death,' swear…before God, by the blood of the ancestors, on my honor and on my life, that I will from this moment until my death be faithful to the laws of this organization; and that I will always be ready to make any sacrifice for it.

Constitution of the Black Hand group

Article 2. The organization gives priority to the revolutionary struggle rather than on cultural striving, therefore its institution is an absolutely secret one for wider circles.

Article 4. In order to carry into effect its task the organization will do the following things:

(2) It will carry out a revolutionary organization in all the territories where Serbians are living:

(3) Beyond the frontiers, it will fight with all means against all enemies of this idea:

(4) It will maintain friendly relations with all the States, nations, organizations, and individual persons who sympathize with Serbia and the Serbian race:…

Document 7

Source: Kaiser William II of Germany and Tsar Nicholas II of Russia, telegrams, July–August 1914

Tsar to Kaiser, July 29, 1:00 A.M.

…An ignoble war has been declared on a weak country. The indignation in Russia shared fully by me is enormous. I foresee that very soon I shall be overwhelmed by the pressure forced upon me…to take extreme measures which will lead to war. To try and avoid such a calamity as a European war I beg you in the name of our old friendship to do what you can to stop your allies from going too far.

Nicky

Kaiser to Tsar, July 29, 1:45 A.M. [This and the previous telegraph crossed.]

It is with the gravest concern that I hear of the impression which the action of Austria against Serbia is creating in your country. The unscrupulous agitation that has been going on in Serbia for years has resulted in the outrageous crime, to which Archduke Francis Ferdinand fell a victim. The spirit that led Serbians to murder their own king and his wife still dominates the country.* You will doubtless agree with me that we both, you and me, have a common interest as well as all Sovereigns to insist that all the persons morally responsible for the dastardly murder should receive their deserved punishment. In this case politics plays no part at all.

I fully understand how difficult it is for you and your Government to face the drift of your public opinion. Therefore, with regard to the hearty and tender friendship which binds us both from long ago with firm ties, I am exerting my utmost influence to induce the Austrians to deal straightly to arrive to a satisfactory understanding with you…

Your very sincere and devoted friend and cousin

Willy

Tsar to Kaiser, July 31

I thank you heartily for your mediation which begins to give one hope that all may yet end peacefully. It is technically impossible to stop our military preparations which were obligatory owing to Austria's mobilization. We are far from wishing war…

Your affectionate

Nicky

Kaiser to Tsar, August 1

Thanks for your telegram. I yesterday pointed out to your government the way by which alone war may be avoided. Although I requested an answer for noon today, no telegram from my ambassador conveying an answer from your Government has reached me as yet. I therefore have been obliged to mobilize my army.

Willy

* a reference to the assassination of the Serbian king in 1903 by the Black Hand

Section II, Part B: Long Essay Question

Time—40 minutes; 1 Question

Directions: Choose EITHER Question 2 or Question 3 or Question 4.

In your response, you should do the following.

- Respond to the prompt with a historically defensible thesis or claim that establishes a line of reasoning.
- Describe a broader historical context relevant to the prompt.
- Support an argument in response to the prompt using specific and relevant examples of evidence.
- Use historical reasoning (e.g., comparison, causation, continuity or change over time) to frame or structure an argument that addresses the prompt.
- Use evidence to corroborate, qualify, or modify an argument that addresses the prompt.

Question 2   *Evaluate the most significant difference between the Italian Renaissance and the Protestant Reformation.*

(RP: Comparison)

Question 3   *Evaluate the most significant difference between the periods 1650–1815 and 1914–1991 in Europe's interaction with the non-European world.*

(RP: Comparison)

Question 4   *Evaluate the most significant difference between the periods 1500–1700 and 1815–1914 in European family life.*

(RP: Comparison)

Practice Exam 1 — Answers and Explanations

MC Answers with Explanations

1. **Answer: B.** HTS: CAUS & DAP; Themes: SCD & CID; KCs 1.2 & 1.4. Though some women, such as Isabella d'Este, did patronize the Renaissance, Knox writes well after that event and clearly seems more concerned with moral issues (A). Knox himself expressed Calvinist dissent within Mary, Queen of Scots's Catholic state, thus eliminating C. The early modern period did witness major economic changes, like rising prices and enclosure, but women generally did not benefit from these (D). This leaves us with B as the answer: women played a key role in spreading ideals of religious reform and this involvement sparked concern among males regarding their proper role in society.

2. **Answer: C.** HTS: CAUS; Themes: TSI & CID; KCs 1.1 & 1.2. A major factor in spreading ideas of religious reform was the printing press, providing an audience for views like Knox's (C). States did exercise increased state control over religion during this period, but only after significant upheaval and even civil war (A). Though B and D originated in the sixteenth century, these developments were not germane to Knox's concerns in the passage.

3. **Answer: A.** HTS: SAS & CES; Theme: SCD; KC 1.4. Here we have a skills-only question that asks you to consider the approaches that historians employ in reconstructing the past. The key in the stem is "ordinary women," whose lives were often dominated by marriage and reproduction, giving us A as the key. B and C show other forms of useful evidence, but these artifacts would be of service primarily to reconstruct the lives of elite women. Many male scientists who made diagrams of female anatomy did so under the assumption and with the purpose of reinforcing female inferiority, making these unreliable as evidence for women's actual lives (D).

4. **Answer: C.** HTS: CTX & DAP; Themes: ECD & SCD; KC 1.4. The chart depicts the generally lower temperatures between 1400 and 1700, termed the Little Ice Age (C). No economic data are shown, eliminating A. Though a portion of this period was known as the Age of Crisis, that term refers to phenomena beyond weather, such as religious upheaval and high crime rates (B). There was no correlation between weather and the Black Death, which preceded the drop in average temperature anyway (D).

5. **Answer: A.** HTS: CAUS; Themes: ECD & SCD; KC 1.4. All of the choices express important features of early modern social and economic life; however, only A resulted directly from the changing weather patterns, as families under economic stress—due to poor crop yields and repeated famine—responded by delaying standard family events such as marriage and children, until conditions improved. Enclosure occurred in response to the growing money economy (B), and serfdom was codified (D) due to the strength of the nobles and weakness of peasant bar-

gaining positions in central and eastern Europe. C is true, but regulation of morality evolved from the goals of religious reformers to apply new dogma to practices.

6. **Answer: D.** HTS: CCOT, MAC, & COMP; Themes: ECD & TSI; KC 4.4. The chart invites us to compare an issue—weather—over two time periods. In the contemporary era, weather concerns revolve around global climate change and the human contribution to it, making the key D. Choices A, B, and C all describe developments after 1945 but are also not relatable to the chart in a direct way.

7. **Answer: D.** HTS: CTX & DAP; Themes: SOP & NEI; KC 1.5. In this passage, Bodin argues for a vigorous use of state power to address a moral issue—witchcraft. During the period of his writings, many theorists, including Bodin, argued for stronger monarchical power over religion and to maintain stability and security (D). Though choices A, B, and C all portray accurate developments during the early modern period, they do not relate directly or are not referenced in Bodin's writings.

8. **Answer: C.** HTS: CAUS; Themes: CID & SCD; KCs 1.1 & 1.4. The focus of the passage is the fear of witches, which led to widespread persecution of those accused between 1550–1680. Prior to the spread of the new scientific methods, most thinkers attributed causation to supernatural forces (A). Of those accused of witchcraft, women comprised about 85% of the total, primarily because of stereotypes that portrayed women as credulous and carnal, thus open to the seduction of the devil (B). Fears during this era were heightened by a fear of community breakdown with the shift from communal to commercial agriculture, rise of a money economy, and unstable prices and food supply (D). This leaves us with C, and indeed, humanist literature did not generally emphasize the danger of witches.

9. **Answer: A.** HTS: CCOT & MAC; Theme: CID; KCs 1.1 & 1.4. As the new scientific thinking based on empiricism and natural laws took hold, elites gradually abandoned folk explanations and the culture of the masses (A). Witchcraft accusations subsided well before the French Revolution (B) and industrialization (C) and positivism (D) in the nineteenth century.

10. **Answer: B.** HTS: COMP, MAC, & CCOT; Theme: SOP; KCs 1.5 & 2.1. Political theorists of the eighteenth century operated within the Enlightenment, which applied the methods of the new science to politics, particularly the notion that it operates according to natural laws (B), as in the writings of Montesquieu and Rousseau. Both periods emphasized the importance of strong state power (A) and the centralization of legal codes (D), though the eighteenth century took the latter further. Though the eighteenth century saw few witchcraft persecutions, outsiders who were perceived as a threat to the state, such as radicals or ethnic minorities, continued to bear the brunt of discriminatory policies, just as perceived witches in the sixteenth century.

11. **Answer: B. HTS: CAUS & DAP; Themes: INT & ECD; KCs 1.3 & 2.2.** This is a straightforward factual question asking about the origins of the slave trade. You may recall that Portugal initiated European contact with the west coast of Africa, which included trade in enslaved persons (B). The other nations mentioned (A, C, D) eventually participated in the slave trade, even surpassing Portugal.

12. **Answer: C. HTS: MAC & COMP; Themes: INT & ECD; KCs 1.3 & 2.2.** It is true that destruction of indigenous cultures in the Americas (A) stimulated the slave trade; however, the slave trade's massive expansion in the seventeenth and eighteenth centuries occurred with the exploitation of unfree labor on American plantations, growing products such as sugar, cotton, and tobacco (C). European powers often converted indigenous peoples to Christianity, yet this practice was not correlated directly with the slave trade. Finally, colonial powers competed for resources (D), but this competition was not primarily over the slave trade.

13. **Answer: C. HTS: CAUS; Themes: INT & ECD; KC 2.2.** The spread of new goods into Europe on the backs of enslaved labor transformed both the economy and the culture. Sugar, tea, coffee, rum, tobacco, molasses—these goods shifted from luxuries to common commodities consumed by the growing middle class (B). African colonization did not occur until after 1850, eliminating A. New political theories also developed during this era but generally not in direct response to slavery (C). Though the trade associated with slavery increased the wealth and power of the bourgeoisie, the nobility continued to dominate positions in government and political power (D).

14. **Answer: C. HTS: CCOT; Themes: INT, CID, & ECD; KCs 2.2 & 2.3.** The Protestant Reformation related minimally if not at all to the slave trade, causing A to drop out. Though the Scientific Revolution eventually led to the Enlightenment, the new intellectual framework itself did not spawn anti-slavery movements. Instead of stimulating opposition to slavery, the Industrial Revolution in fact benefited indirectly from slavery—by producing capital for investment in manufacturing—eliminating D. This leaves C, and indeed, Enlightenment philosophes in their advancement of natural rights came to oppose a practice in such blatant violation of personal liberty (C).

15. **Answer: C. HTS: CAUS & DAP; Themes: CID & SOP; KCs 2.1, 2.3, 3.3, & 3.4.** Mill presents a classic case for personal autonomy from a Liberal perspective—the right for each individual to be sovereign over his or her own affairs. His ideas were inspired by Enlightenment beliefs in natural rights and individualism (as in the writings of Locke, Voltaire, and Montesquieu), as well as many actions of the French revolutionaries, such as the Declaration of Rights of Man (A and B). In addition, Mill shows concern about the "tyranny of the majority," a concern that arose with the development of mass politics (D). However, the Concert of Europe acted primarily as a diplomatic mechanism, and though it might have limited political change, Mill does not condemn its conservatism *per se* (C).

16. **Answer: B. HTS: CTX & SAS; Themes: CID & SOP; KC 3.3.** As noted above, Mill's ideas represent one of the classic expositions of nineteenth-century Liberalism, with an emphasis on individual freedom (B). His argument is based on reason rather than emotion, eliminating A. Mill does not necessarily endorse the elimination of monarchy, one of the central tenets of republicanism (C). Though Mill's ideas may be commensurable with nationalism, he expresses skepticism regarding ideologies that can overwhelm the individual—a danger with nationalism (D).

17. **Answer: A. HTS: CCOT & MAC; Themes: SOP & ECD; KC 3.3.** Each of these developments occurred during the nineteenth century, but it was the recognition by Liberals of the need to address the intractable problems of industrialization, such as poverty and social breakdown, with the powers of the state that transformed its laissez-faire attitude (as expressed by Mill) into a more interventionist approach (A). Choices B, C, and D only indirectly influenced the development of Liberalism, at least in comparison to the pressing problems of industrial development.

18. **Answer: B. HTS: COMP & CES; Themes: CID & SOP; KCs 2.1 & 3.3.** Though Locke lived prior to the age of ideologies, his ideas of contract theory and empiricism are considered the foundations for Liberalism (B). Descartes did not speak directly to political issues (like Mill), dropping out A. Rousseau promoted social contract theories; however, his unique ideas of the General Will would run counter to Mill's fears about the oppressive nature of majority opinion (C). Finally, Mill would likely cite a figure like Robespierre as exactly the type of leader who must be avoided in a state organized around individual rights, since the latter used the power of the state during the French Revolution to curtail liberty (D).

19. **Answer: C. HTS: CTX & CAUS; Themes: SOP, INT, & ECD; KCs 4.1 & 4.2.** All of the choices express causes and the nature of the Cold War. However, the two sources focus on the strong distrust between the superpowers fed by their fundamentally different visions of the world, making C the key. There are no specific references to nuclear weaponry (A). Certainly the US and USSR competed for strategic areas, especially Europe, but these concerns are secondary to the differing ideologies highlighted by the two sources (B). Though the United Nations was created to resolve security issues, the two superpowers never engaged in direct warfare and the "failure" of the UN was secondary to the differences between the rival Cold War blocs (D).

20. **Answer: D. HTS: CAUS; Themes: INT, ECD, SOP, & SCD; KCs 4.1, 4.2, & 4.4.** American aid was channeled through institutions that promoted European unity, which stimulated efforts toward greater coordination of European economies (A). American aid and security guarantees to Europe certainly fostered Western European dependence on the US (B). Economic recovery promoted a higher birth rate (Baby Boom), as families had the means to support more children (C). This leaves D, and although

European states promoted welfare programs, these policies did not directly relate to American aid, particularly since the US did not promote nor adopt them (D).

21. **Answer: A. HTS: CAUS, COMP, & CCOT; Themes: INT, SOP, & ECD; KCs 4.1 & 4.2.** In response to US aid to Western Europe, the Soviet Union worked to organize economic activity in the Eastern bloc, primarily through imposing a central, collective economy on its satellites (A). The reforms mentioned in B came much later with Mikhail Gorbachev (1980s). Both de-Stalinization and the rhetoric of "peaceful coexistence" were attempted under Khrushchev, but that Soviet response was only after those mentioned in A. The Brezhnev Doctrine (D) was articulated in 1968 as justification for crushing the Prague Spring reform movement, once again removed in time from the sources.

22. **Answer: C. HTS: SAS & CES; Theme: SOP; KC 4.1.** This question considers the question of reliability in use of sources. Though all the choices address a potential drawback of the source, C represents the most problematic situation. It is unlikely that an official government publication would promote any position other than the party line. All speeches attempt to persuade (A), but they can still provide useful insights into the attitudes of decision-makers. The lack of specific data in the speech (B) does not present a specific limitation on that type of source, though it would if the source were a statistical report. As for D, most sources require inference and context for interpretation, so this fact would not constitute a problem for the source *per se*.

23. **Answer: C. HTS: CTX & CAUS; Themes: SOP & NEI; KC 1.5.** Unlike the other new monarchies, the Holy Roman Empire suffered from an unusually high degree of localism, being divided into over 300 different principalities, cities, and states. Even with a prestigious title, the emperor struggled to counter these centrifugal forces, as Rosheim relates by the laws regarding Jews (C). Charles did draw from the wealth of Spain, but the passage does not address that particular issue (A). Further, there is no mention or suggestion of Christian humanism (B), nor does the text deal with class conflict (D). Rather, the text shows religious persecution and localism.

24. **Answer: D. HTS: CAUS & CES; Themes: SOP, CID, & SCD; KCs 1.2 & 1.5.** Religious reformers confiscated church lands in Germany; however, Jews did not generally benefit from this practice, eliminating A. Though Luther hoped Jews would convert to Christianity with his reform, he grew disenchanted with Jews when these conversions did not materialize, dropping out B. The status of Jews in most states proved precarious; however, mass emigration occurred primarily in areas like the Iberian Peninsula where the state sponsored campaigns to achieve religious uniformity (C). This leaves us with D, and indeed, the higher degree of concern over religious doctrine during the Reformation tended to increase persecution until the end of the religious wars after 1648.

25. **Answer: B. HTS: CCOT & MAC; Themes: CID, NEI, & SCD; KCs 1.3 & 2.3.** Many of the first treatises arguing for toleration of Jews and granting citizenship emerged during the Enlightenment, with its emphasis on natural rights and secularism (B). The Commercial Revolution increased cultural contact but did not address the status of Jews directly (A). By the Industrial Revolution, Jews in many states had been granted (at least in theory) full civic rights (C). If anything, the two world wars rendered the status of Jews even more precarious, as the unstable conditions fueled anti-Semitism (D).

26. **Answer: A. HTS: CAUS & CCOT; Themes: TSI, NEI & SCD; KCs 3.3 & 3.6.** Anti-Semitism shifted in nature with the popularization of Darwin's theories, as it took on a racial and political focus (A). The undermining of organized religion, particularly Catholicism, would have tended to improve the status of Jews by making religious homogeneity more suspect, eliminating B. Rousseau's glorification of pre-civilization man caused a general questioning of all religions, not supporting or condemning Judaism specifically (C). Marx himself came from a Jewish background (though became an atheist) and many Jews took up socialism/Marxism, but the theory shifted the focus from religion and race toward class as a category of analysis (D).

27. **Answer: B. HTS: COMP & MAC; Theme: SCD; KCs 1.5 & 2.2.** This question relates to the tendency for majority groups to alienate minorities through language, symbols, and depictions, known as "othering." Such groups tended to live in precarious situations and fell prey periodically to persecutions, sometimes popular, sometimes state organized (as with Jews in Russia). Choices A, C, and D capture such marginalized and often powerless groups. This leaves B as the key—though some nobles did experience exile for opposing absolutism, they were not targeted *as a group* and did not suffer from a general lack of social and political power.

28. **Answer: C. HTS: CES & CTX; Theme: SOP; KC 2.1.** The passage conveys two key notions regarding Napoleon: 1) that he accepted the reformulation of the French state by the revolutionaries and 2) that he brought order to the faltering ideals by exercising strong power from above. These principles are most in keeping with enlightened absolutism (C), the embrace of rational reform from the top-down in order to strengthen the state. New monarchs of the sixteenth century preceded such enlightened reforms, canceling out A. Napoleon manipulated religion to gain support but did not claim to derive his power from God (B). Though Napoleon employed popular appeals, he did not have access to the communication and transportation technologies of the twentieth century to exercise total rule, causing D to fall out for chronological reasons.

29. **Answer: D. HTS: CAUS, DAP, & CCOT; Themes: SOP & NEI; KC 2.1.** The historian portrays France amidst chaos prior to Napoleon, thus explaining the appeal of his movement toward central power and order. The situation most responsible for this is expressed by D, which seemed to

require the extreme measures of the Reign of Terror. The other choices (A, B, C) represent more lasting achievements or events of the early (Liberal) phase of the revolution.

30. **Answer: A. HTS: CAUS & CCOT; Themes: SOP & NEI; KC 2.1.** As the reading suggests, Napoleon's success lay in his ability to portray himself as a child of the revolution and to use popular impulses to justify his accumulation of power (A). Though the Napoleonic Code granted some rights to women, they were rendered second-class citizens and stripped of some rights (such as divorce under most circumstances), excluding B. Napoleon did provoke nationalist responses in conquered nations, but this outcome was not intended as a policy (C). Once again, the passage reminds us that Napoleon eschewed popular violence in favor of a top-down regime, leaving off D.

31. **Answer: B. HTS: CCOT, MAC, & COMP; Themes: SOP & NEI; KCs 2.1 & 3.4.** Napoleon initiated a new type of rule that led to the *Realpolitik* practitioners of the later nineteenth century. This characterization includes Cavour (A), Napoleon III (C), and Bismarck (D), all of whom used nationalism and popular appeals to build support for what were essentially authoritarian regimes. However, Metternich, as an old-style conservative who helped overthrow Napoleon, rejected the popular passions of the revolutionary era in favor of unabashed elite rule, hearkening back to the Old Regime (B).

32. **Answer: C. HTS: CTX & DAP; Themes: ECD & SCD; KCs 2.2 & 2.4.** The Fragonard painting portrays the growing "cult of sentiment" surrounding family life and greater resources dedicated to child-rearing with the consumer revolution, as seen by the wealth of the family (D). We see depicted two parents, their two young children, a newborn infant, and likely a wet nurse, indicating a nuclear family, the predominant social unit of this era (A). The title and scene suggest that this space is dedicated to one or more of the children, with parents sleeping separately, a relatively new development in the eighteenth century (B). This leaves the EXCEPT as C, and though illegitimacy increased during this period, it is not portrayed in the painting.

33. **Answer: B. HTS: CAUS; Themes: CID & SCD; KCs 2.3 & 2.4.** This is a straightforward content question, asking for the intellectual causes of new attitudes toward children. Locke wrote a famous treatise, *Some Thoughts Concerning Education* (1693), arguing for a new approach toward children emphasizing psychological over physical persuasion. In *Émile, or Treatise on Education* (1762), Rousseau critiqued the overemphasis on rote learning and urged society to adopt an experiential method of education (B). Though the other sets of thinkers (A, C, and D) listed here also partook of the Enlightenment focus on empiricism and reason, none were noted for writing tracts about childhood or education.

34. **Answer: D. HTS: CCOT & MAC; Themes: ECD, SCD, & SOP; KC 3.3.** The painting depicts a protective and humanitarian attitude toward children. Political ideologies did not generally address the issue of children and their welfare directly, excluding A. Mechanization of production, in fact, often benefited from child labor, the opposite of the stem in this question (B). C represents the best distractor, but movements to aid the poor focused more on issues of class inequality rather than the notion of childhood as a particular phase of human development. This leaves us with D, and indeed, governments eventually passed legislation aimed at protecting children from the rigors of factory labor and to require basic education, at least by the end of the nineteenth century.

35. **Answer: A. HTS: SAS & CES; Theme: CID; KC 2.3.** As noted in Question 32, the new attitude toward children arose in part from the application of scientific principles to issues of social and political reform, known as the Enlightenment (A). Printed materials increased significantly during the eighteenth century, but this fact is not central to the image (B). In addition, the period did see the growth of public venues; however, the painting shows *private* space, eliminating C. No reference or implication regarding religion is portrayed, though skepticism does constitute a feature of Enlightenment thought (D).

36. **Answer: A. HTS: CAUS & CTX; Themes: TSI & SOP; KC 4.1.** All of the choices relate to features of the First World War. Military casualties predominate in most states, excluding B, which refers principally to civilian casualties. The same is true for C. Though military stalemate led to the spread of the war globally (D), this outcome was itself the result of the discrepancy between traditional military strategies (mimicking Napoleon) and new technologies that favored the defensive. Thus, the key is A.

37. **Answer: C. HTS: CAUS & MAC; Themes: SOP, SCD, & CID; KCs 4.3 & 4.4.** With men at the front and with loss of life, women entered the industrial work force to maintain munitions production (A). Due to its tragic nature, World War I spawned a cynical and disillusioned "lost generation" (B). Rather than the French Revolution, it was in fact World War I that severed the hold of traditional elites (monarchies and nobility) on political power (D). This leaves C as the false choice: the Versailles settlement did establish peace but it was directed by the great powers and did not result in a stable Europe, hence the Depression and rise of totalitarian regimes (C).

38. **Answer: B. HTS: CTX & DAP; Themes: SOP, TSI, & ECD; KC 4.2.** The poster depicts and the caption refers to Stalin's Five-Year Plans to collectivize agriculture and accelerate industrial production (B). By the time of this project, Stalin had already purged any threats to his power (A). It is true the Soviet Union controlled the Communist International (Comintern), ostensibly to promote world revolution; however, Stalin preferred to focus on building "socialism in one country" before turning to the spread of Bolshevism (C). Finally, the goals depicted reversed Lenin's New Economic Policy (NEP), which had temporarily compromised with capitalism (D).

39. **Answer: A. HTS: CAUS; Themes: SOP, NEI, & SCD; KC 4.2.** The movement toward collective agriculture led Stalin to steamroll those wealthy peasants (kulaks) who stood in his way, leading to their slaughter (A). The other choices either did not occur or were unrelated to Stalin's forced industrialization. As the lone communist nation, the Soviet Union was isolated diplomatically (B), and even if it was later admitted to the League of Nations, this occurred despite, not because of, Stalin's centralization of power (C). Theoretically, women achieved equality of status with men in the USSR; in reality, women did double duty as homemakers and factory workers, while reproductive rights were curtailed in favor of increasing population (D).

40. **Answer: D. HTS: CCOT & MAC; Themes: SOP & ECD; KC 4.2.** Lenin died prior to the policies depicted, eliminating A. Khrushchev supported de-Stalinization and a movement toward consumer goods; nonetheless, his policies did not dismantle the collective planning of the Soviet system, nor did they meet their goals (B). Brezhnev, who followed the controversial Khrushchev, preached "no experiments" and reinforced the command economy and continued to focus on military and industrial production (C). It was Gorbachev who fundamentally attempted to reconstruct (*perestroika*) the Soviet economy, an undertaking so ambitious that it led to the collapse of the entire Soviet system.

41. **Answer: B. HTS: CAUS & CCOT; Themes: INT & SOP; KCs 2.1, 2.2, & 3.5.** The author addresses the century previous to 1856, which refers to the beginning of the Seven Years War, a major continental and colonial struggle between Britain and France (B). One of the battlegrounds in this conflict was India, with the British emerging victorious and extending their control through the process presented by Innes. The other nations (A, C, and D) had been rivals at one point or another in British history (including Russia in Central Asia during the nineteenth century), but Britain's most consistent rival was France.

42. **Answer: A. HTS: SAS & CTX; Themes: INT, ECD, & SOP; KC 3.5.** Choices B, C, and D all enabled European colonial powers to establish dominance in Africa and Asia, so they could not be presented to colonized peoples as "benefits." However, one claim made by European colonizers was that they modernized the infrastructure of colonized nations by building roads, railroads, and introducing modern sanitation and hygiene (A).

43. **Answer: D. HTS: CCOT & MAC; Theme: INT; KCs 3.5 & 4.1.** Each of the conflicts affected the relationship between European powers and their colonies. The Boer War shook Britain out its half-century of isolation and caused it to seek new allies (A), but it did not radically alter the state of colonial empires. Though the Russo-Japanese War proved that an Asian power could defeat a European power, its effects were not felt across the colonies until decades later, not to mention that Japan used its new modern power to engage in imperialism itself (B). The League of Nations held the promise of self-determination, but it also confirmed mandates strengthening British and French control

over territories in the Middle East, Africa, and the Pacific (C). It was, in fact, the vast devastation and moral failings of the Second World War that severed Europe's hold over its colonies and a reappraisal of their value to European security (D).

44. **Answer: B. HTS: CCOT & CAUS; Themes: INT & SCD; KCs 3.5 & 4.1.** With an EXCEPT question, we are looking for the outlier, and it is B. Former colonial nations did not refuse to participate in the United Nations; in fact, it was one of the few forums where former colonies and developing nations had a voice that could influence the great powers, who dominated the Security Council (B). The other choices represent actions taken by colonized peoples: modernizing economies, such as the Indian textile industry or Egypt building the Aswan Dam (A); establishing national resistance movements, like the Viet Minh in Indochina (B); and emigrating to Europe, seeking jobs along with the European economic miracle (D).

45. **Answer: C. HTS: CES, CTX, & CAUS; Themes: SOP & NEI; KCs 3.3 & 3.4.** Though the revolutions of 1848 both dealt with Italian and German unification, they were more an attempt to overthrow the established order in an effort to establish territorial states. Even though they failed in this goal, this failure set the stage for unification, eliminating A. Industry played less of a role than diplomacy, but if anything, the growth of industry would have facilitated unification by creating a more unified market (B). The dates of the quotes are too early for the pursuit of colonies (D). This gives us the Congress of Vienna, and if you recall, it was this diplomatic settlement (led by Metternich) that stifled the idea of nationalism and retained the division and/or foreign occupation of Italy and Germany (C).

46. **Answer: A. HTS: SAS, CES, & CAUS; Themes: SOP, NEI, & OS; KCs 3.3 & 3.4.** With the failure of Romantic-inspired revolution in 1848, conservatives took up the cause of nationalism, but from the top down. We can see this in the quote by Bismarck (A). The year 1848 represents the end of the Romantic spirit (except for music), canceling out B. Socialism gained influence during the nineteenth century, but that fact does not bear directly upon the changes in nationalism (C). The Crimean War certainly set the stage for unification, but it bears less directly on the *tone* of the sources (D).

47. **Answer: B. HTS: CAUS; Themes: SOP & NEI; KC 3.4.** Diplomacy and warfare produced the modern Italian and German states. This possibility opened with the fall of Metternich's Concert of Europe, aimed at repressing revolutionary nationalism and maintaining the status quo. When the Concert collapsed after 1848, the path opened toward unification (B). Industrialization (A) aided the achievement, but it was secondary to diplomacy. The creation of the Dual Monarchy occurred later (1867) and relates to Austria rather than Italy or Germany (C). Nationalist tensions in the Balkans played a more central role after Germany's rise as a great power and on the eve of World War I (D).

48. Answer: A. HTS: CTX, SAS, & DAP; Themes: CID & TSI; KCs 3.6 & 4.3. All of the choices reflect cultural trends of the era, but upon considering the building, you will likely note its unornamented appearance and use of modern materials, such as glass and steel. This relates most closely to D. The other developments (A, B, and C) do not pertain to this particular building, or do so only incidentally.

49. Answer: A. HTS: CAUS; Themes: TSI & ECD; KC 3.1. As noted above, new building materials allowed for new approaches to architecture, such as skyscrapers (A). Expansion into African and Asian markets coincided with modern architecture, but the latter was not dependent on the former (B). European states did move toward protectionism after 1875; however, this trend did not affect architecture *per se* (C). Same for D—working conditions improved but this was not causally related to new building styles.

50. Answer: C. HTS: COMP, MAC, & CCOT; Themes: CID, SOP & ECD; KCs 1.1, 2.3, & 3.1. Modern buildings like the Bauhaus Building generally lacked ornamentation in favor of an appearance of economic efficiency (C). Choices A, B, and D do not express significant differences between classical and modern architectural styles.

51. Answer: B. HTS: CCOT; Theme: SP; KC 4.3. Prior to the onset of World War I, European culture embraced technological utopianism and the notion of progress. These attitudes were largely undermined by the tragic consequences of the Great War (B). The scramble for colonies in Africa did not appreciably alter the trend of European culture in these directions (A). Though the Great Depression and World War II represented fundamental challenges to Europe (C and D), the tone of disillusionment and wariness of technology had already been established by World War I.

52. Answer: B. HTS: CTX, SAS, & CAUS; Themes: TSI, CID, & SOP; KC 3.6. Bagehot glorifies the importance of competition and struggle in interstate relations, an idea central (at least in biology) to Darwin's *Origin of the Species* (B). Though workers struggled for equality and in Marxism embraced violent revolution, socialism condemned war among states as serving the interests of capital, excluding A. It would be more accurate to argue that attitudes like Bagehot's *caused* the pursuit of colonies rather than vice-versa (C). Though his ideas reflected the growth of mass politics, this development ran parallel to rather than caused the embrace of struggle (D).

53. Answer: C. HTS: CCOT & CES; Themes: CID & SOP; KCs 3.6 & 4.3. Feminists could also be pacifists, but many suffragettes (e.g., Pankhursts) supported the very ideas of struggle and violence Bagehot addresses, excluding A. Both Freud and Darwin tended to undermine the Enlightenment notions of rationality and progress; thus Freud may have endorsed the competitive drive outlined by Darwin as the analog to the *id*, or drive for power (B).

It was not the abandonment of laissez-faire that countered Bagehot's Social Darwinist view; rather, D emerged as a response to such criticisms. We are left with C, and indeed, the immense and pointless destruction of the two world wars led to a more critical outlook toward war and even moved European nations to move toward unity.

54. Answer: B. HTS: SAS, DAP, & CTX; Themes: INT, SCD, & ECD; KC 4.4. One is struck by the multi-ethnic composition of this national soccer team, reflecting the immigration trend following World War II, stimulated by European prosperity (C). New technologies contributed to globalization, but many nations of immigrant origin lacked them, excluding A. The immigrant trend preceded the collapse of communism in 1989 (C). D represents an appealing choice, but its causal relationship (noted above) was more indirect than direct.

55. Answer: A. HTS: CAUS; Themes: INT & SOP; KC 4.1. Many former colonies won independence following the Second World War, though the real wave occurred after about 1960, delayed by concern that former colonies might become communist outposts (A). Separatist violence provoked backlashes, but it often, as in Algeria, was the means to gain independence (B). Choice C expresses an accurate trend but one that was generally unrelated to colonial autonomy. The same is true for D.

SAQ Sample Responses with Commentary

1. **a)** The painting shows many of the features of the Scientific Revolution. On the floor of the Academy, we see a model of the universe according to the new heliocentric theory by Copernicus, a major change in the way people looked at the world. In addition, the scene is filled with many measuring devices, probably to chart the planets and gain knowledge from new astronomical discoveries.

b) Many political figures endorsed scientific discovery as it promoted the idea that their state was the best. In this painting, Louis visits the science academy he founded to learn about its research. Political rulers like him encouraged these discoveries first hand as it also created an aura for the public that they were well rounded in all subjects. Also, since Louis was the Sun King, he wanted to extend his power over Europe through trade and military technology.

c) Since the artist is French, it is very likely that he was hired by Louis XIV to create this image, since most of the artistic work in Louis's absolutist regime focused on Versailles and his government. So of course, he would portray the greatness of France and his royal patron.

This concise response earns all 3 points. First, in Part A the response notes the astronomical model as representing the heliocentric theory of Copernicus. Further, it notes specific objects in the image to highlight the importance of empirical observation and measurement. Next in Part B, the response explains the state's interest in science, such as prestige and military power. Finally, in Part C, it indicates correctly that most artistic patronage emanated from Louis XIV and Versailles, influencing the message of the work. **Score: 3 points**

2. **a)** The Soviet Union was on the brink of collapse in 1989. One example is the Cold War. With all of the money spent on missiles and arms, the Soviet Union could not keep up with the United States and Reagan's infamous "Star Wars" defense shield.

   b) Gorbachev wanted to reform the Soviet Union through structural change. This was known as perestroika. He took actions like increasing consumer products, decentralizing control, and other examples of openness, or glasnost, to fix problems. He did not try to resist the change that was inevitable, and this shows how he was acted upon for the better of the people.

   c) Since the historian is American, it is likely that he supported the US position during the Cold War and is writing from the perspective after the fall of communism. This is clear in the subtle way that he celebrates the end of the America's enemy during that period—the Soviet Union.

Though the response provides an accurate cause of the collapse of the Soviet Union, it is not drawn from the quote, which in the first paragraph, focuses on popular discontent, not issues of national security. No point earned. In Part B, the response briefly but accurately outlines Gorbachev's *perestroika* program and the goals behind it, earning a point. For Part C, the response correctly uses the identity of the historian as American to connect back to the Cold War rivalry and suggest the motivations of his historical analysis. **Score: 2 points**

3. **a)** The Catholic Church first attempted reform with the Council of Trent. This was a meeting of the highest officials in order to address the problems the church was facing, like corruption and indulgences. This meeting came about soon after Luther posted his Ninety-Five Theses and was the first step to solve the problems of division he created.

   b) The Counter Reformation took a long time to respond to the Protestants. But when it did, the Church began to patronize Renaissance works, like Michelangelo's "David," to build enthusiasm once again for the Catholic religion.

c) One result of the Catholic responses was the permanent division of Europe between Catholics and Protestants, with different nations accepting a variety of Christian sects. This made conflict almost inevitable, and so the religious wars dominated politics, ending finally with the 30 Years War and Peace of Westphalia that created more religious tolerance.

For Part A, the response provides an appropriate piece of evidence (Council of Trent), and explains it accurately, earning the point. However, the explanation in Part B incorrectly focuses on Renaissance art, which in general predates the Protestant Reformation; Baroque art would have been a more appropriate choice. Finally, the response recovers to note correctly that the Catholic response led to permanent religious division and eventually warfare, ending with the Thirty Years' War and Peace of Westphalia. **Score: 2 points**

4. **a)** The Revolutions of 1848 were the most significant shift because they introduced the political format of mass politics. Because leaders feared another violent attempt at revolution, they began to create a democratic image to appeal to the public, partly by focusing on the technological advancements of their state.

   b) The Congress of Vienna didn't cause a shift because it failed to stop revolutions as it had aimed to do. If it had succeeded, the Revolutions of 1848 never would have happened. Therefore, the Revolutions of 1848 were more significant as they actually accomplished a true change.

   c) Even with these political changes, one consistent economic pattern during the nineteenth century was the spread of industrialization. It began in Britain, and then other nations saw the benefits of factory production and consumer goods, so they promoted it in their states as well.

Again, this response models a concise approach to the SAQs, providing an accurate explanation for the revolutions of 1848 as a significant shift—introduction of mass politics and savvier political leaders. Next, the response not only argues against the Congress of Vienna but also connects it to the shift (1848) discussed in Part A. Finally, though somewhat general, the explanation in Part C rightly notes the development and spread of industry as one of the consistent features of the nineteenth century, though one might quibble if this represents a continuity or a change. **Score: 3 points**

DBQ Sample Response with Commentary

World War I is a hotly debated topic among historians, probably because it had such important consequences in the twentieth century, like the Great Depression and the rise of the Nazis. There was much nationalism in the period leading up to WWI, especially in the Balkans, where nations like Serbia wanted their independence. Also, nations were seeking colonies in Africa and Asia, creating tensions and potential conflicts all across the world. Meanwhile, industry continued to expand and led to working-class tensions. All of these factors helped create one of the biggest conflicts in history.

World War seems almost unavoidable when we look back on it today. In Document 1, Prime Minister Disraeli recognizes right away that the unification of Germany means trouble for Europe and especially Britain. Because of its size, economic potential, and military strength, Germany, just by existing, disrupted the balance of power. As his nation's leader, Disraeli's goal is to warn the House of Commons that it must be aware of this new threat. However, it was not necessarily inevitable that Germany would cause WWI. After all, Bismarck said Germany was a "satisfied giant" and wanted no more territory. In fact, Bismarck created many alliances, like the Triple Alliance, to help maintain peace in Europe. However, Kaiser Wilhelm II disrupted these policies when he dismissed Bismarck, as portrayed in Document 3. Since this is a British periodical, it may not understand all of the internal conflicts in another country. Whatever its reliability, Bismarck's dismissal put power in the hands of someone who clearly was not fit to rule. This is supported by Document 5, in which the Kaiser takes his usual belligerent stance about a "place in sun," which involved building up the navy and aggressively seeking colonies in Africa and the Pacific. These policies antagonized Britain, who responded by building up their own battleships. The Kaiser probably wants to impress the Regatta Association by showing how committed he is to naval power.

Could WWI have been avoided? As noted above, leaders like Wilhelm II made many mistakes, but he wasn't the only one. France and Russia joined in an alliance once the Kaiser refused to renegotiate his treaty with Russia. Now Germany faced a two-front war, as Document 4 reveals. However, France and Russia were also to blame for their decisions. It's clear that this treaty was secret (so not really for a public audience), and it almost seems like the two powers are eager to go to war, maybe so that France could regain Alsace-Lorraine (which it lost to Germany in 1871) or for Russia to gain territory in the Balkans. Russia should have known that the Balkans was a troubled area, what with Serbia and other small nations seeking independence. This perspective is confirmed by Document 6, a secretive Serbian organization dedicated to overthrowing the Austrian monarchy. In fact, this was the group that assassinated Franz Ferdinand, and its violent approach is clear from its uncompromising and sacrificial language of nationalism. Of course, this document is biased, since it sees the situation from the perspective of an upstart nation that wants to show itself as a power.

The differing perspectives of this question are shown best by the last two documents. Friedrich Engels makes an amazing (and pretty accurate prediction) about how the arms race will eventually lead to the worst war in European history. Engels—the collaborator of Marx—talks about the level of human and material devastation, and he even sees that the total war will topple the old systems of government. However, as a socialist who wants revolution, we would normally take his view with a grain of salt. Maybe he's being "optimistic" about the war to bring the working-class to power; however, he was right. This doesn't necessarily mean WWI was inevitable, and the last piece of evidence that shows this is Document 7, the famous "Willy-Nicky" telegrams. It's clear that each leader wants to avoid war but is reluctant to overrule his generals. They make it seem like they had no choice. But they did have a choice. They might have told military leaders that it is political leaders who make the decisions. Sadly, they rolled the dice, and they created a tragedy—for themselves and all of Europe.

World War I was a tragic situation, probably because it could have been avoided. The effects of the war are seen best in the art that it helped to create. Lost Generation writers bemoaned the human race and talked about alienation and disillusionment in their new works that showed stream-of-consciousness style and amoral characters. Also, Dada became an important art movement, as it poked fun at the entire idea of beauty. For example, Otto Dix, an actual soldier who brought his sketchpad to the front, created horrifying images of smashed faces, prostitutes, begging veterans, and political corruption. All because of World War I.

With one exception, this is an exemplary essay. The response provides adequate background on pre-1914 developments, such as nationalism, imperialism, and industrialization. These references earn it the Contextualization point. Though the response seems to go back and forth with the prompt's two options, it clearly earns the Complexity point through effective use of the documents to show the complexity of causation, often using transitional language to show corroboration (Documents 3 and 5; Documents 4 and 6), modification (Documents 2 and 7), and qualification (Documents 1 and 3). Since the response employs all seven documents accurately toward an argument, it earns both Document Use points. Additionally, the essay offers several successful Source Analysis efforts—Document 1 (purpose), Document 3 (point of view/reliability), Document 5 (pur-pose and intended audience), Document 4 (intended audience), Document 6 (point of view), and Document 2 (point of view/reliability). The Evidence Beyond Documents point is easily earned with multiple uses of content to support an argument, such as the Triple Alliance, Serbia's situation, and Alsace-Lorraine. With a creative twist, the response effectively nails down the Complexity point by extending the "tragedy" of World War I to culture, with a brief yet effective discussion of interwar art and literature. However, the essay never clearly articulated a thesis directly responsive to the question and thus missed the Thesis point. **Score: 6** (+1 for Contextualization, +2 for Use of Documents, +1 for Evidence Beyond Documents, +1 for Source Analysis, +1 for Complexity).

LEQ Sample Responses with Commentary

LEQ 2

The invention of the printing press in 1450 greatly assisted in spreading the Renaissance as well as securing the success of the Protestant Reformation. Martin Luther's nailing of the 95 theses to the Catholic Church's door set the reformation into motion. His continued pressure and criticisms of the corruption in the Catholic church in his texts such as *Freedom of a Christian*, spread like wildfire across Europe. Other reformers joined Luther in a theological movement that resulted in a Catholic revival as well as new Christian doctrines. The fall of Constantinople led many to flee to Italy, and the city of Florence became one that flourished with new thinkers, artists, and architects that all embodied humanist values. Humanists like Leonardo Bruni translated ancient Greek texts to Latin, and the Medici family patronized intellectuals and art. The Reformation was able to create new religious ideas while the Renaissance formed new thinking and values. The Protestant Reformation was a religious movement while the Renaissance was a cultural one but both set the stage for secularism in government.

The Protestant Reformation began with Martin Luther's criticism of indulgences and the Catholic Church. His principles of *sola scriptura*, *sola fide*, and *sola gratia* (by scripture alone, by faith alone, and by grace alone) became the center of the reformation movement. These ideas that the only authority in church is the Bible and that salvation is a gift of god's grace were unheard of. In Luther's *On the Babylonian Captivity of the Church*, he criticized Catholic sacraments with exceptions of baptism and the Lord's supper because those were present in the Bible. Luther sparked a religious movement of a "priesthood of all believers" where reading the Bible was one's way to connect with God, not dependent on the church. His writings inspired other reformers like John Calvin and Huldrych Zwingli. Calvin accepted Luther's theology but placed an emphasis on predestination in which God foreknows and has judged the salvation of people before birth. Zwingli was a radical reformer, who believed the Lord's supper sacrament was symbolic and not the actual body and blood of Jesus. Anaptists were another group that formed amid the religious reform and believed Chrisitianity was an adult choice, so adults had to be baptized. The Protestant Reformation was a time of crisis in faith with new Protestant denominations, and the Catholic Church, which had stood as the sole religious authority in Europe for centuries, was now being fractured. The new interpretations of Christianity and the newly formed lack of religious uniformity classifies the Protestant reformation as a revolutionary theological movement with minimal relative effect regarding the public's social and political views.

On the other hand, the Renaissance was a cultural movement that shifted people's values rather than religious interpretations. The Renaissance invoked a more systematic view of the natural world than a religious, qualitative one. The revival of ancient Greek and Roman classics spread humanist values among the public. Pre-christian literature told a story with humans at the center which led to the idea for humans to take on increased significance with more focus on rewards of wealth and status. Individualism developed with the belief that learning and human affairs should benefit the individual and that the individual's goal is to provide society with intellectual tools that can improve the human condition. Classical influence is present in the columns, arches, pillars, and domes of Renaissance architecture like the Santa Maria del Fiore Cathedral. Humanists were able to exhibit this change in thinking by founding schools for boys and girls with a curriculum of the classics, liberal arts, geometry, astronomy, and poetry. Petrarch is considered the father of humanism and aided in pushing Italy into a new age of learning and individualism through his poetry and writing about humans. Artwork additionally reflected Renaissance values with geometric perspective and the new addition of contemporary or individualist scenes to the traditional biblical paintings. The Renaissance changed the culture of Europeans to one more focused on the individual and learning.

Both the Reformation and the Renaissance were able to set the stage for secularism in government. The Protestant Reformation ended religious uniformity in Europe, and thus caused religious tension, which developed into the religious wars. The Peace of Westphalia ended the long-standing religious conflict which had progressed from religious motives to one of political ambition. The treaty marked the end of future religiously motivated warfare in Europe and church participation in government. Anabaptists, formed as a result of the reformation, even advocated for a separation of church from state. The Renaissance brought a new emphasis on the "now" rather than the afterworld. Classical text's attitude of questioning and glorification of the natural world led to the Scientific Revolution which relied on empirical evidence, mathematical formulas, and natural laws to explain the world rather than religion. This caused many to place a greater importance on science rather than religion which translated to more political power in government. Finally, both movements relied on the printing press to spread their values and invoked discussion.

The response provides a strong introduction, with reference to substantive and relevant background on the Reformation, printing press, fall of Constantinople, and humanism to earn the Contextualization point easily. Though the thesis seems obvious—a religious movement vs. a cultural one—it is germane to the prompt and takes a position. With the body paragraphs, the essay demonstrates a strong, factual grasp of both movements. Especially impressive are references to *theological* issues, such as *sola fide* and the "priesthood of all believers," whereas many responses on this topic will focus on Catholic Church abuses solely. Though the response provides even more specific references for the Reformation paragraph, the body paragraph on the Renaissance actually deploys examples more effectively toward establishing its argument regarding differences. In any case, the response clearly earns both points for Use of Evidence and the point for the Targeted RP. In the conclusion, the response adopts the strategy of examining the "opposing skill" (of similarity) with a high-level analysis of secularism to establish Complexity. **Score: 6** (+1 for Thesis, +1 for Contextualization, +2 for Use of Evidence, +1 for the Targeted RP (COMP), +1 for Complexity)

LEQ 3

In both these periods, European nations tried to dominate other areas of the world. During the 1650–1815 period, Europe tried to set up colonies in the Americas and in Asia, seeking silks, silver, and other goods. The situation was defined by Europe's superior technology, like cannons and joint-stock companies. In the later period, Europe still tried to gain advantage from colonies; however, because of Europe's declining power from the world wars, it was forced to give up its colonies. This decolonization was the major difference between the two periods.

Europe sought many goods and helped expand trade from 1650–1815. This was the age of the Commercial Revolution. One of the greatest powers was the Dutch Republic. With its center based in Amsterdam, the Dutch traded with all areas of the world, even the colonies of other powers. Into Europe flowed new consumer goods, such as coffee, tea, sugar, potatoes, calicoes, and cotton. Many of these products were made on the backs of enslaved persons, imported from Africa and sent to plantations in the New World. This competition for goods created rivalries among European nations, especially between France and Great Britain. These two nations warred over North America, the Caribbean, and India. After the 7 Years War, Britain became the dominant power, but not for long. The French helped the British colonies gain their independence with the American Revolution, and this would set the stage for other revolts based on Enlightenment principles and nationalism.

In 1914, Europe stood at the top of its power, with colonies all over the world. But this would all come toppling down with the two world wars and the Cold War. Even though Britain and France gained mandates after 1918, places like India and Indochina were claiming they should have the same "self-determination" granted to nations that came out of the empires that collapsed at the end of the war. The breaking point came with Europe's utter devastation after 1945. Britain decided on a "partition and run" strategy in places like India, while France tried to hold onto to colonies like Algeria. Now weaker, European nations no longer could hold on to their colonies and instead focused much more on internal problems like recovering from the war. Recovery came with Marshall Plan funds and new institutions like the ECSC and EU.

Though Europe had fewer colonies in 1991 than 1815, it had certainly learned some lessons. By realizing that it's not worth it to waste so much power controlling other nations, Europe focused more on its own problems. This new attitude helped it recover and make a better argument that it was a "civilizing" power.

Here we have a response that conveys a good range of content knowledge and generally uses it in service of analysis. Though the thesis does not consist of a single statement, the introduction clearly outlines differences (and similarities) of the two periods and notes the key difference being "decolonization," earning the Thesis point. In addition, the response provides concise and focused background regarding the Commercial Revolution, joint-stock companies, and the world wars to merit Contextualization. The response provides ample evidence and applies to the argument for both periods, capturing 2 points for Use of Evidence. Though much of the analysis is implicit, the essay adequately accounted for (rather than merely describing) the reasons for the differences in each period, thus gaining the point for the Targeted RP. However, the promise of the first sentence to explore similarities was not pursued in the body paragraphs, nor were any other strategies to extend the argument presented, which means no point for Complexity. **Score: 5** (+1 for Thesis, +1 for Contextualization, +2 for Use of Evidence, +1 for the Targeted RP (COMP))

LEQ 4

We are all born into families, and they define how we live. This was true in both of these periods, 1500–1700 and 1815–1914. In both periods, families were important and had a great influence over social life. However, in the earlier period, families had an even more important role, since people worked together to produce goods, either on farms or in shops. During the later period, families mostly got together to consume things, like meals or to go shopping and have leisure. The most important difference between the two periods, then, was the shift in role of families from production to consumption.

During the period before industry, most people lived on farms and worked together to form a living. As seen in many Bruegel paintings, both men and women brought in the hay and crops. Children were valued for their labor and were often portrayed as little adults in images. Fathers had almost absolute power over the family and looked to have children who could inherit their wealth. For fun, communities did things together, like Carnival, a time when there was much drinking and frivolity. Since there were no shopping malls, people had to find their amusements with each other. This helped build bonds within the community.

In the later period, the Industrial Revolution was changing all of economic and social life. With the advent of factories, families now separated and worked outside the home. Later on, women would control the "domestic sphere" while men labored in factories or offices. This was a big change and in some ways, loosened the importance of families. At first, children worked in factories too, but many states—like England with the Factory Act of 1833—put limits on children working and required them to go to school. When cities began to reform after about 1850, they built places for families to enjoy leisure, such as department stores, museums, and parks, like the one depicted in Seurat's "Sunday on Le Grande Jatte." This painting is unique because it uses dots of color that, when combined, form a complete image of Paris during a beautiful summer day. Most of the painting seems very still—with people fishing, boating, and having a picnic—yet there is some movement, like a girl chasing a butterfly or dogs chasing one another. Impressionist painters focused more on scenes of everyday life like this, which shows how the new leisure activities worked more on a "weekday" basis instead of by the seasons, as before. As we can see, even art reflected changes in family and social life.

The economic issues during each period basically defined what family life was like and what types of leisure pursuits were available. While the later period may have had more choices, it is possible that families were actually closer when they had to depend on each other for survival.

Though uneven, this essay earned all but one rubric point. With its introduction, the essay does identify the key difference of "production" vs. "consumption" as the key difference between the eras, which earns the Thesis point. However, the background provided in the introduction remains too general and ahistorical to earn Contextualization. Next, the second body paragraph clearly provides a higher level of detail and analysis than the first; however, the brief paragraph on the earlier period is on point and does provide a linkage to the agricultural setting of early modern Europe with some specific examples (Bruegel paintings, little adults, paternal power, Carnival). The discussion in each paragraph extends beyond description and links effectively, albeit basically, to the historical context, earning the point for the Targeted RP and 2 points for Use of Evidence. This response earned the Complexity point for the extended art analysis, introducing a new theme (CID), with the Seurat painting, and to a lesser extent, with the Bruegel painting. **Score: 5** (+1 for Thesis, +2 for Use of Evidence, +1 for Targeted RP (COMP), +1 for Complexity)

PRACTICE EXAM 2

Section I, Part A: Multiple-Choice Questions

Time—55 minutes; 55 questions

Directions: Each of the questions or incomplete statements below is followed by four suggested answers or completions. Select the one that is best in each case. Source materials have been edited for the purpose of this exercise.

Questions 1–4 are based on the passage below.

"[W]omen have been able by nature to be exceptional, but have chosen lesser goals. For some women are concerned with parting their hair correctly, adorning themselves with lovely dresses, or decorating their fingers with pearls and other gems…[O]thers wish to gaze at lavish banquet tables, to rest in sleep, or, standing at mirrors, to smear their lovely faces. But those in whom a deeper integrity yearns for virtue, restrain from the start their youthful souls, reflect on higher things, harden the body with sobriety and trials, and curb their tongues, open their ears, compose their thoughts in wakeful hours, their minds in contemplation, to letters bonded with righteousness. For knowledge is not given as a gift, but [is gained] with diligence.

[S]howing your contempt for women, you pretend that I alone am admirable because of the good fortune of my intellect….Do you suppose, O most contemptible man on earth, that I think myself sprung [like Athena*] from the head of Jove*?....For absolutely everything—that which is within us and that which is without—is made weak by association with my sex."

* Roman goddess and god

Laura Cereta, Italian humanist and feminist, *Letter to Bibulus Sempronius: A Defense of the Liberal Education of Women*, 1488

1. Cereta's criticism of the behavior of some women in the passage was most likely caused by the late fifteenth-century trend of the:
   A. persistence of folk beliefs in witchcraft and the supernatural.
   B. increase in luxury items brought about by exploration.
   C. spread of reading materials due to the printing press.
   D. denunciation of the abuses of the Catholic Church.

2. The literary references in the second paragraph best reflect the contemporary cultural trend of:
   A. the growth of civic humanism.
   B. patronage of the arts by elites.
   C. scientific observations of the human body.
   D. revival of classical texts and languages.

3. As reflected in the passage, Renaissance Italy would have been most similar to the rest of Europe in which of the following ways?
   A. The high level of urbanization and economic development
   B. The growth of a new merchant and banking elite
   C. The movement toward centralized monarchy
   D. The continuing importance of hierarchy and social status

4. Cereta's concerns about women were most strongly addressed and changed in the period:
   A. 1517–1648.
   B. 1789–1850.
   C. 1850–1920.
   D. 1920–1945.

Questions 5–6 are based on the passage below.

"There remains simple experience; which, if taken as it comes, is called accident, if sought for, experiment. The true method of experience first lights the candle, and then by means of the candle shows the way; commencing as it does with experience duly ordered and digested, not bungling or erratic, and from it deducing axioms, and from established axioms again new experiments."

Francis Bacon, English natural philosopher, *Novum Organum*, 1620

5. In the passage, Francis Bacon argues for which of the following approaches toward knowledge?

   A. Revival of classical learning

   B. Reliance on mathematics

   C. The inductive method

   D. Astrology and alchemy

6. The method above changed ideas in the sixteenth and seventeenth centuries most significantly in:

   A. astronomy.

   B. medicine.

   C. biology.

   D. chemistry.

Questions 7–8 are based on the passage below.

"5. The Committee of Public Safety is charged to take all necessary measures to set up without delay an extraordinary manufacture of arms of every sort which corresponds with the ardor and energy of the French people. It is, accordingly, authorized to form all the establishments, factories, workshops, and mills which shall be deemed necessary for the carrying on of these works, as well as to put in requisition, within the entire extent of the Republic, the artists and workingmen who can contribute to their success.

6. The representatives of the people sent out for the execution of the present law shall have the same authority in their respective districts, acting in concert with the Committee of Public Safety; they are invested with the unlimited powers assigned to the representatives of the people to the armies."

Levée en masse ("mass levy"), Decree of the French National Convention, August 23, 1793

7. A historian might use this letter as evidence for all of the following EXCEPT:

   A. the growth of citizen armies during the French Revolution.

   B. divisions across Europe caused by revolutionary ideologies.

   C. the exclusion of women from citizenship and legal and economic rights.

   D. an increase in the power of the state during the Reign of Terror.

8. The ideas expressed in the decree remained most consistent under Napoleon with his:

   A. reliance on warfare and mass armies to spread the revolution.

   B. conquest of foreign nations and creation of an empire.

   C. policies of religious toleration and compromise with the Catholic Church.

   D. restriction of women from full citizenship and economic and legal rights.

Questions 9–12 are based on the passages below.

Source 1

"The Humble ADDRESS and PETITION of Thousands, who labour in the Cloth Manufactory.

SHEWETH, That the Scribbling-Machines* have thrown thousands of your petitioners out of employ, whereby they are brought into great distress, and are not able to procure a maintenance for their families, and deprived them of the opportunity of bringing up their children to labour: We have therefore to request, that prejudice and self-interest may be laid aside, and that you may pay that attention to the following facts, which the nature of the case requires.

The number of Scribbling-Machines extending about seventeen miles south-west of LEEDS, exceed all belief, being no less than *one hundred and seventy!* and as each machine will do as much work in twelve hours, as ten men can in that time do by hand, (speaking within bounds) and they working night-and day, one machine will do as much work in one day as would otherwise employ twenty men."

* carding machine in textile manufacture

Petition of Leeds Woollen Workers to Cloth Merchants, Great Britain, 1786

Source 2

"At a time when the People, engaged in every other Manufacture in the Kingdom, are exerting themselves to bring their Work to Market at reduced Prices, which can alone be effected by the Aid of Machinery, it certainly is not necessary that the Cloth Merchants of Leeds, who depend chiefly on a Foreign Demand, where they have for Competitors the Manufacturers of other Nations, whose Taxes are few, and whose manual Labour is only Half the Price it bears here, should have Occasion to defend a Conduct, which has for its Aim the Advantage of the Kingdom in general, and of the Cloth Trade in particular; yet anxious to prevent Misrepresentations, which have usually attended the Introduction of the most useful Machines, they wish to remind the Inhabitants of this Town, of the Advantages derived to every flourishing Manufacture from the Application of Machinery; they instance that of Cotton in particular, which in its internal and foreign Demand is nearly alike to our own, and has in a few Years by the Means of Machinery advanced to its present Importance, and is still increasing."

Letter from Leeds Cloth Merchants, Great Britain, 1791

9. All of the following explain the phenomenon referenced in the sources above EXCEPT:
   A. Britain's ready supply of raw materials such as coal and iron ore.
   B. government intervention in the form of subsidies and regulations.
   C. effective entrepreneurial human capital and credit institutions like banks.
   D. representation of commercial and industrial interests in Parliament.

10. The difference in perspective between the two sources reflects which of the following trends of industrialization?
    A. The persistence of agricultural elites in many areas of Europe
    B. A heightened consumerism as a result of newly available products
    C. Growth of class distinctions between the bourgeoisie and proletariat
    D. Social problems created by rapid migration from rural to urban areas

11. Which of the following sources would a historian most likely research to reach a conclusion regarding the differing interpretations presented in the sources?

A. Blueprints of new industrial machines

B. Data on wages and standards of living

C. Population statistics for industrial cities

D. Journals and letters of industrial entrepreneurs

12. By 1870, most European governments would respond to these issues by:

A. providing an extensive system of social welfare.

B. granting suffrage to all citizens, regardless of wealth or gender.

C. pursuing colonies in Africa and Asia to access key resources.

D. expanding regulation and reforming cities to improve health.

Questions 13–15 are based on the chart below.

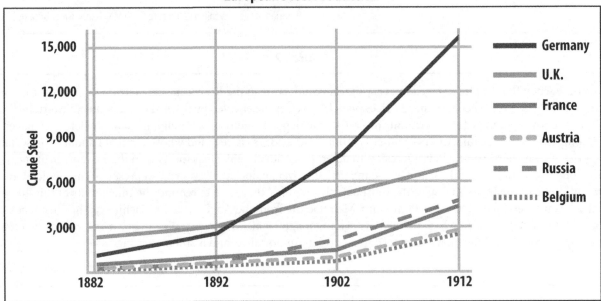

European Steel Production

13. Which of the following developments best explains the overall trends in the chart?

A. Adoption of the mechanization of production and new technologies

B. Steady population growth and resulting emigration to the Americas

C. Ability of working class movements to pressure states for higher wages

D. Increases in agricultural productivity due to introduction of new crops

14. Which is the best explanation for the changes over time in Germany's economic position as shown on the chart?

A. The borrowing of British technology and methods

B. Rivalry with the competing power of France

C. The benefits provided by a unified economy and polity

D. Development of a major colonial empire in Africa

15. All of the following coincided with the developments shown on the chart EXCEPT:

A. the growth of consumerism and advertising.

B. volatile business cycles and periodic unemployment.

C. the spread of Liberal notions of laissez-faire.

D. the pursuit of colonies in Africa and Asia.

Questions 16–18 are based on the passage below.

> "Comrades, in order not to repeat errors of the past, the central committee has declared itself resolutely against the cult of the individual. We consider that Stalin was excessively extolled. However, in the past Stalin doubtless performed great services to the party, to the working class, and to the international workers' movement.
>
> We should in all seriousness consider the question of the cult of the individual. We cannot let this matter get out of the party, especially not to the press. It is for this reason that we are considering it here at a closed congress session. We should know the limits; we should not give ammunition to the enemy; we should not wash our dirty linen before their eyes.
>
> Comrades, we must abolish the cult of the individual decisively, once and for all; we must draw the proper conclusions concerning both ideological-theoretical and practical work."
>
> Nikita Khrushchev, Soviet leader, secret speech delivered at the Twentieth Party
> Congress of the Communist Party of the Soviet Union, February 25, 1956

16. To support his portrayal of Stalin, Khrushchev might have noted all of the following policies EXCEPT:
    A. the liquidation of the kulaks.
    B. the purge of Old Bolsheviks.
    C. the Nazi-Soviet Non-Aggression Pact.
    D. forced labor camps (gulags).

17. A major result of Khrushchev's speech and subsequent policies was:
    A. reforms and revolts within Eastern European nations.
    B. an increase in the arms race between the superpowers.
    C. defeat of the United States in the Korean War.
    D. further efforts toward Western European unity.

18. Which of the following facts, all of which are accurate, would act as the most serious <u>limitation</u> on the speech as a source for Stalin's policies?
    A. Khrushchev was later dismissed (in 1964) by the Soviet leadership for economic and diplomatic failures.
    B. Khrushchev supported Stalin's purges and carried many of them out as governor of Ukraine.
    C. Under Khrushchev, the Soviet Union surpassed the United States in the space race, launching a satellite and the first persons to orbit the Earth.
    D. The Soviet Union controlled the press, establishing a state-run news service and official government newspaper.

Questions 19–22 are based on the map below.

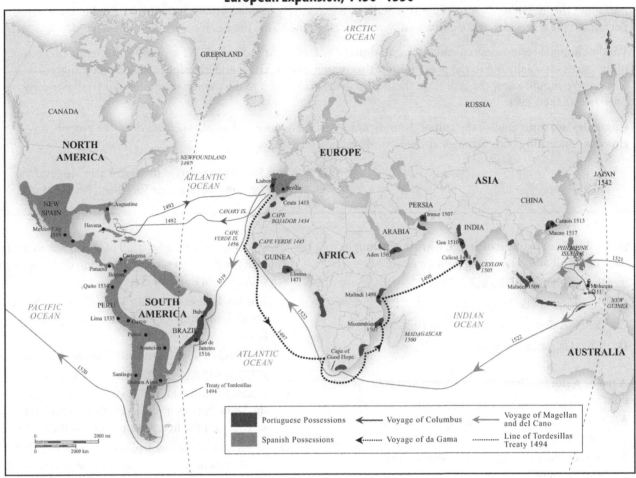

European Expansion, 1450–1550

19. All of the following facilitated the process depicted above EXCEPT:

   A. advances in navigation and map-making.

   B. superior military technology, such as cannons.

   C. the desire for luxury items, such as silks and spices.

   D. a shift in power from the Mediterranean to the Atlantic.

20. The economic theory that came to be associated with the process depicted was:

   A. feudalism.

   B. mercantilism.

   C. capitalism.

   D. monetarism.

21. A major political effect of the process depicted was:

   A. the centralization of the new monarchies.

   B. a decrease in the power of the Catholic Church.

   C. rivalries among European powers over trade.

   D. the outbreak of revolts in the Americas.

22. Which of the following represents the most significant shift in the relationships depicted?

   A. Protestant Reformation

   B. Scientific Revolution

   C. French Revolution

   D. Unification of Germany

Questions 23–24 are based on the image below.

Maria Sibylla Merian, German naturalist and illustrator,
from *The Metamorphosis of the Insects of Suriname*, 1705

23. The illustration above reflects all of the following trends in early modern Europe EXCEPT:
    A. an increasing focus on investigation of the physical world.
    B. the ability of Europeans to interact with overseas environments.
    C. a general improvement in women's economic and legal rights.
    D. the expansion of printed materials, such as books and periodicals.

24. Which of the following figures would have agreed most strongly with the illustrator's method of inquiry and approach toward nature?
    A. Denis Diderot
    B. René Descartes
    C. Aristotle
    D. Karl Marx

Questions 25–27 are based on the passage below.

"Let the business [of marriage] be carried as Prudently as it can be on the Woman's side, a reasonable Man can't deny that she has by much the harder bargain. Because she puts herself entirely into her Husband's Power, and if the Matrimonial Yoke be grievous, neither Law nor Custom afford her that redress which a Man obtains. He who has Sovereign Power does not value the Provocations of a Rebellious Subject, but knows how to subdue him with ease, and will make himself obey'd; but Patience and Submission are the only Comforts that are left to a poor People, who groan under Tyranny, unless they are Strong enough to break the Yoke, to Depose and Abdicate, which I doubt wou'd not be allow'd of here."

Mary Astell, English writer and feminist, *Some Reflections Upon Marriage, Occasion'd by the Duke and Dutchess of Mazarine's Case; Which is Also Consider'd,* 1700

25. Which of the following movements would Astell most likely have drawn from to address marriage practices as described above?

A. Scientific Revolution

B. Commercial Revolution

C. Glorious Revolution

D. Enlightenment

26. Which of the following developments of the eighteenth century would most directly have contradicted Astell's portrayal of family life?

A. The ideas of Jean-Jacques Rousseau

B. Growth of companionate marriage

C. Continued importance of the family economy

D. Rise of in the number of out-of-wedlock births

27. Astell's ideas would parallel most directly in tone and objective the eighteenth-century reform movement of:

A. advocating for more appropriate treatment and education of children.

B. promoting the use of inoculation and vaccination to prevent disease.

C. applying new techniques and technologies to improve crop yields.

D. urging the abolition of the slave trade and slavery in the colonies.

Questions 28–30 are based on the map below.

Europe, 1848

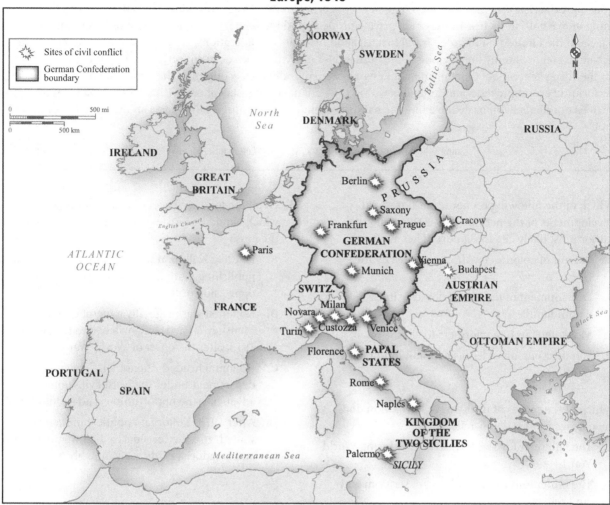

28. All of the following caused the events depicted above EXCEPT:

   A. frustration over the Vienna settlement of 1814–1815.

   B. grievances caused by poor economic conditions.

   C. the effort by France to expand its political influence.

   D. resentment against the persistence of the old regime.

29. Which of the following resulted from the events depicted above?

   A. The reestablishment of the Concert of Europe

   B. A turn toward realism in politics and culture

   C. An alliance of the middle and working classes

   D. The rapid industrialization of eastern Europe

30. The historical situation that shared similar causes as above but resulted in a different outcome was the:

   A. Thirty Years' War and Peace of Westphalia.

   B. unification of Italy and Germany.

   C. Nazi-Soviet Non-Aggression Pact and World War II.

   D. collapse of communism in central and eastern Europe.

Questions 31–33 are based on the passage below.

"The fact that with the consolidation of the capitalist system of production, the marital/family union develops from a production unit into a legal arrangement concerned only with consumption, leads inevitably to the weakening of marital/family ties. In the era of private property and the bourgeois-capitalist economic system, marriage and the family are grounded in (a) material and financial considerations, (b) economic dependence of the female sex on the family breadwinner—the husband—rather than the social collective, and (c) the need to care for the rising generation. Capitalism maintains a system of individual economies: the family has a role to play in performing economic tasks and functions within the national capitalist economy. Thus under capitalism the family does not merge with or dissolve into the national economy but continues to exist as an independent economic unit."

Alexandra Kollontai, Russian revolutionary, "Theses on Communist Morality in the Sphere of Marital Relations," 1921

31. Which of the following economic and/or social developments of the period 1850–1920 would the author most likely cite in support of her analysis?

   A. Pursuit of colonies in Africa and Asia by the Great Powers

   B. Development of the cult of domesticity within families

   C. Movement among reformers to aid the poor

   D. Feminist pursuit of legal, economic, and political rights

32. Which of the causes of the Russian Revolution does the passage most strongly reflect?

   A. The failure of Russia's infrastructure during World War I

   B. The limitations of the abolition of serfdom and land reform

   C. The inability of the tsarist regime to incorporate disaffected elements

   D. Russia's haphazard industrialization and the resulting social inequality

33. Of all the following accurate facts about Kollontai, which would be most useful in providing context for the passage?

   A. In 1908, Kollontai went into exile in Germany after publishing pamphlets that urged Finns to resist the oppression of Russian rule.

   B. Kollontai was originally a member of the Menshevik Party, but switched to the Bolsheviks in 1915, after the onset of World War I.

   C. Kollontai headed Zhenotdel, the women's department under the Bolsheviks, aimed at advancing the opportunities and status of women.

   D. After 1923, Kollontai's political influence waned, and she served as a diplomat in several ambassadorial posts, most notably to Norway.

Questions 34–35 are based on the interpretation below.

"A spirit of collective pacifism possessed them, and made the people content with the lazy approval of high ideals, the verbal condemnation of injustice, chicanery and oppression. Holding all the power, the Western democracies disdained to use it, so long as the status quo was in any way tolerable. The attitude of America was not dissimilar, except that here the League idea was rejected and the Monroe doctrine was still regarded as America's contribution to world peace."

R.H.S. Crossman, British historian and politician, *Government and the Governed*, 1940

34. European culture in the interwar period (1918–1939) most directly reflected the attitude explained in the interpretation with the:

   A. movement toward subjectivity and irony in the arts.

   B. spread of mass communications such as radio and film.

   C. growing influence of the United States in consumer culture.

   D. development of new theories and technologies in science and medicine.

35. All of the following examples support the historian's interpretation above EXCEPT:

   A. the structure and actions of the League of Nations.

   B. western democracies' actions in the Spanish Civil War.

   C. creation of mandates and involvement in the Middle East.

   D. the economic and financial policies of the United States.

Questions 36–38 are based on the map below.

Religions in Europe, ca. 1600

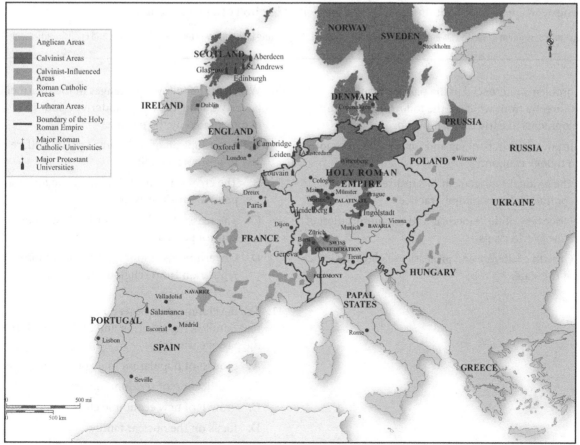

36. Which of the following conclusions regarding sixteenth-century politics can be drawn from the map?

   A. Catholicism was no longer the dominant religion within any major state.

   B. Denmark had become the leading Protestant state.

   C. Calvinism presented a challenge to many Catholic states.

   D. Germany had created a stable state around religious toleration.

37. Which of the following most directly resulted from the situation depicted on the map?

   A. States no longer concerned themselves with religious uniformity.

   B. The Council of Trent reformed clerical abuses and reaffirmed Church doctrine.

   C. Europe's center of power shifted to the Atlantic seaboard.

   D. Religious division led to internal conflict and interstate warfare.

38. The most conclusive resolution to the situation depicted was the:

   A. Peace of Augsburg (1555).

   B. Edict of Nantes (1598).

   C. Peace of Westphalia (1648).

   D. French Revolution (1789).

Questions 39–41 are based on the passage below.

"All the parts of this realm of England and Wales be presently with rogues, vagabonds, and sturdy beggars exceedingly pestered, by means whereof daily happen in the same realm horrible murders, theft, and other great outrage, to the high displeasure of Almighty God, and the annoyance of the commonweal. If a person be duly convicted of his or her roguish or vagabond trade of life…then immediately he or she shall be adjudged to be grievously whipped and burnt through the right ear with a hot iron of an inch around."

Act for Punishment of Vagabonds and Relief of the Poor, parliamentary statute law, approved by Queen Elizabeth I and English Parliament, 1572

39. The problems referenced in the passage resulted most directly from which of the following economic developments in early modern Europe, 1500–1650?

   A. Innovations in banking and finance that promoted a money economy

   B. The gradual replacement of subsistence with commercial agricultural practices

   C. Discovery of the Americas and the importation of New World crops

   D. Growth of literate and professional elites in service of the state

40. Which of the following changes in the treatment of poverty during the early modern period, 1500–1650, is demonstrated by the passage?

   A. The adoption of widespread social welfare benefits to promote equality

   B. The creation of professional police forces and penitentiaries (prisons)

   C. The reassertion by landlords of the right to tax and control peasants

   D. Governments assuming control of moral regulation from religious institutions

41. The development in eastern Europe during this period that parallels the situation and approach addressed in the passage was the:

   A. growth of population to its pre-plague levels.

   B. codification of serfdom into law.

   C. growth of new economic elites.

   D. focus on the nuclear family.

Questions 42–44 are based on the passage below.

"Article 4. It is contrary to the principles of liberty and the Constitution for citizens with the same professions, arts, or trades to deliberate or make agreements among themselves designed to set prices for their industry or their labor. If such deliberations and agreements are concluded, whether accompanied by oath or not, they will be declared unconstitutional, prejudicial to liberty and the Declaration of the Rights of Man, and will be null and void. Administrative and municipal bodies shall be required to declare them as such. The authors, leaders, and instigators who provoked, drafted, or presided over these agreements shall be charged by the police and at the request of the communal attorney will be fined 500 *livres**, suspended for a year from the enjoyment of all rights of active citizenship, and barred from admittance to the primary assemblies."

* the currency of France

The Le Chapelier Law, passed by French National Assembly, June 14, 1791

42. The law above was aimed primarily against the:
 A. economic features of the old regime.
 B. arbitrary nature of absolute monarchy.
 C. powerful position of the Catholic Church.
 D. control of the nobility over offices.

43. Which action of the radical phase of the French Revolution contradicted the principles of the law above?
 A. Requirement of a national military conscription
 B. Execution of the king and Reign of Terror
 C. Imposition of controls on prices and wages
 D. Limitation of women's right to assembly

44. The legislation would have coincided with the nineteenth-century ideology of:
 A. Conservatism.
 B. Liberalism.
 C. socialism.
 D. nationalism.

Questions 45–47 are based on the chart below.

Ethnic Composition of the Austrian Empire, 1910

Language	Number	%
German	11,853,000	22.85
Hungarian	9,944,000	19.2
Czech	6,436,000	12.4
Polish	4,968,000	9.6
Serbo-Croatian	5,495,000	10.6
Ukrainian	3,983,000	7.7
Romanian	3,223,000	6.2
Slovak	1,946,000	3.75
Slovene	1,253,000	2.4
Italian	768,000	1.5
Other	ca. 2,000,000	3.8
Total	**51,869,000**	**100.00**

45. In which of the following ways during the nineteenth century did Austrian rulers attempt to address the situation reflected in the chart above?

  A. Expand territory in the Balkans

  B. Create a Dual Monarchy with Hungary

  C. Ally with Germany and Russia

  D. Abolish serfdom and feudalism

46. In which of the following ways did the Versailles settlement (1919) attempt to resolve the situation depicted in the chart?

  A. The dissolution of empires into ethnically-based nation-states

  B. The attribution of responsibility for World War I to the Central Powers

  C. The creation of a League of Nations to address issues of collective security

  D. The involvement of the United States in European diplomacy

47. The chart above could be used to support most directly which of the following interpretations on the causes of the First World War?

  A. "If not for the system of mutually antagonistic alliances, a regional conflict in the Balkans might have remained limited to the powers with a direct interest in the region."

  B. "The massive increase in armaments and reliance of military leaders and military plans limited the decision-making of political leaders and virtually forced them into war."

  C. "Leaders contemplated global war in 1914 because the principles of Darwin, Freud, and Nietzsche told them that war and struggle were not an evil to be avoided but a force for the good of the race."

  D. "Multi-ethnic empires had survived the twists and turns of history, but they could not escape the trap of nationalism, stoked by agitation throughout the nineteenth century."

Questions 48–51 are based on the passage below.

"The radio will be for the twentieth century what the press was for the nineteenth century. With the appropriate change, one can apply Napoleon's phrase to our age ["the press is the seventh great power"], speaking of the radio as the eighth great power. Its discovery and application are of truly revolutionary significance for contemporary community life. Future generations may conclude that the radio had as great an intellectual and spiritual impact on the masses as the printing press had before the beginning of the Reformation."

Joseph Goebbels, Nazi Minister of Propaganda, speech, August 1933

48. The trend in European history most directly related to Goebbels's analysis was:

   A. the expansion of leisure time.

   B. domination of the world economy.

   C. the growth of mass politics.

   D. conflict among the great powers.

49. Goebbels invokes Napoleon as support for his position. In which of the following ways were the policies of Napoleon and the Nazis under Hitler most <u>different</u>?

   A. Reliance on mass political propaganda

   B. Use of warfare to promote nationalism

   C. Appeal to a charismatic leader

   D. Empire based on racial ideology

50. Which of the following contemporary nations or regimes would most likely have agreed with the methods, if not the goals, identified by Goebbels?

   A. Poland

   B. Spain

   C. Soviet Union

   D. France

51. Hitler and the Nazis exploited all of the following developments in gaining and consolidating power in Germany EXCEPT:

   A. the policy of appeasement by the Western democracies.

   B. fear of a communist takeover and the threat from the Soviet Union.

   C. lack of support for and weakness of the Weimar Republic.

   D. frustration over economic problems such as inflation and unemployment.

Questions 52–55 are based on the quotes below.

- "We want nothing of a world in which the certainty of not dying from hunger comes in exchange for the risk of dying from boredom."
- "How can one think freely in the shadow of a chapel?"
- "The more I make love, the more I want to make revolution. The more I make revolution, the more I want to make love."
- "Professors you are as old as your culture, your modernism is only the modernization of the police."
- "The barricade blocks the street but opens the way."

Graffiti slogans from 1968 revolts in Paris

52. The slogans above reveal all of the following post-1945 issues EXCEPT the:

A. stresses caused by the Baby Boom and expansion of college attendance.

B. influx of guest workers and the changing identity of Europe's population.

C. environmental and ethical concerns over prosperity and consumerism.

D. growth of dissident voices demanding liberation and political rights.

53. The historical development or event that most directly inspired the slogans was the:

A. revival of classical texts during the Renaissance.

B. reform of the Catholic Church in the sixteenth century.

C. development of the New Science in the seventeenth century.

D. attack on the Old Regime during the French Revolution.

54. The twentieth-century development relating to women that most directly parallels the slogans was that women:

A. became increasingly involved in work and mobilization during the world wars.

B. gained leisure time due to advances in mass production and household technologies.

C. were granted the vote and gained positions of leadership in government.

D. experienced increased birth rates after 1945 due to government pro-natalist policies.

55. The movement most similar in its goals and outcomes to the one expressed in the slogans was the:

A. Algerian War for independence.

B. Prague Spring in Czechoslovakia.

C. fall of the Berlin Wall.

D. defeat of the Nazis in World War II.

Section I, Part B: Short-Answer Questions

Time—40 minutes; 3 Questions

Directions: There are four short-answer questions on the exam. Answer Question 1 *and* Question 2, and then choose to answer *either* Question 3 *or* Question 4. Note that the short-answer questions do not require you to develop and support a thesis statement. Use complete sentences; an outline or bulleted list is not acceptable.

Use the map below to answer all parts of the question that follows.

Europe, 1919–1939

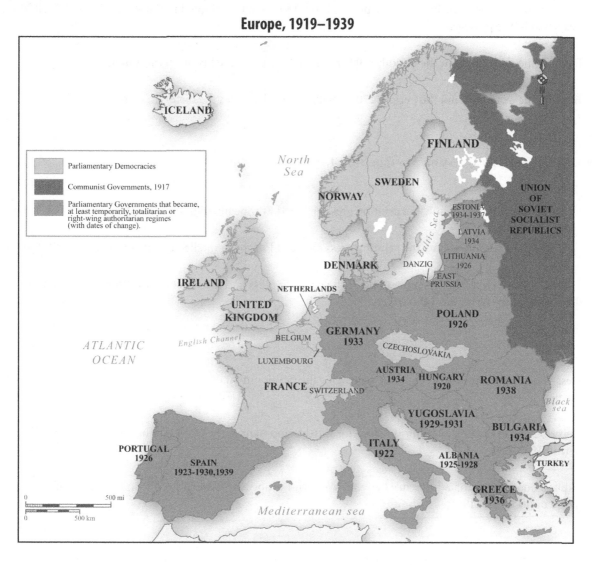

1. a) Describe one example of a <u>political</u> factor that caused the trends indicated on the map.

   b) Describe one example of an <u>economic</u> factor that caused the trends indicated on the map.

   c) Explain one diplomatic or political response to the trends indicated on the map.

Use the interpretation below to answer all parts of the question that follows.

> "A new attitude toward children developed during the eighteenth century....It was a gentler and more sensitive approach to children, one that was part of a wider change in social attitudes: a growing belief that nature was inherently good, not evil, and what evil there was derived from man and his institutions...Children, in a sense, had become luxury objects upon which their parents were willing to spend larger and larger sums of money, not only for their education but also for their entertainment and amusement."
>
> J.H. Plumb, British historian, "The Commercialization of Childhood," 1976

2. a) Describe one intellectual change in the period 1700–1850 that contributed to the attitudes towards children discussed in the passage.

   b) Explain one example from the period, 1700–1850, that <u>supports</u> the historian's argument.

   c) Explain one example from the period, 1700–1850, that <u>undermines</u> the historian's argument.

Answer all parts of *either* Question 3 *or* Question 4.

3. a) Describe one example of how the printing press changed European <u>religious</u> life in the period 1450–1600.

   b) Describe one example of how the printing press changed European <u>intellectual</u> life in the period 1450–1600.

   c) Explain one difference between the effect of the printing press and the effect of any other technological development in the period 1450–1600.

4. a) Describe one example of an <u>economic</u> reason for the development of the Cold War between the superpowers in the period 1945–1991.

   b) Describe one example of a <u>political</u> reason for the development of the Cold War between the superpowers in the period 1945–1991.

   c) Explain one example of a difference between Western Europe and Eastern Europe in the effects of the Cold War in the period 1945–1991.

Section II, Part A: Document-Based Question

Total Time—60 minutes; 1 Question

Directions: Question 1 is based on the accompanying documents. It is suggested that you spend about 15 minutes reading the documents and 45 minutes writing your response. The documents have been edited for the purpose of this exercise.

In your response you should do the following:

- Respond to the prompt with a historically defensible thesis or claim that establishes a line of reasoning.
- Describe a broader historical context relevant to the prompt.
- Support an argument in response to the prompt using at least six documents.
- Use at least one additional piece of specific historical evidence (beyond that found in the documents) relevant to an argument about the prompt.
- For at least three documents, explain how or why the document's point of view, purpose, historical situation, and/ or audience is relevant to an argument.
- Use evidence to corroborate, qualify, or modify an argument that addresses the prompt.

Question 1   *Evaluate the extent to which Romanticism incorporated or rejected the values of the Enlightenment.*

Document 1

Source: David Hume, Scottish philosopher, "Of Miracles," from *An Enquiry Concerning Human Understanding*, 1748

A miracle is a violation of the laws of nature; and as a firm and unalterable experience has established these laws, the proof against a miracle, from the very nature of the fact, is as entire as any argument from experience can possibly be imagined....Nothing is esteemed a miracle, if it ever happen in the common course of nature. It is no miracle that a man, seemingly in good health, should die on a sudden: because such a kind of death, though more unusual than any other, has yet been frequently observed to happen...And as a uniform experience amounts to a proof, there is here a direct and full proof, from the nature of the fact, against the existence of any miracle; nor can such a proof be destroyed, or the miracle rendered credible, but by an opposite proof, which is superior.

Document 2

Source: Jean-Jacques Rousseau, Swiss/French philosopher, *A Discourse on the Moral Effects of the Arts and Sciences*, 1750

We cannot reflect on the morality of mankind without contemplating with pleasure the picture of the simplicity which prevailed in the earliest times. This image may be justly compared to a beautiful coast, adorned only by the hands of nature; towards which our eyes are constantly turned, and which we see receding with regret. While men were innocent and virtuous and loved to have the gods for witnesses of their actions, they dwelt together in the same huts; but when they became vicious, they grew tired of such inconvenient onlookers, and banished them to magnificent temples. Finally, they expelled their deities even from these, in order to dwell there themselves; or at least the temples of the gods were no longer more magnificent than the palaces of the citizens.

....As the conveniences of life increase, as the arts are brought to perfection, and luxury spreads, true courage flags, the virtues disappear; and all this is the effect of the sciences and of those arts which are exercised in the privacy of men's dwellings.

Document 3

Source: Frederick II, "the Great," king of Prussia, *Political Testament*, 1752

Catholics, Lutherans, Reformed, Jews and other Christian sects live in this state, and live together in peace. If the sovereign, actuated by a mistaken zeal, declares himself for one religion or another, parties spring up, heated disputes ensue, little by little persecutions will commence and, in the end, the religion persecuted will leave the fatherland, and millions of subjects will enrich our neighbors by their skill and industry.

It is of no concern in politics whether the ruler has a religion or whether he has none. All religions, if one examines them, are founded on superstitious systems, more or less absurd. It is impossible for a man of good sense, who dissects their contents, not to see their error; but these prejudices, these errors and mysteries, were made for men, and one must know enough to respect the public and not to outrage its faith, whatever religion be involved.

Document 4

Source: Joseph Wright of Derby, British artist, *A Philosopher Giving A Lecture at the Orrery* [mechanical model of the universe], c. 1765

Document 5

Source: François-René de Chateaubriand, French politician and writer, *The Genius of Christianity*, 1802

The forests of Gaul [ancient France] were, in their turn, introduced into the temples of our ancestors, and those celebrated woods of oaks of thus maintained their sacred character. Those ceilings sculptured into foliage of different kinds, those buttresses which prop the walls and terminate abruptly like the broken trunks of trees, the coolness of the vaults, the darkness of the sanctuary, the dim twilight of the aisles, the secret passages, the low doorways,—in a word, every thing in a Gothic church reminds you of the labyrinths of a wood; every thing excites a feeling of religious awe, of mystery, and of the Divinity.

Document 6

Source: Lord Byron, English Romantic poet, *Manfred, A Dramatic Poem*, 1817

I do remember me, that in my youth,
When I was wandering, – upon such a night
I stood within the Colosseum's wall,
'Midst the chief relics of almighty Rome;
The trees which grew along the broken arches
Waved dark in the blue midnight, and the stars
Shone through the rents of ruin….

While Caesar's chambers, and the Augustan halls,
Grovel on earth in indistinct decay
And thou didst shine, thou rolling moon, upon
All this, and cast a wide and tender light,…

As 'twere, anew, the gaps of centuries;
Leaving that beautiful which still was so,
And making that which was not, till the place
Became religion, and the heart ran o'er
With silent worship of the great of old!

Document 7

Source: Casper David Friedrich, German painter, *Wanderer above the Sea of Fog*, 1818

Section II, Part B: Long Essay Question

Time—40 minutes; 1 Question

Directions: Choose EITHER Question 2 or Question 3 or Question 4.

In your response, you should do the following.

- Respond to the prompt with a historically defensible thesis or claim that establishes a line of reasoning.
- Describe a broader historical context relevant to the prompt.
- Support an argument in response to the prompt using specific and relevant examples of evidence.
- Use historical reasoning (e.g., comparison, causation, continuity or change over time) to frame or structure an argument that addresses the prompt.
- Use evidence to corroborate, qualify, or modify an argument that addresses the prompt.

Question 2 *Evaluate the most important effect of the development of capitalism in the period 1450–1650.*

(RP: Causation)

Question 3 *Evaluate the most important effect of the unifications of Italy and Germany in the period 1861–1914.*

(RP: Causation)

Question 4 *Evaluate the most important effect of Europe's economic recovery after the Second World War.*

(RP: Causation)

Practice Exam 2 — Answers and Explanations

MC Answers with Explanations

1. **Answer: B. HTS: CTX, DAP, & CAUS; Themes: INT, SCD & ECD; KCs 1.3 & 1.4.** In the passage, Cereta makes a contrast between women of appearance and women of substance. The former seem to her preoccupied with displaying luxuries, many garnered from the trade with overseas ports (B). No mention is made of folk beliefs (A), nor does Cereta relate her discussion of gender to organized religion, other than references to piety and ethics (D). Rather than criticize women for engaging in intellectual pursuits (promoted by print media), Cereta encourages them in this pursuit, dropping out C.

2. **Answer: D. HTS: DAP & CTX; Theme: CID; KC 1.1.** To bolster her argument, Cereta cites classical figures and texts (D). This was an age of civic humanism, but Cereta draws her attention more to the private behavior of women, excluding A. No mention is made of art patronage (B) or anatomical discoveries (C).

3. **Answer: D. HTS: COMP & MAC; Theme: SCD; KC 1.4.** Because of its uniquely urban setting, Italy provided an environment conducive for the spread of Renaissance ideas, but in this respect it was unique (excluding A). The growth of a new economic elite eventually spread to the rest of Europe, but in the fifteenth century was focused on Italy (B). Italy did not develop a centralized monarchy (due to its thriving city-states), making it different from other states with new monarchies (C). However, social life in all of Europe concerned itself with status and hierarchy, as shown in the passage with women distinguishing themselves by appearance or by the patriarchy that Cereta condemns in the last paragraph (D).

4. **Answer: C. HTS: CCOT; Theme: SCD; KCs 1.4 & 3.3.** Consider when feminism began to emerge as a consistent ideology and to make progress in obtaining rights for women. Of these periods, the strongest case can be made for C (1850–1920), when feminism evolved in response to the nineteenth-century revolutions and when women gained economic rights and the vote (after 1918). The period 1517–1648 saw little progress for women, and though the 1789–1850 period held promise, women's participation in revolutions met with few tangible results (B). Due to the instability of the interwar period and growth of totalitarian governments, the 1920–1945 era marks a holding pattern for feminism, to be revived in the post-1945 era (D).

5. **Answer: C. HTS: CTX & DAP; Themes: TSI & CID; KC 1.1.** Bacon advocates for observation and experimentation, his contribution to the scientific method, also known as inductive reasoning (C). This passage makes no mention of classical learning, which Bacon hoped to surpass by moving toward direct examination of nature, excluding A. Though Bacon's counterpart Descartes articulated a geometric approach to learning, Bacon's focus here is on empiricism, not math (B). No reference is made to folk beliefs like astrology and alchemy (D).

6. **Answer: A. HTS: CCOT & CAUS; Themes: TSI & OS; KC 1.1.** Using the new scientific method of direct observation, astronomers like Galileo and Brahe articulated new theories of the cosmos (A). Though new anatomical discoveries paralleled those in astronomy, these did not yield advances in medicine until much later (B). Though Leeuwenhoek used the microscope to introduce microbiology, these changes were not as profound in altering European worldviews as those in astronomy (C). Robert Boyle also changed the approach in chemistry by using the notion of elements, yet again, these advances did not pose the same challenge as the upheaval in the geocentric model (D).

7. **Answer: C. HTS: SAS & CES; Themes: SOP, NEI, CID, & IS; KC 2.1.** Radical revolutionaries adopted the mass levy to see the revolution through total war against internal and external enemies. The armies are briefly referenced in Section 6; however, the entire law relates to their employment (A). War occurred because of the upheaval caused by dissent over the revolution's course (B). Clearly this law grants the state significant powers to organize the nation for war (D). This leaves C as the EXCEPT outlier, and even though the statement is correct, it does not relate to the passage itself.

8. **Answer: A. HTS: CCOT & MAC; Themes: SOP, NEI & SCD; KC 2.1.** Napoleon succeeded in manipulating nationalism to promote his military and political objectives, reaping the benefits of new citizen armies (A). Eventually the armies of revolutionary France turned the tide and invaded neighboring states, spreading revolutionary ideals. Napoleon did the same; however, this law relates to defense of the revolution, not conquest, excluding B. Choices C and D indicate goals and policies of Napoleon, but neither is indicated or referenced in the law.

9. **Answer: C. HTS: CAUS; Themes: ECD & TSI; KC 3.1.** Both of these sources address, albeit with differing perspectives, the mechanization of textile production, the first phase of the Industrial Revolution. Thus, you are asked, what caused industrialization? Britain's advantages included: access to raw materials (A), an entrepreneurial spirit and advanced credit institutions (C), and representation of industrial interests in Parliament, unlike many continental nations (D). In contrast to continental nations, Britain did not rely upon the active intervention of the government in promoting industry, instead employing a more laissez-faire approach (B).

10. **Answer: C. HTS: CAUS, CCOT, & SAS; Themes: ECD & SCD; KCs 3.1 & 3.2.** The sources reveal diverging perspectives on the mechanization of traditional craft production, or the growth of self-conscious classes, the bourgeoisie (owners of capital) and proletariat (newly unskilled workers), indicating C as the key. No mention is made

here of agricultural elites, crossing off B. Though textile manufacture did produce new consumer goods, that is not the focus of the sources. Social discontent is offered, but it does not arise from migration or urbanization, but instead from the fear workers directed against machines perceived as taking away their traditional crafts (D).

11. **Answer: B. HTS: SAS & CES; Themes: PP & IS; KCs 3.1 & 3.2.** The two passages provide varying perspectives on the standard of living (both material and psychological) produced by the new textile machines. To judge the issue, historians might draw on statistical measures (B). The designs of the machines themselves are not central to the disagreement (A). Since the passage deals only implicitly with urbanization, population measures would not resolve the issue (C). Though the writings on entrepreneurs would provide further data for that group, these would not assist the historian in gaining a more objective sense of the disagreement (D).

12. **Answer: D. HTS: CCOT; Themes: ECD, SOP, & SCD; KC 3.3.** The year 1870 preceded the development of social welfare systems (A). Further, it was not until just before World War I that most states adopted universal male suffrage, and not until after the war (even WWII in some nations) for women (B). European states did pursue colonies for a variety of reasons but not primarily to address social discontent (C). This leaves D, and indeed, most states realized by mid-century that some public health and regulatory measures were necessary to blunt the worst problems created by industrialization.

13. **Answer: A. HTS: CAUS & CTX; Themes: TSI & ECD; KC 3.1.** The chart shows the significant increase in steel production, owing to new methods (Bessemer Process) and the mechanization of production (A). Demographic growth was more likely the result rather than the cause of industrialization, as mechanization supported a higher population, excluding B. Workers did seek higher wages during this period through union activity, but that fact is separate from the increase in productivity (C). Industrialization depended in broad terms on the increase in food supply, allowing for the transition in the labor supply to cities, but this trend does not explain steel production directly (D).

14. **Answer: C. HTS: CAUS & CCOT; Themes: ECD, NEI, & SOP; KCs 3.1 & 3.4.** Germany's level of industrialization in 1882 compared unfavorably to Britain's; however, over several decades Germany reaped the benefits of a uniform economy with standardized weights and measures and central policy direction (C). Certainly Germany borrowed some techniques from Britain, but so did other nations that did not fare as well as Germany (A). France and Germany bore enmity in the fallout of the Franco-Prussian War, but this rivalry focused more around diplomacy and territory, and further, it does not explain German industrialization generally (B). Bismarck pursued colonies tardily and reluctantly and Germany's new colonial empire contributed to its economic expansion minimally (D).

15. **Answer: C. HTS: CAUS & DAP; Themes: INT, ECD, & SOP; KCs 3.1 & 3.5.** Industrialization promoted the growth of a consumer culture in new goods (A); however, it also spawned boom-bust cycles, especially between 1873–1896, leading many governments to abandon free trade and corporations to manage the market through informal arrangements (B). To secure the raw materials needed for industrialization and gain markets for manufactured goods, European powers pursued colonies in Africa and Asia (D). However, as noted above, economic volatility led to the eventual abandonment of a hands-off (laissez-faire) approach, the opposite of C.

16. **Answer: C. HTS: SAS & CES; Themes: SOP & ECD; KC 4.1 & 4.2.** Khrushchev's speech criticizes the excesses of Stalin's policies within the Soviet Union, not foreign policy. This excludes C, as it deals with the agreement Stalin made with Hitler in 1939, primarily due to the western allies' neglect of the Soviet Union. Choices A, B, and D all represent ways in which Stalin repressed various groups in the single-minded pursuit of his goals.

17. **Answer: A. HTS: CAUS; Theme: SOP & NEI; KC 4.2.** Though Khrushchev attempted to keep his critique of Stalin secret, his speech inadvertently inspired resistance to Soviet authority in Eastern Europe, leading to revolts in Poland and Hungary, the latter being crushed (A). The Cold War was defined by an arms race between the superpowers, but this was incidental to Khrushchev's speech (B). The Korean War resulted in a stalemate and ended three years before this speech, eliminating C. The progress toward Western European unity was well under way and generally separate from the policies *within* the Soviet bloc (D).

18. **Answer: B. HTS: SAS; Theme: SOP; KC 4.2.** Since Khrushchev condemned Stalin in his speech, any fact that casts doubt on that central point would be of interest to the historian. Khrushchev did support Stalin's purges, undermining his supposed outrage at Stalin's excesses, making B the key. The others (A, C, and D) would be of interest to a historian, but more likely for other interpretive issues related to Khrushchev or the Soviet Union.

19. **Answer: D. HTS: CAUS; Themes: INT, TSI, ECD, & SOP; KC 1.3.** The map depicts the European outreach toward new goods and colonies. The process was facilitated by the ability to sustain overseas voyages (A), asymmetries in military technology between Europeans and non-Europeans (B), and the pursuit of profit (C). The shift in power to the Atlantic was the *result*, not the cause, of this process.

20. **Answer: B. HTS: CTX, DAP, & CAUS; Themes: INT, ECD, & SOP; KCs 1.3 & 1.5.** New colonial empires required management of their resources from European states, which were guided by the assumption that real wealth required the accumulation of specie, or hard money, known as mercantilism (B). Exploration undermined feudalism (A) by promoting a money economy around trade. Since we are not dealing with free markets or free

trade, C is excluded, though the shift to a money economy laid the foundations for capitalism. Monetarism, or the belief that control of the money supply is the key to economic growth, developed in the twentieth century to address inflation after World War II (D). If anything, the colonial powers importation of gold and silver created unpredictable fluctuations in the money supply.

21. **Answer: C. HTS: CAUS & CCOT; Themes: INT, SOP, & ECD; KC 1.3.** Centralization of monarchies was more the *cause* than the result of exploration, excluding A. The encounter with colonies allowed the Catholic Church (often through the Jesuits) new venues for religious conversion, countering B. The demographic catastrophe in the Americas precluded organized revolts, so these movements did not gain traction until the eighteenth century with the growth of Enlightenment ideals (D). This leaves C, and as the map indicates, several powers sought wealth and colonies, creating conflict and later commercial wars.

22. **Answer: C. HTS: CCOT; Themes: INT, ECD, SOP, & CID; KC 2.1.** The French Revolution spread ideologies of natural rights and self-rule worldwide, best exemplified by the Haitian slave revolt (1790s) and the Latin American move for independence (1810s)—C. The Reformation may have even stimulated further control of colonies through religious conversion (A). Also, the Scientific Revolution provided further technologies, navigational and military, for suppression and control of colonies (B). Finally, the unification of Germany did not reverse this process and even stimulated German pursuit of colonies in the late nineteenth century (D).

23. **Answer: D. HTS: CTX & DAP; Themes: TSI, INT, ECD; KCs 2.2, 2.3, & 2.4.** Here we see precise and detailed illustrations of insects, with the emerging field of entomology. This level of detail comes from a focused investigation of nature (A) and the ability to interact with areas of the world where "exotic" insects inhabit (B). In addition, the eighteenth century witnessed a huge increase in the number and range of printed materials (D), which helped popularize the new science. Despite the drawings being created by a female scientist, women in general did not experience an increase in rights during this era, making C the key.

24. **Answer: A. HTS: CES & COMP; Themes: TSI & CID; KC 2.3.** As a popularizer of the Enlightenment, Diderot urged an empirical and scientific approach to natural and human questions, as laid out in his famous *Encyclopédie* (A). Though Descartes helped establish the scientific method, his contribution lay more in a geometric or a deductive (vs. inductive) method of reasoning (B). The new science suggested by the illustrations generally undermined the Aristotelian world view, eliminating C. Marx argued for a "scientific" socialism in the nineteenth century, but he relied more on grand theories than on experimentation, canceling out D.

25. **Answer: C. HTS: CAUS & CTX; Themes: CID & SOP; KCs 2.1 & 2.4.** Several of these make appealing choices; however, the language Astell adopts involves rebellion against tyranny, pointing to the Glorious Revolution (Astell is British), which had occurred just over a decade before she wrote (C). The scientific revolution did stimulate new theories of politics, but it would have had only an indirect effect on Astell's writings (A). Also, the year 1700 would be too early for the Enlightenment (D). Astell, moreover, does not draw from commerce in her analysis of marriage, excluding B.

26. **Answer: B. HTS: CCOT & CES; Themes: SCD & CID; KCs 2.3 & 2.4.** Each choice expresses an actual development in the eighteenth century. Rousseau's ideas provided support for the unequal gender balance in marriage that Astell condemns (A). Family production as a unit (C) tended to support male control of the family, since men usually directed its labor. The rise of illegitimacy in the eighteenth century does not support Astell's depiction, but it did not contradict either, since it didn't involve marriage itself (D). This leaves us with B, and indeed, the notion that men and women should marry for companionship, rather than for economic pragmatism, tended to elevate the role of women within marriage, counter to Astell's portrayal of it.

27. **Answer: D. HTS: COMP & MAC; Themes: INT, CID, & ECD; KC 2.2.** At the end of the passage, Astell employs language to express women's oppression reminiscent of slavery ("groan under Tyranny" and "break the Yoke"); in fact, the antislavery movement gained steam throughout the eighteenth century owing to arguments from evangelical Christianity and the Enlightenment (D). The closest distracter would be A, but even here, it was not so much that children were oppressed in the household, more that philosophes came to a more nuanced understanding of childhood. Both B and C did occur, but do not relate to the theme of liberation from oppression.

28. **Answer: D. HTS: CAUS; Themes: SOP, NEI, & ECD; KCs 3.3 & 3.4.** The map depicts the spread of revolutionary agitation during the fateful year of 1848. These revolutions stemmed from the political and economic causes expressed by A, B, and D. As usual, the revolutions began in France, reminiscent of the quote, "When France sneezes, Europe catches a cold"; however, revolution in France did not constitute an agenda to spread its political influence, though its new leader, Louis Napoleon, would eventually attempt to do so as emperor. Thus, C is the outlier here.

29. **Answer: B. HTS: CAUS & CCOT; Themes: SOP, NEI, & CID; KCs 3.4 & 3.6.** Rather than reestablish the Concert of Europe, the revolutions of 1848 undermined it, dropping out A. The class conflict that emerged in places like newly republican France revealed the gap between the aspirations of the middle and working classes, which would grow with the rise of socialism (C). Eastern Europe's industrialization was delayed until the twentieth century due to a range of economic and political obstacles (D). With

the failures of 1848, the era of Romantic revolution ended, and a new realism and materialism took its place, as reflected in *Realpolitik*, Darwinism, and Marxism (B).

30. Answer: D. HTS: CCOT, MAC, & COMP; Themes: SOP & NEI; KCs 3.4 & 4.2. The Thirty Years' War was prompted by religion, evolved into a struggle among the great powers, and was resolved with the advent of religious toleration, showing few parallels with 1848 (A). Even with external diplomacy, the unifications of Italy and Germany resulted primarily from internal policies, rather than the spread of ideological discontent, as with 1848 (B). On the eve of World War II, Nazi Germany and the Soviet Union (under Stalin) cynically signed an agreement that gave each a free hand to divide Poland; again, this shows only minor similarities to 1848 (C). However, it was the combination of nationalist resentment against Soviet control of Eastern Europe and poor economic prospects that pushed over the Berlin Wall in 1989, a much more successful outcome than in 1848 but one driven by similar grievances (D).

31. Answer: B. HTS: DAP & CES; Themes: ECD & SCD; KCs 3.2 & 3.3. Kollontai notes how the rise of capitalism shifts families from a unit of production to one of consumption, with women more dependent upon men for material sustenance. To sustain this development, bourgeois thinkers supported the cult of domesticity, extolling women as guardians of the home (B). The passage does not address imperialism, and it is only tangentially related to Kollontai's analysis (A). Though reformers did seek to aid the poor, the text addresses family life in particular, excluding C. Feminists did pursue rights during the 1850–1920, but that fact would not support Kollontai's analysis, since her treatise addresses female inequality (D).

32. Answer: D. HTS: CAUS; Themes: SOP, TSI, & PP; KC 4.2. All of the choices express causes of the Russian Revolution; however, Kollontai's analysis primarily addresses the effects of industrialization and issues of inequality arising from them, which could be extended to other groups (D). The passage does not address Russia's failures during World War I (A), nor issues related to agriculture or serfdom (B). As a revolutionary, Kollontai would have opposed the out-of-touch Romanov dynasty, but the focus of her analysis is not political incompetence but more fundamental economic and social processes (C).

33. Answer: C. HTS: SAS & CES; Themes: SCD & SOP; KC 4.2 & 4.4. Since the excerpt addresses the issue of female equality, any factor that would help understand Kollontai's role would be of strongest interest to a historian—giving us C as the key. The other details of her life (A, B, and D) certainly round out her biography but would not be as central as C.

34. Answer: A. HTS: CES, DAP, & CTX; Themes: INT, SOP, & CID; KCs 4.1 & 4.3. Crossman's interpretation emphasizes the lack of confidence and initiative by the western democracies after World War I. The prewar confidence

in technology and progress had been undermined by slaughter on the Western Front, leading to an embrace of subjectivity and irony in the arts (A). The spread of mass communications did not directly undermine democratic government, though dictators later employed it to establish totalitarian control, excluding B. Though the passage mentions the role of the US, its influence in consumerism was not matched by a diplomatic commitment to European security, as noted in the passage (excluding C). Since the passage deals with lack of confidence, we can eliminate the advance of science (D), which would confirm notions of progress.

35. Answer: C. HTS: CES & CTX; Themes: INT, SOP, & ECD; KCs 4.1 & 4.2. Here we are looking for the outlier—an example that runs counter to the portrayal of the western democracies as on the defensive. Since the League of Nations failed to maintain collective security without the assistance of the United States, we can eliminate A. The western democracies stood aside while fascist Italy and Nazi Germany helped Franco win the Spanish Civil War, arguing against B. Though the US provided loans to Germany, its trade and financial policies helped lead to the Great Depression, excluding D. With the Versailles settlement, Britain and France actually advanced their colonial empires in the Middle East, Africa, and the Pacific, a move that advanced its power, at least temporarily. C is the key.

36. Answer: C. HTS: SAS & CES; Themes: SOP & NEI; KCs 1.2 & 1.5. The map shows the religious division of Europe, with many states facing significant religious minority populations. In states like France, the Holy Roman Empire, and Poland, the dominance of Catholicism was challenged by the spread of Calvinism, later leading to religious warfare (C). Clearly, states like Spain upheld a dominant Catholic position, excluding A. By 1600, England had emerged as the dominant Protestant state, due to its defeat of the Spanish Armada in 1588, which excludes B. Germany's religious division led not to toleration but to the Thirty Years' War in subsequent decades, eliminating D.

37. Answer: D. HTS: CAUS; Themes: SOP & NEI; KCs 1.2 & 1.5. The concern with religious uniformity led in part to the subsequent Thirty Years' War, dropping out A. The Council of Trent ended in 1563, so could not be a result of the situation shown (B). The power center of Europe did shift toward the Atlantic states, but this development owed more to the Commercial Revolution than to religious division. Since the religious divisions depicted were not yet accepted by Protestants and Catholics, warfare dominated the political landscape from 1517 to 1648, making D the answer.

38. Answer: C. HTS: CCOT & MAC; Themes: SOP & NEI; KCs 1.2 & 1.5. The Peace of Westphalia provided for the permanent religious division of the Holy Roman Empire and the independence of Protestant states (Dutch Republic and Switzerland), making it the last of the religious wars (C). Though the Peace of Augsburg divided Germany by religion, it proved a temporary solution, since the Thirty

Years' War took place a century later (A). The Edict of Nantes provided toleration for the Huguenots, but it was revoked by Louis XIV in 1685 (B). Finally, the French Revolution promoted a secular state, but the policies of the radicals repressed religious belief during the de-Christianization campaign, not exactly a solution to religious pluralism (D).

39. **Answer: B. HTS: CAUS & DAP; Themes: ECD & SCD; KC 1.4.** Several early modern developments contributed to the problems of poverty and begging. The expanding money economy produced new forms of wealth, but also caused inflation and stagnated manufacturing wages (A), but the more significant factor was the movement toward commercial agriculture. The break-up of agricultural communities displaced small shareholders, many of whom sought their livelihoods in nearby cities, where they often resorted to begging (B). New World crops would have provided a food outlet to address subsistence problems, excluding C. Choice D represents an accurate development but one largely unrelated to the issue of poverty (D).

40. **Answer: D. HTS: CTX & DAP; Themes: SOP, ECD, & SCD; KC 1.4.** Social welfare provisions were not enacted until the late nineteenth century, so we can cancel out A. The same is true for the developments in B. Landlords did often attempt to revive elements of feudalism, but this phenomenon would have promoted poverty, not resolved it (C). Since Protestants rejected the Catholic notion of good works as a means to salvation, they turned moral regulation and poor relief over to municipalities or states, as shown in this law from England, a Protestant state (D).

41. **Answer: B. HTS: COMP & MAC; Themes: ECD & SOP; KC 1.4.** The text shows the tightening of regulations to achieve a higher degree of social and economic control. In eastern Europe, the correlated development was the codification of serfdom, as in Russia (B). Though the European population reached a post-plague peak in 1600, the law does not deal with this issue directly, excluding A. With its dominance by nobles, eastern Europe lagged in the development of new economic elites, such as merchants or the gentry (C). Not only does the law omit mention of families, eastern Europe was, with its taxation system based on households, more likely to support extended families (D).

42. **Answer: A. HTS: SAS & CES; Themes: ECD, SOP, & SCD; KCs 2.1 & 2.2.** The Le Chapelier Law here abolished the guilds in favor of a free-market system and as such represented an attack on the vestiges of the old regime (A). The role of the monarchy (B) and Church (C) appear nowhere in the law, though they would be attacked with other revolutionary legislation. The Declaration of Rights of Man, cited in the passage, also attempted to remove exclusive noble control over offices, but this law does not address that issue, making D false.

43. **Answer: C. HTS: CCOT & CES; Themes: ECD & SOP; KC 2.1.** During the radical phase, the Committee of Public Safety enacted laws to control wages and prices, in re-

sponse to agitation from the artisans and shopkeepers of Paris (sans-culottes). This ran counter to the free-market system of the Le Chapelier Law here (C). Choices A, B, and D all express actions of the radical phase of the revolution, but they do not bear directly on the economic issues discussed in the law.

44. **Answer: B. HTS: CCOT, MAC, & CES; Themes: ECD & SOP; KCs 2.1 & 3.3.** Of the choices, the ideological framework most likely to endorse the free movement of labor and goods would be Liberalism (B). The other groups' attitudes toward this issue would have ranged from ambivalence (A and D) to hostility (C), leaving us with B.

45. **Answer: B. HTS: CAUS & SAS; Themes: SOP & NEI; KC 3.4.** The chart shows Hungarians as the largest ethnic minority, and indeed, Hungarians briefly established independence during the revolutions of 1848. To appease this largest minority group, the Austrian (German) rulers of the empire allowed for the creation of the Dual Monarchy, providing a high degree of autonomy to Hungarians (B). Any expansion of territory in the Balkans—as with the annexation of Bosnia in 1908—would only further complicate the ethnic situation given in the chart (A). At points after 1871, Austria formed an alliance with Germany and Russia, but this did not directly address its festering ethnic situation (C). Serfdom and feudalism had been abolished in 1848, and though it pleased peasants, it did not address ethnic issues (D).

46. **Answer: A. HTS: CCOT & MAC; Themes: SOP & NEI; KC 4.1.** The Allies fought World War I, especially after US involvement in 1917, with the idea of allowing self-determination, which spelled doom for multi-ethnic empires like Austria, which were broken up (A). Though the Allies blamed the Central Powers and created the League of Nations, these actions did not directly address ethnic issues within states, such as those shown on the chart (B and C). The level of US involvement diplomatically declined with the Senate's refusal to approve the Versailles Treaty and join the League of Nations, and these actions, once again, did not bear directly on ethnicity (D).

47. **Answer: D. HTS: SAS & CES; Themes: SOP & NTI; KC 4.1.** Each of these choices, emphasizing a particular cause of the war, could be supported with examples from the period prior to 1914. But our question deals specifically with the ethnic issues represented in the chart, so the interpretation most closely aligned is D, and not A, B, or C.

48. **Answer: C. HTS: CTX & CAUS; Themes: TSI & SOP; KCs 3.4 & 4.2.** Goebbels focuses on the potential of new communication devices (such as the radio) to alter the relationship between the state and the individual, a major feature of mass politics after 1850 (C). Dictatorships also promoted state-run leisure, but the expansion of leisure in the nineteenth century is only indirectly related to Goebbels's analysis (A). The passage does not address or bear directly upon imperialism (B) or interstate conflict, though Goebbels (as a Nazi) would certainly have an eye toward

this possibility in the future, with the radio as a means to mobilize the German population (D). C is the best choice.

49. **Answer: D. HTS: COMP, MAC, & CCOT; Themes: SOP & NEI; KCs 2.1 & 4.1.** Napoleon and Hitler both appealed to the masses (A), employed warfare to promote internal unity (B), and manipulated their images to gain support for their regimes (C). However, Napoleon, unlike Hitler, did not seek to create a racial empire; his motives were more personal and political. Thus, D is the outlier.

50. **Answer: C. HTS: COMP & MAC; Themes: SOP & TSI; KC 4.2.** Both Hitler and Stalin created totalitarian regimes and employed media to establish a cult of personality, giving us C. The other states ranged from republics to authoritarian regimes, and either did not embrace Hitler's goals (D) or could not mobilize such a high degree of popular support (A and B).

51. **Answer: A. HTS: CAUS; Themes: SOP, NEI, & ECD; KC 4.2.** This question does not require the stimulus, so you can draw directly from your historical knowledge. You may recall that the policy of appeasement *followed* the establishment of Nazi rule, thus rendering it moot as a cause (A). A main pillar of Nazi ideology was anti-Communism, which Hitler used to gain absolute control after accusing communists of starting the Reichstag fire, shortly after he was appointed Chancellor (B). Since the Weimar Republic lacked support from key elites (C) and failed to address (or worsened) Germany's economic problems (D), Hitler was able to promise a strong hand in reestablishing stability, prosperity, and power.

52. **Answer: B. HTS: CTX & DAP; Themes: ECD & SD; KCs 4.3 & 4.4.** These slogans express discontent as part of the 1968 student revolts. As population and college opportunities expanded, universities experienced the stress of overcrowding and rebellion against the bureaucratization of college life—the fundamental causes of the revolts (A). Despite the post-1945 economic recovery, the students condemn the consumerist values of their elders in the slogans (C). Clearly the theme of liberation runs through all of the slogans (D). However, we see no reference to the post-1945 trend of increased immigration from outside Europe, giving B as the key.

53. **Answer: D. HTS: CAUS, MAC, SAS, & CCOT; Themes: SOP, CID, & SCD; KCs 2.1, 4.3, & 4.4.** The key requires drawing a connection across a significant time period. In the slogans one is struck by the theme of liberation, and the movement among those given most closely associated with this theme is D (French Revolution). Though the other movements altered features of European life, they did embrace the rhetoric of violence against the old regime as presented by the student revolutionaries, thus eliminating A, B, and C.

54. **Answer: C. HTS: COMP & MAC; Themes: SCD & SOP; KC 4.4.** Choices A, B, and D all occurred within the context of traditional values and did not necessitate an alteration of values regarding women or give rise to their liberation. Many women returned home after involvement in wartime manufacturing (A). Increased leisure time without access to autonomy would not coincide for women with the desire for liberation in the slogans. Pro-natalist policies reinforced the notion of women as mothers and homemakers (D). We are left with C, and yes, many women gained increased access to positions of power (e.g., Margaret Thatcher) and served increasingly in legislatures (especially in Scandinavian nations). Thus, the students and women both sought access to power.

55. **Answer: B. HTS: COMP & MAC; Themes: SOP, ECD, & SCD; KCs 4.2 & 4.4.** Each of these choices coincides with movements against repression. However, the student revolts in Paris were echoed in that same year (1968) by the Prague Spring, another youth movement aimed against bureaucracy and an out-of-touch government (B). The Algerian War employed a much higher degree of violence and lasted much longer (A). Unlike the fall of the Berlin Wall, the 1968 revolts did not meet with ultimate success (C). The defeat of the Nazis was caused primarily by powerful states marshaling all of their resources, rather than a discontented segment within a state (D).

SAQ Sample Responses with Commentary

1. **a)** One reason for the rise in authoritarian forms of government is the creation of weak democracies during the interwar period as part of the Treaty of Versailles. This would allow for that situation because, in these democracies there was no tradition of democracy and thus they would be susceptible to authoritarian forms of government that were more in line with their tradition.

   b) A second economic reason for the populist authoritarian governments gaining popularity over democracies is the rising distaste for democracy that grew out of the Great Depression. This is no better shown than in Germany under the Weimar Republic. The failures of the Weimar Republic to deal with inflation and unemployment would provide a platform by which the Nazis would use to gain popularity.

   c) One effect that the rise of the Soviet Union had on the diplomacy of Europeans is that it would promote movements toward unity by creating a common enemy. One such example of the unity movements created to combat the USSR is NATO, created explicitly by the US as a part of their containment policy. Although the Soviet Union would actually split Europe in two, the movements toward unity would rise out of the western blocs created to protect against communism and other forms of totalitarianism.

On one hand, the response deals effectively with Part A by explaining briefly how the Treaty of Versailles created fragile states with a limited tradition of democracy. Next, the response explains accurately in Part B how the Great Depression undermined faith in the new Weimar Republic and led to the rise of the Nazis. However, the discussion in Part C errs in invoking the Cold War and NATO, as these examples lie outside of the 1919–1939 era indicated by the map. **Score: 2 points**

2. **a)** One major change in the period 1700–1850 that changed ideas of children were the ideas of Locke and Rousseau, who took Enlightenment principles of reason and progress to stress a more humane and scientific approach toward raising children.

b) Because of growing commerce during this period, there were new consumer goods that parents could purchase for their children—like age-specific books and toys—to help them learn and adapt to the world.

c) These new ideas applied mostly to the upper classes who could afford child-centered products, whereas the lower-class still labored along with parents in agriculture or worse yet, in some of the terrible factories in Britain during industrialization.

Here we have a model of clarity and concision in approaching the task. Despite writing only one sentence for each part, the response earns all three points: for discussing the Enlightenment with Locke and Rousseau for Part A; for noting new consumer goods for children in context of expanding commerce in Part B; and for qualifying the interpretation with an appropriate reference to class differences and poor conditions for children in industry in Part C. **Score: 3 points**

3. **a)** The printing press revolutionized intellectual life by making ideas more easily accessible. During the Renaissance, the printing press allowed for more standard editions of works, like Machiavelli's writings and other Latin and Greek classics. Also, it helped spread the Renaissance to northern areas, such as the Netherlands and Germany.

b) A religious effect of the printing press was the spread of Newton's idea of natural laws. His portrayal of the universe as a giant clock caused people to question the need for an all-powerful God to explain everything.

c) One other major invention of this era was the reliance on gunpowder in warfare. With this development, there was less reliance on noble warriors and the code of chiv-

alry. Both the printing press and gunpowder challenged traditional ways, whether in ideas or in politics, and set the stage for new methods of thinking and fighting.

In this response, we see the dangers of chronological errors. In Part A, the response earns a point for accurately explaining the spread of the Renaissance to the north, as well as the standardization of texts. However, the reference to Newton in Part B is outside the time period (by almost a century) and thus not responsive to the prompt. However, the response recovers with an accurate explanation of gunpowder's effect, albeit with minimal analysis in connection with the printing press: "challenged traditional ways" and "new methods." **Score: 2 points**

4.   Western and Eastern Europe experienced different effects from the Cold War. Because of America's Marshall Plan, the West had an "economic miracle," while Eastern Europe tended to experience domination by the USSR. Their economies were forced to produce goods that benefited COMECON. This shows a major economic reason for the Cold War: America wanted to develop capitalism in their bloc, while the USSR wanted to establish a command system with no free markets. The two superpowers also clashed over Germany, especially Berlin, because it was strategically vital and had been the cause of two world wars. This conflict led to major events of the Cold War, like the Berlin Airlift and the creation of NATO.

Though the format of a paragraph (with no specification of the parts of the question) is not recommended, the response here does answer all parts of the question, even if out of order. First, it notes the differing effects of the Cold War on Western and Eastern Europe, with reference to the Marshall Plan and COMECON (Part C). Next, the response transitions to a brief but sufficient account of the economic differences between capitalism and the Soviet "command economy" (Part A). Finally, in Part B the response explains the importance of Germany and references two specific instances of "clash" there between the superpowers (Berlin Airlift and NATO). **Score: 3 points**

DBQ Sample Response with Commentary

The Enlightenment and Romanticism were two events that occurred back to back, with the Enlightenment expressing control over nature and disproving religion, while Romanticism emphasized a revival of religion and the power of nature. The Enlightenment, which occurred just after the Scientific Revolution, was an attempt of Europeans to apply the methods of the new science, such as empiricism and natural laws, to all areas of human life. This movement encouraged humans to see their power over nature and often disproved religion, because it is not tangible. Romantics, who emerged about a century later, rejected the Enlightenment by reviving religion and discovering the awe that nature possessed.

Europeans' view of nature had traditionally been subjective, as they often followed what they had been told by their religions and other traditional authorities. Some even resorted to folktales and mysticism to dictate the happenings of the universe. However, this changed with the Scientific Revolution and its application to everyday life, which was known as the Enlightenment. With the Enlightenment, the application of fixed laws of nature became prominent within European societies. Artists, such as Joseph Wright (Doc. 4), often reflected this in their works, especially through the impressionism art movement, which experimented with light, shadow and scientific discoveries. This source is an accurate representation of the Enlightenment laws and how they are applied, because of its depiction and detail. The children and adult onlookers seem intrigued by the orrery demonstration, which was a typical response to all information that was being discovered about gaining control of nature. Similar to the painting, many philosophers used the fixed laws of nature to disprove mysteries of the universe, such as miracles. David Hume (Doc. 1) discusses how "a uniform experience amounts to a proof," which cannot be destroyed. His interpretation was a typical one of the time period. He also discovers how miracles "are violations of the laws of nature," which were discovered to be valid during the Scientific Revolution. However, it is not surprising that he would take this standpoint, given that he is a philosopher and intends to support a logical approach to questions. Unlike the two documents, and the Enlightenment approach of nature, Romantics did not see nature to be controlled, but they were in awe of its prestige and power. For example, Document 7 is a painting by German painter Friedrich, which shows a solitary man gazing out at a mysterious landscape, perhaps filled with wonder and awe. Friedrich's painting reflects the classic view of Romantics, who respected nature and wished to become one with it. The views of nature drastically changed from the Enlightenment period to the next century of Romanticism, which was almost a direct response to science.

In addition to fixed laws of nature, the Enlightenment also contained intellectuals who encouraged the idea of the "General Will" of the people and that humans should have choices when it came to religion. Also from the Enlightenment grew Enlightened Despots, such as Frederick II "the Great" of Prussia, who used Enlightenment ideals in their ruling. Doc 3 addresses the fact that politics and religion should not be concerned with each other, and that rulers should not be able to choose their subjects' religion. He also expresses how Lutherans, Catholics, Jews and other religions lived in peace. It is not surprising that Frederick II would express this sentiment, seeing that he is a ruler and wants to spread his popularity among citizens in Prussia. Another enlightened despot, who expressed similar beliefs except with women was, Catherine "the Great" of Russia, who encouraged their better status and education. Although Romantics never really expressed an opinion on religious pluralism and toleration, they encouraged it in an attempt to express religiosity and its greatness. For example, in Doc. 5, Chateaubriand of France discusses the awe that nature brings and expresses through religion by saying that old gothic style buildings and broken tree trunks excite a feeling of "religious awe, mystery and divinity." His works are significant because they expressed the feeling of awe that nature brought to religion, in contrast to the scientist view of the control of nature. Similar to Chateaubriand, Doc 6 is a poem by an English romantic poet, Lord Byron, who was famous for his poetry and controversial lifestyle. His poem, "Manfred" expresses the revival of religion by saying that "silent worship of the Great of Old" would bring wonder and success to the people of Europe. His works expressed the revival of a powerful religion, which was thought to be disproved by scientists, by showing that science and fixed laws were not always the end-all-be-all.

The Enlightenment and Romanticism and their different views on nature and religion show how movements can respond to one another. Romantics revived religion and a sense of awe of the wonders of nature, proving that knowledge doesn't always have to derive from direct science and reason. Romanticism was significant because it gave way to later developments such as Freud's theories that glorified irrationality.

This is a strong response and a model of focused writing. The introduction sets up the question well—earning the Contextualization point for its brief connection of the Scientific Revolution with the Enlightenment—and taking a clear position on the question (Romanticism rejected Enlightenment attitudes about religion and nature) to earn the Thesis point. In the body paragraphs, the student goes on to earn the Complexity point by effective juxtaposition of the documents to show corroboration (Documents 4 and 1) and qualification (Documents 4 and 1 vs. Document 7), as well as with consistent use of historical context to support the analysis of the documents. All 7 documents are used to make an argument on the two movements, earning 2 points for Document Use. Though the student earns the Source Analysis point with examples for three documents—Document 1 (point of view), Document 7 (historical context), and Document 3 (purpose)—the attempt with Document 4 falls short, due to lack of explanation and the inaccurate connection to Impressionism. Finally, Evidence Beyond Documents is earned (minimally) through the reference to Catherine the Great. **Score: 7** (+1 for Thesis, +1 for Contextualization, +2 for Use of Documents, +1 for Evidence Beyond the Documents, +1 for Source Analysis, +1 for Complexity).

LEQ Sample Responses with Commentary

LEQ 2

In the period 1450–1650, Europe was expanding. Christopher Columbus's discoveries were spreading and many nations ventured out into the New World in search of wealth and power, helping to create the Columbian Exchange. This age of discovery led to a push towards the increasing desire of working to make a profit, also known as capitalism. The increase in capitalism led to many effects, such as population growth and a change in gender roles. However, the most important effect of the development of capitalism during this period were the new social classes created, such as the gentry class in England, and the bourgeoisie in France and the Netherlands.

One example of the new social classes created was the gentry class in England. When the rise of capitalism increased in the sixteenth century, the gentry class, made up of middle and high nobility, was at the center of it. Many gentries would increase their property and proceed to lend their land to capitalists, or they would also participate in capitalist activities themselves and try to overthrow the feudal system that was happening in the nation. For instance, Oliver Cromwell was a part of the English gentry class and led parliamentary forces to fight in the English Civil War, which was a war that was aimed at removing Charles I from the throne and abolishing the feudal system.

Another example of the social classes was the French bourgeoisie. The bourgeoisie class of France was a middle class designed specifically for economic and capitalist interests. These people would usually take the place of decreasing old nobility powers and earned their place by the purchase of land and offices. With capitalism slowly rising, King Louis XIV of France also chose bourgeois men as his officers instead of traditional nobility, many of whom soon held very important positions in administration and pushed capitalist practices, replacing feudalism.

Additionally, another one of these new social classes created was the bourgeoisie class in the Netherlands. At the time, the Netherlands were at the center of trade due to them being near the Baltic Sea. As trade increased, there was a shift between a guild system, which was the original system of production, when the Netherlands was dominated by Spanish absolutism, to a capitalist system, up until the seventeenth century. To counter the Spanish, the bourgeoisie revolted against Phillip II's high taxes, who was Spanish king at the time, in an attempt to promote capitalism. Although they weren't as successful in the south, the Northern Netherlands was able to establish capitalist ways, and the bourgeoisie class was able to bring back the economy and become strong.

While the development of capitalism had many important effects that shaped modern Europe, the most important effect had to be the rise of new social classes. The English gentry, French bourgeoisie, and Dutch bourgeoisie all emerged through capitalism in their nation. From this, they were able to establish capitalism, lead the way in reforms and revolution for their nations, and push Europe's economy forward toward capitalism.

Though offering up some errors (effect of gender roles; gentry being part of English nobility), this essay does concisely address the prompt with sufficient evidence. Albeit brief, the Contextualization in the introduction (New World, Columbian Exchange) adequately meets the rubric standard. Also, the essay establishes a clear position in noting the rise of new classes. With three nations represented, the response provides sufficient examples and applies them to the argument to earn both Evidence points. Also, since the essay remains generally focused on its central point regarding classes, it earns the Targeted RP point. However, the mere discussion of three different nations falls short of earning the Complexity point. Perhaps the essay might have explored another effect, such as the population changes noted in the introduction, for the strategy of multiple perspectives. **Score: 5** (+1 for Thesis, +1 for Contextualization, +2 for Use of Evidence, +1 for the Targeted RP (CAUS))

LEQ 3

After the French Revolution, nationalistic ideologies were beginning to peak in the nineteenth century. However, while the Congress of Vienna may have tried to contain riots and revolts within nations that were spurred by Napoleon's policies and ideas, the subsequent Crimean War and the Revolutions of 1848 escalated the urge for unification and decimated the Concert of Europe. Thus, nationalism and the development of *Realpolitik*, a diplomatic method of using mass politics and strategies to increase the power of a nation, caused the unification of Italy and Germany. Nonetheless, since many smaller states were becoming unified, there was a great deal of change in the balance of power as both nations industrialized more efficiently and expanded their armies.

Cavour and Otto von Bismarck both instituted *Realpolitik* approaches to their diplomacy, and therefore, used nationalistic woes to heighten the unification of Italy and Germany respectively. To begin, Cavour strategically made decisions that benefitted the joining of the Italian states. He persuaded France to help Piedmont-Sardinia fight against Austria and won in doing so. As revolutions were taking place in the north, he urged Garibaldi, the leader of the Red Shirts, to use his army and move up the peninsula. Since many people welcomed the unification of Italy, little violence was necessary and it was deemed a nation in 1861. Bismarck also made tactical decisions when the opportunity presented itself. For instance, he partook in three wars that all isolated countries and made Germany easily defeat them. During the Austro-Prussian war, he made sure the surrounding countries did not help Austria, as Bismarck supported the Russian conquest of the Polish revolt, presented France with thoughts of expansion, and gave Italy hope of land. He also provoked France to call war upon Germany with the Ems Dispatch, making it seem as if the king insulted the French ambassador, and easily triumphed in the war. Thus, he used prudent judgments to assist the nation. However, both nations witnessed nationalistic ideologies reach a new height because of its presence in the French Revolution and in the policies of Napoleon, which only promoted the fusion of states.

Nonetheless, since Italy and Germany were unified, their ability to develop a stronger economy and an increase in political standing were promoted, and thus shifted the delicate balance of power. Italy industrialized more efficiently as it was open to new resources that facilitated economic growth, and sustained imperialistic lands abroad. For Germany, Bismarck wanted to get as much power as possible, and made sure he continued to be Chancellor and Prime Minister of State, which gave him control in diplomatic relations. He also tried restricting the growth of the Social Democratic Party by executing welfare programs, which in turn supported the economy. Yet, when the hot-headed Kaiser Wilhelm II dismissed Bismarck, his inability to negotiate and keep peace, and his focus in matching Germany's naval power to Britain's, helped lead into WWI. However, since Italy and Germany unified, their economic and military potential did thwart the balance of power within Europe that was previously set by the Congress of Vienna.

Italy and Germany's unifications were spurred by nationalistic beliefs taking hold and also new methods of political negotiations. As they both partook a larger economic foothold within Europe, their political influence increased. This nationalistic outlook also influenced art and culture of the period. In Delacroix's *Liberty Leading the People*, the artist shows the symbol of the French nation (a vulnerable woman) rallying the people against the oppression of the corrupt monarchy. This is similar to the famous painting of Bismarck at the center of the scene in the Hall of Mirrors as the German Empire is proclaimed. It is clear that nationalism unified states and shaped cultural outlooks.

The response begins with a strong introduction, as the response provides an effective background on the Congress of Vienna, revolutions of 1848, and Crimean War, linking these to the growth of nationalism and impulse toward national unity. Though results are suggested, nowhere does the response take a position on the question—identifying and discussing the *most* important result. For the Targeted RP, the student both describes and explains the reasons for and effects of the unifications, though with stronger detail on Germany with effects, earning both points. Also, abundant examples are provided and, while the essay falls into narration, it brings the analysis back to applying the examples to an argument, earning both Evidence points. To conclude, the essay provides a creative extension of the argument regarding nationalism to an additional theme (CID): the arts. **Score: 5** (+1 for Contextualization, +2 for Use of Evidence, +1 for the Targeted RP (CAUS), +1 for Complexity).

Immediately after World War II, many European countries, especially Britain and Germany, were crippled economically because of the astronomical sums of money they used for the war. This is not even factoring in the amount of money that Germany had to make for reparations. Both countries borrowed large amounts of money from the US, and this plunged them into even greater debt later on. Luckily, both countries regained their former standing and economical power thanks to the US Marshall Plan.

After WWII, many European countries, especially the largest such as Russia, Britain, and Germany suffered from both bombed out cities and destroyed factories, as well as horrible economic deficits. Both Britain and Germany started borrowing large sums from the US, which were funneled back to the US from Germany's reparations. Many countries started printing tons of money, called inflation, to avoid going bankrupt. Though this worked in the short term, it eventually devalued currencies, decreasing the ability of the workers to buy food and clothing even more.

Even after all of these horrible things, Europe's market was able to go back to the way it was, and even surpass its old power. This is largely due to three different reasons: first, Europe wasn't at war anymore, allowing it to sell its goods, which during the war could not really be exported, as well as leaving it open to foreign investment, and, without the Allies (or Axis) destroying factories and fields, the economy could grow back to its pre-war might. Second, the Marshall Plan, named after Secretary of State George Marshall, which pooled money from countries not so badly impacted by the war, and spread that money throughout the other European states, with the exception of Russia and the Eastern Bloc countries, so that they could again rebuild to their former glory. Last, but certainly not least, the Axis stifled the ability of many countries to buy or sell goods, and all of this need for goods built up until the end of the war. Also, as a side note, the pressures and needs of total war prepared the European countries for rebuilding of both their economy and the internal systems, such as apartments and farms, because the machines and techniques used to create bunkers could easily be turned for use by the government to create infrastructure. The change from poverty stricken Europe to economic giant Europe was created by the lessons that Europe learned from all of the nationalist destruction, working toward some unity.

This is because all of the governments tried to think of ways in which to solve the many problems arrayed before them and caused by the war. The states learned how to work together and spread the wealth from the problems caused by total war, and used this new knowledge quite a bit in the future.

This essay suffers from two problems—it conflates the post-World War II situation with that of post-World War I, and it does not address the effects of Europe's economic recovery in any systematic way. An adequate Thesis that addresses the question cannot be found in either the introduction or the conclusion. Since the essay does not address effects in its analysis and provides a confused discussion of causes, it does not earn the Targeted RP. However, the student does provide some relevant examples, despite vagueness and simplifying, to address the question—Marshall Plan, pent-up demand, nationalism to unity. Because of the confusion, the examples are not applied consistently to the thesis, limiting the Use of Evidence point to 1. Finally, without further specifics or explicit connections, the brief conclusion falls far short of the Complexity point. This response serves as a warning to *answer the question asked* as to task, chronology, geography. **Score: 1** (+1 for Use of Evidence).

APPENDICES:
Chronological Supplement—Timelines

To assist in your chronological mastery of the course, you will find three different timelines in this section. With the first timeline, you can identify the major eras and developments by centuries. Next is a list of important dates to provide you with a strong base of chronology that supports your application of HTS. It is strongly recommended that you commit these dates to memory as guideposts. Finally, you can consult the more developed timeline categorized by the themes to make connections across the them and the time periods.

Timeline 1: Important Eras and Developments (by century)

Renaissance—1350–1550

Exploration—1450–1600

Protestant and Catholic Reformations—16th century

Religious Wars—1520s–1650

Early Modern Society—1500–1700

Price Revolution—16th century

Dutch Commercial Dominance—1550–1650

Age of Crisis—1550–1650

Witchcraft Scare—1580–1680

Scientific Revolution—1543–1687

Baroque Art—1600–1750

Conflict between Parliament and King in England—1603–1689

Age of Louis XIV—1643–1715

Absolutism—1650–1750

Commercial Wars—1650–1763

Rise of Prussia—1650–1763

Rise of Russia—1689–1815

Commercial Revolution—17th and 18th centuries

Rococo Art—1720–1760

Rise of the Middle Class—18th century

Enlightenment—18th century

Agricultural Revolution—18th century

Age of Revolutions—1789–1848

Feminism—1790s–1980s

Romanticism—First half of 19th century

Rise of Nationalism—1790s–1914

Unification and Nation-Building—1850–1875

Rise of Liberalism—1830s–1870s

Industrial Revolution—1750–1850

Realism and Materialism—1850–1870s

Second Industrial Revolution—1850–1914

Imperialism—1850–1914

Modern Ideas and Science—1850–1920s

Modern Art—1870–1920

Rise of Modern Society—Second half of 19th century

Totalitarianism—1920s–1945

World Wars—1914–1945

Cold War—1945–1991

European Unity—1945–Present

War on Terror—2001–Present

> ### NOTE
> A century refers to the hundred years numerically **prior** to the number of the century (e.g., the 16th century covers the 1500s).

Timeline 2: Important Dates to Commit to Memory

1348–1351—Black Death

1415–1417—Council of Constance burns Hus and ends Great Schism

1453—Fall of Constantinople; end of Hundred Years' War

1455—Invention of printing press

1492—Columbus encounters America; completion of *reconquista* in Spain

1517—Luther posts 95 Theses

1519—Cortez conquers Aztecs

1534—Act of Supremacy in England creates Anglican Church

1536—Calvin establishes reformed faith in Geneva

1543—Copernicus publishes heliocentric theory

1545—Council of Trent opens

1555—Peace of Augsburg ends religious war in Germany; Charles V abdicates

1588—Defeat of Spanish Armada

1598—Edict of Nantes ends French religious wars

1600—Dutch East India Company founded

1603—Stuart monarchy begins in England

1648—Peace of Westphalia ends Thirty Years' War

1649—Charles I executed in England

1687—Newton publishes *Principia Mathematica*

1688–1689—Glorious Revolution; Peter the Great's reign begins in Russia

1694—Bank of England founded

1713–1715—Peace of Utrecht; death of Louis XIV

1740—War of Austrian Succession begins

1763—Treaty of Paris ends Seven Years' War

1776—American Revolution; Smith publishes *Wealth of Nations*

1789—French Revolution begins

1792—Wollstonecraft begins feminist movement with *Vindication of Rights of Women*

1799—Napoleon comes to power in France

1815—Abdication of Napoleon; Congress of Vienna

1830–1831—Revolution in France; Belgian and Greek independence

1848—Revolutions of 1848; Marx and Engels publish *Communist Manifesto*

1851—Crystal Palace Exhibition in Britain

1857—Britain establishes direct rule of India

1859—Darwin publishes *On the Origin of Species*

1861—Italy unified; Russian serfs emancipated

1871—Unification of Germany; Paris Commune and Third Republic in France

1884–1885—Berlin Conference over imperialism in Africa

1900—Freud publishes *Interpretation of Dreams*

1905—Einstein publishes relativity theory; Revolution of 1905 in Russia

1914—World War I begins

1917—Bolshevik Revolution in Russia

1919—Treaty of Versailles ends World War I

1922—Fascists and Mussolini come to power in Italy

1929—Great Depression begins

1933—Hitler comes to power in Germany

1938—Munich Conference—height of appeasement

1939—World War II begins

1945—World War II ends; United Nations founded

1949—NATO formed

1951—European Coal and Steel Community (ECSC) formed

1953—Stalin dies

1956—Khrushchev's de-Stalinization speech; Hungary revolt

1957—Treaty of Rome creates European Economic Community (EEC); Sputnik launched

1958—Fifth Republic in France under DeGaulle

1961—Berlin Wall erected

1962—Cuban Missile Crisis

1962—Second Vatican Council begins

1968—Student revolts; Czech "Prague Spring" revolt

1975—Helsinki Accords—height of détente

1978—John Paul II elected pope

1979—Soviet Union invades Afghanistan; Thatcher elected prime minister in Britain

1980—Solidarity founded in Poland

1985—Gorbachev comes to power in Soviet Union

1989—Berlin Wall falls and collapse of communism

1991—Break-up of Soviet Union; Balkan conflicts begin in former Yugoslavia

1992—Maastricht Treaty creates European Union (EU)

2001—Terrorist attacks on United States

2002—Euro currency released into circulation

2005—Angela Merkel elected Chancellor of Germany

2009—European debt (euro) crisis begins

2014—Russia annexes Crimea and occupies parts of Ukraine

2015–2016—Terrorist attacks in Paris and Brussels

2016—United Kingdom votes to leave EU (Brexit)

Timeline 3: Key Topics and Events by Theme

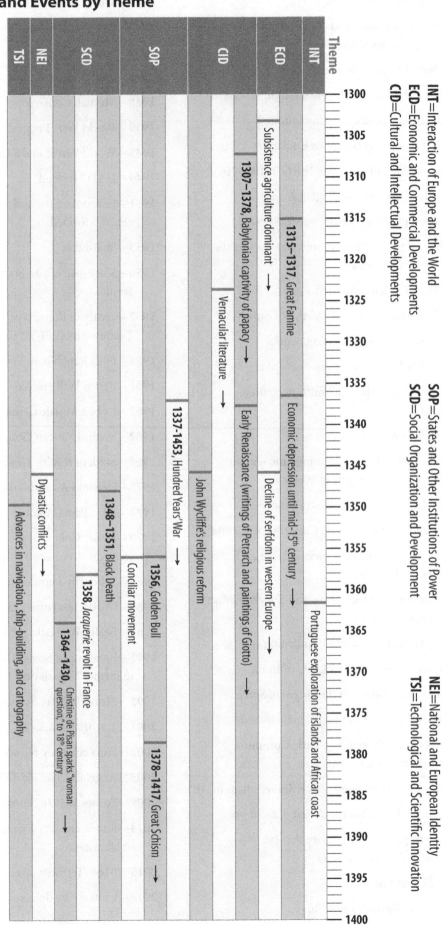

INT=Interaction of Europe and the World
ECD=Economic and Commercial Developments
CID=Cultural and Intellectual Developments

SOP=States and Other Institutions of Power
SCD=Social Organization and Development

NEI=National and European Identity
TSI=Technological and Scientific Innovation

Theme	
INT	
ECD	Subsistence agriculture dominant →
CID	**1307–1378**, Babylonian captivity of papacy →
SOP	**1315–1317**, Great Famine
SCD	
NEI	
TSI	

Economic depression until mid-15th century

Vernacular literature →

Early Renaissance (writings of Petrarch and paintings of Giotto) →

Decline of serfdom in western Europe →

1337-1453, Hundred Years' War →

John Wycliffe's religious reform →

1348–1351, Black Death

Conciliar movement

1356, Golden Bull

1358, *Jacquerie* revolt in France

Dynastic conflicts →

1364–1430, Christine de Pisan sparks "woman question," to 18th century →

1378–1417, Great Schism →

Portuguese exploration of islands and African coast

Advances in navigation, ship-building, and cartography

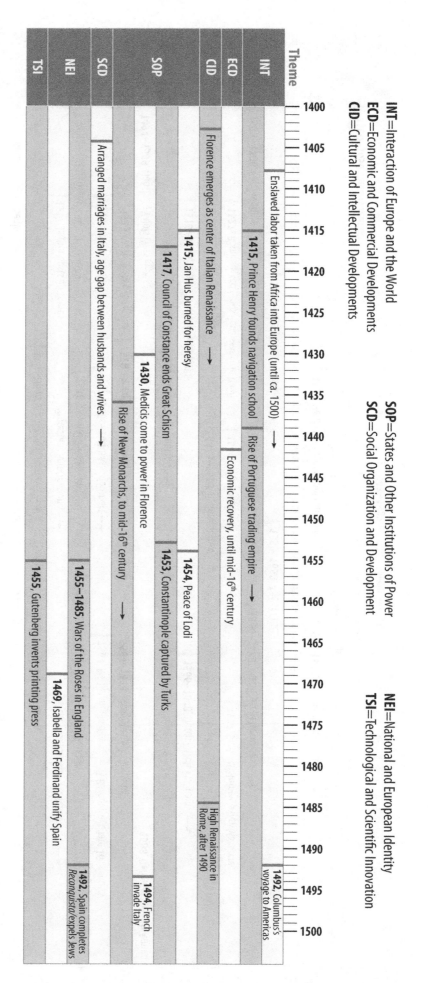

INT=Interaction of Europe and the World
ECD=Economic and Commercial Developments
CID=Cultural and Intellectual Developments

SOP=States and Other Institutions of Power
SCD=Social Organization and Development

NEI=National and European Identity
TSI=Technological and Scientific Innovation

Theme		
INT	Enslaved labor taken from Africa into Europe (until ca. 1500) →	1492, Columbus's voyage to Americas
ECD	1415, Prince Henry founds navigation school	Rise of Portuguese trading empire →
		Economic recovery, until mid-16th century
CID	Florence emerges as center of Italian Renaissance →	High Renaissance in Rome, after 1490
	1415, Jan Hus burned for heresy →	
	1417, Council of Constance ends Great Schism	
	1430, Medicis come to power in Florence	
SOP	Rise of New Monarchs, to mid-16th century →	1494, French invade Italy
	1454, Peace of Lodi	
	1453, Constantinople captured by Turks	
SCD	Arranged marriages in Italy, age gap between husbands and wives →	
NEI	1455–1485, Wars of the Roses in England →	1492, Spain completes *Reconquista*/expels Jews
	1469, Isabella and Ferdinand unify Spain	
TSI	1455, Gutenberg invents printing press	

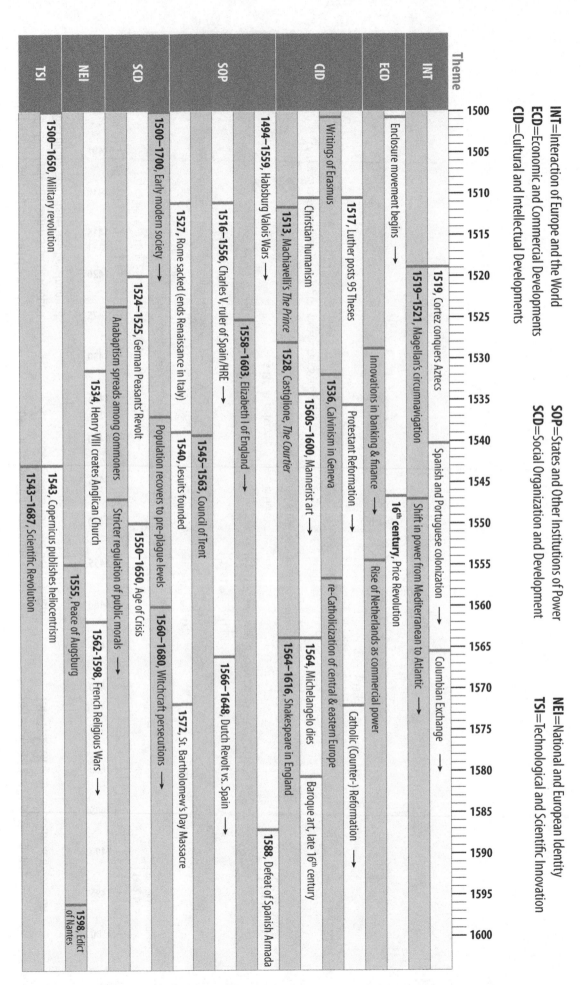

Theme

INT=Interaction of Europe and the World
ECD=Economic and Commercial Developments
CID=Cultural and Intellectual Developments

SOP=States and Other Institutions of Power
SCD=Social Organization and Development

NEI=National and European Identity
TSI=Technological and Scientific Innovation

| | 1500 | | | | 1520 | | | | | | | | | | | | | | | 1600 |

INT
- Enclosure movement begins →
- **1519**, Cortez conquers Aztecs
- **1519–1521**, Magellan's circumnavigation
- Spanish and Portuguese colonization →
- Columbian Exchange →

ECD
- Innovations in banking & finance
- **16th century**, Price Revolution
- Shift in power from Mediterranean to Atlantic →
- Rise of Netherlands as commercial power

CID
- Writings of Erasmus
- **1517**, Luther posts 95 Theses
- Christian humanism
- **1513**, Machiavelli's *The Prince*
- **1528**, Castiglione, *The Courtier*
- **1536**, Calvinism in Geneva
- Protestant Reformation →
- **1560s–1600**, Mannerist art →
- re-Catholicization of central & eastern Europe
- Catholic (Counter-) Reformation →
- **1564**, Michelangelo dies
- Baroque art, late 16th century
- **1564–1616**, Shakespeare in England

SOP
- **1494–1559**, Habsburg Valois Wars →
- **1516–1556**, Charles V, ruler of Spain/HRE →
- **1527**, Rome sacked (ends Renaissance in Italy)
- **1558–1603**, Elizabeth I of England →
- **1540**, Jesuits founded
- **1545–1563**, Council of Trent
- **1560–1680**, Witchcraft persecutions →
- **1566–1648**, Dutch Revolt vs. Spain →
- **1572**, St. Bartholomew's Day Massacre
- **1588**, Defeat of Spanish Armada

SCD
- **1500–1700**, Early modern society →
- **1524–1525**, German Peasants' Revolt
- Population recovers to pre-plague levels
- Stricter regulation of public morals
- **1550–1650**, Age of Crisis

NEI
- **1534**, Henry VIII creates Anglican Church
- Anabaptism spreads among commoners
- **1555**, Peace of Augsburg
- **1562–1598**, French Religious Wars →
- **1598**, Edict of Nantes

TSI
- **1500–1650**, Military revolution
- **1543**, Copernicus publishes heliocentrism
- **1543–1687**, Scientific Revolution

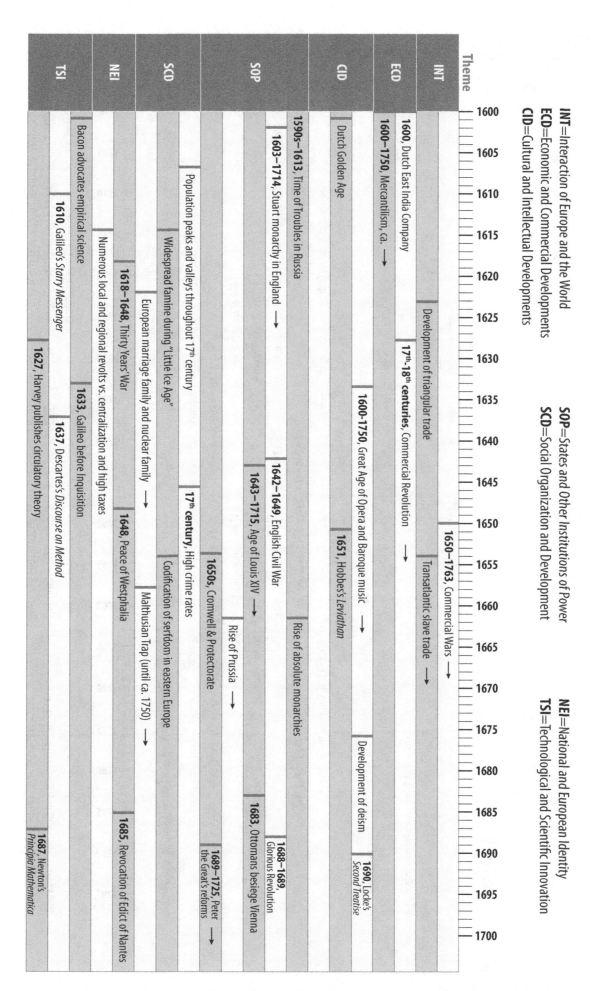

Theme

INT=Interaction of Europe and the World
ECD=Economic and Commercial Developments
CID=Cultural and Intellectual Developments

SOP=States and Other Institutions of Power
SCD=Social Organization and Development

NEI=National and European Identity
TSI=Technological and Scientific Innovation

INT

1600, Dutch East India Company

Development of triangular trade

1650–1763, Commercial Wars →

ECD

1600–1750, Mercantilism, ca. →

17th–18th centuries, Commercial Revolution →

Transatlantic slave trade →

CID

Dutch Golden Age

1600–1750, Great Age of Opera and Baroque music →

1651, Hobbes's *Leviathan*

Development of deism

1690, Locke's *Second Treatise*

SOP

1590s–1613, Time of Troubles in Russia

1603–1714, Stuart monarchy in England →

1642–1649, English Civil War

1643–1715, Age of Louis XIV →

1650s, Cromwell & Protectorate

Rise of Prussia →

Rise of absolute monarchies

1683, Ottomans besiege Vienna

1688–1689, Glorious Revolution

1689–1725, Peter the Great's reforms →

SCD

Population peaks and valleys throughout 17th century

Widespread famine during "Little Ice Age"

European marriage family and nuclear family →

17th century, High crime rates

Codification of serfdom in eastern Europe

Malthusian Trap (until ca. 1750) →

NEI

Numerous local and regional revolts vs. centralization and high taxes

1618–1648, Thirty Years' War

1648, Peace of Westphalia

1685, Revocation of Edict of Nantes

TSI

Bacon advocates empirical science

1610, Galileo's *Starry Messenger*

1633, Galileo before Inquisition

1637, Descartes's *Discourse on Method*

1627, Harvey publishes circulatory theory

1687, Newton's *Principia Mathematica*

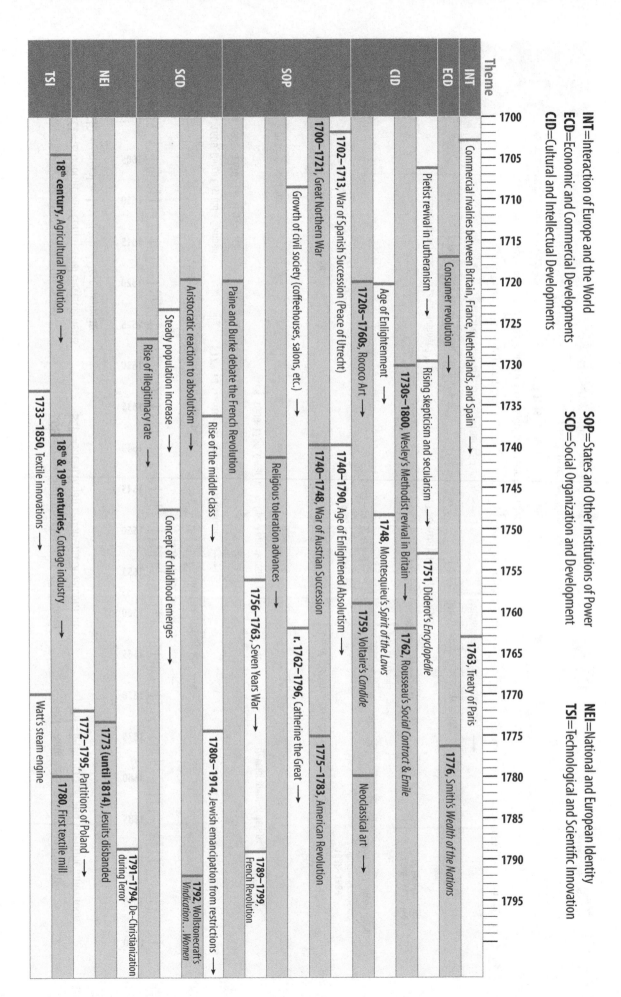

INT=Interaction of Europe and the World
ECD=Economic and Commercial Developments
CID=Cultural and Intellectual Developments

SOP=States and Other Institutions of Power
SCD=Social Organization and Development

NEI=National and European Identity
TSI=Technological and Scientific Innovation

Theme	
INT	Commercial rivalries between Britain, France, Netherlands, and Spain → (1763, Treaty of Paris)
ECD	Consumer revolution → ; Rising skepticism and secularism → ; 1776, Smith's *Wealth of the Nations*
CID	Pietist revival in Lutheranism → ; 1702–1713, War of Spanish Succession (Peace of Utrecht); 1720s–1760s, Rococo Art → ; Age of Enlightenment ; 1730s–1800, Wesley's Methodist revival in Britain → ; 1751, Diderot's *Encyclopédie* ; 1748, Montesquieu's *Spirit of the Laws* ; 1759, Voltaire's *Candide* ; 1762, Rousseau's *Social Contract & Emile* ; Neoclassical art →
SOP	1700–1721, Great Northern War ; Growth of civil society (coffeehouses, salons, etc.) → ; 1740–1790, Age of Enlightened Absolutism → ; 1740–1748, War of Austrian Succession ; 1756–1763, Seven Years War → ; r. 1762–1796, Catherine the Great → ; 1775–1783, American Revolution
SCD	Paine and Burke debate the French Revolution ; Aristocratic reaction to absolutism → ; Rise of the middle class → ; Steady population increase → ; Rise of illegitimacy rate → ; Religious toleration advances → ; Concept of childhood emerges → ; 1780s–1914, Jewish emancipation from restrictions → ; 1789–1799, French Revolution ; 1791–1794, De-Christianization during Terror ; 1792, Wollstonecraft's *Vindication... Women*
NEI	18th & 19th centuries, Cottage industry → ; 1772–1795, Partitions of Poland → ; 1773 (until 1814), Jesuits disbanded
TSI	18th century, Agricultural Revolution → ; 1733–1850, Textile innovations → ; 1780, First textile mill ; Watt's steam engine

Theme Timeline (1800–1895)

INT
- 1790s–1804, Haitian slave revolt
- 1789–1810, Abolition of feudalism in western & central Europe
- 1857, Sepoy Mutiny
- 1870s–1914, Imperialism in Africa and Asia →
- 1884–1885, Berlin Conference →

ECD
- 1830s–1870s, Reforms in Britain
- 1834, Zollverein
- Opium Wars →
- Hungry 40s (potato famine in Ireland)
- Free trade
- 1869, Suez Canal
- Zionism
- 1873–1896, Volatile business cycles
- Decline of laissez-faire

CID
- 1800–1850, Romanticism →
- Protestants split between modernists and fundamentalists
- r. 1846–1878, Pope Pius IX opposes modernism
- 1848, Marx's & Engel's *Communist Manifesto*
- Realism in arts and philosophy
- Positivism →
- Nietzsche's writings
- Modern Art →
- Impressionism

SOP
- 1796–1815, Rise of Napoleon
- Napoleon's Concordat with Catholic Church
- Mass citizen armies →
- 1804–1814, French Empire
- 1830, Revolution in France
- Modern police forces and prison reform
- Liberalism ascendant
- Rise of nationalism →
- 1848–1870, Napoleon III →
- 1853–1856, Crimean War
- 1855–1881, Reforms of Alexander II of Russia
- 1861, Serfdom abolished in Russia
- Anarchist assassinations
- 1862–1890, Bismarck as Chancellor
- 1878, Congress of Berlin
- 1890s, Dreyfus Affair in France

SCD
- Growth of companionate marriage →
- Growth of class identity & institutions →
- Utopian socialism
- Significant population increase →
- Cult of domesticity (Victorian Ideal) →
- Liberalism ascendant
- Mass politics →
- Rise of socialist parties
- Feminism →
- Rise of proletariat and labor unions
- Urban reform movements
- Mass society, leisure, and education →
- Paris Commune & Third Republic

NEI
- 1814–1815, Congress of Vienna
- 1815–1840s, Concert of Europe →
- 1830–1831, Greek/Belgian independence
- Revolutions of 1848
- 1858–1861, Italian unification
- 1862–1871, German unification

TSI
- Industrialization in Britain
- Development of photography
- 1830s, First railroads
- 1851, Crystal Palace Exhibition
- 1859, Darwin's *Origin of Species*
- 1860s, Pasteur's germ theory
- Second Industrial Revolution
- 1880s–1930s, Industrialization of Russia →
- Quantum physics

Timeline (years 1900–1995)

Theme	Entries (in chronological order)
INT	1904–05, Russo-Japanese War; 1905 & 1911, Moroccan Crises; 1919–1940s, Mandate system →; Rise of U.S. as world power; Decolonization →; Postwar international economic institutions
ECD	1900, Boxer Rebellion; Growth of welfare state; 1919–1945, League of Nations →; 1921–1924, New Economic Policy in Russia; 1920s, Hyperinflation in Germany; 1928, Soviet 5-Year Plans,; Great Depression; 1930s, Soviet collectivization; Keynesian economics →; 1945, United Nations; Economic recovery in Western Europe; 1970s, Oil shock and stagflation
CID	1900, Freud's *Interpretation of Dreams*; "Lost Generation" culture; Abstract expressionism; Interwar mass culture and leisure; Existentialism; Pop Art; Postmodernism; Rock music →
SOP	Balkan tensions; 1905, Revolution in Russia; 1914–1918, World War I; 1917–1921, Russian Revolution and Civil War; 1918–1933, Weimar Republic; 1919, Treaty of Versailles; 1922–1943, Fascist Italy →; 1930s, Appeasement; 1933–1945, Third Reich; 1936–1939, Spanish Civil War; 1939–1945, World War II; 1945–1991, Cold War →; 1949, NATO; 1951, ECSC; Marshall Plan and COMECON; 1950s, Khrushchev de-Stalinizes; 1955, Warsaw Pact; 1956, Hungarian revolt; 1957, EEC; 1961, Berlin Wall; 1962, Cuban Missile Crisis; 1962–1965, 2nd Vatican Council; 1968, Prague Spring; 1970s, Détente; r. 1978–2005, John Paul II; 1980, Solidarity in Poland; 1985–1991, Gorbachev →
SCD	Women's suffrage →; Popular Front governments; 1935, Nuremberg Laws; 1939–1945, Holocaust; Postwar Baby Boom; 1960s–1980s, 2nd Wave feminism; 1968, Student revolts; Guest workers; Generation Gap; Gay and lesbian rights →
NEI	Modern medicine, life expectancy rises →; Radio & Motion Pictures; 1960s, Birth control pill; Rise of Green Party
TSI	1903, Airplane; 1905, Einstein's relativity theory; 1927, Heisenberg Uncertainty Principle; 1957, Sputnik; Space race & ICBMs; 1980, Personal computers

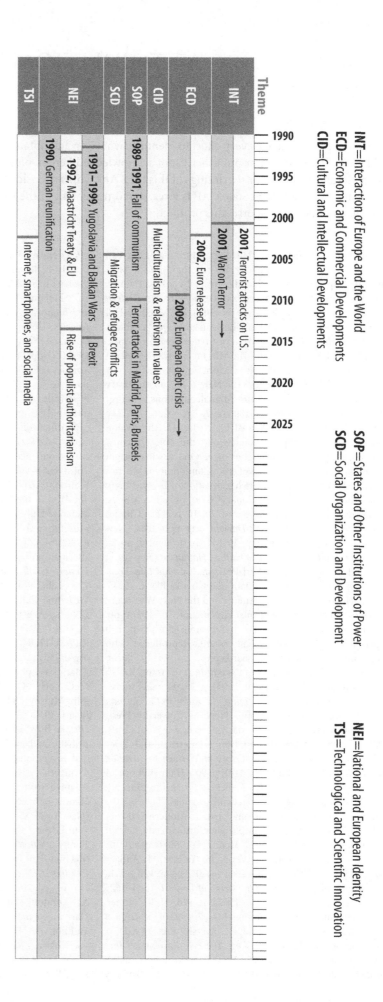

INT=Interaction of Europe and the World
ECD=Economic and Commercial Developments
CID=Cultural and Intellectual Developments

SOP=States and Other Institutions of Power
SCD=Social Organization and Development

NEI=National and European Identity
TSI=Technological and Scientific Innovation

Theme	
INT	**2001**, Terrorist attacks on U.S. **2001**, War on Terror →
ECD	**2002**, Euro released **2009**, European debt crisis →
CID	Multiculturalism & relativism in values
SOP	**1989–1991**, Fall of communism Terror attacks in Madrid, Paris, Brussels
SCD	Migration & refugee conflicts
NEI	**1991–1999**, Yugoslavia and Balkan Wars Brexit **1992**, Maastricht Treaty & EU Rise of populist authoritarianism **1990**, German reunification
TSI	Internet, smartphones, and social media

ATTRIBUTIONS

p. 4, 5 - Rubrics for AP Histories + Historical Thinking Skills, Fall 2015. Copyright © 2019 The College Board. Reproduced with permission. http://apcentral.collegeboard.com; p. 14 - R.R. Palmer, Joel Colton, and Lloyd Kramer, *A History of Europe in the Modern World*, 11th Ed., pp. 56–60. Copyright © 2014 by McGraw-Hill Education; p. 16 - Adapted from Dennis Sherman and Joyce Salisbury, *The West in the World: A History of Western Civilization* (New York: McGraw-Hill Education, 2014); p. 20 - The Miriam and Ira D. Wallach Division of Art, Prints and Photographs: Picture Collection, The New York Public Library. "Burning witches" The New York Public Library Digital Collections, 1886. https://digitalcollections.nypl.org/items/510d47e1-0dc2-a3d9-e040-e00a18064a99; p. 22 - "The Versailles Treaty," June 28, 1919: Part VIII, Article 231. The Avalon Project, Yale Law School, http://avalon.law.yale.edu/subject_menus/versailles_menu.asp; p. 31 - Samuel Wilberforce, "On Darwin's 'Origin of Species,'" in *The Quarterly Review*, Vol. 108 (London: John Murray, 1860); Clemence Royer, preface to French translation of *On the Origin of Species* in Charles Darwin Evolutionary Writings, ed. James A. Secord, (Oxford: Oxford University Press, 2008); p. 32 - Charles Darwin, *The Autobiography of Charles Darwin*, orig. pub. 1887 (New York: Barnes & Noble Books, 2005); p. 33 - Herbert Spencer, *Social Statistics; or, The Conditions Essential to Human Happiness* (New York: D. Appleton and Company, 1873); Karl Pearson, *National Life: From the Standpoint of Science* (London: Adam and Charles Black, 1901); General Friedrich von Bernhardi, Germany and the Next War, trans. Allen H. Powles (New York: Longmans, Green, and Co., 1914); pp. 48-53 - AP European History Course and Exam Description, Fall 2015. Copyright © 2019 The College Board. Reproduced with permission. http://apcentral.collegeboard.com; p. 74 - Jacob Burckhardt, *The Civilisation of the Renaissance in Italy*, trans. S.G.C. Middlemore (London: S, Sonnenschein, 1904); p. 75 - Gerald Strauss, *Luther's House of Learning: Indoctrination of the young in the German Reformation* (Baltimore, MD: The Johns Hopkins University Press, 1978); p. 88 - Potosí silver mine, Historia Americae sive Novi Orbis, CC-BY-SA-4.0; p. 89 - Adapted from Dennis Sherman and Joyce Salisbury, *The West in the World: A History of Western Civilization* (New York: McGraw-Hill Education, 2014); p. 90 - Hajo Holborn, *A History of Modern Germany: The Reformation* (Princeton, NJ: Princeton University Press, 1959); p. 97 - Galileo Galilei. "Letter to the Grand Duchess Christina of Tuscany, 1615," Modern History Sourcebook: Fordham University. http://www.fordham.edu/halsall/mod/galileo-tuscany.asp; p. 98 - Sigerist, Henry E. (1965) *Große Ärzte*, München, Deutschland: J.F. Lehmans Verlag (5. Auflage) (1. Auflage 1958), plate 26; p. 99 - CC0 1.0 Universal (CC0 1.0); p. 126 - J. R. Tanner, *Constitutional Documents of the Reign of James I, 1603–1625* (London: Cambridge University Press, 1952); p. 126 - J. R. Tanner, "Speech to Parliament, 1610," *Constitutional Documents of the Reign of James I, 1603–1625* (London: Cambridge University Press, 1952); p. 127 - Tim Blanning, *The Pursuit of Glory. The Five Revolutions that Made Modern Europe: 1648–1815* (New York: Penguin Books, 2007); p. 128 - Grille du Palais de Versailles, Pothalion, CC-BY-SA-3.0; p. 129

- Peter Horree / Alamy Stock Photo; p. 139 - Adapted from James West Davidson, Brian DeLay, Christine Leigh Heyman, Mark H. Lytle, Michael B. Stoll, *Experience History: Interpreting America's Past* (New York: McGraw-Hill Education, 2014); p. 140 - John Roberts, *Revolution and Improvement: The Western World 1775–1847* (Berkeley and Los Angeles: University of California Press, 1976); p. 141 - Charles W. Colby, ed., *Selections from the Sources of English History*, 55 B.C–A.D, 1832 (London: Longmans, Green, and Co., 1913); p. 152 - Jean-Jacques Rousseau. *Emile, or On Education*, trans., Allan Bloom. (New York: Basic Books, 1979); p. 153 - Thomas Paine, *The Age of Reason, Part the First* (London: Daniel Isaac Eaton, 1796); p. 154 - https://www.nationalgallery.org.uk/paintings/joseph-wright-of-derby-an-experiment-on-a-bird-in-the-air-pump; p. 165 - *Despatches from Paris, 1784–1790*, selected and ed. from the Foreign office correspondence by Oscar Browning Volume II (1788-1790), Camden Third Series vol. XIX; p. 166 - gallica.bnf.fr / Bibloteque nationale de France; p. 167 - Adapted from Dennis Sherman and Joyce Salisbury, *The West in the World: A History of Western Civilization* (New York: McGraw-Hill Education, 2014); p. 170 - © The Trustees of the British Museum; p. 171 - British Library, London; p. 172 - http://is.muni.cz/th/80005/pedf_m/Joseph_II.pdf; p. 174 - Adapted from Dennis Sherman and Joyce Salisbury, *The West in the World: A History of Western Civilization* (New York: McGraw-Hill Education, 2014); p. 177 - Laboratoire et table des raports; lab. & table of symbols. Credit: Wellcome Collection. Attribution 4.0 International (CC BY 4.0); p. 179 - No Artist Identified, "People under the Old Regime," LIBERTY, EQUALITY, FRATERNITY: EXPLORING THE FRENCH REVOUTION, accessed February 21, 2021, https://revolution.chnm.org/d/215; p. 180 - Bibliothèque nationale de France, département Estampes et photographie, RESERVE FOL-QB-201 (119); p. 198 - J.R. McCulloch, "On Wages." in *The Works of David Ricardo* (London: John Murray, 1888); p. 199 - James Harvey Robinson and Charles A. Beard, "The Unification of Italy," in *Readings in Modern European History* (Boston: Ginn & Company, 1909); p. 200 - Yale Center for British Art, New Haven, CT; p. 210 - Adapted from Dennis Sherman and Joyce Salisbury, *The West in the World: A History of Western Civilization* (New York: McGraw-Hill Education, 2014); p. 211 - Adapted from Paul Edward Dutton, Suzanne Marchand, Deborah Harkness, *Many Europes: Choice and Chance in Western Civilization* (New York: McGraw-Hill Education, 2014); p. 214 - Adapted from Paul Edward Dutton, Suzanne Marchand, Deborah Harkness, *Many Europes: Choice and Chance in Western Civilization* (New York: McGraw-Hill Education, 2014); p. 215 - E, J. Hobsbawm, *The Age of Empire: 1875–1914* (New York: Pantheon Books, 1987); p. 227 - F H Hinsley, ed. "Introduction," *The New Cambridge Modern History*, Vol. XI (London: Cambridge University Press, 1962); p. 228 - Charles Darwin, *On the Origin of Species*, The Harvard Classics, Vol 11, Charles W. Eliot, ed. (New York: The Collier Press, 1909); p. 229 - Lithographie von Charles Fichot, *Journal Universel*, 23. März 1872, Seite 205; p. 230 - from MoMA.org, fairuse; p. 236 - from beyondart.at; p. 241 - Cartoon from Punch Magazine, Volume 35, Page 137, 10 July 1858; p. 245 -

Chronicle / Alamy Stock Photo; p. 246 - Lebrecht Music & Arts / Alamy Stock Photo; p. 261 - Adapted from Dennis Sherman and Joyce Salisbury, *The West in the World: A History of Western Civilization* (New York: McGraw-Hill Education, 2014); p. 262 - Siegfried Sassoon, "Does it Matter?" in *Counter-Attack and Other Poems*, (New York: E.P. Dutton & Company, 1918); p. 280 - Sigmund Freud, *Civilization and its Discontents*, James Strachey, trans. And ed. (New York: W.W. Norton & Company, 1961); p. 282 - "The Covenant of the Nations," Yale Law School, The Avalon Project, http://avalon.law.yale.edu/20th_century/leagcov.asp; p. 299 - Ronald Reagon, U.S. President, " Address to Members of the British Parliament," June 8, 1982, https://www.reaganlibrary.archives.gov/archives/speeches/1982/60882a.htm; p. 300 - Angela Merkel, German Chancellor, speech to students at the College of Europe In Bruges, Belgium, November 2, 2010, https://www.coleurope.eu/content/news/Speeches/Europakolleg%20Brugge%20Mitschrift%20englisch.pdf; p. 309 - Adapted from Paul Edward Dutton, Suzanne Marchand, Deborah Harkness, *Many Europes: Choice and Chance in Western Civilization* (New York: McGraw-Hill Education, 2014); p. 313 - Mural of the painting "Guernica" by Picasso made in tiles and full size. Location: Guernica; p. 317 - World History Archive / Alamy Stock Photo; p. 320 - Valéry, Paul. Variété III, France, Gallimard, 1958; p. 339 - John Knox, *The First Blast of the Trumpet Against the Monstrous Regiment of Women*, Edward Arber, ed. (London: University College, 1878); p. 340 - Adapted from Paul Edward Dutton, Suzanne Marchand, Deborah Harkness, *Many Europes: Choice and Chance in Western Civilization* (New York: McGraw-Hill Education, 2014); p. 341 - George L. Burr, ed., "The Witch Persecutions" in Translations and Reprints from the Original Sources of Europeon History, 6 vols. (Philadelphia: University of Pennsylvania History Department, 1898-1912) vol. 3, no. 4, pp. 5-6, Hanover Historical Texts Project, https://history.hanover.edu/texts/bodin.html; p. 342 - William Cowper, *The Poetical Works of William Cowper*, Volume 1 (London: William Pickering, 1843); p. 343 - John Stuart Mill, On Liberty (London:Longmans, Green, and Co., 1867); p. 344 - President Harry S. Truman, Address Before a Joint Session of Congress, March 12, 1947. The Avalon Project, Yale Law School, https://avalon.law.yale.edu/20th_century/trudoc.asp; p. 344 - Andrew Rothstein, ed., *History of the Communist Party of the Soviet Union* (Moscow: Foreign Languages Publishing House, 1960); p. 345 - Chava Fraenkel-Goldschmidt, ed., trans., Naomi Schendowich, trans., Adam Shear, ed., (English Edition). *The Historical Writings of Joseph of Rosheim: Leader of Jewry in Early Modern Germany* (Leiden, The Netherlands: Brill, 2006); p. 346 - Louis Bergeron, *France Under Napoleon*, R.R. Palmer, trans. (Princeton, New Jersy: Princeton University Press, 1981); p. 348 - Adapted from Paul Edward Dutton, Suzanne Marchand, Deborah Harkness, *Many Europes: Choice and Chance in Western Civilization* (New York: McGraw-Hill Education, 2014); p. 350 - James Harvey Robinson and Charles A. Beard, *Readings in Modern European History*, Volume II: Europe Since the Congress of Vienna (Boston: Ginn & Company, 1909); p. 351 - Joseph Mazzini, *The Duties of Man* (London: Chapman & Hall, 1862); p. 351 - James Harvey Robinson and Charles A. Beard, *Readings in Modern European History*, Volume II: Europe Since the Congress of Vienna (Boston: Ginn & Company, 1909); p. 353 - Walter Bagehot, *Physics and Politics: Or, Thoughts on the Application of the Principles of "Natural Selection" and "Inheritance" to Political Society* (New York: The Colonial Press, 1899); p. 355 - https://www.metmuseum.org/art/collection/search/386304; p. 356 - John Lewis Gaddis, *The Cold War: A New History* (New York: Penguin Books, 2005); p. 375 - Margaret L. King and Albert Rabil, Jr., eds., trans., *Her Immaculate Hand: Selected Works by and About The Women Humanists of Quattrocento Italy* (New York: Center for Medieval and Early Renaissance Studies, State University of New York at Binghamton, 1992); p. 376 - Will Durant, *The Story of Philosophy: The Lives and Opinions of the Great Philosophers of the Western World* (New York: Simon & Schuster, 2006); p. 376 - Frank Maloy Anderson, ed., *The Constitutions and other Select Documents Illustrative of the History of France, 1789–1901* (Minneapolis: The H.W. Wilson Company, 1904); p. 377 - J.F.C. Harrison, ed., *Society and Politics in England, 1780–1960: A Selection of Readings and Comments* (New York: Harper & Row, 1965); p. 377 - W.B. Crump, ed., *The Leeds Woolen Industry 1780–1820* (Leeds: The Thoresby Society, 1931); p. 378 - Adapted from Dennis Sherman and Joyce Salisbury, *The West in the World: A History of Western Civilization* (New York: McGraw-Hill Education, 2014); p. 379 - *United States of America Congressional Record: Proceedings and Debates of the 84th Congress Second Session*, Volume 102 - Part 7, May 22, 1956, to June 11, 1956 (Washington, D.C.: United States Government Printing Office, 1956); p. 380 - Adapted from Dennis Sherman and Joyce Salisbury, *The West in the World: A History of Western Civilization* (New York: McGraw-Hill Education, 2014); p. 381 - The Minnich Collection, The Ethel Morrison Van DerLip Fund, 1966; p. 382 - Mary Astell, *Some Reflections Upon Marriage, Occasion'd by the Duke and Dutchess of Mazarine's Case; Which Is Also Consider'd* (London: Printed for John Nutt, near Stationer-Hall, 1700); p. 383 - Adapted from Paul Edward Dutton, Suzanne Marchand, Deborah Harkness, *Many Europes: Choice and Chance in Western Civilization* (New York: McGraw-Hill Education, 2014); p. 384 - Alix Holt, trans., *Selected Writings of Alexandra Kollontai* (Westport, Conn.: Lawrence Hill and Company, 1977); p. 385 - R.H.S. Crossman, *Government and the Governed: A History of Political Ideas and Political Practice* (London: Basis Books by arrangement with Christophers, 1940); p. 385 - Adapted from Dennis Sherman and Joyce Salisbury, *The West in the World: A History of Western Civilization* (New York: McGraw-Hill Education, 2014); p. 386 - *The Statutes of the Realm. Printed by Command of His Majesty King George the Third In Pursuance of an Address of The House of Commons of Great Britain*, Volume the Fourth (reprinted London: Dawsons of Pall Mall, 1965; p. 387 - John Hall Stewart, *A Documentary Survey of the French Revolution* (New York: The Macmillan Company, 1951); p. 388 - Based on A.J.P. Taylor, *The Habsburg Monarchy, 1809–1918: A History of the Austrian Empire and Austria-Hungary* (London: Hamish Hamilton, 1951), Appendix; p. 389 - Anson Rabinbach and Sander L. Gilman, eds., *The Third Reich Sourcebook* (Berkeley: University of California Press, 2013); p. 390 - Ken Knabb, ed., trans., *Situationist International Anthology* (Berkeley, California: Bureau of Public Secrets, 2006); p. 391 - Adapted from Dennis Sherman and Joyce Salisbury, *The West in the World: A History of Western Civilization* (New York: McGraw-Hill Education, 2014); p. 392 - J.H. Plumb, "The Commercialization of Childhood," in Horizon, Fall 1976; p. 393 - David Hume, "An Enquiry Concerning Human Understanding." from *Enquiries Concerning Human Understanding, and Concerning Principles of Morals*, by David Hume (reprinted from the 1777 edition), L.A. Selby-Bigge, ed. (1902), Project Gutenberg, https://www.gutenberg.org/files/9662/old/8echu10h.htm; p. 394 - Jean-Jacques Rousseau, G.D.H. Cole, trans., *The Social Contract & Discources* (London: J.M. Dent & Sons, LTD., 1920); p. 394 - George L. Mosse, Rondo E. Cameron. Henry Bertram Hill, and Mitchael B. Petrovich, eds., *Europe in Review* (Chicago: Rand McNally & Company, 1964); p. 395 - Yale Center for British Art; p. 395 - Viscount de Chateaubriand, *The Genius of Christianity: or the Spirit and Beauty of the Christian Religion*, Charles I. White, trans., (Baltimore: John Murray & Co., 1884); p. 396 - Lord George Gordon Byron, *Manfred: A Dramatic Poem* (London: John Murray, 1817); p. 397 - Hamburger Kunsthalle, www.hamburger-kunsthalle.de.

INDEX

Indonesian Nationalist Party, 294
inductive reasoning, 93
industrial middle class, 188
Industrial Revolution (First), 184–189; France, 187; Germany, 187; Great Britain, 185–187; responses to, 188; social effects of, 188. *See also* Second Industrial Revolution
inequality, 134, 144, 146, 148
infantry, 60, 87, 137, 251–252
inflation, 159, 161, 253, 267
inherited privilege, 156
inoculation, 131, 138, 144
Inquisition, 67, 73, 84, 92, 95; Roman, 73, 92; Spanish, 67, 119
internal combustion engine, 207
Interwar Period, 273–274; high culture, 273; mass culture, 274
International Monetary Fund (IMF), 293
Irish potato famine, 194
Iron Curtain, 286, 292, 303
Iron Curtain speech, 286
iron smelting, 186
irrationality, 222, 273
isolation, 274
Italian Renaissance, 60–61, 121; family structure, 60–61; setting, 60–61
Italy, 60–61, 62, 197, 204, 270

J

Jacobin Club, 159–160, 161
James I, 119, 120
Jansenist movement, 95, 118
Jesuits, 72
Jews, 145, 149, 220, 222, 267, 272, 278–279
John Paul II, 291, 307
Joseph II, 137, 149
Joyce, James, 273
Junkers, 123, 149, 205

K

Kafka, Franz, 273
Kaiser Wilhelm II, 249–250, 254
Kant, Immanuel, 143, 147, 149
Kepler, Johannes, 92
Keynesian economics, 269, 293
KGB, 285, 289
Khrushchev, Nikita, 287, 289

Korean War, 286, 302
Kosovars, 293
kulaks, 259, 272

L

Labour Party, 220–221, 296
laissez-faire, 80, 159, 185, 187, 189, 192; abandoning of, 219, 260
lateen sail, 77
League of Nations, 255–256, 266
leisure, 82, 83, 145, 188, 217, 218, 274
Lenin, V.I., 212, 255, 257–258
Lent, 72
lesbian relationships, 304
liberalism, 191, 192, 194, 219, 220
Liberals, 189, 192, 194, 195–196, 205, 219, 221
limited resources, 187
List, Friedrich, 187
literacy, 62, 72, 143, 145, 218, 305
literature, 202, 226
Little Ice Age, 131
Locarno Pact, 267–268, 275
Locke, John, 95–96, 134, 192
Lost Generation, 273
Louis XIV, 96, 117–119, 120, 121–122, 123, 149, 156, 269
Louis XVI, 157–158, 164, 256
L'Ouverture, Toussaint, 161
Low Countries, 60, 63, 67, 69, 83, 84, 164, 276, 294
Lueger, Karl, 220, 271
Lutheranism, 68–69
Luther, Martin, 68–73

M

Machiavelli, Niccolo, 62, 64
machine guns, 209
Magisterial Reform, 70, 71
Malthus, Thomas, 81, 131, 185
Malthusian Trap, 81, 131
Maginot Line, 268
mandates, 255, 294
Mannerism, 121
maps, 77, 79
Marat, Jean-Paul, 160
Maria Theresa, 123, 137–138, 149
market economy, 136
markets, 136, 185, 208, 209, 268, 285
Marshall Plan, 285–286, 290, 293

Marxism, 203, 257–258, 270, 297
Marx, Karl, 203
Masaccio, 63
mass citizen armies, 249
mass conscription, 160
mass marketing, 303
mass politics, 218–219, 220, 221, 222, 250, 253, 269
mass production, 80, 207
mass society, 217
Matisse, Henri, 225
Mazzini, Giuseppe, 193, 197, 204
mathematics, 91, 92, 93, 94, 95
medical advances, 93, 209, 303
Medici, Catherine de', 84
Medici, Lorenzo de', 62
Medici family, 62, 65
medicine, 93, 118, 144–145, 209, 217, 303
Meiji Restoration, 212
Mein Kampf, 267, 271, 272
mercantilism, 80
Mercator, Gerardus, 79
merchant oligarchs, 133
Metternich, Klemens von, 190-191, 194, 196, 205
Michelangelo Buonarroti, 61, 63, 121
microorganisms, 217
microscope, 93, 96
Middle Ages, 59, 60, 61, 64
middle class, 80, 81, 119, 132–133, 136. *See also* bourgeoisie
Middle East, 253
Middle Passage, 79, 139
military revolution, 87
Millet, Jean-Fran;ois, 202
Mines Act, 194
Mirandola, Pico della, 62
modern corporation, 208
modernism, 222, 224, 226, 306
Monet, Claude, 225
monopolies, 80, 123, 124, 208
Montaigne, Michel de, 79, 94
Montesquieu, Baron de, 147
More, Thomas, 67, 68
Moroccan Crises, 212
music, avant-garde, 307; Baroque, 121, 144; nationalism in, 192, 226; romanticism in, 226; jazz, 79, 274, postwar, 304, protest, 304
Mussolini, Benito, 270–271

N

Napoleon Bonaparte, 161–163; domestic policies, 162–163; educational system, 162; warfare, 163

Napoleon III, 204, 205, 206

Napoleon, Louis, 195

national economic system, 187

National Front Party, 305

nationalism, 162, 163, 192–193, 194, 204, 211, 219, 226, 250, 268, 293

National Liberation Front, 294

national self-determination, 255

national unification, 203–205

native exploitation, 78

naturalism, 63, 68

natural law, 93, 94, 95, 146–148, 151

natural rights, 95, 146

nature, 91, 93–94, 95, 119

Nazi Germany, 271–272, 274, 275, 278

Nazis, 206, 255, 267, 269, 271–272, 276–277, 278; economics, 272; politics, 271; obstacles to power, 272; racial policy, 272; terror, 272

Nazi-Soviet Non-Aggression Pact, 275

Neo-classical, 144

Netherlands, 80, 84–85, 121–122, 189, 295; commercial power, 119; imperialism, 211, 294; *See also* Low Countries

New Economic Policy (NEP), 259, 272

New Monarchies, 64–66

newspapers, 143, 208

Newton, Isaac, 92–93, 94, 96, 222

New World, 67, 69, 78, 79; new crops, 79; new diseases, 79

Nicholas II, 256, 257

Nietzsche, Friedrich, 224, 370

Nightingale, Florence, 204

Nine Years' War, 121

nobility, 70, 117, 132–133, 150, 156, 157, 192; Prussian (Junkers), 123, 149, 205;

nobles of Poland (*szlachta*), 122

nobles of the robe, 65, 81

North Atlantic Treaty Organization, (NATO), 285, 287, 292, 293, 297; France leaving, 296

Northern Ireland, 296, 305

novels, 143, 145, 202, 226, 273, 285

Nuclear Age, 277

nuclear family, 61, 82, 134

nuclear parity, 287, 289

nuclear power, 288, 294, 303–304

O

Old Science, 91

On Crimes and Punishments, 144

opera, 121, 144, 226; houses, 118, 207, 218

oral culture, 143, 145

Other, the, 304

Ottoman Empire, 122, 125, 150, 204, 222, 250–251; Arab nationalism in, 253

P

Palace at Versailles, 117–118, 128

Palestine, 222, 294

Pan-German League, 220

pan-Slavism, 193

parliamentary democracy, 219–220

Partition of Africa, 209

Partitions of Poland, 122, 150

party-state structure, 259

Pascal, Blaise, 95

Pasteur, Louis, 217

Peace of Augsburg, 70, 85

Peace of Westphalia, 86, 123

peasants, 60, 72, 82, 133, 143, 145, 157, 158, 160, 197, 202, 207, 291; kulaks, 259, 272; portrayal in art, 68; Revolt, 69; Russian, 256, 257, 258, 259

perestroika, 289, 290, 292

perspective, in art, 62, 63, 68, 121, 225; geometry, 77

Peter I, the Great, 124

Petrarch, 61–62

Philip II, 70, 71, 83–85

philosophers, 62, 63, 91, 94, 146, 147, 149, 224

philosophes, 146

physics, 92, 223

Physiocracy, 147, 150

Physiocrats, The, 147

Picasso, Pablo, 225–226, 230, 273, 313

Planck, Max, 223

plantation factories, 135

pluralism, 68

poison gas, 252

Poland, 72, 82, 122, 190, 254, 258, 266, 275, 276, 278, in WWII, 276, 279;

nobles of, 122; Partition of, 122, 150; postwar, 284, 291

Polish revolt, 194, 206

political theory, 95

politics, 62, 64–65, 86, 121, 137, 150, 184, 295–297; mass, 218–222, 225, 250, 253, 269; of restoration, 191; of unification, 204–205; Western European, 295–297

popular culture, 143, 145, 304

Popular Front, 269, 275

porcelain, 77, 80, 135, 187

Portugal, 77, 78, 79, 86, 136, 295; colonial empire of, 78, 210, 211

positivism, 202

Post-impressionism, 225

postmodernism, 306

potato, 79, 80, 104, 133, 135, 194; Irish famine, 194

poverty, 82, 117, 133, 134, 187, 221, 303, 305

Price Revolution, 79, 81

Prince, The, 62

Principia Mathematica, 92

printed materials, 73, 143

printing press, 63–64, 67, 69, 96, 208

privacy, 132, 162

producers' cooperatives, 269

proletariat, 188, 203, 258, 259

propaganda, 69, 163, 252, 254, 269, 272, 273, 274, 278, 286

property rights, 164, 185, 257

prostitution, 61, 72, 132, 188

protective tariffs, 187, 208, 220

Protestant, 67, 68–70, 71, 72, 98–98, 118–120, 147, 148, 224, 305, 307

Protestant Reformation, 59, 60, 64, 66, 68–70, 72, 83, 145; causes, 68; social impact, 72

Provisional Government, 195, 254, 257–258

provincial law codes, 159

Prussia, 86, 87, 123, 136, 137, 138, 149, 150, 160, 190, 191, 195–196, 205–206; Brandenburg-Prussia, 118, 123; East Prussia, 255, 275; Frederick II "the Great," 149

Ptolemy, 77, 91

public health, 189, 217, 303; Act of 1848, 189

public health boards, 189

public housing, 218, 219

NOTES

NOTES

Voltaire:
Freedom of rights of Man (supported)
Embraced (Bon Tyrant)
→ Ruler needed to be
educated (Absolute
& Enlightened)

• Had to flee multiple types
• Until pop was edu, there could not be a democracy.
• Writing = Candedo

Absolute Rulers:
• Catherine
• James
• Charels

• Rousseau → Democracy (Most radical)
• Wanted everyone to vote directly for candidate.
• ! education & ! experience (kind of montessori).

Diderot → Did not have "own" ideas, but put into Encyclopedia.
• Wanted to share ideas & spread.
•